CONTINUITY IN HISTORY
AND OTHER ESSAYS

CONTINUITY IN HISTORY AND OTHER ESSAYS

ALEXANDER GERSCHENKRON

THE BELKNAP PRESS
OF HARVARD UNIVERSITY PRESS

Cambridge, Massachusetts

1 9 6 8

FOR HELGA SUSANNA AND MARIA RENATE

Acknowledgments

I am indebted to the following for their kind permission to reprint my essays in this volume:

1. American Philosophical Society, for "On the Concept of Continuity in History," *Proceedings*, June 1962.

2. *Rivista Internazionale di Scienze Economiche e Commerciali*, Milan, for "Some Methodological Problems in Economic History," February 1965.

3. Hugo Hegeland, ed., *Money, Growth, and Methodology and Other Essays in Economics in Honor of Johan Åkerman*, for "Reflections on Ideology as a Methodological and Historical Problem," Lund, Sweden, 1961.

4. International Economic History Association, Geneva, for "Typology of Industrial Development as a Tool of Analysis," *Second International Conference on Economic History, Aix-en-Provence, 1962*, vol. II, Paris, 1965.

5. *Nord e Sud*, Naples, for "The Industrial Development of Italy: A Debate with Rosario Romeo," November 1961.

6. Basic Books, Inc., for "The Modernization of Entrepreneurship," *Modernization*, Myron Weiner, ed., New York, 1966.

7. Cambridge University Press, for "Agrarian Policies and Industrialization, Russia, 1861–1914," *Cambridge Economic History*, vol. VI, Cambridge, Eng., 1965.

8. Harvard University Press, for "City Economies — Then and Now," *The Historian and the City*, Oscar Handlin and John Burchard, eds., Cambridge, Mass., 1963.

9. The Macmillan Company, for "Reflections on Economic Aspects of Revolutions," *Internal War*, Harry Eckstein, ed., The Free Press of Glencoe, 1964.

10. *World Politics*, Princeton, for "The Changeability of a Dictatorship," July 1962.

11. Yale University, for "The Stability of Dictatorships," Harvard Foundation Lecture, April 1963.

The journals listed below were good enough to grant me permission to reprint the review articles and reviews included in Appendices I–III. The name of the author of the book reviewed appears after the name of the journal; the date refers to the issue.

American Economic Review: E. O. Golob (June 1945), John F. Normano (September 1945), Ingvar Svennilson (December 1955), A. I. Pashkov (September 1959), and John U. Nef (March 1966).

American Historical Review: Franco Venturi (October 1953), Oliver H. Radkey (July 1959), N. K. Karataev (January 1962), Valdo Zilli (October 1964), and John M. Letiche (October 1965).

American Political Science Review: Emanuel Sarkisyanz, June 1959.

Economic History Review: Peter Struve (December 1953), Archivio Economico dell'Unificazione Italiana (December 1958), Rondo Cameron (April 1964), Alec Nove (April 1965), Doreen Warriner (April 1966), and Giorgio Mori (August 1966).

Economica: Gino Luzzatto (February 1964) and Everett E. Hagen (February 1965).

Journal of the American Statistical Association: National Bureau of Economic Research, December 1961.

Journal of Economic History: Naum Jasny (Winter 1951), Peter I. Lyashchenko (Spring 1952), Bertrand Gille (Summer 1953), R. Van der Meulen (March 1960), R.E.F. Smith (September 1961), Jerome Blum (March 1964), and Hans Rosenberg (March 1968).

Journal of Political Economy (University of Chicago Press): Theodore Von Laue, December 1964.

Kyklos: R. W. Davies, 1960.

Modern Philology (University of Chicago Press): Vladimir Nabokov, May 1966.

Review of Economics and Statistics: Walther Hoffmann (August 1956) and Erik Dahmén (November 1957).

Slavic Review: Arthur Montgomery, December 1953.

Finally, I am indebted to *Survey*, London, for permission to reprint as Appendix IV, "Study of the Soviet Economy in the USA," January 1964.

Contents

CONTENTS

CONTINUITY IN HISTORY
AND OTHER ESSAYS

Introduction

THIS book is a companion volume to a previously published collection of essays.[1] In the earlier volume, I presented my general approach to the industrial development of Europe in the nineteenth century. I tried to show there, with the help of some case studies, how the industrialization process varied with the degree of backwardness of the individual countries on the eve of their great spurts of industrialization; the industrial evolution of the continent in that period could then be intelligibly conceived as a case of unity in diversity. At the same time, in a number of essays I dealt with several aspects of Soviet economic and social history. The peculiarities of Soviet industrialization served *inter alia* to illustrate the limits beyond which a general approach of this sort cannot be carried without losing most of its explanatory power.

The papers in the present volume should be considered as elaborations of problems discussed in its predecessor. The notion of the great spurt had caused some discussion of the role of discontinuities in economic development. The feeling was often expressed that historical continuity was "good" and discontinuity rather undesirable. The impropriety of normative intrusions into an explanatory framework was matched by considerable conceptual confusion. In the leading essay of this volume, I have tried to distinguish as best I could among the various meanings of continuity and discontinuity, leading up to a clarification of the twin concept as implied in my approach to the industrial history of Europe. The second essay, on methodological problems in economic history, does not deal explicitly with my approach, but what is said there on the role of generalizations in history bears directly on the methodological thinking which underlies and justifies that approach.

1. *Economic Backwardness in Historical Perspective* (Cambridge, Mass., 1962).

Of the essays in Part II the paper on the typology of industrial development (Chapter 4) constitutes a reformulation of my approach, showing how a morphological ordering can be transformed into a causal explanation. Chapter 5, a translation of an oral debate with Rosario Romeo, must be read as a continuation of my discussion of his views in Chapter 5 of the earlier volume. Similarly Chapter 6, dealing with the modernization of entrepreneurship, restates and continues my views on the subject (Chapter 3 of the previous volume) and connects the problem of the entrepreneurial factor in the processes of industrialization with my general views of substitutions for missing prerequisites in backward countries. Chapter 7 provides a rather detailed description of Russian agrarian policies following the emancipation of the peasants in 1861. Here again the main purpose has been to show, as was stated more generally in the earlier volume, how the disabilities of an organization of agriculture that was inimical to industrial progress were overcome through the application of appropriate substitutions. Finally, the little paper on city economies (Chapter 8), though broadly polemical in nature, also deals with modern changes in the location of industries and, by the same token, refers implicitly to the difficulty of applying "lessons" drawn from nineteenth-century experience to current problems of underdeveloped or developed countries.

As for the third part of this volume, Chapter 9 deals with those widespread and hardly tenable generalizations regarding the beneficial effect on industrial development of the revolutionary destruction of "feudal" formations in agriculture. It is bad enough to argue that there are some *necessary* prerequisites, in the absence of which no industrialization can take place. It is worse to regard as a prerequisite of industrialization a factor which, in an important case on the historical record, proved an obstacle to industrial development. Of the last two chapters (10 and 11), the former is a sequel to "Reflections on Soviet Novels," published in my previous volume. It deals with the shy struggle of Soviet novelists against continuing governmental attempts to order and direct, to stifle and censor. It centers on the situation as it existed at the time of the Twenty-Second Congress of the Communist Party in 1961; to bring its story up to date would require a new and different paper. But the chapter must also be seen

2

as a springboard to the one that follows it here. In fact, both essays have emerged from a view expressed in the earlier volume, where I said that the course of Soviet economic history can be most profitably understood in terms of the mechanics of dictatorial power. In particular, in "The Stability of Dictatorships" an attempt has been made to sketch a general historical pattern of the policies of modern dictatorships designed to maintain and to increase their power. In this peculiar set of motivations lies the reason why Soviet economic development, despite some similarities, has stood outside the general pattern of European industrialization in the nineteenth century.

One or two additional remarks on this essay may be added. Although its main purpose was historical analysis, it also dealt with current policies and prospects. The paper was written more than five years ago. In the intervening years, of course, the rift between Russia and China has widened very greatly. The existence of a ruthless enemy of enormous potential power no doubt serves in itself to maintain a crucial stability condition of the Soviet dictatorship. But in other respects the situation is far from clear. As was foreseen in the essay, the measures of economic recentralization have been consummated by the abolition of the regional councils and the re-establishment of industrial ministries. On the other hand, a number of steps have been taken (in 1965) to expand somewhat the area of managerial independence and to provide more rational incentives and yardsticks in some segments of the industrial economy. At the same time, despite some very grave setbacks, there has been evidence of further relaxation in the sensitive field of belles-lettres and literary criticism. Equally important is the fact that for more than three years, since the fall of Khrushchev, the Soviet dictatorship has done without a living "father figure" at the helm, employing Lenin alone as the more remote and intangible object of the inevitable cult of personality. Nor can it be said — though the contingency was suggested in the essay — that such increases in the standards of consumers' welfare as have taken place over the last decade have directly created strong popular pressures upon the regime and have weakened its stability.[2]

2. One cannot be quite sure, but it would seem from the report on the performance of Soviet industry in the first six months of 1967 (*Pravda*, July 16, 1967) that the rate of growth of output of light industry actually exceeded that of heavy

The indirect effects are another matter. I do believe that such strictures of the regime as have found expression in Soviet novels and poetry as well as in protests against censorship and repression are, at least to some extent, the natural consequence of improvements in levels of consumption and of the concomitant decline in the rate of economic growth. For the maintenance of a very high rate of growth served as one of the strongest justifications for the continued existence of the dictatorial system.

Naturally, an exact balance cannot be struck. If I were a political scientist or a sociologist of the modern brand of reckless quantifiers, I should find little difficulty in supplying a precise answer. Taking my leaf from people who can quantify anything, be it alienation, incestuous impulses, or entrepreneurial vigor, I should readily develop a quantitative measure for the stability conditions of modern dictatorships. I should call it "stab," and I should be able to show how many stabs are needed for the minimum stability of a dictatorship, and I could, by adding up the individual stability conditions, arrive at a precise statement regarding the present situation in Soviet Russia as compared with that of five years ago. Unfortunately, however, I come from a profession in which quantification is a serious business. An economist knows that even when he has all the quantitative data, say on change in prices or output, his attempt to quantify the change can still be frustrated by the index-number problem; by the fact, that is, that his yardstick expanded or contracted in the very process of measurements. Thus, all one can say is that some of the classic stability conditions of dictatorial power have become blurred without visibly placing the dictatorship in any imminent jeopardy. If what has been taking place in Russia is an erosion of dictatorship, the process has been so slow as to be almost imperceptible. By the

---

industry. This is a novelty indeed, and will remain important even if the situation were to be reversed in the months to come. One must remember that the relatively faster growth of heavy industry was declared to be a "law of socialist economic development." See my review of A. I. Pashkov's book (Appendix II, item 15).

[As the manuscript goes to press (October 1967), it is reported that the Soviet plan for industrial output for 1968 envisages the following rates of growth: 8.6 percent for light industry and 7.9 percent for heavy industry (*New York Times*, October 11, 1967, p. 1). This announcement, which is justly receiving much attention, bears out the conjecture made here.]

same token, neither the length of this process nor the degree of its reversibility can be foreseen. At any rate, past experience offers no guidance in this respect. Modern history shows clearly enough how dictatorships have tried to assure the stability of their regimes. And it contains the record of their violent downfalls. But — the ambiguous case of Kemal's Turkey aside — a gradual and peaceful transformation of a modern dictatorship would be a historical *novum*, as has been, for that matter, its continued survival for five decades.

I have placed in Appendices I and II reviews of books in the field of economic history and related subjects. The purpose of including them in the present volume is threefold. Some of the books reviewed have been of considerable importance to me. Thus, I have learned much from Walther Hoffmann's study (Appendix I, item 2), and his statistical techniques served me in good stead in preparing the case studies on Italy and Bulgaria for my earlier volume. Erik Dahmén's significant book (Appendix I, item 1) contains the concept of "development blocks," which fits so excellently well with my concept of the great spurt. Franco Venturi's book *Il Populismo russo* (Appendix II, item 7) once caused me to undertake a study of nineteenth-century Russian intellectual history, applying to it my general views on Russian industrialization (see Chapter 7 of the earlier volume). Jerome Blum's magnum opus on the Russian agrarian structure (Appendix II, item 2) deals with a century-long evolution that precedes the sequence of events I treat in Chapter 7 of this volume. On the other hand, several reviews deal with approaches to the economic development of Europe which I consider inadequate, or with interpretations of Russian, French, and Italian economic history which I have been able to criticize from the point of view of my general approach. Finally, some of the reviews cast additional sidelights both on my substantive and my methodological views. The treatment of the concept of necessity in history by Theodore Von Laue and Alec Nove (Appendix II, items 6 and 13) offers examples of what I have in mind. The reviews extend over a very wide field, and their unity is no doubt somewhat elusive. I believe, however, that they will usefully supplement the points I have been trying to make in this as well as in the earlier volume. The review of Nabokov's translation of Pushkin, being altogether special, is housed in a separate appendix (III). It should be noted, however, that problems of translation have a direct bearing on comparative historical studies. They have also been dealt with in Appendix II, item 10. Appendix IV contains a brief discussion of American research on the Soviet economy. It may be added that there is some similarity in the problems involved in organizing Soviet economic research and in building up or rejuvenating the field of economic history in the United States. In either case, the task was, and is, to convert the field into an integral part of the discipline of economics.

I should have liked to conclude this introduction with a critical review of the reviews of my earlier volume. But as I reread the sizable collection of clippings and photostats from journals in this country and abroad, I feel that I must, regretfully, abandon the original intention. To be sure, the individual reviews differed in tone and judgment. In some of them, the praise bestowed on the book went far beyond what I consider to be its merits. Other reviewers were more restrained, and a few approved with grudging irritation that verged on blame. One reviewer (Phyllis Deane) managed to compress in a few short pages a brilliant summary of the book — much superior to anything I could have produced myself. Yet what I have missed was penetrating, thought-provoking disagreement. Some pins and needles there were, but not the scalpel of a probing critic.

There were, however, some complaints not about what I did, but about what I had failed to do. In particular, Ruggiero Romano, in his long preface to the Italian translation of the earlier volume,[3] reproaches me for not having paid sufficient attention to agriculture in backward countries as an obstacle to industrialization; furthermore, he says, my treatment of economic backwardness in Europe casts little light on the problems of currently underdeveloped countries. As far as the former point is concerned, there exists an immense literature on the subject. The fallacious notion of necessary prerequisites of industrialization emerged largely from the belief that, without removal of antiquated forms of agricultural organization, there could be no industrialization. My task was to show that this belief is at variance with the actual historical experience of European countries. Nevertheless, it is possible that Signor Romano will find

3. *Il Problema storico dell'arretratezza economica* (Turin, 1965).

in Chapter 7 of this volume some thoughts on the self-perpetuating forces of stagnation, and in particular the explanation why, given the institutional framework of serfdom, the latter was quite unlikely to disappear simply under the pressure of greater productivity of free as against bonded labor.

The second point touches on the question of lessons from history and is of more general interest. It seems to me that, behind the eagerness to apply what we have learned from the study of given area and period to very different times and climes, there lurks the ancient belief in the basic uniformity of all history, the old search for a simple comprehensive general law of historical evolution. Such views and aspirations lie on the other side of the line that separates serious research from fanciful superficialities. In trying to understand and interpret historical sequences, we must form some generalized hypotheses. But, at the same time, responsible scholarship must be conscious of, and in fact search for, the limits of applicability of its hypotheses. Even within Europe of the period with which I have been concerned, I was confronted with events that did not fit my set of expectations and had to be recorded as deviations. How can one hope that those expectations will be verified when dealing with vastly different social and political frameworks, momentous differences in technology, and far-reaching changes in the patterns of industrial location? Moreover, it should be noted that the very concept of substitutions for missing "prerequisites" sets limits to predictive inferences from history. It is true that such substitutions, once invented, can be imitated or reinvented. But it is equally true that at some point these creative innovations were unprecedented in action and possibly also in thought. In its very nature, what is truly new in history cannot be predicted, although it can be explained *post festum*. This alone should serve as a warning to economic historians against easy extrapolations, which either are likely to remain hopelessly superficial or else will reveal a lack of understanding of the current problems and the limits of historical generalizations. To say this is to reject the idea that history contains prefabricated programs for action. It does not mean, however, that knowledge of previous cases of development is altogether useless. Modern discussion of economic development, vast as it is, has raised few problems that were not raised in one form or another in the course of European industrializations of the nineteenth century. Greater awareness of past developments would have facilitated the search for the relevant questions. But the answers are a very different matter. To repeat what I have said before: "No past experience, however rich, and no historical research, however thorough, can save the living generation the creative task of finding their own answers and shaping their own future." In short, one should not demand of a historical interpretation more than it can reasonably offer. As the French say, the most beautiful girl cannot give more than she has.

To continue, and to conclude this introduction on a lighter note, a couple of sentences from a review of the earlier volume in *The Economist* (London) may be quoted: "The author has a curious doctrine that industrialization always begins with a spurt. Now if it is meant that industry itself grows rapidly, this is the merest arithmetical necessity, since it starts from zero; if a baby grows fast, this is not a 'magnificent achievement.' " [4] I am afraid the curiosity is on the other foot. It seems when discontinuities that some people dislike are too obvious to be ignored or denied, the next thing to do is to declare them arithmetic quirks and to divest them of economic significance. I do indeed believe that industrializations in conditions of European backwardness were characterized by great spurts, that is to say, by a high rate of growth of industrial output. To call this an "arithmetical necessity," however, is quite nonsensical. Zero and infinity, of course, are something very special. But no one is concerned with the "first" industrial plant, and once we do not start with zero the rate of growth is an economic rather than arithmetic problem and will vary with varying economic conditions. Nor, incidentally does a baby start its growth from zero, and there are very excellent biological, and not at all arithmetic, reasons for the speed of early growth. It must be admitted, however, that in making his remarks the semianonymous reviewer [5] was in good company, since similar statements can be found elsewhere in literature coming from quite respectable pens. Unfortunately, repeating a fallacy does not increase its truth content.

4. *The Economist* (May 18, 1963), p. 671.
5. The author of the review obligingly sent me a prepublication copy, explaining that "indiscretion is the best part of anonymity."

Part I

METHODOLOGY

I

On the Concept of Continuity in History

Modo paulatim, modo saltatim.

THE purpose of this essay is to take a closer look at the allied concepts of historical continuity and discontinuity. Their meaning appears often blurred, and their users seem unaware of the existing confusion and its manifold sources. Irrelevant intrusion from alien conceptual structures, inferential sloppiness, and political bias draped in the guise of scientific truth — all these have conspired in tangling the semantic skein. In fact, one cannot suppress the suspicion that it is the very uncertainties of the term which have made it flow so readily from pens and tongues. There is a *prima facie* case for exposing illicit terminological commerce in any circumstance. There is, however, in addition a chance that in the process some unobjectionable and useful concept or concepts of historical continuity will emerge. Beyond that, some light may be cast on the nature of conceptual tools in history or at least in economic history, to which latter discipline this writer's interest is primarily attached.

I

Let us begin with the most common coin in our usage: the customary contrast between "change" and "continuity." When, to quote examples at random, Austria is said to have enjoyed centuries of continuity under the Habsburgs; or when discussion turns to continuity or change in prerevolutionary and postrevolutionary Russia;

or when a Rumanian historian rejects the emigration theory in Rumanian history in favor of the continuity theory — then continuity appears to mean no more than absence of change, that is, stability. There was no change in the reigning dynasty in Austria; Soviet Russia is said to be very much like Imperial Russia; and the Rumanian people, once established north of the Danube, and particularly north of the Montes Serrorum, is asserted to have remained in undisturbed possession of those areas.

So conceived, "historical continuity" may mean two things. It may mean stability of certain elements in an otherwise changing world — Schiller's *ruhender Pol in der Erscheinungen Flucht*; this raises interesting problems concerning interrelationships of the stable and the changing elements in the historical process. But there is another and much broader interpretation of continuity, in the sense of stability as something that is essentially inherent in all human history. This is Schopenhauer's history in the course of which nothing "essential" ever changes, except "names and years": hence a perusal of Herodotus is declared to be altogether sufficient for the "philosophical" understanding of all subsequent history.[1] It makes little difference whether the determining factor is said to be the sempiternal nature of man, or some exterior element, such as climate or the geographical environment that is assumed to be permanently fixed. However justified, such a position comes close to denying the very existence of history. For "changeless history" is a contradiction in terms, and absence of change is just as destructive of history as would be a change that proceeded so constantly, so rapidly, and, most of all, so thoroughly as to leave no discernible relation between successive moments. The point is not whether such change can or cannot be found in actual life. It is rather that the historian — at the peril of losing his subject — must be interested in historical change, that is to say, in the rates of change that lie between zero and infinity.

It does not require long semantic expeditions through the current usages of the term "continuity" to discover that it denotes a good

---

1. Arthur Schopenhauer, *Die Welt als Wille und Vorstellung*, II, chap. 38 (Reclam), 1216–1219. We shall see later that this concept of continuity borders on, or can be redefined into, another which — except at its extreme point — is a much more promising tool of historical research.

deal more than stability. Confused and inconsistent as that usage is,[2] unmistakably it refers time and again to the nature of change rather than to its absence. Hence the phrase "continuous change" is by no means a contradiction in terms; by the same token, the phrase "discontinuous change" need not be pleonastic at all. It is precisely because continuity and discontinuity can relate to a certain kind of change that the two concepts may be expected to prove useful in historical research. In the course of clarifying these concepts, it will be necessary to distinguish a variety of meanings which can be, or have been, attributed to the terms. In so doing, particular attention will be paid to the problem of stability in the rate of change as it relates to modern industrial history — an area in which this writer has conducted a fair amount of research. On the other hand, the intriguing special case of perfect stability in certain respects (zero rate of change) in the midst of an otherwise changing environment will be touched upon briefly, but its discussion must be deferred to another occasion.

Any concept of continuity based on historical change necessarily involves comparisons over time. The precise nature of such comparisons will vary depending on the concept of continuity used and the nature of the historical "matter" to which it is applied. We must assume here that meaningful comparisons over time are possible.[3] The

2. A good example of such confusion is the curious hendiadys "stability *and* continuity" which a recent author uses extensively in referring to the ancientness of our conception of deity. See Gerhard Lenski, *The Religious Factor* (New York, 1961), pp. 304, 306ff.

3. Comparisons over time are seldom unproblematic. It is felt at times that quantitative comparisons are more definite than qualitative comparisons. The distinction between the two is far from unambiguous, and the proposition is open to doubt. "Quantitative" presumably means amenable to measurement. Certain phenomena in history, particularly economic history, are regarded as "quantitative" in their very essence. This is conspicuously true of output, prices, wages, interest rates, income shares, capital stock, and many kindred things. It is true, however, that in order to interpret the change in any of the factors listed, very often recourse must be had to other factors that one will hesitate to describe as quantitative. Moreover, there are many elements of economic life that are but imperfectly quantitative in the sense that only their ordinal values can be established, and even those only in certain favorable circumstances. Still more important is the fact that most of the time even clearly "quantitative" concepts must be redefined for purposes of mensuration. This is particularly true of the application to historical reality of analytical models. Thus, to give an example, the concept of equilibrium in the balance of payments, even

problem then is to establish in what historically significant sense the results yielded by such comparisons may be described as continuous and discontinuous. Before one can approach this problem, however, some persistent misunderstandings must be laid to rest. In our thinking about processes of change, the speed at which the transformation takes place — its rate of change — often occupies a central place. But rate of change is a mathematical concept. It is not surprising therefore that, whenever continuity of historical events is spoken of, the mathematical concept of continuity, clearly or intuitively, is likely to be present in the speaker's mind. This has been a source of considerable confusion. Philosophers, historians, social scientists — they all have been influenced by the concept. Hence a few remarks on the relevance, or rather the irrelevance, of the mathematical concept of continuity to the historian's work cannot be dispensed with.

The mathematician's continuity has the indubitable advantage of being an unambiguous concept, even though it can be defined in a variety of more or less stringent fashions. Here is one of the possible definitions.[4]

---

though a clear quantitative concept in principle, is likely to be redefined in terms of certain movements of gold and short-term capital. Short-term capital, which analytically must refer to the intentions of investors, must in turn be redefined in empirical research in terms of actual durations of investment or in terms of types of credit used. The redefined concept may be viewed as sufficiently close to the original, but the two are not identical and the gap between them is never fully bridged. If the gap is too wide, the redefinition will be rejected as unsuccessful or inappropriate. In the following pages a good deal will be said about continuity in the sense of stability in the rate of change. But unless ways have been devised to define and redefine changing events in such a way as to make it meaningful to apply to them the notion of speed, and to render possible comparisons of the rapidity with which change takes place at varying points of time, the concept of the rate of change, as well as the concept of continuity based on it, will become inapplicable. The point is not only that there are vast areas of human history, such as the whole field of intellectual history, which are ill suited to that particular concept of continuity. A momentous problem is created even with regard to areas of historical research that are "quantitative" par excellence by the historical change in the yardsticks used for measuring aggregate magnitudes, such as industrial output. The index-number problem is a very specific difficulty in problems of measurement of economic growth. But it is useful to keep in mind the fact that whatever the concept of continuity chosen, and whatever the area to which it is applied, the validity of the concept must depend on our ability to construct meaningful temporal comparisons.

4. James M. Hyslop, *Real Variable* (Edinburgh–London, 1960), p. 45. Hyslop

If $f(x)$ is defined in an interval $a \leq x \leq b$, of which x_0 is an interior point, then $f(x)$ is said to be continuous at the point x_0, if $\lim f(x) = f(x_0)$; in other words, if the limit of $f(x)$ when $x \to x_0$ exists and is equal to the value of $f(x)$ at x_0.

This definition can be rendered even more simply by describing a continuous function as one that is "dense everywhere" in the sense of not having, strictly speaking, any contiguous points. For between any two points of such a function an infinite number of additional points can be placed. Stated still more simply, a continuous function is one that can be drawn in its entirety without lifting pencil from paper and which accordingly shows neither "gaps" nor "jumps." [5]

In his book *Die Prinzipien der Wärmelehre*, Ernst Mach, after offering a definition of continuity that is very similar to those discussed in the preceding paragraphs, described it as a "fiction" or as an "arbitrary conceptual construct," and declared it to be altogether unobjectional as such. Yet he went on to say: "The scientist who is not merely concerned with pure mathematics must ask himself whether there is something in nature that corresponds to such a fiction." [6] The somewhat uncertain mood in which the question was asked presumably adumbrated the advent of the new era in physics. But while the attitude of modern physicists to continuity and divisibility has failed to affect historical thinking, and at any rate has as little relevance within the present context as the biologist's views on organic growth,[7] Mach's question is precisely the one which *mutatis mutandis* a historian must ask. Are there historical events that can be said to be continuous within the meaning of the mathematical definitions of the term?

There is one tradition in which the broadest possible affirmative answer to this question is given. This is Kant's deducing the con-

---

goes on to provide a slightly modified definition of continuity for the two end points of the interval.

5. Edward Kasner and James Newman, *Mathematics and the Imagination* (New York, 1940), pp. 54–55; and R.G.D. Allen, *Mathematical Analysis for Economists* (London, 1947), pp. 100–101.

6. Ernst Mach, *Die Prinzipien der Wärmelehre, historisch-kritisch entwickelt*, 3rd ed. (Leipsig, 1919), p. 71.

7. The same is true of the modern mathematical elaborations of the continuity concept, which have made no impact upon social scientists or historians.

tinuous character of all empirical phenomena from the continuity of time and space within which those phenomena necessarily occur.[8] This view was not original with Kant. As Schopenhauer rightly remarks, Kant's position is virtually identical with that of Aristotle, who derived the continuity of change from the recognition of time and space as *quanta continua,* as infinitely divisible magnitudes.[9]

This indeed is the application of the mathematical concept of continuity, and the step from the concept to empirical data may seem invitingly short. To give an example: Those processes of historical change which, at least in principle, are capable of some quantitative redefinition can be presented as a time series of sorts. Such time series usually appear as unbroken lines. If they do not, the observable "gaps" may represent lacunae of information or a change in the unit of measurement, in which case they do not detract from the continuity of events. Alternatively, and more importantly, they can mean cases of temporary nonexistence of events that the time series has categorized into conceptual unity. If our time series depicts a century's output of cotton yarn, there may have been several depression years during which output had fallen to zero. Yet one may well interpret such periods as ones during which the curve of output coincided with the abscissa, along which the "infinitely divisible time" is measured. The curve, then, is still continuous because it can be drawn "without taking pencil off paper." It appears to be infinitely divisible at all points.

Nevertheless, to say that all time series are continuous in this sense is hardly the kind of answer which Mach expected to his question, that is to say, as empirical evidence for the "existence in nature" — and society — of phenomena corresponding to the mathematical concept of continuity. There is a natural, yet fallacious, tendency to extend the properties of a measuring system to the measured object. As Mach pointed out, "one must not assume that everything that is true of a sign, i.e., the number, will necessarily be true of what

8. Immanuel Kant, *Kritik der reinen Vernunft,* ed. Wilhelm Weischedel (n.d., n.p.), II, 210–211.
9. Arthur Schopenhauer, *Über die vierfache Wurzel des Satzes vom zureichenden Grunde, Sämtliche Werke* (Leipzig, 1937), I, 94–95; and Aristotle, *Physics,* V. 3–4 and VI.1–6. Let us abstract here from Aristotle's important distinction between continuity of time and continuity of modification (VIII.8).

is designated by that number." [10] A solar year is indeed infinitely divisible. But the historical time of a year, even though it is measured in terms of the earth's revolution around the sun, neither is capable of nor calls for infinite subdivisions. The divisibility of historical time must find its limits in the human ability to perceive decreasing spans of time. It will find a still sooner limit in the historian's interest in perceiving events occurring within extremely short periods. History certainly is "finite downward." [11]

One must be deceived by neither metaphors nor conventions. When a historian speaks of a "fateful moment" in the history of a country, as likely as not he has in mind a period of weeks or months, if not years. We may be able to determine a minute's output of cotton yarn, but even the efficiency expert in the spinnery may disdain such information. No historian, economic or otherwise, will have his attention arrested by the fluctuations of output over the course of a minute. If he studies seasonal fluctuations he may very well pay much heed to monthly or even weekly data. Students of variations in the productivity of labor in the course of a labor day naturally concentrated on data on hourly output. But whether an output series is based on annual, monthly, or any other figures, the "continuous" time series — the curve of output drawn across the diagram — is nothing but a convention. The historical curve consists of discrete empirical points. The continuous appearance of the curve implies a knowledge about the course of events in the intervals that cannot be substantiated.

To say this is not to deny the usefulness of the convention. It is illuminating indeed to transform the original data by fitting a continuous function to them. Such a transformation is, of course, not peculiar to time series and has nothing to do with the concept of time as a *quantum continuum*. A continuous function can be fitted for many purposes, one of them being precisely the calculation of

10. Mach, p. 76.

11. It seems that the physicist's attitude differs only in degree from that of the historian. Bridgman surmised that "it may turn out that . . . nature will appear to be finite downward." Percy W. Bridgman, *The Logic of Modern Physics* (New York, 1948), p. 94. Bridgman's description of mathematical continuity as a "mental construct" does not seem to be far removed from Mach's "fiction" (*ibid.*, p. 5).

an average rate of change that is implied in the empirical data. It will be noted, however, that the previously stated sequence is reversed. The question as we posed it was the meaning of continuity with respect to comparisons involving *inter alia* the historical rate of change. Now it appears that at least at times we postulate continuity in order to determine the rate of change, because in this fashion it is easier to order the data and to express some of their properties simply and effectively. Obviously, performing such operations cannot possibly be regarded as a positive answer to Mach's question; as a valid test, that is, through which the empirical fact of continuity can be established. Quite the contrary is true. The Aristotelian concept of continuity presented as a general statement about historical phenomena does not lend itself to empirical ascertainment. It is no more than a definitional exercise.

Unfortunately, it has not been treated as such. Very bold and very far-reaching conclusions have been drawn from the concept with regard to the nature and mutual relationship of empirically observable phenomena. In the process, by a convenient *quaternio terminorum*, the meaning of the term has been subtly changed. In addition, following the familiar inferential course from "nature" to "natural law," or from "fact" to "norm," some highly positive values came to be attached to it. First, "continuity" was said to be inevitably present at all times and in all places. Second, it was also declared to be a good thing in terms of "1066 and all that." Obversely, the concept of discontinuity was brushed aside as logically absurd, nonexistent in reality, and ethically reprehensible to boot.

This process, familiar as it is, is hardly good scientific form. It is not pleasant, therefore, to see Schopenhauer blandly identify the "law of continuity" with "the gradualness of all change." [12] Whether Kant got his concept of continuity from Aristotle or from Leibniz is of little interest in the present context It is, however, worth pointing out not only that Leibniz' "continuity" is very Aristotelian, but also that no one could be more emphatic in proclaiming the "gradualness of change" as the "law of continuity" and as a fully verified empirical fact. The famous passage in the *New Essays on Understanding* begins as follows:

12. Schopenhauer, *Über die vierfache Wurzel*, I, 95.

En un mot, les perceptions insensibles sont d'un aussi grand usage dans la pneumatique que les corpuscules insensibles le sont dans la physique, et qu'il est également déraisonnable de rejeter les uns et les autres sous pretexte qu'elles sont hors de la portée de nos sens. Rien ne se fait tout d'un coup, et c'est une de mes grandes maximes et des plus verifiées que *la nature ne fait jamais des sauts*: ce que j'appelois la loy de la continuité.[13]

It is one thing to say that *perceptions insensibles* are of great usefulness; it is another to assert gradualness of change as one of the great philosopher's and mathematician's "best verified propositions." The transition in the preceding quotation from the former to the latter must seem all the more remarkable for not being a gradual one. But the proposition that nature makes no leaps, elevated to the rank of a "law of continuity" and repeated time and again in its Latin version — *natura non facit saltum* — did not fail to exercise its influence upon intellectual history in the two hundred years that have elapsed since the publication of Leibniz' *Essay*.[14] Leibniz had indeed referred to his "infinitesimally small magnitudes" as *fictions utiles*; he distinguished carefully between *petites perceptions* and apperceptions, as he regarded the concept of infinity in the light of "possibility," that is "a necessary condition of actual phenomena and a criterion of their reality" — a clear thought couched in ambiguous language and purporting to describe infinity as a tool of cognition of reality.[15] As such it fitted well with the working assumption of classical physics which postulated infinite divisibility of all physical processes. The methodological function of these concepts was the very reason for which the claim of verification was inherently impossible of establishment. Yet it was Leibniz himself who favored the ensuing confusion by speaking of "verifications" and by presenting examples gleaned from the world of finite perceptions, such as the transition from sleep to wakefulness.[16]

13. *Nouveaux essais sur l'entendement par l'auteur du système de l'harmonie preestablie*, reprinted in *Die philosophischen Schriften von Gottfried Wilhelm Leibniz*, C. J. Gerhardt, ed. (Berlin, 1882), V, 40. See also "Tout va par degrés dans la nature, et rien par saut" (p. 455).

14. Written between 1700 and 1709, the *Essay* was not published until 1765.

15. Ernst Cassirer, *Leibniz' System in seinen wissenschaftlichen Grundlagen* (Marburg, 1902), pp. 203, 207.

16. It is significant that a psychophysical state was mentioned indiscriminately on a par with mathematical constructs of equality as a special case of inequality, or

Once continuity came to be considered an empirical concept, it was natural to relax its original stingency by redefining it into the state of "fairly large similarity" or "fairly considerable proximity" between sets of discrete phenomena, states, or events. Kant very clearly recognized the sleight of hand — or mind — involved in viewing, say, the botanical classification of plants as an empirical counterpart of the *lex continui*.[17] But in the underworld — or at least in the flatland — of everyday language, the discontinuous "jump" from one continuity concept to the other remained unnoticed, and the hybrid conceptual mass was gladly welcomed to the field of social sciences as a most palatable mixture of scientific cognition and social desirability. Alfred Marshall chose the gnomic phrase as an inscription over the entrance gate to his *Principles*. There it did triple duty by referring to Marshall's effective use of calculus as a methodological device, to his belief in the general fundamental gradualness of economic structures and processes of social change, and to his rejection of certain economic policies that seemed to involve an unduly high rate of change. Inevitably, in the minds of readers, the first reference was called upon to lend spiritual support to the other two.

II

Thus, the historian who has gone out to scrutinize the mathematical concept of continuity travels far into strange lands and still is likely to return from his journey empty-handed. Continuity in this

---

of parallelism as a special case of convergence, and so on. See Gottfried Wilhelm Leibniz, *Gott, Geist, Güte, Eine Auswahl aus seinen Werken* (Gütersloh, 1947), pp. 251–252: Also *Essais*, p. 47.

17. Kant, *Kritik der reinen Vernunft*, p. 577. Leibniz, too, referred to the smallness of differences which separate one zoological or botanical species from another (*Essais*, p. 455). Significantly, the Latin version of "Nature makes no leaps" appears to have been used for the first time by Linnaeus in his *Philosophia botanica* (1751). An additional curiosity lay in the fact that the shifted concept was based on contiguity of events or phenomena while, in the mathematical concept, no two points could be truly contiguous. It is another question that in many cases it is the grossness of our perceptive apparatus that creates the semblance of continuity where more accurate machinery would disclose discrete series. But then "contiguous" and "discrete" are arbitrary terms created *ad hoc*. As we shall see further below in discussing "broken" periodicities, the historian can profitably establish "contiguities" between events that are separated by long intervals of time.

sense, or senses, does not appear to be a tool historians can profitably put to work; even when it appears in the empirical guise as gradualness of change, it eludes the crucial problem of mensuration and is so thickly covered with the metaphysical paint of inevitability as to be destitute of all usefulness. In fact, after having busied himself with the concept, a historian may well want to purge himself from the contagion of fallacies, biases, and prejudices which have grown from and around the concept. But should he also purge himself of the concept altogether? The temptation may be strong. Yet by succumbing to it the historian may find himself at a loss for an appropriate lens to view sets of historical sequences in which he cannot help being interested. Scientific terms can be created and banned by the scholar's arbitrary fiat. But our dependence on the existing vocabulary is great.[18] So is the danger that, by excising the term "continuity" from the historian's dictionary of conventional English, less attention will be paid to a complex of problems which, today, have particular actuality in studies of economic history because of our general preoccupation with the problems of economic development of backward countries. It is therefore advisable, after having dismissed the mathematical concept and its various illegitimate progeny, to take a closer look at some of the usages of the concept of continuity which can be viewed as descriptions of empirical reality.

It would seem that five concepts stand out from a large number of possible constructs: (*a*) constancy of direction; (*b*) periodicity of events; (*c*) endogenous change; (*d*) length of causal regress; (*e*) stability of the rate of change. Each of the five concepts refers to historical change and has some points of contact with the others. In fact, the relation at times seems quite close. As a result, the siblings have often been confused with each other. As said before, the present writer happens to be primarily interested in the fifth concept. It is continuity, or rather discontinuity in the specific sense of instability in the rate of economic growth, which serves as a most useful tool in the study of processes of industrialization. To prevent misunder-

18. Alfred Marshall in his wisdom used to stress the need for continuity in this respect. He wrote: "Continuity of tradition is important everywhere; it is nowhere more important than in our use of terms." Marshall, "Distribution and Exchange" (1898), an article reprinted in Alfred Marshall, *Principles of Economics*, 9th var. ed., C. W. Guillebaud, ed. (London–New York, 1961) II, 231.

standings and to isolate continuity in this sense, the five concepts will be discussed in order.

(*a*) Constancy of direction in the evolution of a historical phenomenon is readily associated with continuity. To start with hardly perceptible origins and to pursue the process of growth and expansion to its culmination is the historian's favorite task. Here, to use Goethe's phrase, lies his *wahrer Himmel*. It is a concept that often is blandly used in cases least adapted to quantification, but at the same time it does not call for more than very general ordinal comparisons. Most of the "theories" of historical progress pivot on this concept. H. T. Buckle's view of the steady diffusion of knowledge and comprehension is one of the many instances that are both vague and magnificent: truth marches on "always advancing, never receding." [19] Clearly, the concept need not appear in this chemically pure form. Some setbacks, even fairly regular setbacks, can be easily combined with the concept. This is how the "irresistible" spreading and deepening of democratic government was seen before 1914. But it is precisely the possibility of such a combination that clearly indicates a separation of continuity in this sense from continuity conceived as periodicity. The latter acts as the discontinuous element, breaking the constancy of the direction. So does the change from "rise" to "decline" which starts a new directional sequence, but may be an integral part in a periodic pattern. Similarly, continual change in the same direction can be brought about through endogenous or exogenous processes. Even so, the concept of continuity that focuses upon the length of causal regress does not in any way entail unidirectional evolution. And, finally, constancy of the direction of change does not stipulate constancy in the rate at which the change proceeds. It is compatible with wild fluctuations in that rate.

(*b*) Aristotle used to regard rotary motion as truly continuous — continuous in some more specific sense than the continuity derived from the "continuous" nature of time. It is indeed a time-honored approach to history (or at least to certain segments of history) to view it (or them) as moving along a circular path. From the observation of forms of government by Greek philosophers and

19. See, for instance, Henry T. Buckle, *History of Civilization in England* (New York, 1882), I, 154–155.

historians via Vico's *corsi e ricorsi* to the modern study of the business cycle, to say nothing of very modern and very ambitious attempts to draw circles of whole civilizations, the concern has been with sequences that show periodic recurrence over time. It is the essence of this view that present — or, at any rate, subsequent — experience is understood as a reiteration of past experience, as an articulated movement through more or less well-defined stages, the causal mechanism of propulsion from stage to stage remaining essentially unaltered from rotation to rotation. There may be lively change within each cycle, but the continuity of cyclical repetition focuses on the absence of change.

This view is incompatible with the neo-Kantian image of history as a succession of specific and individual events.[20] By the same token,

20. If we may forget Rickert's grudging admission through the backdoor of his system of that clodhopping conceptual stranger upon whom he bestowed the inelegant name of "relativ-historischer Begriff." See Heinrich Rickert, *Die Grenzen der naturwissenschaftlichen Begriffsbildung, Eine logische Einteilung der historischen Wissenschaften* (Tübingen, 1902), pp. 490–495. But perhaps the concept is worth keeping in mind. It will be remembered that Rickert did not first investigate empirical historical reality and then arrive at the conclusion that it *was* "unique and individual." He left that thankless task to his less sophisticated disciples. Rickert rather defined *a priori* empirical reality as *"nature* if it was viewed with regard to the general" and as *"history* if it was viewed with regard to the particular and the individual" (*Die Grenzen*, Tübingen, 1921, p. 173). The problem was to bestow a name upon a certain selection of phenomena. Starting from his definition, Rickert is in a sense right in protesting that it is "simply logically nonsensical" — *einfach logisch widersinnig* — to try to operate in historical work with general concepts when the task is to understand the reality in its individuality and particularity (p. 174). But under the circumstances the introduction of a generalizing concept — "relativ-historischer Begriff" — into Rickert's view of history seems to testify effectively to the extreme difficulty, if not logical impossibility, of understanding any individuality without the aid of generalizations. The main trouble presumably lies with the belief that empirical reality can be interestingly and importantly treated by pitching "the general" versus "the particular," whereas empirical historical research operates with "gradations of generality," changing from one level of generality to another so that the general and the individual appear as highly relative terms. Something that is general when viewed "downward" may well be seen as individual when the student's eye looks "upward." For the rest, nothing seems more easily forgotten than the fact that Rickert's history is not conceived as *all* history in the sense of being a *comprehensive* past record of man's social life, but only as a specific segment thereof, artificially excised by the knife of a very special approach. The neo-Kantians themselves were eager to abandon the clarity of a stringent methodological position and to discourse as though their "history" has been, or

periodicity does assert the possibility of a scientific approach to history, unless it be pushed to an extreme point at which it either denies altogether or at least greatly reduces the values of all historical interest. On the one hand, the existence of similarities in historical flow is the condition for testing explanatory hypotheses; and to assert periodicity is to assert similarities. But absolute periodicity working with pendulum-like regularity would lead us once more to Schopenhauer's monotonous parade of human bodies which are born, grow, decay, and die as the earth continues upon its diurnal and annual rotations. Whether historical interest can still be attached to such a course of events must no doubt depend *inter alia* on the nature of the cycle, particularly on its total amplitude and the amplitudes of its constituent parts in terms of life spans of those human bodies. It was Schiller who surmised that "alles in ewigem Wechsel kreist," that everything moves along the circle of eternal change. But if the circle is measurable in aeons, the historian may safely neglect its existence. In forming historical concepts one must beware of extremes. What makes continuity as periodicity a worthwhile tool of historical

---

rather should have been, everybody else's "history." Otherwise, the exaggerated emphasis and the emotional tone of the asseverations that historical events are "unique" would be quite ununderstandable.

This footnote is long and may seem to have strayed far afield from problems of historical continuity. This, however, is not the case. For all the difficulties of Rickert's concept of history are nicely epitomized in his treatment of continuity. On the one hand, Rickert uses the concept of mathematical continuity as *the only way* of demonstrating the infinite multiplicity — *die Unübersehbarkeit* — of "all reality in time and space," and hence our inability to treat reality "exhaustively." But after using the concept of mathematical continuity for inferences regarding empirical reality, he proceeds to reject the concept because time and space present a "homogeneous" continuity that is not really *unübersehbar* (presumably in the sense that every event can be generalized by reference to spatial and temporal coordinates), whereas the reality that contains the new and the unknown should be regarded as "heterogeneous continuity" (*ibid.*, p. 28). This is indeed a curious procedure. One might paraphrase Schopenhauer's famous statement on causality and wonder whether mathematical continuity is a cab in which a historian can travel for a brief stretch and then send it home, apparently without paying the fare. But what then is this concept of heterogeneous continuity which is designed to replace the one that had so quickly fallen from grace? We are told: "To start with, every real development is a continuum. When the development becomes divided in certain essential stages, the *gradual* transitions between the stages are eliminated. But the historical science cannot tolerate such gaps and must fill them with causal will (*mit kausalem Wollen*) in such a way that the individual stages are both separated from each

analysis is manageable length of the periods, and also the fact that periodicity requires abstraction and generalization: a certain complex of phenomena must be pared out from the mass of kindred historical tissue. It is precisely the finding of similarities amidst the differences, of recurrences amidst the novelties, which requires the historian in each case to explore the limits separating the one from the other. So viewed, periodicity in history is an object of very unmonotonous study.

Continuity as periodicity is a concept that in most respects is independent from, which means compatible with, the presence or absence of continuity in the other three senses still to be discussed. Clearly, it has no implications at all concerning the rate of change from one stage to the other along the circumference of the circle. To give an example, the transition from one form of government (*Staatsform*) to another, say from democracy to ochlocracy, may take place through gradual degeneration or it may be marked by a violent revolution (so, for instance, a change from tyranny to aristocracy or from oligarchy to democracy).[21] Similarly, an economy may pass almost

other with regard to the values involved *and* tied to each other by dint of the causal nexus" (*ibid.*, p. 326). It is fairly clear that the concept of continuity that finally emerges from this process is related to our concept (*d*) above: it is the causal regress that constitutes the stuff continuity seems to be made of. On the other hand, it is much less clear what kind of continuity — in Rickert's mind — was inherent in historical events before the historian broke it up by carving the notches of the individual stages. Is it simply the continuity of the flow of time that is readmitted once more; or is it the idea of gradualness of change? The latter supposition finds some support in the preceding quotation. except that nothing is said at all as to the type of measurement in terms of which gradualness might be defined. But it is futile to ask the question, for Rickert's reasoning rushes on like Gogol's celebrated troika that storms over the Russian plain without giving an answer as to its where and whence. And all one can conclude from Rickert's confused preoccupation with continuity is that our first concept (periodicity) is altogether alien to him and, we may assume, to the study of history, since it belongs to that of nature. Furthermore, that causal nexus is regarded as one possible concept of historical continuity. Finally, if gradualness of change is used by Rickert for intimating still another concept of continuity, nothing is said concerning its empirical meaning and validity. One then is left with the disheartening feeling that, on the one hand, Rickert's are *a priori* constructs which have nothing to do with the substance of historical processes. But, on the other hand, the nature of historical substance is prejudged in a way that makes refutation impossible and, in addition, the redundance of such a refutation is subtly suggested.

21. It is another matter that "revolution" once used to mean "periodicity," and

imperceptibly from rising prosperity over a high plateau of income generation into slow decline in a long and shallow valley. A change from an "up" to a "down" naturally implies a change in the sign of the rate of change of our *mensuranda*. Still if we abstract from the sign — as we do in a political cycle when we may refuse to evaluate its individual stages — we may speak of stability or near stability of the rate of change. Alternatively, a dramatic financial panic may separate the boom from the slump. Something more about this will be said later, but revolutions and panics, as long as they can be said to have their wonted place in the recurrence of things, are as much an integral part of continuity as periodicity, as are its more tranquil and less conspicuous emanations.

Then there is the possible relation to continuity as endogenous change and as the length of regress. A historian may begin by observing the periodical return of sequences of events. He would be a poor master of his craft, if he failed to investigate the forces which propel the development from arc to arc along its rotary path. One would be tempted to say that he must add analysis to description, were it not for the fact that our usual distinction between description and analysis is a rather clumsy colloquialism. A wholly unanalytical description is fairly unthinkable, and a reasonably complete description is bound to include a reasonably comprehensive analysis. Obviously, such analysis of the cycle can operate with factors that are considered either endogenous or exogenous. At any rate, the concept of continuity as periodicity will frequently involve an examination of the causal chain which extends throughout the cycle. As said before, Rickert appears to think that it is the links of the causal chain which constitute historical continuity. It seems to make very good sense to speak of "temporal continuity" or "spatio-temporal continuity" when the purpose is to explain causality.[22] But there is little to gain by forming a historical concept at that level of generality. Presumably, every historical event can be followed back to the "origin of origins

---

this not only with reference to celestial bodies. Augustine, in combating the "ridiculous notion" (*ludibrium*) of a cyclical course of events, used to describe the latter as *circuitus temporum* or *revolutio saeculorum*. Augustine, *De civitate dei*, XII.14.

22. See R. B. Braithwaite, *Scientific Explanation* (New York, 1960), pp. 308, 310, 317.

and beyond." But this all-pervasive "continuity" is as meaningless operationally as the asserted ubiquitousness of the mathematical concept of continuity. Some specific criteria are necessary if we are to view the length of the causal chain as a finite historical phenomenon. But, in this sense, continuity as periodicity does not imply any statement concerning the duration of the full cycle. Nor is any specific length of the chain in terms of the number of stages within the cycle implied in the concept of periodicity: a cycle that passes through half a dozen stages is no "more continuous" than the one possessing the minimum number of two.

On the other hand, the concept of periodicity appears to approach that of causal regress once we turn away from the individual cycle and begin to explore its historical depth by moving back from one antecedent to another It does seem meaningful to say that the farther we can probe into the receding past, and the greater the number of ascertainable recurrences we find on the way, the greater is the continuity of the cyclical series. This is so because, despite all attempts to exclude the case of the zero rate of change, the ancientness of the present (including *le présent historique*) still lingers in the back of our minds. Nevertheless, the two concepts (periodicity and length of causal regress) do no more than merely touch each other. We may well distinguish between unbroken and broken periodicities. It is one thing to view, say, a century of economic life as a series of ups and downs, every point of time throughout the period having its definite place within one of the successive cycles. It is another to speak of periodicity with regard to recurrent series of events which are separated from each other by long periods that are quite irrelevant from the point of view of the concept. Most of the historical designations that begin with "neo" are of the latter kind, the intervening periods being only negatively, if at all, definable as parts of a "cycle."

Thus, between the successive spurts of government-induced rapid growth in Russia, there were long decades, if not centuries, during which stagnation or decline or relatively slow growth was taking place. Absence of rapid growth was the common characteristic of the intervals. On the other hand, every recurring spurt of rapid growth passed through a number of sequences beginning with the military pressures — often self-imposed — which the government

27

translated into economic pressures upon the population, the spurt finding its end either in the physical exhaustion of the population or in its rising resistance to the continuation of pressure. Another, again negative, way of describing the interval between the spurts may run in terms of absence of military pressures, which meant the relative absence of aggressive designs or defensive fears, or perhaps the ability of the government to solve its power problems with the help of existing economic facilities. The continuity, therefore, consists in the periodic recreation of similar situations, but the causal connection between the individual recurring complexes may be very tenuous and, at any rate, can justly remain outside the purview of the historian. For him, the value of this continuity concept lies in the circumstance that it serves to isolate periods that lie far apart from each other. Therefore it is precisely by neglecting much of the intervening history that the historian is able to make certain situations appear comparable to each other and by so doing create an explanatory mechanism. The latter, incidentally, may be used to move forward or backward in time, so that earlier situations may tend to cast light on later situations or vice versa. Analysis of several recurrences may be mutually reinforcing. That is one of the reasons for which the term "prediction," now in favor with a good many writers, has such a hollow ring when applied to large areas of historical research, and had best remain unused.

(c) Endogenous change is one that is described in terms of a homogeneous set of factors. A concept of continuity in this sense is essentially qualitative and derives from the scholar's approach to his subject through a number of particular theoretical constructs and from his inability to formulate a truly general theory within which there would be no room for exogenous factors. Thus, to give an example, entrepreneurial innovations seen as a driving force in economic development or business cycles appear as an exogenous factor — hence as a discontinuity because the biological or psychological or other factors that are said to determine the relevant entrepreneurial decisions are seen as alien to the economic factor in terms of which the preinnovational and the postinnovational situations are dealt with.[23] Continuity and discontinuity in this sense naturally

23. This is not to say, however, that invention or innovation is necessarily to

are compatible with the other four concepts under discussion here, but should be kept apart from them. It may be noted in particular that in the preceding example the discontinuity of an exogenous change is likely to be accompanied by discontinuities conceived as a considerable change in the rate of change of economic magnitudes. But even in this case the connection is by no means a necessary one, as can be inferred from the discussion under (*e*) below.

(*d*) Enough has been said so far to stress the differences that exist between continuity as periodicity and continuity as a long causal chain. With regard to the latter, it should suffice to set it off against continuity conceived as constancy or relative constancy in the rate of change. As mentioned before, continuity understood in terms of causal chains must mean more than simply the fact that the existence of any given complex of events at any given time can be conceived as having been occasioned by events preceding it in time.[24] This connection of historical events is inherent in the very concept of history. Without it, history and the historian's task have no meaning. Our way of using words strongly suggests that this presumed intelligibility, or connectibility, of history might be described as continuity. Yet what is meant here is not a mental attitude which antedates and underlies all historical research, but concrete decisions to be taken in the process of research. The historian must decide to single out a certain occurrence as the "beginning" of the causal chain.[25]

---

be treated as a case of exogenous change. Marshall's statement on continuity in the preface to the eighth edition of his *Principles* (London, 1938), p. xiii, is a demonstration to the contrary.

24. To say this naturally does not in any way detract from the *interaction* exercised by events coexisting at a given moment. But these relationships do not seem to be pertinent to the concept or concepts of continuity.

25. In one of Chekhov's stories there is a beautiful intuitive expression of the transition from the general idea to the specific concept. A young seminarian had just seen an illiterate peasant woman profoundly moved by his recital of Peter's denials of Christ: "The past — he reflected — is connected with the present by an uninterrupted chain of events, one flowing from the other. And it seemed to him that a few minutes ago he caught a glimpse of both ends of that chain: As you touched one end, the other responded throbbing." Anton Chekhov, *Sobraniye sochinenii* (Collected Works), VII:1888–1891 (Moscow, 1956), 369. Chekhov is said to have regarded this very brief piece ("The Student") as one of his most finished products (p. 515). Also, I. A. Bunin, *O Chekhove* (On Chekhov; New York, 1955), p. 57.

Thus, in discussing the causes of the First World War, the historian may wish to start with the Franco-Prussian War; alternatively, he may select earlier or later events. In all cases, it will be his task to make the selection plausible in terms of the specific strength of the causal chain that is attached, link by link, to the "original" cause. He will have to show how it compares and intertwines with other chains that run in the same direction. There is little doubt that continuity is sometimes thought of in these terms, although the corresponding concept of discontinuity eludes our search. The point to make here, however, is that the length of the chain has no implication whatever for the material it is made of. In other words, leaving aside the unhistorical case of the infinitely rapid change that has no antecedents at all, any speed of development or any change in the speed of development is compatible with events or series of events whose roots can be usefully pursued back into the faraway past.

Thus, to give an obvious example, the causes of the Russian revolution of 1917 may be sought in the great war that broke out in 1914. They may be sought in the failure of the imperial regime to keep the promises granted in the course of the 1905 revolution and in the resentment engendered by Stolypin's attack upon the field commune. While accepting those causal factors, one can convincingly insist on the need for going back farther still and for exploring the formation of the anti-imperial creed of the Russian intelligentsia in the course of the preceding century, particularly in its second half. Yet in many respects that creed was only a reflection of the sentiments and resentments of the Russian peasantry and a consequence of the manner in which the emancipation of 1861 had left the peasantry in the possession of inadequate landholdings in the face of a rapidly increasing population. Even more important, the land hunger of large segments of the peasantry, anchored in the emancipation of the 1860s, must be considered one of the primary reasons for the success of the conspiracy contrived by the Bolshevik Party in the autumn of 1917. But the emancipation settlement itself was one of the tragically delayed actions of the Russian government. If the Decembrists had been successful in 1825, one may have expected perhaps not a sudden but almost certainly a gradual abolition of serfdom. And moving back another six decades or so, one comes to another crossroad in Russian history. It would have been natural for Cathering the Great — and would have greatly enhanced her claim to the attribute — to let the release of the gentry from service obligation (promulgated by Peter III) be followed by the restoration of the previous state of "black" peasantry, placing the peasants, that is to say, again under the immediate tutelage of the state. The Empress' imitation of the Swedish "reversion" (*reduktion*) would have removed the most important barrier to the country's industrial development and would have avoided the creation of an overpopulated and overtaxed countryside.

Parallel with the economic factor runs the political factor. The Decembrists' plans oscillated between a republic and a constitutional monarchy. Introduction of at least some elements of the latter under Alexander I or under Catherine would have started a movement away from absolutism; in the first half of the eighteenth century, the compact between Empress Anna and the members of high aristocracy would have accomplished this much, if the empress had not withheld her signature at the last moment. In discussing matters of that sort, normal rules of evidence are of little use, and the historian's judgment is called upon to decide whether a certain *conditio irrealis* does or does not constitute a grounded historical assumption. Recourse to reasonableness is precariously subjective. In this case, however, the answer seems easier than in others. It does make sense to maintain that both serfdom and absolutism in the eighteenth century were powerful currents in the causal stream that found its estuary in the revolution of 1917; and that in the absence of those currents the stream would have run dry long before the advent of this century.

Thus, the causal chain is in this case a rather long one. In other words, the historian who pursues the origins of the Russian revolution into a fairly remote past will find his efforts well rewarded. But continuity in this sense was perfectly compatible with the greatest possible suddenness of change which marked the events in Russia in 1917. It was likewise compatible with such great accelerations in the course of the historical process as were imparted by the abolition of serfdom and the related reforms in 1861. It would be easy indeed to provide other historical examples pointing in the same direction.

But the negative conclusion is clear enough. As was true of the concept of continuity as periodicity, continuity viewed as long causal regress also has no implications regarding continuity conceived as stability in the rate of change. The latter is a fully independent concept. It must be considered more closely before some general inferences regarding the formation of historical concepts can be drawn.

(*e*) It is obvious, as I have intimated before, that historical illustrations of this type of continuity — and discontinuity — can be most readily gleaned from the area of social statistics, particularly from demographic and economic data. Price movements, changes in large aggregates such as national wealth or national income, growth in the individual sectors of the economy such as agricultural crops, transportation services, and industrial output offer some natural examples. With respect to all these, it is in principle possible to compute the rate of change and accordingly to raise the question about the continuous or discontinuous behavior of that rate. To be sure, lack of data may frustrate the computation. The result may be subject to considerable uncertainties because of structural changes that produce the so-called index-number problem. But within the present context there is no need to go further into this sort of difficulty. On the other hand, the concept of continuity calls for further clarification if its historical significance is to be properly appreciated.

For the purposes of such clarification, it would seem useful to restrict the concept of continuity in such a way as to make it denote "gradualness of change." This is obviously a narrower concept than stability in the rate of change. There is, however, no intention to reinforce, somewhat stealthily, the concept of continuity as stability in the rate of change by not allowing the latter to move too far away from zero. The reason for limiting continuity to the constancy of a *low* rate of change is historical rather than conceptual. The limitation is convenient because — as will be seen from the example chosen — much of the historical significance of the concept derives from viewing situations in which relatively low rates of change prevailed for some time with a fair degree of constancy. *Per contra*, the concept of discontinuity may be similarly restricted to the case of an increase in the rate of change from the previously maintained low level.

But in what terms shall the answer be sought and found? What rate is to be regarded as a low rate? What is a high rate? And what is the operational meaning of constancy of the rate? Whatever the persuasiveness of aphoristic asseverations, perfect stability over time in rates of change, be they high or low, hardly exists in real life. The problem is what variations in the rates can be neglected and what cannot; in other words, what variations are to be still regarded as "continuous" and what variations should be regarded as "discontinuous." It may be tempting to assume that this is merely a problem of an arbitrary choice of terminology. But to do so would be to evade the very essence of the historian's task. Let us explain this by selecting from the previously given list of illustrative possibilities the case of industrial output, that is to say, the growth of product of manufacturing industries and mining.

The period chosen extends from the end of the eighteenth century to the outbreak of the First World War. As we study the available output series for the individual countries of Europe, we observe, with increasing clarity as we move from decade to decade, the reflection in the data of cyclical fluctuations. We may confine our interest to them and examine the degree of continuity in the sense of stability of the rate of change as it combined with continuity in the sense of periodicity. The result will be a morphology of cycles from a particular point of view. The value of such a study will depend upon the intensity with which various elements in the economy tended to vary with the variations in the rates. If, for instance, the flow of innovations, or the life span of individual enterprises, or changes in the scale of plant were associated with the speed and accelerations and decelerations in the growth of output that appeared in the course of the cycle, then it should be possible to formulate some tentative patterns and use them as hypotheses in further research.

The point becomes even clearer if we shift the focus of interest away from cyclical fluctuations and direct our lens to long-term change in industrial output. The following generalization then becomes warranted: In a number of major countries of Europe, industrial development did not proceed at an even pace. On the contrary, after a lengthy period of fairly low rates of growth came a moment of more or less sudden increase in the rates, which then remained at the accelerated level for a considerable period. That was the period of the great spurt in the respective countries' industrial development. Its beginning in several cases coincided with the lower turning point of the cycle, and it benefited in its earlier stages from the forces of cyclical recovery. But the phenomenon in its entirety was altogether different from the cycle. In fact, once the spurt in a given country had gathered momentum, it was likely to continue through the next international depression, unaffected or almost unaffected by it.

The crucial observation, then, concerns a specific "kink" in the curve of industrial output (drawn on a semilogarithmic scale). The rate of growth in the period preceding the kink may have amounted to, say, 2 percent and will have risen in the following period to 6 percent. The rates and the margin between them in the "pre-kink" and the "post-kink" periods appear to vary depending on the degree of relative backwardness of the country at the time of the acceleration. The more backward the country, the sharper was the angle of the kink. There are exceptions to, and deviations from, the pattern in the historical reality of nineteenth-century Europe. But they are of little concern in the context of this essay. What matters here is to establish the meaning and the value of the concept of continuity as related to the rate of historical change.

First of all, it should be noted that, if the historian wishes to observe the specific discontinuity of the kink, he must look for it and he must know how to find it. He will, therefore, have no use for computations of rates of growth given by decades or even quinquennia, but will operate with appropriately selected periods. In other words, he will keep in mind the fact that any curve can be "smoothed" by the use of an appropriate technique in such a way as to eliminate any sign of discontinuity: the constant slope of a fitted curve over a considerable period may easily create the impression of complete lack of changeability. An historian who is out to find stability *à tout prix* has many tools at his disposal to attain his goal, as well as the psychic satisfaction that goes along with it. Furthermore, in addition to selecting proper periods, an appropriate universe must be chosen. If the seat of the great spurt lies in the area of manufacturing, it would be inept to try to locate the discontinuity by scrutinizing data on large aggregate magnitudes such as national income or gross national product.

Clearly, in a very backward country where agriculture accounts for most of the national income produced, even a very considerable and very sudden upsurge in the rate of growth of manufacturing will be unable to produce more than a gentle ripple in the rate of growth of national income. By the time industry has become bulky enough to affect the larger aggregate, the exciting period of the great spurt may well be over.[26]

But these directions for how to go about discovering in historical reality the discontinuity of the great spurt do not yet provide an answer to the question of what changes in the rate of growth are to be regarded as discontinuous or why a search for such discontinuities should be instituted at all. The curious thing is that the two questions can be settled, if at all, by a single answer.

I mentioned before that the sharpness of the kink and a country's degree of backwardness are positively correlated. This does not, however, exhaust the complex of elements related to, and varying directly with, the sudden acceleration in the growth of output. The most important among those elements are the scale of plant and the size of enterprise, the emphasis on producers' goods as against consumers' goods, the concomitant pressure on the levels of consumption of the population, the relative lag of agricultural output, and the use of special institutional arrangements designed to effect a redistribution in the flow of national income as between consumption and investment and, thereby, to cover the capital needs of the nascent industry. Again, there are exceptions and deviations, but the available information suggests that there is a sufficient number of important cases in which the presence of these elements and the intensity with which they appeared were functionally connected with the acceleration in the

26. Walt Rostow's failure to appreciate this point has detracted greatly from the operational significance of his concept of the take-off, which in principle is closely related to the concept of the great spurt as developed by this writer. But the attempt to locate the individual take-offs empirically through national-income statistics was bound to remain unsuccessful, even if, one or two exceptions apart, the long-term national-income statistics possessed some modicum of reliability, which unfortunately they do not as yet. A great deal of additional work, particularly on the conversion of current values to constant prices (deflation), is necessary before national-income series will begin to be usable for the purpose of analyzing long-range economic development. See W. W. Rostow, *The Stages of Economic Growth: A Non-Communist Manifesto* (Cambridge, Mass., 1960).

rate of output, that is, with the kink in the curve To put it differently, since in the master pattern all those elements can be readily shown to vary with the degree of a country's backwardness, the kink in the curve can be seen as one of several essential features of the process of industrial growth during certain periods in the history of the economy within which that growth occurs.[27] And this is indeed the answer designed to slay two questions in one sweep; but it requires some further elaboration.

The answer to the question why continuity — or rather its absence — in a series of industrial output should be a matter of interest to the historian lies precisely in the fact that occurrence of discontinuities in the series has been specifically associated with a number of other factors, which in their totality characterize an important stage in the process of industrialization. From the "observation" of the association, the historian inevitably has had to proceed to an "explanation," to an attempt that is, to pose further questions regarding the interrelation among the factors involved and possibly regarding the relation of those factors to others, still to be discovered. Most of the answers to these questions have been given in terms of the exigencies of the dominant technology as well as in terms of specific advantages inherent in the bigness of plant and enterprise and in the simultaneity of industrial development in a number of appropriately chosen branches of manufacturing. In the process, the historian has been moved to explore how policies of government and other institutions enhanced or obstructed, as the case may be, the operation of the basic economic factors that were intrinsically present in a backward country. And, finally, all historical propositions being "existential" rather than "general," the historian has been moved to establish the spatial and temporal boundaries for the applicability of his approach — a procedure in the course of which he may succeed in systematizing and incorporating at least some of the *prima facie* deviations and irregularities.

27. The lag of (nearly stable) agricultural output behind industrial output, which can be observed in industrial spurts in very backward areas, provides an interesting illustration of a specific continuity in the midst of a period marked by crucial discontinuities. For a less cursory description of the pattern of industrial development as referred to here, see Gerschenkron, *Economic Backwardness in Historical Perspective*, pp. 5–30.

Thus, starting from discontinuity in the form of a sudden acceleration in the rate of growth allows us to move from one question to the other, steadily widening and deepening, discovering and creating the nature of our *explicandum* and delimiting it at the same time. What better measure for the validity of a historical concept can there be than its fertility in research?

But what about the measure of the concept itself? In a very real sense it is identical with the measure of its validity. For the criterion of continuity or discontinuity in a time series of this type consists precisely in the absence or presence of the complex of concomitant factors mentioned before as being associated with the "kink in the curve."

The case of specific discontinuities in the growth of industrial output is no more than one among numerous possible illustrations of the conceptual problems involved. But it is a convenient and an instructive one. It shows first of all with great clarity the distinction between the mathematical and the historical concepts of continuity. The kink in the curve may be never so sharp; the mathematician will still consider the curve to be continuous. On the other hand, the historian, too, may refuse to regard a sharp kink in the curve as necessarily discontinuous. But he will do so for very different reasons. For historical analysis must not be confused with an exercise in elementary arithmetic. In one case, the rate of growth may have suddenly changed from, say, 2 to 5 percent a year without causing the historian to speak of discontinuities; in another case, a change from 2 to 4 percent may justifiably be regarded as a radical breach of continuity. This means that the discontinuity cannot be measured merely in terms of the change in the rate change. The answer will vary depending on the degree of backwardness of the country concerned, because so will the complex of events that occur around the sharp bend in the curve of output. This is not circular reasoning, but creation of usable historical concepts. Such concepts must be judged and measured in terms of the model within which the historian tries to accommodate his material. In terms of the illustrative model as presented in the preceding paragraphs, it makes very good sense to assign varying degrees of continuity to identical numerical values. But a model is a temporary commitment. It will be abandoned as soon as its usefulness has been exhausted. Another model or models will take its place. The new models may or may not operate with any concept of continuity. But if they do, one will not be surprised to find that the criteria of what constitutes continuity — of what is and what is not stability in the rate changes — have varied from model to model.

A few concluding remarks may be in order. At all times and in all cases, continuity must be regarded as a tool forged by the historian rather than as something inherently and invariantly contained in the historical matter. To say continuity means to formulate a question or a set of questions and to address it to the material. This is true of all five empirical concepts of continuity discussed here. Whether continuity is viewed as constancy of direction, or as endogeny, or as periodicity, or as a long causal chain, or as a change in the rate of change — at all times it is the ordering hand of the historian that creates continuities or discontinuities. It is the historian who, by abstracting from differences and by concentrating on similarities, establishes the continuity of events across decades or centuries filled with events that lack all pertinence to the continuity model. It is the historian who decides how far back the causal chain should be pursued and who by his fiat creates its "beginning" as he creates endogenous and exogenous events. And it is the historian's own model in terms of which changes in the rate of historical change are defined.

Those are *prima facie* arbitrary decisions But it is the arbitrariness of the process of cognition. It has nothing to do with the arbitrariness of a meaningless political slogan. Nor has this sort of arbitrariness anything in common with the fallacious attribution of the ideal properties of a yardstick to the real properties of what it is designed to gauge. Concepts are plans for action; they are programs for research. They are created freely, but once created their use is constrained by the requirements of consistency and the rules of historical evidence And they will be known by their fruits, that is to say, their usefulness in organizing empirical data in such a fashion as to obtain meaningful and interesting, though not necessarily positive and final, results.

Those results, too, will vary from topic to topic and period to period. Few individuals are able fully to appraise the significance of a tool of historical research beyond the area within which their own empirical research has proceeded. As indicated earlier, my interests in recent years have been, perhaps all too narrowly, confined to the field of industrialization in European countries in the course of the past century. Within that field, the use of a concept that is attached to changes in rates of growth has opened new possibilities for promising research. It has seemed important, therefore, to formulate a concept of continuity and discontinuity which is properly historical rather than mathematical or metaphysical in its nature, has been separated from false analogies, and has been purged of emotion and preconception. It makes it possible to see economic development as a set of intelligible alterations in rates of growth that proceeds *modo paulatim, modo saltatim,* and to engage in the study of crucial processes of sudden change unbothered by the lovers and haters of revolutions who must find for themselves playgrounds and battlegrounds outside the area of serious scholarship. Yet the concept as presented here has been attached to a rather special model of industrial growth. Nothing would seem more desirable than the construction of still other models for gauging the specific continuities and discontinuities in the process of industrialization.

2

Some Methodological Problems in Economic History

⚜

T HE alleged objective of methodology is to facilitate research. It should explain what questions can be meaningfully posed and what cannot. Unfortunately, some methodological discussions in the field of economic history have failed to perform this useful function. On closer inspection many of the problems raised have turned out to be mere shams, which have tended to obstruct research instead of aiding it. Most of these problems are not peculiar to economic history. They have come from, or at least belong just as much in, the field of any "other" history, be it political, diplomatic, intellectual, or social. At the present time, when so much of the future of economic history depends on greater reliance on economic analysis, it would seem particularly important to clear out of the way some of the methodological misconceptions that inhibit progress in the field.

One might begin with the frequent assertion that all history, and hence economic history, deals with events or sequences of events that are "unique and individual." Such assertions are, of course, correct in the trite sense that economic history deals with actual occurrences, and any such occurrence can be uniquely related to the coordinates of time and space. But the real problem is whether reference to these coordinates is of equally significant interest in all research projects in the field, which obviously is not the case. More basically, assertions of this sort tend to misconceive the nature of cognitive processes. They assume the possibility of knowledge that

40

is not, in some sense, based on generalizations. Finally, and probably most of all, they pervert the meaning and the purpose of all methodological endeavor by supplying *answers* where only *questions* should be asked. It is the business of the researching scholar and not of his methodological adviser to find out to what extent a given set of phenomena differs from or is similar to a set of other phenomena to which it can be meaningfully related. The low level of this type of discussion becomes particularly clear when the economic historian, faced with injunctions against generalizations that in the very nature of his work he cannot obey, seeks protection in such artificial constructs as Max Weber's concept of "ideal type."

In the closing years of the nineteenth century, the neo-Kantian reaction against the confident reduction of all history, including economic history, to a set of simple and ubiquitous "laws" had gained considerable ascendance. Much of the neo-Kantian doctrine *in this respect* was purely definitional, inasmuch as everything that was susceptible to a generalized treatment was regarded as "science," leaving the residual to history This was more than an innocuous play with words because the sleight of hand consisted in the intimation that history so very specially defined was in fact everybody's history.[1]

Under the conditions of the time, Max Weber's introduction of "ideal type" as an instrument of research was an effective way to loosen, if not to shake off, the trammels placed on the work in history and particularly economic history. But sixty years have elapsed since the publication of Weber's celebrated essay, in which the ideal-type method was described as constructing a "one-sided accentuation of one or more points of view" and a "synthesis of a great many diffuse, more or less present and occasionally absent, concrete individual phenomena . . . arranged according to those one-sidedly emphasized viewpoints."[2] The special justification for camouflaging historical generalizations no longer exists. It is no longer necessary to dignify them by an ingratiating name which vaguely suggests some

1. See, e.g., Heinrich Rickert, *Die Grenzen der naturwissenschaftlichen Begriffs-bildung, Eine logische Einteilung der historischen Wissenschaften,* (Tübingen, 1921) For a modern survival of this view of history as an ungeneralizable residual, see G. Spencer Brown, *Probability and Scientific Inference* (London–New York–Toronto, 1957), p. 11: "History is what is left over after the scientist has taken his pick."
2. Max Weber, *The Methodology of Social Sciences* (Glencoe, 1949), p. 90.

relationship to philosophical idealism. For what Max Weber described as ideal type was nothing but the method of abstraction and generalization without which scholarly thinking, as any thinking, for that matter, is altogether impossible: brain biologists rightly inform us that "the brain functions by fitting inputs against models." [3]

The question, therefore, is not whether in economic history one should or should not abstract, but on which *level* of abstraction one should proceed. That naturally is nothing that can be determined *a priori*; it depends entirely on the nature of the research project chosen. But whatever the research project, no economic historian will escape the necessity of forming, implicitly or explicitly, consciously or unconsciously, some sorts of "ideal types." Whatever topic he may touch, he will always find a large variety of possible, more or less abstract, constructs, some of which can be arranged in the order of diminished abstractions so that what appears as an ideal type looking "downward" may well appear as a real type looking "upward." It is not surprising, therefore, to find that the concept of "real type," as introduced by Spiethoff,[4] is only a specific form of an ideal type, as is clear from the definition given: "reality purged of historical uniqueness." A statistical average, say a trend curve of output, may not touch any of the points given by the primary statistical material. It can be more or less abstract than the ideal type of a medieval city, or a modern enterprise, or even an individual entrepreneur.

It is true, of course, that often comparisons of the degree of abstractness are not easy to make. Introduction of a previously neglected but realistically important phenomenon (such as the role of labor unions in wage determination) may make our model less abstract in one respect, but more abstract in others, if comprehension of the new phenomenon requires incorporation into the model of very abstract features. When widely different models are compared, the difficulties of comparison may be even far greater. Some ideal types, for instance, do and others do not lend themselves to presenta-

3. J. Z. Young, *Doubt and Certainty in Science, a Biologist's Reflections on the Brain* (Oxford, 1951), p. 86.
4. Arthur Spiethoff, *Die wirtschaftlichen Wechsellagen: Aufschwung, Krise, Stockung*, I, *Erklärende Beschreibung* (Tübingen–Zürich, 1955), 12.

tion as averages, but the processes of cognition are the same in both cases, and Max Weber was certainly mistaken in arguing that "statistical averages do not require a special methodological elucidation." [5] At all times, our research proceeds in such a way that, from a preliminary study of the "empirical" material, certain generalizing concepts are developed which are applied as a set of expectations to further study of what we call reality or facts, but which in itself cannot be anything but an ideal type at a very low level of abstraction. As Goethe once said: "It is of highest importance to understand that everything factual is already a theory." [6] It is high time, therefore, for economic historians to discard a terminology which once, for tactical reasons, proved very helpful, but was bound to become hopelessly naive with the passing of the specific historical circumstances that originally occasioned and justified its use.

Once this is done, it will become much more difficult to use methodological discussions, not in order to explain how meaningful research can be undertaken, but in order to anticipate its results. Examples of attempts to clothe one's biases and preconceptions in methodological cloaks are not far to seek. In stressing the "unique" character of the historical subject matter, at least some of the writers concerned wish to emphasize the importance of individuals — or rather of certain individuals — in history. That Krupp and Rockefeller or Napoleon and Stalin were highly significant figures in economic history is, of course, a very promising hypothesis. But the actual importance of such individuals cannot be inferred from any methodological proposition. It must be made plausible in every case within the framework of a given set of problems. Depending on that framework, the "great men" can be treated in the light of their individual peculiarities or as members of a larger group. In either case, generalizations will be used, but the nature of the generalizations will vary. Napoleon was no doubt a great man, but his actions may be explained in terms of his genes, or his upbringing, or the general climate of France, or as stemming from his role as a dictator. In the

5. Max Weber, *Wirtschaft und Gesellschaft, Grundriss der Sozialökonomik*, III. 1 (Tübingen, 1922), 10.

6. Goethe, *Maximen und Reflexionen, Schriften zur Naturwissenschaft*, part one, *Sämtliche Werke, Jubiläumsausgabe*, xxxix, 72.

latter case some general hypotheses concerning the behavior of dictators in a modern environment may be found useful and it is an altogether open question how much emphasis is still placed on the "individual uniqueness" of the man.

The concept of continuity in history, which is so readily and so glibly cast about by so many writers, is another good illustration of the same tendency. Continuity, of course, can mean many things.[7] It may mean simply the existence of connections between events that occur in temporal sequence. This is indeed what every historian, economic or otherwise, naturally does, and to claim that continuity in this formal sense is a basic postulate of historical methodology is as harmless as it is trite. It is, however, not harmless at all when, as is too often the case, the concept of historical continuity is vaguely and ineptly derived from its mathematical connotations; in the process it is perverted into the assertion that all change in economic history can be only very gradual, and the assertion, finally, is given a normative twist to the effect that economic change should be only gradual. Thereby, the field of methodological inquiry is in fact altogether deserted. Once more, the historian is told what the results of his research must be, whereas it is precisely the practicing historian's task to determine what the pace of change was, just as it is up to him to fashion for himself appropriate notions in terms of which he can describe the changes that did take place as gradual or sudden. When one reads in a modern book on economic development that certain rapid changes in the course of industrial growth are rejected as implausible because they "violate the principle of continuity and flexibility of growth which derives from general considerations of continuity in history," [8] it shows clearly how methodological propositions that in their very nature can be only formal in character are used as though they supplied information *materialiter*, that is, on the substantive course of history. Obviously, a principle of continuity in history as referred to in the foregoing quotation is a figment of imagination. It has a ring of regrettable plausibility in many ears because it is insinuated by a bold *quaternio terminorum*, in which one concept

7. For fuller discussion, see Chapter 1.
8. Everett E. Hagen, *On the Theory of Social Change: How Economic Growth Begins* (London, 1964), p. 45.

of continuity is surreptitiously substituted for another; and probably also because of a widely spread predisposition to favor gradual over precipitous changes.

The question of determinism which still plagues economic historians is related, though indirectly, to the problem of continuity. Just as it is claimed that discontinuities in history are impossible, very often certain causal interpretations are rejected because they are "deterministic," and hence methodologically unsound, the term becoming little more than a word of abuse. But determinism, too, has been made to mean very many things. Since in some of its connotations it may appear to touch on the justification of applying models of economic theory to economic history, a few words of clarification should be in order.

If determinism means that a perfect, completely exhaustive knowledge of all phenomena would reveal that everything that ever happened — be it the advent of the manorial system, or the rise of medieval cities or that of modern industrialism, including every single manor, city, and factory — could not have happened in any other way, but had to happen as it did at the particular time and place, then determinism is in the nature of inferences drawn from nonexisting and unobtainable sources. Since we cannot know what we would know if we knew, determinism so conceived is on the other side of the line that separates scholarship from metaphysics. If determinism merely means that everything that happens is a link in a causal chain, it is not different from the previously mentioned concept of continuity in the formal sense of the word; this is indeed the hope that sustains all research, but is again something that cannot be established *a priori*. All that can be said is that scholarship consists in looking for such connections in individual cases, but no one can prove that they must exist. When the concept of determinism is extended to argue that a course of events different from the one actually occurring would require different causes, this is quite plausible as a basic assumption and still innocuous in itself. When, however, the final step is made and it is asserted that in fact the causes could not have been different from those actually at work, the proposition is implicit in the first definition of determinism. As a general proposition, it refers to unknowables. In application to individual cases, it

45

means that as a result of research it becomes possible to establish a hundred-percent probability for the occurrence of a certain event. The point is not only that the establishment of the strongest possible probability implying an all-comprehensive theory is not a practical contingency in research, but that here once again an alleged methodological proposition blandly anticipates what can only, if at all, be established by research.

The damage that such notions do actually is greater than appears on the face of it. For in rejecting them one must beware lest, by inertia as it were, too much be rejected. Since, as previously argued, all research consists in applying to empirical material certain expectations, and since such models are not necessarily stochastic in nature, every scholar in the process of his work has occasion to operate with the concept of "necessarily" following sequences as something inherent in his model. This is true whether the model is designed to explain broad phenomena of industrialization of a whole country, or an entrepreneurial innovation, say the introduction of the Thomas-Gilchrist process, or a bankruptcy of an individual firm, even though the nature of the models or their rigidity will vary from case to case. The point, of course, is that every serious scholar in testing his model, which always is a partial explanation, must try to discover the limits of its applicability and will be ready to discard it when those limits have been ascertained. Thus, the logical or hypothetical necessity in the model sense, as has been well shown by some neo-Kantians, has little to do with the broad, truly deterministic concept of "historical necessity." [9] But in the restricted and denaturalized sense of the word, we all may seem to be determinists even though on short notice. This kind of determinism, involving general considerations with regard to testing and discarding of hypotheses, is a genuine methodological problem. Models of economic theory as applied to economic history are as a rule more explicit and rigid than most other generalizations used. As a result, they lend themselves more readily to the unthinking charge of determinism, and the distinction made in the foregoing must be kept in mind if promising research is not be to inhibited or stifled by methodological bogies.

9. See, e. g., Hermann Cohen, *Kants Theorie der Erfahrung* (Berlin, 1918), p. 634. It is another matter that this position is at variance with the previously mentioned views on history by other neo-Kantians.

The materialistic conception of history is usually referred to as an example of determinism in methodological discussions of economic history. It is less clear, however, than is usually assumed that the materialistic conception of history is necessarily deterministic; nor is it certain, on the other hand, that its significance in economic history has not been greatly overestimated. In asserting that the economic infrastructure determines the character of the superstructure, the materialistic conception of history seemed to extol the importance of economic history. At the same time, however, the very emphasis on the relation between economic and noneconomic phenomena has led to an intense preoccupation with questions that are of little concern to economic historians. Whether Rembrandt's paintings or Shakespeare's plays or Tolstoy's novels can be explained by direct or indirect reference to the underlying economic conditions obviously lies outside the purview of economic historians. Nevertheless, the implicit tendency of the doctrine to regard events in the economic sphere as self-contained, so that technology and its evolution are also viewed as endogenous economic factors, does have a definite bearing on the way in which economic history should be studied. But this dogmatic position could not be maintained for long and Engels, in his well-known "four letters," [10] admitted the interaction between economic and noneconomic factors and asserted that the materialistic conception of history claimed only that "in the last analysis" it was the economic element that determined the course of historical events. This was hardly a tenable position. Once the existence of circular effects was granted so that, say, economic factors influenced political factors and the latter in turn affected the economy, the assertion of "last analysis" or "last instance" became impossible. There is no "first" and no "last" in a circle, particularly if the economic reality presents the observer with a multiplicity of intersecting circles and circles within circles. In other words, the problem then becomes truly methodological: to wit, where is it most advantageous for the student of economic history to break into the circle or rather the congeries of intertwined and rolling circles? It is then a moot question whether "starting" with the economic factor will or will not yield optimal results in research. It is true, of course, that as one follows backward along the chains of

10. M. M. Bober, *Karl Marx' Interpretation of History* (Cambridge, Mass., 1948), pp. 306–310.

causation, nearly always a point will be reached where an economic cause will be discovered. But this is not to say that in all cases it will be best either to pursue the investigation to that point or to stop it there. The answer surely will vary with time, place, and area of study. Whereas the repeal of the corn laws in England possibly can be best explained in terms of economic development of the time and the specific economic interests resulting from it, the abolition of serfdom in Russia may be most clearly understood in terms of political interests, forces, and occurrences.

Thus, the materialistic conception of history offers no master key to the elucidation of processes of economic change. It can be easily purged of its deterministic character and become, like any other model, a possible instrument of research, a set of hypotheses subject to test and refutation. So conceived, its stress on economic interests and class conflict certainly can be, and at times has been, of positive value. It is therefore very regrettable that in the hands of many of its adepts, particularly in present-day Soviet Russia where it is forced upon scholars as the only correct approach to research, it has been treated in a most dogmatic fashion. The basic evil of all false methodologies is fully in evidence there, because the results of research are expected to be in accord with a set of ideological pre-conceptions. It aggravates the situation, without altering it essentially, that those preconceptions themselves are liable to change with the changing political situation. The Soviet case is a particularly unedi-fying one. But in principle it is not fundamentally different from the other symptoms of methodological malady discussed in this essay. Whether one preaches determinism and allegedly immutable historical laws, or whether one preaches continuity and regards his-tory as "unique and individual," in either case one misconceives the nature of scholarly inquiry and inhibits its free and normal course. In either case, the purpose is to terrorize the scholar into submission to preconceived opinions, even though there is a formidable difference in the nature and severity of the sanctions applied.

Economic history in the last few decades has been in a state of transition. Partly under the impact of the current interest in economic development and of the resulting increase in the economists' inter-est in past processes of economic change, the character of the discipline

48

has been rapidly changing. It has attracted young men, well-trained economists, able and eager to apply to their research the tools of economic analysis. They have found many important areas the treatment of which has been entirely neglected so far, because the pertinent problems have not been seen and the relevant questions have remained unasked. It would be a pity indeed if this promising work were to be threatened by inane accusations of "economic determinism," which have no meaning beyond their name-calling intent and are not a jot more reasonable than would be the charge of psychological determinism leveled against those who deduce entrepreneurial behavior either from social ambition or lust for power or, even more "deeply," from certain infantile experience.

Postscript

Since the last paragraph of this essay was written, certain changes have taken place and, as a result, the charge of determinism is no longer so readily leveled against attempts to apply theoretical models to the study of economic history. The reason is fairly obvious. Driven by the logic of analytical concepts, modern economic historians have been trying to assess the quantitative significance of a given economic event in a differential fashion, that is to say, by trying to describe the situation as it would have obtained in the absence of that event. In other words, to use the outstanding example: the cost and benefits of such an innovation as the railroads are compared with the cost and benefits that would have been incurred and received by alternative modes of transportation, first and foremost by canals. The method is implied in the apparatus of rational economic choice. Such models are deterministic in the sense that one expects the most profitable choice to be made. It is necessarily predetermined in the model sense. At the same time, exploring what might have occurred, if the next profitable choice had been taken, runs counter to the determinist's belief that the course of history could not have differed from what it actually was. It is true that Marxian writers have from time to time raised the question of what might have happened if Napoleon had never been born, or if the railroad had been invented in Roman antiquity. The purpose of dealing with such subjects invariably has been to show that the historical process would have still unfolded as it did, without any significant change. But this is not the spirit in which modern economic historians inquire into alternatives to the actual. They are trying to gauge the differential impact to be attributed to phenomena rather than to show that it must needs be equal to naught.

Curiously enough, explorations in counterfactual history have not been received with an auspicious eye by scholars who are quite unwilling to accept the metaphysical tenets of determinism. On the contrary, it is said to be an axiom of the historical method that concern with might-have-beens must be avoided. This is hardly a reasonable attitude. As is usual in methodological debates, the tendency is to make dogmatic pronouncements where pragmatic judgments are called for. Nor are the adepts of history in the conditional mood entirely undogmatic when they assert that asking counterfactual questions is at all times the only correct way of writing economic history, and try to bolster up the assertion by saying that any causal statement, by its very nature, is counterfactual.

First of all, it is clear that the question of what would have happened if certain events had not happened is something that very legitimately does excite our curiosity. Take, for instance, the case of Soviet economic development. We have a fairly good idea now about the increase in Soviet industrial output since the inception of the First Five-Year Plan. It is tempting indeed to ask what Russian industrial output might have been today, if the Soviet dictatorship had not been established and its twin policy of collectivization and superindustrialization had not occurred. A satisfactory answer to such a question would no doubt shed a good deal of light on Soviet economic evolution and help us to form an opinion as to its historical significance. The procedure involves taking a set of prerevolutionary (or rather pre-World War I) rates of growth as the starting point and formulating a number of alternative assumptions about the general course of events and its impact on industrial progress. Depending on the outcome of such exercises, we might then say that the comparative Soviet contribution to the country's industrial development has been very large or medium or insignificant, or even negative. A quest for such results is not idle in principle, while in practice everything depends on how plausible one can succeed in making them. The degree of plausibility, we may safely assume, will vary with the magnitude of the problem and the length of the period under consideration. To judge what would have happened to Russian industrial output during the span of a half century if the Bolshevik revolution had not occurred is, of course, a task that should fill the boldest analyst with trembling fear. If it does not, so much the worse for the analyst. Who can presume to say how a non-Soviet Russia would have been affected by domestic labor conflicts and general political unrest; or by the business cycle of the interwar period, and in particular by the depression of the 1930's; or by World War II, which, for that matter, might not have happened at all? Surely, in such a case abstention is the best part of scholarly valor, and what has been published on the subject so far is too unconvincing to be taken seriously.[11]

On the other hand, if all we want to find out about are the effects of a tariff upon a single commodity, say, a few years after the imposition of the duty, we should still have to make assumptions as to the probable output of that commodity in the absence of the tariff, but the results may well satisfy our sense of reasoned adequacy. Even much more ambitious projects are clearly possible, as has been demonstrated by the ingenious and successful attempt to determine what British industrial output would have been by 1914 if the decline in the rate of industrial exports after the 1860's had not occurred. To repeat, the problem is an eminently practical one, involving the exercise of sound judgment. It will not do to declare, as has been done, that preoccupation with problems of this type is not "history." Anything that casts light on past events *is* history, and any attempt to restrict the concept has no meaning beyond revealing the arbitrary predilections and aversions of individuals. Those who object to "counterfactual history" as a matter of principle should note that very often counterfactual operations are concealed in statements that have a perfectly factual appearance and are gladly — at times all too gladly — accepted by everybody. If it is said that by 1910 German industrial output came to equal British industrial output, the proposition, because of the technique of measurement involved, implies the assumption either that German industrial output was produced not in Germany but in the British Isles on the basis of British opportunity costs; or else that British output was produced within the German

11. I must confess that some twenty years ago I made a few extrapolations of the sort suggested here. They indicated that in Russia the extrapolated industrial output would have remained above the actual Soviet output well into the second half of the 1930's. But I never dared spread these results beyond a restricted mimeographed copy.

economic environment. This is as counterfactual as counterfactual can be.

Similarly, certain well-accepted modes of thinking in comparative history have counterfactual aspects. We may argue that in country M a certain factor A_1 appearing in conjunction with factors A_2, A_3 . . . A_n must have had a decisive causal impact on producing effect B, because in country N, where effect B did not obtain, all other factors (A_2 to A_n) were present, but A_1 was not. Here too we are asking the same counterfactual question: what would have happened if a certain factor were absent, that is to say, if a certain event or series of events had not occurred? Again, the answer must be judged in terms of its plausibility. And plausibility will depend on the existence of factors other than A_2–A_n which may have influenced outcome B negatively in country N and positively in country M, as well as on our ability to measure the relative intensity of factors A_2–A_n in both countries.

The likelihood is that in cases of this sort we shall not arrive even at a semblance of exact quantitative results. But the opportunity to use such a test of previously formed, merely qualitative judgments should not be disdained. If it is said that it is difficult enough to form an opinion of what actually happened without investigating what did not happen, it should be considered that at times our judgments upon the *actual* course of history in one area are less plausible than those resulting from counterfactual operations in another area. And it cannot be denied that there are cases in which the plausibility of interpretations of "factual" history is enhanced by looking at its "counterfactual" reverse.

This much has needed saying against unguarded and untenable criticism of some aspects of economic analysis in economic history. But it is one thing to reject such criticism — it is another to accept unnecessarily exaggerated notions in support of counterfactual explorations. It is highly misleading when — in justification of such explorations — it is claimed that a counterfactual proposition is hidden in every causal statement, just as the ancients believed a dryad to be concealed in every tree. This is a deplorable confusion of facts and nonfacts with counterfacts. What is true is that any affirmative factual statement, causal or otherwise, implies a rejection of the negative. If the statement is *operationally* meaningful it can be refuted; that is to say, the alleged fact can be demonstrated to be a nonfact and the search for the true fact can be instituted. As simple examples show, no counterfacts are then involved.

If I merely affirm, "This painting is by Rubens," I am implying that it was not painted by anyone else; but an expert can examine the painting and prove my assertion to be wrong. If I make a causal statement, "The bear died, because I shot it through the heart," I am implying — altogether analogously — that the lethal event was not the result of any ailment or accident to which a member of the ursine family is susceptible and which may cause its sudden death. Again, an investigation can refute my statement. But it will do so not in any counterfactual fashion, but by establishing the *fact* that death was caused not by a bullet, but by a stroke of lightning or a heart infarct; so, too, the art expert may be able to determine the *fact* that in reality the painting in question was done not by Rubens but by one Joe Magee.[12]

All this has as little to do with the case of counterfactual history as flowers that bloom in the spring. Only conventional history in the indicative mood is involved. A counterfactual historian has different problems. He does not deny the fact that I have killed the bear; his purpose is to find out what would have happened to the bear had my shot gone astray. The question may be well worth asking. If I go around bragging that I have liberated the village from a rapacious foe of calves and lambs, it is not without interest to show that, because of extreme old age, the days of the beast were numbered anyway and the value of my exploit must be appropriately reduced.

The case for counterfactual history is damaged rather than helped by confused irrelevant arguments. Once these have been brushed aside, it remains to point out that nothing can be gained by attempts to inflate counterfactual history out of all proportion. It is designed to answer specific questions, and there is no need to present

12. It makes no difference, of course, whether the refutation is merely negative — "Rubens could not have painted that particular picture, because it depicts a historical scene known to have taken place after 1640," and "The body of the bear showed no lesion by a bullet" — or positive, that is, by identifying the painter and establishing the actual cause of death. In either case, facts and not counterfacts are at stake.

it as an integral part of any problem in economic history. There is an infinite number of connections between events and, accordingly, any number of meaningful propositions about events which can keep us safely within the bounds of reality, without having to bother at all about *réalité manquée*. When it is established that the collectivization policy of the Soviet government caused what is known as "the great slaughter"; or that during the runaway inflation in Germany the disparity between the plummeting rate of exchange and the lagging prices worked as an export bounty and, consequently, caused a short-term rise in German exports — in cases of this sort, positive and sufficient enlightenment is produced and economic processes are meaningfully described without any recourse to "what might have been." While many problems do not call for counterfactual analysis, there are others that even preclude it. At any rate, a mass of factual research must be carried out before counterfactual questions can begin to be raised.

There is no intention at all here to deny the utility of counterfactual history when suitably applied. But to minimize the objections to the use of the "unreal" in economic history, the counterfactual method must be used with discretion and moderation. This means first of all that counterfactual history should be essentially regarded as an instrument for the elucidation of relatively short-term changes, preferably in situations where political factors may be largely neglected. Once the period under review lengthens, the number of unconsidered and nonconsiderable factors that bear on the outcome increases fast and the significance of the results diminishes even faster. But even within the short-term analysis, it is most important to erect clearly visible signs as one moves along the inclined plane of diminishing plausibility. Within the much traveled area of cost-benefit analysis, for instance, this means that, in comparing railroads with canals, determination of differentials in user cost appears as the relatively most reliable result obtainable. Even in this case, price deflations and the estimates of cost functions that are involved introduce a good deal of uncertainty. As one tries to refine the differential in user cost by gauging the specific advantages of railroad transportation over canals (comfort, speed, and so on), one moves onto still less certain ground. The land beyond, where attempts are made to measure the comparative impact of both forms of transport upon the economy as a whole, is much less accessible and should be clearly marked as such.

It is likely that certain sins against reasonableness have been committed in some of the relevant recent works. It would be equally unreasonable, however, to judge them too severely. The introduction into economic history of serious economic and statistical analysis is still at its early stages. Much has been and much will be learned. As time goes on, greater restraint will be exercised in counterfactual analysis and also in the use of models of which only small fragments can be actually applied to empirical reality. As economists who have acquired an abiding interest in economic history develop a greater awareness of noneconomic factors, more attention will be paid to the framework of constraints within which economic decisions are taken. But whatever the present shortcomings of what has come to be called "new economic history," there is no doubt that important things have been accomplished and that, at least for some time to come, this is the area in which the most rewarding contributions to economic history can be expected. Very rightly, the feeling is abroad that here lies the still untouched soil which will repay the effort in research by a rich harvest. Periods like this are the star hours in the history of a discipline, and dogmatic criticism, sometimes stemming from inadequate comprehension of the nature of the tools used, should not be allowed to interfere with the work and to dim its promise. Nothing, of course, lasts forever. After a decade or so of assiduous work, diminishing returns will set in, and the lure of new problems and new methods will lead economic historians to other yet undiscernible tasks. The innovators of today may well become the conservators of tomorrow. But this *is* their day, and its splendor should be neither beclouded nor begrudged.

3

Reflections on Ideology as a Methodological and Historical Problem

IDEOLOGY of social movements is a focal point at which the rays of political, economic, social, and intellectual history concur and intersect. But, in addition, ideology of social movements is attractive from a methodological point of view. Being so peculiarly an area of social study, it points to the specific difficulties of such studies as distinguished from those arising in the study of nature. The first part of this essay is devoted to a few cursory observations on some recent methodological pronouncements and should serve as a background for discussing, in the second part, some of the pertinent problems presented by the ideology of social movements.

I

The problem of the position of natural sciences versus social sciences periodically captures and recaptures methodological interest. As often as not, the attempt seems to be to draw a sharp line separating the two branches of study. The curiosity is that the boundary line tends to shift with every new attempt, but still retains its character of an insurmountable barrier. Accordingly, there exists in literature a considerable number of such sky-high barriers of varying position and direction, so that what appears to be natural science in one interpretation may well be seen to belong to the field of social science in another, and vice versa.

The immense doctrinal history of the subject naturally would defy even the briefest summary within the scope of this essay; but two examples from the modern literature may be singled out. Hans Kelsen, the eminent creator of the Pure Theory of Law, sees the distinction in the respective governing principles used by natural science and social science in order to describe the phenomena under study: the principle of *causality* for the former and the principle of *imputation* for the latter. To the extent that a discipline describes human behavior in terms of cause and effect, it does not differ essentially (is not *wesensverschieden*, says Kelsen) from natural science.[1] It is the principle of normative imputation (of an action, that is, to a norm demanding or forbidding that action) which connects actions of individuals in a fashion which is indeed *analogous* to that of causality, but fully *independent* from it, and which constitutes the specific method and circumscribes the proper scope of social science.

On the other hand, F. A. Hayek contrasts the "analytic" method of natural sciences with the "synthetic" or "compositive" method of social sciences. For the latter, *conscious* human action is in the nature of raw data. According to Hayek, the legitimate field of social study is confined to the exploration of the order "that arises as a result of individual action, but without being designed by any individual."[2]

Hence, for Kelsen, social science is first and foremost jurisprudence. For Hayek, it is primarily coterminous with economic theory and preferably oriented toward the serendipities of competitive market equilibria. Either approach would seem to leave social scientists with suffocatingly little room. There is little doubt, for instance, that power can be considered a central phenomenon of human history, a social factor par excellence. Yet deliberate acts to acquire, maintain, or increase power would not be regarded by Hayek as an appropriate area of study in *social* sciences, unless indeed those acts produced reactions which were unforeseen by their authors and presumably ended in failure. Similarly, the whole field of jurisprudence would remain outside the pale, except perhaps for those acts of noncompli-

---

1. Hans Kelsen, "Kausalität und Zurechnung," *Österreichische Zeitschrift für Öffentliches Recht*, VI. 2 (1954), 125ff.
2. F. A. Hayek, *The Counter-Revolution of Science: Studies in the Abuse of Reason* (Glencoe, 1952) p. 39.

ance that go unpunished. *Per contra*, Kelsen would relegate economic theory to the area of natural sciences, assuming, that is to say, that he would be willing to include economics in any *science* whatever. The point, of course, is not that the concept of imputation or that of *Hetero-gonie der Zwecke* as epitomized in economic equilibria models are faulty or useless. Most assuredly, they are not. The trouble rather lies in the desire to forge *one* tool of analysis into a universal passe-partout for all social sciences, and if the key does not open a door so much the worse for the door.

This tendency to distinguish by *one* criterion, and by consequence to fasten *one* specific method upon a bundle of disciplines sloppily circumscribed as social sciences, smacks altogether too much of the long-abandoned search for a simple, comprehensive, and ubiquitous law or set of laws governing human affairs. Not only do the individual disciplines within the social sciences vary greatly from one another, but within each discipline problems are likely to arise, or to be posed, which call for widely divergent methods of analysis. For this reason, the big-bad-wolf words like "scientism" or "mechanistic approaches" are a limitation on comprehension and imagination. They are fully tainted by the ever-lasting temptation of all methodological cogitation to offer final substantive answers where only the tentative mode of posing questions should be under discussion.

All this circumnavigates the problem of ideology rather than bears directly upon it. One way to foreshorten the radius of the discussion is to refer at this point to some modern views concerning value judgments and the peculiar role they allegedly play in social sciences. These views have tended to create confusion and to obscure the very real dangers with which value judgments — be they concealed or unconcealed — threaten the integrity of our disciplines.

The starting point is somewhat remote and at any rate quite unobjectionable. It is quite true, of course, that human action can be "understood" in terms of men's motivations, and that very often it appears attractive and useful to view social phenomena in this fashion. This is likely to give the superficial impression of "deeper" penetration on the part of social sciences. Newton's second law of motion, according to which the rate of change of momentum is proportional to the impressed force, is an experimentally established fact. So are, though perhaps *cum grano salis*, Pareto's law of income distribution or Engel's or Schwabe's laws concerning inverse variation of expenditures for food and housing (respectively) with variations in income levels. In the case of Newton's law there is no scientific, that is, nontranscendental, urge to go "further" into the subject by examining the "innermost" of the impressed force. In fact, renunciation of Cartesian hypotheses marks the birth of classical physics: *Naturam renuntiando vincimus.*[3] But it is not meaningless to ask why the linear income distribution — defined in a certain way — should hold, and it may be bold but not foolish to seek an answer in terms of purposive human action in the course of which incomes are generated. Similarly, the laws formulated by Engel and Schwabe, assuming they are correct, are further explicable in terms of some theory of human wants. All this is undeniable. Yet this is by no means the direction which cognitive processes in social science take *necessarily*; nor is an explanation of a general observation in terms of the properties of the "underlying" forces unknown in natural sciences. This simply means that a proposition may be more or less complete. In the last analysis, therefore, not much remains of these distinctions between natural and social sciences than the semitautological proposition that all human action is a product of human mind and that, accordingly, study of human behavior *can* be conducted as a study of human mind.

Yet this triviality in turn became the starting point for a series of daring semantic exercises. Nothing seems more natural and innocent than to describe purposive human action as evaluative action and to speak of social studies as studies in human values or *value judgments*. But the innocence is quickly lost. Once the magic word is pronounced, the flood gates open and common sense is drowned in inferential confusion. For from the necessity to study the values of man in action one proceeds to regard the value judgments of the scholar who explores human action as a necessary element of social study. Selection of subjects for research is said to be inevitably value-oriented; so are the concepts formed, because they imply selective viewpoints of the material. At the same time, it is pointed out, in problems of public policy not only the ends but also the means to achieve given ends necessarily have values attached to them; hence

3. Oskar Becker, *Grösse und Grenzen der mathematischen Denkweise* (Munich, 1959), p. 27.

the scholar cannot escape concern with value judgments by dint of *just one* choice or one decision; he must go on making them continually.[4]

Thus, through a quick shuffling of the conceptual cards, very disparate things such as selection of subject matter and tools of analysis are placed on a par with a scholar's subservience to some preconceived opinion and, in addition, are lumped together with the value judgments entertained by the objects of the scholar's study.[5] Perhaps one should not be surprised by this tangled skein of concepts. Similar confusion arises in other directions. The rationality of a theoretical model can easily be confused with the rationality of the behavior being studied with the help of the model. Even more pertinent, a model designed to gauge the probability of the occurrence of a certain historical sequence tends to merge with the probability calculus made by the historical figures engaged in that sequence.[6] Thus value judgments, rationality, and historical probability combine to form a *trifolium confusum*, a methodological curiosity, which might reward closer scrutiny on a separate occasion. Here it must suffice to point to the extreme weakness of the case for inescapability from value judgments.

Surely the scholar's processes of selecting his subject and his

4. For an extensive exposition of this point of view, see the methodological writings of Gunnar Myrdal, now conveniently collected and edited by Paul Streeten in one volume called *Value in Social Theory: A Selection of Essays on Methodology*, International Library of Sociology and Social Reconstruction (London, 1958). Less fully but more forcefully expressed, the same thoughts appear in Carl Mannheim, *Ideology and Utopia* (New York, Harvest Book, n.d.), p. 89.

5. Finally, to sweeten the bitter necessity of downright unobjective scholarship, it is also argued that expression of value judgments by the social scientist is not only inevitable but also beneficial. In a spirited defense of value judgments in social science, Arthur Smithies makes the point that policy-making advice can be tendered much more effectively and conveniently if the scientist shares the general philosophy of his advisees and, one must suppose, has taken due care to make the fact known. See Arthur Smithies, "Economic Welfare and Policy," *Economics and Public Policy*, Brookings Lectures, 1954 (Washington, 1955), pp. 3–4. It is incidentally left to the reader's imagination to assume that the scholar's advice in matters of public policy is a desirable thing, which may or may not be the case.

6. It is, for instance, curious to see how Pierre Vendryès, inspired by Cournot (*De la probabilité en histoire, l'exemple de l'expédition d'Egypte*, Paris, 1952), confuses Napoleon's assessments of his own chances to get to Egypt without being intercepted by the British fleet with the historian's attempt to gauge the likelihood of the expedition's being successful.

approach may be, and probably are, a good deal more variegated, at times much more complex and at others much simpler, than would appear from describing them as products of value judgments. A man may elect to write a book on the Sheffield cutlery industry because of his castration complex, or because of his family connections, or because of his class interest, conscious or unconscious, or because of his aversion to class interest, again conscious or unconscious, or because of an accidental discovery of some archival materials, or because he feels that the history of the industry will cast light on some neglected aspects of the industrialization process; or because he hopes through a study of the industry to verify or falsify some previously established hypothesis. The choice of the original hypothesis may have been value-oriented, but the choice of the monograph topic may be dictated by the objective requirement of the testing process or simply by the own momentum of research activities. *Di caso nasce caso e il tempo lo governo*, as Machiavelli used to say. Any number of different reasons is possible. They may be more or less respectable; they may be complementary or mutually exclusive. But to describe them as the "value judgments" of men who produced the knives and the scissors is hardly helpful.[7]

To say that a selection of a subject necessarily involves a value judgment because of the implied exclusion of some other subject may be no more illuminating for the substantive processes of cognition in the chosen subject than a decision in favor of work on that subject as against a chess game or a trout-fishing expedition. Similarly, a decision to play a game of chess rather than fish for trout need not in the least influence the opening and the style of the chess game. It is argued that any selection is incompatible with ideological neutrality and that to preserve the latter one would have to treat "everything" connected with a given phenomenon (such as business cycles). "Everything" about anything, be it business cycles or wages or foreign trade or what not, presumably must mean at the very least the whole

7. It may be true, as Max Weber stressed, that in order to "understand" people's value judgments, the scholar must be *capable* of having value judgments of his own. (See *Verhandlungen des ersten deutschen Soziologentages*, October 1910, Tübingen, 1911, p. 324.) But this debatable proposition is, of course, something *toto caelo* different from letting the scholar's own value judgments invade and pervade his research.

of *social* life, past and present. Clearly, in circumscribing a given phenomenon and paring it from its surroundings, one has to be at least as selective as in circumscribing certain aspects of any phenomenon chosen.

The description of value judgments in social sciences as both inevitable and beneficial is the product of a few hasty and ill-conceived generalizations. At the same time, such description is far from being innocuous. It is quite certain that the temptation to subordinate social sciences to value judgments is particularly strong in our day. We have witnessed the most far-reaching enserfment of social science in totalitarian states. But there are also clouds, already much bigger than a man's hand, in the Western skies. As Popper has pointed out, the real safeguard of scientific objectivity lies in the institutionally anchored unwillingness of the community of scholars to tolerate lapses from objective scholarship.[8] It is precisely this safeguard that is being threatened. The effect of the talk about value judgment must tend to erode those value judgments of the community upon which all scholarship has rested. In the circumstances, it would seem particularly important to resist the present-day reluctance to draw a clear line between scholarly activities and the work performed by scholars in the service of extraneous interests. The scholar's work resembles closely that of a judge. He too will do best to remain *au dessus de la melée* and to separate his work as sharply as he can from his own private opinions and preferences, to say nothing of the opinions and preferences of other people. In this respect, the position of the economist or sociologist does not differ at all from that of the physicist or the chemist.

II

It is one thing to reject arbitrary or imaginary distinctions between the natural and the social sciences. It is another to deny the existence of specific difficulties in the latter. Those difficulties are essentially the result of the opportunities for mutual influence which connect the social scientist and his object. On the one hand, there is the possible effect of published prediction in social sciences upon the

8. Karl Popper, *The Poverty of Historicism* (Boston, 1957), pp. 155–156.

predicted event. Although there is no reason in principle why the prediction cannot take into account — *uno actu* — its own aggregate effect upon human behavior, there is no doubt that thereby a further obstacle to cognition is raised. To overcome it requires collection of additional data and creation of an additional model to accommodate these data. This difficulty, it will be noted, relates only to true predictions. Historical analysis (retrodiction), *in quod fortuna ius perdidit*, is blissfully free from it. On the other hand, there is another difficulty specific to all social study, dealing with the past, present, and future. The reference is to the fact that the objects of social study incessantly characterize themselves. This indeed is a difference in kind.

An active volcano does not try to convince the scientist that in reality it is an innocent molehill. A granite rock does not pretend to be a rhododendron and, as it falls to the flagstones of the piazza from the height of the Leaning Tower, it does not claim to be moved by its own free will rather than by the force of gravity; nor does it deny that it is no longer at rest and that a change in state and locus has taken place. Hamlet's cloud does not seek to impress upon Polonius' mind some changing notions as to its shape; it leaves that to the Prince. By contrast, social actors are rarely mute. Great statesmen and low-order politicians, judges and bureaucrats, bankers and industrialists, labor-union leaders and presidents of chambers of commerce — they all go on describing and interpreting themselves and their actions. This is a blessing and a curse, a fount of enlightenment and a source of confusion. And what is true of the more ephemeral personal statements holds with even much greater force for the long-lived pronouncements by impersonal bodies which somehow contrive to acquire an existence independent of the men who speak and act in their behalf.

When the constitution of Astoria proclaims, in its first article, Astoria to be a democracy or a federal state, this statement may or may not be correct in terms of any reasonable concept of democracy or the federal state. The authors of the constitution may have wanted to deceive the people of Astoria or the opinion of the world. They may have been genuinely mistaken as to the meaning of their actions. Worst of all, they may have been correct at one time and wrong at another. Astoria may have been a ruthless dictatorship when article one was placed on the statute book, but then civilized itself into a rule by the consent of the governed; alternatively, it may have developed in the opposite direction.

All this is particularly true of the collectivities of social actors known as "social movements" and their creeds known as "ideologies." This term inevitably calls for some comment. Ideology no longer is the irritating neologism which, almost 150 years ago, aroused John Adams' indignation. Nowadays it flows from tongue and pen unhesitatingly. Yet its meaning is still somewhat unstable. It no longer means what its sire, Destutt de Tracy, intended it to mean: a science of ideas. As has been true with a number of similar words (such as mythology), the divorce of meaning and ethymology has been complete. And along with the original meaning have faded away also the connotations of impracticability and lack of realism which Napoleon I imparted to the term. The concept assumed a central role in Marxian thinking where it appeared in a double guise, first as identical with superstructure and comprising law and politics, religion and morals, in fact everything that does not directly belong to the economic base of society; and, second, as a specific set of ideas designed to vindicate or disguise class interest. In the former sense, ideology was something possessing a derived rather than an independent existence (a mere "image," a reflection of reality); in the latter sense, the stress lay on deception or at least self-deception ("false consciousness"). "The idea becomes ideology," said Rudolf Hilferding, "as soon as behavior is immediately determined by purposes other than the idea." Those concepts are neither extinct, nor have they remained confined to Marxian sociology. Mannheim's distinction of a "particular conception of ideology" as contrasted with a "total conception of ideology" is an obvious elaboration of Marxian concepts. To be sure, Mannheim does not operate with the Marxian Unterbau-Überbau dichotomy. But the "particular conception" is designed to express skepticism "of the ideas and representations advanced by our opponent" and the broader concept, though more functional and less motivational, still "makes so-called 'ideas' a function of him who holds them, and of his position in his social milieu." In a sense, one has not moved so far away from Destutt de Tracy as one might think. Whereas ideology no longer means the science of ideas, it still appears to mean ideas viewed and organized in such a fashion as to provide a possible subject matter for a science of ideas, a sociology of knowledge.[9] When the notion of "ideas" is restricted to circumscribe a system of beliefs and goals to which a social movement has proclaimed adherence, one arrives at a concept of ideology of social movements which may be usefully discussed within the context of this essay.

One or two conceptual remarks or warnings may be in order. First of all, to speak of a *system* of beliefs or goals need not suggest any internal consistency of the ideas involved. The term system is merely designed to convey that, in some sense, the ideology of the movement is presented and conceived as a unity. The unity may stem from logical consistency or merely from psychological compatibility. Clearly, what is and what is not regarded as compatible is likely to change over time, creating interesting problems for historical interpretation.

Similarly, there is no intention to define the system of beliefs and goals in such a way as to produce a necessary dichotomy between the system and some "reality" of the movement. On the contrary, what matters is to ascertain the changing nature of the connection between ideology and movement. By the same token, the concept of ideology as defined here, broad as it appears, is narrower than it might have been. For it would be possible, of course, to define or redefine either "ideology" or "movement," or both, in such a fashion as to make the two coterminous. This is not intended here and, accordingly, ideology should not be understood to mean *any* beliefs and *any* goals held or pursued by the movement, but solely the *proclaimed* beliefs or goals. In other words, the concern is with the programs of movements rather than with inarticulately held ideas and implicit aims and motivations.

Conceived in this fashion, ideology is the complex of statements a movement makes about itself and by which it wishes to be known both within and without. If those statements are issued and reissued

---

9. See for this paragraph: Emile Caillet, *La Tradition littéraire des idéologues* (Philadelphia, 1943), pp. 1ff; letter by Engels to Franz Mehring, July 14, 1893, reprinted in Karl Marx and Friedrich Engels, *Correspondence, 1846–1895* (New York, n.d.), pp. 510–513; Karl Marx, *Der achtzehnte Brumaire des Louis Bonaparte* (Stuttgart, 1914), p. 34; Rudolf Hilferding, "Probleme der Zeit," *Die Gesellschaft*, I (April 1924), 6; Mannheim, *Ideology and Utopia*, pp. 55–59.

with fair frequency and earnest emphasis, their suggestive power is bound to be great. So is the scholar's temptation to accept them as a faithful character description of the movement. Misconception of the social scientist's object of study and inability to discern pertinent problems are the inevitable result. It is indeed surprising how little *general* work has been done to elucidate the nature of relations that connect a social movement and its ideology. Given the failure on the more abstract levels, it is far less surprising to find much of the special empirical work wanting in depth of interpretation. The Marxian contribution to the subject could not redeem its original promise because of at least two main limitations: (1) the static view of ideology as determined once and for all by a rather unchanging set of economic interests, and (2) the regrettable, though perhaps understandable, reluctance to apply the analysis of ideology to Marxian movements beyond describing them as originating in, and being sustained by, very legitimate economic interests of the laboring classes.

It is stranger to find that writers on sociology of knowledge, stemming as they do from Max Weber and his famous dictum on the applicability of the materialistic conception of history to Marxism and Marxian organizations, have failed to pose the problem dynamically — as one of change over time in the ideology-movement relationship. In fact, as far as this writer is aware, there have been astonishingly few attempts to present some basic hypotheses concerning these dynamic relationships. Beyond all compare, the most important among those attempts is the brilliant pamphlet in which Rosa Mayreder, an Austrian sociologist, some fifty years ago tried to sketch out the "typical course of social movements." [10] Using a concept of ideology very similar to the one circumscribed in the preceding pages, she distinguished the successive phases in the evolution of social movements: (1) ideological phase; (2) organizational phase; (3) power phase. In the first phase, the movement is busy constructing and assimilating its ideology; at that inchoate stage, the movement appears wholly dominated by its system of beliefs. In the second phase, the task of building up the movement as an organized entity requires certain compromises and leads to deviations from the straight ideolog-

10. Rosa Mayreder, *Der typische Verlauf sozialer Bewegungen* (Vienna, 1917; 2nd rev. ed., Vienna, 1927).

67

ical path. In the third phase, it is the exigencies of power exercise that fully dominate action.[11]

Despite the modesty with which Rosa Mayreder presented her scheme, there is little doubt that she regarded it as a "general theory" of social movements, or at least as the first step on the road to such a theory. Nonetheless, the generality of the theory is limited at least in two respects. Clearly, it can refer only to movements that have continued over a very considerable period of time without losing their identity, which in terms of the definitions used here can only mean that the movement has publicly acknowledged its unbroken sameness from the origins onward. And, furthermore, it appears that Rosa Mayreder wrote her essay with the evolution of one political movement in mind: the Social Democratic Labor Party primarily in Germany and in the Austrian monarchy before World War I. It is at least questionable to what extent the scheme was supposed to fit very different political movements such as, say, the Conservative Party in England or the Republican Party in the United States. But the relevance of the scheme for comprehending much in the history of certain labor movements is intuitively quite obvious.

This is not the place to report fully on the extent to which I have found Rosa Mayreder's framework useful and plausible in several historical cases. It must suffice to confine oneself to one empirical though most important example, to wit, the evolution of Soviet Russia, which so often is considered as the specific history of a Marxian social movement. In innumerable books, pamphlets, and articles written by reputable scholars, in speeches made by celebrated statesmen, the perennial tendency has been to explain the Soviet govern-

---

11. Some twenty years later, Bertrand Russell developed a not entirely unrelated trichotomy: "Organizations that have a long career of power pass, as a rule, through three phases: first that of fanatical, but not traditional belief, leading to conquest; then that of general acquiescence in the new power which rapidly becomes traditional; and finally, that in which power, now used against those who reject tradition, has again become naked. The character of an organization changes very greatly as it passes through these stages." (Bertrand Russell, *Power, a New Social Analysis*, New York, 1938, p. 82.) It may be seen that power and ideology appear somewhat commingled in the preceding quotation, inasmuch as the distinction between "traditional belief" and "traditional power" is elusive. But the distinction between fanatical and traditional belief is not and seems to be quite in line with the spirit of Rosa Mayreder's hypothesis.

ment's actions — which directed and determined the processes of change in the country — as stemming from a body of beliefs that reasonably, meaningfully, and illuminatingly could be described as Marxian ideology. It must be granted, of course, that distributive imputation of historical events or sequences of events to a number of competing factors remains an uncertain enterprise at all times. And yet those who placed exclusive stress upon the one factor of Marxian ideology should at least have been given pause by considering the ease with which most important sequences in Soviet Russian history can be plausibly explained without any reference to the motivational force of Marxian ideology. This is particularly true of Soviet economic history. The great landmarks separating the successive stages in the evolution of the Soviet economy and marking the changes in the grand policies pursued, as well as most of the specific technical and institutional arrangements that have been evolved, are readily explicable in terms of the exigencies of given situations or in terms of the mechanics of power.[12] One must consider, on the one hand, that crucial decisions were frequently made in order to meet the threat of circumstances in conditions where the very existence of the Soviet government was in grave jeopardy. Such, no doubt, was the situation from which the decision emerged to embark upon the collectivization of agriculture and very rapid industrial growth. On the other hand, the idea that a consistent and unambiguous program for action — be it prerevolutionary or postrevolutionary — could have been extracted from a body of thought, known as Marxism, was fantastic in itself. Otherwise, it would have been quite incomprehensible that formidable discussions on the subject could have developed within the ruling Bolshevik group, every member of which had been raised and steeped in Marxian doctrines.

The truth of the matter is that Rosa Mayreder's pamphlet, the first edition of which was published several months before the October Revolution, now some fifty years after that revolution reads like a succinct summary description of the intervening years. It is hardly necessary to do more than to equip oneself with a list of things that have been designated as being "Marxian" in Soviet Russia. It will

12. For an elaboration of this point of view, see Gerschenkron, *Economic Backwardness in Historical Perspective*, pp. 188–197.

appear at once that the concept comprises anything and everything the Soviet government ever stood for or stands for now. And since in the course of time the policies of the Soviet government induced it to approve of a great variety of very disparate things, it is not surprising at all to find a conglomeration of wildly inconsistent policies, ideas, and value judgments unblushingly lumped together under the name of Marxism.

When confronted with phenomena of this sort, a social scientist should naturally try to separate the meal from the bran, the truth from the pretension, and to discover not only the actual function of ideology but also the reasons for stubborn nominal continuity in the face of substantive change. In his previously quoted study, Bertrand Russell expressed the opinion that "it is advantageous to have beliefs which are in accordance with facts." [13] Whatever can be said in support of this position from various points of view should not blur the inference that the survival of ideology beyond its policy-determining stage, in other words, the discrepancy between belief and facts, is likely to have been advantageous to some interests. There is little doubt that leaders of social movements have found it useful to create an impression of ideological continuity either because the open acknowledgment of change would have deprived the movement of an important solidifying force, or else because such an acknowledgment would have weakened the position of the leaders who had led the movement upon roads unforeseen by, and perhaps incompatible with, the original system of beliefs. It is certainly curious to see that a most radical social movement such as the Bolshevik Party, which carried out the most far-reaching and most rapid change that ever occurred in the history of Russia, has been most anxious to suppress any appearance of change in its ideology.

It is perhaps even more surprising that a formally, though of course not substantively, analogous process can be easily discerned in a number of socialist movements in Western Europe. The discrepancy between the acknowledged belief and the policy pursued began growing almost from the moment when social-democratic parties and the labor unions that stood close to them saw the prospects of immediate practical success through action in parliaments, municipalities,

13. Russell, p. 151.

social-insurance institutions, factories, and other enterprises. But the original ideology has been steadfastly maintained through nearly two generations, and it is only now, years after the end of the Second World War, that serious attempts are being made to discard the traditional mode of thinking — or speaking. In conditions of total-itarian monopoly of all communication media, outdated ideologies are not in danger of being exposed and subverted by criticism as long as they continue to be used as the calling cards of the regime. But it is quite striking that democratic movements in democratic countries could, for long decades, separate their policies from their ideologies. Presumably, the reasons must be sought not only — and possibly not primarily — in the oligarchic structures of political parties, the strength of which (as Michels has shown) must not be underestimated even within very democratic movements; at least as important may be the fact that, while leaders and adherents of the movement deem to draw benefits from ideological stability, the opponents of the movement welcome the movement's refusal to acknowledge the change because the traditional ideology constitutes a more convenient target for attacks. What the movement would need in such circum-stances is a balancing of advantages accruing to the movement against those accruing to its opponents. Even if the psychological readiness to carry out such a calculus were not a problem in itself, absence of a finely calibrated gauge would make calculations of this sort fairly impractical, until the differential has become so large as to force itself upon the naked eye. Since a given ideological appeal often exercises both a positive and a negative effect because of the opposite reactions of different strata of the population, the situation is less paradoxical than it might appear at first glance.

Considerations of this sort do no more than scratch the upper-most surface of the problem. Obviously, no real progress can be achieved until a general framework has been developed with whose help a set of expectations can be established and a series of meaning-ful questions formulated.

Within such a framework, a good deal more would have to be accommodated than the general fact of ideological stability. One would have to explore those changes in ideology which are still compatible with the image of stability and, in fact, make such stability possible. For without grafting certain new and possibly varying elements upon the central trunk of ideas, the discrepancy between belief and action would become too obvious and impossible of maintenance. Nor could one leave out of consideration the techniques of power struggles within the movement. Again, the situation is complex, if not paradoxical. The leaders of the movement preserve the orthodox ideology because they think it offers certain real or imagined advantages. At the same time, however, the disparity between belief and deed exposes the leaders who are responsible for the deeds to the charge of abandoning or betraying what they themselves are eager to represent as the fundamental system of beliefs and the ultimate goals of the movement. Thus, struggles for power within the movement are always likely to revert to traditional ideology, whose vitality may easily be enhanced thereby. Clearly, an organizational split of the movement which leads to competition for power between the two groups can have very similar effects. The intensity of ideological adherence then tends to rise and fall with the intensity of the competition and with the magnitude of the threat emanating from the radical group. And what is true of conditions within a given movement, and of relations between two branches of a previously unified movement, may even apply to two countries, as appears with increasing clarity from the story of the relations between Soviet Russia and Communist China. The Chinese fervor in preaching what in Peking they are pleased to call orthodox Marxism no doubt makes it more difficult for the Russians to move away from a "creed outworn." At any rate, the picture of ideological stability and growing discrepancy between belief and fact must be complemented by a good many additional traits showing the ups and downs and the back and forth of the elements involved. And, finally, much thought must be devoted to the study of circumstances which surround the eventual expiration of a traditional ideology, particularly if its abandonment should occur discontinuously by a change in a party program or by a similarly conspicuous manifestation. Naturally, the resolution or elimination of a problem is part and parcel of its history.

It may be in order at this point to summarize the simple conclusion that emerges from the preceding reflections. It has been their main burden that the persistent search for arbitrary, unduly abstract, unduly sharp, and mutually exclusive lines of separation between natural and social sciences has tended to blur the comprehension of, and curtail the interest in, an area that is truly peculiar to social science: to wit, the self-characterizations of the objects of social study.

Some years ago, a president of the American Historical Association sought to encourage young historians to apply in their research the methods and results of psychoanalytic study.[14] This is not the place to debate the value of that suggestion. In particular, psychoanalysis may prove to be of very limited help for elucidating the problems discussed in this essay. At the same time, there is little doubt that those concerned with the large problems of intellectual and ideological history in relation to social movements would stand to benefit greatly from emulating the task that has been performed by psychoanalysis. For the social scientist, too, must first of all *learn to listen* to the objects of his study. And in order to be able to listen *understandingly* he must, like the psychoanalyst, develop a general theory that he can use for organizing and interpreting what he is told. It has been the purpose of this essay to emphasize the urgent need for such a theory.

14. William L. Langer, "The Next Assignment," *American Historical Review*, LXIII (January 1958), 283–304.

Part II

*PROBLEMS IN
ECONOMIC HISTORY*

4

The Typology of Industrial Development as a Tool of Analysis

THERE is something pleasantly rejuvenating about the ways of conferences. Writing under an assigned title inevitably brings back to mind the sunny days of adolescence when one was composing Gymnasium essays on preordained subjects such as "Differences in English, French, and German Romanticism" or "Objectivism and Subjectivism in the Russian Novel." Then, as now, the assignation of the theme limited the writer's freedom more severely than one might think. For the nature of the treatment of the topic had been subtly anticipated. No one ever dared argue that the so-called romantic writers had best be treated as individuals without being pressed into the respective national collectivities. It would not have done at all to suggest that there might be other and less inept criteria for evaluating the prose of the Russian *ottocento*. The theme was not to be quarreled with. It seems that the present conference has adhered to the venerable practice of the high-school essay. Also here the imposition of the title has inescapable substantive implications. It so happens that this writer is quite unreluctant to accept them. But they deserve to be made explicit.

A typology is made of types. To speak of the typology of industrial development, therefore, precludes at least two conceivable views of industrial development. If one believes that industrialization, wherever it occurred, was characterized by perfect — or at least very far-reaching — uniformity, there would be nothing significant to say

Note. This paper was presented in 1962 at the convention of the International Economic History Association, Aix-en-Provence.

77

about *types* of industrialization, since only one significant type would be in existence. One tree does not make a forest, and one type does not add up to a typology. On the other hand, if every discernible — or at least every interesting — phenomenon of industrial history were altogether *sui generis*, the number of such phenomena would equal the number of "types" thereof, and attempts at constructing a typology would be defeated from the opposite end by the infinite variety of the empirical material.

Neither of the two extremes has failed to leave its mark upon historical research. Some philosophers' view of history as being composed of nonrecurring and nongeneralizable phenomena may have been no more than a somewhat disguised definitional exercise. This certainly was the case with Heinrich Rickert.[1] Yet his spirit was and still is strong upon many a practicing historian. One might have thought that economic historians, because of the nature of their material, should have remained impervious to the lure of the unique in history, but much that has been written in business history clearly reveals the attractiveness of the approach.

Nor must one underestimate the strength of the temptation that pressed in the opposite direction. To emulate natural science, to find a simple formula to cover a very large number — perhaps the "totality" — of the relevant phenomena, appeared a most worthwhile task to many historians of the last century, and the aspirations have not been altogether abandoned in our own time. In the field of economic history, the multifarious "stage" schemes offer the obvious case in point. True, the criteria of the classification differed from author to author. The individual scheme may have pivoted around the predominant mode of economic activity, or the seat of political regulation of economic life, or the distance separating producers and consumers, but all those (and several other) cases had one crucial feature in common: the assumption that, at least in the aspects covered by the given scheme, economic life developed in obedience to a general law that was valid for all times and climes. In some cases the assumption was made tacitly; in others — Bruno Hildebrand's is the outstanding example — it was stated with emphatic clarity. In our own day, Rostow's attempt to view modern economic growth as pro-

1. See Chapter 1, note 20.

ceeding in accordance with a definite pentametric rhythm is indeed limited — or hedged — by some references to choices and deviations from normalcy, but its general purpose has been to stress the ineluctable ubiquitousness of the five stages of economic growth. When everything is said and done, it is fair to say that for Rostow, as for List or Schmoller, there is only one type of economic development.

It has been characteristic of the schemer of stages from List to Rostow to present his own scheme as circumscribing the totality of economic development. The present writer is constrained to deal with just one facet of economic development: industrialization. But the main difference lies elsewhere. The point to be made here is that one must move on a plane of generalization located between the two extremes discussed in the preceding paragraphs. In other words, we must in the first instance be willing to look for generalizable variabilities, for differences in industrial development that may be said to constitute *types* of industrial progress. Once this is done and such types have been successfully discovered, we shall begin to wonder how seriously we have to take the term "typology." If we are going to be serious about it and if, accordingly, there should be some logos to every typology, we shall have to ask whether all, or at least some, of the types we have successfully discovered can be conjoined into unified patterns.

To do so does not at all mean that the extreme approaches are necessarily "wrong" in any meaningful sense of the term. Since any approach of this kind (claims to the contrary notwithstanding) inevitably deals not with the unmanageable and incomprehensible "totality" of the phenomena but with sets of abstractions, different approaches yield different insights, and it is in terms of those insights that the value of an individual approach must be judged. The results need not be commensurate. What must be avoided, however, is the elevation of a given approach to the rank of a dogma. And as soon as the dogmatic belief in the inevitable sameness of industrialization processes has been discarded, the discovery of a number of variabilities exacts little effort. In fact, the problem is to exercise reasonable self-restraint and to abstain from finding too much. For typology as an analytical tool in the treatment of industrial processes in all ages and all societies would be a topic far exceeding this writer's competence.

79

Analysis and fact are relative or rather correlative terms. There is little point in a general discourse that is unrelated to empirical material. Hence the following discussion of historical variabilities leading up to their analytical significance will be confined to modern (largely pre-1914) industrial history of Europe. This qualification must be kept in mind.

As one looks for such variabilities within the area and period specified, some of them present themselves in the convenient shape of contrary pairs. A few may be listed in the following. An industrialization may be classified as:

1. autochthonous or derived;
2. forced or autonomous;
3. concentrating on producers' or consumers' goods;
4. occurring within an inflationary or a stable monetary environment;
5. involving merely quantitative changes or being in addition characterized by far-reaching structural transformations;
6. proceeding continuously or discontinuously;
7. proceeding in conditions of progress in agriculture or of stagnation, if not retrogression;
8. motivated primarily by economic or by political aims.

It is not claimed that those variabilities have been chosen entirely at random. The typology to be constructed obviously has cast its shadow before. It can be claimed, however, that most of the pairs listed are not likely to be ignored in any serious study of contrasts in European industrialization that can be observed across the map and over time. There are, of course, other variabilities, which are not so easily susceptible to being arranged in pairs. Rather they emerge from more or less arbitrary divisions of concrete data. But before we turn to them, something more must be said about those mentioned in the preceding paragraph. It seems best to discuss them in order.

1. The distinction between an autochthonous and a derived industrialization is of obvious importance in modern industrial history. It is premised upon the assumption that in many cases political boundaries are of fundamental significance for the study of processes of industrialization. In other words, the state is taken to be the ap-

propriate unit of observation in many of such studies. Those cases are regarded here as autochthonous. A "derived" industrialization is one for which this assumption does not hold. The economy of the country in which a derived industrialization takes place is closely tied up with the economy of some other larger and more advanced country or countries. The timing and the character of such industrialization are essentially determined by this connection. Under suitable conditions, such an industrialization had to overcome fewer obstacles, was less expensive, and proceeded in a relative absence of stress and strain. The composition of the growing output, its rate of growth, the pressures upon levels of consumption, and many other features of the process tended to be much more favorable to the population than was true, in otherwise comparable circumstances, of autochthonous industrializations. Derived industrialization is something that remained peculiar not simply to a small country, but to a small country in an appropriate geographic position and populated by men able and willing to apply modern methods of cultivation, that is to say, to act in the fashion of rural populations in more advanced countries. It is in this sense that Denmark's industrial evolution in the nineteenth century may offer a case (or at least some elements) of derived industrialization. The crucial fact in Danish economic growth was the transformation in agriculture which occurred largely at the behest of the English market. The increase in labor productivity in agriculture and the consequent growth of incomes were the main driving force in the creation of Danish industry. It largely determined the composition of Danish industrial output. Foreign competition in conditions of trade unimpeded by tariffs and other restrictions further reduced the range of commodities which the domestic industry could produce in order to satisfy the demand of the farming population. It is sufficient to allude to those general circumstances in order to make it clear that derived industrialization must be regarded as exceptional rather than predominant among European industrializations. One will not go wrong in supposing that a small country with lower standards of popular education and lacking easy communications with capacious markets abroad would be quite unable to reproduce the Danish model within its own confines. The industrial history of Bulgaria offers a convincing confirmation of that supposition. A *minori ad maius,* one may assume further that it would be in vain to expect derived industrialization in any major European country. Indeed, the mere juxtaposition of such magnitudes as national income and foreign trade or capital imports from abroad shows that, as a practical proposition, a large country could not be pulled into industrial growth by the mere momentum of one or several advanced countries. To repeat, the predominant type of European industrialization was perforce autochthonous.

2. Was it also autonomous rather than forced? A "forced" or a "forced draft" industrialization is one in which significant portions of the process were accomplished by those who had the right to force and to enforce, that is to say, by the holders of political power. There is no doubt that, if one is willing to go sufficiently far back in the economic history of Europe, elements of forced industrialization appear to have been nearly ubiquitous, although greatly varying in intensity from country to country. This is meant when a fairly long historical period is described as the age of mercantilist policies. This essay, however, is concerned with modern industrial history. Much is to be said, therefore, for starting conventionally with the industrial transformation in England in the second half of the eighteenth century. If this be the "beginning of modernity," then taking Europe as a whole it would be impossible to write the subsequent industrial history of the continent without placing due emphasis upon the role of the state. But that role was far from homogeneous. There is little doubt that in some cases the state obstructed industrial development either for ideological reasons or because of the influence of vested interests that feared economic or social losses as consequences of industrialization. A government that was earnestly bent upon suppressing an industrial upsurge did not find it difficult to achieve its aim. In such circumstances, a change in governmental policy could indeed be regarded as a prerequisite of successful industrialization. Such a change of heart was naturally followed by a good many measures designed to demolish the state-created hindrances to industrialization. The problem, however, was the *positive* policy of the government once the antagonistic attitude was abolished. And in this respect, two types of policy do stand out.

On the one hand, there was the policy that aimed at creating a suitable environment for industrial enterprises. This was done mostly by establishing an appropriate legal framework, but also by supplying social-overhead capital and beyond that, perhaps, efficient services, mostly in the area of transportation and communication, as well as by taking regulating measures, mostly in the field of monetary and foreign commercial policies. On the other hand, there was the complex of policies through which governments became directly concerned with the establishment and conduct of industrial enterprises. If the state refrained from running state-owned enterprises, it could still profoundly influence the entrepreneurial and managerial decisions of industrial firms by providing them with investment funds, by acting as a large buyer of their products, by assuring them of a steady supply of labor, and by subsidizing their current operations through various devices. It is only the second type of policy that is to be regarded as "forced" for the purposes of this discussion. There is little doubt that forced industrialization in this sense was regarded in Europe before 1914 as being at variance with the dominant value system and was widely rejected as leading to an "artificial" or "unsound" growth, these terms having penetrated so deeply into European vocabularies that their metaphorical character was rarely, if ever, perceived. But there is equally no doubt that forced industrialization (or significant elements thereof) played an important part in important areas of the continent before World War I. To admit this naturally raises a number of questions. Most notably, a historian would want to know to what extent and for what length of time forced industrialization — as compared with its autonomous counterpart — resulted in significant variations in the quantitative and structural aspects of the process. Problems of this sort should provide ample justification for distinguishing these two types of industrialization.

3. The distinction between types of industrialization according to the varying relation between output of producers' goods and output of consumers' goods is a quantitative one. Hence "high" and "low" in this context are relative terms that must be understood through the medium of suitable interspatial or intertemporal comparisons. But the economic significance of the distinction is obvious, if for no other reason, because of the close relation that exists between the share of producers' goods in the incremental output of industry and

the rate of growth of industrial output as well as the opportunities for the process of growth to continue unreduced for a fair length of time. The fact that "investment for investment's sake" is an economically possible process is basic for the study of any industrialization in which the problem of sustained effective demand is not continually solved by the growing expenditures of the consumers. This aspect of the matter is *sui generis* in the sense of being independent of the physical properties that producers' goods display in the process of production and of the effect of growing stock of capital upon productivity of labor. It is still another question whether these effects of a relatively large share of producers' goods in total output are enhanced or curtailed according to whether the reservoir of available technological progress tends, at any given time, to favor producers' goods over consumers' goods or vice versa. One may assume, therefore, that quantitative variabilities of this type are very likely to be associated with significant variations in many important features of industrial development.

4. The differences in industrial progress that are associated alternatively with the falling or steady (perhaps even rising) value of money have many facets. Persistent inflationary processes are bound to affect propensities to save, patterns of consumers' expenditures, time horizons of investors, and many other forms of economic decisions and attitudes. Alluring hypotheses have been advanced regarding the differential behavior of entrepreneurs whose formative years were overshadowed by inflationary or deflationary developments. In the present context, however, the distinction may be made to revolve around monetary developments that were occasioned by processes of industrialization rather than the other way round. Differences in this respect are bound to occur, depending on the nature of supply of capital disposition to the nascent industry. Assuming a closed economy, inflationary tendencies will result from the employment either of previously accumulated claims against current national income or of newly created purchasing power that has been placed in the hands of the entrepreneurs. In either case, competition in the market will ensue through which labor and raw materials will be bid away from consumer-good industries or, more generally, from old ("preindustrialization") industries. *Per contra,* industrial develop-

ment that is financed either by voluntary (rather than forced) and current (rather than previously made) savings or by politically engineered transfers of purchasing power from consumption to investment can, in principle, proceed in stable monetary conditions. Clearly, the intensity of inflationary pressures in the former cases will depend on the scope of the industrial development and the efficiency displayed in the process, as well as on the length of the gestation periods, the nature of the finished goods produced, and the secondary pressures generated by the original increase in the rate of investment. It is furthermore clear that this distinction between the two types of industrial development is unlikely to stand in isolation but is likely to be associated with other distinctions, in particular with the first three discussed in the preceding pages. As said before, the mutual relationship of the individual types and their conjunction in a consistent pattern is the main problem to be considered here and will be dealt with at the end of the essay.

5. An industrial development that is merely quantitative and is not accompanied by structural changes may appear as an altogether unrealistic case. It is certainly true that any industrialization that changes the share of industrial output in total national output will entail structural changes within the economy as a whole. But what is being referred to here is confined within the sphere of industrial development proper, that is, relates to changes in the output of manufacturing and mining. So conceived, at least the industrial evolution of Bulgaria between the beginning of the century and the end of the interwar period offers an interesting case in point. Over the period, an expansion of output took place that was far from negligible; yet most qualitative indicators, such as size of plant and enterprise, composition of industrial output, productivity of labor, and the like, remained by and large unchanged. The existence of such a type of industrialization, sometimes described as "growth" versus "development," is of interest here because it suggests that structural changes of this sort are unlikely to take place, unless the rate of growth exceeded a certain minimum level. That minimum level no doubt varied from country to country and from situation to situation, but as long as the rate of growth remained below it, the opportunities for industrialization remained imperfectly utilized.

6. Continuity and discontinuity in industrial development can be defined in a number of ways. Thus, to give a few instances, continuity has been used to mean stability conceived either as a complete absence of change or at least as existence of certain stable elements in the midst of change; at other times continuity has been made to refer to periodic recurrences of industrial upswings and depressions; frequently, it was used to refer to an uninterrupted direction of change (growth or decline) of phenomena; then again, continuity appears to denote the quality of being rooted in an ancient past, not in the sense of stability but in the sense that a given situation can be profitably explained in terms of very long chains of causal regress; and, finally, continuity seems to refer to a relatively smooth as against a relatively jerky development It is the last concept that probably bears most tellingly upon problems of modern industrialization. The distinction between continuous and discontinuous types of industrialization can be promisingly related to that concept. It is obviously premised upon quantitative measurements of magnitudes such as industrial output, capital investment, numbers of workers employed, and the like. But, as I have noted, it has little in common with the mathematical concept of continuity. A historically useful concept of discontinuity — or continuity — must have a different meaning. There is much to be said for basing it on a sudden change in the rate of change of an appropriately selected economic series, say industrial output. Clearly, in historical reality every time series is studded with sudden accelerations (and decelerations). The historian will have to decide which of those accelerations can be reasonably and profitably described as constituting a discontinuous type of industrial development. First of all, in order to isolate the phenomenon, the historian will have to organize his material in an appropriate fashion. Presumably, he will reject unsuitable averages which disguise the course of the evolution by casting it in the artificial mold of quinquennia or even decades. *Prima vista,* his decision will depend on the quantitative significance of a given acceleration. But beyond that, one may surmise, he will be willing to speak of discontinuities only in those cases where the accelerations he finds appear to be specifically conjoined with other features of the process. To the extent that this is true, a discussion of an individual type of industrialization is *concep-*

tually possible only against the background of an extended treatment of other types as well.

7. The role of agriculture in the process of industrialization may be more or less active. Very often, it has been assumed that a "revolution" in agriculture must precede a "revolution" in industry. The underlying reasoning has been based on a simple deduction. In order to supply the growing industrial labor force with foodstuffs, agricultural output must be kept stable at the very least. If most of the industrial labor force comes from the villages, productivity of agricultural labor must perforce increase. In addition, agriculture is said to act as the growing market for industrial goods. Thus, it is alleged, the role of agriculture in the process of industrialization cannot be anything but active. Unfortunately, in application to the industrial history of Europe, the reasoning constitutes a drastic simplification, if not distortion, of actual historical processes. There is little doubt that in some situations industrial development on a considerable scale took place, while agricultural output hardly kept pace with the growth of the population. There was no significant increase in the productivity of labor in agriculture, and disposable farm income was declining. The curtailing of the peasants' purchasing power may have gone so far as to lead, at least temporarily, to depletion of the capital stock in agriculture. It is another facet of the same situation that in such conditions the income gradient between agriculture and industry was achieved not through increased workers' incomes in industry, but through reduced farmers' incomes in agriculture. The crucial fact is precisely that decrease in peasant income and increase in agricultural productivity were historical alternatives within the European area as a whole. The difficulty of achieving increases in productivity in the face of falling farm incomes conspired with ignorance and inertia of the peasants to push the development in certain countries along the much less attractive channel of pressure on, rather than progress in, agriculture. Naturally, as a general proposition, some combination of the two forms of industrial development is not inconceivable. Nor is it unthinkable that in some cases importation of foodstuffs from abroad can offer still another alternative to improvements in agriculture. At the same time, greatly increased imports of certain agricultural products may be an integral part of

schemes designed to rationalize production in agriculture. But all this should not obscure the basic significance in European history of the two types of industrial development: the one in which agriculture partook as an active partner, deriving profit from the process while furthering and sustaining it, and the other in which agricultural population played the passive role of an exploited object.

8. Distinguishing between economic and political motivations does not necessarily supply an unambiguous conceptual pair to which two types of industrialization can be readily attached. A government may do a great deal to promote the cause of industrialization. It may do so because in its estimation the creation of an industrial apparatus and the concomitant increase in economic potential of the state will increase the power of the latter. In this sense, the motivation of the industrial policy of the government is clearly political. This however, may leave the actual character of the process rather unchanged, inasmuch as the bulk — or even the totality — of entrepreneurial and managerial decisions may continue to be determined by the profit motive and related considerations. The situation will change when the government begins to determine areas of industrial pursuits that are to be promoted and goes on to influence such choices as the average length of the gestation period in the industrial economy. Still, up to a point, the government may be said to do more than to reinforce and accentuate tendencies that have asserted themselves even in the absence of governmental intervention. It is one thing, however, to see governments favor large industrial enterprises because control of investment funds advanced by the treasuries cannot be effectively exercised over large numbers of small firms, or because compact investment operations offer better opportunities for bureaucratic corruption. It is another thing when, as a result of governmental policies, the nascent industry is largely placed in the service of immediate military needs of the state by concentrating chiefly upon the construction of strategic railroads and production of armaments. But even in this case the distinction is a relative one in the sense of being based upon varying "amounts" of this kind of governmental activity. The difference is divested of its quantitative character and becomes absolute, as it were, when continued high rates of industrial growth, conceived *in abstracto*, become one of the stability conditions of power exercise. This indeed may be regarded as an independent,

politically motivated type of industrialization — which, of course, does not mean that high standards of technical and economic efficiency cannot be properly observed in the course of such an industrialization as long as the guiding principles of governmental policy remain unaffected thereby.

The foregoing discussion must suffice to illustrate the "contrary pairs" as types of industrial development. It does not, of course, exhaust the reservoir of contrary pairs which can be interpreted as alternative types of industrial development. There are, however, other varying aspects of industrialization which can be suitably seen as belonging to different types of the process without appearing as simple dichotomies. One or two illustrations should be in order.

When discussing inflationary and noninflationary types of industrial development, reference was made to different modes of providing the needed capital disposition. To repeat what has been said above in a slightly different form, four types of industrial development can be easily distinguished with regard to the sources of industrial capital: (1) it may come from industrial profits that are being plowed back into investment and from voluntary savings out of current incomes earned in other segments of the economy; (2) capital may come from previously earned incomes; (3) credit creation by the banks is still another source; and (4) capital may be obtained through the budgetary operations of the state. It is obvious that each of the four types of financing, if predominant in industrialization, will imply a specific institutional framework of the industrializing economy. A host of questions is inevitably raised as to whether, and if so to what extent and in what way, entrepreneurial attitudes and decisions are affected by the source of funds the enterprise receives for investment. Clearly, such attitudes and decisions can relate to very crucial areas of entrepreneurial activity, such as mergers and amalgamations with other enterprises, determination of the appropriate time horizons, and so forth.

To give another example: There are fairly pronounced differences between systems of beliefs that have played their role in various European countries as "industrialization ideologies." The term ideology in this context must be used in a broad sense, comprising both the way in which industrial activity was vindicated (leaving aside the question whether justification was undertaken in good or bad faith) as well as motivations of certain economic actions or failures to act (acceptances). So conceived, it is easy to distinguish: (1) an ideology that placed central emphasis upon "man's desire to do the best he could for himself and those about him," letting him find the serendipities of economic equilibrium and economic progress on the road to the fulfillment of that desire; (2) an ideology according to which industrialization was expected to usher in the golden age of social justice and — alternatively or concomitantly — to enhance national power and national prestige; and (3) an ideology according to which industrialization was to be regarded as a harsh but ineluctable process that developed in obedience to unalterable historical laws and was to be crowned in the more or less distant future by an optimistic historical denouement.

There may well be some hesitation to distinguish types of industrialization in terms of the prevailing ideological justifications or motivations. Economic factors seem better suited for the purpose than such normative constructs, whether they appear with or without the syncretic admixture of causal inevitabilities. In the present context, however, the problem is not that some types of industrialization relate to aspects that are believed to be more crucial to the process than others. What really matters here is that, as one looks over the range of dichotomies or trichotomies adduced in the preceding pages, it becomes fairly clear that the significance of each individual type or set of types is greatly enhanced if it can be shown to be regularly associated with a number of other types or sets of types. In other words, the problem, as previously stated, is to conceive the process of industrialization as a unified but well-articulated pattern, that is to say, to advance from a consideration of types to a typology of industrialization.

To move from the former to the latter, however, is a somewhat complex procedure. What any typology needs — if it is to be worthy of its name — is an organizing principle that is the actual instrument of unification. As was adumbrated earlier, a priori the number of conceivable organizing principles is unlimited. So is a priori the number of the conceivable underlying types. In reality, however, limitations do exist. Partly they stem from the inadequacies of our knowledge and imagination. But there are also other difficulties that restrict our freedom to choose and to organize. On the one hand, in each case the nature of the organizing principle determines the line that separates usable and nonusable types. On the other hand, the available types must be adjusted to the needs of the typology and, moreover, once an organizing principle has been fastened upon, it almost inevitably will require creation of new types that had not been thought of before. Thus, it is in a limited sense only that one can regard the types as the raw material from which typologies are fabricated. The relation is one of interaction between the two constructs. It is still another problem that, once a given typology has been developed, the limits of its applicability will serve to gauge the significance of the device as a tool of historical research. In the process of searching for the boundaries of a typology, many types that have been excluded in the process of its formation may come back to life. In the remaining portion of this essay, the attempt will be made to offer an example of a typology of industrialization and to illustrate with its help the relationships touched upon in this paragraph.

In selecting the typology for the purpose, it is convenient for the present writer to remain within the area of his previous research and his previous generalizations in the field.[2] In fact, it is doubtful that any other course is really open to him. This means that he must ask leave to choose the degree of a country's backwardness on the eve of its industrialization as the organizing principle. From this point of view, it should be possible to take a different look at some of the types of industrial development that have been discussed earlier.

For simplicity's sake, let us refer in the following to the organizing principle of our typology as "D." In the following, D is used as the independent variable.

The higher D
1. The sharper was the "initial" kink in the curve of industrial output (plotted in a appropriate manner) and the more sustained was the following great spurt of industrialization;
2. the greater was the stress on producers' goods as against consumers' goods;

---

2. From this point on, the text follows and expands the summary of my approach as presented in the "Postscript" in *Economic Backwardness in Historical Perspective*, pp. 353–364.

3. the larger was the scale of industrial plant and enterprise;

4. the greater was the pressure upon the levels of consumption of the population;

5. the less active was the role performed by agriculture as market for industrial goods and as an area of increasing productivity of labor;

6. the more active was — up to a point — the role of banks and, beyond that point, the role of the state as promoters of industrial development.

If the foregoing points of propositions present a tenable view of important features of the industrial development of Europe, the question arises in which sense they can be regarded as comprising various types of industrial development. In other words, what types and what kind of types can be subsumed under D? Since D is a quantitative concept and since (with one exception) the dependent variables associated with it are expressed in quantitative terms, it is clear also that such types of development as may be distinguished will be quantitative in nature. This means that upon scrutiny of the available material some dividing lines must be cut through it, in the first instance with respect to D itself. Let us assume that, in the light of the available historical information, it seems reasonable to operate with three classes of D, yielding:

1. advanced areas where D was very low;
2. areas of medium backwardness;
3. areas of very considerable backwardness.

Let us regard these three classes as so many distinct *types* of industrial development.

It will be noticed at this point that this classification has an immediate bearing upon what has been said above with reference to one of the contrary pairs. If "eve of the industrialization" is interpreted in terms of a subsequent more or less sudden increase in the rate of growth of industrial output, and if continuity has been defined in terms of an absence of such an increase, then the previously discussed type of "continuous" industrialization must remain outside the present classification. Continuous industrialization may serve to indicate one of the limits of the present typology, but will not be an integral part of it. From the point of view of this typology, all industrial development that is accommodated under its wings is discontinuous.

At the same time, industrial development can be more or less discontinuous: the sudden rise in the rate of industrial growth may be larger or smaller After having ascertained the changes in rates of growth which pertain to countries in each of the three classes with regard to D, it is possible to obtain three groups or ranges, that is to say, three "types" of industrial development with regard to the acceleration that initiated this development. The same operation can then be performed with regard to the intensity and duration of the great spurt of industrialization; the share of producers' goods in the output of the nascent industry; the average scale of plant and enterprise; the changes in the levels of consumption; the changes in the productivity of farm labor and in the rate of growth of farm purchases of industrial goods. Finally, the role of special agents in the course of industrialization can be built into the general typology in such a way that in countries of considerable backwardness the government can be ascertained to have made a major contribution to both the supply of capital and the supply of entrepreneurial guidance to industrial enterprises; in countries of medium backwardness the same role was performed by investment banks; in the most advanced countries recourse to such special agents could be avoided. It might be possible to develop some quantitative indicators in order to compare the relative contributions of banks and governments. Still, in our list of the dependent variables, this case must be regarded as an exception (as mentioned before) in the sense that the qualitative differences between the different types of institutional arrangements have no counterparts in the other variables discussed.

Assuming that the operation, as described, is successful and that sufficiently large portions of the empirical material can be satisfactorily organized in this manner, the result will be a unified scheme comprising three main types of industrial development, every one of which is to be treated with reference to six or seven subtypes. The differences between the same subtype in each of the main types are uniformly related to the same organizing principle, as naturally are also the differences among the main types. Accordingly, what has been presented here may be viewed as a genuine typology at least in the formal sense of the term. But the typology may also claim to possess a fairly strong substantive or explicative texture. To put it differently, the degree of relative backwardness (D) used as an organizing principle may be said to satisfy our sense of reasoned adequacy because D can be viewed as the factor *causing* the variations in the individual subtypes, and accomplishing this not only across space but also over time. In other words, the typology can be expanded in such a way as to include changes in the degree of relative backwardness that occur in the process of industrialization. This is most easily demonstrated with reference to the last subtype discussed, that is, the role of special agents supplying capital disposition to industry. It is indeed instructive to see how, under the pressure of diminishing backwardness, sources of industrial finance tended to shift over time. In areas of medium backwardness, reinvestment of industrial profits replaced the original reliance on banks as the source of capital disposition. In areas of considerable backwardness, the sequence was more complex: the government budget came to be replaced by the banks, and then banking credit in turn began to be supplanted by the plowing back of profits earned by the industrial enterprises.

Thus seen, the organizing principle — the change in D — is also an explanatory principle. This, of course, is not the place to go into detail and to append reservations and qualifications. No more has been needed in this context than a schematic view of some of the tendencies that were in evidence in Europe before 1914. The only purpose has been to supply an illustration of the intertemporal regularities that occurred in response to changes in the organizing principle upon which my typology has been erected. And it must be noted that, once a typology of industrial development has been constructed, it may well be expanded into stagelike sequences. For it is only the usual unilinear stage concept that is incompatible with a typological ordering of the material.

It is of some interest to confront the typology of industrialization as presented here with the previous listing of selected types of industrial development. Some of the latter have been incorporated in the typology with a minimum of change or adjustment. This is true of the predominant role of producers' versus consumers' goods as distinct types of industrialization. It is true of the variations in the role of agriculture as well as of the variations in the sources of industrial capital supply. It is somewhat less true of the distinction

94

between "autonomous" and "forced" types of industrial development. In the typology the contrast is perhaps mitigated by the introduction of intermediate positions between the extremes (the role of the banks), and it is certainly attenuated by the change over time from forced toward autonomous types of development. (A similar statement, incidentally, could be made with regard to the "ideological" types, even though ideology has not been explicitly mentioned in our discussion of typology. Also here changes over time from the relatively "stronger" to relatively "weaker" ideologies of industrialization could be observed to occur as a function of changes in D.) In all these cases, however, the individual types have been placed within a unified explanatory framework.

At the same time, it is worth noting that other types listed have not been incorporated in the typology. This has been true of such juxtapositions as autochthonous versus derived industrializations; or continuous versus discontinuous developments; similarly, distinctions between economic and political motivations or structural versus non-structural changes remained outside the typology. It has been already mentioned that all the cases subsumed under the typology have been viewed as discontinuous. In very much the same way, all these cases have been viewed as autochthonous, and, finally, political motivation, to the extent that it has been admitted within the typology, has been assumed to do no more than merely reinforce the economic motivation. Political motivation, therefore, was not seen as becoming the predominant and permanent force in shaping the course of industrialization. And, of course, an extensive multifarious change in economic structures has been postulated as an intrinsic element of the typology. This, however, does not mean that the excluded cases should be regarded as irrelevant from the point of view of the typology. Rather they should be viewed as limitations upon the sphere of its applicability. As such, these cases are essential for appraising the value of the typology as an analytical tool in historical research.

No one, and least of all the present writer, would want to exaggerate the possible positive contribution of such a tool. The typology as presented here has been distilled from the industrial history of certain European countries during a period that came to a close with the outbreak of the First World War. It is thus delimited both in space and in time. Moreover, even in countries to which its propositions may be said to apply to a considerable extent, significant deviations from "typological normalcy" have been registered. Italy, for instance, is one interesting case in point. It must not be forgotten that, after all, the generalizations that have been organized in the typology are based on a very small number of discrete cases.

At the same time, however, the positive feature of the typology should not be overlooked. One of the dangers in historical research of this kind lies precisely in the temptation to overextend the scope of the generalization. This is usually done either at the price of historical accuracy or at the cost of jettisoning significant historical matter. Seen in this light, the geographic and chronological boundaries of our typology need not necessarily be viewed as its deficiency.

Moreover, even within the narrow scope there are complex problems of limitations. The organizing principle of a typology emerges from a given nucleus of historical material and at the same time is "verified" by it. Up to a point, therefore, a typology is not a "tool of analysis." Strictly speaking, it is analysis itself. Constructing a typology means analyzing a certain complex of historical situations and events. Taking the explanatory interest that inheres in the organizing principle as given, the value of a typology in the first instance will depend on the size of the original "nucleus," the area from which the typology developed and to which it naturally applies.

As we move beyond that area, the question is raised what other historical situations and events, not yet studied, can be sheltered under the same organizing principle. It is at this point that the typology is converted into a set of expectations and becomes a tool of analysis in the proper sense of the term. Clearly, whenever the expectations are satisfied and the area of applicability of the organizing principle is widened, the value of the typology is further enhanced. It would be quite unwarranted, however, to assume that negative results are necessarily destitute of analytical interest. As one discovers deviations from the expected standards, it is first of all important to identify them as such. For such an identification has, or at least can have, independent cognitive value. The next question then is whether it is possible to systematize the deviations in such a way as to qualify or expand either the organizing principle of the typology or the propositions in which it is encased and upon which stands the structure of main types and subtypes as exemplified in this essay. The result would be a more comprehensive and a more satisfactory typology. It may do better service as a tool of analysis when still untrodden ground is approached. It may also lead to additional insights in revisiting previously covered territory. In the end, however, the point will be reached where the deviations from what is expected have become so pervasive and far-reaching that no useful purpose can be served in trying to match them with an alien organizing principle. This does not mean a refutation of the old typology. Historical generalizations are not universal propositions that are falsified as soon as a single black swan has been observed. Our hypotheses are not "lawlike." They are "contingent" and they must be treated as such. Verifying historical generalizations and establishing the area of their validity are identical operations. And it is by pushing a proposition, an approach, a typology, to the limits of its applicability that its value can be fully appraised. If, in the process of discovering the discrepancies between old expectations and new materials, the historian is moved to institute the search for a new organizing principle leading to a new typology and new ways of research, the old system of types and subtypes may indeed be said to have doubly justified itself as a tool of historical analysis.

At the same time, it must be stressed that the preceding discussion has not been intended to vindicate a single typology of modern industrial history. The purpose has been to illustrate with the help of one possible case some of the conceptual and architectural problems involved. Whether the particular example chosen will or will not directly stimulate other approaches, it is to be hoped that other typologies will be constructed, and it is reasonable to expect a good deal of further elucidation from a confrontation of several typologies. It has been well said that we usually start by classifying problems and then proceed to classify ways of classifying problems. Perhaps something in the nature of a typology of typologies of industrial development will eventually come within our grasp, permitting new questions to be raised and new answers to be found in the never-ending process of research.

5

The Industrial Development of Italy:
A Debate with Rosario Romeo

GERSCHENKRON: Needless to say, I greatly appreciate this opportunity to meet Rosario Romeo in person and to exchange ideas with him. The most fruitful way of starting the discussion would probably be for me to concentrate on those matters where certain disagreements exist between my views and his. For I could easily spend two or three hours talking about those aspects of his book with which I am in perfect agreement. By contrast, a quarter of an hour or so should suffice to circumscribe the area of my dissent. Thus I can be brief and leave Professor Romeo plenty of time for his rebuttal.

When I speak of disagreement or dissent, I have essentially two points in mind. First of all, there are concepts, or sets of concepts, which I find it difficult to accept. And proceeding from conceptual — or perhaps merely semantic — problems, I arrive at somewhat different evaluations of Italian industrial history. I should like therefore to say a word or two about our conceptual differences before discussing the substantive problems and the hard facts of industrial development.

The conceptual problems essentially relate to an old Marxian idea which of late has celebrated some well-deserved resuscitation in our literature. The reference is to the concept of original accumula-

Note. This debate, presented here in my translation from the Italian, was organized by Svimez and took place in Rome in July 1960. The book mentioned in the first paragraph is Romeo's *Risorgimento e capitalismo* (Bari, 1959); see also "Rosario Romeo and the Original Accumulation of Capital," in my *Economic Backwardness in Historical Perspective,* pp. 90–118.

tion of capital, also known as primitive or preliminary accumulation. Marx himself left the concept in a state of some confusion, as I have tried to point out elsewhere.[1] It was, however, an interesting idea and in fact an exciting historical intuition; it is regrettable that, after having presented a brief sketch, Marx abandoned the main line of approach and allowed himself to be deflected into a discussion of enclosures. This was a blind alley as far as the development of the concept was concerned, even though one can readily understand the political reasons that tempted and propelled Marx in that direction.

Naturally, everybody is his own master in forming his own concepts, and there are many possible ways to define the concept of original accumulation. I should like to present briefly three possible ways of looking at the phenomenon. First of all, we can define original accumulation in monetary terms, that is to say, as previously accumulated claims against current national income. "Previously" in this sense means not only that the accumulations result from past national income, but also that they antedate the period of industrialization. The accumulations must be in such a form that they can be readily converted into effective claims against current national income. When the time is ripe and "the hour of industrialization strikes," they can be quickly aroused from their prolonged sleep and put into active entrepreneurial hands to be used for the deflection of resources from production of consumers' goods to production of producers' goods. The function of original accumulation then is to change at a strategic moment the distribution of national income as between consumption and investment. What is implied in the concept is precisely the idea of the "hour that strikes," of the "strategic moment," that is to say, of the beginning of industrialization. Of course, there is something artificial in placing a dam of this sort across the continuous flow of history. In a way it is our own work. In speaking of "the beginning of industrialization," we assert that at this point certain definite changes have taken place, important enough for us to regard what lies beyond that point as a new historical period. It is in this sense, involving the plausibility of our historical judgment, that we speak of an original or previous accumulation.

1. *Economic Backwardness in Historical Perspective*, pp. 33–38.

But this is only one of the possible concepts. We can construct another one which has nothing to do with previously accumulated claims. The accumulation can derive from current income. If we persist in speaking of original accumulation, we do so because income to be devoted to the purpose of investment in industry comes from branches of the economy that are nonindustrial, we might say pre-industrial. The originality or previousness of the accumulation then lies in its distinction from accumulation in a fully developed industrial economy, where industrial profits constitute the primary source of industrial investment. In this sense particularly there is something "previous" about savings derived from agriculture — the original branch of the economy — which are used to finance the new, non-traditional economic pursuits. This is still a monetary concept of accumulation, but it differs from the first *inter alia* because it does not involve any processes of forced savings. Depending on the circumstances, the concept may possess independent usefulness in clarifying historical sequences.

There is, finally, a third concept of original accumulation. Unlike the first two, it is not related to the sources but to the use made of the funds. If they are employed in sectors of the economy which in some sense can be regarded as specific preindustrial investments, that is to say, as a precondition or prerequisite to industrial development, then we may speak of previous accumulation — this time not in monetary terms, but in real terms and thus in a different and very specific sense. It seems to me that Romeo has ignored the first concept of original accumulation and has combined the second and third into a new unified concept, upon which he bestows the name of primitive accumulation of capital. So far so good. The procedure is perfectly sound and unexceptionable. As said before, any concept may do. The proof is in the eating, in the enlightenment that can be derived from the concept, and there is little doubt that Romeo has been able to make good use of his own conceptual creation.

Let me note in parentheses that Romeo's welding together of the two concepts of original accumulation has distinct advantages from the point of view of statistical measurement If we are faced with a situation where savings made in agriculture — be they voluntary or exacted through taxes — are channeled into other economic activities, it is very probable that, given appropriate statistics, we should be able to measure the quantitative importance of these processes with very little difficulty. But the first concept of original accumulation is much more refractory as far as empirical application is concerned. The concept involves forced savings in the specific sense of the term, and forced savings — whether a result of original accumulation or of credit creation by banks — entail changes in relative prices and, by the same token, require use of complicated and hazardous techniques of deflating current values. It is always precarious to estimate *ex ante* processes from *ex post* data. But the difficulties are not insuperable. And, at any rate, to say that a concept is difficult of application does not mean that it is in principle nonoperational. It can still be very illuminating even if it resists precise and comprehensive statistical measurement. We may still collect enough partial and approximate information to justify some meaningful conclusions and to enable us to say, for instance, that in England in a certain period a fair portion of financing of the nascent industrial enterprises was obtained by utilizing, in one form or another, previously accumulated wealth and by unleashing processes of forced savings with their specific effect on relative prices.

Returning now to Romeo's concept and to his application of it to the industrial history of Italy after the Unification, it seems to me that he is primarily interested in what nowadays is often described as "infrastructure." This is not a very elegant term. On the other hand, "social overhead capital," which may sound better, is rather misleading since it is never quite clear what actually is "social" and "overhead" about the stock of capital created in this fashion. And elegance apart, there is something all too suggestive or autosuggestive about the term "infrastructure." The moment you use it, things begin immediately to look impressively logical, in fact, much too logical to make for convincing history. There are things that are at the bottom and things that are on top, and naturally the former must come first. Who would think of starting a house with the roof? Clearly, you must start with the foundations. Similarly, development must begin with infrastructure to be followed by superstructure, that is, by constructing and equipping factories and hiring labor.

Before speaking of the empirical disabilities of this approach, let me say that Romeo's case is well defined. He shows clearly how in the 1860's and 1870's Italy succeeded in getting from agriculture, through voluntary contributions and taxes, funds that were used to finance railroad building. In this fashion, Romeo says, a prerequisite was created for the subsequent industrialization that took place in the eighties. The proof, then, of the whole argument is the spurt of the eighties.

The industrial expansion of the eighties has become somewhat controversial since the publication by Benedetto Barberi of his "Indagine statistica," [2] according to which the decade of the eighties was marked, if anything, by a decline of output rather than by the considerable increase I believe to have ascertained through my own researches. But pending further research and the presentation of Barberi's computations, I see no reason to change my position and, accordingly, am quite willing to accept Romeo's view on the course of industrial events in the eighties. This then, as I see it, is Romeo's story of Italy's industrial development in the three decades after the Unification. I hope I have presented it fairly, and very fortunately he will be able here to correct any wrong impression of his views I may have given.

Now it seems to me that there are primarily two difficulties with Romeo's scheme, as I tried to point out in my earlier essay on the subject. First of all, there is the relative insignificance of the savings supplied by agriculture. I agree that agriculture did well in the first two decades after Unification and that there was a considerable expansion of agricultural output — this is out of dispute. What is dubious is the volume of savings made available; furthermore, neither the volume of public works nor that of investment in general was in any way remarkable during this period. In other words, the events that Romeo has described and their interrelationship are correctly observed, but their quantitative importance was much too small to have had any significant effect.

I should like to offer still another consideration, which I did not mention, but probably should have mentioned, in my essay. On the basis of my studies of industrial development and particularly of

2. "Indagine statistica sullo sviluppo del reddito nazionale dell'Italia dal 1861 al 1956," *Annali di statistica*, IX (Rome, 1957).

railroad construction, I have come to believe that the problem of capital supply for the railroads in European countries (France, Germany, Italy, and pre–1914 Russia) did not present extraordinary difficulties. I realize, of course, that railroad construction was an expensive business, and perhaps nowhere more so than in Italy. A few days ago I traveled once more by train from Bologna to Florence across the Apennines, and once more I could not help marveling at the tremendous achievement of burrowing those innumerable tunnels through the proud rock of the mountains. And yet, once the initial aversion to the innovation was overcome, funds to cover the stupendous cost were readily found. Not so in industry. While capital from foreign and domestic sources flowed into railroads, capital for industrial investment was timid and reluctant. This difference impressed me particularly in my observations of the Italian capital market as it operated around the turn of the century. The investors certainly had pronounced preferences for railroad securities over industrial paper. Hence the creation of the infrastructure was much less of a problem than is implied in Romeo's presentation.

I must return now to industrial development in the eighties, which plays such a crucial role in Romeo's scheme. In appraising that decade, much depends on the kind of spectacles through which one wishes to look at the events. If you favor rosy spectacles you might say: "After all, it was quite a spurt. True, the rate of growth was not very high but still, such as it was, it kept up for a fair number of years." On the other hand, using grey spectacles the picture you get is less encouraging. And there are good reasons for choosing the grey hue. There *is* such a thing as a great spurt of industrialization, which is not to be confused with normal cyclical fluctuations. A great spurt, a tidal wave, once it starts rolling, tends to pass through an international depression with almost no loss in speed and impetus. This at least is what we have learned from the industrial experience of Europe. Now what occurred in Italy in the eighties certainly was not a great spurt of the kind just described. The expansion went on for a while, then stopped and was followed by one of the most difficult decades in the economic history of the new state. Those years were marked by banking failures and a general lack of confidence in the economic future of the country. This situation led toward the end of the decade to widespread political unrest. Taking all this into consideration, it is difficult indeed, if not impossible, to describe the Italian experience of the eighties as a specific great spurt of industrial development. If, for example, Russian industrialization between 1885 and 1900 *was* a great spurt, then the Italian upswing of the eighties was a phenomenon of an altogether different order. Italy had to wait for another ten years, until 1895–96. Then the great spurt came, bringing along with it a radical structural transformation of Italian industry. The spurt did possess such great momentum that the Italian economy remained essentially undisturbed by the great European depression of 1900. To be sure, there was some unpleasantness — enforced shifts in foreign commerce, shrinking of export markets — but the spurt was great enough to carry the country through the depression without any significant reduction in the rate of growth.

I believe, therefore, that the historical problem presents itself as follows: Why was the upswing of the eighties so short-lived? In trying to answer the question, I think it useful to recall the first concept of original accumulation and to use it as background for discussing Romeo's second and third concepts. As I see it, the crux of the matter is that the upswing of the eighties began in conditions of very considerable relative backwardness. At the same time, the first concept of original accumulation, based as it is on previously amassed wealth, is peculiar to more advanced countries. Such countries were able to develop methods for channeling the previously accumulated funds into the proper hands, and to do it through special institutional arrangements or thanks to favorable general attitudes of relevant groups of the population. (Let me add here something I should have said earlier, namely, that one of the advantages of the way Romeo uses his concept is that he does not simply speak of savings and availabilities of funds, but tries to ascertain whether and how such funds actually found their way into investment projects. Hence his model is fully developed and ranges from the creation of surpluses to their use in railroad construction and public works).

But once we keep the first concept of original accumulation in mind, concepts two and three appear to be closely related to it. What I mean is that Romeo's two concepts can be regarded as *substitutes* for the first and more fundamental concept of original accumulation.

For those concepts should not be regarded as prerequisites of industrialization in the same sense that concept one can be. What took place in Italy, in a very important sense, was not creation of prerequisites but substitution for missing ones. Since "previous wealth" was inadequate or could not be attracted into industry, it was necessary to have recourse to savings produced by current national income in general, and agricultural income in particular. These processes of substitution are far from simple. In fact, as I have said, the greater the degree of a country's backwardness on the eve of its industrialization, the more complex are the patterns of substitution for what may be regarded as prerequisites in more advanced countries. Hence we find that, in a country like England, previously accumulated funds came forth and were made available to industrial entrepreneurs partly through the stock exchange, but even more so by family relations, friends, people interested in developing and utilizing certain inventions, and so on. In a backward country, such processes are much less in evidence, and accordingly recourse to various patterns of substitution becomes much more important. This is the point at which I find myself farthest away from Romeo. For I believe that the substitutions (which are implied in his concepts two and three) simply were not quantitatively strong enough to launch the Italian economy upon the road of the great spurt, upon the road, that is, of a high rate of growth sustained for a sufficiently long time to create major structural changes in the industrial economy.

Italy had to wait for ten long years. Why? I believe that what the country was waiting for — to put it teleologically — was the disappearance of the old banks and the creation of an atmosphere more propitious for the appearance of a new factor. Personally, I attribute very great importance to the arrival of German financial institutions in Italy in the middle of the nineties. The German banks came to Italy essentially for two reasons. The first is precisely because the old Italian banks, including the most significant of them, the Credito Mobiliare, had disappeared. These banks had been less interested in industrialization and much preferred to invest in city housing. Housing in itself is, of course, a respectable area of investment, and it is not up to me to express a political opinion here as to whether building up Rome at that particular time and at that speed was or was not a good thing. The emphasis on *edilizia* in Rome may have been "natural" in terms of the historical situation and as such, so to speak, "inevitable." But the effects of this policy are perfectly clear: concentration on housing prevented a generous and far-sighted industrial policy on the part of the old banks. Moreover, having their origins in French rather than German tradition, they never succeeded in becoming an efficient instrument of industrial financing, as did the German banks — those jacks of all trades, veritable department stores in the field of banking. When the old banks were swept away by the economic crisis, the great opportunity came for a new start. The German banks could both gather the flotsam of industrial enterprises that had been connected with the old banks and launch into new ventures, unimpeded by the competition of the defunct banks.

The second reason for the coming of the German banks is that a historical period was then drawing to its close in Germany. German industry, after a period of rapid growth, was less and less in need of aid and guidance from the banks. Industry was becoming self-reliant and independent. True, this evolution did not reduce the banks to the status of their English counterparts, for the German banks were always to remain *sui generis* by comparison. But by 1900 the period of the banks' ascendancy over German industry was over, and hence the banks had much reason and incentive to begin large-scale exports of their capital and of their rich experience in the field.

Perhaps I may be allowed to insert a few words on certain aspects of the functioning of the new banks in Italy. [The late] Gino Luzzatto made extensive excerpts from the archival material of the Banca Commerciale in Milan and very kindly allowed me to consult his papers. In examining them, I could not help being greatly impressed by the boundless energy with which the Banca plunged into the business of creating and financing important Italian enterprises. Since the Italian directors of this bank were accountable to headquarters in Germany, their correspondence is most revealing of their methods and intentions. At least two conclusions can be drawn. At times it is said that Italian economic development started slowly and belatedly because the Italian bourgeoisie was not permeated with the right spirit — because, as Einaudi would have said, there were no *principi mercanti*, no proud heroes of industrial adventure, but only small men, parochially limited and destitute of great ideas. This is clearly and emphatically not the impression I received from my study of those archives. From the very beginning, the German directors of the Banca Commerciale were fascinated by the availability in Italy of men possessing entrepreneurial vision and constructive ideas. What troubled them was something else — the fear lest such men allow their imagination to carry them beyond the boundaries of prudence and circumspection. In other words, one might say that Italian entrepreneurs were viewed by the Banca Commerciale as corresponding much more to the entrepreneurial image of Werner Sombart than to that of Max Weber. The bank's solution often consisted in letting an enterprise be led by an Italian entrepreneur, supported by a German manager or at least by a German chief accountant. In this way they felt the audacity of an innovating entrepreneur could be combined with, and held in check by, the accountant's rational calculus.

The second point that emerges from the correspondence is, if anything, even more surprising. As one scrutinizes the literature of the period, one finds it very hostile to the penetration of the German banks into Italy. Contemporaneous articles both in professional economic journals and in more popular periodicals, the daily press, public opinion in general, were unanimous in viewing German banking with great suspicion. In left and right circles alike, there was a general tendency to regard the newcomers as spearheads of German imperialism. It was therefore extremely curious to see how quickly the German directors in Italy assimilated the environment. The process of their "Italianization" was rapid indeed. Time and again one finds in the correspondence insistent orders from Germany to appoint a German director for this or that industrial enterprise. But the German representatives in Milan resisted such orders, pointing out that such an appointment would not be favorably received in Italy; moreover, it was entirely unnecessary to appoint foreigners to such posts since native Italian talent was abundantly available and the Italians were perfectly able to manage their own affairs. It seems that, relatively soon, the Germans in Milan began to grow more and more independent of German capital and were even anxious to establish contacts with France in order to use French capital as a counterpoise to the German influence.

At any rate, as one studies the story of the new banking in Italy after the mid-1890's, one can only admire the vigor, the perseverance, and the optimism with which these men went about their business. They proceeded exactly as they had in Germany, applying the lessons they had learned so well through the trials and errors of several decades. They took care of an industrial enterprise from its establishment on, supported it over a number of years, collected a number of similar enterprises, waiting patiently for the opportune moment when they could be welded together into a really significant entity; they opened generous lines of short-term credit to their fledglings, knowing full well that the short-term funds would be invested long, into fixed capital. But, at least in the early years, they had the assurance that their German principals would bail them out if something went wrong, and they assumed that in a very desperate situation they could count on aid from the Banca d'Italia. These expectations provided sufficient guarantees for them to engage in "unsound" operations and to conduct them in Italy with the same measure of success that they had had in Germany.

My main point is that these activities of the banks were a strategic factor. They were the real substitution for the missing prerequisites and must be held responsible, more than anything else, for the fact that Italy finally, after 1896, had its great spurt. For this reason, I believe that Romeo's concepts two or three, however interesting and original, do not really touch on the crucial factors at work in that period.

All this does not mean, of course, that I disagree with Romeo as far as the original motivation of his book is concerned. He started from a survey of Marxian historians in Italy after the last war and found them to stand under the strong influence of Antonio Gramsci. Romeo opposed the thesis according to which everything would have been just fine in Italy, if only an agrarian reform upon the French pattern had been carried out. Here I find myself in agreement. He has criticized effectively the inconsistency in operating with two "half problems": the industrial revolution in England and the political revolution in France. The two very different phenomena have been very confusingly merged into a hybrid construct of necessary prerequisites, intimating that economic development everywhere must conform to the model of English industrial history, while agrarian reform and the political transformation must follow the French pattern and "feudalism" must be destroyed exactly as it had been in France. I believe, and I am sure Romeo will agree, that feudalism in this sense is not an operational term and that the relation between the preindustrial institutional framework and industrialization is much more complex than is suggested by the bland use of simplicist formulas. Gramsci and the Italian historians who follow him have failed to notice that many retarding factors, those behind the slow economic development in postrevolutionary France, had their origin in the extent to which the small family farm had existed in France. It is altogether possible that the Jacobins bear some measure of guilt for the disabilities of French economic growth in the nineteenth century.

It may be in order for me to mention one more area of agreement with Romeo: the fundamental fact that there was an impressive industrial development in Italy between 1896 and 1914. What happened during those years must be neither belittled nor exaggerated. It must be viewed with a clear sense of proportion. On the one hand, nothing is more unfair than to speak of the "little Italy of the Risorgimento" or of the mediocrity of the Italian bourgeoisie, which allegedly proved unable to launch a substantial economic offensive. On the other hand, it may be true that the period failed to produce very great business leaders, even though some entrepreneurs did leave a permanent imprint upon the economic history of the country; at the same time, the rate of growth did not quite reach levels that might have been expected on the basis of the general condition of the country. Between the extremes there is much room for the view that, such as it was, the great spurt after 1896 did entail a magnificent transformation of the Italian economy. This much is certain. But, for the rest, it must also be recognized that we have not done much more than scratch the surface and that much deeper study of the relevant facts and problems is called for. To give just one example, there is still the previously mentioned unresolved divergence between Barberi and myself with regard to the behavior of the index of industrial output in the eighties. Who knows? Perhaps Barberi is right and there was no upswing at all during that decade. Clearly, further research is urgently needed. And thus one has every reason to welcome the fact that this area of study has aroused the interest of a man of Romeo's talents. I do hope that he will continue his research in the direction he has so felicitously inaugurated, and that we may expect from him further work as fruitful and stimulating as his previous studies.

Romeo: I wish to thank Alexander Gerschenkron for the attention he has devoted to my book — an attention which, I believe, should be attributed not so much to my conclusions as to my attempt to pose certain questions, upon which his own studies have cast much light. The questions under discussion certainly deserve a much more penetrating analysis than the one they have received so far. I should like, therefore, to thank Professor Gerschenkron not only in my own name, but also in the name of many Italian scholars who have so greatly appreciated his contribution to the study of problems that have been hardly touched upon by our research in Italian economic history.

It is precisely the complexity of the problems that Gerschenkron has raised here which makes it difficult for me to reply to all of his points; or, I should say, renders it difficult to give expression to all the trains of thought he has stimulated in my mind. Gerschenkron has here added important new elements to the problems treated in his last year's essay in the *Rivista storica italiana* and elsewhere. I shall confine myself, therefore, to a few aspects of the problem which seem to me to be most essential.

Gerschenkron has said that, of the three senses in which the concept of original accumulation can be understood, I have preferred to use the two last concepts, combining them into one. (Let me add in parentheses that I have never intended to use the concept of original accumulation in the strict Marxian sense, and I have said so explicitly.) On the other hand, Gerschenkron thinks that the proper key to the understanding of Italian industrial development can be found precisely in concept number one, which I have excluded. The concept refers to savings already existing in the Italian economy around the middle of the nineteenth century and their use for industrial investment, that is, their transformation into a factor of production, or capital in the real sense of the term.

Indeed, I am not inclined to overestimate the volume of savings in Italy that antedated her capitalist development. Although it is true that money for railroad construction was found with relative ease, it is also true that at the beginning those large investments had been made possible only with the help of large financial institutions abroad or through government intervention. The latter either took the direct form of railroad construction, or proceeded through concessions equipped with profit guarantees and contributions to the cost of operations. In this way investments, which in terms of strict private accounting would have been neither sufficiently secure nor sufficiently promising, were rendered attractive and economically possible. Still, despite this reservation, Gerschenkron is certainly correct when he stresses the central importance of the moment when pre-existent savings, which had eschewed industrial employment in the past, begin to turn to it. This is the meaning of his emphasis on that phase in Italian economic history which is marked by a new type of banking investment in industry, and is closely connected with economic development during Giolitti's era. But to pose the question in this way immediately leads to the next question: What determined this change in the direction of investment?

In order to answer this question, it is necessary to clear the air of a misunderstanding that perhaps is the only one remaining between me and Gerschenkron. It refers to my evaluation of economic significance of the period 1881–1887 in Italian history.

In fact, I have never regarded the eighties as the time of radical industrial transformation of the Italian economy. As I have explicitly stated, my starting point has been the index of industrial output constructed by Gerschenkron. According to his findings, the critical period of Italian industrial development, our "industrial revolution," falls between 1896 and 1907. But the years 1881–1887, to my mind, show with particular intensity the process that characterized the whole flow of Italian economic history from 1860 till the beginning of the industrial revolution in 1896. I am referring to the modernization of the economic structure, to the replacement of old modes of production by new ones, to the appearance of new forms of marketing, to the creation of a network of infrastructures, and so on. To be sure, if we look at the growth of Italian national income in the years before

1896 (rather than before 1888), we are certainly struck, as is Gerschenkron, by the insignificance of the quantitative change in national income and, in particular, the industrial contribution thereto. But there is a real danger that, by riveting our eyes exclusively to the quantitative aspect of the matter, we fail to notice the transformation in the structure of productive processes. Let me give an example that, to my mind, appears especially convincing. As is generally known, production of ferrous metals in Italy was declining in the second half of the nineteenth century because the industry's charcoal-fed blast furnaces were unable to stand the competition of French and English iron and were being closed down one after the other. Output of Italian pig iron plummeted. But then there appeared a new demand for pig iron with the opening of new and modern blast furnaces in Terni. The total volume of iron output in the period is small, resulting as it does from the expansion of output of modern plants and from the decline of the old ones. However, the economic significance of the process should not be measured in aggregate terms. The total volume of output may have remained unchanged, but it makes all the difference in the world if a large part of that output is no longer produced by an antiquated and declining industry, but by modern and efficient plants.

Analogously, the economy went through a process of decline in the putting-out system. There is plentiful evidence that the processing of materials, particularly that done by peasants in their homes, gradually diminished. As the volume of their output fell from year to year, its place was taken by the volume of output produced by the new textile mills. Naturally, the output of the mills does not appear to rise very fast, because the aggregate figures also reflect the shrinking of the putting-out system. But, in reality, the rate of growth of output of modern plants is much higher than appears from data for the whole industry.

More important than quantitative increases in output, however, were the complex consequences of the application of new methods, which became evident quite a while before the advent of the industrial revolution. The latter cannot begin unless it is necessarily preceded by changes, or at least by initiation of changes, in a number of economic relationships. Previously dominant positions must be undermined. And this is precisely what took place, slowly but steadily, in the decades before 1896. Now, in causing these transformations, a central role was played not so much by pre-existing savings — which, as Gerschenkron reminds us, were still reluctant to move spontaneously into industry — but rather by incomes from current outputs. These incomes were either impounded by the state through taxation or else accumulated by landowners and agrarian entrepreneurs through pressure upon payments to agricultural producers before the advent of the agrarian crisis (which in Italy came around 1880). These funds then were used to finance public works in close collaboration with a number of important foreign firms. It was this capital whose job it was to demolish old economic structures, thereby rendering possible, that is to say, economically profitable, investment of private savings (both current and pre-existing) in industry, whether directly or through the medium of the big banks that came after 1894 and combined the normal functions of commercial banking with those of the *crédit mobilier*.

In fact, if we neglect these antecedents, the phenomenon of the industrial revolution itself becomes rather incomprehensible. There are, of course, various interpretations of Italian economic expansion in the second half of the nineties. We may neglect the alleged widening of peasant markets for industrial goods, which is said to have come after the agrarian strikes, for this development belongs to the period after 1900 and cannot be used to explain the original recovery. More convincing among these interpretations is the reference to the level of prices in world markets (which started rising precisely in 1896) and to the stimulating effect of price increases first upon exports and then upon the whole economic system. But there had been periods of rising prices before, for instance between 1849 and 1874, that is, before the Great Depression, which did not elicit any response on the part of the Italian economy. Why then was the effect so radically different after 1896? Obviously it was because, in the interval, things came into being that had not been in existence earlier. And, indeed, there had occurred a commercialization of the Italian economy, a general modernization of the organization and the modes of production, so that new economic structures had emerged which *were* able to respond to the stimulus of rising world prices.

In the earlier period, when our economy was largely insulated from international markets, the foreign impulses were not felt and the beneficial effects did not materialize.

Gerschenkron, on the other hand, assigns the role of strategic factor in the Italian great spurt to another factor, to wit, to the appearance of new banks of the mixed German type and to their activities within the Italian body economic. Everything he has said in this respect is of extraordinary interest in view of the decisive role played by these banks in our industrial system, not only before the First World War but also after it until the very beginning of the world depression in 1929. But even then we must ask ourselves whether the activity of the banks should not be seen in relation to the structural changes in the Italian economy of which I have spoken earlier. It would seem to me that the banks could not have performed in the same way within an economic framework that existed, say, in the seventies, when collecting deposits and passing them on to industry would have been a much more arduous task. Suffice it to see, for example, what institutions such as the Credito Mobiliare Italiano or the Banca Generale were doing prior to 1894. Of course, they were not banks of the German mixed type, and they were much less adapted to the job of industrial investment. But if we compare their activities with similar institutions abroad, say with the French Crédit Mobilier, we easily see that their investment policies were kept at a level below what could have been reached even within the then-existing banking structure. To be sure, both the Banca Generale and the Credito Mobiliare (for which we have better documentary evidence) had a certain importance in the industrial evolution of the country. But the effects on the whole were small. If we look at the most important sectors of Italian manufacturing at the time, for example, the textile industry, by far the most significant one, it is clear that it developed almost entirely independently of the banks. The old branches of manufacturing, such as silk, wool, linen, and foodstuffs — with the exception of the cotton industry — all continued to be more independent of the banks than the branches created later in the period dominated by the Banca Commerciale, the Credito Italiano, the Banco di Roma, and the Società Bancaria Italiana. Where we find a closer connection between investment of bank capital and industry after 1896 is always in the new sectors of the industrial economy, such as ferrous metals, machinery, chemicals, and electricity.

Hence if we concentrate our attention on the new factor, on the appearance of the mixed bank of the German type in 1894, the basic question still remains: Why did the new banks begin their activity at that point and not earlier? I do not believe that this question can be satisfactorily answered simply by reference to the new orientation of Italian foreign policy, that is to say, by reference to Crispi's asking the German government for assistance in establishing a new bank designed to defend Italian government securities against short-selling speculations on the stock exchange in Paris. I believe that in reality the innovation came when domestic conditions had matured to assure it of a durable success. This is shown by the fact that the first newcomer — the Banca Commerciale — was quickly followed by others which proved no less successful. This success expressed itself in a performance for whose historical significance in our economic development I must refer you to the lucid exposition by Professor Saraceno, which does not need much additional elaboration.

Thus, to my mind, the significance of the pre-1896 period in Italian economic history lies in the creation of preconditions for modern economic development. For some thirty years after 1896, this development pivoted on the powerful activities of banks. No more than the preconditions were created before 1896, because considerable increase in our national income, and especially in industry's contribution to it, came only after that date. What happened in the years 1881–1887 was the first appearance of large-scale enterprises in industry and, for the first time, a considerable quickening of the rhythm of industrial growth. Gerschenkron's index confirms the increases in output that occurred in the eighties, although the data of our Central Institute of Statistics show a different picture. As between the two indices I believe that Gerschenkron's is closer to the truth. I am not saying this for reasons of statistical techniques, since I should not deem myself qualified to decide on the relative merits of two highly competent technical studies. But I am saying this, as it were, for general historical reasons. For we have evidence on the industrial expansion in Italy between 1881 and 1887 from a large multiplicity of sources. It is attested to in economic literature and in political literature. We can infer it from the foundation dates of many enterprises and the opening of many plants. The fact of expansion is made clear to us from purely literary sources depicting the change in customs and social life in general, and particularly in the large cities of the North. It is true that from 1888 to 1895 the Italian economy went through a very grave crisis. But from a proper point of view, those years, characterized as they are by the abolition of old systems of banks of issue, by the reform of monetary circulation, and by the disappearance of the old banks of the *crédit mobilier* type, are in reality a period of transition from the phase of preconditions to that of the actual "industrial revolution." In these intervening years the old structures that had exhausted their usefulness were removed, and others, better adapted to the needs of the new epoch, were formed. In saying this I do not wish, of course, to indulge in hindsight justifications, and to deny the grave hardships and the retardation that the depression inflicted upon the economy of the country.

This is the essence of the fleeting thoughts that were occurring to me as I listened to Gerschenkron's exposition. And once more I wish to thank him in the name of all those in Italy who approach those problems not in the spirit of ideological schematism, but moved by the desire and will to understand how things really happened.

Gerschenkron: Let me first of all thank Professor Romeo for his kind words. For the rest, I shall try to be brief. I am not sure that I can readily accept Romeo's vision of a slow, and perhaps not easily perceptible, structural change which, he says, preceded the actual start of industrialization. In general, as far as concerns the industrial development of backward countries in Europe of the nineteenth century, I am rather suspicious of any attempt to find too much orderly sequence in that process. First, it is said, certain prerequisites are created; then certain structural changes take place; then there is a purge of things that do not belong in the new age, and so the putting-out system and other preindustrial formations are eliminated and the land is cleared for industrialization. Up to a point, all this is plausible and, in fact, appears extremely logical. I have said myself that the disappearance of the old banks was a step on the road of industrial progress. But when it comes to structural changes, in particular the elimination of small artisans and domestic industries, I am not at all sure that the industrialization of a backward country proceeds in this way. Something of the sort Romeo describes certainly did take place in England. There the industrial revolution ushered in the textile age, and the textile industry then looked back upon a long premodern history: single artisans, artisans united in craft guilds, merchant employers, and so on. In England, the modern factory had to compete against all these preindustrial formations before it could assert itself.

Now, one advantage of a backward country — and the great spurt in Italy came a century or so after England's — is precisely that it can channel its major industrial effort into sectors where preindustrial formations either are few or do not exist at all. In the machinery industry or the chemical industry, but particularly in the former, there are no preindustrial formations. The field is wide open. And if Italy, in fact, did witness a considerable upswing of her textile industries, this was a rather abnormal phenomenon and essentially the result of the protectionist policy of the Italian government, a policy altogether ill advised and misguided from the point of view of the country's economic development. Moreover, I believe that the same is true with regard to the production of iron and steel. Of course, there were political problems, political ambitions, ideas relating to the position of Italy as a great power. But if one may abstract from politics and confine oneself to economic factors, then we should ask in which way the rate of industrial growth in Italy could have been maximized. Then, I believe, the answer is clear. We cannot escape the conclusion that Italy had no economic interest in promoting the iron and steel industry, the huge consumer of coal that had to come from afar, doubling its price between Newcastle and Genoa. So Italy never should have tried to build up an iron and steel capacity of such dimensions. But the structure of the Italian tariff, particularly in the early years of protectionism, was clearly oriented to the protection of iron and steel at the expense of the most promising Italian industry — that is, the machinery industry, whose development therefore came later together with the chemical and automobile industries.

Incidentally, as far as the automobile industry is concerned, let me record another surprising — and this time negative — impression I received while studying the archives of the Banca Commerciale. The bank failed to appreciate the importance of the automobile industry for the economic development of the country. Apparently it considered the new vehicle as something primarily for the racing sports, at best a luxury item. The otherwise sharp-eyed bankers showed a blind spot when it came to discerning the immense potentialities of producing motor cars within the Italian socioeconomic environment.

But more surprising than what the banks did not do is what they did do. In a country like Italy, one could have reasonably expected the state to play — for some time — a considerable role in furthering industrial progress. I have the suspicion that Romeo and I do not quite see eye to eye on this point either. He finds merit with the industrial policy of the government, whereas my judgment of it is rather negative. And let me say that, as a matter of principle, I have no objections, no objections at all, to state intervention. The contrary is true. I do believe, however, that the policy of the Italian government in this area was quite inadequate. Given Italy's degree of backwardness, protection of grains was much too expensive and burdensome a policy. It was ill advised even in a country like Germany, but there at least the country was already sufficiently developed to be able to pay the price, and the grave damage was political rather than economic. In Italy, agrarian protection was folly, just as it was folly to subsidize industries that proved such a heavy drag on the country's development (and I have more in mind than the iron and steel industry). If the government was not ready to pursue a constructive, rational policy of protection, it would have done better to have crossed its arms and remained inactive. If the Italian government had pursued a reasonable policy in the beginning of the eighties, it is quite likely that the promising beginning would not have been nipped in the bud in the decade's second half. The process could have continued, and it would have continued if it had been supported by a sufficiently large demand for industrial goods on the part of the government and if, on the other hand, provision had been made for an adequate supply of capital both through credit institutions and through the state budget.

118

What was needed was precisely substitution for the missing prerequisites. It was not made, and this was a serious failure. When the banks came, they played a decisive role, and on this we are in agreement. In a sense, though, the banks were but a second-best solution. If the banks had been properly supported by government policy, the great spurt after 1896 may well have become even greater in speed and scope. As I said before, Romeo sees a logical sequence of things: first the prerequisites, that is to say, the infrastructure; then changes in structure; then development. It is difficult for me to discern this straight line in the industrial evolution. I believe that we can explain why development in Italy did not follow that logical course. As long as the period of railroad construction was underway, it would have been relatively easy to provide the nascent industry with the external economies and the growing demand it needed. During the eighties, given appropriate government support, industry would have benefited from concomitant railroad building. But the opportunity was allowed to pass unutilized. When the great spurt came, the railroad network had been essentially completed. One could possibly argue that this was all to the good, since in this fashion capital was released for industrial investment. But such an argument would misconceive the nature of the Italian capital market, which was divided in water-tight compartments — hence, as Romeo says, it was easy to secure funds for the railroads and difficult to obtain them for industry. When railroad construction was completed, the funds that theoretically could have begun flowing into industry in actual fact shunned industrial employment: they either went into local savings banks to be used for municipal public works or else went abroad in exchange for foreign securities. This is a clear example of how complex are the processes of substitution in a backward country. Things that are *first* logically may be *last* historically. The "prerequisites" to a process and the process itself can be so completely interconnected and intertwined that it is impossible to disentangle the skein. And it is in this sense that Italy in the eighties, as it were, missed the bus. The industrial transformation that came a decade later was less impressive than it might have been otherwise — perhaps only a pale reflection of what the upswing of the eighties could have been, if it had been properly guided and supported.

Let me add that this aspect of the process is assuming more and more importance in my general cogitations about Europe's industrial development in the nineteenth century. At the same time, I am less inclined to adhere completely to my previous and perhaps too rigid view according to which growing relative backwardness is accompanied by *steadily* increasing advantages from the point of view of the country's subsequent industrialization. I used to think that, the more delayed the beginning of the great spurt, the easier it would be to profit from these accumulations of advantages. This is often the case. But I also believe now that greater attention should be devoted to what may be called the peaks, the optimal points in this process. The advantages of backwardness do indeed accumulate until they reach a certain high point; such a point was reached in Italy in the eighties. Once the point was passed and railroad construction was over, however, the advantages diminished and vested interests, such as iron and steel and probably also cotton textiles, became strong enough to influence the policy of the government in a less than perfectly desirable way. The favorable moment was lost. A period of depression came during which it was not the advantages but the disadvantages of backwardness that dominated the scene.

The rhythm of these ups and downs no doubt relates to a large variety of factors. A technological innovation of strategic importance (railroads, automobiles, electrical power) may be of crucial importance in determining the location of the optimal points. These fluctuations in advantages and disadvantages of backwardness deserve a good deal of study. Italian industrial history before 1914 can teach us many useful things in this respect. And it is quite likely that similar relations can be discovered during the same period in other European countries.

Romeo: If I have understood Gerschenkron rightly, he maintains that my presentation of processes of economic change in Italy suffers from too "orderly" a view of the various phases of that change. He thinks that the eighties gave the Italian government a unique, nonrecurring opportunity to upset this orderly succession of phases. Had the development started then, it could have concentrated on machinery as against textiles and thus would have upset the normal

English pattern of development; this is not advisable in a backward country arriving on the industrial scene at a time when the machinery industry is in a dominant position.

What separates me from Gerschenkron is possibly a difference in points of view, which in turn reflects differences in purpose and interest. He is primarily eager to gather data and observations for the construction of a general theoretical model of economic development. What matters to me is, above all, to understand the historical process as it occurred in Italy. It is this difference in interests that has caused a certain shift of ground in our discussion, away from the original problem. Gerschenkron's assertion that in the eighties there was given an opportunity for a development that could not be recaptured later, and that the Italian government failed to grasp that opportunity, raises a number of problems that deserve deeper probing. Thus, for instance, one could ask whether the conditions for industrial development were really present, as long as both the railroad network and the commercialization of the economy which the railroads stimulated were still so far from completion. It is a matter of debate whether capital liberated by the completion of the railroads went into local banks or savings banks, which notoriously invested their deposits in local ventures; or whether the capital — I am referring to private Italian capital — did not actually continue to move within the ambit of the financial market in close proximity to industrial investment. Above all, it is permissible to ask whether it is in order in a historical discussion to lament that the Italian state of the eighties did not pursue the policy advocated by Gerschenkron, a policy based upon activation of public demand and creation of more effective instruments within the framework of the budget as well as upon an intensified building of infrastructures. (In this connection, let me say in parentheses that in those years expenditure for public works reached the highest percentage of total expenditures ever experienced in the whole history of the Kingdom.) In particular, the tariff policy of the state would have had to be altogether different. It seems clear to me that many of the measures referred to by Gerschenkron would have required a conception of governmental policy that was as yet quite alien to the economic culture of the nineteenth century. Gerschenkron himself shows clearly in his writings how governments developed effective policies of substitution only in the most backward countries, such as Russia. In countries that were more advanced, such as Germany and Austria-Hungary (and partly France), the task of substituting for the free market, in the effort to catch up with England, fell to the banks. When everything is said and done, I do not believe there is much reason to be astonished that the government and the ruling economic class in Italy pursued policies similar to those followed in countries that were in so many respects much closer to Italy than to imperial Russia, where an entirely different political and institutional system was in existence. It is true, of course, that a better tariff policy could have been pursued; but even with regard to the tariffs I believe, as I have said elsewhere, that from the vantage point of the present it is difficult to doubt the legitimacy of Italy's iron and steel industry, despite the manifold strictures of it from free traders, radicals, socialists, and others.

Something else is more important, however. Even if we went so far as to assume the correctness of all the strictures made by Gerschenkron with regard to Italian economic policy of the period, we would be able to do no more than identify a number of accelerating factors that were *not* present in the economic system. But this would not take us a single step farther along the road of understanding those factors which promoted the development that actually took place in historical reality. If what we are looking for is not what might have been a more effective industrial evolution, but what was the actual historical development, we must ask a series of questions. What were the results that Italian economic policy, despite all its errors, succeeded in achieving? Was there a destruction of old productive structures and the formation of new ones, and, if so, how did it proceed? Was there actually a process of commercialization in the Italian economy? This is the stuff Italian economic history is made of, and the history we are investigating is the history of Italian industry, which was shaped by the tariff policy such as it was and not by a different tariff policy — by a *given* relationship between the economic policy of the state and industrial activity rather than by any other.

Gerschenkron is right in stating that in reality things do not proceed in an orderly way. By this, I assume, he intended to say that the ordinary course of events — in which machinery construction comes after textiles and modern enterprise comes after domestic industries — could have been changed by a different policy of the government. But the fact remains that Italian economic history did in fact follow a certain order. This, by the way, does not mean that the process was free of complexity. It is not true that the old forms had to disappear — both in production and in distribution — before the new ones could appear on the scene. In reality, both the appearance of the new and the disappearance of the old were so closely interrelated as to constitute one indissoluble process. It is difficult indeed to distinguish in that process what came first and what came afterwards. A certain order does exist in the historical process, but only in the sense that we can ascertain factors as being more important than others and that, after a certain time, we can see this order reversed.

To return to the principal point: Gerschenkron has maintained that the policy of the Italian state basically retarded rather than promoted the economic development of the country. He says that if the state had confined itself to mere police functions, if it had been just a night watchman's state, if it had left the economy of the country to its own devices, development would have been more rapid. Yet even for him who accepts this now *in toto*, the fact remains that there was in fact an economic development and that it occurred in given historical circumstances. If the policy of the state proved a retarding factor, then we should not look at the retarding factor, precisely because it cannot explain how development did come about. We must look at those factors responsible for the development that actually took place. In other words, if we want to understand historical reality, we must look not so much at factors that obstructed development but at those that brought the development into being. To be sure, not even then is it possible to separate neatly the accelerating and retarding factors, which are very closely intertwined. But in the logic of our approach the principal factors are those which created the historical reality. If we look only at the factors that impede industrial development, we should know all the reasons for which industrial development does not take place, but still would know nothing of the reasons for which it actually occurs, and the latter are precisely the things we have wanted to learn about.

I have nothing else to add. But I should like to repeat that it would be very pleasant to have another opportunity of discussing these problems with Professor Gerschenkron.

Postscript

At a conference of Italian and Soviet historians, held in Moscow in 1964, Professor Romeo returned to the subject matter of the foregoing discussion. Unfortunately, his references there to my views on Italian industrial development are likely to give a distorted impression of my position. Hence a few words of clarification should be in order. Romeo said in Moscow that I "have denied that there was an industrial development in Italy after 1880" and he asserted further that such a denial was inconsistent with my own index of Italian industrial output, which clearly showed the fact of industrial development.[3] In making these misleading utterances (different in both tone and substance from his statements in the foregoing debate), Romeo regrettably failed to make clear that the point at issue between us is not a "denial" on my part of the short-lived upswing of the eighties, and still less that there was *some* industrial development between 1861 and 1896, but the question whether that upswing can be reasonably regarded as a great spurt of industrialization, comparable to what occurred in the years following 1896. It is quite possible, however, that this failure on Romeo's part to do justice to an opponent's views is unintentional, and due to a limited understanding of the scope of the historical problem under discussion, as was evidenced by his second rejoinder in our debate. He is in error in believing that a given rate of growth in an economy is merely the result of the accelerating factors at work. It is the composite result of both the accelerating and the retarding factors. And the latter are just as much an integral part of any historical evolution as the former. It ill behooves a historian of Romeo's talents to retreat behind Ranke's

3. "Atti del primo convegno degli storici italiani e sovietici, Mosca, ottobre 1964," in *I Quaderni di rassegna sovietica*, I (1965), 125–127.

"wie ist es eigentlich gewesen," a phrase that was not too felicitous coming from the pen of a great historian and then became fully meaningless when repeated *ad nauseam* by countless mediocrities. For the problem I was trying — alas unsuccessfully — to make clear to Romeo was not "wie es uneigentlich hätte sein können"; it was not an attempt to state what might have happened. The problem rather was to appraise the actual rate of industrial growth in Italy; that is to say, to ask whether the actually achieved rate of growth was or was not in line with the fundamental conditions in Italy on the eve of its great spurt. And if, using appropriate comparative material, I have come to believe that the rate of growth was lower than might have been expected, this inevitably impels one to search for an explanation of the fact — an explanation that must be looked for in the historical reality of Italy of the time. To forgo raising such questions and to abstain from attempts to answer them would mean refusal on the part of the historian to appraise the significance of the phenomena he claims to analyze. When it comes, therefore, to the question why the Italian government pursued its ill-advised economic policy, the reason may lie either in the government's incompetence and inability to withstand the pressures of vested interests, as I believe, or in the restraints imposed by the Western Zeitgeist, as Romeo believes. But whatever the answer, the fact itself is most relevant and directly pertinent to the understanding of Italian industrial history *as it actually occurred*.

I do not believe, therefore, that Romeo is right in saying that our disagreements stem from my interest in a general theoretical model of industrial development while he confines himself to exploring the industrial history of Italy. It is true indeed that I think we can perceive the industrial evolution in Europe in the nineteenth century as an intelligibly diversified unity, although the set of simple generalizations with which I have operated hardly deserves to be called theory. But the main point Romeo has failed to see is that such value as these generalizations possess lies precisely in raising relevant questions which help us to understand and evaluate the processes of industrialization as they occurred within the confines of individual countries.

Rosario Romeo has started a most deserving line of research. It would be very unfortunate if resistance to an imperfectly understood criticism should cause him to constrain his work within unduly narrow limits and make him shun important and exciting aspects of a subject to which he has made such a promising initial contribution.

6

The Modernization of Entrepreneurship

☙❦❧

M OST people will agree that the emergence of modern entrepreneurs has been an integral part of the great economic transformation known as the historical process of industrialization The question
I wish to consider is twofold: (1) What are some of the distinguishing "modern" features of industrial entrepreneurs, particularly in
the early stages of that transformation? (2) How did those characteristics come about? In dealing with these questions, I shall be
thinking mostly of the area of European industrializations, which
should give us sufficient scope for both generalization and differentiation.

There are many ways to define an entrepreneur, and scholars
have been arguing for a long time, often heatedly and confusingly,
about the relative merits of this or that definition. For our purposes,
it is sufficient to say that entrepreneurs are people whose task it is
to make economic decisions. Naturally, there is hardly any economic
activity that does not involve decisions. The man who spends his
working day sorting out big and small oranges is involved in a
continual process of decision making. But there are big and small
decisions. The big decisions refer, for instance, to what shall be produced and how it shall be produced; what goods should be bought
and sold, where and when, and at what price; whether output shall
be kept constant, or whether it should be increased or reduced; and
so on. All such decisions are entrepreneurial decisions.

There have been entrepreneurs in this sense at all levels in all
periods of economic history. A peasant in a backward agrarian country

who decides when to start plowing, what to sow, and when to reap makes entrepreneurial decisions. So did a Venetian merchant in the sixteenth century who decided what kinds of spice he should buy in the East and then carry across the Alps and whether Augsburg in Germany or Lyons in France was the most promising market for his wares. Very broadly speaking, such decisions are not different from those of an executive in a modern American plant — say, in Wilmington, Delaware — who has decided to concentrate on the production of a new vibration-absorbing material or from those of an automobile factory in Detroit that has decided to add a small car to its list for the next fall.

But, despite a certain similarity of all entrepreneurial decisions performed in all times and climes, we all know intuitively that the differences among the cases just mentioned are enormous. Entrepreneurship on a medieval farm or in a guild-dominated artisan shop in Perth or Strasbourg of the fifteenth century, or even in a large wool-processing mill in Flanders of the same period, is in many important respects not comparable to entrepreneurial activities in the modern age, from the eighteenth century onward, when rapid industrial progress, spreading from one country to another, became the characteristic feature of economic life, primarily in Europe and North America. Let us try to make some of these differences explicit.

For one, modern industry requires large amounts of fixed capital. In other words, it demands construction of buildings and acquisition of machinery whose contribution to output must be utilized over a considerable period of time. This means that an industrial entrepreneur must look far ahead into the future. His time horizon must be high. To be sure, even in preindustrial times, there were merchants who loaded and dispatched ships on long sea voyages, waiting many months, perhaps a year, for the reappearance of the vessel and the sale of the return cargo. But even this relatively long stretch of time, during which the merchant's capital was tied up in his risky venture, was not comparable to the average life span of modern machinery; nor did transactions of this sort ever begin to assume, within the total volume of goods and services produced, a significance remotely comparable to the share of industrial output in the national income of a modern country.

With the heightening of the time horizon, also, something else happened that was at least indirectly related to it. Industrial entrepreneurship became a lifetime occupation. A merchant in preindustrial days who had accumulated a sizable fortune would be strongly tempted to say farewell to his mercantile pursuits, acquire a landed estate, and attempt to elevate himself into the ranks of the gentry. A modern industrial entrepreneur in Germany or England often liked to see his children marry into a noble family; he was sensitive to the social prestige and the amenities of a country house, but in valuing those things he did not cease to be what he was, that is to say, a modern industrialist.

Connected with what has been just said and partly following from it, there were other differences. The contacts between a merchant and his customers were often fleeting affairs, once-over transactions. Hence the urge was strong, indeed, to deceive the buyer as to the quantity and quality of what he purchased. *Caveat emptor* — it is the buyer's lookout — warned the Roman law, and the idea of dishonesty became fully associated in the popular mind with trade and traders. Various etymologies reflect the connection. In German, for instance, the verb for exchange is "tauschen," but if two little dots are put over the "a," the word becomes "täuschen" and means to deceive. In French, the similarity between "truc" and "troc" — trick and barter — reflects the same connection; and the etymological origins of the very term "barter" in English, as in several Romance languages (whence the word came), point to cheating and deception. In Russian, an often quoted popular proverb used to advise: "If you do not cheat, you will not sell," which only repeated in a pithy form something that had been said time and again since the days of Ecclesiasticus.

It is not claimed, of course, that the modern industrialist entrepreneur has been at all times a paragon of impeccable probity. He was not. But it is fair to say that the permanence of his activities, the closeness of relations with the customer established by installation of equipment and delivery of spare parts, the very fact that so much of modern industrial output was sold, not to an amorphous mass of anonymous buyers, but to other industrial entrepreneurs — all these factors necessitated a much more scrupulous attitude toward the buyer. Furthermore, and no less important, modern industry was largely based on a well-developed credit system. The price at which a modern entrepreneur got his capital disposition — that is, the interest rate — had to be relatively low, which it could not be if the service of the debt included high-risk premiums. If there was to be an industrial entrepreneurship, its standards of commercial honesty perforce had to be high.

Finally, modern industry was inseparable from technological and organizational progress. New ways of doing things were continually emerging. Very few modern industrial entrepreneurs were truly great innovators, in the sense of being the first to apply a revolutionary, unprecedented technique. Most of them were imitators, a part of what Schumpeter called the "secondary wave," which spread a new signal innovation over broad segments of the industrial economy. But, as everyone who has ever worked inside a modern enterprise knows, the distinction between the innovator and the imitator is a very uncertain one. Every imitation requires a great deal of energy to overcome inertia, to abandon the accustomed way of doing things. It raises a million technical and economic problems that must be solved. And they will not be solved unless there are alert minds to welcome the new and to see the solutions and strong wills to carry the tasks to successful termination. No comparable problems, no comparable pressures to tackle them, had existed before the advent of modern industry.

Thus, modern industrial entrepreneurship has specific features that could not have been easily discovered to any similar extent and in any similar intensity in the preindustrial periods. We can now turn to an attempt to deal with the second question asked earlier. How did these features come about? What is the historical process in the course of which entrepreneurship became modernized so that the proper functioning of modern industrial enterprises could be assured? This is a question that used to exercise — and still does exercise — very many scholars, and a considerable literature of the subject has been created. As I see it, the most interesting problems in this discussion are related to the broader problem of prerequisites of modern industrialization. This calls for a brief digression.

According to a widespread view, which has been particularly

popularized and dramatized by Walt Rostow, the times of rapid industrial progress — the great spurts of industrialization — were preceded, country by country, by a more or less protracted period during which the "preconditions" of modern industrialization were created. Such preconditions or prerequisites are taken then so seriously that some scholars are willing to speak of "necessary and sufficient" preconditions, just as in a logical definition one speaks of conditions that are necessary and sufficient in order to define a given object. Thus, it would be argued, certain agrarian reforms involving a change in the system of land tenure, abolition of restrictions on the personal freedom of the peasantry, and increase in the productivity of agriculture were necessary prerequisites for subsequent industrialization.

Or it would be asserted, particularly by Marxian writers, that a previous accumulation of wealth over considerable historical periods was a necessary precondition for financing the capital investment of entrepreneurs during great industrial spurts. In either case, the inference is that, where such preconditions were not established, no industrialization could take place. But such arguments and assertions, presented as propositions of ubiquitous validity, do not stand up under the test of confrontation with the empirical material, even within the relatively restricted area of Europe of the nineteenth century. In important cases, considerable industrial development took place despite the absence of the allegedly necessary prerequisites, however logical the sequence of events scheduled in an abstract scheme may sound to the ear of an uncritical listener. For, analytically speaking, the attempt to convert logical conditions into historical preconditions is hardly more than a sleight of hand, a coarse analogy that insinuates into the argument the concept of historical necessity — which is something that lies on the other side of the line separating scientific pursuits from metaphysical speculation and political propaganda. And, historically speaking, the concept of necessary prerequisites fails because economic life is pregnant with many alternative solutions, so that in countries where the so-called prerequisites were not present, various substitutions for them have been developed in the very course of industrial development. This was true of the lack of proper agrarian reforms, as it was true of the lack of preindustrial accumulations of wealth, even though Soviet scholars are still busy trying to find "original accumulation of capital" in every country that ever went through the process of industrialization.

This brief discussion of prerequisites of modern industrialization has a direct bearing on entrepreneurship. Is the creation of modern entrepreneurship a prerequisite of modern industrial development? And is this creation itself a protracted historical process, in the course of which the prerequisites for modern entrepreneurship are created? The first of these questions is very often based on a misunderstanding. When people say, "Of course entrepreneurs are a prerequisite of industrialization. How else could you industrialize without them?" they are again confusing preconditions with conditions. Entrepreneurs use capital and hire labor in order to produce industrial goods, but this is the very stuff industrialization is made of; these are the very conditions of any reasonable definition of industrialization. But what we are talking about is not a definition or a description of industrialization, but a historical process, more or less lengthy, in which the prerequisites of modern entrepreneurship are created. And this, indeed, is a real problem that calls for more extended discussion.

It is not difficult to argue that, in *some* countries, things may be discovered which make us think that certain features of modern entrepreneurship have roots in the fairly remote historical past of those countries. Take, for instance, the experience of master artisans in towns dominated by the craft guilds in the late Middle Ages. There is no doubt that in many cases the institutional framework of the craft guilds — their rules and regulations and their ideology — served to inform the guilds' membership with an instinct of workmanship, with pride in the quality of their work, and, by the same token, with the idea of honesty in dealing with the customers: that is to say, with a characteristic we have already found to be very germane to modern industrial entrepreneurship. All this began centuries before the year 1517, when Martin Luther started the Reformation by nailing his theses on the door of a church at Wittenberg.

But there is no reason to deny that Prostestantism, particularly in its Calvinist branch, tended to promote the attitudes of honesty and thrift, lifetime dedication to one's work, and interest in innovation, even though it remains entirely a moot question to what extent it was the doctrines of the Protestant churches rather than adherence to a penalized minority, be it the Huguenots in France or the Non-conformists in England, that determined the attitudes. Nor is it clear that people did not tend to espouse Protestant persuasions *because* they had certain attitudes. Still, it is quite reasonable to say that in *some* countries, in the course of their preindustrial history, certain habits of thinking originated from several sources that provided a propitious climate for the exercise of modern entrepreneurial attitudes. There is nothing wrong, therefore, in considering those habits of thinking where they actually occurred as prerequisites for the emergence of modern entrepreneurship in the countries concerned. Yet we must be very wary of generalizing such findings and regarding them in any way as necessary prerequisites.

It is precisely this, however, that is done by several sociologists and psychologists who are trying to develop general theories of modern industrialization, with particular stress on the entrepreneurial element therein. One body of such theories tends to emphasize the dominant value system of the society within which industrial development takes place. It is argued that, unless the value system that prevails is such as to bestow social approval upon the role played by the entrepreneurs, they cannot succeed, and modern industrial development will not occur or at the very best will be hopelessly retarded. Thus, a change in the values of the society as a whole is regarded as a necessary prerequisite for the deployment of modern entrepreneurial activities and, by the same token, for industrialization. Generalizations of this sort are in obvious conflict with the facts.

Economic history, within the European framework, provides many cases where magnificent entrepreneurial activities were conducted in the face of a dominant value system that was violently opposed to such activities and continued to regard the working of the land that brought forth the blessing of its fruit as the only economic activity pleasing in the eyes of the Lord. Theories of this sort are wrong, but they are not entirely useless because they do help to raise the interesting question of how the lack of social approval was overcome or, to put it differently, what substitutions, if any, were found for the absence of social approval as a prerequisite of modern entrepreneurship.

There is an even more comprehensive theory for the emergence of modern entrepreneurship, which combines social and psychological factors and tries to establish the necessary prerequisites in a grandiose historical scheme comprising many centuries. It is argued that modern entrepreneurship requires replacement of the "authoritarian personality" of traditional society by the "innovational personality" of modern society. In either case, the personality is said to be the product of the methods of childraising in the four or five years after birth. It is further claimed that the change is brought about by the upper group's withdrawal, at some point, of status respect from the "common folk." Thereby the traditional society is disrupted, and the common folk spend many hundreds of years in a state of "retreatism." During that period, the parent-child relationship experiences profound changes and the methods of childrearing are fundamentally altered, so that in the end — in the very long end — the innovational entrepreneurial personalities emerge from the lap of society, and modern economic growth can begin.

It is easy to see the difference between the two theories just sketched. While the former considers that what the entrepreneurs need is simply approval of their activities under the dominant value system of the society, the latter envisages a thoroughgoing metamorphosis of personality formation in the society at large. But this is not the only difference. Theories that center on "social approval" can be criticized because, in many societies, stratified and complex as they are, approval by some groups is paralleled by disapproval by others; and a single system of dominant social values is little more than a fiction. Still, the historical record shows societies where traditional agrarian beliefs have survived fairly unchanged into the modern period and are accepted, at least superficially, by groups that are rather far removed from the tillage of the land. Russia in the late nineteenth century may serve as an important example of such a society.

But the point is that, with respect to this theory, it is still possible to get some empirical data in order to see how well or how badly it squares with the facts. On the other hand, the theory claiming basic changes in the methods of infant rearing and in parent-child relations over long centuries defies any empirical testing, which would require, within the meaning of the theory, psychoanalyzing huge samples of dead men who are unable to tell their tales on an analyst's couch. All we can say is that, by looking at the treatment of infants and young children in a number of countries that had gone through very successful periods of industrialization and have produced considerable entrepreneurial figures (such as Germany or Sweden before World War I), it is very difficult to discover any striking progress in this respect. Thus, the theory is little more than a figment of speculative imagination, and this particular attempt to view the emergence of modern entrepreneurship as a very prolonged process requiring creation of certain definite necessary prerequisites may be shelved as altogether unconvincing.

When general theories fail us, we must return to a more modest, but also more effective and more enlightening, way of looking at the creation of modern entrepreneurship. What has been said before about substitutions in other areas of industrial development for missing prerequisites should give us some guidance also with respect to the problem of entrepreneurship. As we take a closer look at those substitutions, we are able to say that they were not randomly distributed about the map of nineteenth-century Europe. On the contrary, there was a rather clear relationship: The more backward a country was on the eve of its big industrial spurt, the fewer prerequisites of industrialization it had and the more widespread and intensive was the use of substitutes for such prerequisites. Another way of putting it is to say that, in the more advanced countries, the preindustrial history presented a rich and colorful picture whereas the industrial history was relatively simple. By contrast, the preindustrial landscape of backward countries was rather barren, and the history of their industrializations much more complex and variegated, precisely because it was shot through and dominated by substitutions of many kinds.

Let us apply this generalization to the field of modern industrial entrepreneurship. A backward country such as, say, Russia in the last decades of the nineteenth century no doubt suffered from many disabilities in this respect, as it did in others. The number of able entrepreneurs was relatively small, their time horizon limited, their standards of commercial honesty deplorably low; and entrepreneurial activities were viewed with suspicion by both the mass of the populace and the intelligentsia. In a less backward country such as, for instance, Germany in the middle of the last century, most of those negative features were also present, even though in an attenuated form — in particular, the tradition for honesty in commercial dealings was fairly high, probably as a result of the craft-guild experience in the past centuries.

One cannot go amiss, therefore, in saying that in either country the prerequisites for modern entrepreneurship were nonexistent or present to a quite insufficient extent. And yet Germany in the second half of the century went through a magnificent industrial upsurge that brought her abreast of England, the "workshop of the world." Russia before 1914 did less well than Germany in absolute terms, but its great spurt of industrial development in the eighteen-eighties and particularly the eighteen-nineties is a matter of historical record, and the rate of industrial growth it achieved in those years was far above anything attained by Germany. How could that happen in the face of the disabilities just mentioned? The answer is that in both countries men succeeded in developing specific substitutions.

The inadequacy in the numbers of available entrepreneurs could be remedied or substituted for by increasing the size of plant and enterprise above what otherwise would have been an optimal size. In Germany, the various incompetencies of the individual entrepreneurs were offset by the device of splitting the entrepreneurial function: the German investment banks — a powerful invention, comparable in economic effect to that of the steam engine — were in their capital-supplying functions a substitute for the insufficiency of the previously created wealth willingly placed at the disposal of entrepreneurs. But they were also a substitute for entrepreneurial deficiencies. From their central vantage points of control, the banks participated actively in shaping the major — and sometimes even not so major — decisions of the individual enterprises. It was they who very often mapped out a firm's paths of growth, conceived far-sighted plans, decided on major technological and locational innovations, and arranged for mergers and capital increases. To some extent, although less effectively, similar pressures were brought to bear upon Russian entrepreneurs by the imperial bureaucracy — that is to say, first and foremost, the Ministry of Finance, which in other respects also provided substitutions like those incarnated in the German banks and altogether pursued very similar policies of industrial expansion. In Russia, of course, the quantitative and qualitative deficiencies of entrepreneurs were also alleviated by importation from abroad of foreign entrepreneurial talent, although the over-all extent thereof should not be exaggerated.

And, finally, the lack of social approval of entrepreneurs, that is, the existence of sentiments and values unfavorable to them, was overcome to a considerable extent by the fact that the power of the state — the judicial machinery as well as the police and the army — was used to protect the entrepreneurs and their interests from hostile social forces, to say nothing of many statutory provisions that pursued the same purpose.

The conclusion, therefore, must be that the processes of modern industrialization are much too variegated to allow of simple generalizations. Those processes in general vary with the degree of backwardness of the countries concerned. And this is as true of modern entrepreneurship as of other factors in industrial progress. It is simply factually incorrect to hold that, in countries in which the historical roots of modern entrepreneurship were weak or even nonexistent, no industrial development could take place. It could, and did in fact, occur because human ingenuity discovered a number of ways to substitute for the missing and allegedly necessary prerequisites.

But something else is of great importance. With the spurt of industrialization also begins a rapid process of transformation of entrepreneurs as their ranks are speedily increasing. For more important than all historical prerequisites of modern entrepreneurship is the effect on entrepreneurs of being passed through the training school of industrialization. Few things are more surprising than the great change in values, attitudes, and standards experienced by the Russian entrepreneurs over just one generation between the eighteen-eighties and the years preceding World War I. An astonishing process of modernization took place, not before but in the very course — and as a consequence — of a spurt of industrialization.

These two conclusions, taken together, do help us to understand the historical record of European industrialization in its graduated diversity. But, in addition, they also contain a message of some encouragement for the currently underdeveloped countries. In their case, too, the lack of entrepreneurial talents and the absence of historical roots of modern entrepreneurship need not be an obstacle that cannot be overcome by ingenuity, dedication, and, above all, a reasonably short passage of time after a serious industrialization effort has been launched. There is, of course, no such thing as "industrialization gratis." Industrialization always was and will remain a costly business. Still, one may perhaps express the hope that, in the currently underdeveloped countries, "substitutions" will be discovered that may prove less unpleasant and more equitable than were some of the devices applied in the backward countries of Europe in the nineteenth century.

7

Russia: Agrarian Policies and Industrialization, 1861—1917

⚜

I

THE ABOLITION OF SERFDOM

THE abolition of serfdom provides a natural starting point for an essay devoted to Russian agrarian policies in their relation to industrialization. The act concerning the emancipation of the peasantry and the imperial manifesto that proclaimed the event to the people bear the date of February 19, 1861. In many historical writings, that day of the Julian calendar (March 3, 1861, according to the Gregorian time reckoning) is said to mark the dividing line between two periods in Russian economic history, sometimes loosely referred to as feudalism and capitalism. At the same time, both liberal and Marxian historians frequently stress the "inevitability" of the emancipation, even though in so doing the former think in terms of an irresistible march of human progress while the latter point to the dialectical contradiction between productive forces and traditional relations of production.

It is certainly true that many contemporaries, among them no less an authority than Emperor Alexander II himself, held that the emancipation was bound to come sooner or later.[1] Nevertheless, from

1. Aleksey Popelnitski, "Rech' Aleksandra II skazannaya 30–go Marta 1856–go goda moskovskim predvoditelyam dvoryanstva" (Speech Made by Alexander II on March 30, 1856, before the Marshals of the Moscow Gentry), *Golos Minuvshego* (1916), no. 5–6, p. 393.

the point of view of an historical approach which attempts to interpret the *concrete timing* of events, the fact that they would have occurred at some indefinite point of time would be hardly significant, even if "historical inevitability," and by the same token "historical evitability," were operational concepts rather than *qualitates occultae.* Moreover, there is little evidence that in the decades preceding the emancipation the institution of serfdom had become incompatible with the growth of agricultural output. In fact, the weight of evidence points the other way, as has been impressively shown by Peter Struve, who cast grave doubts upon the usual sweeping generalizations.[2] It certainly cannot be maintained as a general proposition that forces within the productive system of agriculture led to the progressive disintegration of serfdom, causing it to "fall of its own weight." This is not surprising. An agricultural system based on serf labor may be much less productive than one where free labor is employed. But from the point of view of the individual estate, *once the allocation of some lands to the serfs is taken for granted,* the differential in productivity between serf labor and free labor must become quite formidable before it becomes profitable to discard the serf laborer whose services are available gratis and to replace him by the more productive, but also more expensive, free laborer.[3] But it is even more difficult to argue that "the nascent capitalism" changed the agrarian structure to suit its own needs. Divested of its anthropomorphic quaintness, the statement must mean that some men ("bourgeoisie"), propelled by their own economic interests, caused other

2. Peter Struve, *Krepostnoye khozyaystvo: Izsledovaniya po economicheskoy istorii Rossii v XVIII i XIX vekakh* (The Serfdom Economy: Explorations in Russian Economic History in the Eighteenth and Nineteenth Centuries; St. Petersburg, 1913), esp. pp. 102ff.

3. It could be argued, as indeed does Struve (p. 149), that further progress in agriculture was premised upon railroad construction and that the maintenance of serfdom was incompatible with railroadization. Yet his argument apparently refers not to the early 1860's, but to some indefinite point in the future, and the incompatibility between railroad construction and serfdom was far from being an absolute one. In addition, it was the absence of railroads that protected agriculture in the less favored areas to the north of the black-earth belt, even though the *podvodnaya povinnost'*, that is, the possibility of using gratis peasant labor during the winter months for transporting grain by peasant wagons and peasant horses, certainly tended to lengthen somewhat the radius of the marketing area accessible to the individual estates.

men ("statesmen" or "bureaucrats") to bring about the emancipation of the peasantry in order to remove a block to the industrial development of the country. It would be futile, however, to look for any such connection, given the weakness, inexperience, and inarticulateness of any group in mid-century Russia that might be reasonably described as "bourgeoisie."

The statement might be reread to mean that the Russian government, perhaps inspired by the economic development of the West and recognizing that industrialization would greatly increase the military power of the country, deliberately decided to abolish serfdom in order to create a socioeconomic framework (production relations) within which the new technological and economic opportunities (productive forces) could be much more fully utilized. So reinterpreted, the spirit of autonomous economic necessity is thoroughly exorcised out of the emancipation act. It becomes a political decision of the men in charge of the Russian government. The question then is whether, and if so, to what extent, was the disenserfment predicated upon the desire to promote the industrialization of Russia.

The desire to maintain and to increase the power of the state by improving the efficiency of the country's economic system manifested itself at a number of important junctures throughout Russian history. Thereby economic development tended to become a function of changing military necessities, proceeding in a curiously jerky fashion. When, for the sake of defense or aggression as the case may be, and especially following serious defeats in foreign wars, the government attempted to raise the economic activities in the country to a level more consonant with the power policy of the state, Russia went through a period of economic reforms designed either to increase output or at least to change the distribution of the given output of goods and services in favor of the state. In earlier centuries, this policy had contributed in a decisive manner to the process of enserfment of the Russian peasants by assigning masses of peasants sitting on "black" (that is, taxable but otherwise free) lands to the *pomeshchiki* (seigniors) as compensation for their services to the state.

On the other hand, once the military pressure subsided and Russia's foreign position appeared secure, the government tended to curtail its own activities in promoting economic development. The period after the death of Peter the Great was characterized by a long series of Russian military and political successes in the foreign field. The steady pressure upon the Turks, the appearance of Russian Cossacks in Berlin during the Seven Years' War, the partition of Poland, which made Russia contiguous with Prussia and Austria, the conquest of Finland, Napoleon's ignominious retreat and the subsequent entry of Russian troops into Paris, the suppression of the Hungarian revolution by the troops of Paskevich — all these seemed to mean that the reforms of Peter the Great, in conjunction with the moderate economic growth during a century and more after his death and with the rapid increase of population in the huge country, had sufficed to assure Russia of a strong position within the concert of powers. Herein may lie one important reason for the Russian government's failure to attack the problem of serfdom after the original connection of the institution with the country's military and economic development had been severed in the second half of the eighteenth century.

The Crimean War imparted a severe blow to the serene image of Russia's strength. It revealed Russian inferiority in many crucial respects. The Russian men-of-war were no match for the English and French navies, and their conversion into submarine reefs was the only use to which they could be effectively put; the primitive Russian rifle was primarily accountable for the loss of the crucial battle of Alma; the supplies of men and ammunition to the besieged Sebastopol were hindered by the poverty of the transportation system. In the minds of the emperor and the higher bureaucracy, the course of the war and its outcome left the feeling that once more the country had been allowed to lag too far behind the advanced nations of the West. Some degree of modernization of the economy was indispensable for regaining a strong military position. It seemed clear, at the same time, that some change in the peasant status must be assigned a very high, perhaps the highest, priority on any list of requisite reforms. It is tempting to say that to this extent one element at least of a traditional pattern of Russian economic history tended thus to reproduce itself.

Unfortunately, the attitude of the Russian government toward economic development was neither as strong or as unambiguous as might be concluded from the foregoing paragraph. In addition, whatever such motivations existed, they tended to be overshadowed by a different set of considerations. Count Valuyev, one of the most powerful figures of Alexander II's administration, frankly expressed in his diaries the feeling that "the goal of self-preservation of autocracy" was "perhaps predominant" in the decision to liberate the peasants.[4] It is undeniable that there was much reason for concern. The war had greatly enhanced the unrest among the serfs. In its course, rumors that the hour of liberation was near were rife throughout the countryside. It was said that Napoleon had repented of his failure to abolish serfdom in 1812 and had returned to Russia to correct the past omission. It was said that military conscription, or even merely participation in railroad building, bestowed freedom from serf status on the persons concerned. The state of fermentation in the villages seemed to adumbrate a widespread peasant rebellion, perhaps a repetition of the Pugachev uprising of 1773 which had shaken the empire to its foundations. For long decades, the fear of such a rebellion had caused the government both to refrain from any serious reform, which might have rekindled the long-pent fire into an uncontrollable conflagration, and to keep pondering ways and means by which serfdom, and with it the perennial danger to the political stability of the empire, could be gradually eliminated. In 1839, speaking of the problem of serfdom, the chief of the imperial secret police expressed the view that "it is necessary to start somehow, and it is better to start gradually and cautiously rather than wait until things should be set in motion from below, that is, from the people." [5] That piece of competent advice given to Nicholas I was almost verbally repeated in the celebrated speech by his son Alexander II, in March 1856, the first governmental announcement of the planned reform. In addressing the representatives of the Moscow gentry, less than a fortnight after the Peace of Paris had been proclaimed, the emperor explained that the reform was necessary because of "hostile feelings between the peasants and their owners," and added: "It is, therefore, much better for it [the liberation or changes in the system] to happen from above rather than from below." [6]

4. P. A. Valuyev, *Dnevnik, 1877–1884* (Diary: Petrograd, 1919), p. 190.
5. *Krest'yanskoye dvizheniye, 1827–1869 gg.* (The Peasant Movement), ed. E. A. Morokhovez (Moscow, 1931), I, 32.
6. *Golos Minuvshego* (1916), p. 393. It may be added that the concept of

This was a strong and clear statement, and one would look in vain for an equally unambiguous and authoritative pronouncement seeking to justify or explain the impending reform by reference to the need to raise the country's economic potential. The requirements of what Georg Knapp, in a somewhat different context, used to call "imperial propaganda" among the gentry may be presumed to have caused special stress to be laid on the dangers of peasant violence. Pointing at the much more long-run and much less tangible promise of economic development would hardly have sounded very persuasive in the ears of a gentry audience. Moreover, it might be argued that political stability in itself was to be regarded as a crucial prerequisite for economic development, so that the two motivations were not entirely unconnected.

Such considerations, however, do not seem to carry much weight. It seems much more important that certain aspects or areas of economic development were viewed by the government with suspicion and apprehension. Railroad construction seems least objectionable. A change had taken place in this respect since the days of Nicholas I when Kankrin, his perennial, powerful, talented, and narrow-minded minister of finance (1823–1844), used to refer to railroads as "a malady of our age" and to fear lest railroad construction should raise the rate of interest, cause excessive mobility among the populace, and favor the spread of egalitarianism.[7] If Alexander II's father still agreed with his friend, Francis I of Austria, who regarded the railroads as harbingers of the revolution,[8] the young emperor had to take risks. After the Crimean defeat, the military importance of a

---

"revolution from above" goes back to the time of the Prussian agrarian reform, when it was formulated by Altenstein and Hardenberg. See Leopold von Ranke, *Denkwürdigkeiten des Staatskanzlers Fürsten von Hardenberg*, IV (Leipzig, 1877), pp. 8* 116

7. Georg Kankrin, *Aus den Reisetagebüchern, 1840–1845* (Braunschweig, 1865), I, 23, 141 "This mode of traveling increases the equality among the social estates, a subject on which there is much to say in the interest of the so necessary social hierarchy." Presumably, because of considerations of this sort, a high-ranking member of the Russian bureaucracy, as late as the last decade of the century, used to transport his horses and carriage on the train with him and would leave the train at the penultimate station, in order to make a fitting entry into the capital. See Wladimir von Korostowetz, *Graf Witte, der Staatsmann in der Not* (Berlin, 1929), p. 29.

8. "Na, na, damit ist's nichts, da käm' mir höchstens die Revolution ins Land." Viktor Bibl, *Der Zerfall Österreichs* (Vienna, 1924), II, 66.

swiftly growing railroad network could be ignored no longer. Nor was the growth of commerce and banking considered undesirable. But the rapid growth of factory towns seemed another matter. Creation of large industrial centers threatened, in the parlance of the time, to infest Russia with "the cancer of the proletariat." The government was eager to lay the ghost of peasant rebellions; it was unwilling to conjure up the menace of urban revolutions. Political stability appeared best assured by the traditionalism of an agrarian structure and not by the restless changeability of modern industrialism.

Among the vocal forces in Russia in the second half of the 1850's, there was none whose pressure might have caused the government to shift toward more deliberate policies in favor of industrialization. The nobility and the gentry, taken as a group, were never interested in the large-scale industrial growth that threatened their pre-eminence within the Russian body social. The Russian intelligentsia was largely radical, and political stability was not among its ideals. It opposed the regime of autocracy and advocated a mode of emancipation of the peasantry which went far beyond what was acceptable to the government. But in its aversion to industrialization and its espousal of the — alleged or actual — value system of an agrarian society it was, though for very different reasons, surprisingly close to the position of the government.[9]

Distribution of emphasis among competing motivations must remain uncertain. Yet some tentative conclusions may be gleaned from the preceding pages. It is in a twofold sense that the emancipation of the peasantry must be viewed as an essentially political act: first, because of the implausibility in this case of any model that would assign the role of the "original cause" to impersonal economic processes; second, because the primary concern of the government was to obviate outbreaks of peasant violence with their threat of catastrophic consequence to the regime. The economic lesson of the defeat, while not forgotten, was obfuscated both by the immediate political peril and by the fear of long-term dangers resulting from far-reaching economic changes. To be sure, whatever the motivations,

9. See Gerschenkron, "Economic Development in Russian Intellectual History of the Nineteenth Century," *Economic Backwardness in Historical Perspective*, pp. 152–187.

the emancipation of the peasantry was to become the first long step in the process of clearing the stage for industrialization. But for the speed and character of that process and, by the same token, for the industrialization itself, it was of considerable significance that it had been initiated almost as an incidental and not quite desirable by-product of a political action oriented to other goals and inspired by other considerations. In 1861, the time of deliberate subordination of agrarian policies to the needs of industrialization lay still far away in the future. In the course of the following presentation an attempt will be made to support and to amplify these preliminary suppositions, through a review of the actual procedures by which the bonds of serfdom were relaxed, and to trace briefly the changing character of agrarian policies in the decades following the great reform.

THE REFORM AS A PREREQUISITE TO INDUSTRIALIZATION

Historically, there are essentially two main facets to a thorough-going agrarian reform: first, the replacement of various forms of communal cultivation of land by an individualist system of cultivation and, second, the abolition of the traditional obligations of the peasants to the landowners. An agrarian reorganization has come to be regarded as a major prerequisite of modern industrialization. Ideally, it is supposed to increase the productivity of agriculture so that its growing produce will allow shifts of population out of agricultural areas and will support the increasing numbers of men engaged in nonagricultural pursuits. At the same time, it is supposed to eliminate, or at least to reduce, the traditional restraints on the mobility of the agrarian population and its freedom to exercise a free choice of occupation. Such a reorganization can be the result of a slow disintegration of the traditional system of agricultural production, essentially under the impact of economic forces, perhaps coupled with some subsidiary action on the part of the state. Where such disintegration has not taken place and the traditional system is well anchored in the existing legal order, an action of the state, an agrarian *reform* alone can open the road to an economic transformation in agriculture.

With regard to the latter, the nature of the reform will vary

147

with the nature of the peasantry's obligations. But the character of such obligations can differ. Schematically, it is useful to follow an established convention in distinguishing two extreme cases. On the one side stands the system as it emerged over large parts of Western Europe as a result of commutations of labor services into payments in kind or in money, with a concomitant cutting up of the lord's demesne. On the other side stands an agricultural economy where such commutations either never took place or were undone by recommutations; and the lands were divided into lands let over to the peasantry (or the peasant village as an entity) and lands retained by the lord, while the peasantry remained under the obligation to provide man and team services on the demesne. The two types of agrarian relations are traditionally designated by the German terms *Grundherrschaft* and *Gutswirtschaft*, although the phenomena so described are by no means confined to German areas. In the former case, the landowner no longer exercises an entrepreneurial function. In the latter case, the landowner has retained such functions and, moreover, the peasant's and the landlord's economies are closely interwoven by the sameness of labor supply and, at least in part, of capital. It is obvious that the agrarian reformer faces a different problem in the two cases. In the case of *Grundherrschaft*, the task is relatively simple. If so desired, the reform can be carried out at a stroke of the pen, by decreeing the cessation of quitrent obligations on the part of the peasantry. If a drastic dispossession of the landowning group is not desired, various types of redemption procedures can be devised. But the reform, however executed, is confined to the sphere of income distribution and does not impinge upon production. True, a change in income distribution in favor of the peasantry may indeed affect agricultural output by changing the rate of investment on farms or by improving productivity of labor by better nutrition. But those are secondary effects, and presumably they are likely to be positive.

The case of *Gutswirtschaft* is very different. There, a sudden cessation of obligations on the part of the peasantry is bound to have a far-reaching effect upon agricultural output. If the lords are left in undisturbed possession of their land, the productive processes are likely to be upset by the changes in labor supply and the diminution of available capital, because the artificially maintained allocation

148

of factors of production as between the peasant's and the landlord's economies presumably implied a less than optimal supply of both labor and capital to the former. There may be, therefore, a strong temptation in the course of such a reform to *reduce* the area of peasant-tilled land in order to maintain the supply of labor to the estates of the lords. If, on the other hand, the reform under such conditions involves a confiscation of the lord's lands in favor of the peasantry, the elimination of the entrepreneurial guidance by the lords in itself is apt to produce dislocations of production. In addition, both the productivity of agricultural labor and the intensity of its connection with the market will probably be affected by the change in the scale of farming operations. Barring a violent revolution, the reform of such a system is therefore likely to be a protracted process which extends over decades and in the course of which the nexus conjoining the two economies is slowly relaxed. Unlike the case of *Grundherrschaft*, the effects of a reform breaking up the existing *Gutswirtschaft* are much more difficult to predict. Whether they are positive or negative on balance will depend on the tempo of the reform and the size and economic strength of the productive units as they are created and consolidated in the course of the reform.

Thus, from the point of view of its effect upon industrialization, a reform of peasant obligations in the conditions of *Grundherrschaft* is likely to be of secondary importance, and interest must center upon removal of limitations on the personal and entrepreneurial freedom of the peasantry. By contrast, a reform of peasant obligations in conditions of *Gutswirtschaft* can result in a significant promotion or a considerable retardation of industrial growth.

The reality in any country naturally was much more complex than the two simplified types just described. Here it must suffice to point out that serf-labor services were practiced in Russia in nearly all areas where serfdom existed, even though the regions where they predominated mostly lay within the huge black-earth belt girding the country from west to east. As a rule, the peasants came to work with their teams and plows and harrows. This in itself predetermined the character of the reform as an extremely complex operation. The reformers had to face problems such as the relative extent of peasant and large estate land, or the continued supply of labor to the large estates, and any solution adopted was bound to exercise considerable influence upon the subsequent economic development of the country. In addition, both the economic — and political — backwardness of the country and the belatedness of the reform imparted certain peculiarities to the situation. Some of these peculiarities, though not completely absent from the economic history of countries west of Russia (particularly Prussia), tended to appear in Russia in a much accentuated form.

It is one thing when peasant serfdom exists in conditions of political disintegration. It is another when, as was the case in Russia, the institution stands under the protection of a modern well-developed central government. Because serfdom in Russia was a modern institution in this sense, it became possible for the status of serfs to deteriorate to the point where in many respects it became indistinguishable from that of a slave. Sales of serfs, with or without land, in families or individually, were an established commercial operation.[10] The serf owner could transfer the serfs at will from work on the land to house services; he could freely select among the serfs recruits for the army, and he could punish a recalcitrant serf by deportation to Siberia. Behind the power of the serf owner stood the power of a ubiquitous government. What matters most for the context of the present essay is the effect of these conditions upon development of nonagricultural pursuits. On the one hand, the pomeshchik could establish factories on his lands and man them with serf labor. No "custom of the manor" restrained him from such a course. On the other hand, the serf who left the village in order to seek employment in urban areas enjoyed no change in his legal status. The city air did not make free automatically, whatever the length of sojourn within its confines. The imperial police at all times stood ready to return a serf to the village, if he tried to overstay the leave granted by the pomeshchik. Children of the serf born in the city assumed hereditary serf status just like their village-born brethren. Only purchase of freedom from the owner could terminate the serf relation. This meant that commutations of labor services into money payments

10. It was only in 1833 that sales of individuals without families were forbidden. See *Svod zakonov rossiyskoy imperii* (Code of Laws of the Russian Empire; 1857 ed.), vol. IX, article 1082.

in Russia were not just a process confined to agriculture. Also the serf who gained his livelihood in the city was under the obligation to pay regular quitrents, the magnitude of which was determined by the owner and liable to change at will. For the minority of serfs who contrived to acquire some fortune in the city, the payment of quitrents was not nearly as burdensome as the uncertainty of status and the resulting difficulty to make economic decisions for any longer period ahead. Naturally, conditions in this respect varied from case to case. A serf of a very wealthy owner of thousands of serfs enjoyed a greater degree of security because of the less personal and more institutional character of the relations between the serf and the bureaucratized estate management. Still, it may be surmised that the time horizon of entrepreneurial decisions, which in general is relatively low in backward countries, was further pressed down in the case of serf-entrepreneurs, a not unimportant retarding factor for economic development in general, and in particular for industrialization where the investment in fixed capital calls for relatively long-term decisions.

On the other hand, for those serfs living in the cities who were engaged as industrial laborers, the obligation to pay quitrents was of primary importance economically. In conditions where the wage level in industry was close to subsistence level, the existence of the serf-owners' claims upon the wage earners' income may have meant either that industrial enterprises had to pay more dearly for their labor or that the pressure upon the standard of living expressed itself in lowered productivity of the laborer. In either case, the quitrents to the pomeshchik constituted a tribute of industry to the serfowners and as such a trammel upon industrial development.[11] Accordingly, owing to the belatedness of the reform, its authors had to include within their purview existing conditions and immediate effects that would have been negligible otherwise.

As a result of Russia's economic backwardness, the need for a reformer's paying heed to the effects of the reform both on productivity and on the marketing ability of agriculture was considerably enhanced. First of all, in conditions of economic backwardness the

11. It must be considered, on the other hand, that in some cases the serf owners' pressure for high quitrents may have tended to increase the supply of manpower to urban occupations.

first stages of industrialization are likely to include a rapid initial spurt, involving considerable accretions to the industrial population within a relatively short period and requiring, therefore, a corresponding increase in indigenous food availabilities. Moreover, the very occurrence of the spurt is largely premised upon the possibility of the backward country's importing capital in real form (machinery) and know-how. Even though part of these imports may be financed by foreign loans, the balance must be financed by exports of agricultural products. Under such conditions a reform, if it is to serve as a basis for the subsequent industrialization, must be such as to be conducive to rapidly increasing marketed produce, which in turn must be based on increased productivity of agriculture or at least on such a redistribution of income within agriculture as to make for the growth of marketed products.

At the same time, an agrarian reform in conditions of backwardness cannot be regarded as a prerequisite for industrialization in the same chronological sense in which one is wont to use the term in applying it to more advanced countries. If the economic situation in a backward country on the eve of an industrial spurt may be described as one of tension between "what is" and "what can be," between the actual conditions of stagnation and the potentialities for economic development, then it is quite likely that the shock of agrarian reform will increase the tension beyond the breaking point and unleash considerable processes of industrial change long before the reform has had time to work itself out and fully to achieve those effects that are so often regarded as preconditions to industrialization. In other words, in such conditions, the job of clearing the decks for the battle of industrialization continues throughout the battle. This simultaneity of the two processes (which succeed each other in an "ideal type" model and were indeed much more clearly, though far from perfectly, separated in the history of more advanced countries) is bound to affect both the course of the industrial evolution and that of the agrarian policies subsequent to the reform.

In addition, and to a large extent for reasons already mentioned, in Russia the clearing of the decks was accompanied by a good deal of cumbering of the decks. As if the basic economic problem of severing the gentry and the peasant economies had not been complex enough, the mechanics of autocratic power, the government's fears and predilections, and the whole interplay of political and economic backwardness tended to obscure and confuse the course of agrarian policies in the country.

II

THE EMANCIPATION ACT AND RELATED MEASURES

On the eve of the emancipation, the peasantry which was in bondage to the pomeshchiki in European Russia and Siberia numbered about 22 million, or 53 percent of the Russian peasant population.[12] Various categories of state peasants (*gosudarstvennyye krest'yane*) and peasants belonging to the imperial family (*udel'nyye krest'yane*) constituted the remaining 47 percent.

Although an extensive presentation of the formidable legal framework within which the emancipation was encompassed and conducted is neither possible nor necessary here, five main aspects of the reform will be dealt with in the following: (1) The emancipation proper, that is, the change in the personal juridical status of serf peasantry; (2) the provision of serf peasants with farmsteads, farm plots, and field lands, and the obligations resulting therefrom; (3) the establishment of peasant ownership over farmsteads and lands; (4) measures taken to increase the productivity of agriculture; and (5) the institutional framework within which the peasants released from bondage were to be placed. Finally, something will be said on the position of peasants other than the manumitted serfs.

12. The figure resulting from the Tenth Census of 1857–1859 (the so-called *Desyataya Revisiya*) was 10,696,139 male souls and 11,283,794 female souls, or 21,979,932 peasants of either sex. Out of this number, 1,467,378 peasants were in the category of house servants (*dvorovyye*). A. Troynitski, *Krepostnoye naseleniye Rossii po desyatoy narodnoy perepisi, statisticheskoye izsledovaniye* (The Serfdom Population in Russia According to the Tenth Population Census, a Statistical Inquiry; St. Petersburg, 1861), pp. 49, 57. A. G. Rashin, *Naseleniye Rossii za sto let, 1811–1913 gg.* (The Population of Russia During One Hundred Years, 1811–1913; Moscow, 1957), gives a slightly higher figure for the number of male serf peasants (10,858,400) and a considerably higher figure for the total male peasant population (23,658,400); according to these data, the percentage of bonded male peasantry in the total male peasant population was only 45.9 percent (p. 34).

CIVIL STATUS

Article 1 of the fundamental Emancipation Act proclaimed: "The bondage rights over peasants settled on gentry estates and over estate servants (*dvorovyye*) are abolished forever." [13] This was a truly momentous stipulation by virtue of which the bonded peasants ceased being the "baptized property" of the pomeshchiks, to use Alexander Herzen's celebrated phrase. Apart from certain special restrictions to be discussed below, the peasants became equal in civil status with the members of other "taxable estates."

Thenceforth, the former serfs became subject to the existing general laws regarding family matters; in particular, conclusion of marriage ties no longer required the pomeshchik's consent.[14] The peasants became free to enter into any lawful contractual obligation; to establish enterprises in commerce and industry, to acquire membership in craft guilds and merchant guilds, and to engage in gainful pursuits as artisans and craftsmen; [15] to sue and to be sued in matters of civil law and to proffer charges and safeguard their interests in criminal matters, except that acts or omissions of their former owners antedating the emancipation could not be made object of lawful suits by former serfs.[16]

The change in the legal status of the peasantry before and after the emancipation was great indeed. It is true, however, that the pre-emancipation status had been a good deal more variegated and flexible than can be concluded from the terse stipulations of the code. These stipulations were essentially the result of a series of restrictive measures gradually passed in the course of the eighteenth

13. "Obschcheye polozheniye o krest'yanakh vyshedshikh iz krepostnoy zavisimosti" (General Statute Concerning Peasants Released from Bondage; cited in the following as *OP*), in *Polnoye sobraniye zakonov rossiyskoy imperii* (Complete Collection of Laws of the Russian Empire), XXXVI (1863 ed.), no. 36657, cited in the following as *PSZ*.

14. *OP* article 21. Even though the serf owners were prohibited by a law issued in Peter I's time (1722) from enforcing serf marriages (*Svod zakonov rossiyskoy imperii*, 1857 ed., article 1032), the practice of compulsory marriages was widespread throughout the existence of serfdom.

15. *OP* article 23.

16. *OP* article 24.

century. Thus, by the Act of 1730, peasants were prohibited from acquiring real estate; in the following year they were excluded from participation in government contracts and in the farming out of taxes and monopolies. In 1761, peasants were enjoined from issuing bills of exchange and could no longer provide collateral for borrowed funds in an officially recognized form without the written consent of the pomeshchik. The literature of the subject, perhaps because of the authors' juridical background and perhaps also because of their hostility to the system of serfdom, tended to picture the peasantry as an undifferentiated servile mass, destitute of any property rights.[17] The nineteenth-century reality differed considerably from such a picture. Without going into detail, it must be said that serfs, even before the emancipation, engaged in trade and entered into contractual obligations not relating to real estate. They could sue and suits could be brought against them. To be sure, the position of a serf-entrepreneur was precarious. His contractual partners had to apprehend at all times that a decision on the part of the owner to return him to the land might make it impossible for him to fulfill his obligations toward them. An act passed in the nineteenth century obliged the pomeshchiks not to separate a serf-merchant from his business for the purpose of sending him as a recruit to the army or of deporting him to Siberia,[18] but the law did not prevent the owner from ordering the serf's return for purposes other than the two just stated. The legal inability to sign bills of exchange and to offer mortgage securities no doubt limited the scope of active and passive credit transactions accessible to a serf engaged in business and, by the same token, limited the scope of his opportunities. Yet, even with regard to real-estate property, it has been shown that very considerable land purchases were effected by serf peasants in the name of the owners.[19] In this fashion, some serfs individually or jointly with others even came into actual ownership of other serfs. In addition, in 1848 an act was adopted under the terms of which landed properties could

17. The exceptions were few and far apart. A distinguished position among them belongs to the classic of N. I. Turgenev, *La Russie et les Russes* (Paris, 1847).

18. *Svod zakonov rossiyskoy imperii* (1857 ed.), article 1137.

19. Cf. V. Kashin, "Zemlevladeniye krepostnykh krest'yan" (Land Ownership of Serf Peasants), in *Krepostnaya Rossiya, sbornik statey* (Serfdom in Russia, Collected Essays; Leningrad, 1930).

be acquired and sold by the serfs in their own names, with the consent of the pomeshchik and provided that the lands were not settled by other serf peasants.[20]

It must be noted, however, that modern historical research has discovered land transactions on the part of serf peasants essentially on very large estates alone. Partly this is the result of absence (or destruction) of well-organized archives on smaller estates. But bureaucratically managed large estates quite naturally tended to widen the rights and scope of the economic activities of their serfs; on smaller estates such opportunities either were not offered at all or were greatly restricted in comparison.

Furthermore, the Act of 1848 remained largely unknown to the peasants, and the number of purchases and sales carried out under its terms between 1848 and 1861 remained very limited.[21] The serfs continued to buy land, houses, and market stalls in the name of the owner. Such a procedure, however, was not without obvious hazards. The law did not countenance the rights of the peasants to the land fictitiously purchased in the name of their owners. The Act of 1848 expressly refused recognition of any claims on the part of the peasants to real estate acquired in the name of the owner prior to 1848. Such a recognition was left to voluntary action by the owner of the serfs who had purchased the properties. The Emancipation Act established a special procedure for arbitration and final recourse to a division of the Ministry of the Interior for adjudging such claims on the part of the peasants. But the Act of 1861 also stipulated that such claims must be made within ten years *after the date of purchase*, making it impossible for the peasants to acquire title at least to properties bought between 1848 and 1851, and in practice even to some properties bought between 1851 and 1861 because of the curiously retroactive character of this statute of limitations. In addition, the peasants were handicapped by a further provision which confined the type of adducible evidence to written documents that seldom existed.[22]

If before emancipation the pomeshchik had some incentive to

20. *Svod zakonov rossiyskoy imperii* (1857 ed.), article 1138.
21. P. P. Semenov Tyan-Shanski, *Memuary, epokha osvobozhdeniya* (Memoirs, the Epoch of Liberation; St. Petersburg, 1915), III, 259.
22. See *OP* article 32 and appendix to it, 1–8.

see the economic strength of his peasants increased by land purchases, his interests in this direction were in many cases diminished after the emancipation, and the temptation to counter the expropriation of "baptized property" by appropriation of lands belonging to that property was certainly great. Though a quantitative assessment is impossible, and in some cases voluntary settlements between peasants and their pomeshchiks may have led to satisfactory results, it is not without significance that the extent of lands claimed by the peasants and assigned to them by the Ministry of the Interior was strikingly small.[23]

These provisions are important within the context of this essay, although not so much because of the obvious discrimination involved. The reduction of peasant lands in favor of the gentry, which must be presumed to have resulted from this regulation, may not have been very large. But what matters primarily here is rather the adverse educational effect of the provisions. Great emphasis has been justly placed in processes of industrialization of backward countries on the need for improvements in the standards of honesty and in the willingness to abide by the obligations assumed. The flagrant breach of good faith and the disregard for property rights involved in the stipulations of the acts of 1848 and 1861 certainly were a most inadequate way to instill respect for property and inviolability of contracts into a population among which very vague views of proprietary rights and a firm tradition of fraud were only too widespread.

Quite frequent in conditions of economic backwardness, such attitudes had been fostered and intensified in Russia by several traits of the serfdom system itself. On the one hand, the peasant population never seemed to recognize the pomeshchik's right of ownership over the land. Whether for religious reasons or because of tenacity of collective memories carried over from the pre-serfdom era, the peasants regarded the land as being under no human ownership ("the land is God's") and its produce reserved to its tillers, unless they simply viewed themselves as the rightful owners. Such views were no doubt greatly aided by the fact that it had required a long historical process to convert the temporary fief (*pomest'ye*), granted to the

23. Y. E. Yanson, *Sravnitel'naya statistika Rossii* (Comparative Statistics of Russia; St. Petersburg, 1880), II, 147.

pomeshchik for a consideration in terms of his services, into an allodial holding. They were further supported by the customary mode of reckoning a pomeshchik's wealth not by acres but by the number of "male souls" in his ownership. At the most, the peasants might be willing to consider the lord's demesne on which labor services were performed as his rightful possession, but the lands allocated to the peasantry were surely viewed as peasants' land, and this view was fully supported by the conventions of everyday language distinguishing between *barskaya zemlya* (the lord's land) and *krest'yanskaya zemlya* (the peasants' land). Against deeply rooted beliefs of this kind, it mattered little that the language of the positive law was absolutely clear and unambiguous. "Lands appertaining to pomeshchik villages as well as peasants' houses erected on such lands belong to the pomeshchik." [24] Nor did the legally approved practice of selling peasants without land individually or in large groups for resettlement (*na vyvod*) on new lands in the southern or eastern regions seem to impair the peasantry's fundamental attitude.

Furthermore, in the everyday life of the serf village, the products of forests and orchards were generally regarded by the serfs as *res nullius*. Lumbering in the lord's forests and grazing cattle on his fields were regular occurrences, certainly not at variance with the moral code of the peasantry and far from obsolete half a century after the reform.[25] Finally, the labor services themselves presented plentiful and fully utilized opportunities to practice deceit and evasion of orders and regulations. It took a long time for Russian industrial laborers of serf origin to shed the attitudes so firmly implanted during their adolescence in the villages. And the beliefs or behavior of businessmen — artisans, merchants, and industrialists — small or large as they might be, were not dissimilar. Under these conditions, the authors of the Emancipation Act, starting as they inevitably must from the assumption of the lord's ownership over all the land purchased or inherited by him, should have been particularly careful to protect the private property of the peasants where they were free to do so.

24. *Svod zakonov rossiyskoy imperii* (1857 ed.), article 1138.

25. D. S. Flekser, *Okhrana sel'skokhozyaystvennoy sobstvennosti* (Protection of Property in Agriculture; St. Petersburg, 1904), pp. 6–7.

As will be shown, however, the legal treatment of the claims to lands purchased by the peasants was by no means the most important instance of the government's failure to introduce modern concepts into the agrarian sector of the economy. More will be said about it in discussing the role assigned to the village commune within the framework of the emancipation procedure. It also will be shown that, in a not insignificant measure, the civil status of the peasantry as established by the Emancipation Act was curtailed again by the preservation and strengthening of communal relationships in agriculture. Nevertheless, neither the trammels resulting from those relationships nor the fact that portions of the serfs either legally or virtually had been able to act as fairly independent agents prior to the emancipation should obscure the great change in status wrought by the emancipation provisions. It opened opportunities for occupational social mobility to the peasantry as a whole, thus widening tremendously the basis from which both labor and entrepreneurs for non-agricultural pursuits could be recruited. In this sense, the emancipation did serve as a precondition for the subsequent economic development. Whatever strictures can be raised against the reform should not make one forget that thereby nearly 40 percent of the population of the country were liberated in their economic decisions from the gentry's tutelage, which at best was designed to serve narrowly conceived interests of the group and all too often was exercised in a willful fashion in obedience to passing moods and fleeting whims.

PEASANT AGRICULTURE VERSUS GENTRY AGRICULTURE

Emperor Alexander II, like his predecessors on the throne, carried the official title of "Samoderzhets Vserossiyski" — the Autocrat of All the Russias. By the time of the emancipation, the original meaning of the term connoting a ruler not subject to a foreign suzerainty had faded away, and Russian autocracy came to mean absolute sway on the part of the sovereign. Assuming for a moment that the emperor's power was actually unrestrained and that he could decide at his discretion among different types of reform, one might review the main choices he may have reasonably considered. At one extreme stood the possibility of confining the reform to the abolition of bondage proper, leaving the gentry in undisturbed and unencumbered possession of the land and letting members of both groups, the peasants and the gentry, arrive individually as free contracting parties either at agreements ranging from short-term sharecropping to long-term money rent tenancy or at a simple wage-labor relation. At the other extreme stood the possibility of expropriating all the lands in the possession of the gentry and of distributing them among the individual peasant households according to some predetermined pattern. In view of Russia's subsequent economic history, one might also mention the possibility of expropriating the land in favor of the state in order to organize government-run or -supervised farms, using the peasants either as wage laborers or as tenants, but at any rate distributing the produce between the state and the tillers of the soil, and perhaps utilizing the government's share of the produce in such a way as to assure the speedy economic development of the country.

It is sufficient to mention such alternatives in order to see that, to all practical intents and purposes, none of them was within the range of the autocrat's free decision. The relations between the emperor and his bureaucracy on the one hand and the gentry on the other were far from being simple and straightforward. Over the past and still fairly recent history of autocracy hung the shadow of palace revolutions and regicide, as well as that of the Decembrists' uprising, engineered by members of the nobility and gentry. If the Russian gentry had had the opportunity for representation and organized expression of opinion even to the moderate degree accorded to the Austrian *Stände* in Metternich's time, it is almost certain that frictions similar to those that developed in Austria in the 1840's would have made their appearance in Russia. Yet, when all is said and done, the gentry was the very backbone of imperial power. To expropriate the gentry and thus deprive it of its social basis as the landowning class in the country would have left the imperial government in a most precarious and probably untenable political position. Viewed over a very long period, such a policy might have served to save and perpetuate the dynasty, but only on the implausible assumption that the government would not have succumbed in the short run to the opposition of the gentry and to the concomitant disintegration of the civil service and the officer corps. Such a policy would have forced the emperor into an alliance with the radical intelligentsia. Again, in the long run, such an alliance might have helped the intelligentsia to shed its radicalism, but in the short run it would have further weakened and disorganized the imperial power. No one could expect the emperor to adopt a policy that would have been even more far-reaching than had been that of the French Convention.

Compared with these political necessities, economic considerations could not appear very important. But they, too, if any heed had been paid to them, would have legislated against an expropriation of the gentry. Even if an indemnification of the gentry for all its lands were a feasible budgetary measure, such a policy would have meant committing for a long time to come a sizable portion of national income to a group deprived of any participation in productive processes, even though some of the funds might have been used to repurchase the alienated lands and others might have been employed toward a realization of Belinski's old dream to convert the gentry into a bourgeoisie.[26] In addition, though perhaps paradoxically, a radical abolition of large landed property throughout the country was likely to retard rather than hasten the growth of a bourgeoisie.

By the same token, nationalization of the expropriated lands, too, was an extreme political implausibility. But even if expropriation had been politically feasible, nationalization of the land and creation of government-owned and -supervised estates was not in the stars. At no time between Peter the Great and Stalin could such a measure have entered the purview of practical politics, and least of all in the third quarter of the nineteenth century. However backward Russia's political structure was in comparison to that of Western Europe, the impact of the Zeitgeist upon it was irresistible. With economic liberalism prevailing in the West, anything even remotely resembling the *kolkhozy* or *sovkhozy* of Soviet Russia or the military villages of Arakcheyev's time would have been inconceivable in terms of the predominant contemporaneous ideology.

On the other hand, to transform the peasantry into a class of landless laborers would not have been necessarily inconsistent with such an ideology. But the imperial government, haunted by the fear

26. *P. V. Annenkov i ego druz'ya* (P. V. Annenkov and His Friends; St. Petersburg, 1892), p. 611.

of peasant rebellions, never could consider effecting such a transformation by the one fell blow of the Emancipation Act. That the peasants' provision with land had to be assured in the first instance was therefore one of the axioms underlying the emancipation procedure. Accordingly, the freedom of the autocratic government being limited at both extremes, the actual solution could have been only one of compromise. In some fashion, the interests of the gentry and the interests of the peasantry had to be recognized.

From the point of view of a government that was both conservative, in the sense of wishing to minimize the injection of new elements into the body social and economic of the country, and liberal, in the specific sense of wishing to minimize the government's interference with peasant–gentry relations, a relatively simple, or rather least complex, solution suggested itself almost naturally. It was incorporated in the "Imperial Message" of November 20, 1857, to the governor-general for the governments (or provinces) of Vilna, Kovno, and Grodno. This message was intended to serve as a guiding light for the preparation of the reform. The document expressly recognized that the gentry were to retain the right of full ownership over the land but not over farmhouses and plots, which were to be let to the peasants for permanent use; in due time (over a period of twelve years) the houses and plots were to be acquired by the peasantry through a special redemption procedure. At the same time, the pomeshchiks were to be placed under the obligation to supply the peasantry with the extent of land necessary in given local conditions to assure its livelihood. In exchange, the peasants were to pay quitrents or perform labor services for the landowners.[27] It was believed that the exact extent of mutual obligations had best be left to voluntary agreements between the parties concerned. In this way, it was assumed the status quo would be largely preserved and the government

27. *Zhurnaly sekretnago i glavnago komitetov po krest'yanskomu delu* (Minutes of the Secret and Chief Commissions on the Peasant Question; Petrograd, 1915), I, 27–35; *Materialy dlya istorii uprazdneniya krepostnogo sostoyaniya pomeshchich'ikh krest'yan v Rossii v tsarstvoyaniye Imperatora Aleksandra II* (Materials for the History of Abolition of Serfdom of Gentry Peasants in Russia During the Reign of Emperor Alexander II; Berlin, 1860), I, 140–141. Also A. A. Kornilov, *Ocherki po istorii obshchestvennago dvizheniya i krest'yanskago dela v Rossii* (Essays in the History of Social Movements and the Peasant Question in Russia; St. Petersburg, 1895), pp. 170–171.

would interfere as little as possible in the relations between the two groups. In fact, the very innovation implied in the pomeshchiks' surrendering the farmsteads (houses and plots) to the peasants could be expected to strengthen traditional ways by keeping down the migration movements which otherwise might have imperiled the flow of labor supply to the gentry. At the same time, the future would remain unprejudiced for any final solution. It might be possible in the end to follow the East Elbian pattern and by gradually reducing the extent of lands allotted to the peasantry, substitute wages in money or in kind for the quitrents. The reform thus would end in a process of engrossing similar to that carried out in Prussia's eastern provinces through a number of decades after the original reform of 1807–1816. The Prussian agrarian reform in the end conferred substantial benefits upon German industrialization. The Junker estates proved to be a capacious reservoir of labor supply to industries in western Germany, while for several decades exports of grain from those estates steadied the German balance of payments and facilitated imports of machinery and equipment. There is no evidence that these consequences were intended by the authors of the Prussian reform, and Thomas Hardy's Spirit Ironic might well view the process as another instance of "the groping tentativeness of an Immanent Will." If the Prussian model had accepted in Russia, the Immanent Will in all likelihood would have produced similar results and would have played its irony upon the makers of the Russian reform as well. It is therefore crucial for the understanding of the Russian reform that it did not follow the trail blazed in Prussia, even though assertions to the contrary have not been infrequent.

What effectively precluded the Prussian solution in Russia was the emperor's change of mind, which took place after the message already referred to. It is not necessary to discuss here at length the reasons that caused the change beyond mentioning the role of the gentry from provinces situated north of the black-earth belt, among whom those of Tver were particularly vocal. In those areas, serfdom as an agricultural institution had been in a rather precarious position. The quality of the soil was poor; a large part of the gentry lived away from its estates either in one of the two capitals or in the local urban centers. The lack of entrepreneurial energy made it difficult

to compensate for the poverty of the resource endowment by introducing technological innovations, even if the traditionalism inherent
in serfdom had not obstructed such innovations. Partly as a result of
absentee ownership, the importance of labor services in those areas
was much smaller than that of quitrents, and a sizable portion of the
peasantry paid the rents out of earnings made outside agriculture.
Since, finally, the customary level of consumption of the northern
gentry was high and not easily reducible, the indebtedness of the
gentry to government mortgage institutions grew *pari passu* with the
sinking profitability of the estates. A liberation of the peasants upon
the principles of the Imperial Message would have further deteriorated the lord's position by depriving them of quitrent income from
those former serfs who lived in the cities and would not return to
the village to accept a land allotment. At any rate, since their lands
represented a diminishing source of wealth and the burden of debt
was pressing, many of the gentry felt that the emancipation should
be conducted in such a way as to provide them with sizable one-time
income, out of which it would also be possible to repay their debts.
The reform, therefore, should allow — or perhaps even compel —
the peasants to acquire the lands allotted to them and make the
government finance the operation. Once conceived, this solution was
pressed with a great deal of energy. After a brief period of resistance,
the emperor acquiesced in the demands and thereby changed the
character of the emancipation in two most significant respects. (1)
Not only the farmsteads, but also the field lands were to be allotted
to peasants in *permanent use*.[28] (2) A special Redemption Statute
regulated the procedure for the acquisition of the allotted lands by
the former serfs. Something more will be said about it below.

This turn of events effectively obviated an eventual creation of
a mass of landless peasants. A *landowning* peasantry, along with a
landowning gentry, was to become a fundamental trait of the Russian agrarian structure, even though the nature of peasant ownership
over the land was to be of a very special kind and far removed from
the simple concept of individual property. For the question of relation between the emancipation and the subsequent economic development of the country, it must be noted that a momentous decision

28. *OP* article 12.

affecting those relations for a long period of years to come was taken essentially to satisfy the immediate needs of one segment of the gentry.

ALLOTMENT AND QUITRENT

The decision to make the allocation of land to the peasantry an irrevocable one imparted particular significance to the question of what kind of land, how much of it and on what conditions the peasantry should receive. The original intention to leave these questions to voluntary agreements of the pomeshchik and his peasants in each individual case was indeed introduced into the Emancipation Act.[29] But in reality the principle of nonintervention on the part of the state could not be maintained. On the one hand, provision had to be made for cases where such agreements failed to materialize. On the other hand, the government could not accept with equanimity agreements by which the economic power of the peasant household was reduced, by inadequacy of land allocation or by imposition of two heavy a compensation to the landowner, to such an extent as to make it impossible for the peasantry to fulfill its tax obligations. Accordingly, the General Statute was accompanied by four Local Statutes in which as a rule a minimum size of land allotment per male peasant — "per soul," in the official parlance — was set, below which the individual agreements could not go.[30] The land allotment was gen-

---

29. *OP* article 6.

30. One Local Statute referred to the provinces situated in Great Russia, Belorussia, and Novorossia: "Mestnoye polozheniye o pozemel'nom ustroystve krest'yan vodvorennykh na pomeshchich'ikh zemlyakh v guberniyakh velikorossiyskikh, novorossiyskikh i belorousskikh" (Local Statute Concerning Land Arrangement of Peasants Settled on Pomeshchik Lands in the Great Russian, Belorussian, and Novorossian Governments; cited in the following as *MPV*), *PSZ*, XXXVI (1863 ed.), no. 36662. The other Local Statute referred to three Little Russian governments: "Mestnoye polozheniye o pozemel'nom ustroystve krest'yan vodvorennykh na pomeshchich'ikh zemlyakh v guberinyakh malorossiyskikh: Chernigovskoy, Poltavskoy i chasti Khar'kovskoy" (Local Statute Concerning Land Arrangement of Peasants Settled on Pomeshchik Lands in Little Russian Governments: Chernigov, Poltava, and a part of Kharkov), *ibid*, no. 36663; cited in the following as *MPM*. Two more Local Statutes were issued: one for the so-called western provinces and the other for the so-called northwestern provinces: "Mestnoye polozheniye o pozemel'nom ustroystve krest'yan vodvorennykh na pomeshchich'ikh zemlyakh v guberniyakh Kievskoy, Podol'skoy i Volynskoy" (Local Statute Concerning Land Arrangements of Peasants

erally described as consisting of "field lands," without further specifications concerning inclusion of woodlands, meadows, and pastures. It is very important for a proper grasp of the Russian peasant economy after the reform that in very many cases the composition of the allotment turned out to be quite unbalanced. The way chosen for determining the minimum allotment was complex and devious. It may be illustrated briefly with reference to the most important Local Statute, that for the Great Russian, Belorussian, and Novorossian provinces. What was determined in a geographically differentiated manner was not the minimum, but either the maximum or the "prescribed" allotment per soul. It was not permitted to reduce by voluntary agreements the actual size of the allotment below one half of those maximum or prescribed allotments.[31] Moreover, in the zones where a maximum allotment was set, and the actual amount of land in the hands of the peasantry at the time of the emancipation (that is to say, of pomeshchik land allotted to the peasants by the pomeshchik during the period of serfdom) was below one third of the maximum allotment, the pomeshchik was under obligation to increase the size of the actual allotment to the level of one third of the maximum allotment.[32]

On the other hand, and this was the purpose of introducing the concept of maximum allotment (rather than setting the minimum allotment directly), should the pre-emancipation allotment be found to be in excess of the maximum allotment, the pomeshchik was given the right "to cut," as the term ran, the permanent allotment down to the size of the maximum allotment.[33] Thus, if the pre-emancipation allotment was somewhere between the maximum and the minimum allotment, then in the absence of voluntary arrangements the pre-

Settled on Pomeshchik Lands in the Governments of Kiev, Podolsk, and Volyn) and "Mestnoye polozheniye o pozemel'nom ustroystve krest'yan vodvorennykh na pomeshchich'ikh zemlyakh v guberniyakh Vilenskoy, Grodenskoy, Kovenskoy, Minskoy i chasti Vitebskoy" (Local Statute Concerning Land Arrangement of Peasants Settled on Pomeshchik Lands in the Governments of Vilno, Grodno, Minsk, and a part of Vitebsk), *ibid.*, nos. 36664 and 36665. Important provisions of the last two acts, however, were altered after the Polish uprising of 1863, as a punitive measure against the Polish gentry.

31. *MPV* article 121.
32. *MPV* article 16, note 1, and article 19.
33. *MPV* article 18.

emancipation allotment was to be regarded as the permanent allotment under the emancipation procedure. This general rule, however, was infringed in favor of the pomeshchiks by some additional stipulations. If the aggregate pre-emancipation allotments were more than twice as large as the pomeshchik land proper (that is, the demesne constituted less than one third of the total land area, waste land never counted), then again the pomeshchik had the right to reduce the permanent allotment in such a way as to raise his own holdings to one third of the total, provided, however, that thereby the permanent allotments to the peasantry were not reduced below one third of the legal maximum allotment. In the steppe areas, where the peasants were to be given land in permanent allotment according to the "prescribed" size of allotments, the prescribed allotments could be reduced to the point necessary in order to leave the pomeshchik one half of the total land.[34] Thus, the government's role in determining the division of the land between the two groups proved quite far-reaching. In addition to protecting the peasantry against insufficiency of land, the Emancipation Act also protected the gentry's possession of land by setting a floor below which those possessions should not fall, without consent of the individual owners. The conservative idea of freezing the pre-emancipation division of lands into a permanent arrangement was allowed to be broken from two sides. On balance, the additions to and subtractions from the status quo of pre-emancipation allotments as they emerged from the emancipation settlement can be summarized in Table 1.[35]

A diminution of 4.1 percent in the amount of land available to the peasantry cannot be considered very substantial. The total percentage, however, disguises the fact that the subtractions and additions were very unequally distributed among the various areas of the country. The elimination from the computation of the eight western provinces, where the predominantly Polish gentry was being discriminated against, changes the picture very considerably. Those eight provinces accounted for about 90 percent of all additions to peasant lands carried out in the course of the emancipation settlement. If they are ex-

34. *MPV* article 22.
35. P. A. Zayonchkovski, *Otmena krepostnogo prava v Rossii* (Abolition of Serfdom in Russia; Moscow, 1954), pp. 206–207. One desyatina equals 2.7 acres.

Table 1. Change in Peasant Land Allotments (43 provinces)

Land under peasant tillage before 1861 (desyatinas)	Land permanently allocated to peasants under the emancipation procedure (desyatinas)	Decrease compared with pre-emancipation allotments	
		(desyatinas)	(percent)
35,196,734	33,755,658	1,441,076	4.1

cluded, the extent of land lost by the peasantry in the 1861 settlement increases to 13 percent. This figure again disguises the fact that the "cuts" were much more substantial in black-soil and steppe areas than elsewhere. In the sixteen provinces in that region, the peasants before the emancipation had 13,093,000 desyatinas allotted to them, of which they lost through the emancipation 3,059,400 desyatinas, or about 23.3 percent. The percentage cuts in the less productive non-black-earth provinces were accordingly smaller. Again, it would be difficult to attribute this result to considerations relating to the economic development of the country. An explanation in terms of relation between the government and the gentry is much more plausible. Under the pressure of the gentry in non-black areas, the emancipation went far beyond mere abolition of personal bondage. The gentry in the fertile black-earth regions whose economic position was much more favorable, owing to the greater profitability of land cultivation there, had little reason to approve a more radical reform; under these conditions the opportunity to reduce the allocation of valuable lands to the peasants provided some compensation for the disturbance by the reform of an economically satisfactory order of things and tended to reconcile the gentry of these regions to the idea of emancipation.

From the point of view of industrialization, an evaluation of the reform will have to take into consideration, first the further development of agriculture on landed estates which were thus increased in size and, second, the significance of the diminished economic power of the peasant economy. The latter must be considered in conjunction with the general budgetary position of the government and the fact that the income of the peasantry was the main source of government revenue, the gentry being largely free from tax obligations. The distribution of land, however, was not the only way in which the emancipation affected the peasant economy. Equally important was the assessment of obligations placed upon the liberated peasantry in payment for the land, together with the problem of purchasing the allotted lands from the gentry under the rules established in the emancipation statutes.

Just as the authors of the Emancipation Act refused to leave the question of land allotments to voluntary agreements without setting certain limits, partly for reasons of social policy and public interest and partly for other reasons, they introduced into the Local Statutes stipulations concerning the maximum amounts of labor services and quitrents to be defrayed by the peasantry for the land allotted to them. Accordingly, the amount of labor services to be performed was limited in the Great Russian Local Statute to 40 male and 30 female working days per year per "maximum allotment per soul." [36] The Little Russian Local Statute contained similar, even though more differentiated, stipulations.[37] Only 60 percent of this workload was to be performed during the summer.[38] The landowner was given the right to ask for team services rather than mere labor services at his discretion, thus assuring for the area of the Great Russian statute (except in the southern steppes) the continued supply of draft animals to the demesne. For labor services performed with the help of peasant teams, a ratio of team days to "pedestrian" days was established in the Great Russian statute.[39] It should be noted, however, that after a transition period of two years, the peasants received the right to convert labor services into quitrents without consent of the landowner.[40] Taken in isolation, this provision might be taken to suggest that, in the opinion of the authors of the reform, the separation of the peasant and the pomeshchik economies was an easy matter, to be accomplished within a very short period. But such a conclusion would be premature. Other measures, to be referred to later, were designed to guard the pomeshchiks indirectly against too sudden interruptions or diminutions in the flow to their lands of peasant labor and peasant capital.

36. *MPV* article 189.
37. *MPM* article 195.
38. *MPV* article 193; *MPM* article 198.
39. *MPV* article 201.
40. *MPV* article 236; *MPM* article 234.

The quitrents, like the labor services, were determined in the Local Statutes as maximum amounts not to be exceeded in the voluntary agreements between the two parties. They were set for the maximum allotment with considerable differentiation by areas and sub-areas. A curiosity of the arrangement was that, in cases in which the actual allotment was smaller than the maximum allotment, the quitrents due were not reduced proportionately to the reduction in the land area of the allotment. Vaguely justified in the committee discussions on the reform by reference to the "law of diminishing returns," the quitrent for the "first" desyatina of the maximum allotment was set in such a way as to be higher in all cases than that for the "subsequent" desyatinas. Thus, for example, for some of the non-black-earth regions the quitrent for the maximum allotment of, say, 4 desyatinas was set at 10 roubles; the quitrent for the "first" desyatina was to be 5 roubles; for the "second" desyatina 2.50 roubles and 1.25 roubles for each of the remaining two desyatinas. In this way, the burden of quitrent on an actual allotment of the size of one half of "maximum allotment" amounted not to 50 percent, but to 75 percent of the total quitrent for the maximum allotment.[41] For allotments in black-earth areas, the same principle was maintained, but the gradations were somewhat flatter. Viewed as a taxation on income, this principle of regressive taxation was introduced to increase the yield in quitrents per unit of land, particularly in non-black-earth regions.[42] The stipulation, however, was primarily devised because of fears that the peasants might be reluctant to accept a *full* allotment, expecting to lease the additional land at a lower price.

Finally, the quitrents could be raised by one rouble per soul, upon representation by the pomeshchik, for a number of reasons, including the proximity to the village of a larger urban settlement or a port city that gave peasants an opportunity for making substantial nonagricultural profits.[43] By this provision, the principle that the

41. Cf. *MPV* article 168.

42. It is true that, by a special stipulation in villages in which before the emancipation only quitrents were paid and no labor services were performed, quitrents for the permanent allotments could not exceed their pre-emancipation level (*MPV* article 170; *MPM* article 178). But since cases of pure quitrents were rare and some labor services were performed in most cases, the restrictive value of this stipulation remained small.

43. *MPV* article 173; *MPM* article 181.

quitrents represented payment for land use was *pro tanto* abandoned, and a participation of the pomeshchiks in industrial and other nonagricultural earnings of the peasantry was rendered possible. On the other hand, some provisions were also introduced designed to reduce, in the absence of voluntary agreements, the existing quitrents or quitrents set in accordance with the Local Statutes in several instances, including cases in which the peasants received particularly poor or distant lands.[44] The level of quitrents was to become of particular importance in connection with the redemption procedure through which the lands allotted to the peasants for permanent use were to pass into their permanent ownership. At any rate, according to the Local Statutes, the obligations of the peasantry, including the quitrents, were to be set for twenty years, after which period a revaluation should become possible.

The foregoing description of land allocation and peasant obligations provides but a summary view of a most complex set of provisions. The execution of these provisions no doubt involved a task of formidable proportions. In the eighteenth century, beginning with Empress Elizabeth's reign, the government proceeded to determine the boundaries of gentry estates. But it abstained from crossing those boundaries in order to examine the inner working of the estates. Except in the western regions, both the land allotments and the size of peasant obligations had been left in pre-emancipation times to the discretion of the owners, and the government had abstained not only from regulating those relations, but even from obtaining any reliable and comprehensive information concerning them. The only exception was Paul I's limitation of labor services to three days per week, a limitation, however, that was never enforced by the government.[45]

Accordingly, for most of the area of the empire there was nothing comparable, for example, to the *Urbaria* set up in Austria in the second half of the eighteenth century. The authors of the reform (the "drafting commissions") carried out an *ad hoc* census of sorts and, as a result, operated with essentially unverified data on the extent

44. *MPV* article 174; *MPM* article 182.
45. Law of April 5, 1797. *Svod zakonov rossiyskoy imperii* (1857 ed.), IX, article 1046; and V. I. Semevski, *Krest'yane v tsarstvovaniye Imperatritsy Yekateriny II* (Peasants During the Reign of Empress Catherine II; St. Petersburg, 1903), I, xiii.

of land under peasant cultivation and the nature of peasant obligations. It is doubtful whether they had at their disposal a really adequate basis for appraising the actual significance of the reform provisions and for judging the extent of the change to be brought about.
At any rate, for the implementation of the emancipation procedure,
it was necessary therefore to determine in each individual case, village
by village, the size of the existing division between the demesne and
peasant land and the extent of peasant obligations. Since, moreover,
the emancipation procedure allowed for redistribution of fields, difficult problems of evaluation were bound to arise. A machinery for a
practical solution of these problems had to be set up. Briefly it operated
as follows.

The first step in each case was the composition of the separation
brief or "establishment charter" (*ustavnaya gramota*) in which the
emancipation settlement was to be incorporated. This was left to the
pomeshchik who could carry out the task either alone or jointly with
his peasants. The charters were then to be submitted to special peace
arbitrators, who were to be elected by the local gentry from its ranks
every three years. The peace arbitrator (*mirovoy posrednik*) had
to examine the establishment charters for their conformity with the
provisions of the Local Statutes and, if the document had not been
approved by the peasants, to submit the charters to them and to
attempt to achieve an agreement between the two parties. Regular
sessions consisting of arbitrators of a given district served as court of
appeal in the case of disagreement, and so did in the last instance a
bureaucratic body which was to be set up in each government center
under the chairmanship of the governor.

There is no question that in this fashion a great deal of the implementation of the reform was laid in the hands of the gentry. It
should be clear that the pomeshchiks in many cases could derive considerable benefits from understating the extent of the pre-1861
allotments and from overstating the level of the pre-1861 quitrents
in the establishment charters. The personality of the arbitrator was
crucial. To ascertain the existing conditions and to "establish" the
peasants' allotments and obligations required much good will, patience,
and a valiant effort. Yet even given all these qualities and assuming
the arbitrator's complete objectivity, much depended upon the peasants' ability and willingness to articulate their position. Conditions in

this respect varied greatly from village to village. It appears that in very many cases the peasants believed that a second, the "real," emancipation was still to come, and they often were unwilling to participate in an operation that appeared to them a mockery of their ideas of right and justice. Accordingly, they refused to cooperate and to sign the charters, with the result that the settlements as submitted by the arbitrator to the arbitrators' session in all likelihood were more prejudicial to the peasants' interests than they would have been otherwise.

The determination of existing quitrents was particularly arduous. Sometimes, the pomeshchiks had traditionally set the quitrents at too high a level because of the equally traditional propensity on the part of the peasants to pay less than the full amount of their obligations; sometimes arrears from previous years had been simply included in the current year's quitrents. To the extent that very primitive systems of rotation (such as *perelog*) were in use, it was as good as impossible to determine the size of the peasant lands. In the steppes of the extreme south where land was abundant, the pomeshchik did not mind the peasants' cultivating *po silam* ("within the limits of their ability"), as the expression ran, provided of course that the obligations to the pomeshchik were fulfilled. But also in areas of the traditional three-field system the task all too often was far from easy. The quality and the location of the lands to be "cut" from, or added to, the allotment were a matter of much argument, even in absence of attempts to let waste lands pass for arable.

In addition, the scarcity of geodetic personnel was a serious matter. The number of official experts was quite insufficient for the purpose, and the arbitrators frequently had to have recourse to voluntary helpers whose standards of competence were lower but whose ability to resist temptation was greater than that of the civil servants. Finally, the pressure of the gentry upon the arbitrators was very great. Leo Tolstoy, who served one year as an arbitrator (May 1861–May 1862), was threatened with both criminal prosecution and bodily violence, even though he claimed to have conducted operations in "a most unemotional and conscientious manner." [46]

The quality of the arbitrators began to deteriorate noticeably

46. Leo Tolstoy, *Polnoye sobraniye sochinenii* (Complete Works), *Pis'ma* (Letters), LX (Moscow, 1949), 415 — also pp. 403, 405, 416, 433; and XLVIII 2nd ser.; *Dnevniki* (Diaries; Moscow, 1952), pp. 37–38.

some time in the 1860's. Yet the arbitrators of the "first echelon," who were appointed immediately after the proclamation of the emancipation act and who supervised the bulk of the charters, received a good deal of praise from quarters that were either unprejudiced or prejudiced against the arbitrators. The consensus is that a good many of them were moved by idealistic motives, and their choice by the authorities was premised upon fears of peasant violence in response to inequitable treatment in the charters. As it turned out, the charters were biased in favor of the gentry and did tend to accentuate the traits of the law which placed the peasants at a disadvantage. Nevertheless, one may not go far wrong in saying that in general the arbitrators prevented the execution of the reform from degenerating into a further blatant discrimination against the peasantry. At the same time, it must be remembered that there was not much alternative to the procedure actually employed and that the imperial bureaucracy was neither numerically adequate nor competent to tackle a task of this nature. Whatever may be said of class and group interest, it would seem that the arbitrators, precisely because they were members of the landowning gentry themselves, could display a degree of independence and integrity which would have hardly been matched by a lower-rank imperial chinovnik.[47]

THE REDEMPTION OF ALLOTMENTS

The quitrents, determined in the manner described above, were supposed to remain unchanged for twenty years, when a reassessment could take place upon request either of the peasants or the pomeshchiks. But this provision never became effective. The reason was that over the period a radical change took place with regard to the juridical nature of the land allotments. Thanks to the redemption

47. The legal provisions on implementation of the reform were laid down in: "Polozheniye o gubernskikh i uyezdnykh po krest'yanskim delam uchrezhdeniyam" (Statute Concerning Government and District Institutions for Peasant Matters) and "Pravila o poryadke privedeniya v deystvie polozheniya o krest'yanakh vyshedshikh iz krepostnoy zavisimosti" (Rules on the Manner of Execution of the Statute Concerning Peasants Released from Bondage), *PSZ*, XXXVI (1863 ed.), nos. 36660 and 36661. A valuable analysis of a fairly large sample of establishment charters is contained in P. A. Zayonchkovski, *Provedeniye v zhizn krest'yanskoy reformy 1861 g.* (Implementation of the Peasant Reform of 1861; Moscow, 1958).

procedure, most of the land allotted to the peasantry passed over into the ownership of the latter, thus discontinuing the payments of quitrents or rather transforming them into redemption payments to the state.

The main features of the redemption procedure may be summarized as follows:

(a) The redemption of the farmstead in principle was left to private agreements between the pomeshchik and the peasants. If no such agreement could be arrived at, the peasant could request redemption against the will of the pomeshchik. In these cases, the Redemption Act provided a four-step scale of the amounts to be regarded as quitrents for the farmstead out of the total quitrent per soul set for an allotment. Each village was to be assigned to one of the four points on the scale. A multiplication of the quitrent for the farmstead by 16.67 — that is to say, a capitalization at 6 percent — yielded the value of the farmstead per soul to be paid to the pomeshchik. Thereby the peasants' ownership over the farmstead was established, and further payments for the allotment as a whole were to be diminished by the amount of quitrent on the basis of which the value of the farmstead had been computed. The role of the government in this case did not extend into financing the purchase, and was confined to its supervision and registration.

(b) The purchase or redemption of the land allotment could not be initiated against the will of the pomeshchik. On the other hand, it could be initiated by the pomeshchik against the will of the peasants. In this way were protected the interests of the gentry in areas where they were anxious to get rid of their land as well as the interests of the gentry in those areas where they were unwilling to part with the land permanently. The emperor refused to accede to the proposals to make redemption compulsory upon request of the peasants, since he regarded such a procedure as equivalent to a forcible expropriation.[48] As the redemption eventually was made compulsory, the effect of this provision was to slow down somewhat the process of passing lands into peasant ownership.

(c) In the case of the land allotment as well, the principle of relying on voluntary agreements was maintained. However, in cases

48. Semenov Tyan-Shanski, *Memuary*, III, 211.

in which the redemption procedure had been forced upon the peasants, the value of the land was to be computed by a capitalization, at 6 percent of the quitrents set for the allotment.

(*d*) Whether or not the value of the allotment was computed, the government undertook to finance 80 percent (and sometimes only 75 percent) of the value obtained. If the farmstead had not been purchased by a separate agreement, the quitrent referred to the whole allotment, that is, land and farmstead. The pomeshchik then received 5 percent (later raised to 6 percent) interest-bearing bonds for four fifths of the computed value minus the amounts retained for the liquidation of the existing indebtedness of the pomeshchik to government mortgage institutions. Other outstanding obligations of the pomeshchik to the state (tax arrears, etc.) were to be satisfied in the first instance out of the nonbonded portion, if any, of the purchase price to be paid by the peasants to the pomeshchik, but in case of its inadequacy such obligations, too, were deductible from the bonded portion of the purchase value. If the redemption was carried out against the will of the peasants, the pomeshchik could not claim additional payments in excess of 80 percent of the computed value. (A number of deviations from the norm just described were provided for, but may be disregarded here.)

(*e*) Peasants who had purchased the allotments with government aid were placed under the obligation to pay to the Treasury annually 6 percent of the total sum advanced by the government for a period of 49 years. As read from the annuity tables, this involved an annual interest burden of about 6 percent, and at that time (and until 1879) still was the maximum permissible rate of interest.[49]

In view of the general use that was made of the redemption opportunities in the decades following the emancipation, the provisions of the Redemption Act must be considered the final instrument

---

49. See Konstantin Pobedonostsev, *Kurs grazhdanskago prava* (A Course in Civil Law), III (St. Petersburg, 1896), 95. The preceding summary of the redemption provisions has been gleaned from "Polozheniye o vykupe krest'yanami vyshedshimi iz krepostnoy zavisimosti ikh usadebnoy osedlosti i o sodeystvii pravitel'stva k priobreteniyu simi krest'yanami v sobstvennost' polevykh ugodi" (Statute Concerning Redemption by Peasants Released from Bondage of Their Farmsteads and Concerning Government Aid for the Acquisition of Field Lands by These Peasants), *PSZ*, XXXVI (1863 ed.), no. 36659. See esp. articles 2, 3, 4, 11, 14, 15, 29, 32, 35, 36, 64, 65, 66, 113, 114.

through which the peasant family farms were irreversibly established in Russia — irreversibly, that is, within the framework of the empire. It required the "second revolution from above," to use Stalin's somewhat unoriginal description of the collectivization of the 1930s,[50] to change the base laid by the Redemption Statute. Without the redemption provisions, it is at least conceivable that upon the reassessment of the peasant's obligations to the landlord, which was to take place in the early 1880s and for which no restrictive provisions were included in the reform, the pomeshchiks might have tried by steep rises in quitrents to induce the peasants to relinquish the allotments given to them for "permanent use."

It is not quite easy to appraise the burdens involved in the redemption provisions, for the weight of those burdens was liable to change with the basis of comparison chosen. The secular drift of land values was upward. Lositsky compared the redemption values with the average land prices in free traffic during the years 1854–1858 and 1863–1872.[51] The often-quoted results of this comparison are striking, as can be seen from Table 2.

Table 2

	Allotment land in thousands of desyatinas (1)	Value of allotment land at free-market prices in millions of roubles		Value of allotment land at redemption valuations (4)	Column (4) as percentage of column (3)
		1854–58 (2)	1863–72 (3)		
Non-black-earth provinces	12,286	155	180	342	190
Black-earth provinces	9,841	219	284	342	120
Western provinces	10,141	170	184	183	100
Total for the three regions	32,268	544	648	867	134

50. J. Stalin, "Otnositel'no marksisma v yazykoznanii" (On Marxism in Philology), *Bol'shevik*, XXVII (June 1952), 92. See also above, p. 144.
51. A. E. Lositsky, *Vykupnaya operatsiya* (The Redemption Operation; St. Petersburg, 1906), pp. 16, 38–39. The free-market prices were computed for the individual provinces and weighted by the extent of allotment land in each province. The data do not refer to the country as a whole.

It would perhaps be more justifiable to compute the allotments at prices which also take into account the period 1873–1882. But an average price for the whole period 1863–1882 would be only about 10–11 percent higher than the price for 1863–1872.[52] What happened after 1882 is of less interest. At the beginning of 1881, no less than 84.7 percent of former serfs had become owners of their allotments, most of them (almost 93 percent) through the established redemption procedure.[53] Moreover, at the end of 1881, the original redemption procedure was amended by being made compulsory for the Great Russian and Little Russian provinces, and those peasants became owners of their allotments as of January 1, 1883.[54]

Apart from the choice of the appropriate price period, it should be clear that a partial computation of this sort, which applies an average provincial price to lands differing widely in quality and location, cannot be regarded as too precise. Nevertheless, granted their average character, free-market prices as given by Lositsky for 1863–1872 do not seem too *low* as appears from computations from other sources.[55]

If Lositsky's computations are accepted as generally indicative of comtemporaneous land prices, they reveal a very considerable overvaluation of the allotments in terms of prices current at the time. If one compares Table 2 with Table 1 above, a curious contrast is noticeable. While the pomeshchiks in the black-earth regions succeeded in reducing the peasant land allotments much more effectively than the pomeshchiks of the non-black-earth regions, it was the latter who

52. Computed on the basis of land price data given by V. A. Kosinski, *Osnovnyye tendentsii v mobilizatsii zemel'noy sobstvennosti i ikh sotsial'no-ekonomicheskiye faktory* (Basic Tendencies of Mobilization of Landed Properties and Their Socioeconomic Factors; Prague, 1925), p. 78.

53. Computed from data given in Zayoynchkovski, pp. 272–274.

54. *PSZ*, vol. I up to December 31, 1881, no. 585. For "western governments" such an amendment was introduced as early as 1863, after the Polish uprising.

55. The combined average price for both black-earth and non-black-earth governments implied in Table 2 for 1863–1872 comes to about 21 roubles per desyatina. This is *higher* than the price per desyatina given by Kosinski, p. 78. According to this source, the average price per desyatina in 1863–1867 was 14.73 roubles and in 1868–1872, 20.44 roubles. Similar data (14.62 and 19.52 roubles, respectively) are given in V. V. Sviatlovski, *Mobilizatsiya zemel'noy sobstvennosti v Rossii, 1861–1908* (Mobilization of Landed Property in Russia; St. Petersburg, 1911), pp. 81–84.

benefited most from the overvaluation of the allotments. In one case, the peasants had to give up the land; in the other, they obtained the land but at a price nearly 100 percent over and above the current market price. Since such a solution was well adjusted to the different interests of the gentry in the two regions, it is difficult not to conclude that it was these interests that consciously or unconsciously had been taken into account by the authors of the reform in determining the size of the allotments and the extent of the peasants' obligations, and thereby indirectly fixing the level of the redemption values.

The redemption values having been yielded by a capitalization of the quitrents at 6 percent, the overvaluation of the redemption values may have been the result either of too low a capitalization rate or of too high quitrents, or both. The reasonableness of the capitalization rate for an operation of this nature is difficult to determine.

The actual rate of interest (net of taxation) on domestic government loans in paper roubles issued in the 1860's varied between 4.40 and 4.82 percent.[56] More pertinent perhaps is the fact that some years later the actual rate of interest on mortgage bonds sold at the St. Petersburg bourse varied between 6.5 and 7 percent.[57] Choice of the latter rate (if it were permissible) would, of course, have lightened the burden of the aggregate debt by some 14 percent. At any rate, it is clear that variations within a plausible range of interest rates could not begin to account for the total overvaluation of redeemed lands. Moreover, the capitalization rate was the same for black-earth and non-black-earth regions. It was the same also in the "western provinces" where, for reasons stated, the redemption values were not overvalued at all and, if anything, were lower than the market values; this is particularly so if one considers that the redemption in those areas was completed much earlier than in the heartlands of the empire. It must be assumed, therefore, that the quitrents in non-black regions had been set at too high a level in relation to the prevailing market

56. Walter A. Knoop, *Die verzinsliche russische Staatsschuld* (Berlin, 1907), table 2, appendix.

57. Tsentral'ny Statisticheski Komitet, *Statisticheski vremennik rossiyskoy imperii, sbornik svedenii po Rossii za 1883 god* (Central Statistical Commission, Statistical Timebook of the Russian Empire, Collection of Data for Russia for 1883; St. Petersburg, 1886), ser. III, 8, p. 286.

prices of the allotted lands. This conclusion is further reinforced by justifiable doubts as to the extent to which free-market values correctly reflected the productive values of the land. Because of the social prestige attached to the land, and for another reason to be discussed presently, the market land values tended to lie above the capitalized net-yield values. At the same time, free-market lands were not suffering from the various restrictions to which allotment lands were subject. Thus, the actual overvaluations of the allotments in terms of yield values (*Ertragswert*) may have been even higher than is shown by the figures in Table 2. It is therefore not surprising that in the emancipation acts the legislators had considered it necessary to stipulate that for nine years (counting from February 19, 1861) the peasants were obliged to continue to hold the allotment,[58] a situation the pomeshchik then could render perpetual by initiating the redemption procedure unilaterally. As Count Witte rightly remarked, the discrepancy between market values of land and the quitrents imposed made it imperative, "so to speak, to tie the peasants to the land" while emancipating them.[59] In default of such a stipulation, many peasants may have preferred cheap leases to expensive allotments. It is another question that increases in land values in subsequent decades were to change the lease-redemption price ratios very radically.

On the other hand, a point must be stressed here which, for whatever reasons, has not been made with sufficient clarity in the literature of the subject. Taken in isolation, the redemption provisions were highly advantageous to the peasantry since they did not involve much of an *additional* burden. If the government had financed the full redemption value of the land, the peasants would have simply continued to pay to the government what previously they had to pay to the pomeshchiks. Under this condition, the right of ownership in the land (as distinguished from the right of permanent use) would have been received gratis. This follows from the fact that the annual installments amounted to 6 percent of land values computed by capitalizing quitrents at the same rate of interest:

58. Cf. *MPV* article 120.
59. S. Yu. Witte, *Zapiska po krest'yanskomu delu* (Memorandum Concerning the Peasant Question; St. Petersburg, 1904), p. 45.

$$\frac{\text{quitrent} \times 100}{6} = \text{discounted present value of land}$$

$$\frac{\text{quitrent} \times 100 \times 6}{6 \times 100} = \text{annual installment} = \text{quitrent}$$

It is true, however, that in general the government financed only 75–80 percent of the computed land value. This meant that in cases where the pomeshchik forced the redemption procedure upon the peasants and the latter were free of any direct payments to him, the redemption dues were 20–25 percent *lower* than the quitrents as set down in the establishment charters. In this case, the annual purchase payment was below the quitrent. If the redemption stemmed from mutual agreement between the pomeshchik and the peasants, the latter had to arrange for direct payment of 20–25 percent of the computed land value, amounting, that is, to a sum from 3⅓ to 4⅙ times the previous quitrent. In some cases, this additional payment was burdensome. Even when it was carried out in annual installments, the period of amortization was shorter than that of the redemption debt, while the interest rate may have been a good deal higher; at times, interest payments — and even the principal itself — were exacted in terms of labor services; some pomeshchiks tried to enforce the obligations by stipulating draconic fines for delays in payment. But such cases seem to have been quite exceptional. Installment payments up to twenty years would be granted without requiring any interest charges. Frequently, fairly large portions of the debt were forgiven from the outset. At least partial defaults were not rare, and in some cases the pomeshchiks tried to create an incentive for punctual discharge of obligations by making gifts of arable or forest or pond land with the proviso that in case of default the gift should return to the creditor-donor.[60] By and large, it is unlikely that the aggregate annual burden was higher than the previous quitrent. When all is said and done, it is clear that the procedure adopted made it very attractive to the peasants to enter into the redemption arrangements. The trouble lay not in those arrangements, but in the original determination of excessive quitrents.

An intermediary conclusion, significant from the point of view

60. See Zayonshkovski, *Provedeniye*, pp. 318–360.

of the effects of the reform upon industrialization, may be drawn at this point: *The peasantry released from serfdom received insufficient allotments of land, for which it had to pay a disproportionately high purchase price.*

According to the competent estimate of Yanson, made about a decade and a half after the reform, a peasant household in the black-soil areas needed about 5 desyatinas per soul in order to be able to provide itself with an amount of grain needed for bread consumption and to maintain two horses, one cow, two sheep, and one hog. Such an allotment would not allow of outside purchases of textiles, salt, and sugar, agricultural equipment, payment of taxes and redemption dues, to say nothing of other expenses. In the non-black-soil areas, where the yields were lower, an allotment of about 8 desyatinas would be necessary for mere subsistence.[61] Viewed in light of these computations, the actual allotments of the peasants released from bondage were, as a rule, very considerably below the subsistence minimum.[62]

Considering the differences in productivity of the soil, even the higher allotments in the non-black-soil areas were in general below the computed minimum. On the whole, almost three quarters of the peasantry received allotments per soul that were below 4 desyatinas.[63]

The conclusion is inescapable that the release from bondage was not accompanied by the creation of an economically strong peasantry. Its chances to gain economic strength in the decades following the reform depended, first, on the possibility of increasing the yield per unit of land. Second, the peasant economy could try to remedy the

61. Y. E. Yanson, *Opyt statisticheskago izsledovaniya o krest'yanskikh nadelakh i platezhakh* (Essay on a Statistical Investigation of Peasant Allotments and Payments; St. Petersburg, 1877), pp. 25, 65–67.

62. The average allotment per male soul in desyatinas in some of the southern provinces were as follows: Kursk, 2.2; Kazan, 2.7; Voronezh, 2.4; Poltava, 1.9; Ryazan, 2.9; Penza, 2.5; Saratov, 2.8; Tambov, 2.5; Tula, 2.7; Simbirsk, 2.7. In the northern provinces, the allotments were higher: for example, Vladimir, 3.8; Moscow, 3; Pskov, 4.8; Tver, Yaroslavl, 3.8. Only in a few provinces were the allotments above 5 desyatinas: Novgorod, 5.8; Vologda, 5.3. *Statistika pozemel'noy sobstvnenosti i naselennykh mest yevropeyskoy Rossii* (Statistics of Landed Property and of Populated Places in European Russia), Vypusk I–VIII (St. Petersburg, 1880–1885).

63. The total number of 10,039,800 peasants who received allotments can be broken down by the size of the allotment as follows (*ibid.*, Vypusk I, 1880, p. xliii):

insufficiency of allotments by increasing its landholdings through purchases or renting arrangements and by offering its labor for hire within and outside agriculture. Third, peasants could engage in independent, nonagricultural pursuits, such as domestic industry, handicrafts, and others. The extent to which some of these opportunities could be utilized depended on a great number of factors, including the general movement of agricultural prices, the agrarian policy of the government with regard to taxation and its interest in promoting the agricultural economy, and the strength of certain institutional obstacles to economic progress that will be discussed shortly. For the time being, it seems fair to conclude that the smallness of the peasants' landholdings, in conjunction with the high financial burdens imposed through the redemption procedure, made it extremely unlikely if not impossible for the peasantry, in the time following their release from serfdom, to constitute a strong and growing sector of the internal market for industrial commodities. There is no indication in the official deliberations preceding the reform that this effect of the reform had been given any consideration.

MEASURES TAKEN TO INCREASE PRODUCTIVITY

It is one of the characteristic features of the Russian agrarian reform that its main weight rested on concerns other than the modernization of agricultural production. Nevertheless, some provisions in this respect are contained in the Local Statutes. Most importantly, they refer to the right of the pomeshchik to request, before February 19, 1869, a separation of the commons and a consolidation of the de-

Size of allotment in desyatinas	Number of peasants	Percent of total
Below one	544,884	5.5
1–1.5	548,453	5.4
1.5–2	784,414	7.8
2–3	2,828,882	28.2
3–4	2,613,435	26.0
4–6	2,239,334	22.4
6–10	413,059	4.0
Over 10	67,339	0.7
	10,039,800	100.0

183

mesne out of the open fields. On the other hand, the peasants were expressly deprived of the right to claim any change in the open fields or commons, leaving such changes, including divisions and consolidations, to voluntary agreements between the pomeshchiks and the peasants.[64] Furthermore, the pomeshchiks were given the right to request, at any time prior to the redemption, exchange of any part of the land allotted to the peasants in the case of discovery on those lands of useful minerals, or for the purposes of drainage, irrigation, establishment of river ports, road building, and the like. The peasants were to be given equivalent lands adjacent to the lands retained by them.[65]

No definitive statistical picture based on archival materials has yet been presented. It is therefore impossible to speak with complete assurance of the use that was made of those provisions. But P. A. Zayonchkovski has supplied some relevant, although incomplete, data for selected provinces. His presentation would seem to justify the following conclusions: such separations and consolidations as were carried out affected a relatively small part of the existing estates. The pomeshchiks in black-earth governments showed much more interest in the opportunities afforded them by the law than did their counterparts outside the black-earth belt. Because of the one-sided character of the provisions, the scope of separations and consolidations undoubtedly was narrower than it would have been if the peasants, too, had been given the right to demand readjustments. This was so for both obvious and less obvious reasons. In fact, the surfeit of discrimination proved self-defeating. Since such actions as were initiated had been dictated by the interests of the pomeshchiks, the resistance of the peasantry to them was considerable. After a few cases of violent disturbances, the Ministry of the Interior issued a secret ordinance directing chiefs of provinces (*gubernatory*) to *obstruct* separations and consolidations. No less important seems the fact that, after a brief flurry of interest in such rearrangements, the pomeshchiks relapsed into inertia and failed to take advantage of the law during the prescribed period. Finally, in many cases it may not have been rational for the pomeshchik to ask for consolidations.

64. *MPV* articles 64, 65; *MPM* articles 56, 57.
65. *MPV* articles 93, 94, 95; *MPM* articles 87, 88, 89.

Having his lands commingled with those of the peasants very often presented him with certain specific advantages, which may have been deliberately reinforced by a carefully determined configuration of the cuts under the emancipation procedure. If the latter were selected in such a fashion as to encircle the peasants' lands and to impede access to them, the pomeshchik received important nuisance possibilities to use against the peasants. By exploiting them he could increase the peasants' willingness to offer their labor and to reduce their wages for work performed. It was credibly reported that in some areas the availability of such means of pressure was a most important element in determining the market value of an estate.[66]

To take it all in all, appreciation of the economic value of enclosures was not conspicuous in the thinking of the authors of the reform. Naturally, as far as peasant lands proper were concerned, the stipulations of the reform acts extended no inducements for the elimination of open fields. The opposite was the case. For the institutional framework within which the peasants were placed militated directly against any improvements in this respect.

THE INSTITUTIONAL FRAMEWORK

The problem of enclosures, or rather consolidations, of peasant land was almost inextricably connected with the problem of the Russian field commune. The field commune did not exist in Baltic areas. Its share in total peasant landholdings amounted to less than 15 percent in the formerly Polish areas of the Ukraine on the right bank of the Dnieper; even in Belorussia and in the Ukraine on the eastern bank of the Dnieper, that percentage did not rise above 33–40 percent. But in the steppes of Novorossiya and the easternmost area of the Ukraine, the village communes held between 80 and 90 percent of all peasant land and in the regions populated by Great Russians, including the eastern steppes, the percentage of individual landholdings in total peasant land rarely exceeded 3–3.5 percent.[67]

66. Zayonchkovski, *Provedeniye*, pp. 113–119. For the last-mentioned point, see particularly the classic by A. N. Engelgardt, *Iz derevni* (From the Countryside; Moscow, 1937), pp. 291, 350–351.

67. K. R. Kachorovski, *Russkaya obshchina* (The Russian Field Commune; Moscow, 1906), p. 74.

As seen by the legislator, the basic features of the Russian field commune (*obshchina*) were two: (1) periodic repartitions of the field lands among the individual households, and (2) the institution of joint responsibility of the members of the commune for its tax obligations to the government.[68] The criterion by which land allocations to the households were carried out varied from region to region and also over time. Allocation of land according to the number of census souls (male members, independent of their age) or to the number of workers per household, or to the number of "eaters" (all members of a household), or to the number of married couples, were all in use. The quantity of the land per unit used was equalized by allotting to each unit an equal number of strips in each subdivision of the open fields. The differences in the quality of land were taken into account as far as possible by the strip allocation. To the extent that some inevitable differences remained, they were supposed to be equalized over time by so-called shifts, that is, by periodic rotation of strips in the individual shots (*Gewanne*). The pronounced egalitarian character of the Russian field commune certainly is the trait that sharply distinguishes it from the land-use systems in Western Europe. The obshchina was based on the open-field system in the sense that the former was inconceivable without the latter.

The authors of the reform could not altogether ignore the problem of the obshchina. In their deliberations, strong voices were raised which condemned the institution as incompatible with the requirements of modern farming and quoted Western experience and literature in support of their views.[69] This opinion found its expression in article 36 of the General Statute, which reads as follows:

Each member of a village commune can demand that out of the landholdings acquired as communal property a quantity of land corresponding to his contribution to the acquisition of this land be separated out into his individual ownership. If such a separation should appear impractical or impossible, the commune has the right to satisfy the peasant wishing to leave the commune by a sum of money arrived at by agreement or by an official evaluation.

68. *OP* article 113, note.

69. N. P. Semenov, *Osvobozhdeniye krest'yan v tsarstvovanye Imperatora Alekandra II* (Liberation of the Peasants in the Reign of Emperor Alexander II; St. Petersburg, 1890), II, 383.

This stipulation, however, which on the face of it seemed to provide for a simple and easy exit from the commune, remained without practical significance. In the first place, the Redemption Statute immediately restrained the possibility of transforming shares in communal property into individual property, in its oft-quoted article 165:

Until the redemption loan has been repaid, the separation of land to individual householders out of lands acquired by the commune is not permissible except with the consent of the commune. However, if the householder desirous of separation should pay to the District Treasury the whole redemption debt falling on his land, the commune is obliged to separate out to a peasant who has made such payment a corresponding amount of land, if possible in one locality [that is, consolidated], at the discretion of the commune; until the separation takes place the peasant will continue to use the land he acquired as a part of communal lands.

It must be noted that even for the case of repayment of the redemption debt before maturity, the above provision does not enforce the consolidation of the land, leaving the commune at liberty to carry out or not to carry out such a consolidation. The difference in this respect between the rights conferred upon the pomeshchik and those conferred upon the prospective individual peasant owner is quite obvious. Naturally, the cases of premature repayment could not be expected to be numerous. To all practical intents and purposes, the stipulation reflected the legislator's desire to preserve each existing commune for 49 years after the initiation of the redemption procedure. Thus, the opportunity to combine the reform at least with some inducements for the modernization of the land-use system over a large part of the country remained unutilized. It was idle to insist, as was often done in the literature, that given certain favorable conditions, the obshchina as a whole could adopt more productive systems of rotation and improve the techniques of cultivation. In Russian reality, the general shortcomings of the strip system were further aggravated by the temporary character of land use and the strong disincentive to improve a piece of land that sooner or later was to be transferred to another household. By erecting a barrier to the dissolution of the individual's ties with the commune, the reform tended to preserve, if not reinforce, the traditionalism and the inefficiency of peasant agriculture.

187

In fact, some main elements of the institutional framework created by the reform tended to buttress the communal element in agriculture. The basic administrative unit as established by the reform was the *mir*. In general, the mir was the political counterpart of the obshchina. The mir, however, was not made to coincide necessarily with the village but rather united the former peasant serfs of the same pomeshchik, which meant that at times one village could contain several independent village communes. The establishment charters setting forth the land allotments and peasant obligations, while using the "soul" as a unit of computation, were prepared for the collectivity of the peasants in the mir. This was true not only for the cases of field communal organization, but even for the areas where such an organization did not exist. Only in the latter cases were the holdings of the individual households specified in the establishment charter. The redemption of land, again, was carried out by the mir collectively; true, where the obshchina did not exist, redemption by individual households was possible, but joint responsibility (*krugovaya poruka*) for the payment of taxes, the fundamental trait of the obshchina, was extended also to village communes where land was held by the individual households and not by the field commune. Where the redeemed land was held by village communes and where *ad hoc* groups were formed for the redemption of the land, the payment of installments on the redemption debt was again secured by joint responsibilities.[70]

Last and not least, the special protection under which the obshchina was placed expressed itself in the voting procedure prescribed for the mir. The rule laid down required the decisions to be made by majority vote. However, decisions on repartitions of land and on the abandonment of the obshchina and its replacement by individual hereditary land use could not be adopted except by a two-thirds majority. The basic traditionalism of the peasantry thus received strong legal support. A minority could obstruct the dissolution of the obshchina and render obedience to rational economic calculations all but impos-

70. See for the foregoing *OP* articles 40, 187: "Polozheniye o vykupe." Articles 34, 35, 127, 131: "Pravila o poryadke privedeniya v deystviye polozhenii o krest'-yanakh vyshedshikh iz krepostnoy zavisimosti" (Rules Concerning the Order of Implementation of Statutes on Peasants Released from Bondage), *PSZ*, XXXVI (1863 ed.), no. 3661, article 23.

sible. That the same restriction applied to land repartitions reflected the doubts on the part of some members of the bureaucracy concerning the economic advantages of the obshchina. In subsequent years other attempts were undertaken to preserve the obshchina while reducing the frequency of repartitions. Something of this nature had been proposed by the liberal opinion in the country.[71]

The inconsistency of the solution [72] points to the fact that the arrangement adopted by the reform must have been deliberately premised upon considerations other than concern for economic progress within peasant agriculture. At least some of them appear with sufficient clarity from the materials available on the preparation of the reform. Partly there was the desire to conserve an institution whose historical roots — though probably wrongly — were believed to lie in a very remote past.[73] Partly there was the feeling that without the obshchina no strong mir would be possible, the economic field commune being regarded as the necessary basis for a well-functioning administrative village commune. A strong mir was of primary importance from the government's point of view. Prior to the emancipation, the pomeshchik exercised the police powers in the villages. The General Statute preserved these powers, but they were to lapse shortly through the redemption procedure. It was argued, therefore, that "at the present moment the obshchina organization is indispensable for Russia; the people need a strong power which would replace the power of the pomeshchik." [74] Moreover, the pomeshchik had been the government's tax collector and was subject to fines for delays in payments. To assure the continued flow of tax revenue was a task

71. K. D. Kavelin, *Publitsistika, sobraniye sochinenii* (Writings on Public Policy, Collected Works; St. Petersburg, 1903), II, 163, 164, 177, 181, 184.

72. It may be noted, however, that the concept of repartitions in the law apparently did not refer to the rotation of strips within the arable, but to radical reallotment of the land because of changes within the member households. Cf. A. A. Leontiev, *Krest'yanskoye pravo, sistematicheskoye izlozheniye osobennostey zakonodatel'stva o krest'yanakh* (Peasant Law, a Systematic Treatise of the Singular Features of the Peasant Legislation; St. Petersburg, 1909), p. 194.

73. "No, gentlemen, I shall not allow you to break asunder our history . . . We have the obshchina and accordingly we need it, and must preserve it." This was the position of the most influential chairman of the Editorial Commission which drafted the reform statutes, Y. I. Rostovtsev; see Semenov, *Osvobozhdeniye krest'yan*, II, 383.

74. Semenov, I, 95.

for which the bureaucracy was quite unprepared. And the problem was not simply the payment of taxes. If it were, the collective responsibility of the mir might have sufficed. It was rather to assure that the productive resources were divided among the individual peasant households in such a way as to make it possible for each household to pay the tax. The poll tax (*podushnaya podat'* — the soul tax) being the mainstay of peasant taxation, the egalitarianism of the communal land allocations provided the government with a system that, at least in theory, both justified the poll tax and at the same time greatly simplified the mechanism of its collection.

The very fact of separating the peasant and the gentry economies was bound to enhance the repartitional feature of the obshchina. Before the emancipation, general repartitions were less important, as long as the pomeshchik had land reserves at his disposal and was willing to use them to satisfy the needs of *net* additional numbers of married couples in the village. If the peasants were on labor services rather than quitrents, the pomeshchik would also add an appropriate amount of land to his own arable. By contrast, the aggregate allotment of a village remained constant once and for all after the emancipation. Communal land purchases apart, repartition was then the only method to take care of population increase while maintaining equal land allocations.[75]

Similarly, considerations of expedience suggested making the mir rather than the individual peasant a party to the basic separation procedure between the pomeshchiks and the peasantry and also to the redemption procedure, which like the poll tax was based on equal payments per soul. For the period preceding the redemption, as long as the peasants were still under obligation to pay quitrents to the pomeshchik or to perform labor services for him, it was felt again that confronting the pomeshchik with the resistance of the unorganized individual households would make it impossible for him to overcome that resistance and to enforce compliance with the stipulations of the establishment charter.[76] That lack of organization for a group can be

75. N. Brzheski, *Obshchinny byt i khozyaystvennaya neobezpechennost' krest'yan* (Obshchina Life and the Peasants' Lack of Economic Security; St. Petersburg, 1899), pp. 3–4.

76. A. A. Kornilov, *Krest'yanskaya reforma* (The Peasant Reform; St. Petersburg, 1905), p. 125; also *Zhurnaly sekretnago i glavnago komitetov po krest'yan-*

a source of both strength and weakness is a rather general phenomenon. In the late 1920's it was precisely the amorphous force of the unorganized peasantry that imperiled the Soviet government and caused it to assume the grave risks of collectivization.

In addition to basic conservative aversion from change and to considerations of fiscal and economic expediency, there was in the minds of the government the conviction that the obshchina was the foundation on which the political stability of the empire rested. The obshchina, which assured to every peasant a share in the land, seemed a strong barrier against unrest and upheavals. Haxthausen, the great admirer — and in some sense the literary "discoverer" — of the Russian obshchina, had stressed the conservative character of the field commune forcefully and eloquently.[77] This view became automatically accepted as the guiding principle of Russian agrarian policy for many decades to come. Only in this light is it possible to understand later acts of legislation and administration designed to protect the field commune against disintegration. It required the shock of the experience of peasant unrest in the early years of the new century, culminating in the 1905 revolution, to cause the government to abandon its deeply anchored attitude to the obshchina. It must be admitted, however, that the mere fact that the government's obshchina policy was proved wrong nearly half a century later does not mean that it necessarily was erroneous for the early decades after the emancipation. The vision of statesmen anywhere rarely transcends the horizon of a few years.

It is true that, as its immediate effect, the reform provoked a good deal of resistance, disobedience, and unrest. With the publication of the reports to the emperor of the minister of the interior for

---

skomu delu (Minutes of the Secret and Chief Commissions on the Peasant Question; Petrograd, 1915), I, 298.

77. The field commune "preserves the social and political virtues; it preserves the feeling of belonging together, of community, brotherhood, and equality under the common authority, of justice, of love for the home and the fatherland." "As long as this system exists, no hereditary proletariat can emerge and form itself in Russia." August Freiherr von Haxthausen, *Die ländliche Verfassung Russlands* (Leipzig, 1866), pp. 416, 420. During the period of the preparation of the reform, Haxthausen entered the debate with a pamphlet written in French so as to make it easily accessible in St. Petersburg: *De l'abolition par voie legislative du partage égal et temporaire des terres dans les communes russes* (Paris, 1858), which was much noted at the time.

the years 1861–1862, a very detailed picture is available. The basic principle of the reform declaring all land to be property of the pomeshchiks certainly caused fairly general dissatisfaction. In the course of preparation of the establishment charters, there was local friction and at times violence. As mentioned before, attempts at separations and consolidations were another source of discontent. But the main reason for disorders lay in the transitional stipulation of the General Statute, according to which for two years the pre-emancipation status was to continue unchanged. Most of the trouble that came after the proclamation of the act had been caused by the refusal of the peasantry to go on performing labor services for the gentry. Once the preparation of the establishment charters was completed, the disorders ceased and in general peace and order were restored to an extent unknown before the emancipation.[78]

Nevertheless, the authors of the reform, while not necessarily changing their conclusions, might have at least raised in their discussions the general question of the tenability of the obshchina arrangement in the long run and its compatibility with the needs of the country's economic development. In the decade of the 1850's, when their deliberations were conducted, the birth rate was reaching a new high (52.4 per 1000; it had been 43.7 in 1801–1810). True, mortality rates also reached an unprecedented high (39.4 per 1000) in that decade, thus illustrating impressively the backwardness of the country. But the two rates still yielded a rate of population increase of 1.3 percent per year.[79] The authors of the reform, as shown before, had curtailed perceptibly the landholdings of the obshchina. Other things remaining equal, this rate of increase of population meant that two decades after the reform the extent of the land available per capita would be further reduced by some 25 percent. Under the serfdom

78. Akademiya Nauk SSSR, *Otmena krepostnogo prava, doklady ministrov vnutrennikh del o provedenii krest'yanskoy reformy, 1861–1862 g.* (Academy of Sciences of the USSR, The Abolition of Serfdom, Reports of Ministers of Interior on the Execution of the Peasant Reform: Moscow-Leningrad, 1950).

79. Brokgaus i Efron, *Entsiklopedicheskii slovar'*, XXVII, "Rossiya," 92. Rashin believes that the increase in mortality at least in part was spurious, being the result of improved records of deaths. His own estimate for the annual increase in population during the decade of the 1850's is only a little lower than that given in the text — 1.22 percent (pp. 38–42).

system, as we have seen, the pomeshchik in those regions where land was plentiful would increase peasant allotments to accommodate the mir for the growth of population. With the end of serfdom, this possibility was eliminated. There is no evidence that the government gave any serious consideration to the problem of how the increase in population and the concomitant diminution of landholdings per capita was to affect the obshchina as the basis of political stability in the country.

That the preservation of the obshchina in a strengthened form legislated against increases of output on peasant lands was recognized by some of the authors of the reform. But the prevailing attitude was very similar to that of Haxthausen, who argued that "for the moment" agricultural progress within the peasant economy was not needed, since the extent of arable land was fully sufficient to feed the population, as was witnessed by the fact of grain exports. Agricultural progress, he claimed, knew no cure against crop failures and the resulting famines. At any rate, progress could not be achieved on peasant lands because it was the large estates that must begin improvements and carry them a long way before the peasants' interest in imitation could be aroused. Before that happened, half a century might elapse. It is therefore not the peasant economy but the gentry economy where one could expect such little progress in agriculture as was needed and was feasible. As a result of the emancipation, the Russian gentry would be forced to assume entrepreneurial leadership of the estates and to improve their productivity.[80]

It is again plausible to assume that Haxthausen's rather unguarded generalizations well summarize the government's ideas on this aspect of the reform. If agricultural progress was to be confined to the gentry economy, then the economy of the peasants should be made to act as a subsidiary to the former providing it with the needed cheap labor force. The insufficiency of allotments and the high obligations imposed upon the peasantry were bound to produce this effect, except that the peasantry could have sought to abandon the land and turn to nonagricultural pursuits. It would seem that an additional motivation in making the mir and the obshchina an integral part of the reform was the desire to prevent a flight from the land.

80. Haxthausen, pp. 420–423.

This is the point where the connection between the reform and the subsequent economic development is most direct and immediate.

The Emancipation Act, in its General Statute, laid down a set of rules governing the peasant's right to abandon the mir, the most important of which must be listed here. First and foremost, the peasant had to waive forever his right to communal land allotments and to the use of the commons. He had to discharge all tax payments to central and local authorities, including all arrears up to the end of the current calendar year, and this not only for himself but for the household as a whole. He could not leave without the express consent of his parents.[81] As if the foregoing provisions were not sufficiently stiff, they were further reinforced by the stipulation of article 173 of the Redemption Act, which reads as follows:

When the land has been acquired from the pomeshchik by the village commune as a whole, the single members of that commune have the right to be dismissed from the commune upon payment of one half of the principal debt on the state redemption loan falling upon the holding of the respective member, provided that the village commune would assume the guarantee for the payment of the other half of the debt.

The peasant had the right, however, to sell or to take apart and carry with him the farm buildings.

A small freeholder in England, if he found the cost of enclosing his land too high, could sell his holding and by doing so acquire some funds which would permit him to start a business venture elsewhere, or would at least serve to cover the transfer cost. The Russian peasant had not only to abandon his lands, but to make a sizable payment toward the redemption of the land he was relinquishing. That the consent of parents was difficult to obtain for a son whose departure meant a diminution of the land available to the household should be clear.

The requirement that tax arrears must be paid up before the dismissal likewise made departures from the commune very difficult. An inflexible stipulation of this sort was obviously ill advised from the point of view of the government's fiscal policy, because the arrears might reflect — as they often did — the paucity of the land allotment and the general economic weakness of the household; in such cases a

81. *OP* chap. 5.

conversion of the arrears into a personal obligation of the departing member of the commune would have constituted the last chance for the government to protect its revenue. It is worth noting in this connection that one of the prescribed ways for dealing with tax arrears was the right of the mir to send either the head of the arrear-accumulating household or one of its members into outside employment, either within the district or, with the consent of the arbitrator, even into other "not too remote" provinces.[82] At least this legal stipulation, which introduced forced labor into the workings of the mir, justified the view expressed by some of the authors of the reform during their deliberations that the preservation of the obshchina meant substituting bondage to the mir for bondage to the pomeshchik.[83]

Temporary departures from the village and voluntary assumption of outside employment were possible, but such departures, until 1894, required the statement of the elected head of the mir that he saw no objections to the issue of a passport to a member desirous of going away. The same was true of extensions of the validity of passports. The right to raise objections also implied the possibility for the local powers to determine at their discretion whether a passport was to be issued for a period of six months only or for longer periods not in excess of three years.[84] Since the nature of the objections was not specified by the law, and no travel or sojourn outside one's own district was permissible without a valid passport, this meant that even temporary absences of the members of the mir were premised upon consent of the mir. Moreover, in case of nonpayment of the redemption installments, the arbitrator was given the right to prevent the mir from issuing a passport or extending the validity of old passports.[85]

It was not until three decades after the reform, in a period in which the policy of the Russian government was deliberately hitched

---

82. *OP* article 188.

83. Kornilov, p. 290. In addition, in cases of arrears the mir could be compelled by the arbitrator to force the members with arrears into outside employment (Redemption Act, article 129).

84. Svod ustavov o passportakh i beglykh" (Code of Statutes Concerning Passports and Fugitives), articles 141–142.

85. Redemption Act, article 129.

to the goal of rapid industrialization, that a certain liberalization of these stipulations was carried out. Under the Passport Act of 1894, the validity of a normal passport was extended from one year to five years. Passports could be issued despite the existence of arrears, at the given village commune, provided it gave its consent to the issue of the passports. But the consent of the head of the household was necessary both for the issue of the passport and for its extension. Upon request of the head of the household, an issued passport could be rescinded if the mir supported the request. Similarly, the issued passport was rescinded if the bearer had been elected to one of the positions within the mir or to a higher stage in peasant administration. The decisions of the mir, however, required the consent of a government representative and could be reversed by a special judicial process. If the passport was rescinded, the bearer was, within seven days, to be deported by the police to his village. A peasant's passport also contained information on his taxpaying status, and discovery of arrears likewise led to the confiscation of the passport and forcible deportation.[86] Thus, the extent of liberalization was moderate to say the least, and even the legislation of the 1890's stipulated the consent of the mir to its members' assuming work away from the village. It stressed the role of the *pater familias* in giving or refusing permission to the would-be absentee, and in general maintained the link between the urban worker and the mir, hence opening the door for various financial pressures by both the mir administration and the head of the household. Even where either power had no true economic reason for retaining a man, it was tempting to make the absentee's continued sojourn in the city dependent upon exacting a share from his earnings. His position as an urban laborer remained precarious.

If industrialization requires formation of a labor force which accepts the discipline of the factory and acquiesces in the lifelong exercise of a nonagricultural occupation, the reform in its aspects just discussed certainly tended to retard the process of formation of such a labor force in Russia.

It may be argued that this process was bound to be particularly difficult in Russia. The habits of perfunctory labor for others, formed

86. "Ustav o passportakh" (Statute Concerning Passports), *Svod zakonov rossiyskoy imperii*, XIV (1903 ed.), articles 22, 29, 30, 31, 32, 46, 49, 60.

in the fields of the pomeshchik, were not easily eradicated and certainly survived the emancipation. Also the Russian climate with its short and uncertain summers forced the Russian peasant to work in sudden spurts, followed by long periods of inactivity, a rhythm that agrees ill with the clocklike regularity of factory work and its requirements for an even effort, day in day out. Even today, Russian factories are still plagued by *shturmovshchina*, the mad rush at the end of each plan period after earlier months of laxity and indifference. This is generally regarded as a result of the Soviet plan system, with its exaggerated targets for output. But the phenomenon also has roots in the nature of agricultural work in a country where, time and again, only a superhuman exertion over a very short period could save the crop and prevent starvation. It is not surprising that under such conditions regular application was despised as "German," as "un-Russian," whereas the quick record performance, if possible involving risk and bravado on the part of the performer, was an object of great admiration. Even while combating *shturmovshchina*, the Soviet government attempted to utilize this traditional attitude to work in the *stakhanovshchina* and in this way to find a limited place for it within the modern industrial environment.

In these circumstances, the urgency to cut the umbilical cord between the city worker and the land was great. But, far from cutting the cord, the reform tended to reinforce it and, in addition, to direct the nutritional flow through it from the city laborer to the land rather than the other way round.

Thus, neither the widening of the country's food basis nor the increased supply of labor to nonagricultural branches of the economy was deliberately promoted by the Emancipation Act. The insufficiency of land allotments and the heavy financial obligation imposed upon the peasantry did not create a steep gradient for the flow of labor; this was so mainly because of the preservation and strengthening of the role of the village commune. The latter, oriented as it inevitably was upon traditional methods of cultivation, effectively prevented increases in the productivity of labor. Besides, the very system of distributing land in accordance with the manpower available to the households — the most frequent criterion of repartition — meant that the households in order to secure the relatively scarce factor (land)

197

had to hoard the relatively abundant factor (labor). This prevented rational use of those factors and made for rural overpopulation. The weakness of the peasant economy as a source of demand for industrial goods and the difficulties in industrial labor supply were the natural consequences, which in turn were bound to affect the character of the country's industrialization.

The high labor–land ratios within the peasant economy were said to favor the gentry. The question may be raised whether the assurance of cheap labor to the large estates was not a dangerous gift. The artificial pinfolding of peasants within the confines of the villages was likely to disembarrass the pomeshchiks from the bothersome need to introduce technological improvements and to raise the capital-output ratios on their estates. The reform undoubtedly went very far in this solicitude for the pomeshchiks. And yet, to some not easily measurable extent, the discrimination in favor of the gentry was an expression of basic necessities inherent in the conditions with which the reformers had to deal. As explained before, the separation of the two economies was bound to be a slow and painful process. On the face of it, the establishment charters in conjunction with the redemption procedure had made a quick severing cut. But, in reality, all the basic features of the reform — the inadequacy of the allotments, the high level of obligations, the restrictions on the peasants' mobility — served to cushion the shock of the reform upon the economy. It is another matter that the cushion was cut much too large and stuffed much too generously, and was not removed when its choking and stifling effects upon the patient became clearly apparent.

THE ASSIMILATION OF STATE PEASANTRY

The emancipation of the pomeshchik serfs presents a convenient vantage point for casting a brief glance at the category of state peasants (adding a few words about the smaller category of those peasants who belonged to the imperial family). The legislation of 1861 regarding the gentry serfs is connected with the government's policies vis-à-vis the state peasants both *pro passato* and *pro futuro*. What was done in 1861 tended to assimilate the position of the former serfs to that of state peasants. By contrast, in the decades that followed the emancipation it was the state peasants who in their turn were being assimilated to the position of the emancipated peasantry, particularly with regard to the redemption provisions. The tendency of the governmental policy was toward a gradual obliteration of the historical differences which existed among the individual categories of Russian peasantry.

The state peasants were formally constituted as a separate estate (*sosloviye*) by the decrees of Peter the Great issued between 1719 and 1724. As a result, the huge group, containing numerous subdivisions by historical origin, came to comprise all the peasants who neither had been given in bondage to the gentry nor were regarded as falling in the category of palace peasants, the property of the emperor. Throughout the remainder of the eighteenth century, the numbers of state peasants were diminished by gifts of peasant-populated lands to the nobility and gentry; on the other hand, the "estate" received a considerable influx from the secularization of church lands and from territorial acquisitions. With the succession of Alexander I to the throne, the practice of donating peasants was discontinued. Thenceforth, the numerical strength of the group depended mainly on the birth and mortality rates and, to a small extent, on the exodus into the two other "taxable estates," the merchants and the *meshchane*, the lowest non-rural group.

Such an exodus was possible. For the civil status of state peasants was a good deal more liberal than that of the pomeshchik serfs. As was true elsewhere (in Prussia, for instance), the conditions on state domains had been modernized long before the government proceeded to a thorough reform of the relations between obliged peasants and private estates. In fact, it was a peculiarity of the Russian development, resulting from the belated introduction of serfdom, that the power of the pomeshchik over his serfs was still being increased and consolidated at a time when the state had begun to improve the civil status and the economic position of its own peasants. By the third and fourth decades of the nineteenth century, the Russian state peasant, at least in principle, had acquired fairly ample rights to engage in commercial and industrial pursuits, to move away from the villages for temporary and long-term absences, and to abandon the state peasant estate for good, even though the last action presupposed fulfillment of a number of requirements and the resistance of the obshchina and bureaucracy formed serious obstacles. Through a series of reforms, carried out between 1837 and 1841, the administration of the state peasantry was somewhat improved and was entrusted to a Ministry of State Properties, created for the purpose. P. D. Kiselev, the author the reforms, remained for many years in charge of the new ministry and, later on, in the 1850's, attempted to re-adjust the "quitrent tax" payments, to which the state peasants were subject in addition to the poll tax, by changing the tax from a "per soul" to a "per unit of land" basis and by taking the quality of the land in various geographic areas into account, thus moving the quitrent tax in the direction of a tax on income. Finally, an attempt also was made to increase the amount of land in the possession of the peasantry, although this occurred, if at all, to a very modest extent. On a national average, the "per soul" allotment tended to decline as the population grew. Still, there is little doubt that in the years immediately preceding the emancipation the state peasantry's dues were much lower than those of the gentry peasants, whereas its land allotments were at least equal to, and probably in excess of, those of the serf peasantry.[87] It is clear after what has been said about the course of the emancipation of the serfs that, as a result of the reform, the position of the state peasant with regard to land availabilities and possibly also with regard to money payments became even more favorable than that of the former serfs. For the serfs' position deteriorated at least as far as their land allotments were concerned, while the state peasants did not lose any land.

Suffice it to add, with regard to the peasants owned by the emperor, that in most respects their position was intermediate between the state peasants and the gentry peasants. This is certainly true of their civil status and the amount of dues to which they were subject. As far as the former is concerned, the imperial peasants before 1858 frequently could not marry without consent of the authorities; the

87. See, on the preceding, the standard work by N. M. Druzhinin, *Gosudar-stvennyye krest'yane i reforma P. D. Kiseleva* (The State Peasants and the Reform of P. D. Kiselev), I (Moscow-Leningrad, 1946); II (Moscow, 1958). For a comparison of dues and land allotments of peasants belonging to different categories, see II, 133, 214.

barriers against their leaving the villages, even for seasonal work, were high, and, unlike the state peasants, imperial peasants could not acquire real estate except in the name of the administrative agency in charge of imperial peasants (udel'noye vedomstvo); even disposition over chattels was by no means free from orders and injunctions. In 1858, their legal status was formally assimilated to that of state peasants, but the administration remained separate and the practice was slow to change.

It is a moot question to what extent the authors of the Emancipation Act of 1861 were influenced by the Kiselev reform. Druzhinin, in his previously quoted book, is eager to answer the question in the affirmative.[88] Be that as it may, there is no doubt that the civil status of the liberated peasants became essentially the same as that of the state peasants, and that the stress on the village commune and joint responsibility in the legislation of 1861 also had been anticipated both in the long practice and in the more recent legislation with regard to state peasants. It is, however, equally true that, while catching up with the state peasants in some respects, the former serfs had moved ahead of them in others; this was particularly so with reference to the juridical position of the ex-serfs with regard to the land. It could, of course, be argued that the preservation of the obshchina reduced to mockery all right of *individual* ownership within the village commune. Still, the liberated peasantry, as collective units, received the land "in permanent use," and then by virtue of the redemption provisions the rights of ownership became vested in them. By contrast, the juridical position of the state and imperial peasants was altogether inarticulated. Differences of this sort were bound to lead to invidious comparisons and to discontent on the part of the less privileged groups. Before the emancipation, the Russian gentry felt quite uneasy over any improvement in the position of peasants other than the gentry serfs; it tried very hard to oppose Kiselev's reforms for the state peasants. Similarly, it proved difficult for the government to avoid an adjustment in the legal position of state and imperial peasants once the arrangements under the emancipation acts began to be carried out.

It is not surprising that particular haste was shown to regulate

88. *Ibid.*, II, 551–566.

the conditions of imperial peasants. Peasants who were the personal property of the emperor could not be treated less well than gentry peasants without casting dark shadows on traditional popular images. Accordingly, the statute concerning the imperial peasants was published in July 1863, at about the time when the mass of the establishment charters of the former serfs was being approved.[89] The statute explicitly referred to the "principles adopted in the legislation of 19 February 1861" and proceeded to grant the imperial peasants all the personal rights which had been bestowed upon the gentry serfs. Furthermore, the lands of their allotments were to become their property after two years. During those two years, as was true of gentry serfs, establishment charters would be issued, under the terms of which the imperial peasants essentially were to be given the "maximum" allotment (see above) while basically the payment of the same quitrents was to continue for 49 years, as "redemption payments" to which the provisions of the Redemption Act of the gentry serfs were to apply.[90] The arbitrators were to play the same role in drawing up the charters as they had in the case of gentry serfs. In one respect, the imperial peasants were placed in a preferred position, inasmuch as the redemption of the land was automatic for them — it did not become generally obligatory for the lands of the former serfs until two decades later. At the same time, the legislator stipulated that, whenever the quitrents of the imperial peasants exceeded those of the gentry peasants, a downward adjustment was to take place. For the rest, with regard to the obshchina arrangements, tax payments, and opportunities for leaving the village commune, be it for temporary sojourns or permanently, the assimilation to the position of the liberated gentry peasants was far-reaching indeed.

The analogous problem with respect to state peasants was less speedily resolved. Nothing reveals the confusion existing over prop-

89. See "Vysochayshe utverzhdennoye polozheniye o krest'yanakh vodvorennykh na zemlyakh imenii gosudarevykh, dvortsovykh i udel'nykh" (Imperially Approved Statute Concerning Peasants Settled on Lands of Imperial, Palace, and Udel'nye Estates), *PSZ*, 2nd ser. XXXVIII, part I, no. 39792, June 26, 1863 (St. Petersburg, 1866). The differences between imperial, palace, and udel'nye peasants were narrowly technical and are of no significance in this context, where the terms have been used interchangeably.

90. Articles 1, 2, 3, 4, 5, 8, 38, 77.

erty concepts more than the fact that the question of ownership of the lands allotted to the state peasants became subject to prolonged deliberations within the government. The force of those who believed that the lands in question belonged to the peasants proved too weak to determine the substance of the legislation; but it was sufficiently strong to exert a negative influence which, curiously enough, worked to the disadvantage of the state peasants: the redemption of their lands was postponed for a considerable period, and even the first incomplete solution was not attempted until 1866.

In January of that year, the validity of the General Statute of February 1861 was extended to apply to all the categories of state peasants. Thereupon, on December 1, 1866, an imperial ukase to the Senate was published concerning the "Land Arrangements of State Peasants." [91] The preamble to the ukase explained that as early as March 1861 the Minister of State Properties had been instructed to prepare appropriate legislative drafts concerning the application of the emancipation acts to the state peasantry, "to a degree that will be recognized as possible and necessary for additional enhancement of their economic conditions." The uncertainty of this language well reflected the vacillating uncertainty of governmental policies.

The act solemnly announced that the village communes of state peasants were to receive formal title to all the lands which had been in use by them. The name selected for the title was an unusual one: *vladennaya zapis'*, which may be rendered as "possessional entry." The adjective chosen had the double advantage of connoting to the juridically learned the absence of the right of ownership and implying precisely that right in the common Russian usage of the day. At any rate, the peasants were obliged to requite the possessional entry, which was to be handed over to them in the presence of a peace arbitrator by continuing payment of the quitrent tax. The quitrent tax, slight changes apart, was to remain fixed at its previous level for twenty years; at the end of that period the rate of the tax could be changed, though only by a legislative measure. It was possible to

---

91. "Imennoy danny Senatu . . . o pozemel'nom ustroystve gosudarstevennykh krest'yan v 36 guberniyakh" (Imperial Ukase to the Senate . . . Concerning Land Arrangements of State Peasants in thirty-six Governments), *PSZ*, 2nd ser., part II, no. 43888, November 24, 1866 (St. Petersburg, 1868).

redeem the quitrent tax wholly or in part by a capitalized payment but the government extended no assistance in this respect, and the legislation even failed to specify the rate at which the tax should be capitalized. The ukase in question applied to only 36 provinces. Its failure to provide for a redemption procedure was all the more striking since, a few months later, the state peasants in the nine western and northwestern provinces had their quitrent tax changed into redemption payments at the low price of a 10 percent increase in quitrent tax, the payments to continue until January 1, 1913. Thereby the state peasants, or rather the state peasant communes, in those provinces were elevated to the rank of full owners of their lands. Accordingly, they were not given a "possessional entry" but a document obscurely described as *dannye* — which may be translated as "the facts." [92] Quite obviously, the desire to secure the allegiance of the peasantry in western provinces against the Polish gentry had determined the differential treatment. The awkwardness of a discriminatory policy might well have caused the government to reconsider its decision not to embark upon general redemption of lands of state peasants in the heartlands of Russia. But no such reconsideration took place. The uncertain juridical position of the state peasantry continued for another two decades when, after the abolition of the poll tax, the quitrent tax (including the so-called forest tax for utilization of the woodlands within the village allotment) was to be raised by two thirds and transformed into redemption payments; but the increased amount was not to exceed the previously imposed sum of quitrent tax *and* poll tax. The redemption payments were to continue for 44 years until February 1, 1931. Premature redemption was possible at the capitalization rate of 5 percent, the lower percentage (6 percent for the gentry peasants) designed to provide some compensation for the increase in land values since the 1860's.[93]

92. "Imennoy danny Senatu ukaz o pozemel'nom ustroystve gosudarstvennykh krest'yan v 9 guberniyakh" (Imperial Ukase to the Senate Concerning Land Arrangement of State Peasants in Nine Governments), *PSZ*, 2nd ser. XLII, part I, no. 44590, May 16, 1867 (St. Petersburg, 1871).

93. "Vysochayshe utverzhdennoye mneniye Gosudarstvennago Soveta o preobrazovanii obrochnoy podati byvshikh gosudazstvennykh krest'yan v vykupnye platezhi" (Imperially Approved Opinion of the Council of State Concerning the Transformation of the Quitrent Tax of Former State Peasants into Redemption Payments), *PSZ*, 3rd ser. VI, no. 3807, June 12, 1886 (St. Petersburg, 1888).

From a juridical point of view, the measure just described must appear vulnerable to criticism. There was some good sense to the celebrated remark made by I. S. Aksakov, a conservative thinker, who claimed that to let the state peasants redeem their lands was very much like forcing an oak to redeem its own roots.[94] From the economic point of view, however, different aspects of the problem appear to stand out. The whole post-emancipation arrangement with regard to state peasants amounted essentially to the maintenance of a specific source of government revenue at a constant flow. The transformation of the quitrent tax into redemption payments was, as far as fiscal policy was concerned, nothing but the creation of a new title — and a new name — for an old revenue, coupled with the need to find, in a remote future, either new revenues or still other names for an old one. For unlike the case of the gentry peasants, the redemption of state peasant lands did not involve any corresponding interest-bearing bond issue on the part of the Treasury. Similarly, the elevation of the state peasants from possessors to owners did not confer upon them any additional right of disposition over their lands.

This does not mean, however, that the measures adopted after the emancipation with regard to state and imperial peasants were of little consequence for the economic development of the country. To the extent that the state peasants found themselves in a somewhat better position than the gentry peasants, the pressure upon them to abandon agriculture in favor of industrial occupations was smaller. As the population kept increasing, so did the numbers of former state peasants or their descendants willing to join the urban labor force. But the process of assimilation to the position of gentry peasants, and in particular the redemption of the lands, redounded to a further strengthening of the obshchina arrangements and to an erection of additional barriers to migrations out of agriculture. At the same time, the material position of the state peasantry, despite their relative superiority over the former gentry peasants, was quite insufficient to allow for a considerable and expanding demand for industrial goods. The restrictions on economic progress inherent in the very existence of the obshchina arrangements constituted an impediment

94. See Nikolai Barsukov, *Zhizn' i trudy M. P. Pogodina* (Life and Works of M. P. Pogodin; St. Petersburg, 1904), XVIII, 16.

to a high rate of income within agriculture and would have done so, even if the last quarter of the nineteenth century had not been so generally unkind to agriculture.

With the series of measures described here, the process of forging the main groups of the Russian peasantry into one estate was essentially completed. To be sure, differences in origins continued to be reflected in varying levels of wealth and income. But the agrarian policies of the government, as they were expressed in subsequent legislative acts, envisaged a unified homogeneous group whose problems could be treated as such. Whatever the merits or demerits of this attitude, it tends to throw the nature of those policies into a clear perspective.

III

AFTER THE EMANCIPATION

THE CHARACTER OF RUSSIAN INDUSTRIALIZATION
AND THE AGRARIAN REFORM

A historian who is interested in the relation that exists between agrarian reform and the process of industrialization must first attempt to decompose the reform into its constituent elements. He will then try to ascertain whether, and to what degree, each individual element under investigation tended to promote or to impede industrial development. This has been attempted in the foregoing. Such a procedure is justifiable and, in fact, indispensable. It would be unwarranted, however, to assume that merely by separating the accelerating from the decelerating factors, by identifying them as such, and by trying to gauge their relative importance, one can arrive at a complete appraisal of the bearing of the reform upon the course of industrialization. Historical reality is complex. The effects of a measure of economic policy, such as an agrarian reform, are not necessarily given once and for all. They may be enhanced, but also neutralized or even overcompensated, by adaptive steps taken in response to the challenge of the original measure. In the process, not only the rate of growth but also its character are likely to be affected. It is with this in mind that the effects of the agrarian reform in Russia must be observed.

The concept of an agrarian reform as a historical prerequisite of industrial development has been touched upon above. There has been a somewhat unfortunate tendency to regard such a reform as representing the "abolition of feudalism" and therefore as a necessary, if not sufficient, condition of modern industrial development. But the implied view of a uniform process of industrialization, repeating itself persistently from area to area, is difficult of maintenance when confronted with broad empirical material. In many areas, industrial development took place without the creation of conditions which on the basis of some limited historical experience (British economic history, for instance), reinforced by some deductive reasoning, have come to be regarded as prerequisites of industrialization. As so often in the history of human affairs, the cognitive value of a concept lies in finding the limits of its applicability. To regard an agrarian reform as a prerequisite of industrialization is not to establish a narrow set of dogmatic expectations but, on the contrary, to ask what pattern or patterns of substitutions may be expected to materialize in compensation either for the absence of an agrarian reform or for those disabilities, from the point of view of industrial development, with which an imperfect agrarian reform has been burdened.

It is indeed not the concept of prerequisites but the concept of substitutions for lacking prerequisites that appears useful in understanding Russian economic development during the period under review.

As I have said before, the more backward a country, the more likely it is that the early stages of its industrialization will be characterized by a sudden violent spurt of growth in investment and output. The requirements of rapid and manifold growth tend to increase the strain on the available resources, to enhance, by the same token, the disabilities of a backward economy, and to institute a search for ways and means of overcoming those disabilities. As a result, the pattern of industrial development in a backward country contains a number of features that appear quite unorthodox from the point of view of the more advanced country which (because of better endowment in material and human resources and a more adequate institutional framework) could have easily afforded a very high rate of growth but, in fact, was content with a much more gradual evolution. It is in this light that the effects of the Russian agrarian reforms of the nineteenth century must be seen.

The agrarian legislation of the 1860's was not followed by rapid industrial development. The abolition of serfdom and the upsurge of industrial growth were separated by nearly a quarter of a century. The intervening period, showing a very moderate rate of industrial expansion, was dominated by the construction of railroads, as well as by the implementation of the judicial and administrative reforms that undoubtedly had an important bearing on Russian economic development. From the second half of the 1880's, however, industrial growth was stepped up and throughout the decade of 1890 gathered momentum, attaining an average annual rate of more than 8 percent. Whatever the deficiencies of the emancipation arrangements, they did not prevent a spurt of industrial development whose speed had few, if any, counterparts in the industrial history of the major countries of the world.

The positive sides of the emancipation acts must not be underestimated. The reform of the civil status of the gentry peasantry was bound to affect the economic life of the country; among other things, it certainly widened the reservoir from which entrepreneurial talent could emerge. The increase (as a result of the "cuts") of the lands belonging to large estates tended to raise the share of marketable — and exportable — produce in total agricultural output, an important factor both for the expansion of urban populations and for strengthening the balance of payments, adjusting it to the needs of industrialization. There is, furthermore, no doubt that through the mechanism of redemption payments the role of the money economy was greatly increased. At the same time, the abolition of the exclusive privilege to own men on the part of a group that was traditionally averse to industrial development was bound to weaken the group and to reduce its power to resist economic progress. Above all, the psychological impact of the abolition of serfdom was enormous. The disappearance of an institution which more than anything else had tended to make Russia different from the West inevitably acted as a strong stimulus to the further westernization of economy and society, and this to a large extent meant rapid industrial development.

Against this must be held the negative aspects of the reform, set forth in section II. Among them two stand out: the limitation upon the flow of manpower to industrial areas and the obstacles to an increase of agricultural output. Either directly or indirectly, both effects stemmed from the preservation and the strengthening of the obshchina, and elimination of those limitations would have required revision of the government's policy vis-à-vis the obshchina. Other, perhaps less tangible, disabilities were likewise connected with the obshchina. As shown before, the emancipation acts failed to lay the basis among the peasant population for a firm concept of individual property suitable to the needs of a modern industrial economy. A peasantry whose own property rights had been trodden underfoot throughout the history of serfdom had no respect for the property of others. The emancipation provisions tended to perpetuate those attitudes in a variety of ways, but perhaps most notably and effectively through the perpetuation of the communal arrangements.

Because of some peculiarities of Russian intellectual history, the crucially adverse role of the obshchina in its effects upon the industrialization of the country has remained curiously unemphasized. The Populists tended to glorify the obshchina and were not interested in industrial development. The Marxians, on the other hand, were so eager to show that the obshchina was in the process of rapid disintegration, as a result of the wealth and income differentiation that had been going on within it, that they came to treat the institution as a *quantité négligeable* as far as current developments were concerned. Liberal opinion should have been most vocal in denouncing the obshchina. But the liberals were constitutionally weak in Russia, and most of them were tinged by populist sympathies. Finally, until a later volte-face, the conservative circles supporting the government — the intellectual "junk dealers," to use Count Witte's expression — were by and large in favor of the obshchina. After the volte-face — to be described further below — had taken place, the obshchina became an object of sharp criticism on the part of the bureaucracy and of pro-government writers; but the latter stood so far outside the main stream of Russian intellectual life and were regarded with so much distrust by public opinion that they succeeded in influencing neither the contemporary publicists nor the later historical appraisals of the period, least of all current Soviet historiography which, peculiarly inert, has continued to reproduce the logomachies of the 1890's. Viewing the problems of economic development in Russia from a vantage point located in the second half of the twentieth century, and unaffected by the value judgments and prejudices of the time, it is virtually impossible not to regard the maintenance of an archaic form of land ownership and land utilization as a strategic factor in understanding the peculiarities of Russian industrial development toward the close of the last century.

The more backward on the eve of its industrialization was a country in nineteenth-century Europe, the more pronounced was the tendency to compensate for its manifold disabilities by relying on the great advantage of borrowing modern technology from abroad, and by concentrating especially on those branches of industrial endeavor in which the recent flow of technological innovations abroad had been particularly vehement. The outstanding feature of nineteenth-century technology was its pronounced labor-saving character and its inherent tendency toward increased capital–output ratios. In this way, a backward country could master, or at least attenuate, its difficulties in forming a force of reliable and skilled labor, while auxiliary operations (loading, transporting, and so on) in the factories could still be left in very primitive technological conditions and entrusted to an unskilled and unsteady labor force. Solving in this way a basic problem of an industrializing backward economy did not, however, eliminate the shortage of labor as a very serious deficiency in the process. Nowhere did this appear so clearly as in Russia. The basic fact is that industrialization in Russia, if it was to take place at all, could proceed only at a very high rate of growth. From the point of view of the individual Russian entrepreneur, this was reflected in the fact that the profitability of each labor-saving innovation depended in the last analysis on the rapid expansion of output in the commodity in question. In other words, the change in factor proportions implied in the technological innovation could justify itself only in a rapidly expanding econmy, that is, through increased use not only of capital but also of labor. Much depended therefore on the availability of additional labor at a fairly constant marginal real wage. But it was precisely this consummation of entrepreneurial plans that was frustrated by the structure of post-emancipation agriculture. Because of it, labor supply to Russian industry was inadequate in quantity and inferior in quality. If industrialization was to proceed, the recourse to labor-saving innovations had to be increased even further and, along with it, the capital intensity of the growing industrial output. There lies the explanation for the paradoxical situation that a country, so poor in capital and holding much of its preaccumulated wealth in hands that would not make it available for industrial ventures, contrived to build up, during the spurt of the 1890's, a modern industrial structure many areas of which in technology and capital equipment compared favorably with those of economically advanced countries. A specific substitution process had taken place. Taken in isolation, the obshchina restrictions on labor mobility were an obstacle to industrial progress. But once a "creative adaptation" to the disabilities engendered by the emancipation was carried out, it is impossible to say whether those disabilities on balance had decelerated or accelerated the industrial development in Russia. All that can be said is that the character of the industrialization process was much affected thereby, and that many of the peculiar features inherent in it were further emphasized and accentuated.

The problem of agricultural output and its expansion was not entirely dissimilar, although the solution found was much less attractive. Given the institutional limitations on the increase of agricultural output, the forcible redistribution of the existing output in the interest of industrialization was a possible solution. More will be said presently about certain aspects of such policies. Suffice it to note here the tendency of such policies to be short-term in character. This is clearest when the redistribution of output directly or indirectly extends beyond net output into the area of gross output, so that it affects those portions which should be dedicated to the maintenance of capital or even, in one form or the other, begins to reduce directly the share of capital goods available to agriculture. Obviously, the process of making the farmers destitute could not continue indefinitely. Discontent was growing. Thus, the very success of industrialization tended to create a force that was adverse to it and threatened to render its continuation difficult, if not impossible. Industrialization needed political stability and presumably was making for it in the long run. But for the time being, it was leading to a highly unstable situation. There is little doubt that the cataclysms of the 1905 revolution were organically connected with the years of industrial transformation that had preceded it. There is equally little doubt that it was the threatening disintegration of the empire in the storms of peasant rebellions and the mass strikes of factory and communications workers that caused a revision in agrarian policy. At length, the agricultural structure was to be adjusted to the needs of an industrializing economy.

The decks were to be cleared, but not before the decisive engagement had been fought.

BETWEEN REFORM AND REVOLUTION

Russian agrarian policies between 1861 and the period of revolutionary disturbances around 1905 were oriented to three closely interrelated purposes: (1) to correct for certain excesses resulting from the emancipation arrangements, (2) to widen the sphere of application of those arrangements, and (3) to deepen it, partly by closing loopholes that became apparent with the passage of time. Measures falling under (2) essentially involved assimilation to the emancipation arrangements of peasant groups other than gentry peasants, and were discussed above. The other two aspects may be briefly touched upon here.

The effect upon a growing peasant population of inadequate land allotments and burdensome financial obligations began to force itself upon the attention of the government in the 1870's. This was the period in which the laissez-faire attitudes of the Russian government, short-lived and limited as they were, were still gaining in importance. Free-trade policies fitted well into the needs of the pre-spurt period, and the end of the 1860's had seen the passage of a very liberal tariff. It is not surprising, therefore, that the special government commission entrusted with the study of the peasant question seriously considered reversal of the governmental policy with regard to the village commune. Yet the reasons of social and political expediency which were believed to argue in favor of the obshchina prevailed over considerations of economic efficiency. Nor was anything done until the very end of Alexander II's reign to relieve the peasantry's tax burden, which was obviously incommensurate with the profitability of the farms. The accumulation of tax arrears was allowed to go on unchecked. In 1876–1880, the tax arrears for the country as a whole amounted to 22 percent of the budgeted revenue from direct taxes, but in some areas the percentage rose to 33, 36, and even 46 percent.[95] It was only in the last years of the reign, after

95. N. Brzheski, *Nedoimochnost' i krugovaya poruka sel'skikh obshchestv* (Tax Arrears and Joint Responsibility of Village Communes; St. Petersburg, 1897), p. 393.

a terrorist's bomb had shaken the Winter Palace in St. Petersburg, that the government moved to abolish the very unpopular excise tax on salt.[96] After the assassination of the emperor in March 1881, his successor saw the imperative need for some major demonstrations of good will toward the peasants. Accordingly, the tax burdens began to be adjusted downward to more realistic levels. The poll tax — since Peter I the main pillar of the budget — was abolished, first (1881–1883) for landless peasants and for those peasants who received, after 1861, the so-called gift allotments, which were far below the minimum needed for self-sustained farming; and in May 1885 for all categories of peasants in European Russia.[97] It was resolved to forgive portions of the accumulated arrears, and the reductions were announced on solemn occasions, such as the Coronation Manifesto of 1883. Still in 1881 — the year of Alexander III's accession to the throne — the level of the redemption payments was permanently reduced, the diminution amounting to 16 percent in Little Russian provinces and to one rouble per allotment in Great Russian provinces. The different mode of computing the remission apparently was designed to disguise a much less generous treatment of the Great Russian peasantry; the Little Russian peasantry was in immediate proximity to the favored peasantry of the western government. But the remission was not insignificant and, in addition, smaller special reductions were carried out in localities where economic conditions were particularly unfavorable.[98] Altogether the reductions amounted to 9.2 percent of the debt.[99]

96. Brzheski, *Obshchinny byt*, p. 13; Valuyev, *Dnevnik*, pp. 63–129.

97. The tax was abolished for all former gentry peasants and imperial peasants as of January 1, 1886. The poll tax of state peasants was abolished as of January 1, 1887. "Vysochayshe utverzhdennoye mneniye Gosudarstvennago Soveta ob otmene podushnoy i preobrazovanii obrochnoy podati" (Imperially Approved Opinion of the State Council Concerning Abolition of the Poll Tax and the Reform of the Quitrent Tax), *PSZ*, 3rd ser. V, no. 2988, May 28, 1885 (St. Petersburg, 1887).

98. "Imennoy danny Senatu . . . o ponizhenii vykupnykh platezhey" (Imperial Ukase to the Senate Concerning Reduction of Redemption Payments) and "Vysochayshe utverzhdennoye mneniye Gosudarstvennago Soveta, o vykupe nadelov krest'yanami . . . i o ponizhenii vykupnykh platezhey" (Imperially Approved Opinion of the State Council Concerning Redemption of Allotments by Peasants . . . and Concerning Reduction of Redemption Payments), *PSZ*, 3rd ser. I, nos. 576 and 577, December 28, 1881 (St. Petersburg, 1885).

99. J. Polyakoff, *Die bäuerlichen Loskaufszahlungen in Russland. Mit beson-*

Along with correcting excessive consequences of the emancipation arrangements in the fiscal fields, a modest attempt was made to remedy the scarcity of peasant land by the creation of the so-called Peasant Land Bank, which was to help finance purchase of land by loans to village communes and cooperatives (not individuals!).[100] The bank was not expected to enter the land market as a buyer. Still, it came to play some role in the process of the very gradual transfer of gentry lands into the hands of the peasantry through the medium of the free market. Neither this process nor the tax reductions, however, changed in any significant way the main elements of the situation as it emerged from the emancipation settlement. The pressures were to be reproduced, on an even larger scale, several years later when the great spurt of industrialization began. By the middle of the 1890's, the arrears almost equaled the annual direct tax estimates (95.2 percent). In the eastern regions they exceeded those estimates nearly one and a half times; and even in the central black-earth region the tax arrears were 25 percent higher than the taxes.[101]

As far as the government's help with land purchases is concerned, the bank, during the first crucial nine years of its existence, increased the extent of peasant land by only 1.2 percent. The unaided purchases of the peasants were much more significant.[102] On the other hand, the endeavor of the government was to reinforce the peculiar features of the emancipation settlement in some important respects.

Among the measures of peasant policy passed within the first year of Alexander III's reign was the belated generalization of the redemption procedure: it was rendered compulsory and imposed upon all those gentry estates in which the lack of a voluntary agreement between the peasant and the pomeshchik, and the unwillingness of the latter to force redemption upon the peasants at a loss of at least 20 percent, had prevented initiation of the redemption procedure. By that time, the bulk of the former serfs — more than 85 percent — had

---

derer Berücksichtigung ihrer Bedeutung innerhalb des russischen Reichsbudgets (Munich, 1916), p. 40.

100. "Vysochayshe utverzhdennoye polozheniye o krest'yanskom pozemel'nom banke" (Imperially Approved Statute Concerning the Peasant Land Bank), PSZ, 3rd ser. II, no. 894, May 18, 1882 (St. Petersburg, 1886).

101. Brzheski, Nedoimochnost', p. 413.

102. Kornilov, Krest'yanskaya reforma, p. 227.

changed to redemption status. The measure of 1881, therefore, had only a limited significance and was designed to remove the bias of the 1861 legislation which had given the pomeshchiks, but not the peasants, the right to demand redemption.[103] It may be noted that, since the peasants who redeemed the land under the act of 1881 did not have to pay the 20 percent of the capitalized quitrent value, the arrangement actually amounted to a 20 percent reduction in dues for the peasants concerned.

The establishment, in 1889, of the institute of rural (district) chiefs (*zemskie* [*uchastkovyye*] *nachal'niki*) might perhaps be regarded not as a deepening of the emancipation arrangements, but as the reverse. It is true that the rural chiefs, who could dismiss or jail for a short time any member of the village administration, essentially served to subordinate the organs of peasant self-government, which had been set up by the legislation of 1861, to the Ministry of the Interior. The rural chiefs' wide powers comprised also all those that had been vested in peace arbitrators. Yet it must be considered that the initial idea of a peace arbitrator as a public-minded independent mediator between opposing interests (who could be dismissed only by an act of the Senate) hardly applied to the men who filled that office even as early as the second half of the 1860's, after so many of the original peace arbitrators had resigned to become justices of the peace. Moreover, the power of the arbitrator over the self-governing institutions of the peasantry had kept increasing from year to year. It was still in the early 1870's that a sharp observer of conditions in the post-emancipation village could maintain that the "arbitrator was everything" — meaning that his influence with the self-governing bodies in the village and his power for good and for evil was almost unlimited.[104] Finally, and most importantly, the very nature of the emancipation settlement, implying as it did agricultural overpopulation and the alternative between no industrialization at all and industrialization through a much accentuated, strenuous, and costly spurt, called for strong police powers over the village communes and

---

103. "Imennoy danny Senatu . . . o vykupe nadelov" (Imperial Ukase to the Senate Concerning Redemption of Allotments), *PSZ*, 3rd ser. I, no. 575, December 28, 1881 (St. Petersburg, 1885).

104. Engelgardt, *Iz derevni*, p. 119.

individual peasants, unless the goal of industrialization was to be abandoned by the government. Paradoxical as it may sound, the obshchina, with its specific consequences for the economic development of the country, required a counterpart of strong police power over the villages. In a situation where much depended on the government's ability to tax the peasantry, and where the police had to be called upon since the reform of 1874 to make certain that the tax-collecting job was properly done,[105] the institution of a strong *zemskii nachal'nik* was much more consonant with the spirit of the emancipatory legislation than the originally nursed idea of leaving the administrative, and also the lower judicial, functions in the villages to the inhabitants. This might have been possible in an industrialization pulled along by the rising demand of a prosperous peasantry. Such an industrialization was not very likely to occur in Russia in any circumstances, but least of all after the reform of 1861 turned out to be what it was. An industrialization that strained the country's political stability to the breaking point would have collapsed in its initial stages without the strong arm of the government, which for an astonishingly long time succeeded in keeping the manifestations of peasant discontent within the bounds of the tolerable.[106]

The abolition of the poll tax in 1885 had provided some limited relief to the peasantry and necessitated some readjustments in the structure of the Russian budget. It might have meant more than that. For with the removal of the "egalitarian" poll tax there disappeared a strong argument in favor of the egalitarian obshchina arrangements. The existing direct taxes, such as the land tax, the redemption payments, and the various local taxes, were naturally adjusted, or at least easily adjustable, to the size of an individual peasant's or a household's landholdings. A relaxation of the restrictions upon exit from obshchina might have been expected to follow. This, however, was not the case. It is true that joint responsibility for taxes was maintained. This

---

105. "Vysochayshe utvershdennoye polozheniye ob izmeneniyakh v ustroystve mestnykh uchrezhdenii po krest'yanskim delam" (Imperially Approved Statute Concerning Changes in the Organization of Local Institutions for Peasant Matters), *PSZ*, 3rd ser., part I, no. 53678, June 27, 1874 (St. Petersburg, 1876).

106. "Polozheniye o zemskikh uchastkovykh nachal'nikakh (Statute Concerning Rural District Chiefs), *PSZ*, 3rd ser. IX, no. 6196, July 12, 1889 (St. Petersburg, 1891).

extended beyond obshchina villages to villages of individual ownership, but it could not be gainsaid that egalitarian land use and joint
responsibility went well together. At the same time, general political
reasons may have been even more important in determining the
government's policy. At any rate, the government refused to draw the
consequences from the abolition of the poll tax. In fact, it took the
opposite course and proceeded to provide additional props for the
institution of the village commune. By several legal measures the
government further deepened the specific features of the emancipation
settlement.

The first act to be mentioned in this connection refers to divisions
of property within the households of obshchina members. Under the
rules laid down in 1886, such divisions could not be carried out
without the consent of two thirds of those eligible to vote at a village
meeting (*sel'skii skhod*). The veto of the meeting (or, for that matter,
of the head of the household) was definitive, while a permissive vote
could still be reversed by an appeal to the rural chief.[107]

To some extent, the measure was dictated by the desire to prevent
creation of family units that were too small for efficient farming and
for orderly discharge of tax obligations. It must be noted, however,
that a farming unit that was too small within the obshchina may have
been of perfectly satisfactory size outside the obshchina, after the
household carried out technological changes that had been impossible
under communal arrangements. Thus, the considerable increase in the
influence of the obshchina (and that of the *zemskii nachal'nik*) over
the individual household was a necessary consequence of the basic
inefficiency of the village commune.

Much more important, however, were two other measures, taken
within the last year or year and a half of Alexander III's reign. One
of them was designed to remove a real or alleged threat to the
existence of the obshchina, and the other was intended to increase the
economic efficiency of the institution.

107. "Vysochayshe utverzdennoye mneniye Gosudarstvennago Soveta o poryadke
razresheniya semeynykh razdelov v sel'skikh obshchestvakh v kotorykh sushchestvuyet
obshchinnoye pol'zovaniye mirskoy polevoy zemley" (Imperially Approved Opinion
of the State Council Concerning the Procedure for Permission of Household Divisions
in Those Village Communes in Which Exists Obshchina Utilization of Communal
Field Lands), *PSZ*, 3rd ser. I, no. 5578, March 18, 1886 (St. Petersburg, 1888).

By an act passed in June 1893, the government stipulated that at least twelve years must pass between communal repartitions of lands. In the interval between repartitions, the obshchina lost the right to carry out current readjustments by taking land away from some households and giving it to others; the few exceptions from the rule included the undiminished right of the obshchina to take land away from a household that had been remiss in paying its taxes. Furthermore, a peasant household that had improved its allotted land was to receive, at a repartition, either the same land or else a compensation in one form or another for the loss of improved land. The decisions of the obshchina in all these matters could be contested by appeal to the *zemskii nachal'nik*. There was something paradoxical about this attempt to preserve and solidify the obshchina by curtailing an essential feature of the institution. For the rest, the positive effect of the measure was slow to materialize for a number of reasons. First of all, it did not provide an immediate deterrent to repartition because, even if the government had wanted to apply the act retroactively, it would have been hampered by the nearly complete absence of records concerning past repartitions. On the other hand, the prospect of being compensated for improvements made during the tenure of an allotment failed to serve as an incentive, because of the uncertainty of the compensation and the difficulty of making it commensurate with outlays. Therefore, the new system did not remove the impediments to introducing improvements either before the twelve-year period started running or as the end of the period came near and, most notably, after the expiration of the period (when a repartition could take place anytime). It was a sign of progress that the government had recognized one of the basic deficiencies of the obshchina. The attitude implied in the act was much better than the traditional tendency to claim that there was economic value to periodic repartitions: the run-down land of a poor and indolent peasant coming under the care of a thrifty and industrious tiller would quickly recover its productive forces.[108] Beyond this, not much could be said in favor of the act.[109]

108. A. A. Rittikh, *Zavisimost' krest'yan ot obshchiny i mira* (The Dependence of Peasants upon the Obshchina and Mir; St. Petersburg, 1903), p. 49.

109. "Vysochayshe utverzhdennoye mneniye Gosudarstvennago Soveta ob ut-

The second act, far from betraying any concern over the economic value of the obshchina, was frankly concerned with its preservation. It will be remembered that, under the terms of the Redemption Statute, the consent of the commune was required before an individual peasant could leave the commune; if, however, the individual householder had paid the whole redemption debt attached to his allotment, the commune was bound to permit his departure, if possible consolidating the various strips of the allotment into one compact holding.[110] During the "goodwill era" of the 1880's, the government took care to clarify the legal situation concerning the liquidation of the redemption debt before maturity. The view that the individual peasant wishing to hasten the repayment of the debt had to pay the original sum (*sic*) despite previous installment payments was declared invalid, and only payment of the outstanding balance was required.[111] Thereby, repayment of the redemption debt before maturity ceased to be an outright economic impossibility. The trend of land values continued upward. By the beginning of the 1890's, what once used to be very high redemption values had come to be exceeded by current land values. One might suppose, therefore, that it would be profitable for the individual peasant to repay the redemption debt, leave the obshchina, and then sell the land to an outsider who as likely as not might have advanced the redemption money in the first place. This, however, did not occur: partly, the peasants' helplessness in economic matters may have been responsible; partly, the reason may have been that in Russian conditions high land values were *not* derived from correspondingly high yields. At any rate, before 1882 the number of allotments redeemed before maturity was altogether negligible (47,000), and it could not have been otherwise in view of the legal confusion just mentioned. After 1882, the rate of repayments before

verzhdenii pravil o peredelakh mirskoy zemli" (Imperially Approved Opinion of the State Council Concerning Acceptance of Regulations for Repartitions of Obshchina Lands), *PSZ*, 3rd ser. XII, no. 9754, June 8, 1893 (St. Petersburg, 1897).

110. Redemption Statute, article 165.

111. See "Vysochayshe utverzhdennoye mneniye Gosudarstvennago Soveta a poryadke zacheta osobykh vznosov predstavlyayemykh v uplatu kapital'nykh dolgov krest'yan po vykupnym ssudam" (Imperially Approved Opinion of the State Council Concerning the Mode of Crediting Extraordinary Payments Made in Settlement of the Oustanding Principal of the Peasant's Redemption Debts), *PSZ*, 3rd ser. II, no. 752, March 23, 1882 (St. Petersburg, 1886).

maturity was stepped up, but still remained quite low; by 1891 no more than about 182,000 allotments of about 889,000 desyatinas were so redeemed by members of the village communes. If one adds to the number the 317,000 desyatinas redeemed by peasants outside of village communes, no more than about 1.2 percent of the total allotment land of peasants of all categories would appear to have been redeemed. In addition, it might be noted that, out of the land redeemed before maturity, no more than 12/100 of one percent was sold to outsiders.[112] It seems to be fairly clear that the majority of peasants who redeemed their lands prematurely did it not for the sake of selling them. The redemptions appear to have been caused by the desire to escape from the obligations inherent in joint responsibility and perhaps to receive a free hand for choosing methods of cultivation.

There is no doubt that in the early nineties the movement was quantitatively quite insignificant. Still, one could reasonably assume that, where the redemption payments proceeded regularly and the outstanding balance became smaller from year to year, the rate of redemption before maturity would be stepped up. The government, however, refused to wait until the tendency became pronounced. The obshchina was so important an element in the government's policy that any threat to it had to be smothered at once. Accordingly, by an act passed in November 1893, the government proceeded to revise the stipulations of article 165 of the Redemption Statute. Henceforth, as long as the redemption of all communal lands was not completed, the individual peasant could no longer redeem his land before maturity without the express consent of the commune, that is to say, without an affirmative vote of two thirds of all those entitled to vote at a village meeting. At the same time, the act went on to prohibit sales of allotment land by communes to anyone but persons of legal peasant status. Not only was the commune to be maintained, but also the increase in nonpeasant, that is, bourgeois, landholdings was to be prevented.[113]

112. Rittikh, pp. 76–86.
113. "Vysochayshe utverzhdennoye mneniye Gosudarstvennago Soveta o nekotorykh merakh k preduprezhdeniyu otchuzhdeniya krest'yanskikh nadel'nykh zemel'" (Imperially Approved Opinion of the State Council Concerning Certain Measures to Prevent Alienation of Peasant Allotment Lands), *PSZ*, 3rd ser. XIII, no. 10151, November 14, 1893 (St. Petersburg, 1897).

Finally, the new passport statute must be mentioned in this connection. The act, one of the last important measures of the reign, contained some liberal features, but at the same time accorded well with the two measures just discussed in that it gave the obshchina and the head of the household considerable powers over the absent member and opened to them subtle opportunities for pressure and blackmail.

While the legislation tried to maintain the institutional status quo, the economic condition of the peasantry kept deteriorating. The last quarter of the nineteenth century brought along with it hard times for agriculture everywhere. But in Russia the difficulties were greatly compounded by the pressures of forced-draft industrialization. Prices of agricultural products began falling in the early 1880's. In the following years, it was the so-called gray cereals, the specific peasant crops of rye and oats, which suffered most grievously. If the prices for rye and oats are taken to equal 100 in 1881, the index stood at 42 and 56 respectively in 1894. The price of red grains — winter and spring wheat — was fairly well maintained until the end of the 1880's, although from then on it too started falling very rapidly indeed.[114] Those price levels were unprecedented within the memory of the contemporaneous peasant generation, and the brief recovery of prices in the famine year 1891–92 was as catastrophic for the peasant economy as were the preceding and following price declines.

At the same time, the agricultural population kept increasing. Between 1867 and 1898, the rural population increased from about 56 to more than 80 millions, that is, at an annual rate of 1.2 percent. From 1877 to 1898 rural population must have grown by at least 25 percent.[115] The peasantry managed, between 1877 and 1905, to increase the land at their disposal by about 15 percent. This was done through purchases, about one fifth of which were financed by the

114. Departament Zemledeliya i Sel'skoy Promyshlennosti, *Sel'skockhozyaystvennya statisticheskiya svedeniya* (Department of Agriculture and Rural Industry, Agricultural Statistical Data), issue III, *Stoimost' proizvodstva glavneyshikh khlebov v yevropeyskoy Rossii* (Cost of Production of the Most Important Cereals in European Russia; St. Petersburg, 1890), p. xii; and P. L. Lyashchenko, *Istoryia narodnogo khozyaistva SSSR* (History of the National Economy of the USSR; Moscow, 1948), II, 90.

115. Computed from Rashin, *Naseleniye Rossii za 100 let*, pp. 46, 98.

Peasant Bank.[116] Thus, the per capita availabilities of peasant land declined not inconsiderably. In order to compensate for the deficiency, the peasants had to have increasing recourse to the leasing of gentry lands. But even the 6.7 million desyatinas which were under leases by peasants in 1901 were insufficient to bring the per capita availabilities back to the penurious levels of the 1860's and 1870's.[117] Land purchases made under the pressure of the dwindling land reserves drove up land values at a time when the prices of land products were declining. If in the period 1868–1877 the average price per desyatina was 19.1 roubles, it had risen in 1888–1897 to 42.5 roubles.[118] It is true that the tendency of yields per acre was clearly upward. Yet it was strongly pronounced on gentry lands and relatively weak on peasant lands; many of those increases were achieved by reducing sheep grazing in favor of cereal cultivation on the virgin lands of the south, a process from which the peasant economy received little benefit; on the other hand, the yields were increased within the peasant economy by plowing up valuable meadow and pasture lands, thus reducing the basis for cattle farming and the supply of manure to the economy and paying a disproportionately high price for the improvement in yields. The improvement in the seed-harvest ratio which was noticeable over the period, changing from an average of some 25 to about 17 percent of the crop, was likewise the result of changes in gentry farming. Within the peasant economy the waste of seeds was still very high.

Nor could the peasant economy improve its position by introducing technological innovations. The lack of capital and the deficiency of appropriate forms of credit provided a serious obstacle. The primitive wooden Russian plow — the *sokha* — remained dominant over wide areas of the country. Apart from financial considerations, introduction even of a simple Western plow was hampered not only by

116. W. von Swyatlowski, *Der Grundbesitzwechsel in Russland, 1861–1908* (Leipzig, 1909), pp. 116, 128.

117. *Statisticheskiya svedeniya po zemel'nomu voprosu v yevropeyskoy Rossii* (Statistical Data on the Land Question in European Russia; St. Petersburg, 1906), p. 41.

118. Peter Lokhtin, *Sostoyaniye sel'skago khozyaystva v Rossii sravnitel'no s drugimi stranami* (Conditions of Russian Agriculture in Comparison with Other Countries; St. Petersburg, 1901), pp. 4–7, 15–17.

the depressing effect of the obshchina and by the ignorance and indolence of its members, but also by the consideration that peasant farms with their inadequate draft power were unable to introduce the more efficient but usually also much heavier machinery.[119] The number of horses in peasant agriculture was pitifully small. According to the 1899–1901 census no less than 29.3 percent of peasant households had no horses at all, while the percentage of households with only one horse amounted to 42.7.[120] Between 1888 and the census of 1899–1901, the number of horseless households in European Russia (except in the southern and eastern steppes) increased 22 percent; the number of households with only one horse increased 25 percent; the crucial number of households with two and three horses was 4 and 35 percent down, respectively. The most important capital good of the peasant economy was not maintained.[121]

In the last quarter of the nineteenth century, Russian agriculture, taken as a whole, made a valiant effort to keep the per capita output constant. But it failed. The per capita index of output of wheat and rye developed as follows (in fifty provinces):

1870–1874	100.0	1891–1895	95.1
1883–1885	97.1	1896–1900	97.2
1886–1890	92.3		

Deducting the quantities exported abroad further deteriorates the picture:

1870–1874	100.0	1891–1895	91.9
1883–1885	95.3	1896–1900	94.5
1886–1890	86.1		

The share of exports in total output had grown under the pressure of government policies.[122]

---

119. Ministerstvo Zemledeliya i Gosudarstvennykh Imushchestv, *Sel'skokhozya-stvennyya statisticheskiya svedeniya* (Ministry of Agriculture and State Properties, Agricultural Statistical Data), issue XI, *Primeneniye i rasprostraneniye v Rossii sel'skokhozyastvennykh mashin i orudii* (Application and Diffusion of Agricultural Machines and Implements in Russia; St. Petersburg, 1903), esp. pp. 1–24, 119–128.

120. *Statisticheskiya svedeniya po zemel'nomu voprosu v yevropeyskoy Rossii,* 1906, p. 27.

121. Peter Maslov, *Agrarny vopros v Rossii* (The Agrarian Question in Russia; St. Petersburg, 1908), p. 9.

122. The preceding two sets of figures were calculated from Raymond W. Gold-

One must consider the prominent role of the large estates in the increases of total output that did take place; it is also important to take account of the fact that, along with an increase in exports, there was also a considerable increase in marketing of products to the cities whose population was rapidly growing and whose bread consumption was considerably above that of the peasants. It is then difficult to escape the conclusion that the bread consumption of the rural population in the 1890's reached a very low point, even if one abstracts from the disaster of the great famine in 1891–92.

As prices for agricultural products fell, the prices of industrial products sheltered by the high protectionist tariff of 1891 were rising. In addition, prices of commodities purchased by the peasants were greatly increased by the rise in indirect taxes from 16.5 million roubles in 1881 to 109.5 million roubles in 1895; in the same year, the direct taxes *including* redemption payments were a good deal higher than they had been in 1881, despite all the reductions of the good-will era. The alcohol revenue likewise increased during the period, although less drastically.[123] It is quite true that a very small segment of the peasantry managed to develop prosperously in the face of all handicaps. But the vast majority of the peasant population, with the terms of trade turning sharply against it, found the tax burden intolerably heavy and the rise in output quite inadequate. As the net money yields of peasant farms were falling and the land values rising perversely, while the capital stock of the farms was in danger of depletion, the situation of the peasantry became precarious indeed. The political effects of this evolution could not be postponed forever. For the time being, nevertheless, the government remained committed to its policy and was unwilling to do more than to grant a few fleeting concessions.

Throughout the decade of the 1890's, the government remained concerned with the growing arrears of the redemption payments. The famine years 1891 and 1892 resulted in doubling all tax arrears, raising them from 51.1 million roubles in 1890 to 102.8 million

smith, "The Economic Growth of Russia, 1860–1913," appendices A–1, A–2 (mimeographed); and Lyashchenko, *Istoriya narodnogo khozyaystva SSSR*, II, 144. I am grateful to Professor Goldsmith for permission to use his study.

123. *Ministerstvo Finansov, 1802–1902* (The Ministry of Finance; St. Petersburg, 1902), II, 640–641.

roubles in 1892. By a special ukase, the redemption arrears in the provinces struck by crop failure were postponed till 1902.[124] Thereupon, by an act passed in 1894, legal prerequisites were created for deferment and installment payment of the accumulated arrears.[125] Two years later, another measure was passed designed to provide the possibility for a new amortization plan, involving alternative new repayment periods of 28, 41, and 56 years for one portion of the outstanding redemption debt; the remaining portion could thenceforth be postponed until after the end of the amortization period of the former portion. Later on, in 1899, the administrative procedure for providing relief in the individual cases was simplified, but the length of the extended new amortization period was limited to 28 years, upon the insistence of the Minister of Finance.[126] Without this amendment, the amortization period of the redemption debt would have exceeded 100 years.

It will be noted that the redemption payments were a source of considerable trouble for the government during the period under review. Their capacity to produce arrears was greater than that of any other tax. There is no question but that the redemption payment was an exceedingly unpopular tax, having had its origin in juridical views that were quite unacceptable to the peasantry. It was a very expensive tax. The cost of collecting the redemption payments was about five

124. Brzheski, *Nedoimochnost'*, p. 413; Polyakoff, pp. 58–59.

125. "Vysochayshe utverzhdennoye mneniye Gosudarstvennago Soveta o poryadke otsrochki i razsrochki nedoimok vykupnykh platezhey" (Imperially Approved Opinion of the State Council Concerning the Procedure for Deferment and Installment Payment of Redemption Arrears), *PSZ*, 3rd ser. XIV, no. 10328, February 7, 1894 (St. Petersburg, 1898).

126. For the two measures, see "Vysochayshe utverzhdennoye mneniye Gosudarstvennago Soveta o merakh k oblegcheniyu sel'skim obyvatelyam vsekh naimenovanii uplaty vykupnogo dolga" (Imperially Approved Opinion of the State Council Concerning Measures to Relieve Payment of the Redemption Debt for Peasants of All Categories); "Vysochayshe utverzhdennoye mneniye Gosudarstvennago Soveta ob izmenenii zakona 13–go maya 1896 goda o merakh k oblegcheniyu sel'skim obyvatelyam uplaty vykupnogo dolga" (Imperially Approved Opinion of the State Council Concerning Amendment of the Law of May 13, 1896, Concerning Measures to Relieve Payment of the Redemption Debt for Peasants of All Categories), *PSZ*, 3rd ser. XVI, part I, no. 12933, May 13, 1896 (St. Petersburg, 1899); and XIX, part I, no. 16983, May 31, 1899 (St. Petersburg, 1902). Also *Otchet po deloproizvodstvu Gosudarstvennago Soveta za sessiyu 1898–1899* (Report of the Procedings of the State Council During the Session 1898–1899; St. Petersburg, 1899), p. 439.

times higher than that of all other taxes.[127] The tax in 1903 amounted to only 6.4 percent of the total net tax revenue. The coronation of Nicholas II in 1896 provided the occasion for a manifesto in which, along with various amnesties, all the accumulated arrears for payment of the land tax were forgiven; the land tax rates were reduced by half for a full decade, and all the ancient arrears arising out of the poll tax and quitrent tax which had been abolished in the 1880s were forgiven.[128] But neither the regular redemption debt nor the arrears accumulated in connection with that debt was touched upon in the manifesto. Rather than "forgive" any part of them, the government preferred to handle them through a normal legislative act, which it did one day earlier (see note 126 above). Nor, for that matter, was any part of the redemption payments forgiven in a previous manifesto of the new reign, where it was stipulated that a portion of the incoming redemption payments should be earmarked for the purpose of increasing the capital of the Peasant Bank.[129]

There is little doubt that, if the government had wanted to disembarrass itself of this unpalatable, costly, and insignificant tax, it could easily have found an appropriate substitute. If it failed to do so and preferred to go on inventing ingenious schemes for relief and readjustment, it must have been guided by special motives. There is indeed every reason to believe that the government clung to the redemption payments because their cessation would have removed the legal ties holding the obshchina together. At the same time, another connection must be emphasized. It is difficult to probe into the story of policy measures with regard to the redemption payments without

127. This, at least, was true in 1903, the ratio of the cost of collection to revenue being 29.6 percent for redemption payments and only 5.9 percent for all the other taxes. See Polyakoff, p. 257.

128. "Manifest o darovannykh v den' svyashchennago koronovaniya ikh imperatorskikh velichestv milost'yakh" (Manifesto Concerning Mercies Adopted on the Day of Coronation of Their Imperial Majesties), *PSZ*, 3rd ser. XVI, part I, no. 12936, May 14, 1896 (St. Petersburg, 1899).

129. "Manifest o vsemilostiveyshe darovannykh milostyakh i oblegcheniyakh po sluchayu brakosochetaniya yego imperatorskago velichestva gosudarya Imperatora Nikolaya Aleksandrovicha" (Manifesto Concerning the Most Graciously Accorded Mercies and Reliefs on the Occasion of Conclusion of the Marriage of His Imperial Majesty the Sovereign Emperor Nikolay Aleksandrovich), *PSZ*, 3rd ser. XIV, part I, no. 11035, November 14, 1894 (St. Petersburg, 1898).

receiving the strong impression that, in addition to the general reasons determining the pro-obshchina policy of the Russian government, there was also a very powerful special reason: namely, the vested interest of the Ministry of the Interior, which was in charge of the entire police machinery of the country.

The great spurt of industrialization in the 1890s signified an enormous expansion of the Ministry of Finance. It was natural that with the passage of time many a function previously exercised by the police would be taken over by appropriate organs of the Ministry of Finance. The institution of tax inspector (*podatnoy inspektor*) had been created by Minister of Finance Bunge as early as 1885, but it was only in 1892 that the Ministry of the Interior began for the first time to allow some cooperation with the inspectors in matters of tax collection. The shift to indirect taxes that was taking place inevitably reduced the role of the police in matters of tax collection. A reform of the direct taxes and the introduction of an income tax would have diminished that role further. But an income tax seemed undesirable in the early stages of industrialization, when the attempt was to increase rather than decrease the incomes of industrial entrepreneurs. In fact, an income tax was not instituted until 1916. Yet the threat was clearly perceptible, and the preservation of the traditional taxes whose collection required archaic methods of police compulsion, including corporal punishment, and the existence of the village commune whose members were tied by joint responsibility seemed to aid the Ministry of the Interior in warding off the encroachments upon it by the Ministry of Finance. The conflicts between the two ministries affected a great many fields, such as taxation policies, passport regulations, and labor policies.[130] They eventually culminated in the attempt of Count Witte, the great Minister of Finance in the 1890's, to modernize the basic political structure of the country by the introduction of a constitutional system of government.

It must be noted, however, that in the 1890's the Ministry of Finance was slow to take an independent attitude on the problem of agrarian policies. As Witte admitted himself, in the beginning of his

130. The Ministry of Finance favored moderate social legislation while the Ministry of the Interior was to embark upon organization of labor unions by the police.

career as a minister of finance, he was only superficially acquainted with agrarian problems and was generally in favor of the obshchina because he regarded it as a traditional Russian institution.[131] It was only after the turn of the century that Witte, moved by the depressed state of agriculture, began to "probe the ground" concerning abolition of both redemption payments and joint responsibility, and declared in the State Council that the Ministry of Finance did not need joint responsibility and the job of tax collecting should be transferred from the police to the organs of the Ministry of Finance.[132] It was then that special commissions began to study the problem of conditions in agriculture, one of them organized under Witte and a competing one set up by Pleve, the all-powerful Minister of the Interior. It was also by that time that Witte's policy of industrialization had come under open attack by the Ministry of the Interior. Witte was accused of having placed agriculture under too great a strain. In this, the Ministry of the Interior was seconded by the Ministry of War, which felt that a policy that impoverished the peasantry was prejudicial to the military interests of the nation. For it weakened the human reservoir of the army and, by reducing the horse population, depleted the army's source of drafting power.[133]

But all this was merely adumbrated during most of the 1890's. Witte, at that time, was glad to leave the peasantry to the revenue-extracting powers of the Ministry of the Interior and was content to participate in compromise solutions which reflected the status-quo policy of the Ministry of the Interior with regard to taxes and agriculture, and particularly the redemption payments, but at the same time provided for greater participation by the Ministry of Finance in supervisory and advisory capacities. The series of measures concerning redemption payments must be regarded as representing such compromise solutions. So also was the reform of tax collection from village

131. Witte, *Vospominaniya*, I, 446.

132. *Ibid.*, p. 473. It would have been quite in order for Count Witte to mention in his Memoirs that as late as 1899 he still voted in the State Council for the preservation of joint responsibility. At that time, the attacks upon the institution came from the members of the Council. Witte was a consummate politician, and the strategy of his relations with the Ministry of the Interior was very complex. Cf. *Gosudarstvennago Soveta, 1898–1899*, pp. 459f, 466.

133. This was a reproduction under different conditions of the Louvois-Colbert controversies. See Kuropatkin, *Dnevnik*, p. 30.

communes which was carried out in 1899, under the terms of which the rural chief was responsible for *postoyannoye ponuzhdeniye* (unceasing coercion) in tax matters while the tax inspector was to check on the inflow of revenue. True, the passage of this measure had been preceded by lively debates in the State Council; and the measure itself, though again proclaiming the principle of joint responsibility for taxes on village communes, introduced individual responsibility for village communes with less than sixty "per soul" allotments.[134] But this was no more than a little dent in the walls of the agrarian policies of the 1890's. To preserve the obshchina until liquidation of the redemption debt, to prolong the period of amortization of that debt so as to protect the obshchina, and at the same time to continue holding the peasantry in the vise of ruinous aggregate taxation — those were the guiding principles of the government's agrarian policy of this period. Modernization of industry and preservation of an archaic structure in agriculture were not very harmonious goals, though not necessarily inconsistent or impossible. But their attainment presupposed a good deal more patience than the Russian peasant was willing to muster. In the stormy years that marked the beginning of the new century, a long series of concessions to the peasantry had proved necessary before the government succeeded in smothering the revolutionary fire. It was then ready to draw an historical inference from the barely averted threat in the form of a complete volte-face in its agrarian policy. It remains to describe both the concessions and the reorientation of policy.

CLEARING THE DECKS AFTER THE BATTLE:
THE GREAT VOLTE-FACE

The great industrial spurt of the 1890's ended in the depression year 1900. The slump has been variously reported as an overproduction crisis, a financial crash, or the result of unfavorable economic conditions outside Russia, particularly in Central Europe. Any of

134. "Vysochayshe utverzhdennoye polozheniye o poryadke vzimaniya okladnykh sborov s nadel'nykh zemel' sel'skikh obshchestv" (Imperially Approved Statute Concerning the Mode of Collecting Taxes Imposed on Allotment Lands of Village Communes), *PSZ*, 3rd ser. XIX, part I, no. 17286, June 23, 1899 (St. Petersburg, 1902).

these explanations would be incomplete, and in fact quite superficial, without taking into consideration the exhaustion of the taxpaying capacity of the peasantry. For the first time since the days of the Emancipation Act, peasant unrest assumed major proportions. Between 1900 and 1902, the acts of violence and disobedience grew in both number and intensity. They declined somewhat in 1902 and 1904 and rose to unprecedented peaks thereafter. There was illegal occupation of gentry lands and parks for grazing purposes; villagers in large groups invaded the gentry forests for wholesale fellings; barns on the estates were broken into and ransacked; the owners were subject to threats and bodily injuries; the peasants plundered the country houses and let "the red cock fly over the roofs," watching in exultation as the hated imitations of French chateaux and Georgian manors went up in flames. To complete the picture, one must add the strikes of land laborers for higher wages and collective refusals to pay the leases that had been agreed upon. The government had long developed a simple technique for dealing with peasant violence or resistance. An army detachment would be sent into the riotous village, dispersing the crowds, if necessary by the use of firearms, arresting the ringleaders, staging mass whippings, and then departing with peace and order re-established. Those methods were efficient enough as long as riots were few and far apart. When they became a nearly ubiquitous mass phenomenon, with large segments of the government forces deflected by the war in the Far East, and, when in addition peasant rebellion coincided with a widespread strike movement in transportation, communications, and manufacturing, the revolution was at hand.[135]

The revolutionary wave reached its crest with the Moscow uprising in December 1905. From then on, the government gradually recaptured many lost positions. By the autumn of 1906, order was largely re-established and maintained, although by a combination of physical and judicial brutality that was unprecedented in the modern history of the country. In the field of agrarian relations, the great

---

135. For descriptions of peasant unrest, see Peter Maslov, *Krisis krest'yanskago khozyaystva i krest'yanskoye dvizheniye* (The Crisis of the Peasant Economy and Peasant Unrest; St. Petersburg, 1908); also V. I. Picheta, *Istoriya krest'yanskikh volnenii v Rossii* (History of Peasant Unrest in Russia; Minsk, 1923), chaps. 12–14; S. M. Dubrovski, *Krest'yanskoye dvizheniye v revolutsii, 1905–1907* (The Peasant Movement During the Revolution; Moscow, 1956).

attack of the peasantry upon the lands of the gentry was beaten back. The government refused to acquiesce in the various expropriatory schemes that were supported far to the right of the radical socialist groups and parties.[136] And yet the postrevolutionary situation was far from being a simple return to the status quo *ante revolutionem*. A number of irreversible changes had taken place in the interval, which profoundly affected the conditions of peasant agriculture. The most important of those changes were embodied in several measures, to be briefly mentioned here.

Abolition of joint responsibility. In February 1903, an imperial manifesto deplored the troubled character of the times, which "hindered the attempts to improve popular welfare," ordered initiation of studies directed to improve the position of agriculture, and emphasized that unchanged adherence to the principle of the obshchina system must be the basis of such studies. The manifesto announced that the activities of the Peasant Land Bank (and of the Gentry Bank) would be placed in the service of further consolidation of the "fundamental principles of Russian rural life," and steps would be taken without delay to abolish the institution of joint responsibility, which was said to have been "restrictive" upon the peasantry.[137] Indeed, a fortnight later joint responsibility was abolished for most of the country's provinces. Payments of current direct taxes and of accumulated arrears both became a responsibility of the individual peasant household.[138] It will be noted that this removal of an institution that had been regarded, in the legal definition, as an essential element of the obshchina was conjoined with the solemn assurance that the obshchina arrangement would continue unabated.[139]

136. In particular, by the Liberal Constitutional Democrats (the so-called Cadets). A lifetime later, Maklakov, an outstanding leader of the party, described its platform on forcible alienations of land as "the gravest (spiritual) sacrifice of Russian Liberalism." V. A. Maklakov, *Iz vospominanii* (From Memories; New York, 1923), p. 222.

137. "Manifest o prednachertaniyakh k usovershenstvovaniyu gosudarstvennago poryadka" (Manifesto Concerning Plans for Perfecting the Political Order), *PSZ*, 3rd ser. XXIII, part 1, no. 22581, February 26, 1903 (St. Petersburg, 1905).

138. See "Vysochayshe utverzhdennoye mneniye Gosudarstvennago Soveta ob otmene krugovoy poruki po uplate okladnykh sborov . . ." (Imperially Approved Opinion of the State Council Concerning Abolition of Joint Responsibility for Payment of Direct Taxes), *ibid.*, no. 22629, March 12, 1903.

139. *MPV* article 113, note. A few months later, when the Senate was instructed by an imperial ukase to review the existing legislation concerning the peasantry "on

Accumulated arrears and corporal punishment. The disorders in rural areas continued, and the birth and baptism of a male heir to the throne gave the government the opportunity to issue a special manifesto by which to forgive — in one fell swoop — all the arrears that had accumulated as a result of failures to pay on time both the redemption payments and the state land tax on allotment lands, as of the crown prince's day of birth.

At the same time and by the same act, the peasant population was made exempt from corporal punishment, thus, it was explained, completing the gradual exemption of the population, "estate by estate," from this particular method of law enforcement. The two measures were closely related, inasmuch as administration of whipping had been very widely used by the police in its efforts to reduce the amounts of the accumulated arrears.[140] In fact, along with the public sale of the domestic utensils, clothing, bedding, and cattle of the villagers, lashings were the principal instrument the authorities employed to remedy the situation. As a rule, the punishment was applied to the delinquent debtors themselves, but in the past the police had frequently interpreted the principle of joint responsibility in such a manner as to permit wholesale and indiscriminate whippings of punctual and unpunctual taxpayers alike.

The abolition of redemption payments. After the general political strike in October 1905 had forced the government's hand, and constitutional rights, including a representative assembly — the Duma — had been accorded the population by the manifesto of October 17, 1905, the continuation of peasant unrest resulted in the publication of the manifesto of November 3, 1905, which declared that continua-

---

the basis of the main principles of 1861," there was again reference to the "inviolabil-ity" of the obshchina system and the necessity to preserve the peasantry as a special estate and to maintain the inalienability of the allotment lands. "Imennoy vysochayshii ukaz danny Senatu, ob uchrezhdenii gubernskikh soveshchanii po peresmotru zakono-datel'stva o krest'yanakh (Imperial Ukase Given to the Senate Concerning Establish-ment of Provincial Conferences for a Review of the Legislation Concerning the Peasantry), *PSZ*, 3rd ser. XXIV, part I, no. 23860, January 8, 1904 (St. Petersburg, 1907).

140. "Manifest o milostyakh darovannykh v den' svyatago kreshcheniya nasled-nika tsesarevicha i velikago knyazya Alekseya Nikolayevicha" (Manifesto Concerning Mercies Accorded on the Day of the Holy Baptism of the Crown Prince and Grand Duke, Aleksey Nikolayevich), *ibid.*, no. 25014, August 11, 1904.

tion of acts of violence in the villages would not be tolerated. It proceeded to announce the resolution to reduce the redemption payments for peasants of all categories by 50 percent during the year 1906 and to abolish them altogether as of January 1, 1907. As of the latter date, 670.3 million roubles had been repaid by the peasantry out of an *originally* scheduled total of 2,012.1 million roubles.[141] The state peasants had been transferred to redemption status nearly one generation after the former serfs. Accordingly, they were the chief beneficiaries of the cancellation of redemption payments: their forgiven debt, amounting to 765 million roubles, was more than twice as large as the remaining debt of the former serfs.

Along with reducing the financial burden of the peasants, the government also wished to reduce the impetus behind the seizures of gentry lands by the peasantry. The same manifesto, therefore, announced a forthcoming increase in the capital of the Peasant Land Bank and an increase of the bank's loans to 90 and even 100 percent of the purchase value of land in cases of landless peasants or peasants with very little land at their disposal.[142]

Equalization before the law. A comprehensive ukase, passed in the autumn of 1906, bestowed upon the peasantry a number of rights that had been withheld, although enjoyed by most other groups of the population. The restrictive provisions concerning division of property within families were deleted from the statute book. So was the prohibition against the signing of bills of exchange by peasants who did not own real estate outside the obshchina. A peasant could no

---

141. Polyakoff, p. 55.

142. *PSZ*, 3rd ser. XXV, part I, November 3, 1905 (St. Petersburg, 1908): (1) no. 26871, "Manifest ob uluchshenii blagosostoyaniya i oblegchenii polozheniya krest'yanskago naseleniya" (Manifesto Concerning Improvements in Welfare and Relief in the Conditions of the Peasant Population); (2) no. 26872, "Imennoy vysochayshii ukaz danny Senatu ob umen'shenii i posleduyushchem prekrashchenii vykupnykh platezhey s krest'yan byvshikh pomeshchich'ikh gosudarstvennykh i udel'nykh" (Imperial Ukase to the Senate Concerning Reduction and Subsequent Discontinuation of Redemption Payments by Former Gentry Peasants, State Peasants, and Imperial Peasants); (3) no. 26873, "Imennoy vysochayshii ukaz Senatu, ob oblegchenii zadachi krest'yanskago pozemel'nago banka po sodeystviyu k uvelicheniyu ploshchadi zemlevladeniya malozemel'nykh krest'yan" (Imperial Ukase to the Senate Concerning Alleviating the Task of the Peasant Land Bank in Contributing to Increases in the Area of Land Ownership by Peasants with Little Land at Their Disposal).

longer be punished for acts not regulated in the Statute Concerning Justices of the Peace. He could no longer be given by the village commune into forced employment as a punishment for failure to pay his debts. Most importantly, the peasants received the right to choose freely a place of permanent residence. In receiving passports they no longer were dependent upon consent of the head of the household or the village commune. The latter lost its right to recall absent members of the commune, and a source of extortions by family and commune against members working away from the village was at length stopped. Finally, passports could be issued without limit of time; for the first time, the threat was removed that had hung continually over the peasant away from home — the threat, that is, of becoming a *bespasportny*, a passportless outlaw, and of being forcibly deported to the home village where alone a passport could be renewed.[143]

The measure did not altogether abolish the "peasant estate." A subject of the tsar was still identified before the authorities as a peasant, or a nobleman, a civil servant, a merchant, a town dweller. There was still no equality in judicial and administrative organization as between town and country. But the most blatant aspects of the discrimination against the peasantry were abolished; the juridical power of the village commune over the peasant was broken, and the legal barriers to free mobility were removed. If one considers that only two years earlier the Autocrat of All the Russias had proclaimed the necessity of conserving the peasantry's character as a special estate, the change is striking indeed. The preamble to the decree claimed it to represent the consummation of the emancipatory plans of Alexander II. In some sense this was not necessarily wrong, but all the stress on broad historical continuity could not undo or even obscure the several decades of strenuous government efforts designed to

---

143. The act contained a number of other stipulations which are of less interest in the present connection. It may be noted that it was passed as an emergency decree under the terms of the famous article 87 of the Fundamental Acts; the government obviously wished to make the article palatable by using it for the introduction of a very popular measure. For the complete text of the decree, see "Imennoy vysochayshii ukaz danny Senatu ob otmene nekotorykh ogranichennii v pravakh sel'skikh obyvateley i lits drugikh byvshikh podatnykh sostoyanii" (Imperial Ukase to the Senate Concerning Abrogation of Certain Limitations on the Rights of Rural Residents and Persons Belonging to Some Other, Previously Taxpaying Status), *PSZ*, 3rd ser. XXVI, part I, no. 28392, October 5, 1906 (St. Petersburg, 1909).

keep the peasantry within the pinfold of its estate, separated as much as possible from the rest of the population. On the eve of the 1905 revolution, the juridical position of the peasantry was, if anything, more specific than it had been four decades earlier. To anyone who, treading the path of easy historical generalizations, has regarded the changes worked by the French Revolution as the prerequisite for modern industrial development, the sequence of events in Russia must be bewildering indeed. In the preamble just referred to, the emperor spoke of the principles of civil liberty and equality before law. Russia's industrialization had gone very far before the general political framework began to be seriously reformed.

In more than one respect, the complex of legislative measures just discussed touched directly upon the problem of the village commune. Establishment of personal responsibility for tax payments, abolition of supervision over division of family property, liberalization of passport regulations, and particularly the cancellation of the redemption debt — all these seemed to curtail the power of the obshchina over the individual or, at least, to restrict its functions. Yet those changes did not necessarily prejudge the future of the obshchina in Russia. If the government had still felt that the obshchina represented the traditional, and hence stabilizing, element within the Russian body social; if it had still believed that it prevented impoverishment of, or at least made poverty tolerable [144] for, the mass of the population and satisfied some general postulates of egalitarian justice, it would still have been quite possible to place the Russian village commune under renewed and perhaps even increased legislative protection. To achieve such protection, it would have been necessary to

144. The qualification is important. It was in this sense that Konstantin Pobedonostsev, the strongest spiritual beacon of Alexander III's reign, viewed the obshchina: "There are problems of grand policies which it is dangerous to solve exclusively on the basis of abstract principles of economic freedom. Land is a commodity which it is perilous to throw upon the free market. One may . . . endeavor to establish economic freedom and get the freedom of pauperism instead which everywhere has been the worst form of slavery . . . So far the mass of our peasant population finds itself in a condition in which what matters is not savings but daily bread . . . In such a state of affairs only the obshchina can save the peasant from impoverishment and keep a shelter over his head; or rather in his very pauperism — which is a normal phenomenon with us — to keep away the danger of death from starvation. The obshchina makes it possible to till the land without capital expenditures and to do it anyhow [koye kak — the Russian equivalent of the Italian pressappochismo]." Pobedonostsev, Kurs grazhdanskago prava, I, 477–480.

adopt a number of special policy measures designed to block separation from the obshchina. Keeping the peasants' allotment lands within the obshchina could still have been made quite consistent with the rights of free travel and settlement as assured by the postrevolutionary legislation.

Such might have been the policy of the Russian government if it had continued to adhere to its pre-1905 position. But this was not the case. In July 1906, when the first elected Russian Duma was dissolved after a lifespan of only three months, the emperor dismissed Prime Minister Goremykin and elevated to premiership P. A. Stolypin, who had been Minister of the Interior under Goremykin. This was the crucial turn of events. Before joining the cabinet, Stolypin had served as the governor of Saratov province, with its overwhelming predominance of the obshchina. He had had plentiful opportunity to witness the behavior of the allegedly conservative obshchina members during the long months of agrarian disorders in 1905. In a secret report to his chief, the Minister of the Interior, Stolypin expressed the view that revolutionary agitation was but the proximate cause of peasant unrest. The root of the evil lay in the poverty of the rural population. Yet increasing the extent of peasant lands would not solve the problem, Stolypin believed, because in very many cases it was peasants with large allotments who were found wrecking and setting fire to gentry estates. The solution was to create "a class of small proprietors — this basic cell of the state and in its very nature an adversary of all destructive theories." [145] There is thus very little doubt that the police aspect of the problem, that is to say, the new view of the obshchina as fostering rather than suppressing unrest and violence, was at the origin of Stolypin's views. A strong-willed man, Stolypin was not given to half measures. "The point is that I do not admit any concessions, be they large or small. I believe that what is needed is real action and real reforms," he wrote in a letter to D. N. Shipov, an outstanding representative of very moderate Zemstvo liberalism. [146] "It was the age of disorders," he said four years later looking back upon the years 1905–1906. "The gentry estates

145. Printed in N. Karpov, *Agrarnaya politika Stolypina* (Stolypin's Agrarian Policy; Leningrad, 1925), pp. 172–173.
146. D. N. Shipov, *Vospominaniya i dumy o perezhitom* (Memoirs and Thoughts of Things Lived Through; Moscow, 1918), p. 470.

were in flames or lay in smouldering embers . . . That was the time for decision, not for cogitation . . . The political disorder had its roots in the soul of the people [*v narode*]; they were nourished by social disorder . . . It was necessary to destroy the cause of causes . . . to establish for the peasantry a new socioeconomic order." [147] In that position, Stolypin undoubtedly was supported by large numbers of the gentry, whose attitudes toward the obshchina underwent a radical change. The obshchina may have been a source of cheap agricultural labor and obshchina members may have paid high rents for gentry lands, but those advantages paled into insignificance when protection of gentry property from destruction by ax and fire at the hands of communal villages became the pressing problem. The problem as to whether Stolypin's motivations were primarily those of a nobleman or of a faithful servant of the state need not concern us here.[148]

At the same time, however, it should be mentioned that by 1906 the anti-obshchina sentiment had grown considerably. The special conference set up in 1902 under Witte to study the needs of agriculture was handicapped by the imperial pronouncement that the obshchina must remain inviolate. Nevertheless, after one year's work the provincial and district committees of the conference produced a severe catalogue of communal shortcomings and suggested various reforms, including easier exit from the commune. Witte, in his Memorandum Concerning the Peasant Question (1904), had to go through considerable tergiversation in order to demonstrate that inviolability of the obshchina meant refraining from compulsion designed to make the peasants remain in the obshchina or leave it. He argued strenuously that the reformers of 1861 had accepted the obshchina as a temporary expedient, and for the rest proceeded to

147. *Gosudarstvenny Sovet, Stenograficheskii otchet* (The State Council, Stenographic Report), session V, meeting 25, March 15, 1910, pp. 1137–1138.

148. The role of the gentry was strongly stressed by P. N. Milyukov, who regarded the change in the gentry's position vis-à-vis the obshchina as having determined the government's change of mind. In particular, in two gentry conventions held during 1906 the views expressed resembled very closely those contained in Stolypin's secret report, quoted above. *Gosudarstvennaya Duma, tretii sosyv, stenograficheskiye otchety* (The Third State Duma, Stenographic Reports), 1907–1908, 2nd session, part I, October 31, 1908, and November 5, 1908, pp. 627–628, 774 (St. Petersburg, 1908).

criticize the institution, the admiration of which, he said, had long preceded the understanding of its nature; he stressed the obshchina's incompatibility with economic progress and "culture" in general. The obshchina had been traditionally viewed as an infallible vaccine against the "scourge of the proletarianization." Now Witte described it as converting large numbers of the population into paupers and subtly argued "the at least exterior resemblance" between the obshchina and the "theoretical constructions of socialism and communism." This, however, was rather accidental in the memorandum. Its main stress lay in the economic sphere: it exposed the communal ills and advocated the transition to economic individualism in agriculture.[149]

It is worth noting that Pleve, the powerful Minister of the Interior, tried to obstruct the work of the special conference. He succeeded in putting the latter into a state of prolonged hibernation, and in establishing a competing conference on the problem of agriculture within the Ministry of the Interior. After Pleve's death at the hands of revolutionary terrorists, Witte's conference was revived. Interestingly enough, at that time the most radical position against the obshchina was taken by a representative of the Ministry of the Interior, Gurko, who pleaded to proceed against the obshchina with the same vigor with which Witte had proceeded to build up the industry of the country. Gurko also tried to make Goremykin, who was in charge of still another commission to aid agriculture, abandon the traditional view, but was unsuccessful. It was Stolypin's advent to power that marked the end of a period. As a result of the gradual turning of bureaucratic opinion away from the obshchina, a good deal of preparatory work had been accomplished in the form of preliminary legislative drafts. Stolypin could, and in fact did draw upon this reservoir. On the other hand, it would be wrong to assume that Stolypin benefited much, if at all, from the more profound intellectual roots of the recent opposition to the obshchina. Witte and Stolypin seemed to have arrived at similar negative positions. Yet a significant difference between the two leading Russian statesmen of the period persisted. Witte was not averse to combating the revolutionary upheavals by increasing the peasants' landholdings, and caused work to be done regarding plans for compulsory alienation of portions of

149. Witte, *Zapiska*, pp. 10, 22, 30, 81–90.

gentry land. Stolypin, on the other hand, considered such an alienation altogether undesirable and unacceptable. But important as this
was, the main difference lay elsewhere: while Witte considered the
obshchina a problem pertaining to the industrial development of the
country, Stolypin's interest in industrialization was marginal, to say
the least, and he was explicit in regarding the land as "the only
source of our welfare." Even in his celebrated Duma speech, in which
he contrasted the "drunken weaklings" among the peasantry with
"the strong and the intelligent" and declared the government's intention to have its "wager" placed on the latter rather than the former, it is perfectly clear that economic individualism essentially meant
for him no more than creation of strong *points d'appui* for the government in its struggle against the revolutionary forces.[150] The historical
analogy is irresistible. It was the fear of a peasant war that led to the
emancipation of the serfs in 1861. It was the belief in the political
value of the obshchina that caused its perpetuation in 1861 and was
responsible later on for the series of special measures designed to protect it from disintegration and decay. The positive effects of the emancipation upon industrial development were never paramount in the
minds of the reformers of 1861. Once more, the decision to withdraw
the government's protection from the obshchina and to hasten its
dissolution was motivated by political considerations. Once more, the
age-long primacy of politics over economics in Russia had asserted
itself.

The act of November 9, 1906, issued as an emergency decree
(under article 87 of the Constitution), appeared under a modest
title which hardly did justice to the significance of the measure:
Imperial Ukase to the Senate Concerning Supplementing Certain
Stipulations of the Law Presently in Force Regarding Landownership and Land Utilization of Peasants.[151] It was true, as was mentioned in the preamble to the act, that with the cessation of redemption payments (as of January 1907) the restrictive legislation passed in

---

150. *Gosudarstvennaya Duma*, meeting 27, December 5, 1908 (St. Petersburg,
1908), pp. 2282–2283.

151. "Imennoy vysochayshii ukaz danny Senatu o dopolnenii nekotorykh postanovlenii deystvuyushchego zakona kasayushchegosya krest'yanskago zemlevadeniya i
zemlepol'zovaniya," *PSZ*, 3rd ser. XXVI, no. 28528, November 9, 1906 (St. Petersburg 1909).

the 1890's had become inapplicable. By the same token, the peasant members of the obshchina had acquired (under article 36 of the General Statute, also known as article 12 in other editions) the right of free exit from the obshchina. In such a case, the peasant was to receive as his personal property an extent of land commensurate with his participation in the redemption of those lands. Obviously, it was no easy matter, and in fact impossible, to measure the exact degree of a peasant household's participation in an operation that in many cases had lasted for more than four decades; also, a household's contribution to the redemption payments varied with the size of the family and the extent of its landholdings, to say nothing of its ability to evade the obligation to pay by accumulating arrears that were later forgiven.

Stolypin's solution to the problem was simple and drastic. First of all, it established the right of all heads of households in village communes to demand at any time a formal transfer into their personal ownership of a portion of communal lands. That portion was to be determined as follows. In village communes that had had no general land repartition for the last 24 years, the peasant wishing to leave the obshchina could claim all the allotted lands currently under his utilization. In those village communes in which there had been general repartition during the last 24 years, the same rule prevailed, except that households found to have more land under their utilization than would be allotted to them on the basis of the criteria used during the last repartition would have to pay for the difference at the average redemption price at which the given obshchina had received the land. Those leaving the obshchina would retain current rights in common meadows, woods, pastures, and so on. The obshchina was expected to comply with the request of a member wishing to leave it within one month, the communal decision requiring no more than the majority of those present at the meeting. If the obshchina failed to act within the prescribed time, the *zemskii nachal'nik*, that is, a subordinate of the Minister of the Interior, was to act instead of the obshchina.

In addition to receiving the formerly communal lands into private ownership, the head of the household was given the right to demand at any time consolidation of his lands into one compact piece.

If the demand was made at the time of a general repartition, the obshchina had to comply unconditionally; at other times, it could retain the lands by compensating the owner at a price that was either mutually agreed upon or fixed by a rural court. Finally, it was stipulated that by a two-thirds vote of those entitled to vote, a village commune was given the right to abandon the open-field system and to carry out wholesale consolidation of the lands utilized by the member households.

These main features of the act of 1906 were further elaborated and codified with greater care in the law of 1910, which was no longer an emergency decree but was duly passed by the Duma and the State Council.[152] In particular, the new law introduced the principle of certain automaticity by stipulating that village communes to which land had been allotted before 1887, and in which no general repartitions had taken place since the time of allotment, were to be regarded as having changed over to individual ownership. The members of such communes simply retained all the lands under their utilization at the time when the 1910 law was promulgated.[153]

It should be clear that the two acts just referred to were much more than a mere interpretation and elaboration of the old article 36. The authors of the new acts actually did not attempt to find out what had been a household's share in the aggregate redemption payments. They decided to favor the *beati possidentes* who may have held the land for a very short time or else may have consistently dodged their obligations. They were given the right to purchase excess landholdings in their possession at the average redemption prices, which once had been very much higher than market prices but which, as a result of the great boom in land values, came to be just a fraction of current

152. "Vysochayshe utverzhdenny, odobrenny Gosudarstvennym Sovetom i Gosudarstvennoy Dumoy zakon ob izmenenii i dopolnenii nekotorykh postanovlenii o krest'yanskom zemlevladenii" (Imperially Sanctioned Law, Approved by the State Council and the State Duma, Concerning Changes in, and Supplements to, Certain Stipulations Regarding Peasant Land Possession), *PSZ*, 3rd ser. XXX, part, I, no. 33743, June 14, 1910 (St. Petersburg, 1913).

153. This stipulation substituted for the previous distinction between communes in which repartitions did or did not take place within the last 24 years. That distinction was dropped in 1910, and all the communes in which a general repartition had occurred were subject to the general procedure which had been prescribed in 1906 for communes in which a repartition had taken place less than 24 years earlier.

market prices. Article 36 gave the village communes the option of compensating a member wishing to leave the commune in terms of money rather than land. The new acts confined this right only to cases in which the member wished, in addition to separation from the commune, consolidation of his lands; and even in the latter case, the option was withdrawn in cases of general repartitions. Perhaps the most important element of the new legislation was the strong procedural position accorded to the organs of the government. The rural chiefs could press for the speediest dissolution of the bonds that tied the individual peasant to the obshchina. There is hardly any doubt that the eagerness of subordinate officials to show the greatest possible number of exits from the obshchina was very great. Cases of threats and use of force by the authorities were not few. Although Stolypin kept urging the provincial governors to apply great energy in carrying out the act of 1906, at times the local authorities seemed even to exceed his instructions.[154]

It must be assumed that Stolypin's acts provided an effective instrument for a considerable reduction of the obshchina's role in the agrarian structure of the country. Along with the obshchina, it must be added, another traditional institution was also placed under the government's fire: the ancient concept of family property was not recognized by the laws of 1906 and 1910. It was the head of the household, rather than the family unit, who was to acquire full proprietory rights over the lands separated out of the obshchina.

It would be altogether wrong, however, to assume that because of the nature of the laws and the way in which they were implemented the obshchina in Russia was doomed to quick extinction. Despite the many expressions of contrary views, the obshchina in Russia was not in a state of general disintegration. Hence even a blow as strong as the one imparted by Stolypin failed to prove completely annihilating. Between November 1906 and May 1915, more than 30 percent of the total number of heads of households in village communes declared their intention of leaving the commune; almost 22 percent of all heads of households in village communes were separated out of the obshchina

154. Zenkovski, *Pravda o Stolypine*, p. 37. Cf. Stolypin's marginal note, "how silly!" on the report concerning jailing of a peasant who had voiced objections to the 1906 act (Karpov, p. 182).

and became individual owners of the allotment lands. The corresponding percentage of lands owned by those former obshchina members was above 16 percent. The discrepancy between the two percentages reveals the fact that the number of those who had less than the average allotment of land was considerable among the departing obshchina members. This should not be surprising. As a result of Stolypin's legislation, a peasant, wishing to abandon his land and to emigrate into the city or another part of the country, could for the first time sell the land and acquire the wherewithal to finance his move away from the village. It is true, however, that the sellers were still restricted, in that sales of allotment lands to nonpeasants were forbidden. On the other hand, there were many well-to-do peasants who had accumulated more allotment land than was their due and were anxious to establish their individual rights over those lands by a quick exit from the obshchina. For the rest, the regional variation in departures was very considerable, the outlying areas in the south, southwest, and west showing the highest percentages — peasants in the center, the east, and the southeast were much more reluctant to leave. In general, the annual data clearly revealed the explosive nature of the rush out of the obshchina on the part of those who had wanted to leave it for a long time, including those who had repaid the redemption debt before maturity and were forcibly retained within the obshchina by the legislation of the 1890's.[155] The number of newly established proprietors in the years 1908–1910 amounted to almost 72 percent of the total figure of departures for 1906–1915; the corresponding figure for the years 1911–1913 was only 20 percent. At the later rate (at which the annual departures amounted to about 1.5 percent of the 1906 number of communal heads of households), it would still have required a considerable number of years to reduce the original number by, say, 50 percent, even though the process would have been abridged by the existence of those obshchinas to which the "automacity" procedure applied and where, accordingly, no separation procedure took place and simple ownership certificates sufficed; but also the rate of issue of ownership certificates had greatly declined after 1911.

The separation of communal lands into individual ownership

155. The above percentages were computed from the data given in S. M. Dubrovski, *Stolypinskaya reforma* (Stolypin's Reform; Moscow, 1930), pp. 150, 152.

precluded further repartitions, but did not per se terminate the communal open-field system with its large number of strips distributed over many shots. The destruction, or at least diminution, of the open-field system was part and parcel of the plan to create a group of economically strong — and hence politically conservative — class of peasant proprietors. It is not surprising, however, that consolidations of land into compact holdings lagged behind mere separations into private ownership, while establishment of homesteads (*khutor*), implying moves out of the nucleated village, lagged behind simple consolidations. Altogether, about 60 percent of the separated allotment lands appeared to be consolidated in one form or other by January 1, 1916.[156] It must be mentioned, however, that the government effort to introduce something resembling the enclosure movement into the Russian agrarian scene went a good deal further than can be judged from the preceding figures. By an imperial decree issued early in 1906, a special Committee for Matters of Land Organization was established centrally, with appropriate provincial and district committees functioning under the main committee.[157] Thus, all lands bought through or with the help of the Peasant Bank were surveyed and consolidated by the committee. To mediate among owners of all descriptions, whether they were individual peasant owners or communal land holders or gentry owners, with the aim of consolidating interlaced lands of villages and private persons, was the direct responsibility of the committee.[158] In addition, under the terms of a comprehensive act passed in 1911, the local committees were empowered to carry out compulsory consolidation of intermingled landholdings upon request of the parties concerned, provided the committee regarded the existing conditions as economically prejudicial.[159]

156. *Ibid.*, p. 191.

157. "Immennoy vysochayshii ukaz danny Senatu ob uchrezhdenii komiteta po zemleustroitel'nym delam . . ." (Imperially Approved Ukase to the Senate Concerning Establishment of a Committee for Matters of Land Organization), *PSZ*, 3rd ser. XXVI, no. 27478, March 4, 1906 (St. Petersburg, 1909).

158. "Nakaz zemleustroitel'nym komissiyam" (Instruction to the Land Organization Commissions), N. T. Volkov, *Sbornik polozhenii o sel'skom sostoyanii* (Collection of Acts Regarding Rural Status; Moscow, 1910), articles 68–97, pp. 482–493.

159. "Vysochayshe utverzhdenny i odobrenny Gosudarstvennym Sovetom i Gosudarstvennoy Dumoy zakon o zemleustroystve" (Imperially Sanctioned Law, Approved

The consolidation policy was pursued with a good deal of vigor; the interest of the peasantry in the abolition of the strip system and in providing clear delimitations of property or possession was considerable. More than six million households asked for consolidation of allotment land between 1907 and 1914. Unlike the case of exits from the obshchina, there was no visible decline in the annual number of demands for consolidation until the outbreak of the war in 1914.[160]

History was not particularly generous to Stolypin's reforms. War and revolution prevented them from attaining their full impact. True, not all of Stolypin's legislative work was lost in the collapse of the old regime. It is surprising indeed to see how strongly the first land code of Soviet Russia was influenced by the acts of the late empire.[161] Throughout the 1920's, the policy of land consolidation was pursued along the lines drawn by Stolypin. In fact, from a narrow point of view, even the collectivization of agriculture may be seen as the consummation of Stolypin's land-consolidation policies.[162]

For the rest, everything was different. The revolutionary expropriation of gentry lands which occurred in 1917 was precisely what Stolypin's policies had tried to avert. Even during the years of the NEP, the Soviet government merely tolerated the strong elements among the peasantry. The early beginnings of the collectivization policy, with its search for someone in the villages the government could rely on, bore some formal resemblance — with the opposite political sign — to Stolypin's policies. But, apart from the obvious fact that collectivization was to seal the fate of economic individualism

---

by the State Council and the State Duma, Concerning Land Organization), *PSZ*, 3rd ser. XXXI, part I, no. 35370, May 29, 1911 (St. Petersburg, 1914).

160. Ministerstvo Zemledeliya, Departament Gosudarstvennykh Zemel'nykh Imushchestv, *Otchetnyya svedeniya o deyatel'nosti zemlestroitel'nykh komissii na pervoye yanvarya 1916 goda* (Ministry of Agriculture, Department of State Land Properties, Reported Data Concerning the Activity of Land Organization Committees as of January 1, 1916). See table entitled "Vnutrinadel'noye zemleustroystvo, obshchiye svedeniya" (Inner Allotment Land Consolidation, General Data; Petrograd, 1916).

161. For instance, provisions regarding separation from the obshchina in the land code (articles 135 and 136) were almost bodily lifted from article 34 of the 1910 act.

162. See *"Zemel'ny kodeks RSFSR, sobraniye uzakonenii"* (Land Code of the RSFSR, Collection of Legal Norms), 1922, no. 68, *Sobraniye kodeksov RSFSR* (Collection of Codes of the RSFSR), 3rd ed. (Moscow, 1925).

in the villages, the crucial difference lay in the interplay of agrarian and industrial policies. The purpose of Soviet collectivization, as it evolved after some initial uncertainties, was to place Russia's agriculture at the service of a new spurt of industrial development, unprecedented both in length and in intensity. By contrast, Stolypin's reforms came after a spurt of industrialization had come to an end. It is this sequence that determines the historical locus of Stolypin's reforms.

IV

CONCLUSION

Actors on the political stages like to justify their action in terms of historical continuities. It is not surprising to find that Stolypin's agrarian legislation was presented by its authors as the natural consummation of the emancipation of the serfs in 1861. Indeed, Stolypin's stress on economic individualism appeared to be logically connected with the transformation of the human cattle into free men. And the course of events in some Western countries, primarily in France, seemed to demonstrate that abolition of ancient restraints upon the peasantry "naturally" led to the establishment of an economically strong and independent peasantry. The revolution from above began with the emancipation and ended with the acts of 1906–1910. Nevertheless, the claim that there was a straight line connecting the reforms of the early 1860's with those of Stolypin must be viewed with caution. To repeat a conclusion reached earlier, the emancipation acts indeed established the family farm in Russia, but not as a strong and prosperous economic entity. Granted that the economic bonds between the peasant economy and the gentry economy could be undone only gradually, the whole course of agrarian policies following the emancipation revealed a remarkable lack of interest in the progress of Russian agriculture. The result was a pattern of relations between agriculture and industrial development that was not easy to understand, for instance, in terms of the traditional views of English economic history. In England, in Paul Mantoux's oft-quoted words, "The growth of great industrial centres would have been impossible if agricultural production had not been so organized as to provide for the needs of a large industrial population, and agricultural production, on the other hand, could not have developed had not the industrial districts supplied adequate markets with growing numbers of consumers." [163] No interaction of this sort was apparent in Russia before Stolypin. The supply of produce to the cities was largely achieved through the pressure upon peasant incomes; and Russian industry did not rely upon the growing demand for industrial goods by a prosperous agriculture, but upon demand for investment goods that was largely supported by the government. Taking the policy vis-à-vis the obshchina as given, the only clearly visible alternative to the way in which industrialization occurred in Russia in the 1890's was no industrialization at all. By the same token, an agrarian reform carried out by this or that West European pattern may have been an important precondition for certain types of industrialization, but its lack in Russia did not prevent a very considerable industrial development from taking place there.

Yet, though an agrarian reform was not a *pre*requisite of industrialization in Russia, it may have been — *sit venia verbo* — its *post*requisite. Great spurts of industrialization in pre-1914 Europe did not last forever. Unless artificially impeded, normalization of conditions of growth was likely to occur as the very consequence of the progress made during the great spurt. In Russia, the end of the period of rapid industrialization was dramatically punctuated by revolutionary disorders. When Russia emerged from the troublous years of war and revolution, the continuation of previously used patterns of substitution in industrial growth was clearly impossible. In particular, the state could not resume its role of providing both demand and capital for industry. Nor could the policy of strong fiscal pressure upon the peasantry continue after the revolution. The period of easy budgetary spending was over. In the years between the 1905 revolution and the outbreak of the First World War, a financial policy of cautious deflation was designed to keep the budget under strict control and to close the great gaps torn by the war against Japan and the struggles against revolutionary upheavals. The spontaneous economic forces that had developed during the years of the great spurt began to take over functions previously performed by the state. This inevitably meant that some of the more costly substitutions for the deficiencies in the supply

163. Mantoux, *The Industrial Revolution of the Eighteenth Century*, p. 190.

of suitable labor and for the lack of appropriate markets had to be abandoned. They were outside the purview of institutions oriented upon profitability calculus.

It has been argued here that Stolypin's reform was essentially oriented to political rather than economic aims. From the point of view of its author, the effect upon the industrial development of the country was merely incidental to his main purpose. This, however, does not detract from the significance of the reform for the subsequent industrial development. During the years 1906–1914, growth of industrial output could be resumed, and it proceeded at a reasonably high rate of 6 percent a year. It would seem that this result, unaccompanied as it was by the urging of the government, could not have been attained without the simultaneous modernization of conditions in agriculture. While contributing to the resumption of industrial growth, Stolypin's reform also seemed to influence its character. Greater availability of labor rendered possible greater stress upon labor-intensive industries; relaxation of fiscal pressures upon agriculture and the formation of a group of strong consumers within the peasantry tended to reduce, at least to some extent, the previous emphasis upon heavy industry. To the volte-face in agrarian policies corresponded a momentous change in the nature of industrial processes.

Thus, nearly half a century after the emancipation of the serfs, economic development in Russia seemed to fall into patterns that resembled more closely the historical models of Western Europe. Yet this belated — and abortive — "normalization" should not obscure one's vision or obliterate the memory of the road that had been traveled in the interval. At the end of this survey of Russia's agrarian policies, the observer cannot overlook the fateful errors of judgment and the mental indolence and narrow-mindedness that caused them. But at the same time, in viewing the course of the country's industrial evolution, he cannot fail to be impressed by the ingenuity, boldness, and strong-willed action that was able to offset, if not turn to advantage, many a hesitation and blunder perpetrated in the field of agriculture. It is in this juxtaposition of two divergent lines of policy that lies the complexity of the story, which defies any simple interpretation, as does the unintended denouement of Stolypin's reform.

8

City Economies — Then and Now

▰▰▰

A specific difficulty in social science stems from the frequent desire of the scholar to elevate his favorite species to the rank of a genus or a well-liked genus to that of a family. A zoologist may be very fond of tigers, but he still would hesitate to claim that they alone compose the cat family. Robert Lopez' reference to the Egyptian symbol for the city — the cross within a circle, the wall and the crossroads — is admirable both because it is so illuminating for some types of medieval towns and because it illustrates the urge to let a favored *sub*category drop its prefix.

No one would want to quarrel with the appropriateness of the circle. No one will deny that the nature of some important medieval cities is very properly intimated by a symbol standing for a market that serves long-distance trade. But are we really sure that there were no medieval cities for which other inscribed symbols may be much more suitable? Is it just the cross, and always the cross, we want to put inside the circle? It is not difficult to think of a few different symbols that could be placed there very fittingly: a compass or a hammer; perhaps a chisel; a weaver's shuttle or a tailor's needle. In other words, is it legitimate in discussing the medieval city to forget so completely the industrial development that took place within its walls and that determined decisively the character of so

Note. These comments were made at a conference on The City in History convened by the Joint Center of Urban Studies in Cambridge, Massachusetts, August 1961. The two papers to which reference is made are "The Crossroads within the Wall" by Robert S. Lopez and "The Economic Significance of the City" by Shigeto Tsuru.

many, though by no means all, towns in medieval Europe? To repeat: also in this connection, the circle is of crucial importance. The
texture of the circumvallation was as much of the spirit as it was of
stones and mortar. If the medieval city had not been pared out from
its environment, both physically and spiritually, it never would have
become a powerful engine of economic change, a landmark in the
industrial history of Europe.

One might be tempted, perhaps, following Shigeto Tsuru, to
discuss that change in terms of the external economies created and
effectively utilized in the city. To be sure, we are all masters of our
own terms, and we can call external economies whatever we please.
This particular case, however, seems to be much too big for the concept and strains it beyond all limits of reasonableness. The most
striking innovation in medieval cities was the emergence of a new
attitude toward manual labor. Perhaps for the first time in the history
of Western civilization, the stigma traditionally placed upon manual
labor was obliterated. The work of the artisan became respectable,
sometimes eminently so. In the process, that work became surrounded
by a number of highly significant social attitudes. Nowadays, through
a somewhat humorless misunderstanding of Max Weber's playful
hypothesis, these attitudes are usually presented as the effects of
Protestantism and are causally related to the rise of capitalism. This
is a regrettable historical distortion, which works havoc with the
chronology of the social history of Europe. For it was precisely within
the institutional framework of the medieval cities, antedating by
several centuries the emergence and diffusion of Protestantism, that
new attitudes toward labor, the product of labor, and the consumer
of that product came into being. Like freedom, thrift and steady industry also seemed products of the "city air." True, the individual
artisan absorbed them from the outside, "externally," as it were. But
to relate them to external economies, to their impact upon the volume
of inputs designed to produce a given output or upon the cost of
given inputs, would not begin to do justice to the great transformation taking place, which implied an altogether new concentration
upon high-quality outputs produced by a newly motivated force.

To some extent, this process of change took place in all medieval
cities in Western and Central Europe. Its full fruition was reached
in those towns where, mostly in the course of the fourteenth century,

the craft guilds succeeded in obtaining a considerable measure of influence in the political life of the town. In important areas, such as the Flemish or the Italian cities, that influence remained small, but nothing can be gained by generalizing Antwerp or Florence into the paradigm of all medieval towns. That would excise from the industrial history of Europe a rich chapter whose contents reached far into the future. In the much more recent past, it made a good deal of difference whether a country did or did not go through that specific experience of medieval industrialization. It is a quite defensible proposition to say that, at the turn of this century, a country such as Russia found the road of industrialization much more arduous precisely because she had never been through the training school of medieval craft guilds. As a result, irregular work habits, carelessness and negligence, low time horizons, and frightening dishonesty remained endemic in Russia, constituting persistent handicaps to economic progress. Things that in Germany had been learned long before the advent of modern times, Russian entrepreneurs and workers, trades and artisans, had to absorb painfully in belated haste in the midst of a rapid and costly spurt of industrial development.

It is, however, precisely the story of Russian industrialization and urbanization that strongly forces upon us the recognition that the concept of external economies is, at best, only one among a number of possible keys to the understanding of modern city development. The more backward countries on the European continent were plagued by exactly the same problem which other and more advanced regions had faced much earlier, that is, by the creation of the "city man." Much water had to go down under the arches of city bridges before the urban dweller was ready to strike roots in the city — to say farewell forever not only to sunsets and roses, but also to the irregular, weather-determined pace of work — to accept the discipline of the factory, and to begin to find substitutes in the city newspaper and technical and political pamphlets for the abandoned folklore, the songs and fairy tales, of his native village. Again, this transformation is to some extent expressible in terms of external economies; but it implies a broad dynamic view of urbanization that is very different from the abstract economy to which the tame textbook concepts of external economies — and diseconomies — are applicable, however useful those concepts may be in themselves.

251

On the other hand, if from the processes of city growth in relatively backward countries or areas we turn to the fully developed modern countries, many of the economic advantages of the cities appear to be a story of yesteryear. The economic difference between the city and the countryside is no longer what it used to be. The external economies of the city have lost much of their charm. The result is a new process of change which takes the textile factories out of the traditional urban environment of Lowell and Lawrence, Lynn and Salem, and transposes them to the rural areas of South Carolina. The same change is visible everywhere. We can see it, for instance, in Vorarlberg, the westernmost province of Austria, where rural populations in the isolation of high Alpine valleys perform the job of industrial labor in factories enclosed in those valleys, and perform it in the most efficient way with the help of the most modern machinery.

We do not have to travel so far from Cambridge, Massachusetts, to see the new, the "unurban," way of doing things. All that is necessary is to move some sixty or seventy miles northwest into southern New Hampshire. As we do it, we must cross the "electronic route," that is, Route 128, the circular artery that surrounds Greater Boston and is studded with electronics factories. These may still be considered as lying within the economic *Weichbild* of Boston. But in New Hampshire you see everywhere, amidst little towns with a population of some fifteen hundred people and in still smaller villages, factories representing the last word in modern technology. They produce electronic equipment, micro-ballbearings, and precision instruments, and are based altogether upon indigenous labor in those villages.

Now what has made all this possible? The fact that the native of a New Hampshire hamlet does not require any change in his general philosophy or any upgrading in his general education in order to become an efficient factory worker is only one of the factors involved. The difference between the rural man and the city man has all but vanished, in very relevant respects. But surely no less important is the tremendous rise in incomes in what Tsuru persists in calling a capitalist society. (It would have been, incidentally, quite in order for him to consider that many things which are now regarded as diseconomies are only viewed as such because incomes have risen and men's wants have changed as a result.) Along with the rise in incomes, there have been certain specific technological changes.

The locational pattern of a New Hampshire factory is very simple. The raw materials and semifabricates are brought in by road. The finished materials leave the factory by the same road, unless the daily output is taken each evening to the local post office and airmailed to the customers, as is done, for instance, by a micro-ball-bearing factory whose annual sales go into many millions of dollars. The degree of fabrication per weight unit has become so high that cost of transportation would be a negligible item, even if the weight losses of raw materials were not so small. The factory can look for its labor force within a radius of some ten to fifteen miles. This is possible because every worker has a car at his disposal. At the same time, the high level of national income has not only created a superb road network, but also has enabled the states and towns to set aside sufficient resources for maintaining the roads and keeping them open through the hardships and hazards of a New England winter. Finally, the availability of cheap electric power, reliably supplied, provides the last element in this highly decentralized pattern.

This, then, seems to be the modern trend. Tsuru's presentation would have gained if he had paid more attention to it. On the other hand, I am somewhat dubious about his suggestion that comparisons between capitalist and socialist societies may be illuminating in the studies of urban policies to be pursued now. I am not at all sure that the nineteenth-century dichotomy of capitalism and socialism deserves any place in a serious scholarly discussion in the second half of the twentieth century. It may be time to forget about this head of Charles the First. If the rising incomes and technological progress are the main ingredients of change, we may expect them to assert themselves whether the institutional framework be called socialist or capitalist.

To say this, however, is not to deny a specific point. I take it that, when Tsuru speaks of socialist countries, he wishes to include Soviet Russia among them. If this be the case, I am willing to admit that the government system that exists in the Soviet Union constitutes an effective hindrance to an industrial flight from the city, as I have described it in the foregoing paragraphs.

Let me digress for a moment. The industrial laborer in New

Hampshire finds very modern shopping centers, which include large supermarkets, erected in the midst of forests and lakes. In addition, the factory, anxious to keep the labor force satisfied, maintains connections with discount houses in order to provide the workers, and that perforce means everybody living in the area, with durable consumers' goods at low wholesale prices, thus introducing a new and very efficient system of distribution. This is part and parcel of the decentralized locational pattern. Such a pattern is still largely impossible in Soviet Russia — first of all because supermarkets and self-service systems presuppose a level of income that allows the individual family to own an automobile and a refrigerator. It is impossible, second, because out of a given per capita income in Russia a much larger share is devoted to investment and military expenditures, at the expense of consumption. This is the policy of the Soviet government, to which a decentralized industrial pattern, including decentralized living conditions of the labor force, is hardly acceptable. A dictatorial government prefers to see people live in large city blocks, in apartments through the walls of which sound travels freely (as one knows from multifarious references in Soviet novels), and where appropriate supervision of the inmates can be exercised by the appropriate authorities. It is doubtful, therefore, that those interested in urban policies in the United States have anything to learn from Russia; it is equally doubtful that Soviet Russia can afford to learn anything from recent developments in the United States.

It is true, of course, that these developments are still passing through their early stages. The dead hand of the past loosens its grip but slowly, and the conventional cities are going to be with us for a long time to come. Naturally, a great deal will depend upon the rate of economic growth in the United States. If we succeed in achieving and maintaining a high rate of growth, the process of decentralization will proceed at an accelerated pace because a growing portion of the accretions to output is likely to be produced in the new locational environment. In more than one sense, this process is the consummation of a chain of events which began some six or eight centuries ago in the medieval cities of Europe. The "circle" is no longer necessary. It is going to disappear, but it is unlikely to be forgotten. For it has served mankind well, and truly great things have been accomplished within its charmed circumference.

Part III

THE POLITICAL FRAMEWORK

9

Reflections on the Economic Aspects of Revolutions

⁓⁓⁓⁓

"Revolution" is a vague and equivocal term. In its common usage it seems to hinge, in an uncertain and sometimes bewildering fashion, on certain modes of behavior — such as violence — or on certain elusive interpretative concepts — such as discontinuity. Through the use of assimilative imagery, the term has been extended to processes of change in various fields, yielding *inter alia* kindred concepts of industrial, scientific, and technological revolutions. Similarly, the upward trend of commodity prices in the sixteenth century has been dramatized by describing it as a "price revolution." For present purposes, such extensions will be neglected, and the definitional difficulties inherent in the political mother concept will be circumvented by forcing a historical reference to events commonly recognized as revolutions to serve in lieu of a precise definition. Accordingly, the problems raised are those that have emerged from, or can be related to, actual historical experience, most notably in France and Russia.

To be manageable, the topic must be narrowed still further. There is no intention here to draw in the following what might be described as the "total economic balance of revolutions." The question whether revolutions "pay" must go unanswered. Still less should anything said here be regarded as an attempt at appraising the social and political effects of revolutions, either in themselves or in their impact upon the economy. The purpose is more modest: to concentrate on the agrarian sectors of the economies of countries passing through revolutionary convulsions and to express some groping thoughts on the causes and particularly the long-run economic effects of developments within those sectors and of the policies pursued with regard to them in the course of the revolutionary period.

While the subject of this essay is thus restricted, it seems useful to reflect on these matters against the broad background of the Marxian view of revolutions. It is a peculiarity of this view that it attempts, on the one hand, to establish a bond between economic interests and ideology and to present the former as the "real" cause of revolution; on the other hand, ideology is treated as a program for the revolution and, by the same token, as predetermining the effects of a successful revolution. In the process of evolution from feudalism to capitalism and from capitalism to socialism, revolution occupies its pre-established place, first as a bourgeois revolution and then as a socialist one. It is, then, the function of political revolutions to mark the transition from one economic system to another, and as such to be an integral part of economic history. There is no need in this context to dwell on the admixture of teleological elements in what presents itself as a causally determined system. Nor is it relevant to point out that noneconomic causes of revolutions may be most plausibly considered along with — or even in precedence of — economic causes. Neither a "complete" explanation of revolutions nor the general adequacy of the materialistic conception of history is at issue here. The usability of Marxian concepts is to be discussed only in relation to the limited area of agriculture and, as far as possible, in the light of concrete historical experience.

It seems natural, therefore, to begin by looking at the agrarian conditions that prevailed on the eve of the French Revolution and at developments in agrarian policy that took place during its course. Those conditions were described by the men of the revolution as "feudalism" and their own actions as abolition of the hated system. These semantic preferences are readily understandable. When Emperor Joseph II of Austria, in 1781, abolished by a famous edict the existing restrictions on the personal freedom of the Austrian peasants, he did not hesitate to present his actions as *Aufhebung der Leibeigen-*

schaft. Since the Austrian peasant of the eighteenth century had not been *owned* by the seignior in any meaningful sense of the word, the phrase was misleading and was aptly styled "a bit of imperial propaganda." The use of the term "feudalism" in speeches and edicts in France, from Mirabeau to Napoleon, was open to similar objections. What was feudalism? Was it a totality of very complex, very subtle, and very inconsistent relationships, both harmonious and antagonistic, embracing widely disparate and incommensurate elements — in short, Marc Bloch's *Société Féodale*? But no one needed a revolution to melt away the snow of yester-ages. A system based on land grants for the consideration of homage and service, with provision for analogous subinfeodations, of course, did not exist in eighteenth-century France. Was feudalism a system of seignorial rights over the labor or product of labor of enserfed peasantry? Such rights were more than a historical memory, but they had undergone a formidable transformation. The remnants of serfdom on the eve of the revolution were small indeed. The *corvée* obligations had been greatly reduced. To an overwhelming extent, the demesne had been divided among the peasants, and the labor services performed on the demesne had been commuted into money payments — even though a variety of contingent obligations and monopolistic compulsions were preserved and regional variations were very great.[1] There is little doubt that the nature of those payments and other obligations was not entirely alien to normal economic rent. Indeed, the distinction between "feudal" rent and "economic" rent is not easy to grasp. Was the peculiarity of feudal rent that it was fixed once and for all, as the *cens* certainly was? That would imply, in concrete historical terms, that the *cens* was a feudal rent *because* its real value was being reduced over the centuries by the falling value of money, denoting an improvement in the position of the peasant — surely, a curious criterion.

Or were the payments feudal because in so many cases the peasants were the "actual" owners of the land for which the payments were made? This conclusion of Loutchisky's research on the owner-

---

1. In general, as was clearly observed by Turgot, the peasants' burdens seemed to grow with the distance from Paris. See Otto Fengler, *Die Wirtschaftspolitik Turgots und seiner Zeitgenossen im Lichte der Wirtschaft des Ancien Régime* (Lucka, 1912), p. 13, and *Oeuvres de Turgot*, E. Daize and H. Dussard, eds., II (Paris, 1844), 68–69.

ship rights of the French peasants is generally accepted today.[2] As an "actual" owner, the French *censitaire* was a hereditary occupant of the land and was entitled to lease or sell it, even though such a transaction required payment of additional imposts to the seignior. Again, the argument is curiously paradoxical. It is apparently the very extent of the peasants' emancipation from the powers of the seigniors that defines the relationship as feudal. On the other hand, the degree to which a social phenomenon should be viewed in terms of its origins must depend on the extent of the change that has taken place in the interval. If the whole fief had been retained by the seignior as his demesne and the peasants converted into sharecroppers, the relation would not have been viewed as feudal, even though the origin of the seigniors' rights in the land may have been — and in many cases certainly was — feudal in the unambiguous juridical sense of the word.

Leaving aside specific budgetary discriminations in favor of the nobility and neglecting marginal survivals, it is not easy to say precisely what was feudal in the economic structure of prerevolutionary France. Normally, though not very explicitly, the position is taken that the liberation of the peasant from his obligation toward the seignior must be regarded as the abolition of feudalism because it implies the strengthening of the peasant economy and a strong and independent peasant farm is "unfeudal" by definition. There is every reason to remain aware of the difficulties inherent in such a definition. Assume, for instance, promulgation in the 1770's of a legal act circumscribing the rights of the *censitaires* roughly within the then existing scope and describing those rights as statutory tenant protection, thus limiting the seigniors' rights of ownership while leaving the determination of the rental payments to contractual agreements. Such an act would have placed the ownership rights of the seigniors on a new basis and, in addition, would have attached to them modern ideas of social legislation. From an economic point of view, it would be difficult to find anything feudal in this arrangement. It must be noted, however, that the rents agreed upon under such conditions most likely would have been greatly in excess of the "feudal pay-

2. J. Loutchisky, *L'Etat des classes agricoles en France sur la veille de la Révolution* (Paris, 1911).

ments." Such deterioration in the position of the peasants and the obverse improvement in that of the seigniors would have constituted the only economic change vis-à-vis the feudal situation. We obviously move on very uncertain ground. Nevertheless let us, for the sake of the argument, accept the conventional way of equating creation of an independent peasantry with the abolition of feudalism. In fact, it is primarily this conception of the historical process that underlies the view that the French Revolution, a bourgeois revolution, stands as a historical landmark on the road from feudalism to capitalism.

Before we explore the further implications of this position, a few words may be said on the forces that must be held responsible for the agrarian antiseignorial policies in France. There is on record a long and persistent controversy about how far popular misery should be included among causes of the revolution. As is true of most long-lived debates, the opposing views are in reality never mutually exclusive. It is true that the position of the French peasantry in the eighteenth century was much better than it had been in preceding periods. It is also true that it was a good deal more favorable than the position of the peasantry in most, if not all, other countries on the European continent. On the other hand, the standards of living were low, and it was not very difficult for postrevolutionary historians like Taine to gather a sufficient number of illustrations, which in the minds of readers in the nineteenth century added up, somewhat unhistorically, to an impressive mosaic picture of abysmal misery.[3] More importantly, it is impossible to deny the findings of Labrousse that a general economic deterioration in the last prerevolutionary decade made the economy very vulnerable to the crisis, which began in the second half of 1788.[4] The so-called feudal or seignorial reaction, resulting *inter alia* from the revisions of the manor rolls (*terroirs*) and from attempted revivals of some claims that had fallen into desuetude, may have further contributed to the deterioration in not entirely negligible measure. De Tocqueville did not have the benefit of Labrousse's findings, and he did not attribute exaggerated importance to the restoration of hunting rights, the renewed insistence on observation of

3. H. Taine, *Les Origines de la France contemporaine,* II, "L'Ancien Régime" (Paris, 1910), bk. V, chaps. 1, 2.

4. C. E. Labrousse, *La Crise de l'économie française à la fin de l'ancien régime et au début de la Révolution,* I (Paris, 1943), xxxix–xl.

banality privileges, the *triage* or *cantonnement* encroachments upon the commons, and other developments of this kind. But he had a truly magnificent grasp of the mechanics of discontent. He understood that it was economic prosperity itself that hastened the advent of the revolution. He knew that "it is not always by going from bad to worse that one tumbles into a revolution. It happens most often that a people after having suffered most oppressive laws, without complaint and perhaps even without awareness, turns vehemently against them once the pressure has begun to lighten." [5] This profound insight, which incidentally it is useful to keep in mind in judging many a situation of our own time, should have sufficed to explain the extent of the peasants' discontent on the eve of the revolution — without any further reference to the subversive ideas of the age and the possible role of the country lawyer, let alone the village priest, in spreading them. But De Tocqueville's view is powerfully reinforced by modern research. Once the alienation of which he speaks had taken place and begun to generate discontent, any downward turn of the path of well-being was bound to exacerbate the feelings of ire and disaffection. It is therefore not at all surprising that in the streams of discontent whose cascading confluence brought the flood of revolution, the mass movements of the peasantry played a decisive role. As Georges Lefebvre has it, "the peasant uprising is one of the most distinctive features of the Revolution in France." [6] The attitude of the revolting peasants was an essential determinant of the dramatic events on the night of the fourth of August, when the ideas of the Enlightenment provided as much illumination as the distant glare of the burning chateaux. It was this attitude that after August 10, 1792, and even more so after June 2, 1793, led to abolition without compensation of all the seignorial rights that contemporaries were pleased to describe as feudal.

Still, it is only one side of the picture. For the French Revolution is said to be a bourgeois rather than a peasant revolution. Much of the stress on the prosperity of the eighteenth century, and the somewhat reduced emphasis on popular misery in the works of such historians as Jean Jaurès and Albert Mathiez, comes precisely from viewing the

5. *L'Ancien régime et la Révolution*, E. Pognon and J. Dumont, eds. (Paris, n.d.), p. 238.
6. *The Coming of the French Revolution* (New York, 1960), p. 113.

revolution as the triumphant advent to power of a rapidly rising and economically very successful class. There can be little doubt that the agrarian legislation of the French Revolution and the structure of agriculture that emerged from it differed in some respects from what they would have been if the peasants themselves, rather than the "friends of the people" in the Jacobin Club, had written the texts. It is true, as Jaurès says, that the urban leaders of the revolution were at times afraid of peasant violence and sought to moderate and restrain it.[7] But it was the town, rather than the country, that was responsible for some radical changes in the organization of agricultural production. For the bulk of the peasantry, while abolishing the privileges of the seigniors, would have preferred to preserve the manifold communal features and collective usages inherent in the prerevolutionary agrarian system. In a sense, then, some obstacles to the introduction of technological progress in agriculture were removed.

It is at least doubtful to what extent this outcome was produced by the economic interests of the bourgeoisie. Was the set of values that dictated the Jacobins' policies reducible to those interests? If so, it was certainly not in the direct manner in which the moral indignation of the peasants over seignorial encroachments was reducible to, or derivative from, *their* economic interests. The peasants' economic discontent and the economic discontent of the urban middle class do not seem to be elements of quite the same order. Obviously, many a knotty problem must be solved before concepts such as bourgeois ideology, economic interests of the bourgeoisie, Jacobin policies, and bourgeois revolution have been rendered operationally manageable and have been combined into a clearly articulated whole. For the limited purposes of this essay, it may suffice to have pointed to those difficulties and, for the rest, to accept the vague concepts of bourgeois revolution and bourgeois agrarian policies, just as we have accepted the uncertain and ambiguous concept of feudalism. The question then is to what extent the revolutionary policy of abolishing the feudal system — for which the peasants fought and which the bourgeoisie put on the statute book — was a favorable condition for the post-revolutionary development of French capitalism. It seems fair to say that there is a widespread readiness to answer the question in the

7. *Anthologie de Jean Jaurès*, Louis Levy, ed. (London, 1947), p. 114.

affirmative — particularly in Marxian analyses of the period. In fact, the case of France is regarded as a paradigm, a general model from which inferences for other countries can be drawn. The most impressive instance is the discussion of Italian economic development in the nineteenth century.

A few years ago the able Italian historian, Rosario Romeo, surveyed some recent contributions by Marxian scholars to the history of the Italian Risorgimento and its aftermath.[8] Romeo was struck by the virtual unanimity with which the relative weakness of capitalist development in nineteenth-century Italy was attributed to the failure of the left wing in the Risorgimento movement to emulate the Jacobin example — by abolishing large-scale agrarian ownership and establishing a strong landowning peasant class that would have provided powerful popular support for the Italian bourgeoisie. It was claimed that the Italian bourgeoisie's coming to power (*andata al potere*) was not preceded or accompanied by recourse to the people (*andata al popolo*) in the form of a far-reaching agrarian reform. Accordingly, the bourgeoisie proved unable to create for the nation an efficient political structure, unencumbered by local particularism on the one hand and cosmopolitan catholicism on the other. Without such a framework, the economic growth of the country was slow and Italian capitalism fell far short of its potentialities. This thesis, which goes back to the influential writings of Antonio Gramsci,[9] imputes far-reaching consequences to a specific difference between the French Revolution and the Italian Risorgimento, to wit, the fact that the movement for national unification in Italy missed its opportunity to become a bourgeois revolution. A prerequisite for capitalist development failed to materialize. The Risorgimento remained "une révolution manquée."

It is nothing if not amazing to observe the ease with which generalizations of this sort are accepted without much curiosity about how they can be tested, as well as about the probable results of such tests. In fact, the volume of empirical material that is ignored in such exercises in comparative history is considerable. Even with regard to

8. *Risorgimento e capitalismo* (Bari, 1959).
9. *Il Risorgimento* (Turin, 1949).

seignorial rights before the French Revolution, one should not over-look the cases where the existence of such rights permitted a more efficient utilization of the available land resources. The cases of the seigniors' leasing timber-cutting rights in the forests or grazing rights in the commons to wealthy and enterprising tenants frequently brought about exploitation of forest and pasture lands that was more rational and more productive, even though it was introduced under the cover of "feudal" privileges.[10] Lefebvre was quite correct in stressing the "conservative" aspects of the agrarian revolution of 1789 in France. "The peasant destroyed the feudal regime, but he consolidated the agrarian structure of France." [11] He might well have added that in getting rid of the feudal regime the peasants *uno actu* got rid of economic phenomena usually described as capitalistic. The neat dichotomy of feudalism and capitalism is decidedly blurred when one descends from the heights of unduly dogmatic conceptualizations to the lower levels of abstraction.

There is no doubt that the picture of the revolution's introducing capitalism into France would be much more convincing if French economic development in the century following the revolution were characterized by brisk and steady growth. That, however, was not the case, particularly in the long interval between the end of the Napoleonic wars and the advent to power of Napoleon III. With one reservation, the period of both the Bourbon Restoration and the so-called Bourgeois Monarchy must be regarded as one of relative stagnation.[12] The 1850's brought a spurt of rapid economic development, most notably in the fields of railroad building and manufac-

10. Georges Lefebvre, "La Révolution française et les paysans," *Études sur la Révolution française* (Paris, 1954), p. 256.

11. *Ibid.*, p. 257.

12. A study by Jan Marczewski, "Some Aspects of the Economic Growth of France, 1660–1958," *Economic Development and Cultural Change*, IX (April 1961), 369–386, casts a different light on the course of French economic development, suggesting in particular a relatively high rate of growth between 1825 and 1844. This result must cause surprise, since it is at variance with much of the quantitative and qualitative information available thus far. As long as the raw materials underlying the calculations and the calculations themselves, including the derivations of the weights used, have not been published, one must confine oneself to a reference to Marczewski's study. Nevertheless, it may be in order to add that, even if one were to accept his data as impeccably correct, the rates of growth communicated would still be below those reached for comparable periods in either England or Germany.

turing; but the upsurge could not be sustained, and the French industrial economy continued at a rather slow pace until some acceleration occurred in the years immediately preceding the outbreak of war in 1914.

What are the causes of this unimpressive performance? Clearly, it is implausible to explain a complex phenomenon of retardation continuing over a very long period by reference to one or two decelerating factors. The range of such factors may well extend from the pattern of resource endowment to the scale of preferences of a housewife in Paris or Dijon. Still, in reviewing them, it is impossible to overlook the conditions in French agriculture. There can be no doubt that the French family farm deserves a place of distinction in the array of hindrances and handicaps placed in the path of French economic development.

First of all, the French farms proved a very inadequate source of labor supply for the cities. The French farmer clung to his land. When torn away from it, he would move to the next local town, still eschewing a distant and irrevocable migration and always watching for opportunities for return to the land. It is not surprising that poetry in France has produced nothing comparable to Goldsmith's *Deserted Village* or to Verhaeren's melancholy vision of the dying countryside in Belgium ("la plaine est morne et morte et la ville la mange."). The French exodus from the land was very small throughout the whole first half of the nineteenth century. It did accelerate during the century's second half, but at no time did it become in the least comparable to the *Landflucht*, the rush from the large estates in East Elbia, of embittered landless laborers in search of better and fairer lives in the coal mines and the steel mills of the Ruhr Valley. At the same time, for a number of reasons closely connected with revolutionary and Napoleonic legislation, the desire to purchase additional land always seemed to rank highest in determining the economic decisions of the French peasantry. Thus, its proverbial thrift meant abstention from buying additional consumers' goods; yet little of the savings was used for the acquisition of capital goods such as machinery and fertilizers in order to intensify the processes of agricultural production. As a result, the French peasantry not only failed to aid industrial development by providing it with cheap and disciplined labor (as did the Junker estates in Prussia); it also failed to act as a large and growing market for industrial products.

One must beware of attributing everything in the agricultural structure of nineteenth-century France to the revolution. It is certainly true, as we have intimated, that the French Revolution in many respects simply marked the last stage of a development that had been continuing for centuries. But this point serves, if anything, to reinforce an inescapable conclusion: to further the cause of economic progress in France an entirely new direction in agrarian policies was needed. Hence, the positive economic effects of the revolution must be sought outside the sphere of agrarian relations. Abolition of internal customs and other economic measures designed to produce the economic unification of the country are probably most relevant in this respect, even though there, too, the revolution largely continued the policy of the absolute monarchy that it had overthrown, as Napoleon in his *Code Civil* continued the policy of the revolution.[13]

13. It is interesting that Engels draws a sharp contrast between the French Revolution and the English Revolution of 1688. The latter, he says, resulted in a compromise between the landed interests and the capitalists. It preserved the continuity of the common law. In France, he goes on, the battle was fought to the bitter end; the last vestiges of feudalism were swept away, the break with tradition was complete, and a masterly adaptation of the legal framework to modern capitalist conditions was created through the *Code Napoléon* — Friedrich Engels, *Die Entwicklung des Sozialismus von der Utopie zur Wissenschaft* (Berlin, 1951), pp. 25–26. It is difficult to interpret the postrevolutionary economic histories of the two countries in the light of that contrast. While France gloried in the proper prerequisites for economic development, England excelled in the thing itself. In one of his novels, Italo Calvino speaks of "un paese dove si verificano sempre le cause e non gli effetti." France seems indeed to have been a country well endowed with causes but sadly lacking in effects. Marx, of course, kept open a dialectical loophole: "The roots which the small scale farm had struck into the French soil deprived feudalism of all nutritional supplies." "But in the course of the 19th century" a change took place. The young and vigorous peasant farm (*die jugendfrische Parzelle*) turned into the old and decrepit peasant farm (*die überlebte Parzelle*), an easy prey for the capitalist usurer. See Marx, *Der achtzehnte Brumaire des Louis Bonaparte* (Stuttgart, 1914), pp. 105–108. The peasantry was seen as having assured the predominance of capitalism, only to be subjugated and swept away by the latter. "*Code Napoléon* has become a code of distraint and foreclosure" (*ibid.*). But the French peasantry refused to accept the dialectical solution. It remained on the stage, thus forcing the Marxian interpretation to shift its ground rather unmetaphorically. For if one looks at modern Marxian literature on the subject, it appears that, rather than to abandon a good hypothesis because of obdurate facts, it has become customary simply to abstract from the English Channel and to regard the French Revolution as a natural

It is much less certain how we should appraise the economic effects of the changed social and political position of the bourgeoisie. It is easy to repeat a familiar sequence: The bourgeoisie is the class vitally interested in capitalist development; the revolution increased the power of the bourgeoisie in France; ergo, the revolution enhanced the prospects for capitalist development. However great the suggestive force of that syllogism, it appears to be a fact that the Bourgeois Monarchy was characterized by a most narrow-minded economic policy. The bourgeoisie was in power or at least stood close enough to the seat of power, but it was perfectly content to perpetuate in France a hothouse atmosphere in which antiquated and inefficient enterprises were maintained at high cost, while new plants and enterprises lacked both the sting of competition and unobstructed connection with foreign countries for the importation of capital goods and know-how. Adam Smith knew well how shortsighted and detrimental the behavior of vested interests can be when they are using political power for economic purposes. He would not have been impressed by stolid syllogistic exercises; nor would he have been surprised by a historical experience that was clearly at variance with those exercises. If these connections are less clearly understood than they should be, the reason probably lies in the unwillingness to define "capitalism" in such a way as to make falsification of statements about it possible. If capitalism is defined as a system based on private ownership of capital goods and the existence of hired labor which is divorced from ownership of capital goods, then it is certain that all or nearly all industrial growth in nineteenth-century Europe was capitalist growth. It is then some quantitative yardstick — be it growth of national income, or industrial output, or capital stock, over-all or per capita, or the numbers of gainfully employed — that must be taken as a measure of capitalist development. It is by a standard of this sort that the capitalist development in France appears to have been disappointingly slow.

It is precisely by quantifying his concepts that Rosario Romeo was able to place the Gramsci thesis within an operational framework and to demonstrate that the failure to carry out an agrarian reform in

---

political counterpart of the Industrial Revolution in England. In this way, one could, in good conscience, forget the negative effects of the revolution upon France's economic development.

Italy tended to aid rather than to obstruct the capitalist development in Italy, inasmuch as "unreformed" large-scale agriculture provided a basis for the creation of social overhead capital in the Italian economy, to an extent that a reformed peasant economy never would have been able to match. Romeo may have exaggerated the significance of the economic upswing that occurred in Italy after the unification. By the same token, he may have exaggerated the extent of the contribution the large estate owners made to the capital formation of the period. There can be no doubt, however, that Romeo was doubly correct in putting the problem into a form in which the arguments become refutable and in making very plausible, again in quantitative terms, what an agrarian reform would have meant for the economic development of Italy.

It can be argued that this discussion applies at least to some aspects of the revolutions that occurred in Russia during this century. While abolishing personal subjection (serfdom or slavery) of the peasants and bestowing upon the peasantry ownership rights to part of the land that had formerly belonged to the seigniors, the emancipation of the peasantry in 1861 preserved and, in fact, reinforced a number of archaic communal traits in the Russian agricultural structure. In addition, land allotments were small, and the financial burdens placed upon the peasants very heavy. The subsequent increase in population inevitably led to further deterioration. For about a quarter of a century after the emancipation, Russia developed at a fairly slow rate, building its railroad network and expanding the scope of its industrial activities. Then, from the second half of the 1880's on, came a period of rapid industrial growth. Proceeding largely under the impulse and tutelage of the government, the great upsurge exerted a very considerable pressure upon the standard of living of the Russian peasantry and, to some extent, possibly even caused some depletion of agricultural capital. As the new century began, there was a body of large and rapidly growing discontent among the peasantry. The numerous local disorders culminated in the general cataclysm of the 1905 revolution.

Again, I do not intend to ascribe that revolution to economic causes alone. The points that must be stressed here involve the similarities and dissimilarities between the Russian and the French revolutions. Peasant unrest, no doubt, constitutes a common element, but its causes appear to differ considerably. If the French peasant rebellions were the complex result of both the long-run progress and the short-run economic crises, the Russian peasantry suffered from the combined effect of the emancipation settlement and subsequent government policies designed to bring about the industrial growth of the country. Clearly, the relationship between peasant discontent and economic development was more intimate and complex in Russia than in France. In the long run, economic development in Russia could have been expected to lead to improvement in the position of the peasantry. But in the short run, it was precisely the economic development of the country that added so greatly to the burden of the peasantry. In France before 1789, the cessation of economic progress contributed to the growth of the peasants' discontent. It is true that the depression of 1900 cut short the great spurt of Russian industrialization in the 1890s. Yet the revolution of 1905, to the extent that it was a peasant rebellion, was a protest, not against the depression, but against the prosperity that had preceded it. Whatever may have been the role of the weak and disorderly French budget, with its inequitable tax system, in bringing about the revolution, the effect is hardly comparable with that of the Russian budget, which was neither weak nor disorderly at the turn of the century. But its pressure upon the income levels of the peasantry was formidable, and in its effects even assumed at times the nature of capital levies. Also in France, as in Russia, industry was favored by both sides of the budget, and as a result some capital movements from agriculture into industry are said to have taken place before 1789. It would, however, be a gross exaggeration to depict French industrial progress in the eighteenth century as proceeding at the expense of the French peasantry.

In this sense, the Russian peasant's attitude toward economic development was a great deal more negative than that of the French. The latter was hurt by certain forms of large-scale exploitation in agriculture, but he could watch economic development outside agriculture with equanimity and, in fact, with satisfaction. The Russian peasant was grievously affected by the industrialization of the country, even though his hostility was directed against the traditional enemy — the landowning gentry — and expressed itself in time-honored fashion by acts of arson, forest destruction, illegal grazings, and high-handed land seizures. At the same time, to a much greater degree than had been the case in France, the vast majority of the Russian peasantry was anxious to preserve its communal organization of land tenure. That organization, with its periodic repartitions of land and underlying ideas of equality and collective ownership, was even more "unmodern" than had been the open-field farming in the manorial villages of medieval Europe, where rotation of strips among the village households was not practiced. It would seem therefore that, at least as far as the role of the peasantry goes, there is little justification for describing the 1905 revolution as a "bourgeois revolution."

It is indubitably true that much of what happened during the upheavals of 1905–06 can be meaningfully characterized as attempts by leaders of commercial and industrial groups to obtain for themselves a greater degree of influence upon governmental processes. The problem, however, is the use they would have made of their power with regard to the country's economic policy in general and agrarian policy in particular. In this context, it is quite significant that, after the revolution, steps designed to bring about the abolition of the Russian field commune were carried out by Stolypin. He was the man who had engineered a coup d'état in defiance of the constitution that the emperor had granted at the height of the revolutionary cataclysm; it was his energy that stamped out the remnants of revolutionary fires, and it was he, more than anyone else, who was responsible for maintaining the system of absolutism under the new veneer of pseudo-constitutionalism. On the other hand, it was the representatives of Russian liberalism, in particular the leaders of the so-called Cadet Party, who fought Stolypin's measure, because it was designed to destroy the egalitarian character of Russian villages and to favor the economically strong elements among the peasantry at the expense of the weaker majority.[14] The French bourgeoisie, while liberating the peasantry from various burdens, could insist on abolition of communalism in agriculture. Such a course was not readily open to groups

14. See the speeches on the subject by P. N. Milyukov, which he made in the Third Duma. *Gosudarstvennaya Duma, tretii sozyv, stenograficheskiye otchety* (The Third State Duma, Stenographic Records), 1907–1908, first session, part I, November 16, 1907 (St. Petersburg, 1908), p. 301; and third session, part I, October 10, 1909 (St. Petersburg, 1910), p. 22.

that can be fairly described as representing the Russian bourgeoisie. The reasons were partly ideological: whatever the economic interests may have been, they could not obliterate the strong feeling of compassion for the peasantry and the traditional respect for the principle of collectivity and egalitarianism. Furthermore, weighty practical reasons militated against such a policy, because no political party anxious to obtain popular support could possibly commit itself to a position against which the sentiments of the peasantry were so violently engaged.

The economic effects of the 1905 revolution in the area under discussion were essentially twofold. A considerable alleviation in the financial position of the peasantry took place owing to the cancellation of land-redemption payments, abolition of joint responsibility of the villages for tax obligations, and other measures. In fact, the removal of corporal punishment within the peasant estate — which followed an analogous measure for the gentry estate with a lag of about one hundred and fifty years — must also be regarded, unironically, as a measure of fiscal policy. For that form of punishment and the threat thereof had been traditionally used to hurry tardy taxpayers. Thenceforth, it certainly was more difficult for the government to continue its policy of forced-draft industrialization based, as it was, on keeping the peasants under strong and steady pressure. On the other side of the ledger stood, first, the abolition of the various statutory discriminations against the peasant estate and, second, the acts directed against the field commune. Measures of this sort no doubt had a positive aspect as far as economic development was concerned. They tended to increase the supply of labor available to the growing industry and, in the long run, would have led to improvements in methods of cultivation and to increases in agricultural productivity. Even though the revolution, in a very real and central sense, was a protest against previous industrial development, what happened in its course or as its consequence thus tended to favor subsequent industrial evolution.

It is far from easy, therefore, to draw a balance of the effects of the 1905 revolution and to append to it a simple label like "bourgeois revolution." At least as far as Stolypin's reform was concerned, the Prince of Denmark had once more absented himself from *Hamlet*: as said before, the most radical "bourgeois" measure of doing away with archaic survivals in agriculture was adopted in the teeth of "bourgeois" disapproval. Nor is it without interest that a study of the motivations of the authors of the reform reveals with considerable clarity that the probable effect of the reform upon industrial development was the least important consideration in their minds. The measure was adopted for political purposes on the basis of a very disappointing political experience. The field commune had been considered by the government as the impregnable fortress of rural conservatism, a pillar of the throne. Yet during the revolution the wildest excesses against gentry property occurred precisely in the areas where the field commune predominated. Stolypin understood the lesson. Like so many agrarian reforms in other countries, Stolypin's reform was carried out without any thought of its impact upon the country's industrial or "capitalist" development. The measure may qualify as a bourgeois measure, but it was dictated neither by the economic interests of the bourgeoisie nor by a desire on the part of the government to favor those interests.

Finally, another consideration may be in order. The years between 1906 and the outbreak of World War I were a period when — after the caesura of revolution — the industrial growth of the country resumed and proceeded at a fairly high rate. The government's contribution to the process was astonishingly small, particularly in comparison with its decisive role during the last decade of the nineteenth century. But can this revival of industrial activities be regarded as a result of the revolution? This view seems very questionable indeed. Probably nothing was so important in causing the postrevolutionary economic upsurge in Russia as the legacy of the preceding upsurge, during which capital stock had been accumulated, labor skills acquired, and labor discipline "internalized," while the entrepreneurs learned to think in terms of higher time horizons and to use rational and more complex cost calculations. No one can study the performance of the Russian economy in those two periods without feeling that between them there occurred something in the nature of a graduation, on the part of Russia's industrial economy, from the government-instituted — or at least government-supervised and government-subsidized — school of industrialization. By comparison, the favorable effects of the revolution appear to be of little weight, particularly if one sets off against them its negative effects. Among the latter, in addition to the previously mentioned reduction of the government's capability to tax the peasantry, one must mention the necessity to provide, in the postrevolutionary budgets, for a greatly increased service burden. For large loans had been contracted in order to cover the high cost of suppressing the revolutionary disorders. The result was the deflationary policy inaugurated after the revolution, which contrasted so strongly with the openhanded habits of expenditure in the 1890's.[15] We may say, therefore, that after the revolution the vastly decreased reliance of Russian industrial growth upon government aid and encouragement was, in part, a natural process; in part, however, it was the unintended consequence of revolutionary disturbances. To that extent, the revolutionary effects included a rate of industrial growth that was lower than could have, and probably would have, been the case in the absence of revolution. In the long run, it is true, Stolypin's reform could have been expected to help sustain Russia's economic growth and also further to normalize its character by strengthening the peasants' demand for industrial products. But the long run was cut short by the outbreak of World War I.

Within the area of problems with which this essay is concerned, the picture does not, therefore, favor any simple conceptual convention. Neither the agrarian policies of the French revolution of 1789 nor those of the Russian revolution of 1905 can be properly described as "bourgeois" revolutions directed against feudalism and carried out by the bourgeoisie in the interest of the bourgeoisie to further the development of capitalism. On the other hand, it is possible to suggest that in some respects at least the Russian revolution of 1905 showed more pronounced positive tendencies for economic development than its great predecessor. The reason is likely to lie in the varying degrees of relative economic backwardness in the two countries at the times of their revolutions. This writer has ventured the proposition that the processes of modern industrialization are the richer and the more complex the higher the degree of backwardness in a given country on the eve of its great spurt of industrialization, which, if one wishes, may be called its industrial revolution. Arguing by unwonted reverse analogy from an economic to a political phenomenon, we may hazard

15. It was the policy of what V. N. Kokovtsov called "budgetary modesty . . . the only correct policy for a country living beyond its means." *Gosudarstvennaya Duma*, November 27, 1907, p. 612. Kokovtsov, at that time Stolypin's Minister of Finance, became in 1911 his successor as Premier.

a similar proposition about the economic attainments of political revolutions: the more backward a country, the more likely it is that a political revolution will carry out, or at least attempt to carry out, a larger program of economic measures. This expectation is partly the result of the fact that, in an advanced country with a rich prerevolutionary history, a great many measures of modernization are adopted in the course of gradual evolution. In a more backward country, the poverty of the preceding history has left a legacy of *réformes manquées* for the revolution to put into effect.

This proposition is reinforced by the consideration that, in a backward country, successful execution of industrialization policies requires more than simply introducing the institutional framework that suffices for the purposes of industrialization in an advanced country. It would be attractive, though in the nature of an excursus, to illustrate this relationship by a somewhat indirect personal comparison of two historical figures placed in a similar position vis-à-vis the approaching revolutionary storm: Turgot and Witte. It must suffice here to indicate the main points of such a comparison. The personal differences between the two men need not be overlooked. Voltaire would not have called Witte — as he called Turgot — the most learned man of his age. For Witte's original contribution to economic doctrines was nil, while Turgot's doctrinal influence extended far into the nineteenth century. But there is also an impressive set of similarities. Both statesmen towered high above their contemporaries in vision, resolution, and resourcefulness. They both tried to meet the threats of revolution. Each failed and was eliminated from the scene by a weak and incompetent monarch about the same number of years before the fall of the dynasty provided belated justification of his foresight and his warnings.

And yet one must still discern the vast difference in the magnitude and complexity of the respective tasks. We may assume that Turgot's six edicts of 1776 would have gone far toward reducing discontent. A further arrangement concerning partial redemption of seignorial rights probably would have greatly diminished the likelihood of a successful revolution. A merely negative policy of abolition might well have sufficed. By contrast, Witte, in his economic policy, had to do a great deal more than simply to remove obstructions from the path of economic progress. We may say that, in a general political situation resembling Turgot's, he had to pursue policies strongly reminiscent of Colbert's. Those policies are costly, and their fruits ripen slowly. It is not only that, in trying to forestall the revolution in the long run, one increases its danger in the short run. In order to carry out positive policies of this type, certain negative measures, most desirable in themselves, must be postponed.

Witte's attitude toward the obshchina is a case in point. In his Memoirs, he explains at some length his changing views on the subject. Originally, he says, he was favorably disposed toward the institution because he regarded it as an ancient product of the Russian or Slavic genius. He goes on to say that Bunge, his predecessor — one step removed — in the Ministry of Finance, explained to him the economic drawbacks of the field commune and caused him to change his mind on the subject. Yet he did nothing to reduce the scope of the institution. On the contrary, he supported, in the middle 1890's, a measure designed to stop up a loophole and prevent peasants of certain description from leaving the field commune. In fact, he went so far as to persuade the very reluctant emperor of the usefulness of the measure.[16] Witte himself tends to explain his actions as the result of inexperience. It is, however, much more plausible to assume that the Minister of Finance did not dare abolish the field commune precisely because of his ambitious budgetary policy. The commune was in fact a fiscal agent of the government and played an important part in the process of tax collection. In a backward country with an inefficient bureaucracy, a considerable lapse of time was required before a modern tax-collecting mechanism could be built up. In addition, the change presupposed a protracted struggle between the Ministry of Finance and the Ministry of Interior, whose police force was in charge of collecting taxes from the communes.[17] We must once more conclude that economic development in a very backward country

16. S. Yu. Witte, *Vospominaniya* (Memoirs; Leningrad, 1924), I, 446, 455–458.

17. It was only toward the end of his service as Minister of Finance that Witte stated that the apparatus of his ministry was able to collect the taxes from the rural population without having to rely on the help of the communes and the institution of joint responsibility. It is also of interest that, despite Witte's conversion and his many statements on the economic importance of individualism, his criticism of Stolypin's legislation in the State Council was severe. In his memoirs, he predicted that "much innocent blood will be shed" in consequence of that legislation. *Vospominaniya*, II, 343.

is a most complex matter. To expect political revolutions in such countries to exercise simple and straightforward economic effects is even more unrealistic than are similar expectations for more advanced countries — in which the economies are so much more complicated, but problems of policy *per contra* so much simpler.

We must still say a few words on the Russian revolution of 1917 and its economic aftermath. In every real sense, the overthrow of the imperial regime and the subsequent establishment of the Soviet dictatorship were the results of the war. As Witte — and probably Stolypin — understood so clearly, one thing that the Russian government as it emerged from the revolution of 1905 could *not* afford was to engage in major military conflicts. It is true that, after 1905–06, the process of Russian westernization in the economic field proceeded continuously and smoothly, as never before. Still, a number of years of a steady rate of growth were needed to raise the population's income above levels conducive to passive resignation or violent protest — and to continue the gradual process of transferring the gentry's lands to peasant hands before the muzhiks' craving for more land would cease to result in periodic riots and rebellions. For the time being, the tensions, while diminishing, remained great. In addition, the political structure was extremely shaky. There is little doubt that the question of widening the rights of the Duma at the expense of the monarch would soon have become acute and that it would have required an enormous application of skill and wisdom to solve the problem without skidding into another revolutionary crisis. In the circumstances, it was utter folly and incredible shortsightedness to view the war in the light of the brief outburst of patriotic sentiment that marked its beginning; yet we may assume that this view played a large part in the minds of the emperor and those in his immediate environment.[18] The illusion persisted despite the lessons of the Russo-Japanese War.[19]

18. It is revealing indeed to recall Nicholas II's words to one of his provincial governors at the beginning of the Russo-Japanese War: "Now you will find your work to be much easier." He went on to explain to the governor, who did not at once grasp the emperor's meaning, that subversive tendencies were bound to be choked in the resurgence of patriotism. S. D. Urusov, *Zapiski gubernatora* (A Governor's Notes), *Kishinev, 1903–1904* (Berlin, n.d.), p. 210.

19. How much of an illusion it was has been vividly recalled recently by General Spiridovich, a police officer who, in 1914 and thereafter, was in immediate charge

The revolution of 1917 in St. Petersburg in its first moments resembled *la guerre des farines* of Turgot's times. But, once started, all the disappointments and grievances, all the resentment and discontent broke into the open and with them appeared all the problems that, in peacetime, were susceptible of gradual solutions but now demanded immediate and radical settlement. This reaction was particularly true of the land question. It was not the land hunger of the peasants that had caused the revolution but, once the old powers had fallen, the land problem overshadowed everything else and, in particular, rendered impractical the continuation of the war. If the war was to continue, immediate action by the Provisional Government would be necessary to nationalize all gentry lands and to keep them in an undivided fund until after the end of the war, when an orderly division could take place. This solution, which is so readily suggested by easy hindsight, would have presented the administration of the fund with problems of economic exploitation of the gentry estates that probably were insoluble or nearly insoluble in terms of the practical possibilities of the moment. At any rate, no such dams were erected by the Provisional Government, and the seizure of gentry lands by the peasants — as well as mass desertions from the army by peasants who were eager to take part in that seizure — proceeded with an elemental force. This violent appropriation must be regarded as by far the most important economic consequence of the 1917 revolution. It was its approval and encouragement of this process that carried the Bolshevik Party to power in the fall of 1917.

What kind of revolution then occurred in Russia in 1917? Was it a bourgeois revolution? Or was it a socialist revolution? We can suggest that the radical change in the land-labor ratio in the peasant economy was bound to retard for a number of years, if not stop altogether, the flow of labor to nonagricultural employment. Strength-

of the emperor's personal security. The patriotic wave in 1914 never seemed to climb higher than it did in August 1914, when the imperial family, following the tradition for declarations of war, went to Moscow and participated in a number of ceremonies. Even at that solemn moment, Spiridovich's agents, spread through the dense crowds, brought to him a considerable number of "terse but expressive" popular sayings on the subject of the imperial family, particularly in relation to the ominous figure of Grigori Rasputin. A. I. Spiridovich, *Velikava Voyna i fevral'skaya revolyutsiya, 1914–1917 gg.* (The Great War and the February Revolution; (New York, 1960), I, 16–18.

ening the peasant economy was bound to affect the composition of the country's industrial output in favor of goods that may be described as "peasant harvest goods" and would have consisted primarily of mass consumers' goods and cheap farm implements. We might also describe such goods as "low-investment goods." The long-run effect, once the ravages of war and revolution were repaired, would have been to produce a perhaps steady, but fairly low, rate of economic development. In other words, in its very essence the revolutionary movements of 1917 deserve to be described as neither a bourgeois nor a socialist revolution but as a peasant revolution, even though the concept does not readily fit into conventional conceptual schemata. That is not to forget either the advent to power in November 1917 of a political party that regarded itself as a socialist party or the fact that, under the pressure of circumstances, that party proceeded to nationalize most of Russia's industrial and financial enterprises. Neither of those events would have justified regarding it as an emanation of "socialist revolution." The Bolshevik government throughout the 1920's can reasonably be considered a vicegerent, tolerated by the mass of the peasantry. The ownership conditions outside agriculture remained subject to change as the Bolshevik government — in a historical rather than constitutional sense — remained subject to recall.

It is only when Stalin successfully launched his policy of collectivization and superindustrialization that the historical period initiated in 1917 reached its termination. Rilke's prophecy with regard to the Russian peasantry — "Weit schreiten werden welche lange sassen in ihrer tiefen Dämmerung" — remained unfulfilled. For the march of the peasantry was stopped, and the effects of the peasant revolution of 1917 were undone by what Stalin himself once called a revolution from above and what, to all intents and purposes, amounted to a counterrevolution. One is free, if one desires, to describe that counterrevolution as a socialist revolution. Yet, before doing so, it may be useful to consider first that the house that Stalin built and that, despite some alterations, the Soviet dictatorship still inhabits has little in common, in its architecture and interior decoration, with the traditional concept of socialism as it was developed in the course of the nineteenth century. No less important is that, in carrying out his counterrevolution and embarking upon a policy of a high rate of investment, sustained far beyond what may have been justified by military threats from Germany, Stalin and his government were primarily moved by the mechanics of dictatorial power.

There is no doubt that Stalin's dictatorial counterrevolution resulted in a rate of industrial growth in Russia that was unprecedented in the country. And this is perhaps the note on which these reflections can be suitably ended: it seems to reinforce the conclusions that have forced themselves upon us throughout these pages. The economic meaning of such terms as "bourgeois" or "socialist" revolution and of their relationship to the subsequent course of economic change is most elusive. On the other hand, there is nothing ambiguous or elusive in the description of the French and Russian revolutions as "agrarian." In both countries, the peasants formed the mass of the population. May one not assume that in those conditions any popular movement against the established regimes was bound to fail, unless it not only enjoyed the support of the peasants but to a very large extent *was* a peasant movement? Assumptions of this kind may be accepted or rejected. However plausible, they are not part of the historical record. But it is a matter of historical record that the French and Russian revolutions went far toward satisfying the desires of the peasantry and that in so doing they placed serious obstacles in the path of subsequent industrial development. This conclusion appears to be valid whether that development is described as bourgeois or nonbourgeois, as capitalist or socialist. Historical processes are complex, and attempts to integrate the story of economic development with that of political revolutions are likely to fail, as soon as one moves from the realm of easy abstractions to more concrete levels.

The foregoing remarks have been confined primarily to French and Russian illustrations, with a side glance at Italy. It would be illuminating to evaluate the French and Russian experience against the background of economic development of those countries where, in the nineteenth century, agrarian policies were much better adjusted to the needs of industrialization. In particular, contrasting comparisons with England and (for a limited period) Germany would offer additional confirmation of the views expressed here. This task, however, must be reserved for another time.

I O

The Changeability of a Dictatorship

Dictatorship is destiny.

T HE following reflections have been occasioned by the Twenty-Second Congress of the Communist Party of the USSR (October 1961). The purpose is to try to grasp the nature and gauge the extent of the change between the Russia of today and the Russia of Stalin's time. Naturally, no more can be done within the scope of a brief essay than to indicate some of the areas that may be relevant in this connection and to arrive at some provisional conclusions. In looking for those areas, various curiosities and incongruities of the Moscow congress may serve as guiding beacons.

I

Some of these incongruities are more conspicuous than others. Thus, no one could possibly fail to notice the strange fate that befell the main business of the great gathering. Ostensibly, the congress had been convoked in order to discuss the new party program, "the program for building the Communist society." [1] Once more the vision of

Note. The present tense as used in this essay and the facts mentioned in it as current refer to the time of writing, that is, to the late fall of 1961. To repeat what has been said in the Introduction (pp. 2–3 above), no effort has been made to bring the story up to date. For the essay should be seen as an attempt to move, through contemporaneous analysis of the Soviet scene at an important juncture, to a more general explanatory framework, which then is further developed in the following essay (Chapter Eleven).

1. *Programma Kommunisticheskoy Partii Sovetskogo Soyuza* (Moscow, 1961), p. 6.

the ultimate goal was to be conjured up. The consummation of long yearnings, the redemption of ideological promises, the end justifying long and appalling miseries, were pronounced to be within the grasp of the living generation. Much time was indeed devoted to the subject. And yet this is hardly what the Twenty-Second Congress will be remembered for. There is little doubt that in the card catalogue of history the congress will be filed under the headings of "Critique of Stalin, Stalinists, and Stalinism" and "Power Struggle with China." The nakedness of the latter was somewhat disguised by leaves fallen from Albanian fig trees. The former, by contrast, was moved from the twilight of secret meetings into the bright sun of full publicity. The past and the present had vied with the future, and the day was theirs.

It is quite consistent with this result, though perhaps a trifle less obvious, that an attempt was made in the program and at the congress to extend the present into the future, as it were, by claiming that the great change to come required absence of change in the meantime. Stalin, it was revealed, had no correct conception of the prerequisites of a Communist society. He believed the road to be much shorter. In particular, he did not appreciate the necessity for first laying "the material-technical basis" for the Communist system. He did not understand that only "after having fully exhausted the progressive role of socialist principles was it possible to attain the full establishment of communist principles." [2]

As nearly as one can understand the meaning of such pronouncements, they purport to stress the necessity for continuing for the next twenty years the high rate of industrial growth and the stress on producers' goods, and for leaving essentially unchanged the very considerable inequalities in the income structure. Because Stalin failed to grasp those necessities, his last study on *The Economic Problems of Socialism*, once acclaimed as a work of genius, is now found to be woefully deficient and altogether unsuitable to "serve as the basis of the new program of the Communist Party of the Soviet Union." [3]

These strictures seem rather undeserved by the fallen idol. Stalin did specify a long list of preconditions that must be fulfilled — in accordance with Marx, he said — before "it will be possible to pass from the socialist formula . . . to the communist formula," and,

2. Speech by Mikoyan, *Pravda*, October 22, 1961, p. 7.
3. *Ibid.*

what is more, he steadfastly kept asserting the "law" according to which a higher rate of growth of output of producers' goods than of consumers' goods is a necessary condition of economic growth. "Without the predominant growth of producers' goods it is altogether impossible to achieve economic growth." [4] As a theoretical proposition, the law was sheer nonsense, since a positive rate of growth can conceivably be achieved with a zero (or even a negative) rate of net investment. But as a principle of practical action it was eminently important, expressing the will to continue the policy of investment for the sake of investment while keeping down the levels of consumption as much as possible.

It is true, of course, that after Stalin's death his successors were unable to continue Stalin's policy in all its grim severity. The struggle for power that went on behind the smoke screen of collective leadership forced the participants to court popular favor by conceding some increases in the output of consumers' goods. The Stalinist Malenkov, who promised to fulfill the Fifth Five-Year Plan for consumers' goods in four rather than five years, was overthrown by Khrushchev, allegedly because of Malenkov's failure to recognize the vital importance of heavy industry in the process of growth. But the anti-Stalinist Khrushchev continued Malenkov's policy of keeping the rate of growth of output of consumer's goods above that which had prevailed in the days of Stalin's rule. On the other hand, Khrushchev faithfully retained Stalin's policy of letting producers' goods grow faster than consumers' goods. According to the long-run estimates for the next two decades, the share of consumers' goods in total industrial output is scheduled to fall from 32.2 percent in 1960 to 25.7 percent in 1980. "Heavy industry," Khrushchev added, "always played and will continue to play the leading role in the growth of output." [5]

Almost exactly nine years before Khrushchev's performance at the Twenty-Second Congress, his hapless rival Malenkov, then the heir apparent of the Kremlin, was presenting the main address to the Nineteenth Congress. Stalin's previously mentioned study had appeared a short time before, and Malenkov's speech was interlarded with generous quotations from it. He stressed, therefore, the "pre-

4. Joseph Stalin, *The Economic Problems of Socialism* (New York, 1952), pp. 53, 61.

5. Khrushchev's speech, *Pravda*, October 19, 1961, p. 3.

dominant growth of producers' goods" and reminded the congress that "Comrade Stalin has issued insistent warnings against frivolous haste in the transition to higher economic forms without prior creation of necessary preconditions for such a transition." [6]

This time it was Khrushchev and Mikoyan who continued the traditional line. Neither criticism of Stalin's detailed views about the road to communism nor the addition of further "qualitative preconditions" (such as growing socialization of incomes) in the speeches of the present masters must be allowed to disguise a basic fact: an economy of high consumers' levels and general abundance would ill agree with the continued existence of totalitarian dictatorship.[7] Dictators have a vested and vital interest in keeping the elusive goal within sight but out of reach. This means that as the Soviet economy develops, more and more stringent preconditions for the advent of the communist society must be laid down. At the Twenty-Second Congress, Stalin was accused by Mikoyan of having unduly simplified the transition to communism. But if there was one thing for which Stalin could be trusted, it was for a fine sense of the mechanics of power. If he were still alive and in power, he could be relied upon to add some complications to the alleged simplifications and to see to it that the eternal goal would remain *on* the horizon but also would move *with* the horizon.

It is not my purpose to discuss the reasons for the savage vehemence with which the rulers of the Soviet state have turned against the past — which after all is also their own — and against some of their former associates. Continuation of the power struggle within the Communist Party, connections between the opposition to Khrushchev and the Chinese government, and above all the dire need of any dictatorship to have enemies to combat, to say nothing of rankling memories of past humiliations and rivalries — all these, severally and together, are some possible reasons for what happened

6. G. M. Malenkov, "Otchetnyi Doklad XIX S'ezdu Partii o rabote Tsentral'-nogo Komiteta VKP(b)" (Report to the Nineteenth Congress of the Party on the Work of the Central Committee of the All-Union Communist Party [Bolsheviks]), *Bol'shevik*, no 19 (October 1952), pp. 58, 60.

7. With regard to the qualitative preconditions, many a Soviet citizen must have wondered whether the prospect of receiving gratis from the government a variety of things, ranging from children's clothing to housing, implied an improvement in the standard of living or merely a further limitation of the freedom of choice.

after the 1961 congress. The ejection of Stalin's body (assuming that no mere import from Madame Tussaud's had been on exhibition in the mausoleum); the change of the name of a city, the battle for which has been deeply engraved into recent history as the great turning point of the last war; the revelation of some flagrant cases of inhuman cruelties committed by Stalin and his associates (even though what was presented was no more than a few well-selected samples, and the horrible statistics of murders in the cellars of the secret police and deaths in remote prison camps, which must run into many millions, have been withheld) — these events could not help capturing the imagination of the world. But the rapidly unfolding change in some areas must not blind us to its absence in others. The elements of stability are no doubt less dramatic, but they may be more important for grasping the nature of the present-day government in Soviet Russia and for plotting the course it is steering. In fact, the question must be raised whether the sound and fury of de-Stalinization has not been accompanied by a powerful process leading in the opposite direction, one of the functions of the former being to deflect attention from the latter.

From what has been said above, it would seem indeed that very little has changed in the attitude of the Soviet rulers toward the establishment of communism. Khrushchev quite naturally inherited from Stalin the position that *mutatis mutandis* had been preassigned to both of them in Ivan Karamazov's Legend. As said before, it does not require searching study to see the stability of that position as well as to perceive its natural corollary — the grand line of economic policy to be pursued. Nevertheless, some telling details have perhaps failed to receive the attention they deserve. Thus one should not overlook Khrushchev's momentous reference — dropped in passing — to the need to observe strict "proportionalities" in economic development and to the "important role to be played in that respect by the recently formed enlarged economic regions and the councils that have been organized in those regions for coordinating and planning the work of the *Sovnarkhozy.*" [8] The regional economic councils, about one hundred of them, were set up in May 1957 and endowed with far-reaching competence in administering the industry of the individual

8. Khrushchev's speech, *Pravda*, October 18, 1961, p. 6.

regions. Since the Sovnarkhoz assumed the functions formerly exercised by the economic ministries in Moscow, its establishment was an act of radical decentralization of industrial organization.

It was and, to some extent, still is popular to explain this change as a natural result of the preceding economic growth: Soviet industry, it was said, had reached, quantitatively and qualitatively, a level at which it had become so complex as to defy and defeat centralized administration. It is quite probable that Soviet industrial enterprises work more efficiently if they receive general guidance and supervision from a local center rather than from Moscow. It is even conceivable that maximum efficiency would be reached with the minimum of direction from above, be it central or local. But it is not at all clear that, from the point of view of the Soviet government, such gains in efficiency are not more than offset by other factors.

First of all, decentralization under conditions of continuing scarcities of consumers' goods almost inevitably shifts the activities of many enterprises toward better satisfaction of the needs of the local population and away from the production of producers' goods; there was plenty of evidence of how difficult it was for the Soviet government to obtain secure knowledge as to what was really going on within individual enterprises. It is true that the Sovnarkhoz finds itself closer to the enterprise and may know more about its inner workings; but it is also true that the local authority has much less incentive to uphold the national plan and is naturally much more interested in its own region.

It would be most surprising if, for instance, the regional authorities failed to tolerate various barter transactions among the enterprises within the region. Such barter transactions, deflecting goods from their planned routes, are bound to enhance regional autarkies. Dealings of this sort may indeed have served to lessen the rigidity of the plan and by the same token to alleviate difficulties in interplant supplies — that perennial weakness of the Soviet economy. This presumably was the reason why they were not stamped out by Stalin and his secret police, even though their existence must have been gall and wormwood to the central planners and to the dictator himself. Within the centralized framework, however, their extent could be held in check. At all times, the various barter transactions, apart from being a source of illegal enrichment for the managers, also tended to affect the composition of output in favor of consumers' goods, which were transmitted to local consumers in various ways — often in the form of effective incentive or merely "popularity" wages paid by the managers of industrial enterprises.

Furthermore, decentralization inevitably diminishes the reliability of statistical and other information that is made available to the central planning authorities. Khrushchev had plenty of opportunity to complain bitterly about the deceptions practiced on him by local agricultural authorities. It would be improbable in the extreme if very similar problems had not arisen in the field of industrial reporting. There is little doubt that, since the decentralization, Soviet industrial statistics as published by the central authorities must be taken with even greater caution than before.

It is therefore not surprising that the dangers and hazards of decentralization began to be discussed in the Soviet press almost as soon as the measures concerning industrial reorganization were initiated. The old word, *mestnichestvo*, which in the sixteenth century was mostly used to describe the order of precedence of Russian boyars at official functions and became charged with the connotation of squabbling pettiness, has been revived in new semantic guise to mean "localism," the remembrance of its old derogatory meaning readily merging with new disparagements.

If the Soviet government has been so keenly alive to what must appear to it as the negative features of decentralization, the question arises as to why decentralized organization was introduced in the first place. Are we really to believe that it was done in order to increase the efficiency of Soviet industry and that the undesirable consequences of the new arrangement were simply underestimated by Khrushchev? Such an error is highly improbable because of the long preceding history of local evasions of the central plan. There was a body of painful experience that any Soviet leader was unlikely to ignore. It is much more plausible to assume that decentralization was introduced, in full knowledge of the risks involved, as a temporary measure designed to accomplish a specific purpose — the demolition of the bureaucratic staffs in the numerous economic ministries. Those staffs had been largely built up by, and were loyal to, men who turned out to be Khrushchev's enemies. The establishment of the Sovnarkhoz should therefore be considered as the first step on the devious road to the creation of a new bureaucracy loyal to the victorious group. The setting up of the new councils in the enlarged regions was the second step.

These councils are expected "to coordinate and to plan." Altogether, seventeen of them have been established. Though the original regional councils have been preserved, there can be no doubt at all that important functions of the latter have been — or will be — transferred to the new councils. It is curious to see attempts in the Soviet press to present the new organizations as something that has been in existence in Soviet Russia for almost forty years.[9] These claims of continuity are, of course, unjustifiable, even though their political purpose is fairly obvious. This *is* an important innovation, a thorough upheaval of a recent and much praised reform. It is in fact not unlikely at all that, after some period of lingering uncertainty, the sovnarkhozy will disappear altogether. Those units, it should be noted, are large enough *not* to enjoy whatever advantages of proximity to individual enterprises were available to the smaller units. On the other hand, they are still too far removed from the center of government to satisfy the needs of the dictatorship. The arrangement, therefore, may be safely regarded as an intermediate one. The reinstitution of economic ministries in Moscow in one form or another may be expected to occur as the final step in the complex maneuver. If this interpretation is correct, what on the face of it appeared as

9. For instance, *Sovetskaya Belorussiya*, July 1, 1961, p. 2. It appears that the joint ordinance of the Central Committee of the Communist Party and of the Council of Ministers establishing the regional councils was passed sometime in May 1961. *Pravda* (February 23, 1962) at length broke its silence on the subject ("in response to readers' inquiries") and devoted twelve columns and an editorial to a discussion of the reform. Though the sovnarkhozy are praised as the "most practical form of industrial organization," they are criticized because of both "localist" tendencies and inability or unwillingness to eliminate excessively long hauls. The paper is obviously anxious to soften the blow. The same issue contains selected replies of functionaries of the sovnarkhozy to *Pravda*'s questionnaire on the reform. It is noteworthy that all the replies carefully refrain from answering the question as to how, in the opinion of the respondent, the reform will affect the activities of the sovnarkhozy. The delay in discussing the reform and the character of the discussion seem to testify rather clearly both to the importance of the change and to the existence of considerable opposition to it.

de-Stalinization may well upon closer examination emerge as a considered step on the road to re-Stalinization.

There is an inveterate tendency to approach Soviet developments in terms of long-range historical speculations gleaned from Western experience. These speculations stress the dominant role of the economic or, rather, the technological factor and its determining impact upon the course of events. This is a comforting view. Naturally, technology is the area in which the differences between Soviet Russia and the West are at a minimum. It is tempting to think that "in the end" all other parts of the Soviet body social will adjust themselves to the requirements of technology. In this fashion, the Russian evolution seems to become comprehensible. Whatever the strange deviations, the final outcome will be a society closely resembling that of the West. Walt Rostow's thought moved along similar lines when he tried to accommodate Soviet Russia within his universal scheme of economic development.[10]

The trouble with this sort of view is its failure to understand the modus operandi of a totalitarian dictatorship and, in particular, the mechanics of power within such a system. Once the role of power is properly evaluated, it becomes extremely likely that under the specific Russian conditions a decentralized industrial structure would be untenable, even if the local authorities were not trying to circumvent or to distort the general intentions of the government. For dictatorial power tends to erode unless it is maintained intact through an incessant series of acts of command followed by corresponding acts of obedience. It is for this reason that dictators so often allow themselves to fall prey to the *fascinatio nugacitatis*. The concern with detail, including the trifling detail, is irresistible. This is the force that caused Napoleon to keep dispatching orders from his battlefields to the far corners of subjugated Europe — from the plains of Russia to the Kingdom of Naples — in order to assert his will regarding the importation of a parcel of textiles or the establishment of a small machine shop. Decentralization means delegation of power, and delegation of dictatorial power means its diminution. If decentralization and dictatorship are found side by side, it is safe to predict that in

10. W. W. Rostow, *The Stages of Economic Growth: An Anti-Communist Manifesto* (Cambridge, Mass., 1960), pp. 93–105.

the long run one of them will give way. In this particular case, the run has not been very long.

Two areas of Soviet policies have been touched upon so far. In one — that of basic economic policy and attitudes toward establishment of a communist society — the main principles of Stalin's era seem to have remained unchanged. In the second, it appears that the change that did take place was deliberately made as a prelude to its unmaking at a later date; the change, as it were, was a prerequisite for a return to stability. But there is also a third area where the change that occurred was spontaneous rather than a well-premeditated political maneuver. This area is Soviet literature, and it is instructive indeed to take a somewhat closer look at its treatment at the Twenty-Second Congress.

II

In a beautiful and proud poem, Friedrich Schiller once described the neglect of German literature at the courts of the German princes. No Augustan or Medicean age, he said, had ever smiled upon the poets of the German *settecento*. The great work was not created in the shadow of the throne. The result was a free art defying and scorning the trammels of imposed rules.[11] This poem is of consider-

11.   Kein Augustisch Alter blühte,
    Keines Medizeers Güte
    Lächelte der deutschen Kunst.
    Sie ward nicht gepflegt vom Ruhme,
    Sie entfaltete die Blume
    Nicht am Strahl der Fürstengunst.
    Von dem grössten deutschen Sohne,
    Von des grossen Friedrichs Throne
    Ging sie schutzlos, ungeehrt.

    . . . . . .

    Rühmend darf's der Deutsche sagen,
    Höher darf das Herz ihm schlagen:
    Selbst erschuf er sich den Wert.
    Darum steigt in höherm Bogen,
    Darum strömt in vollern Wogen
    Deutscher Barden Hochgesang.
    Und in eigner Fülle schwellend
    Und aus Herzens Tiefe quellend,
    Spottet er der Regeln Zwang.

able historical moment. Written at the pinnacle of German literary history, it is informed by a high sense of independence and achievement. It is very tempting to accept it as the voice of the German *tiers état*, extolling freedom from the state and rejecting *l'art poétique*, that literary analogue to Colbertian economic regimentation. Indeed, there may be much plausibility in such an interpretation.

The Soviet experience, however, is very different. The "proletarian" art in Russia cannot complain of neglect and indifference by the state. The history of the past decades offers convincing testimony to the contrary. And the present time is no exception. While setting the pace of the country's further economic growth, sitting in judgment on Stalin and selected Stalinists, and settling down to a war of attrition with Albania, the congress still found time to listen to a number of speeches dealing with the Soviet literary scene. What then were the attitudes revealed in those speeches, and in what respects did they differ from those prevailing during the lifetime of the now defamed and de-monumented tyrant?

The very first discussion speaker, following Khrushchev's two impressive demonstrations of durative oratory, was P. N. Demichev, the first secretary of the Moscow city committee of the Communist Party — in other words, the city boss of the capital. He dealt with some problems of economic development of the city and its housing problems, formulating as the "immutable law" of Soviet economic growth "the achievement in the interest of society of *maximal* results at *minimal* costs." From this piece of time-honored logical illiteracy, Demichev moved over to discuss alcoholism, delinquency, and rowdyism — which served as a rational approach to the problems of Soviet literature:

A great role in the formation of the new man must be played by literature and art. In the last few years, their importance in the Communist education of the people has kept growing. There is an undeviating process of consolidation of the creative forces in the service of party principles. This is the result of the powerful impact of our building up the Communist society; it is the result of the wholesome creative atmosphere which surrounds the life and work of our people. This is due to the Party, to its Central Committee, and personally to Nikita Sergeevich Khrushchev, who with much care and attention has been educating writers and painters and helping them to reach a deeper understanding of complex phenomena of life and to correct their mistakes before it is too late. It is a pleasure indeed to notice that contemporaneous themes have taken leading positions in all genres of literature and art. Many a work of art has been created in which the heroic deeds of Soviet people, their thoughts and their yearnings, have been imprinted.[12]

This is a most satisfactory picture, suggesting an unprecedented flowering of the Russian literary genius. Nine years earlier, addressing himself to the same subject, Malenkov said as Stalin listened: "A most important, an indispensable, part of Soviet culture is literature and art. We have attained great achievements in the development of Soviet literature, theater, and movies. This is clearly demonstrated by the Stalin Prizes which every year are awarded to many talented figures in those fields." [13]

This, too, was praise, but it was brief and restrained. It was not surprising, therefore, that Malenkov continued with a couple of passages that were not laudatory at all. They deserve to be quoted at length:

Nevertheless, it would be incorrect not to notice behind the great achievements of our literature and art very considerable shortcomings. The point is that, despite all success in developing literature and art, the ideological and artistic level [14] of many works is still insufficiently high. In literature and art there still appear many mediocre, nondescript, and sometimes simply trashy products that distort Soviet reality. The many-sided, bubbling life of the Soviet society is depicted in the work of some writers and painters in a listless and boring fashion. There are still some defects in as popular an art form as our cinema. We know how to produce good films of great educational significance. But such films are few. Our cinematography has all the opportunities for producing good and diverse films, but those opportunities are poorly utilized.

It is necessary to remember that the ideological and cultural level of the Soviet man has risen immeasurably; the taste of the Soviet man is formed by the Party, which in the process of education uses the very best works of literature and art. Soviet people do not tolerate anything that is nondescript, nonideological, or not genuine. They expect much from our writers and artists. In their works our writers and artists must scourge the

12. *Pravda*, October 20, 1961, p. 2.
13. Malenkov, p. 43.
14. It should be noted that in Russia, which lends itself to Greek-like compounds, the word used is *ideologico-artistic*, the language itself, as it were, revealing through a forced unnatural union the real crux of the problem.

vices, the drawbacks, and the pathological phenomena that exist in our society; they must reveal in positive artistic images the new type of men in all the magnificence of their human dignity; in so doing, they will further the creation within our society of characters, customs, and traditions that are free from the vicious cancers grown by capitalism. But our novels and short stories and our plays and movies still avoid certain creative forms, such as, for instance, the satire. It is incorrect to think that Soviet reality offers no targets for the satirist. What we need are Soviet Gogols and Shchedrins [15] whose satirical fire would burn out of our life all that is negative, that is decaying and dying and retards our progress. Soviet literature and Soviet art must boldly show the contradictions and conflicts of our life. It must skillfully use the weapon of criticism as an instrument of education . . . Our painters and writers . . . when engaged in their creative work of producing artistic images must remember that the typical is not only what one can see frequently; typical is what reveals most fully and clearly the very essence of a given social force. For a Marxian-Leninist the typical is by no means some statistical average . . . The problem of the typical is a political problem . . . The duty of our writers, painters, composers, and movie workers is to study more profoundly the life of the Soviet society and create considerable artistic works that are worthy of our great people.[16]

Perhaps the most remarkable aspect of the preceding quotation is the unconsciously self-satirical character of the loud clamor for satirical command performances; Malenkov spoke at a time when it was difficult indeed to write satire in Russia. The most recent examples of satirical art in Soviet Russia — in particular, the two novels by Ilf and Petrov, and Zoshchenko's short stories — had been withdrawn from bookselling and booklending circulation after the last war and were unknown to the younger generation. One is uncertain as to which was most naive in Malenkov's text — the urgent invitation to the writers to be bold; or the serene assurance that Soviet life was not so perfect as to be out of the satirist's reach, coupled with the severe admonition not to concentrate too much upon unpleasant reality, which might indeed be all-pervasive and yet "not typical" at all; or, finally, the belief that dictatorial exhortation and appeal to duty could produce works of art along with machine tools and diesel locomotives. Nothing can surpass the naiveté of the hard-boiled.

15. The reference is to N. V. Gogol (1809–1852) and to M. E. Saltykov-Shchedrin (1826–1889).
16. Malenkov, pp. 43–44.

Stalin's regime had destroyed Russian literature. Its path was strewn with the dead bodies of poets and novelists. *Quis tulerit Gracchos de seditione quaerentes?* Who could stand Malenkov complaining of the downfall of Russian art? The answer to the great satirist's question is that the Romans could not, but the Russians did.

Let us return to the Twenty-Second Congress, to Demichev and his praise of Soviet authors so carefully and so effectively trained in Khrushchev's courses in creative writing. The unwary reader is all ready to attribute the satisfactory position of Soviet literature to the break with the Stalinist past. But disappointment is just around the corner. For Demichev also let his praise be followed by complaint and stricture. He, too, deserves to be heard fully:

> But our reality which hastens toward communism expects even more from art and literature. In our immediate proximity, in mills and factories, on state farms and collective farms, in scientific laboratories and on construction sites, toil thousands of men who have covered themselves with glory. They are the builders of communism. Their lives deserve to be depicted colorfully and vigorously. Nevertheless, in literature, on the screen, on painters' canvases, we sometimes observe nothing but pale, inexpensive shadows, characters drawn outside of time and space. In particular, there are the complaints leveled against those working in the most popular of arts — the cinema. Studios in Moscow and elsewhere have issued a number of good pictures, but very often we get films that are weak both ideologically and artistically." [17]

This is striking indeed. So far the correspondence between the two speeches in structure, substance, and even vocabulary is very close. Did Demichev, too, then proceed to issue orders to the writers, painters, and movie producers to engage forthwith in bold, creative, preferably satirical, activities? He did nothing of the sort:

> The Party has always emphasized that the political and ethical education of the people proceeds in the course of unrelenting struggles with the poisonous bourgeois influences. Against the background of our rich spiritual life and of our achievements in literature and art, it is particularly intolerable that certain immature writers, painters, composers — young people, as a rule — suffer from such diseases as pseudo-innovationalism and formalism in art. True, their number is infinitely small, but if the illness is not stopped at its incipience, it may become dangerous . . . [Carried away by] a grotesque play of colors and shadows, by pretentious rhymes and sounds,

17. *Pravda*, October 20, 1961, p. 2.

some of our creative workers are prevented from perceiving the emaciated hopelessness and the ideological vacuousness of the contemporary bourgeois culture. And there are also some people who are trying to cover absence of talent and industry with a screen of pseudo-innovationalism. And the most surprising thing is that some of our considerable writers and art specialists fear to appear old-fashioned; they flirt with those seekers after novelties and try to speak their language. Those mistakes in the creative activities of writers and painters stem from inadequate knowledge of life. It is impossible to write of Communist labors and of the great accomplishments of Soviet people simply by observing reality through the windows of one's Moscow apartment or through brief creative inspection trips.

This is a fairly complex situation, at least on the face of it. At the same congress at which Malenkov is denounced as one of Stalin's henchmen, laden with full measure of guilt for the dictator's heinous crimes, a high party official makes pronouncements on art and literature that appear to have been cribbed from Malenkov's speech delivered under Stalin's auspices. Of course it makes no difference whether in fact an act of plagiarism was committed (permissible, for the rest, under the laws of warfare, as a trophy taken from the defeated enemy), or whether it was the spiritual affinity reinforced by the standardized jargon that produced the bewildering result. But the confusion becomes complete when it is realized that the plagiarism, if it be one, had to remain abortive: the end of Malenkov's statement could not be included in Demichev's speech *because it would have been much too liberal* for the needs of those who had been so eagerly engaged in pillorying Stalin's rather illiberal policies. The point is that, even as it was denouncing the misdeeds of the past, the congress proceeded to mount an attack against contemporary Soviet figures in the literary field.

Demichev's speech had sounded the clarion call. Its notes were then repeated and varied upon by other speakers. In particular, E. A. Furtseva, who occupied in the Soviet cabinet the position of Minister of Culture, insisted that the main reason for the large number of "mediocre and simply weak works" produced lay in the remoteness of writers from the life of the people. She went on to divulge "very important data," showing that "for instance, in the Russian Federal Socialist Soviet Republic [by far the largest of of the USSR], out of a total of 2,700 writers, no less than 1,700 resided in Moscow or

Leningrad." And she proceeded to advocate a dispersal of that concentration by urging the writers (and painters) to betake themselves
to virgin lands in the east and other remote corners of the country.[18]

The leader of the Komsomol, S. P. Pavlov, claimed that Soviet
youth welcomed books and films which contain "the great truth about
the Soviet man" and present "heroes in whom one wants to believe
and whom one wants to imitate." But Soviet youth, he explained,
rejects works in which primary attention is devoted to the adventures
of a pitiful, tiny group of "scrofulous youths." Pavlov then referred
to the journal *Yunost'* (Youth), in which, he said, those strange tendencies had become pronounced, and he also upbraided some movie
directors who had shown unwarranted haste in deciding to film two
novels published in *Yunost'*.[19] Similarly, M. A. Sholokhov, a central
figure in Soviet literature and, on the speakers' tribune of the congress,
a faithful reproduction of Sholokhov's own creation — the clowning
old Shchukar [20] — turned serious for a moment to refer to Furtseva's
"truly horrifying figures" concerning the writers' preference for residence in the large urban centers and preferably in Moscow, and he
too stigmatized *otryv ot zhizni*, the writers' isolation from real life,
as the main source of their literary inadequacies and shortcomings.
These similarities are hardly coincidental. There is little doubt that
they reflect obedience by the speakers to a common set of instructions. The purpose of those instructions was well summarized by
Propaganda Chief Ilichev, who, after providing some further revelations of acts of censorship and suppression committed by Stalin, went
on to say: "The contemporary situation presents the ideological workers [*sic*] with higher and qualitatively different demands. What are
these demands? First of all, ideological work must make the greatest
possible contribution to the creative upsurge which the whole Party
is experiencing at present. Propaganda and agitation, the press, radio,
television, popular lectures, *literature and art* — the whole ideological
front must be converted into a more active factor for transforming
all sides of life of Soviet society in the spirit of Communist principles." [21] Thus Russian novelists and playwrights — the ideologi-

18. *Pravda*, October 22, 1961, p. 2.
19. *Pravda*, October 25, 1961, p. 5.
20. Sholokhov, *Podnyataya tselina* (Virgin Land under Plow; Moscow, 1960).
21. *Pravda*, October 26, 1961; italics added.

cal workers — need not live in fear of neglect. They will not be left alone, and the Soviet government will redeem the promise of the party program "to take unrelenting care to assure the flowering of literature."

III

As one reads the oratorical efforts which have been summarized in the preceding section, one cannot help wondering what reaction these speakers produced in the minds of the delegates to the congress and, particularly, in the minds of the many millions of readers of the Soviet newspapers that, day in and day out, carried the stenographic records of the proceedings. Naturally, the thoughts expressed were not new to them. They had heard them stated many times in the course of decades. They also have come to know full well that repetitiveness is an apparently indispensable technique of totalitarian policy, and they must still remember how for many years the festive Proclamation for the First of May contained an entirely unchanged formula — uncharming in its simplicity — requiring writers and artists to continue producing works of great artistic value. Moreover, the slogan has not changed much in recent times.[22] And yet the incongruity of the situation and the tristesse of the involuntary humor were only underscored by Sholokhov's deliberate gaiety and could not possibly pass unnoticed. As Stalin's crimes were told and the story of atrocities unfolded, one victim of the dictatorship

22. For instance, *Pravda*, April 24, 1949, p. 1: "Workers in literature, art, and cinematography! Keep increasing the level of your workmanship. Keep creating new highly ideological artistic works, worthy of the great Soviet people." The 1961 proclamation, too, invited the writers and the artists to "fight for high ideological character of [their] works and for artistic workmanship, for close inseparable connection of literature and art with the life of the people, with our age" (*Pravda*, April 9, 1961, p. 1). The words "our age," it may be added, are a somewhat free translation of the Russian term *sovremennost'*, which literally means "contemporaneousness." It is interesting that the meaning of the term has been discussed in recent Soviet writings. The official interpretation is to regard as "contemporaneous" only novels, plays, films, etc., which depict present-day Soviet life. A broader and freer view includes in the concept "everything that excites us today," so that, for instance, *Othello* or *The Idiot* may make more "contemporary" motion pictures than jejeune scripts dealing with Soviet reality. See Akademiya Nauk SSSR, Institut Istorii Iskustva, *Yezhegodnik Kino, 1959* (Academy of Sciences of the USSR, Institute of History of Art, Cinema Yearbook, 1959; Moscow, 1961), p. 11.

remained altogether unmentioned: the unprecedented decline of Russian literature; the transformation of a great art stemming from a great tradition into a mechanical process of mass-fabricating products according to patterns prescribed by the dictatorship and varying in response to its changing needs. This was the inevitable result of turning writers into "ideological workers."

It should be quite in order at this point to select from the large number of usable cases just one illustration of this process of ordered creation. Nothing can serve the purpose better than a reference to Feodor Panferov and one or two of his novels. Panferov was a celebrated Soviet writer of considerable fertility and small literary gifts. He achieved his first big success in 1930 when he published the first two parts of his collectivization novel (*Bruski*), and added two more parts during the 1930's. After the war he wrote *Bor'ba za mir* (Struggle for Peace), a novel dealing with an automobile factory in the Urals which earned him the Stalin Prize of 1947. The heroes of that novel reappear in still another, *V strane poverzhennykh* (In the Land of the Defeated), whose action takes place in Germany; in 1949 this novel received the same high distinction. Thereupon Panferov quickly forged the third link in the chain, returning in 1949 to the Ural factory in his novel *Bol'shoe iskustvo* (The Great Art).

After the end of the war, Stalin's dictatorship became increasingly concerned with the independence and self-assurance of managers of industrial enterprises in the Soviet Union. In addition, the purges and the victorious war left the Soviet government without enemies, that much-needed grease for the wheels of smoothly functioning dictatorial machines. Naturally there was the United States, but it was far away and its quality as an enemy was unduly abstract. A campaign against managers accompanied by a controlled wave of anti-Semitism seemed a very natural remedy. Panferov's novel rose to the needs of the hour. In its center the author placed one Kokorev, who was being sent to the Ural factory to replace the former manager — the hero of the preceding novels — who was believed to have perished in a German prison. During the war Kokorev had done wonders managing an automative factory and supplying the urgently needed tanks and trucks. But after the war the negative qualities of the man — his egotism, his rude treatment of the workers, his contempt for collective institutions — became an object of bitter criticism. His dismissal could have been a simple matter. Yet, in obedience to his political task, Panferov lets the process of showing up the inadequacies of the manager and getting rid of him pass through the following stages:

(1) Arrival in the factory town of an American woman who is a journalist and a spy and who, for purposes of disguise, wears a riding habit and carries a horse whip.

(2) A conversation between the woman and Kokorev, the manager, in the course of which she tells him that his brother, the owner of a large steel mill in the United States, is dying and wants Kokorev to go to America in order to take over the plant.

(3) A meeting of the factory committee at which the workers' complaints against the manager are discussed. At the meeting, which follows closely upon the manager's conversation with the American spy, a member of the secret police reports the overheard contents of that conversation and adds "as though by the way" that the manager's real name is not Kokorev but Rosenzweig, whereupon the manager is beaten up by the workers.

(4) Several police examinations of Rosenzweig, who is shown as using idioms and mannerisms usually regarded as Jewish.

(5) Further revelations by the secret policeman, who has discovered that the manager's true name is not Rosenzweig after all, but Nielson: a native American, he had bought his Russian passport from the son of an anti-Soviet émigré (a former owner of a sugar factory) by the name of Rosenzweig.

(6) Thereby the Jewish episode is finished, "the enemy of the people" — as Kokorev-Rosenzweig-Nielson is called — disappears, and the novel ends with the miraculous return from a German prison of the positive hero of the previous novels, who used to be the director of the factory and who answers to an undisputed and irreproachable Russian surname. He is joyfully received by the workers and by his wife, whose reputation Kokorev, the perfidious enemy of the people, had tried to ruin by casting aspersions on her marital faithfulness.[23]

The novel clearly demonstrated that managerial arrogance could well serve as *prima facie* evidence of espionage and, in a non-committal way, planted in the reader's minds some germinating ideas regarding connections between Jewishness and treasonable propensities. To use a favorite Soviet expression, it was "ideologically well-horseshoed." There is no doubt that this collection of patent absurdi-

23. For the preceding, see the first edition of the novel, *Bol'shoe iskustvo*, in *Oktyabr'*, XXVI (November 1949), 3–143.

ties, written in the flattest possible language and having no literary value whatsoever, is an excellent example of the average Soviet novel of the period.

Five years passed after the first publication of the novel. In the interval occurred the death of Stalin. It was preceded by the "doctors' plot" and followed by their rehabilitation. The atmosphere in 1954 differed in some respects from that of 1949. Open anti-Semitism was no longer desired and, in addition, the industrial manager was no longer the prime target so far as the government was concerned. Other enemies were emerging to satisfy the system's needs. In the struggle for power within the ruling group, the discussion had shifted to the merits and demerits of the bureaucrats in the economic ministries in Moscow.

In 1954, when a second edition of Panferov's novel was published, the situation in some respects was still obscure, but Panferov had no difficulty in engineering the appropriate changes. First of all, the suggestive Rosenzweig episode was eliminated. Furthermore, the main onus was shifted from the shoulders of the manager to his assistant, who had maintained relations with the United States; he was the native American by the name of Nielson and had bought a Russian passport from a certain Popov. But the manager — Kokorev, now without aliases — is still dealt with severely: it was from his safe that his assistant had abstracted some secret documents and smuggled them abroad. Kokorev must bear the full measure of responsibility for having trusted the wrong man, and so he is solemnly punished by dismissal from the factory, expulsion from the Communist Party, loss of six medals, and withdrawal of the previously accorded titles of "general" and "hero of socialist labor." In addition, he suffers a heart attack.

In this form the novel could be reprinted in an edition of Panferov's collected works in 1959. The additional changes that had to be made by then were minor. In 1954 it was still in order to let some undisputable verity ("Learning is always good") be preceded by a pious: "As Stalin says." In the 1959 edition, the authorship of the truism was no longer revealed.[24] But Panferov did not stand still.

24. Panferov, *Bol'shoe iskustvo* (Moscow, 1954), p. 306; and *Bol'shoe iskustvo*, in *Sobranie sochinenii* (Collected Works), v (Moscow, 1959), 314.

He continued to change with the times. In 1960, shortly before his death, he published the fourth volume in the series, *Vo imya molodogo* (In the Name of Youth).[25] There he was ready to attack the policies that had been pursued by the economic ministries in Moscow as a "peculiar form of feudalism," impervious to control and supervision and designed to extract from the State as much as possible. "Only people infected to the core by lust for power . . . could oppose so furiously the creation of the sovnarkhozy."

The elimination of Stalin's name was accompanied in this novel by a positive reference to the new power: "One could gauge the speed of the country's life from the actions and speeches of the first secretary of the Central Committee of the Communist Party. All his speeches were good in themselves; they were free from undue simplifications, they were reasonable and cordial, calling upon every honest person to dedicate himself to the last drop to the great general surge for the construction of the material and spiritual basis of the communist society. But even apart from this, the speeches and the activity of Nikita Sergeevich Khrushchev — who already began to be lovingly referred to by the common people as 'Our Nikita' — were amazingly many-sided."

Once more Panferov's lucky ideological horseshoes proved firmly nailed. One can be fairly certain that, if he were able to prepare yet another edition of this novel now, the oblique criticism of Stalin in the preceding quotation would give way to some very direct pronouncements. There may be some legitimate doubt as to the propaganda value of Panferov's implausible concoctions. But there can be no doubt that the aim of the official policy, as revealed at the 1961 congress, is to preserve the character of Russian literature as it existed under Stalin — pegged at the level so perfectly gauged by the aforesaid concoctions.

It must be kept in mind, however, that the point at issue is not simple "preservation." For certain very significant changes in Russian literature did take place after 1953, when Stalin had been called to his account. One aspect of those changes probably is the publication of works by the victims of Stalin's terrorism — by those who perished in the cellars of the secret police or the concentration camps and by

25. In *Oktyabr'*, XXXVII (July and August 1960).

those who survived after long years of enforced silence. The extent of the liberalization must not be exaggerated. Pasternak's *Doctor Zhivago* is still inaccessible to Soviet readers except in typescripts that pass from hand to hand. Nor have Mandelstam's poems seen the light of day in Russia. Neither his earlier, merely premonitory *Tristia* nor his later real *Tristia*, written in the despair of his own exile, have been published. But there have been two editions of a slim volume of the poetry of Akhmatova, who was allowed to indicate in a preface that she had never stopped writing.[26] A collection of Babel's short stories appeared; so did a novel by Bruno Yasenski. After years of suppression, the Soviets reissued the satirical novels of Ilf and Petrov, as well as a single volume containing some of the more placid short stories of Zoshchenko. It will be remembered that Akhmatova and Zoshchenko were singled out by Zhdanov in 1946 in his infamous condemnation of writers and poets. Those destroyed or muted by the Soviet dictatorship (leaving the field free to the cacography of the Panferovs) had been remarkable original talents. The return of their works to the shelves in bookshops and libraries is no mean occurrence. Even absurd editorial prefaces criticizing the satirists for being too subtle, and at the same time defending them — or, rather, defending the editors themselves — against any suspicion of disloyalty, cannot detract from the significance of this resurrection.[27]

Moreover, there has been a relaxation of the strict injunctions against the treatment of love in literature except in the form of a union of two highly virtuous people whose private feelings and actions are thoroughly collectivized and at all times kept in strict accordance with the rules of dictatorial morality. By being permitted to acknowledge the existence of some irregularities in the marital life of otherwise very "positive" heroes, the post-Stalin literature was rendered somewhat more human. The new freedom was eagerly seized upon,[28]

26. Anna Akhmatova, *Stikhotvoreniya* (Poems; Moscow, 1961), p. 10.

27. Ilya Ilf and Evgeni Petrov, *Sobranie sochinenii* (Collected Works), preface by D. Zaslavski. Also B. Galanov, *Il'ya Il'f i Evbenii Petrov, Zhizn' i tvorchestvo* (Life and Work; Moscow, 1961), pp. 132, 191–192.

28. See my "Reflections on Soviet Novels," *Economic Backwardness in Historical Perspective*, pp. 318–340. It might be in order to mention at this point that a parallel process took place in Soviet cinematography. In Soviet writings on the subject, it is freely stressed that the Twentieth Congress (1956) marked a turning point. After that date "'attempts to substitute . . . sham idyls for real conflicts" were abandoned,

revealing a surprising coarseness of mores hidden beneath the varnish of the earlier writings.[29]

Finally, and most important, literature in some measure has become the vehicle for expressing certain views of general political significance — trying to feel out, as it were, the limits of the possible. In this category falls, for instance, the poetry of Yevgeni Yevtushenko, who claimed once to possess "the talent of fearlessness" [30] and whose name was never mentioned at the congress, but whose physical, sartorial, and poetic irregularities, as well as unwholesome popularity, were the obvious target of some acrimonious remarks.

In the same category belong the rather short novels that appeared chiefly in *Yunost'*, the journal that was named and specifically attacked at the congress. The heroes of most of these novels are adolescents and young men. None of the novels seems to be a piece of great writing, but very many of them are true "novels" in the etymological sense of the word. They are permeated by a spirit of frankness and freedom from the deadwood of standard types, characteristics, prob-

---

and interest in "the ordinary common man and his everyday life" became a characteristic feature of motion pictures produced in the second half of the 1950's. *Yezhegodnik Kino, 1959*, p. 7.

29. Even a writer like Panferov could not resist the temptation to discuss in his latest novel, *Vo imya molodogo*, some interesting aspects of female anatomy and to report various conversations held in matrimonial and adulterous beds, while still dealing with the pernicious greed for "original accumulation of capital" (a Marxian concept that he revised to include such things as acquisition of a small house) and with the no less pernicious tendencies in abstract art. V. Kochetov, who, among Soviet writers, is the undisputed leader of the back-to-Stalin movement, fully agrees with Panferov on the social evils produced by private home ownership, but refuses to go quite so far in matters of sex. With regard to the latter, he prefers a cautious negative method. Thus he likes to place a high party functionary in close proximity to an attractive woman (whose charms have been prominently displayed by the author) and then to tell in fair detail all the things which the functionary might have done if not restrained by virtue and position. This unhumorous Soviet version of W. Busch's delightful story, *Der heilige Antonius von Padua*, appeared in Kochetov's novel, *The Secretary of the Obkom*, which is his most recent effort to freeze over the "thaw" in Soviet literature. This novel, which incidentally contains a thinly disguised vituperative caricature of the poet Yevtushenko, was published in the summer of 1961; a few months later Kochetov was awarded the Lenin Prize for his contribution to Soviet literature. Cf. *Sekretar' obkoma*, in *Zvezda*, no. 8 (1961), p. 55; also *Literaturnaya gazeta*, February 6, 1961, p. 1.

30. See *Yabloko: Novaya kniga stikhov* (The Apple: A New Book of Poems; Moscow, 1960), p. 6.

lems, and situations, which appears altogether new against the background of the nauseating sameness of the official literature. There is a simplicity, an immediacy, and a naiveté about the writing in *Yunost'* that is most refreshing. This is reflected in the language and the style. Thus one of the novels that evoked official displeasure at the congress tells its story in a manner that is an obvious but possibly unconscious imitation of *Huckleberry Finn*.[31] Accordingly, there is no hesitation in *Yunost'* about employing the atrocious but often very colorful slang used by young people. As happens so often, the true rendition of speech leads to a truthful rendering of its content. The young personages exhibited in the novels are rebelling against authority in state, school, and family. They want to escape from the boredom of compulsory virtues to be displayed while trotting along predetermined tracks of life. Hence the novels themselves are in the nature of controlled rebellions.

Some of the actions described are in the category of frank rowdyism. They show that the Soviet Union, like every country that went through the last war, is burdened with the legacy of that war. Juvenile delinquents in the United States, the English Teddy boys, the French *blousons noirs*, the German and Austrian *Halbstarken*, the Italian *teppisti* or *ragazzi di vita*, and the young *khuligany* in Russia may be taken to be phenomena that are closely related in both causes and symptoms. It is revealing to be shown in Soviet novels the seriousness of disciplinary problems in Soviet high schools — for example, the pupils' nasty habit of ruining an hour of instruction by open rioting in the classroom.[32] Relations between high-school boys and openly criminal elements and molestations of couples in the streets by hoodlums are candidly described.

But there is much more to this literature than exposure of the seamy side of Soviet life. The novels do deal with the thoughts, aspirations, and value systems of the young generation. When one of the youngster heroes says, "We have no theories!"; when a young physician in another novel expresses his disgust of all those sickening "high-

31. N. Zeleranski and B. Larin, *Mishka, Serega i ya*, in *Yunost'*, nos. 7 and 8 (1959).

32. The procedure has a special technical term to describe it — *sorvat' urok* — which has been taken over from pre-dictatorial political jargon, where it referred to the deplorable practice of noisily obstructing the mass meetings of political opponents.

falutin' words," all those "verbal fetishisms," and his friend declares
to have thought about the matter and understood that it was all
"bluff" — their views are an open challenge to a state that forces
every one of its subjects into an ideological straitjacket. For "theories"
and the "high-falutin' words" obviously refer to the totality of official
values. The young people are eager to escape from it all. Hence many
of these stories deal with running away from home and school, from
discipline and duty. Thus not only in style but also in content they
are Huckleberry Finn stories. This does not necessarily mean that
the flight carries them beyond the point of no return. They may
eventually make their peace with the system. But they do proclaim
their right to seek and to err and to hack out their own paths. They
refuse to be wholly impounded by the tasks of economic development;
they wish to withdraw from the "grayness" of Soviet dogmas into
the eternal philosophical problems of life and death. Theirs is a flight
from pressure to conform, and a fleeting scene of a small crowd in
the park gathered around a loudspeaker emitting the hackneyed
phrases of official patriotism becomes a disgusted protest against
Gleichschaltung: "The faces in the listening crowd somehow are all
identical." So does the expression of indignation on the part of a
young man at the customary way of voting at Soviet meetings, when
hands are raised mechanically while people's thoughts are far away:
"Are we some kind of robots, or what?" [33]

These are quite new tones. To write in this fashion means much
more than a mere widening of the range of topics that can be treated
in literature. It is very different, therefore, from the previously mentioned innovation of Soviet erotica.

There is no simple relationship between the interests of a dictatorship and the public treatment of sex. A very strong dictatorship

33. See, for the preceding, the second novel that suffered official disparagement at
the congress: Vasili Aksenov, *Zvezdny bilet* (Ticket to the Stars), in *Yunost'*, no. 6
(1961), pp. 6, 20, and 7 (1961), p. 52. Also Aksenov, *Kollegi* (The Colleagues;
Moscow, 1961), pp. 6, 18. Let us add that it would seem tempting but hardly warranted to relate the fermentation in Soviet Russia to the exploits of the beat generation in the United States. There is no "raggedy madness and riot" about Soviet
youth. They do not seem to include any "holy goofs" of Dean Moriarty's ilk. Nor
is there much doubt that Soviet writers have a sense of touching upon problems that
pervade the young generation throughout the country, while Jack Kerouac, in *On
the Road* (1957), is quite conscious of dealing with peripheral oddities.

will tend to be very restrictive for a number of reasons. Sex offers a predestined field for prohibitions and injunctions and, by the same token, a natural area for self-assertion of dictatorial power. Moreover, the dictators are likely to assume that any looseness in matters of sex may loosen behavior in other areas, and in particular may affect the political discipline of the ruled. Besides, they may fear lest preoccupation with sex effectively deflect attention from tasks set by the state. But a dictatorship that has been weakened, say, by a prolonged succession crisis may welcome some injections of prurience into literature as the lesser of two evils — as an alternative to treatment of political problems and some opposition to the dictatorial system and to the conformity of behavior it exacts. It is therefore not quite clear to what extent the rediscovery of sex life in recent Soviet literature is the result of a spontaneous response to the opportunities of the post-Stalinist period; and to what extent it is a shrewd governmental device to direct that response into the least undesirable channels. The fact that Panferov became a major contributor to the subject naturally would make one incline to the latter supposition.

But what about the future? Must we assume that the liberalizing attempts will be nipped in the bud — that *Yunost'*, for instance, will receive the pedagogically trained supervisor for whom there was a clamor at the congress, and thereafter will quickly publish a series of novels featuring model youngsters worshiping Khrushchev while decrying the cult of personality? Must we assume that the congress has spoken and that *Roma locuta, causa finita est?* A categorical answer to these questions would seem at least premature.[34]

At one of the last sessions of the congress, A. T. Tvardovski replied to some of the criticism directed against literature. He spoke of what had been accomplished since the "turning point" of the Twentieth Congress, at a secret session of which Khrushchev had made his first anti-Stalin speech. He mentioned the many whose "literary name" and whose place in the history of Soviet literature had been restored. But he also insisted on saying frankly that some habits of

34. The character of *Yunost'* changed perceptibly in the months that followed the congress. Moreover, the editor of the journal, V. Katayev, has been replaced by Boris Polevoy, whose record provides assurance that the journal will be safely prodded back into the pinfold of Soviet conformity.

thought, literary practices, and manners of writing formed under Stalin still persisted; that "boldness, straightforwardness, and truthfulness" were often lacking; and that one could discern "immoderate bragging" about the positive aspects of Soviet life, a desire to "varnish the picture" and to avoid discussion of imperfections and disabilities. Tvardovski argued that literature should not be confined to depicting life in factories and on collective farms; that literature may legitimately deal with very personal sides of the everyday life of men and women, their joys and griefs, "with life as it exists in all its complexity." And he went on to suggest that the domicile of a writer may not be the prime factor in determining his quality.[35]

That a truism of this kind could have been presented as a liberating truth once more reveals what four decades of Soviet rule had done to Russian literature and to Russian spiritual life. But the important point is something else. The sessions of the congress went on for many days; hour-long speeches were made; millions of words were spoken. And yet in all that verbal flood, with two exceptions, one could not discover a solitary incident of argument and counterargument, of anything resembling a debate, even a trace of differing opinion. One of those exceptions does not properly count in this context, the Chinese dissent on Albania. The other exception, produced by a native Russian and possessing such a high scarcity value — a tiny island in an ocean of conformity — was precisely Tvardovski's defense of the rights of a freer literature.

How should one appraise Tvardovski's action? Was it an act of suicidal boldness, of magnificent civil courage? Tvardovski has been editor-in-chief of *Novyi mir*, which has acquired a somewhat liberal reputation. The journal published, for instance, Ehrenburg's carefully balanced memoirs in which the praise of Mandelstam and Babel — victims of Stalin — is nicely counterpoised by the author's rejection of *Doctor Zhivago*. But no one would accuse *Novyi mir* of undue recklessness, and Tvardovski knows well from long experience the fears and circumspection that guide the pens of Russian writers. His long epic poems, "Horizons beyond Horizons," has gone through some very important changes. To the 1954 edition of the poem

35. *Pravda*, October 29, 1961, p. 7.

there was added a moving description of Stalin's death: "unfathomable sorrow," "silent grief," "a beloved father," "the happiness of having been Stalin's contemporary," "the cruel day and hour when disaster struck"—all the solemn paraphernalia of an official dirge were mixed into the poem, imperceptibly tempered by a brief concessive clause admitting that "at times" Stalin's "ruthless *pravota*" — infallibility (literally, "his being right") — was "hard to take." [36] But in the new edition that appeared after the Twentieth Congress the chapter on Stalin was thoroughly revised. "A son of the Orient," he was said to have exhibited the features of a "ruthless and cruel *nepravota*" — fallibility (literally, "his being wrong") — and there was a quick reference to Stalin's crimes, the slightest hint that Stalin's death may have been hastened by powers other than fate or nature. But there was also a forcefully expressed unwillingness to forget that it was Stalin's foresight that had built the factories and moved them into trans-Uralian safety; it was his will that had inspired the country in the fateful years of the German war; and no one had a right to sit in judgment on Stalin — least of all the poets who had sung his glory and had been crowned with his laurels.[37]

Possibly now, after this congress, a still further revision, less judicious and more judicial, will appear. One may wonder why Tvardovski had to refer to Stalin's death at all in the early version of the poem. Was it in response to an outside order or to an inner compulsion, some sort of a hypnotic trance? Was it simply a conditioned reflex, or did it result from a long habit of thought or, rather, from its suspension? Whatever the explanation, under conditions of totalitarian rule, the question that André Gide addressed to his *confrères* fifty years ago, "Il est donc si difficile de se taire?" clearly must be answered in the affirmative. At any rate, Tvardovski does not seem to be a man to rush blindly into a mortal fray. The congress rewarded his speech with strong manifestations of approval. One may assume that he will get away with his refusal to conform. But will Russian literature retain its precariously established right to deviance? This is much less predictable.

36. A. T. Tvardovski, *Stikhotyoreniya i poemy* (Lyrical and Epic Poems; Moscow, 1954), pp. 589–590.

37. A. T. Tvardovski, *Sobraniye sochinenii* (Collected Works), III (Moscow, 1960), pp. 340ff.

IV

The Twenty-Second Congress has been an important landmark in the history of the post-Stalinist dictatorship. It greatly enhanced the consolidation of that dictatorship. This, no doubt, must be seen as Khrushchev's personal triumph. It would be futile to belittle the importance of the personal qualities of the leader in such a system. In particular, it makes good sense to attribute much of Stalin's terror to Stalin's daimon. So far, the absence of a comparable phenomenon in today's Russia has been the most decisive mark of momentous change. In this, as in some other respects, Russia has traveled far since the days of Stalin. At the same time, however, it is tempting to assume that there are certain stability conditions of a totalitarian dictatorship that are less personal and more objective in nature.

To function properly, a dictatorship, as has been said before, needs enemies, preferably of the tangible kind. The public dethronement of Stalin created a reservoir of Stalinists which it will take a long time to exhaust, particularly if the leadership continues to abstain from Stalin's unwise propensity to commit irreparable acts, so that one and the same person can be purged several times over, as was Molotov in 1957 and then again in 1961. It may be assumed that the conflict with China, now brought into the open, will keep bursting forth periodically. And, finally, there is still the cold war with the West.

In addition, a dictatorial government must perform what in the eyes of the population appears to be an important social function, which either could not be performed at all or not nearly as well in the absence of dictatorial guidance and pressure. The postponement of the advent of a "communist society" beyond the foreseeable future means that the government will continue the policy of high investment, and it remains to be seen whether or not the government will resume Stalin's policy of systematic underfulfillment of production plans with regard to consumers' goods. Furthermore, one may expect that the reversal of the decentralization movement will continue and increasingly assure the dictators of an opportunity to issue innumerable permits and prohibitions directly affecting individual lives and concrete situations all over the country, and in this way to exercise their privilege of ruling and of being obeyed.

The stability of a dictatorial government of this type is greatly enhanced by veneration of the dictator's wisdom and energy, as well as of his fatherly benevolence. It is a good thing for his eye to be "exceedingly kind and gentle. A child would like to sit in his lap and a dog would sidle up to him," as Ambassador Davis once wrote of Stalin.[38] There has been enough rewriting of past history in Russia to represent Khrushchev as one of the major engineers of victory in the last war; there has been a sufficient number of quotations from Khrushchev's speeches in learned books in various fields of scholarly endeavor; the glorifications in *Pravda* and *Izvestiya* have been faithfully echoed in the provincial press; and the stream of personal adulation of Khrushchev at the Twenty-Second Congress showed that in this respect also the wind hath returned upon its circuits, and still another stability condition of the dictatorship has been fulfilled. One can safely assume that Khrushchev's protest at the congress against a cult of personality will not change the nature or direction of ineluctable processes.

And then there is the requisite of an ideology that at least has the appearance of being monolithic. There can be no doubt that the complex enterprise of debating and adopting a new party program was embarked upon mainly because of the desire to rebuild the ideological structure, some parts of which had fallen into disrepair after Stalin's death, and in the process of reconstruction to imprint upon the edifice the individual features of the new architect.

Can literature expect to remain a lone anomaly in a system that is being so vigorously propelled back to normalcy? The deviant tendencies discussed in the preceding sections may seem paltry when viewed from the intellectual remoteness of a democratic country. Under Russian conditions, they have a considerable significance, which is first and foremost political. No one since Stalin's death had uttered such plain criticism of the system as did the unheroic heroes of the Soviet novels of the early sixties. This, after all, is well in accordance with the great nineteenth-century tradition of Russian literature. Although a "gentry literature," it was even farther removed from throne and court than the German literature of the preceding century. Much of it, though by no means all, was a literature of

38. Joseph E. Davis, *Mission to Moscow* (New York, 1941), p. 357.

social critique and political accusation. Tvardovski's admonition at the congress to Russian writers to remain faithful to their great predecessors of the past century may therefore have been charged with more political meaning than appeared on the surface.

In the light of such considerations, the dispersal of the writers from Moscow and Leningrad appears less absurd. It may be missing the point to argue that the artistic value of literature is likely to grow rather than decline in the atmosphere of mutual stimulation and encouragement that exists in the large cities. It makes little sense to mention the historical role played by Moscow and St. Petersburg in this respect or to refer to Chekhov's advice to young writers, including Gorki, to go to the capital and live among literary people. For the problem is an exquisitely political one — to wit, to get rid of a deviant group that may become quite dangerous politically. There have been signs and near miracles. Enthusiastic gatherings of thousands to listen to recitals of poetry with libertarian overtones would be disquieting to any police state, even if those gatherings did not create bad traffic problems in the streets of Moscow, requiring the regulating intervention of mounted police. What was therefore discussed at a congress was in fact a mild form of camouflaged exile. Sending Russian writers and poets into remote parts of the country is, of course, a policy of which Stalin was a most effective adept, but by no means the originator.

It thus seems reasonably clear what the Soviet dictatorship fears and what it wants with regard to literature. If it can have its way, literature once more will be *gleichgeschaltet* and, by the same token, another stability condition of totalitarian dictatorship will be fulfilled. Once this has happened, it would again become possible for the government to clamor with impunity for more boldness in literature, as did Malenkov in 1952.

Whether and when and how completely that goal will be reached must depend on the future strength of the regime, which, of course, remains an unknown. The factors discussed here may be very important, perhaps even indispensable, in the long run for the maintenance of the dictatorship. Yet it is fairly clear that they cannot suffice in themselves. Much must depend on forces that act and react far from the light of publicity, through the councils of the ruling group, the loyalties — and disloyalties — of the higher bureaucracy, and the leadership of the army and the secret police. Surprises are always possible. Perhaps the temptation to indulge in metaphorical borrowings from different and more precise contexts and to speak of stability conditions should have been resisted. Nevertheless, looking over the road that has been traversed, one can only marvel at the vigor and the persistence of forces that have tended to preserve unchanged or to restore the traditionally essentially elements of the Soviet system.

To paraphrase Heraclitus, one might repeat the motto chosen for this article and say that dictatorship, rather than the dictator's character, is destiny. In other words, the dictatorship must be as it is or not be at all. Its long-run changeability appears limited indeed. This, however, can be no more than a very tentative conclusion. In particular, one should not rely upon it too heavily when speculating about the future of Russian literature. On the other hand, after what happened at the 1961 congress and after the experience of the last few years, it may be safely assumed that the vicissitudes of Russian literature in the years to come will offer excellent opportunities for testing the validity of that conclusion.

II

The Stability of Dictatorships

Nec unquam satis fida potentia, ubi nimia est. — Tacitus

I AM afraid I must begin with apologies. First of all, my very choice of topic calls for a plea for indulgence. It is an extraordinary occurrence in one's curriculum to be given the privilege of lecturing under the auspices of the Harvard Foundation at Yale University. I felt that an extracurricular event might justify an extracurricular theme. Hence instead of speaking here on some problems of economic history, which is the daily bread of my professional life, I have decided on a topic that indeed has strong economic implications, but essentially lies in the field of political science and political history. And yet, while I could not resist the temptation, I know that professional boundaries rarely can be crossed with impunity, and I can only hope that the penalty of disapproval will not be unduly severe.

In addition, what I have to say here is exceedingly simple and probably will seem quite unsophisticated. Any adult living in the second half of our unhappy century has been richly provided both by recent history and by events still unfolding before our eyes with all the material that is needed in order to formulate the few generalizations I am about to present here. If, nevertheless, I make bold to encroach upon your time and to tax your patience by betraying Polichinelle's secrets and by revealing La Palice's truths, it is because

Note. In reading this essay, the reader should keep in mind that it has been left unchanged as it was written in 1963 and, for the rest, refer to the relevant observations made in the Introduction (pp. 2–5 above).

of my feeling that, in much of the current discussion, things that should have been obvious have been allowed to become obscured and distorted. It is another question that no interpretation of the type I am trying to offer can be truly conclusive. As shall be made clear later, there will always remain some room for alternative interpretations.

It will not take me long to state my thesis. I believe that a modern dictatorship has one primary aim and that is maintenance and, by the same token, increase of its power. I also believe that this power at all times — though to a varying degree in varying situations — is jeopardized by doubt. The subjects — or, rather, the objects — of dictatorial rule are perennially moved to ask the simple but deeply probing and profoundly disturbing questions: Why should there be a dictatorship? Why should it continue in power? However aggressive the actions of the dictatorship, in a very real sense it always finds itself on the defensive.

The problem of justifying the state is as old as man's preoccupation with the phenomenon of government. It seems to me that over the course of history two forms of government stand out as having elicited a long-run acceptance that was largely independent of the character — one might say, contents — of governmental activities: a hereditary monarchy that claimed divine sanction and whose legitimacy was reinforced by the ancientness of its tradition; [1] a rule based upon the active and effective consent of the governed. The decisive fact is that a modern dictatorship finds itself deprived of these all-comprehensive, because formal, instruments of justification.[2] It must therefore establish its vindication through appropriate actions. Upon

1. Naturally, I am abstracting here from the rational considerations that were advanced for or against a hereditary system, such as avoidance of dangers inherent in recurring struggles for succession, counterpoised by the disadvantage of surrendering the power of the state to the mercy of biological and other hazards. See, for intstance, Georg Simmel, *Soziologie* (Leipzig, 1908), p. 516.

2. There is, of course, no intention to suggest that monarchies were not overthrown, once the specific justification lost its power over the minds of men; nor that a democracy in an hour of crisis and demoralization may not go so far as to vote itself out of existence. Once the formal justifications are no longer accepted, either form of government must seek to avert the perils threatening it by appropriate policies. But the passage in the text refers to what may be called monarchical or democratic "normalcy," and it is the normalcy of modern dictatorship that is under discussion here.

those the stability of the dictatorship depends. A modern dictatorship is therefore permanently at work trying to assure what may be called the stability conditions of its power.

Let me list briefly what I believe to be the most important among those stability conditions:

1. Maintenance of a permanent condition of stress and strain
   a. by the existence or creation of enemies both internal and external, and
   b. by imposing upon the population gigantic tasks that exert strong pressures upon its standards of well-being or, at least, greatly retard improvements in those standards.
2. Incessant exercise of dictatorial power.
3. Creation of an image of the dictator as an incarnation of supreme wisdom and indomitable will power.
4. Reference to an allegedly unchanged and unchangeable value system by which the actions of the dictatorship are justified (including perhaps adherence to an ultimate goal, the attainment of which will render the dictatorship unnecessary but which is steadily kept in an appropriately distant future, although still within sight of the living generation).
5. Proscription of any deviating values and beliefs, coupled with threats and acts of repression, sustained and implemented by appropriate organizational devices.

Before I start elaborating upon this list, one or two cautionary remarks may be in order. For one, the concept of stability conditions may appear to be taken over from theoretical physics via economic theory. But the borrowing, if it be one, is at best terminological rather than substantive, and the concept has little to do with the sense attached to it in either discipline. Equilibrium in things political or social is largely if not wholly a metaphorical notion. Its precise meaning eludes me. All that I mean, and can reasonably mean, by stability conditions is that absence thereof creates or is likely to create a situation which threatens a modern dictatorship with the danger of disintegration and possibly sudden overthrow.

The second point is even more important for the understanding of what follows. I have spoken so far of modern dictatorship *tout court*, without circumscribing it, except indirectly, and particularly without specifying the actual historical cases I have in mind. Let it be said that, for the time being, I understand a *modern* dictatorship to be a system of dictatorial government which cannot derive its claim to power from an ancient tradition, or at least from a close and effective alliance with a strong traditional power. The very tendency of a modern dictatorship to be totalitarian, or at least to approach totalitarianism, precludes the continued existence of such a traditional power.[3] For the rest, such research and such thought as I have devoted to the subject have revolved around the Soviet dictatorship in Russia. There is no doubt that the stability conditions I mentioned forced themselves upon my mind in the course of those studies. If I persist in speaking of modern dictatorship rather than confining myself to the Soviet case, it is not because I want to present here a general theory of dictatorship, but rather to convey my strong feeling that a number of features that strike one's eye so forcibly in dealing with the Soviet political system appeared also in several comparable cases. The main purpose of speaking in more general terms is to reinforce my interpretation of the Soviet dictatorship by discussion of related cases, even though, I feel, the explicatory effect is reciprocal and the Soviet experience does cast some light on dictatorial policies that were pursued in other countries and at other times.

I

To return at length to the stability conditions set forth earlier, I should like to select a few significant aspects of Soviet policies and relate them to the generalizations I have advanced. Let us first look at the investment policies of the Soviet government. If I were to summarize in a single sentence the results of the economic policies in Russia during the quarter of a century between the First Five-Year Plan and the death of Stalin (1928–1953), I might put it as follows. As research of American scholars has shown, over that period industrial output increased perhaps sixfold, while the level of real wages decreased by perhaps as much as 20 percent. Real wages, of course,

3. Totalitarianism, of course, is an approximate concept which never fully means what the word implies. The *totality* of human relations, if we take the word seriously, will always escape the most penetrating invasion on the part of the state. As Georg Simmel pointed out, "The elimination of any spontaneity in a subordinate position is in reality much rarer than one might assume from popular speech which uses very freely such terms and phrases as 'compulsion,' 'no other choice,' 'absolute necessity,' and so on. Even in the most cruel and oppressive states of subordination, there usually exists a considerable measure of personal freedom." *Soziologie*, p. 135.

are not an exact measure of levels of consumption because of increases in numbers of gainfully employed per household — what is known as "the participation rate" — as well as because of increases in social services to individuals. But when everything is said and done, we find that in 1953 per capita consumption may have been some 25 percent above 1928, from which figure some, and by no means inconsiderable, deduction must be made for the losses in leisure and domestic comforts brought about by a rise in the participation rate.[4] Whatever measure we take, the gap between the growth of output and the growth of consumption is truly stupendous. The Soviet economy of the period may be justly described as an investment economy in which consumption was not the ultimate goal of production but, on the contrary, the inevitable cost to be incurred grudgingly in the process of continued growth.

It is, therefore, not surprising that the postulate that the rate of growth of investment goods should be higher than that of consumers' goods was solemnly enunciated in Soviet Russia as a "law of socialist economic development," as a condition of growth. Naturally, as an economic proposition the law crumbles to nothing under a minute's reflection, because growth can take place whatever the relation between the rates of growth of investment goods and consumers' goods. It is true, however, that by pursuing the policy of *growing* investment rate, the Soviet government has been able to offset a good many retarding factors at work within the Soviet economy and to maintain for long years after the last war the rate of industrial growth at levels only insignificantly below those attained in the 1930's. Moreover, given the Soviet system, there is no *economic* reason why the Soviet government could not continue this policy for years on end, producing investment goods in order to produce still more investment goods and letting the rate of consumption in national income approach negligible percentages.

More important, however, is something else. Although the law is absurd economics, it is very excellent dictatorial politics. In the long run, nothing serves so well to maintain the conviction that the dictatorship fulfills a useful social function as the continuation of great

---

4. See Abram Bergson, *The Real National Income of Soviet Russia since 1928* (Cambridge, Mass., 1961), pp. 250–252.

investment plans and the atmosphere of stress and strain created in the course of the implementation of those plans. It is paradoxical indeed that the dictatorship has to hurt the population in order to elicit acquiescence in the system. But this, as we shall see, is neither a new insight nor the only paradox of dictatorial rule.

After Stalin's death, the Soviet government, caught in the throes of the succession crisis, was unable to maintain this policy in its grim purity. As internal struggles for leadership weakened the power of the dictatorship, some increases in the supply of consumers' goods became necessary. Stalin's first successor, Malenkov, promised completion of the then current plan for consumers' goods (under the Fifth Five-Year Plan) within four years; he was overthrown, as it was claimed, because of his inability to recognize the priority of heavy industry in the process of Soviet growth. His successful rival, Khrushchev, could not avoid keeping the rate of growth of consumers' goods above that which prevailed under Stalin, but he continued — despite a moment of hesitation — to emphasize his adherence to the aforementioned law. Indeed, the rate of growth of producers' goods not only has been persistently higher than that of consumers' goods, but the gap between the two rates has been widening over the last few years. It is true that great promises regarding increases in consumers' welfare have been made, but such promises were included in every one of Stalin's five-year plans since 1928 and were broken with monotonous regularity. The point is not that the recent increase in consumers' goods will necessarily peter out. It is only that, as long as it continues, it denotes the continued instability of the dictatorship.

Along with the investment policy, the organization of the Soviet economy appears directly pertinent to the problem of dictatorial stability. This is the question of centralization versus decentralization. After Stalin's death, a far-reaching attempt at decentralization was made when, in 1957, most of the economic ministries in Moscow were dissolved and the administration of Soviet industry was placed in the charge of some hundred-odd regional economic councils (*sovnarkhozy*), leaving only the function of general planning to the center. The step was hailed by many outside Russia as a natural consummation of the preceding industrial growth of the country. The Soviet economy, it was argued, had become much too large for efficient centralized guidance. Those observers must have received a rude jolt when after a few years the course was changed again: first, in 1961, a number of regional supercouncils were set up to guide and coordinate the activities of the sovnarkhozy, and thereafter, in the fall of 1962, the sovnarkhozy themselves were greatly enlarged and their numbers drastically reduced. At the same time, the curious reorganization of the Communist Party by splitting its structure into parallel agricultural and industrial hierarchies provided more direct channels for the flow of central guidance to the industrial enterprises. Finally, in March 1963, a new agency was created, the Supreme Council of the National Economy of the USSR (the Supreme Sovnarkhoz) to which the State Planning Committee (Gosplan) and the previously established Sovnarkhoz of the USSR were subordinated. The Supreme Sovnarkhoz was equipped with rather unlimited powers; those powers extend not only to industry and construction, but to any state agency "regardless of its subordination." The various "state committees" for the individual branches of industry, most of which had been set up at various times in 1961–62, were either placed directly under the Supreme Sovnarkhoz or under one of the central agencies, subordinated to the Supreme Sovnarkhoz.[5] Thus, after two years passed in the flux of a recentralization movement, the Soviet economy found itself just about where it was before 1957. It is true that in April 1963 Khrushchev still spoke against direct subordination of industrial enterprises to the state committees.[6] Nevertheless, the reforms of March 1963 came very close to the resurrection, albeit under different names, of the economic ministries in Moscow as they existed in Stalin's time. The wind hath returned upon its circuits. But why was the circuitous road chosen at all? Why this zigzagging policy? It is at least plausible to assume that the decentralization in the first place was dictated not by considerations of economic efficiency, but by the urgent need of the victorious group to do away with the

5. See *Pravda*, March 14, 1963, p. 1, and *Current Digest of the Soviet Press*, XV (March 27, 1963), pp. 3–5.

6. Speech, *Pravda*, April 26, 1963, p. 2. [It will also be noted that Khrushchev's dual organization of the Communist Party was likewise abolished by his successors. Moreover, with regard to the relative rates of growth of output of consumers' and producers' goods (as mentioned in the preceding paragraph), the reader's attention is called to the change in this respect which took place in 1967. See above, Introduction, note 2.]

bureaucracy in the economic ministries that had been raised and steeped in loyalty to Khrushchev's enemies. It took a long time to rebuild reliable bureaucratic staffs at the center. The creation of the new organizational framework in Moscow can be taken as a sign that the job was accomplished at length. Once this was done, the return to centralized normalcy was the natural result.[7]

It is a moot question how great are the losses in economic efficiency involved in recentralization. In the long run, one must keep in mind the immense technological potentialities for centralized planning inherent in large-scale electronic computers. The main point, however, is something else. For more important than economic efficiency is — to use Thomas Hardy's phrase — the economics of vitality or, I should say, of viability of dictatorship. It is my belief that in dictatorships delegation of power means its diminution. Decentralization of decision making must needs lead to the erosion of that power. And power is the resource that a dictatorship must husband above all other resources.

Stalin's unrelenting concern to invent enemies in order to annihilate them covered with blood the pages in the book of his reign. One may admit freely that many aspects of his crimes cannot be understood without the help of psychiatry. And yet it is the dictatorship's — rather than the dictator's — thirst for enemies that cannot be quenched as long as the system continues in existence. Stalin initiated, in the fall of 1945, the policy of the cold war, but the cold war outlived its author. In order to pose as the defender of the nation from foreign threats, the Soviet government has untiringly conjured up one crisis after the other. The dangerous road has led from Berlin to Korea, from Korea to the Middle East, from the Middle East back to the Far East, from there again to Berlin, and from Berlin to Cuba. But the struggle against the West has not been sufficient. The United States, unwillingly enough, has obliged the needs of the Soviet dictatorship by playing its role in the cold war. But it could not do a perfectly satisfactory job. America is far away, and, between the crises, the image of the "imperialist enemy" has tended to become blurred in the minds of the population despite all efforts of vituperative

7. The final abolition of the sovnarkhozy after Khrushchev's fall was the consummation of the evolution sketched here.

journalism, supine scholarship, and a crowd of servile writers of novels, plays, and poetry. Search for enemies at home could not be dispensed with. Thanks to the new methods used by Khrushchev, no irreversible acts were committed so that, in dealing with the alleged or real opponents of the regime, the same men have been purged twice over, leaving the door open for further reiterations of the procedure. Anti-Semitism is kept just below the surface of public life, when it is not allowed to break into the open sporadically through announcement of capital punishment meted out "for crimes against the state" to persons readily identifiable as Jews. An internal enemy, against whom the aggressions and the hatreds of an oppressed population can be deflected, is no doubt much more tangible and effective from the point of view of dictatorial needs — unless indeed a new and a better external enemy can be discovered. China pressing upon her food reserves and adjacent to huge and sparsely populated Soviet areas — some of them relatively recently parts of the Chinese Empire [8] — is threatening to reproduce the Soviet performance in economic development at a still faster tempo, because enriched by the Soviet Russian experience. Propelled by even more virulent demand for antagonism and conflict, it may soon come to provide all the hostility that the Soviet dictatorship wants.

But might one not think that the ostensible sameness of the official ideologies in the two countries should militate against the likelihood of a conflict between them? That such a question should be asked betrays a fatal misunderstanding of the functions of ideology within the dictatorial system. Soviet ideology is frequently described as "monolithic." This is an awkward and perhaps misleading term. To be sure, as said before, it is essential for a stable dictatorship to admit of no competing value systems, and even transcendental thoughts and sentiments that wander beyond the grave are as a rule highly suspect to it. But if the term "monolithic" is taken seriously in its etymological and lexical meaning, Soviet ideology quite patently is not hewn from a single rock of uniform consistency. In a protracted process that is as old as the Soviet government, the Marxian ideology of the revolutionary period, already then muted by Lenin, underwent

8. It was only in 1858–1860 that Russia acquired from China the regions north of the Amur and west of the Ussuri rivers.

a long evolution in the course of which, under the pressure of exigencies of changing situations and the specific power interests of the dictatorship, most disparate and contradictory elements came to be conjoined under the unchanged original name. Thus, a doctrine that has stressed the role of objective impersonal forces in history found itself in cohabitation with the shameless veneration of Stalin; an internationalist ideology proved compatible with rabid stress on Russian nationalism; Marxian stress on increasing returns, so deeply imbedded in the system, became readily associated with attacks upon gigantomania; the strong egalitarian strain in Marxism was no impediment to the acceptance of a policy of enormous wage differentials.

The point is that it is not Marxian doctrine or Marxian ideology that in any way has determined the policies of the Soviet government. On the contrary, any Soviet policy was immediately described as "Marxian" by the virtue of the very fact of its being pursued. The official ideology in Russia, therefore, constitutes a hybrid mass, the function of which is merely to vindicate what is being done for reasons that have little if anything to do with the original ideology. It is, of course, not surprising at all that the Soviet government has not attempted to rid itself of the fiction of a unified, internally consistent, and unchanged ideology. The semblance of ideological continuity is a strong stabilizing factor within the dictatorial system. It may appear curious to see that a most radical social movement such as the Bolshevik Party, which carried out the most far-reaching and most rapid change that ever occurred in the history of Russia, has been most anxious to suppress any appearance of change in its ideology. But the seeming paradox only serves to underscore the advantages which a dictatorial regime derives from a system of belief that in its original form was associated with a large humanitarian movement of the past century and that encompasses a final goal which, even though quite incompatible with the nature and interests of the dictatorship, is clearly useful to the regime as long as its attainment is kept at a never attainable future distance.

Thus, official Soviet ideology has been so thoroughly transformed both in function and in contents and has become so flexible and so easily adaptable to the changing needs of changing policies that, far from being an impediment to Chinese-Russian dissensions, it is being used effectively to fan the fire of controversy. In fact, the sameness of the jargon employed by both sides and the use of identical authorities to support the opposing points of view must needs provide an additional irritant to the struggle.[9]

At any rate, the Soviet ideology in its present form is well suited to serve the power interests of the dictatorship and can be relied upon to support whatever enmities in whatever direction those interests may wish to pursue. There is no question, however, that within the Soviet Union the strength of the official ideology has lost some of its previous vigor in consequence of events that took place after Stalin's death. What is called in Russia today the cult of personality was itself a perhaps incongruous, but an integral, part of the official ideology. It has been proclaimed that Stalin committed many a grievous "mistake." But Stalin was identical with the state to an extent that Louis XIV never was. The cult of personality was also the cult of the state. If the state could err so flagrantly, serious doubt is cast on the principle of absolute devotion to the state — the very foundation of the Soviet value system. Indeed, one has merely to leaf through the pages of Soviet literature over the last five years or so to see how far-reaching the effects have been, and how in particular the members of the young generation have strongly emphasized the theme of conflict between individual personality and the claims upon it and the actions against it by the "coldest of all cold monsters," to use Nietzsche's phrase — a conflict in which the sympathies of the authors, and presumably those of many readers, are very unevenly distributed.

De-Stalinization thus broke away some of the carrying pillars in the ideological edifice. It was clearly the purpose of the program of the Communist Party adopted at the Twenty-Second Congress, after extensive country-wide discussions, to repair the damage and to inject new life into the creed outworn. At the same time, as the myth of Stalin's infallibility was being destroyed, earnest attempts were made to equip the public image of Khrushchev's with similar traits of supreme authority over areas ranging from authentic interpretations of works of Marx and Lenin to victorious strategy in the historical

---

9. In addition, of course, the very existence of an opponent operating within the same ideological framework should make it impossible for the Soviet government to discard that framework, even if it were willing to do so.

battle in and around a certain town on the Volga River and to problems of correct aesthetic standards in the arts. In the field of ideology then, as in the other fields, the regime tried to restore the stability conditions that are the requisites of the unimpaired exercise of dictatorial power.

II

As said before, the concept of stability conditions has been distilled from the historical experience of the Soviet Union. I have touched on some of the problems confronted and the techniques used by the Soviet government in its efforts to secure its position. At first glance, those problems and techniques look strange, perhaps implausible, and one may tend to doubt that thinking in terms of such stability conditions is the proper avenue to the understanding of the modus operandi of the dictatorship. And yet, as one looks at the classical literature on the subject of tyrannical governments; as one reads and rereads the sayings of men who were deeply concerned with the problem of power and observes the motivations and actions of other dictators, the sense of strangeness and implausibility vanishes. The apparent paradoxes dissolve into natural — and somewhat trite — verities, and one begins to feel to have broken through open doors, curtained as they may be by ignorance and muddled thinking.

Nearly twenty-four centuries have passed since Aristotle's *Politics*. But as one peruses its pages devoted to the problems of tyrannical government, one is struck by the modernity of his insights, which incidentally are draped as matter-of-fact counsels to tyrants.[10] In order to secure his power, a tyrant must keep the population in poverty so that the preoccupation with daily bread leaves them no leisure to conspire against the tyrant; he must multiply taxes and engage in great investment projects; he must conduct foreign wars and maintain domestically an atmosphere of distrust and mutual suspicion.[11] One marvels how close the great Stagirite came to de-

10. In discussing these pages, Theodor Gomperz rightly wondered at their curious Machiavellian tone. "Nowhere else in his *Politics* does Aristotle assume such a relativistic position." *Griechische Denker*, III (Berlin and Leipsig, 1931), p. 167.

11. Aristotle, *Politics*, book V, chapter 11. For the historical connection between tyranny and investment projects, in particular public works assuring full employ-

scribing the stability conditions of Soviet dictatorship and how much of what he said was repeated through the ages by other men on the strength of their own experience. Take the rulers' love of poverty — for their subjects. Richelieu (and his ghost writer), who knew well that "power was the most necessary thing to assure the greatness of kings and the happiness of their reigns," put the problem succinctly in the Cardinal's Political Testament: "All the statesmen agree that it would be impossible to contain the peoples within bounds of duty, were they to become too prosperous." [12]

This is a clear but perhaps incomplete statement. For the great dangers to a dictatorial regime stem not alone from a relatively high level of well-being of the population, but even more from improvements in those levels. This connection could not escape De Tocqueville's sharp eye. The French, in the years before 1789, "found their conditions all the more intolerable because they had improved." [13] It is connections of this kind Talcott Parsons had in mind when he wrote, with reference to the Soviet dictatorship, that "a state of continuing emergency is less threatening than its relaxation." [14] The increased supply of consumers' goods in Soviet Russia is likely to provoke effects much more complex than a burst of enthusiasm on the part of a grateful populace; so is the relaxation of the dictatorial grip upon minds and sentiments which has occurred since 1956. *We* may require the help of Richelieu and De Tocqueville to discern the intricacies of the situation. But the men who stand at the helm of the Soviet dictatorship, the graduates of Stalin's seminars in practical politics, are not in need of literary illuminations. Who can hope to rival their understanding of power and the techniques of power? We must assume that they are fully aware of the threats to the stability of the regime and anxious to do what they can to restore it.

But also for us, in our attempts to comprehend the motivations

ment at subsistence levels, see Hermann Gottlob Plass, *Die Tyrannis in ihren beiden Perioden bei den alten Griechen* (Leipsig, 1859), 352–365. On the role of distrust in the Soviet regime, see Khrushchev's speech, *Pravda*, April 26, 1963, p. 1, where he declared it to be the duty of every Soviet citizen to act as a watchful policeman.

12. Louis André, ed., *Testament politique du Cardinal Richelieu*, (Paris, 1947), pp. 253, 372.

13. Alexis de Tocqueville, *L'Ancien régime et la révolution* (Paris, 1961), bk. 3, chap. 4.

14. Talcott Parsons, *The Social System* (Glencoe, 1951), p. 532.

of the Soviet dictatorship and in plotting the course it is steering, a glance at the actual practice of other dictatorships may be more important than general interpretations. Unhappily, modern history has provided us with a large legacy of experience upon which we may draw for enlightening parallels: Napoleon I, Hitler, perhaps Napoleon III or Mussolini — despite all the differences among them, the common traits are undeniable. They all shared the common dynamics of power exercise. To stand still was to decline. Stable power meant growing power. Hobbes spoke of mankind's "perpetual and restless desire of power after power" because, as he said, the power man has at present cannot be assured without acquisition of more.[15] Whatever the validity of the statement in the general form that Hobbes chose to give it, it describes well the devil who, in Mr. Wickfield's words, finds mischief still for busy dictatorial hands to do.

In the bleak years on St. Helena, Napoleon, reviewing what he called once "the novel of my life," returned time and again to the search for the fateful error that had caused his downfall. The widest possible variety of possible causes is scanned at various times: his own ambition and his fiery temperament; an intrigue of Empress Josephine that prevented his marriage with a Russian grand duchess and so "changed the course of history," for such a marriage would have precluded war against Russia; the failure "to destroy Prussia" after Jena; the failure to dismember Austria after Wagram; the failure to make peace after the battle of Dresden; the exclusion of Murat from the battle of Waterloo because of a personal resentment; wrong decisions on domestic policy during the hundred days. All imaginable things, big and small, cross Napoleon's mind in those conversations on the Little Island, of which now, since the discovery in the 1940's of General Bertrand's Copybooks, we possess a most faithful and uninhibited record. In the course of that melancholy review, even a little joke escapes the unhumorous man: "the greatest mistake," he says, "was to have lost at Waterloo."[16]

15. Thomas Hobbes, *Leviathan* (London–New York, 1952), part 1, chap. 11, p. 79.

16. See Général Bertrand, *Cahiers de Sainte Hélène: Journal, 1816–1817* (Paris, 1951), pp. 23, 210, 246; *Journal, 1818–1819* (Paris 1959), pp. 96, 97, 108, 228, 260; *Journal, Janvier 1821–Mai 1821*, p. 38. Also Comte de Las Cases, *Le Mémorial de Sainte Hélène* (Paris, 1961), I, 539, 893, and II, 171; Général

But what seemed to Napoleon the cardinal error and to which he returns incessantly in those conversations is still something else: the unfinished business of the war in Spain.[17] He said: "That miserable war was my ruin. All the circumstances of my disasters are tied to that fatal knot. The Spanish war enhanced my difficulties; it divided my forces; opened a flank to the English army, and destroyed my moral standing in Europe." But why did he embark upon the Spanish adventure at all? Several reasons are advanced, none of them too convincing: the destiny of France demanded it; Spain had to be punished because in 1806, when Napoleon was engaged in Prussia, it "almost declared war on France"; in the crisis in which France found herself in the great cause of the new age against the rest of Europe, Spain could not be left behind.[18] More is mentioned: "I began the war in Spain, because I believed France to be less safe than it actually was." [19] But this admission of an error of judgment is no more convincing than the rest of the reasons. The real motivation for the invasion of Spain must be sought elsewhere. When John Quincy Adams served as ambassador of the United States at St. Petersburg, Chancellor Rumyantsev related to him (in February 1812) a conversation he had had with Napoleon. "Tranquility," Rumyantsev said, "is not in his nature. I can tell you in confidence that he once told me so himself. I was speaking to him about Spain and Portugal and he said to me: 'I must always be going. After the peace of Tilsit where could I go but Spain? I went to Spain because I could not go anywhere else.' " [20]

This is indeed a plausible explanation. It is supported by the very weakness of any alternative interpretation. Lefebvre, for instance, claimed, and Sainte-Beuve agreed, that the heir of the revolution, the target of "all the hatreds of the past" (*de toutes les haines du passé*), simply could not find a place to stop in his struggle against old

Baron Gourgaud, *Sainte Hélène, Journal inédit de 1815 à 1818* (Flammarion, Paris, n.d.), I, 135, 202, and II, 112.

17. *Journal, 1816–1817*, p. 148; *Journal, 1818–1819*, pp. 114, 229; *Journal, Janvier 1821–Mai 1821*, p. 35.

18. Las Cases, I, 610. The text of this passage on Spain appears in different editions with slight variations, some of which have been used in the text.

19. *Journal, 1816–1817*, p. 148.

20. Charles F. Adams, ed., *Memoirs of John Quincy Adams*, II (New York, 1874), 338.

Europe.[21] But such abstract constructs do not stand up in the light of empirical knowledge. It is true, as Alexander I wrote in 1804, that Napoleon's "most powerful weapon consisted in the common opinion that the cause of France was the cause of liberty and welfare of the people." [22] But that was the weapon which Napoleon was never compelled to use and which, in fact, he used more and more sparingly as the years passed. He refrained from applying the weapon in Prussia after Jena and did not even employ it when its use might have made all the difference between victory and defeat, as in Russia in 1812.[23]

The choices were not "Europe's." They were Napoleon's, and he knew that well. "I was," he said once on St. Helena, "the greatest of all the sovereigns of Europe. The alliance with me was eagerly sought by the greatest reigning houses. I ruled as a master in almost all the capitals of Europe. I made kings." [24]

If Napoleon could not "stop," it was not because "old Europe" would not let him. Nor was it because of his "nature," as Rumyantsev suggested, or because of his fiery temperament, as he said himself. Nor is it easy to attribute crucial importance to the dream of World Empire, which at times he called a "universal dictatorship." Not that he had not thought in such terms. "Who in my place would not have wanted it?" he asked upon his return from Elba. He even had an answer to Cineas' demonstration to Pyrrhus of the futility of world conquest: "Et après tout, à quoi bon? To build up a new society and to save [Europe] from great misfortunes." [25] But more significant than the admission is Napoleon's profound aversion from long-range

21. Armand Lefebvre, *Histoire des Cabinets de l'Europe pendant le Consulat et l'Empire* (with a preface by C. A. Sainte-Beuve), I (Paris, 1866), xxxvi.

22. Sergey Soloviev, *Imperator Alexandr Pervyi, politika, diplomatiya* (Emperor Alexander I, Politics and Diplomacy; St. Petersburg, 1877), p. 65.

23. Now for the first time after a long interval Soviet historians have been willing at least to touch — though very lightly indeed — on the hopes of the Russian peasants that the Napoleonic invasion might bring about the end of serfdom and on the peasant uprising engendered by the invasion. See A. N. Kochetkov, "Partisanskaya voyna" (Guerrilla Warfare), *1812 god, K stopyatidesyatiletiyu otechestvennoy voyny, Sbornik statey* (1812, To the 150th Anniversary of the Patriotic War, a Collection of Papers; Moscow, 1962). But Napoleon refused to become "le roi d'une Jacquerie." Benjamin Constant, *Mémoires sur les Cent Jours* (Paris, 1961), p. 134.

24. *Journal, 1816–1817*, pp. 44–45.

25. Constant, p. 135; Las Cases, I, 250–251, and II, 517; Plutarch's *Lives*, Loeb Classical Library (Cambridge, Mass., 1950), IX, 386–389.

plans and his deep belief in the merits of instantaneous decisions, on the battlefields as well as in diplomacy. He had the horror of Jomini's scientific strategy, of conducting campaigns according to "rules of the general staffs." "War," he kept saying, "is a matter of momentary decisions": *La guerre est l'affaire du moment.*[26]

What mattered was to act. *On s'engage et puis on voit.* And if the action was to lead to a domination of the world, it was unpremeditated — *sans calcul,* as he said, and because the road led in that direction, "step by step." [27] But the source of the urge to act lay neither in the personality of the dictator nor in his ambitious schemes. If he could have rooted his rule in the consent of the governed or in the legitimacy of ancient descent, if only, as he put it, he could have been his own grandchild, the compulsiveness very likely would have disappeared. He made attempts in both directions. The plebiscites were meant to provide the democratic sanction, to create the "new legitimacy in the spirit of the new doctrines." [28] The concordat with the papacy (1801) and the consecration by Pope Pius VII (1804), as well as the marriage with the daughter of the oldest ruling dynasty in Europe, were steps in the other direction. All were in vain. The two plebiscites were mocked by the everyday workings of the police state. The concordat did not prevent the quarrel with the Pope and the excommunication of the Emperor. Beneath the make-believe veils of democracy and legitimacy lay the perennial fear of what Napoleon himself once called a *contre-brumaire,*[29] lay the real need to create and recreate the social function of the dictatorship by creating and recreating enemies, acting to produce the crises which in turn justified action, by endangering France in order to be able to rescue her, by continually maintaining the glory of the reign — its vindication — by the glories of the successive campaigns.

26. *Journal, 1818–1819,* pp. 176, 322. Gourgaud, II, 457.
27. Las Cases, I, 441.
28. Las Cases, I, 391.
29. Las Cases, II, 303. The "least relaxation" of his power, he believed, might have produced the dreaded upheaval. In the days after Austria's defeat at Wagram, at the very acme of power, Napoleon still feared that France might turn against him and he upbraided Fouché — in a letter from Schönbrunn — for conscribing national guards in certain sensitive areas in France "Men begin to wonder, the minds are aroused, and the least incident may produce a crisis." *Correspondance de Napoléon I* (Paris, 1864), XIX, 521.

Hence the Napoleonic fear of being late: "In our time," he said to a Russian diplomat (Kurakin), "events chase each other so quickly that the opportune moment, once missed, will escape forever." [30] Hence the conviction that decay was the only alternative to expansion, a view expressed with terse vigor in the French memorandum to Prussia in 1805, when Napoleon tried to secure that country's cooperation in the war against Austria: "It has been often said that a state that does not grow declines; that proposition was never more rigorously true than in the present age . . . The occasion is truly unique. Centuries may elapse before a similar opportunity presents itself." [31] This is the true expression of the Napoleonic philosophy of action except that, of course, it was Napoleon himself who largely was the cause of the swift movement of events.

However true it may have been that Napoleon's mind, in the words of a modern historian, "was congested with alternatives" when it came to choosing between different actions, he never saw any alternative to action. Hence, to quote the same historian, his immense "capacity to work" was "a nervous complaint, almost we might say, the equivalent of St. Vitus Dance," which extended indiscriminately to all things, be they grandiose troop movements and creation of new statehoods or minute administrative decisions.[32] And the latter are no less significant than the former, because they stem from the selfsame source. Napoleonic history shows with particular clarity how unwilling a dictator is to delegate power; how well Napoleon understood the basic dictatorial maxim that power — that elusive, intangible, and yet so real thing — is maintained through unremitting exercise. The capacity of his brain made it possible, but his position made it necessary, for him to go on exercising his will so as to regulate, often from faraway parts of Europe, the establishment of a small workshop, or the shipment of a parcel of textiles from the Duchy of Berg to the Kingdom of Naples, or the curriculum of a school, or the program of a theater, or the number of horses to run at the races in Paris. The smallest details — an ordinance of the police, a minor item in the budget of a municipality, a family problem of an individual citizen —

---

30. Soloviev, p. 208.

31. Leopold von Ranke, *Aktenstücke zu den Denkwürdigkeiten des Fürsten von Hardenberg* (Leipzig, 1877), p. 158.

32. Herbert Butterfield, *Napoleon* (New York, 1962), pp. 24, 33.

nothing escaped, as Count Mollien put it, "his restless vigilance lest a particle of power should slip from him." Everything was absorbed by his "insatiable need to be the center of all, the only principle of action and propulsion upon every person and every object." [33] Very similarly, Stalin used to call up, in the small hours of the morning, managers of far-flung industrial enterprises all over the country in order to upbraid them because of a flawed delivery or to issue a decision with regard to a new line of production. Even so, Khrushchev on his frequent inspection trips entered into the trivial problems of a sovkhoz or factory. Absentee dictatorship cannot last, and absolute power and the rule of law, be it even laid down by the absolute power itself, are at opposite poles.

Therein lies, it may be added parenthetically, the fundamental difficulty of deistic conceptions. To envisage the deity as having created, once and for all, the all-comprehensive law for the universe means to extol the magnificence of creation, but at the same time it means to dethrone the divine power in favor of the human brain that can grasp the operation of the law. It is not surprising, therefore, that a deeply religious man like Newton was pleased when he discovered certain instabilities in planetary motions which he could attribute to the will of God.[34] And it showed a profound intuitive understanding of the problem when the much lamented Swedish writer, Stig Dagerman, in a posthumously published fragment "A Thousand Years with God," made God visit Newton's house and abolish there the law of gravity. Absolute power must be unpredictable, and its intervention must be frequent if not incessant.[35]

Butterfield says: "We may feel at times that if he [Napoleon] could have taken a holiday . . . he might have been saved." [36] But that feeling would lead us astray. Dictatorial power knows no vacation from danger. There is no salvation for dictators in following Pascal's advice and staying put in their rooms. There is no choice between

33. Comte Mollien, *Mémoires d'un ministre du trésor public, 1780–1815* (Paris, 1898), I, 40. This is the view of a man who was in an excellent position to observe Napoleon as an administrator and whose memoirs are an important source for the economic and financial history of the reign.

34. See Gerd Buchdahl, *The Image of Newton and Locke in the Age of Reason* (London and New York, 1961), p. 6.

35. Stig Dagerman, *Tusen år hos Gud* (Stockholm, 1954), pp. 13ff.

36. Butterfield, p. 33.

perilous action and fatal inaction, and there is little point in charging Napoleon, as Butterfield does, with a lack of skill for allowing himself to get involved in the peninsular war. He followed the paradoxical course of keeping his hold on France by taking the war-weary country into war; by seeking, as he had done before, security in perennial insecurity.[37] Napoleon's famous words addressed to Metternich after the victorious battles of Bautzen and Wurschen in 1813 sound like a further elaboration of his statement to Rumyantsev: "Your sovereigns, born to the throne, may suffer twenty defeats and still keep returning to their capitals. I cannot. I am an upstart soldier. My rule will not survive the day on which I have ceased being strong and feared."[38] The paradoxes of Soviet policies should appear less striking in the light of French history in the early years of the past century.

It would not be too difficult to detect similar connections in the

37. Nevertheless the utopian vision of a blissful future was not altogether foreign to Napoleon's mind. The time would come, he claimed, when universal peace would reign supreme; when all his efforts would be dedicated to "improving the condition of the whole society"; when a corps of carefully selected do-gooders (*espions de la vertu*) would aid him in discovering and removing hardships and injustices; and when "the great European family" would bask in the sun of true civilization, united by common principles, common currency, and a common code But Napoleon also knew that those were "chimerical dreams"; for still another war, still to be won, would always come to stand between him and his *beau idéal* — just as in Soviet Russia new tasks must be ever interposed between the present and the attainment of the ultimate goal. Las Cases, II, 49, 220, 545–546.

38. Richard de Metternich, *Mémoires, documents et écrits divers laissés par le Prince de Metternich*, I (Paris, 1886), 148. Metternich himself observes elsewhere in his memoirs: "One of his keenest and constant regrets was not to be able to invoke the principle of legitimacy as the basis of his power. Few men have felt more strongly than he how much an authority lacking that basis must remain precarious and fragile and how readily it exposes itself to attacks" (p. 283). It was natural for Metternich to appreciate this point. What he could not be expected to understand as well was that Napoleon, in his recourse to wars, had to overcome not only the population's growing reluctance to bear the burdens of military adventures, not only the people's craving for political freedom, but also the spirit of what Benjamin Constant aptly termed the "age of commerce which must of necessity replace the age of war." *De l'Esprit de la Conquête, 1813* (Paris, n.d.), p. 15. Also, Constant, *Mémoires sur les Cent Jours*, p. 65.

It should be added that in his feverish domestic activity, just as in his aggressions abroad, Napoleon was well aware of the difference between himself and the legitimate rulers. He explained once why he was spending so much time on administrative matters by saying that he could not reign as other princes did; his special position imposed extraordinary duties. Mollien, II, 139.

history of the third Napoleon, even though on an appropriately diminished scale, corresponding to the size of the protagonist. The great constructions, the plebiscites, the play with socialist ideas, the assurances that *l'Empire c'est la paix* and the willingness to engage in three major wars, to say nothing of other military adventures — all those are the familiar elements of a dictatorial regime. Napoleon III recognized clearly, and Bismarck, who was not exactly a tyro in questions of power, understood him well, the function of foreign wars in the play of domestic policies.[39] But he was unable to maintain the state of permanent tension needed for the stability of dictatorial power. Hence, the main interest of his regime in the present context lies in the protracted process of the disintegration of the dictatorship, a period imperfectly labeled as "Liberal Monarchy." The Mexican expedition and the disaster of the war against Prussia were as much attempts to halt and reverse that process as the constitutional reforms and increasing discontent were its manifestations.

The experience of the Nazi regime in Germany, no doubt, is much more illuminating for our purposes. In 1962 a British historian presented to the world a new interpretation of the causes of the Second World War.[40] Taylor's critique of the British appeasement policies contains nothing that has not been said many times before, but his thesis, which tends to exonerate Hitler, is that war broke out in 1939 because of diplomatic blunders committed by both sides: the fatal British guarantee to Poland in March 1939 and Hitler's one day's delay in launching a diplomatic maneuver. This is not the place to discuss Taylor's methods as a historian, in particular his brushing aside or ignoring altogether the evidence that militates against his thesis, while gladly admitting the same type of evidence when it accords with that thesis.[41]

39. See Bismarck's report on his conversations with Napoleon III in 1857. Otto Fürst von Bismarck, *Gedanken und Erinnerungen,* I (Stuttgart, 1898), 179.

40. A.J.P. Taylor, *Origins of the Second World War* (New York, 1962).

41. It is curious that Mussolini, cogitating on the origin of the war in his temporary exile on a Sardinian island, propounded views that were very similar to Taylor's as far as Britain was concerned, but was willing to go a good deal further in blaming Germany. In speaking of his attempts in the last hour to avert the conflict, he says: "[My] efforts failed. The responsibility for [the war] falls almost equally upon the British and the Germans; on the former for having given guarantees to Poland and on the Germans for having built a powerful military machine and for

Nor is the point at issue Taylor's general view of history, which he expresses by stating that Hitler's decisions in 1939 are "capable of rational explanations, and it is on these that history is built." And he adds contemptuously: "The escape into irrationality is no doubt easier." [42] This view reveals the frequent confusion between rationality of explanation and rationality of the behavior that is to be explained [43] (which, of course, does not mean that there are no other ways, alternative to Taylor's, of viewing Hitler's actions as rational, that is, purposive within his specific context). Least of all should one reproach Taylor for having abandoned his previous appraisal of Hitler as "the greatest of demagogues, confident of his powers, marching *somnambulistically* to world conquest"; [44] or to charge him with inconsistency in the later book because of his references to Hitler as a gambler who "plays for high stakes with inadequate resources." [45] Nor is, finally, the problem whether at that particular moment Hitler really wanted war, or whether he acted in accordance with a precise schedule. It is very probable that, like Napoleon, Hitler very often did not know precisely where he was going, but like Napoleon he knew that he must keep going.[46] For what really matters in this context is Taylor's inability to appreciate the strength of forces that push a modern dictatorial regime into continual dramatic action; an action that is perfectly rational per se, once the dictator's *cupido dominandi* — his lust for power — is accepted as being the primary motivation of dictatorial decisions, as being in the words of Tacitus

---

being unable to resist the temptation of setting it in motion." Benito Mussolini, "Pensieri Pontini e Sardi," *Opera omnia,* XXXIV (Florence, 1961), 286.

42. *Origins,* p. 216.

43. The same confusion frequently prevails with regard to the value judgments of the historian as distinguished from those of his actors as well as with regard to probabilistic assessments by the historian of consequences of certain actions which are confused with the probability calculus employed by the authors of those actions. Cf. Chapter Three above, p. 61.

44. A.J.P. Taylor, *Bismarck, The Man and the Statesman* (New York, 1961), p. 271; italics supplied. For the rest, Hitler himself once declared to "walk with somnambulistic certainty . . . in obedience to the commands of Providence," which is a rare case of a sleepwalker reporting on his own experience. Max Domarus, *Hitler, Reden und Proklamationen, 1932–1945, kommentiert von einem deutschen Zeitgenossen* (Würzburg, 1962), I, 606.

45. *Origins,* pp. 75, 251.

46. Las Cases, II, 545, 618.

"cunctis adfectibus flagrantior," which we may translate as "more important than all other sentiments and motivations." [47] But it is impossible to abstract from the very essence of a dictatorial regime without distorting its history. It is therefore not surprising at all to find Taylor painting a picture of a Hitler who possessed immense reserves of patience, was a master in the game of waiting, never took the initiative, and preferred to remain passive until the desired fruit fell into his lap. [48]

In reality, every year after Hitler's accession to power was marked by a crisis. The year 1934 brought the internal upheaval of June 30 and the first attempts at subverting the Austrian government. In the following year, conscription was introduced. In 1936, Hitler marched into the Rhineland. In 1937, he rehearsed in Spain and developed plans for attack on Austria and Czechoslovakia, as we know from the so-called Hossbach memorandum. [49] In 1938, came the invasion of Austria — a step that, according to Taylor, Hitler took "unintentionally" [50] — and the Munich agreement. Finally, 1939 saw the final destruction of Czechoslovakia, the onslaught on Poland, and the outbreak of the war. Those were years of permanent crisis. Nothing could be more misleading than to garb Hitler in the clothes of Bismarck, the man who indeed knew how to bide his time and could well afford to do so as a servant of a legitimate ruler. By contrast, Hitler could not wait and, as full employment was re-established and the memories of the depression began to fade, the urge to act, to create one crisis after another, was bound to become keener and keener. Taylor himself makes much of the deadline for the invasion of Poland, which Hitler had set and from which he could not back down unless he was able to present the generals, who were "watching sceptically," with "something solid" — the same generals who, again according to Taylor, less than a year earlier insisted that Germany was not ready for a general war and talked of overthrowing Hitler lest

47. Tacitus, *Annals*, bk. 15, chap. 53.
48. *Origins*, pp. 71, 72, 84, 108, 137, 142. The origin of the "waiting theory" presumably lies in Hitler's boasts to his intimates which have been mentioned in Weizsäcker's memoirs. Ernst von Weizsäcker, *Erinnerungen* (Munich-Leipzig-Freiburg i.B., 1950), pp. 224, 239.
49. Domarus, I, 748–756.
50. *Origins*, p. 150.

he lead the country over the brink.[51] If Taylor had connected the two observations, he might have begun to grasp some of the pressures to which an ostensibly omnipotent dictatorship is exposed, as well as the ever-present tendency to escape from danger into danger.

The pressures, of course, need not be patent and tangible. Apathy on the part of the population and its growing indifference to the system may not constitute any visible and immediate threat to the safety of the regime. And yet it is likely to create a stifling climate for the dictatorship and spur it into action. This in itself may provide sufficient explanation for Mussolini's escapade in Ethiopia, which in a review Taylor attributes to an "absurd desire to build an empire in Africa"; in his book he describes "the background and the significance" of the Ethiopian war as "still something of a mystery." [52] Croce once warned historians against taking easy "refuge in mystery," and seeming absurdity may make excellent dictatorial logic, as presumably does the more recent Chinese attack upon India.[53]

Much more penetrating is the interpretation of dictatorial action left by a man who had risen high in Hitler's Germany, and who after the war suffered the well-deserved punishment for the manifold crimes committed in the service of the dictator. Hans Frank, the erstwhile governor general of Poland, used the time of his imprisonment to do some hard rethinking about the gruesome historical drama, the last act of which brought him under the gallows of Nuremberg. Some of his conclusions bear directly upon our problem:

51. *Origins*, pp. 171, 275. Weizsäcker claims that preparations for Hitler's arrest were made twice during the Munich crisis (September 13 and 27, 1938) and again in October 1939 (pp. 193, 270).

52. A.J.P. Taylor, review in *The Observer*, December 30, 1962; *Origins*, p. 87.

53. Benedetto Croce, *Nuovi saggi di estetica* (Bari, 1926) p. 36. It may be added that by the early thirties important segments of Italian public opinion had become thoroughly disillusioned with Fascism. The fear of social upheavals, in the wake of the occupation of factories, had faded away, while the original laissez-faire policies of the regime — its *liberismo* — had receded into the background. What remained were the effects of the depression against the background of which Mussolini's oratory appeared more and more *buffo*. The expansion in Africa and the establishment of the empire were designed to provide much needed justification for the dictatorship. In these terms, the policy was undeniably successful, even though for a limited time. No wonder that plans for an Ethiopian campaign began to be nursed by the Italian dictator probably as early as 1932. Christopher Hibbert, *Mussolini* (Milan, 1962), p. 95.

With Hitler's accession to power on January 30, 1933, the critical struggle of the National Socialist Party against the other political parties was essentially over. But at that point began the much more difficult internal crisis of the Party's own existence within the State which it had come to dominate. It is curious that the very term "party" became meaningless after the advent to power and, particularly, after its coalition with the Nationalists was dissolved. For the concept of a "party," meaning "a part," necessarily presupposes the existence of other parties. In the absence of such parties, the natural task of any genuine party, that is, competitive struggle with them for political power, is no longer possible . . . Since the visible enemies in the shape of other parties were no longer there, and since every party must needs have enemies in the conflict with whom it renews its vitality, the National Socialist Party proceeded to create such enemies . . . so as to utilize its otherwise unused energy reserves and in order to vindicate its own existence.[54]

This inside view of the workings of a dictatorship, on the part of one of Hitler's foremost henchmen, is valuable. To be sure, Frank prefers to speak of vitality — the German term he uses is in fact *Lebenswärme* — instead of power. He also has a distorted view of the role of "enemies" in a democratic system, a view based on his own experience gleaned during a period when the German democracy was in a state of disintegration. But he does point to a basic problem of dictatorial rule: the perennial need for justification for its existence and the creation of enemies in an attempt to find such justifications.[55] A dictator cannot rest on his laurels as Bismarck did after 1871. This is the crux of the situation, the common ground trodden by all modern dictatorships, despite the manifold differences that so obviously separate them.[56]

54. Hans Frank, *Im Angesicht des Galgens* (Munich-Gräfelfing, 1953), pp. 185–186. The preceding quotation has been somewhat compressed and slightly changed in translation, to remove some obscurities of expression, but without doing any violence to the author's meaning.

55. It should be mentioned in this connection how persistently Hitler viewed his foreign policy and his warlike engagements as a natural continuation of the preceding struggle for power within Germany. Henry Picker, *Hitler's Tischgespräche im Führerhauptquartier*, 1441–42 (Bonn, 1951), p. 187; Weizsäcker, p. 129; Hermann Rauschning, *Gespräche mit Hitler* (Zurich, 1950), p. 255; Domarus, p. 39.

56. Two more remarks on the Hitler dictatorship may be in order. It is curious to see Frank accuse Hitler of perverting the ideology of the Nazi movement by abandoning the original party program, so that whatever Hitler pronounced was National Socialist by definition. "Whatever the Führer orders is German" (pp. 184,

III

No historical interpretation is truly cogent. Alternative interpretations are always possible. One might feel tempted to explain the actions of some dictators by reference to the economic conditions in which they found themselves. Few would claim that Napoleon's continental system was the goal rather than an instrument of his power policies. One may argue that the need to increase the economic potential of the country in the 1930's was the prime mover behind Stalin's policy, but such an explanation would carry much less conviction if applied to the situation after the end of World War II. Or it might be argued that Hitler was pushed onward by his view that Germany could not prosper unless its Lebensraum were greatly widened. But to explain Hitler's policy in terms of Malthusian population pressures is to overlook his frank willingness to create such pressures for political purposes. He said: "It is our good fortune that we have a surplus of children. Because this creates misery and misery compels to act." [57] It was not the stress and strain, or at least a sincere belief in their existence, that forced Hitler's hand. Stress and strain were needed to justify expansionist policies. As always in a dictatorship, politics had primacy over economics.

There are those who prefer to see the dynamics of dictatorial power as mainly engineered by the personal characteristics of the dictator. They cannot be shown conclusively to be in error. Who will want to quarrel with Goethe's pronouncement that Napoleon was "daimonic in the highest degree," [58] or hesitate to apply it to Hitler or Stalin? Boundless ambition, often sustained by the belief in one's star or the equally mystic sense of mission, the gambler's instincts, perhaps self-destructive yearnings, may be sufficient to explain dic-

---

189). The parallel is obvious. The second point is this: no one can read Hitler's table talks without receiving the strong impression of his hatred and fear of the German bureaucracy, because it acted as an intermediary between Hitler's orders and their impact upon the population, and in so doing applied pre-established rules and abhorred exceptions. Hence his preference for the Gauleiter, to whom the words of command could be transmitted directly and executed without delay, thus offering the proper channel for the continual and unpredictable assertion of dictatorial will. Picker, pp. 203, 250.

57. Picker, p. 323.
58. Goethe, *Gespräche mit Eckermann*, March 2, 1831.

tatorial action. As Thomas Hardy makes his dictator confess: "Some force within me, baffling mine intent, / Harries me onward, whether I will or no."

Yet it would be difficult to deny that, whatever the intensity of ambitions, they result in different actions in different circumstances and within different social frameworks. It should be considered that Bismarck's daimon did not push him into permanent action, and the apparently undaimonic Khrushchev, for a fateful moment, made the world tremble on the very edge of the nuclear precipice. In thinking about these matters, one cannot help feeling that concentrating on the soul of a dictatorial ruler leaves us far short of an explanation that would satisfy our need for reasoned adequacy.[59]

Weak ambition and dictatorship are indeed an unlikely combination. But it is precisely a strong ambition, an insatiable lust for power, that endows a man with an ability, quite uncanny at times, to perceive what devices he must use if power is not to slip from his grasping hands. It makes sense, therefore, to put the problem in Heraclitic terms and to surmise that dictatorship is destiny, rather than the character of the dictator. And that may be the deeper meaning of the Napoleonic saying: "Politics is destiny." [60] It seems to me that the cursory look at the other dictatorships enhances the plausibility of the view according to which the Soviet dictatorship was and still is engaged in an attempt to create or recreate the stability conditions of its power.

Unfortunately, it is easier to understand the nature of these efforts than to perceive, however dimly, their likely outcome. One contingency can indeed be excluded with a good deal of assurance. The Soviet dictatorship is approaching the half-century mark in its history. But it would be rash indeed to assume that the mere passage

59. Just so, in scrutinizing stability conditions it would be quite inadequate to fasten all attention upon the personal appeal of the dictator. When, for instance, Max Weber describes the Napoleonic rule as a "purely plebiscitarian charismatic power," he obviously neglects Fouché's role in the system as well as the dictator's policy of conjuring up national dangers and the unremitting insistence of asserting his will both *in magnis* and *in minimis*. Max Weber, *Wirtschaft und Gesellschaft*, Grundriss der Sozialökonomik, III. 1 (Tübingen, 1948), pp. 141–142.

60. Goethe, "Paralipomena zu den Annalen," *Sämtliche Werke*, Jubilaeumsausgabe (Stuttgart–Berlin, n.d.), XXX, 414; also Napoleon's letter to Fouché of December 31, 1806, *Correspondance de Napoléon I* (Paris, 1863), XIV, 127.

of time — its growing ancientness — can of itself put an aura of legit-imacy around it and thus liberate it from the unrelenting search for conspicuous social function and for the vindication that goes with it. Political scientists, particularly in Germany, liked to speak of the "normative force of the factual," which is a generalized form of the special proposition, current since the days of Callicles, that power justifies itself.[61] Yet in modern conditions the mere existence of dic-tatorial power does not crown it with popular approval. It is true that modern industrial society — despite assertions to the contrary — does not automatically preclude dictatorial rule. But in such a society the active participation of the population in the process of policy forma-tion is the only system of government that carries its own justifi-cation.[62] It is extremely doubtful that years of totalitarian education of the young are likely to change the validity of this proposition. Nor is the weakness of an established democratic tradition an argument against it. Lack of democratic traditions may indeed make it very difficult for a country, however industrialized, to assure proper func-tioning of democratic institutions. Such a lack, however, does not prevent modern man's fundamental rejection of a heteronomous rule and his deep yearning for liberty. Sham elections are just as ineffective to satisfy those yearnings as would be a resurrection of some artificial construct, such as the fiction of a Hobbesian *civitas instituiva*. It is in this sense that one must speak of "modern" dictatorships, even though

61. See, for "die normative Kraft des Faktischen," Georg Jellinek, *Allgemeine Staatslehre*, 3rd ed. (Berlin, 1929), pp. 337–340; Adolf Menzel, *Beiträge zur Ge-schichte der Staatslehre*, Akademie der Wissenschaften in Wien, Sitzungsberichte, vol. 210:1 (Vienna–Leipsig, 1929), p. 71; Plato, *Gorgias* (Cambridge, Mass., 1925), pp. 384–386.

62. This does not preclude the possibility in less developed countries for dictator-ships to function without any recourse to dynamic policies of justification, as long as they succeed in allying themselves with a strong traditional power. It is enlight-ening, therefore, to see how in Spain, once the hand of the Church began to withdraw from the Franco regime, the signs of weakening, if not disintegration, set in. On the other hand, in those modern dictatorships whose power is derived rather than original, the search for stability conditions may appear in a much attenuated form, as has been obviously the case with some of the Communist countries in Eastern Europe. Finally, an actual and persistent danger of foreign aggression by another dictatorship may in itself provide such strong justification for the dictatorial regime as to enable it to permit fairly far-reaching measures of decentralization, as well as a certain relaxation in other respects. This, no doubt, has been true of Yugoslavia since Tito's break with Stalin.

the conditions of their stability were so clearly perceived by the ancient Greeks and even though Machiavelli dealt with the distinction between *principati novi* and *principati ereditarii*, between young and hereditary rules, in the very first pages of *Il Principe*.

For the rest, however, everything is open. The shock that the stability of the dictatorship received by Stalin's disappearance was a rude one. We see clearly how the regime has been trying to recover the lost ground.[63] It fully realizes that every rise in the supply of consumers' goods, instead of evoking the gratitude of the population, only serves to underscore the inadequacies of the standard of living and provokes urgent claims for still further increases; but every improvement in the supplies of material commodities raises the inevitable problem of the fatal shortage of the immaterial commodity called liberty. The Soviet government knows full well that an omnipotent rule must be ubiquitous and incessant. It must be in a position to issue words of command, day in day out, and thus assert its power through a never-ending stream of individual decisions. That has been the purport of recentralization. The will is all there. But the chances of success are far from perfect. The nuclear age sets limits to military adventures, although, as the example of the Cuban missile episode shows, it does not preclude and indeed favors creation of moments of extreme tension. The conflict with China can indeed provide alternative opportunities for years to come, and purges of real or fictitious "pro-Chinese" factions in Russia may helpfully link external and internal enemies.

Yet the question is whether the process of relaxation that started in 1956 has not reached the point of no return. As one reads some of the more recent works in Soviet literature — novels, plays, and poetry, but also travelogues, recording foreign impressions, and

63. As one ponders over these matters, one cannot help feeling that Pitirim Sorokin's generalization of Herbert Spencer's and Le Play's formulas is at best a half truth. It is indeed plausible that, as a result of great emergencies and cataclysms, certain — not all — societies may experience a totalitarian transformation. But when Sorokin goes on to complete the "formula" by saying that "conversely, each time a society's major emergency decreases, [its] economic, political, ideological, and cultural systems undergo a de-totalitarian reconversion," he obviously omits the ability and the need of dictatorial systems to perpetuate or to recreate the state of emergency. "Reply to My Critics," in *Pitirim A. Sorokin in Review* (Durham, 1963), pp. 465–466.

literary criticism — one sees on the one hand how in some of these works an attempt is made to undo the damage by stressing the positive contributions of Stalin's era and by seeking to re-establish the climate for the unquestioned acceptance of the regime. On the other hand, one also sees tendencies that have pointed strongly in the opposite direction. Until recently, those tendencies were clearly on the increase, and some of the things that appeared in print went far beyond criticism of Stalin's policies and touched on very fundamental aspects of the current situation.[64] The government has been trying hard to turn the rudder. In October 1961, at the Twenty-Second Congress, vitriolic attacks were launched against the new trends in literature and cinema. But the effects were virtually nil. Then another and much stronger campaign got under way. In March 1963 Khrushchev, for the second time within three months, admonished the novelists, poets, and painters to fall in line.[65] Thereafter, as in Stalin's time, the pages of Soviet newspapers became filled with ecstatic expressions of admiration for Khrushchev's stand by authors, composers, and painters. Some (but not all) of those accused of errors and deviations offered public recantations and promised to reform. A few of the offending writers were moved into faraway provinces, thus executing at length the demand for dispersal of writers that was raised at the Twenty-Second Congress and reviving a Russian tradition that had been established ages before Stalin.[66] The plenary meeting of the Central Committee

64. An unfavorable comparison of a minor aspect of everyday life in Soviet Russia with its counterpart in the West may seem a trifling matter. In reality, however, the potential snowballing effect of such comparisons is very considerable. In particular, the step to similarly unfavorable comparisons of collective farms with individual farming abroad is invitingly short. This is shown by the astonishingly frank piece on a Soviet kolkhoz by F. Abramov, which was published in January 1963 in the Soviet journal *Neva* under the title "Vokrug da okolo" and appeared in English translation under the title *One Day in the "New Life"* (New York, 1963). It is worth noting in this connection that in an otherwise rather conservative novel an army general is made to say: "We are eliminating the cult of personality, doing away with the glorifications, closing down the concentration camps . . . But what about the ruined village?" Cf. Alexander Chakovski, "Svet dalekoy zvezdy" (The Light of a Far Star), *Oktyabr'*, no. 12 (1962), p. 22.

65. *Pravda*, March 10, 1963, pp. 1–4; also the speech by Ilichev in *Pravda*, March 9, 1963, p. 2.

66. *Current Digest of the Soviet Press*, XV (May 29, 1963), p. 9. Even earlier, some writers appear to have been forcibly committed to mental institutions: *The Observer*, May 12, 1963.

in June 1963 was devoted entirely to problems of "ideology" and thus continued the pressure.

All this may mean the end of the "liberal" period. Nevertheless, the final outcome is uncertain. The abused writers had been read avidly. They were admired, if not worshiped, by many. The cake of liberty was small but its taste was sweet, and it is not clear at all that the forces of criticism have been decisively defeated and subdued. In addition, any succession crisis, if and when one occurs, is bound to inject new unpredictabilities. A new weakening of the regime may lead to a desperate attempt to take the highest risks and, true to precedent, gamble all in order not to lose all. But it also may mark the point beyond which the disintegration of the dictatorship will proceed irresistibly at an accelerating pace. In a situation of this kind, prophecies are out of place. We cannot say whether the Soviet government is engaged in rear-guard actions to cover retreat or whether it will succeed in regaining the heights of power. But a conditional assessment is another matter. Whatever the future may bring, the renewed strength of the Soviet dictatorship — or its decay — will depend on its ability — or the lack thereof — to restore the stability conditions which have been the subject matter of this essay.

APPENDICES

INDEX

APPENDIX I

Reviews: European Economic History

A SCHUMPETERIAN ANALYSIS OF ECONOMIC DEVELOPMENT *

In some of the recent writings devoted to the late Joseph Schumpeter, one finds a few wondering comments on the absence of a "Schumpeter School" in economics. The present study by Erik Dahmén of the Stockholm Handelshögscholan must be viewed either as an exception to or as the first long step toward a refutation of the observation underlying those comments. For, in a very real sense, Dahmén is a Schumpeterian. Whereas the immediate stimulation appears to have come from Johan Åkerman, it is Schumpeter's spirit that dominated and guided the formidable research effort which now lies encompassed in the 700-odd pages of Dahmén's book.

The title of the study gives at best a very approximate idea of its contents. It is not an "entrepreneurial study" in the sense of placing the main weight of emphasis upon personality, value judgments, and activities of individual entrepreneurs. Although Dahmén's work has much to say to scholars whose interest is specifically "entrepreneurial," it is essentially a study of economic development in the Schumpeterian sense of the word. From Schumpeter comes the author's pre-eminent interest in observing and understanding the processes of economic change; from Schumpeter comes the basic belief that those processes cannot be revealed by methods of analysis dealing in economic aggregates, that attention must be focused on what happens within the individual enterprises, and that the concept of innovation provides the clue to the secret of economic development. From Schumpeter

---

* Review of Erik Dahmén, *Svensk industrielle företagarverksamhet, Kausalanalys av den industriella utvecklingen 1919–1939* (Entrepreneurial Activity in Swedish Industry in the Period 1919–1939), with an English summary, 2 vols. (Stockholm: published under the auspices of Industriens Utredningsinstitut, 1950).

derives the emphasis on new versus old enterprises in the process of growth; and from the same source, finally, comes the interest in the relation between cyclical fluctuations and economic development. In fact, the study might be described as an attempt to pit some of Schumpeter's suppositions, or intuitions, against the industrial history of Sweden in the interwar period. But such a description probably would be unfair, for two reasons. It would not do justice to the considerable originality displayed by the author; and Dahmén — at least in this study — is not an economic theorist, but an economic historian in the sense that he is much less interested in the *verification* of a theoretical model than in its *application* to empirical material.

The basic concepts with which Dahmén operates are rather few. He distinguishes first of all between what is, from the point of view of the individual enterprise, a process of "market creating" (*marknadsutvidgning*) or "market filling" (*marknadssugning*). It is the former that is engendered by economic innovations. The author distinguishes between innovations involving creation of new commodities and those involving change in production methods. He also separates primary, or original, innovations from secondary innovations designed to improve upon already existing commodities or productive processes. Finally, in viewing the process of economic development, he attributes great importance to what he calls "development blocks," to the fact, that is, that, essentially for reasons of technological and economic complementarities, rapid development requires the cooperative effort and coordination of a large number of entities, often spread over several industrial branches. Even though the author speaks of "the problem of balance in development," his concept is only indirectly related to Nurkse's "balanced growth," since the author's main concern is with the supply side rather than with the demand side. In Dahmén's thinking, development blocks are the vehicle for the consummation of a significant innovation. He views the history of the creation of such development blocks with particular attention. A development block *in statu nascendi* appears to him as shot through with specific weaknesses, "structural tensions" in his language, and it constitutes an important link between cycle and growth analysis.

Equipped with that set of tools (to which perhaps his own concepts of "malinvestment" and "the negative effects of growth" might be added), Dahmén proceeds to investigate the course of Swedish industrialization. His short treatment of the pre-1914 period to a large extent is designed to illustrate the role of development blocks in long-term growth. After the slow start, he finds the development gathering speed rapidly from the 1870's on, suffering a setback in the early 1890's and then proceeding with renewed vigor until the end of the period in 1914.[1] The latter subperiod was characterized by the existence of many "completed development blocks," which had been still in the process of creation during the former subperiod. Cumulative effects were released, and the result was a somewhat more rapid and even growth in the decades preceding the outbreak of World War I. From this point of view, the author regards the cyclical fluctuations after the 1880's essentially as disturbances brought in from outside rather than generated within the Swedish economy (I, 88).

In approaching his actual topic — Swedish industrial development in the interwar period — the author presents first a general statistical survey of growth of output, profitability, and the changing significance in the total for individual industrial branches. The purpose is to classify those industries as either progressive, stagnating, or regressive. Despite some inevitable arbitrariness, the author's formulation of the three concepts on the basis of the empirical material is altogether reasonable. Proceeding then from industry to industry, Dahmén tries to reveal in each case the specific "driving forces" at

1. It may be remarked here that the statistical data shown for the development of the individual industrial branches do not quite confirm the author's view that the great industrial spurt began in the 1870's. As far as this reviewer can see, for the majority of industrial branches the commencement of rapid growth falls into the 1880's; while for a smaller number of branches that grew swiftly in the 1870's, this rapid development was but a continuation of a growth, the beginning of which antedated the decade of the 1870's. It is true, however, that the picture is blurred, first, because some of the data on output are given in kronor, presumably at current prices, and, second, by the author's aversion to ratio scales. The reason is said to be to avoid the exaggerated impression of very rapid growth in the initial period as long as output is quantitatively small. But apart from the fact that those high initial rates are not just a freak of the percentage calculus, but possess an economic significance of their own, there is no justification at all for presenting growth data pertaining to the interwar period along an arithmetic scale. The lack of logarithmic diagrams has rendered absorption of the material more difficult, for at least one reader.

work — that is to say, to relate the rate of progress, positive or negative as it may be, to the presence or absence of market-creating activities or market-filling responses of the respective enterprises; and thereafter to associate the market-creating activities either with the introduction of new commodities or with new production methods. As could not be expected otherwise, the empirical material shows some resistance to being pressed into a rigid classification. Several times the author has to point out (I, 134, 144, 150) not only that market-filling and market-creative situations appeared conjoined, but also that the two forces need not be independent of each other, in the sense that the pull of market may cause, or at least facilitate, the innovational push into the market on the part of the enterprises. This difficulty is probably more than just a beauty blemish in a classificatory picture, since it impinges on the basic problem of what Dahmén calls "causal analysis." Still, as far as the classification of industries is concerned, the attempt seems quite successful, and the reader emerges from the discussions of Part Two with a good deal of knowledge of the pre-dominant forces within the individual industries.

In some respects Part Three, contrasting the "new" and the "old," must be considered the central portion of the study. It is here that Dahmén deals with the problem of "birth, growth, and death of enterprises" in the interwar period. This again involves construction of empirically usable concepts of the enterprise (essentially defined by the author as a productive entity), as well as of its beginning and end — problems to which the author finds quite satisfactory practical solutions. His vast empirical material is summarized in the following five ratios: (1) percentages for the number of new enterprises (enterprises that began between 1919 and 1939 and were still alive in 1940) in the total number of enterprises in existence in 1939; (2) the percentage ratios of workers in new enterprises in 1939 to the total number of workers in 1939 both in new and in old enterprises (those already in existence in 1919); (3) the ratios of the number of workers in new enterprises to the increase (or decrease) in the number of workers in the old enterprises between 1919 and 1939; (4) percentages of the number of old enterprises in 1919 which went out of existence after 1919 in the total number of (old) enterprises in 1919; and (5) the percentage ratios of the number of workers in 1919 in the old enterprises that disappeared after 1919 to the total number of workers in (old) enterprises in 1919. All these ratios have been computed for no less than twenty-six groups and sixty-one subgroups of industries.

A couple of brief comments may be in order at this point. Some question may be raised about the choice of 1919 as a basis for the comparison, a year doubtless still in the shadow of the abnormal conditions prevailing during 1914–1918. Furthermore, it will be noted that no measure has been constructed to gauge the death rate of new enterprises. Finally, it must be emphasized that the relative importance of new enterprises (ratios 2 and 3 above) as well as the death rate of old enterprises (ratio 5 above) is measured by the number of workers in the respective enterprises in relation to the larger totals. This method apparently requires at the very least the assumption that, within each industrial group or subgroup, the labor-output ratios were fairly equal as among the new and the old enterprises. To the extent that the assumption does not hold, the meaning of the ratios becomes somewhat elusive; and to the extent that there were significant differences in this respect as among the individual groups or subgroups, the value of intergroup (or subgroup) comparisons of the ratios tends to be diminished. It is regrettable that data on net outputs of individual enterprises could not be used instead. Given their unavailability, Dahmén's method must be accepted as the best solution in the circumstances.

The statistical findings just described are then conjoined with the results obtained in Part Two on the classification of industries with regard to the major driving forces prevailing within them. The extremely interesting result may be summarized with regard to progressive industries as follows: (p. 194): (1) In industries characterized by market-creating forces in consequence of introduction of *new commodities*, the share of new enterprises in the total number of enterprises in 1939 was very large, and varied between 50 and 80 percent; at the same time, the number of workers in the new enterprises in relation to the total number of workers in those industries in 1939 was also quite high, although the respective percentages in all cases were below those obtained for the number of new enterprises. (2) In industries characterized by strong market-creating forces in consequence of introduction of *new methods of production*, the share of new enterprises in the total number of enterprises in 1939 was much smaller than in the previous case, and so was the share of workers in new enterprises in the total number of workers in such industries in 1939. (3) Finally, those industries that were dominated by the pull of the market showed as a rule high ratios of the number of new enterprises to those of all enterprises in those industries in 1939, although not quite as high as in the first case; the ratios of the number of workers in new enterprises to the number of all workers in such industries tended to lie somewhere between the high ratios in case (1) and the low ratios in case (2).

These results seem to reveal that, despite a rather lively rate of formation of new enterprises in the growing Swedish industries of the interwar period, the old enterprises by and large managed to retain a predominant position with regard to the size of labor force employed. It is more than likely that the position of the old enterprises would appear even stronger if the relative growth of the two groups had been measured by the amounts of value added within the respective industries. This conclusion is further strengthened by Dahmén's general finding that the old enterprises as a rule were the seat of pioneering innovational activities, and this was so not only in industries where innovations in productive methods were pre-eminent, but also in industries characterized by introduction of new commodities. Dahmén is quite emphatic on this point (I, 197). Thus, Schumpeter's supposition that innovations as a rule are launched by new men in new enterprises does not hold for Sweden of the interwar period. On the other hand, the data described under (1) above do point with considerable clarity to the existence of a strong Schumpeterian secondary wave following the introduction of new commodities by old enterprises. It is interesting that Dahmén found cases where old enterprises that had launched the innovation abstained from advertising it too widely in order not to provoke the start of the secondary wave before they had succeeded in bringing about some reductions in cost of production (I, 236). Nevertheless, in general, "secondary innovations" — further improvements upon primary innovations — were frequent in both old and new enterprises. It must be added that the lack of a strong secondary wave following innovations in methods is perhaps not surprising, for in general imitation of new commodities should be a good deal easier than that of new methods of production.

Dahmén did not confine his effort to the quantifiable aspects of the problem. In a rather detailed presentation, he proceeds to deal descriptively and analytically with the process of enterprise formation in the individual industries, trying to trace differences between industries with high and low rates of enterprise formation. At the same time, he attempts to elucidate the character of new enterprises and to ascertain the nature of their relation to old enterprises (competition or complementarity, direct organizational affiliation or independence, and such). An impressive amount of material derived from special literature, and particularly from the author's questionnaires, personal interviews, and correspondence, has been organized to throw light on conditions in the individual industries. The treatment of these industries, however, is somewhat uneven, since the volume of information obtained varied from industry to industry. It is especially the important machinery industry, along with the forest industries, woodworking industries, and clothing industries, that comes in for fuller treatment. Much information is provided in these sections on the "death" of enterprises, the changing range of output (Dahmén has developed a Linné-like scale, 1–10, for measuring the degree of specialization of individual enterprises), and the effect of monopolistic compacts on the process of enterprise formation. With regard to the latter, his conclusion is that cartels and other similar restraints on trade rarely impeded the formation of new enterprises, although they tended to thwart their further development.

After an interesting attempt to connect the locational changes in Swedish industry with his findings, Dahmén winds up his presentation by a discussion of the size and types of capital supply in the new enterprises. His computation of the share of investment in new enterprises in the total (he makes it 38 percent) is one of the very few occasions in the study where the crudity of the method casts a severe doubt on the significance of the result. (He assumes that within each industry investment is proportionate to the number of workers, and aggregates the data for individual industries by using fire-insurance values for weights). But the data on the sources of finance are important. They show the predominant significance of the entrepreneurs' own funds in the formation of enterprises; by contrast, recourse to the stock exchange was quite limited. On the other hand, the role of bank loans was far from negligible (particularly during the 1930's). As one might have expected, it is rather clear, though not stressed by the author, that bank loans tended to play a much greater role in metalworking and forest industries than in industries producing textiles or foodstuffs. The same is true of the cases of recourse to stock issues. The ubiquitous fact of the banks' short-term loans being actually used for long-term investment is duly recorded by the author for Sweden of the interwar years. Of some significance is his conclusion that it was easier to obtain capital in order to start a new enterprise than to make possible its further growth (pp. 328–329, 334, 335).

In the second volume of the study, Dahmén has assembled, with exemplary completeness, the basic statistical data that underline the text of Volume One. It might be added that only a portion of the material contained in Volume Two has been fully worked into the text volume. This is particularly true of the separate computations for the two halves of the interwar period. Since the preceding attempt to summarize the contents of Dahmén's study has been necessarily fragmentary, the interested reader may profitably peruse the English summary appended to Volume One. With a modicum of help from the dictionary, those who do not read Swedish should find the statistical diagrams and tabulations throughout the study quite accessible.

As said before, Dahmén's book is first and foremost a contribution to Swedish industrial history in the interwar period. It is at the same time a contribution to the scholarly (though politically not always quite neutral) controversies on the relative merits and demerits of the two interwar decades. Against those who pitch the deflationary 1920's against the expansionist 1930's stand the economists who point to losses sustained by Sweden in the 1930's through increases in the degree of autarky and through an income distribution less propitious to investment and growth. As Erik Lundberg has shown, comparison of the rates of industrial growth in the two decades is difficult, the result varying with the choice of the respective base years.[2] Dahmén avoids taking sides in the controversy. He is conscious of using a special

2. Erik Lundberg, *Konjunkturer och ekonomisk politik* (The Business Cycle and Economic Policy; Stockholm, 1953), chap. 2, esp. pp. 57–64.

approach which leaves important factors outside his purview. Still, from the point of view of his approach, the separation of the two decades appears spurious. For in his view, the 1920's are characterized by the formation of important development blocks, the consummation of which fell into the 1930's. Accordingly, the 1920's appear burdened with many structural tensions, which were then eliminated in the following decade.

For those in whose minds the prosperous twenties are contrasted with the hungry thirties, the Swedish discussion may appear somewhat unreal. The fact is, however, that the Great Depression in Sweden never assumed the severity or the persistence it had in other countries, and the process of recovery was quite spectacular. Whether the explanation lies with the government's Keynesian policies — "Keynesian," that is, *ante litteram* — or with the quick revival of the foreign demand for wood products, or with the play of forces stressed by Dahmén, or, as is quite probable, with all these factors in varying degrees, is less important for present purposes.[3] Nor is it of interest here to inquire whether a different economic policy pursued in the 1920's might not have hastened the process of creation of development blocks and might not have enhanced the prosperity of the later 1920's, which in Sweden, according to Dahmén, was far from being as general as appeared to superficial observers (I, 368). What matters rather is that the absence of a prolonged depression in the 1930's has made it possible for Dahmén to attempt a treatment of the Swedish interwar period not as a cyclical analysis but as a study in economic development. Different economic conditions in the 1930's might have easily blurred the long-term factors so as to make them unrecognizable, even to Dahmén's keen eye. It might still have been true, as our author holds, that Sweden at the end of the 1920's stood at the

3. Incidentally, Dahmén's apparent belief that only an approach to economic development which centers upon the individual enterprise may be regarded truly as a "causal analysis," while an analysis that runs in terms of aggregates could not be so designated, seems to this reviewer to be at variance with the maturity of methodological judgment displayed throughout his study. Since the *ultimate* cause in a continuous and interacting process is not an operational historical concept, it must depend on the judgment, needs, and purposes of the historian as to just what factor in what "model," or combination of models, he should turn into a causal agent, into a "driving force," in his attempt to observe and to interpret the course of events and the processes of economic change.

threshold of an industrial growth comparable to that which began in the 1890's, but the verification of this hypothesis would have remained much less plausible. So would have Dahmén's belief that the economic difficulties in Sweden during the early 1930's had been caused not by too much but by too little industrial investment in the 1920's (I, 373). Almost inevitably, the interesting idea of approaching the cycle through a treatment of growth would have bogged down.

Thus, Dahmén's approach in some respects has been facilitated by the peculiarities of the Swedish economic scene in the interwar period. Nevertheless, the importance of this book far transcends the boundaries of the author's own country. There is little doubt that the concepts and methods developed by Dahmén could be most profitably employed in the study of other countries and other periods. In particular, this writer, who in his own work has laid a good deal of stress on the degree of backwardness and the importance of "big-ness" in relation to the great initial upsurge of industrial development in various European countries of the nineteenth century, feels that he has much to profit from extending his studies in the direction suggested by Dahmén's approach. In fact, it is just possible that, given availability of material, Dahmén's methods might prove of even greater fruitfulness when applied to earlier stages of industrial-ization. To some extent, Dahmén's interest in the formation and growth of new enterprises within the mature Swedish economy of the interwar period has not been fully rewarded. The smallness of the new enterprises (which in Dahmén's apt expression often were just the "underbrush" of industrial growth), their imitative rather than creative character, their frequent subordination in one way or other to the old established firms, and the pre-eminence of the "live-lihood principle" rather than of the "profit principle" in a goodly number of cases studied by Dahmén could not help detracting some-what from the significance of one of his central emphases. Very dif-ferent results are likely to obtain for the less developed countries of our day or for the earlier periods of the history of advanced coun-tries, including the United States, and it is to be hoped that serious attempts along these lines will be made. For this reason alone, a translation into English of this trail-blazing study would seem emi-nently desirable.

In addition, Dahmén's study should be of particular interest to those devoted to the entrepreneurial approach to economic history. This study contains a good deal of interesting information on the Swedish entrepreneurs. Thus, the author points out the narrow social basis for recruitment of Swedish entrepreneurs prior to 1914 (which, incidentally, runs counter to another Schumpeterian supposition), and his research reveals a considerable widening of that basis in the inter-war period: with the general democratization of the Swedish social milieu and with rising educational standards, the number of entrepreneurs originating from the ranks of industrial labor tended to increase noticeably; the author has something to say on the attitudes and the modes of behavior of such entrepreneurs. Or, to give another example, Dahmén registers the fact that during the interwar period "men with ideas" preferred to take jobs with the established enterprises, which could place both capital and an efficient sales organization at their disposal, rather than start uncertain enterprises of their own; in addition, the policies of the banks tended to reinforce such preferences. These examples could be multiplied, even though the author's interests in this direction have remained in the background of his study. But the study as a whole provides an incomparable framework for those who are seriously interested in the study of the economic significance of entrepreneurial behavior. The concept of development blocks and the vicissitudes of their creation raise, for example, the question of the degree to which individual entrepreneurs are able and willing to think in terms of such development blocks and of the extent to which their behavior will be modified thereby. The story of many an entrepreneurial failure could be meaningfully written against the background of Dahmén's "structural tensions." The changes in the rate of enterprise formation and in the death of enterprises could be further elucidated by the study of entrepreneurial behavior in various historical situations. To understand entrepreneurial attitudes in advancing and shrinking industries would shed further light on the very processes of progress and retrogression. A study of entrepreneurial evaluations of market-filling forces and the impact of these evaluations on their readiness to innovate, and by so doing to widen the market, may put to test the value of Dahmén's dichotomy of "market pull" and "push into the market." Almost every finding of Dahmén's can be turned into a question directed to the entrepreneurial approach to economic history. In order to achieve economically significant results, the adepts of that approach need above all firm knowledge of aspects of economic development which are both significant in themselves and congenial to the approach in the sense that they can become promising objects of "entrepreneurial" explanations. To have shown them the road to such a knowledge is probably not the least merit of this remarkable book.

BRITISH INDUSTRY, 1700–1950 *

The appearance in English of this basic study, first published in Germany nearly three decades ago,[1] is a most welcome event. For the book is unique in the literature of the subject in that it embodies an index of British industrial output for a period extending over two and a half centuries. The coverage of the index, which for the year 1700 comprises just six series, widens gradually, and the index comes to embrace finally more than fifty series of manufacturing output, to say nothing of a number of nonmanufacturing series that the author utilizes in the interpretation of his findings. The construction of the index must have involved a truly formidable effort on the part of the author who, apart from some limited assistance with computations, carried out his task singlehandedly. The book, therefore, is a real tour de force of old-fashioned individual research. Probably any other approach would have been unsatisfactory; only from a thorough penetration into the source material could have emerged the innumerable ingenious devices that were necessary in order to transform the scattered multifarious data into uniform output series.

The method used for the construction of the index is relatively simple. The physical series for output of individual commodities have been combined arithmetically by using value added estimates for

* Review of Walther G. Hoffmann, *British Industry*, *1700–1950*, trans. W. O. Henderson and W. H. Chaloner (Oxford: Basil Blackwell, 1955).

1. Walther Hoffmann, *Wachstum und Wachstumsformen der englischen Industriewirtschaft von 1700 bis zur Gegenwart*, Probleme der Weltwirtschaft, 63 (Jena, 1940).

weights. The period 1700–1935 was divided into seven weighting periods.[2]

The weight computations were made by constructing direct estimates from data on employment and wage rates and adjusting them upward so as to include the other elements of value added; alternatively, where data on gross value of output (value of product) were available, value added was computed on the assumption that the *ratios* of value added to value of product in the respective British industries were the same as in the United States; accordingly, the data of early American censuses were utilized.

The author did not confine himself to a mere presentation of the index but attempted a series of interpretations and drew a number of conclusions. Some of these may be summarized as follows:

1. The average rate of industrial growth in Great Britain was relatively low in the first eight decades of the eighteenth century and amounted to some .7–.8 percent per year (pp. 29, 34). Thereafter, it rose very considerably, the average rate for the period 1781–1913 being 2.8 percent per year. Within this period, the rate tended to be above 3 percent prior to 1855 and below that figure thereafter (p. 33). (All these rates represent slopes of straight lines fitted to the logarithms of the index series.[3] Output per employed person doubled between 1841 and 1911 (p. 38).

2. By multiplying his output index for each year by the corresponding index number of (a) a retail price index and (b) a price index for finished manufactured export goods, Hoffmann obtained two estimates of what he calls an index of net value of output. This index, he says, "makes it possible to estimate the influence of the gen-

2. The weighting years are 1740, 1783, 1812, 1850, 1881, 1907 and 1924. For the English edition a further period 1935–1950 was added by linking the author's index with the data of the *London and Cambridge Economic Service*. This expansion of the index period, however, is largely ignored in the text, the discussion being essentially limited to the original period 1700–1935.

3. Hoffmann devotes a somewhat lengthy discussion to the method of computing the rates of growth. Given the length of his index period and sub-periods and the rapidity of change that took place, it does not really make much difference what particular method is chosen to compute the rates. Under these circumstances the compound interest formula probably would do just as well, and it is even doubtful whether too much would depend on the appropriate choice of initial and terminal years.

eral trend of prices on the economy." He found that volume of net output and its value tended to move together very closely except in periods of great military disturbances (such as the Napoleonic Wars or World War I — pp. 219, 51).

3. With regard to the rates of growth of individual industries or subgroups of industries, the author found for the period 1820–1914 a higher rate of growth for producer-goods industries than for consumer-goods industries. Similarly, "new" industries tended to grow faster than "old" industries. The former maintained an average rate of 4–5 percent per annum, whereas the latter grew at a rate of 1–2 percent.

4. In examining the fluctuations of British industrial output (after having smoothed his curves twice by ten-year moving averages), Hoffmann believes to have discovered a twenty-year symmetric cycle, both for total output and for most of the component industries. He proceeds to explain this specific fluctuation in terms of the average life of machinery in conjunction with the observation that replacement of old plant and expansion of plant tend to be carried out simultaneously and, in addition, are bunched during prosperous years.

5. The individual industries typically have tended to pass through two successive stages marked by rising and then falling rates of growth; certain industries reached a third stage in which the rate became negative. The author notes that in some cases long periods of decline were reversed; his explanation of the phenomenon runs in terms of special circumstances (p. 202). With regard to large subgroups of industry, the author registers the fact that the decline in the rate of growth in consumer-goods industries set in earlier (around 1830) than in producer-goods industries (around 1850). Hoffmann is careful not to commit himself to more than a working hypothesis with respect to the similar course of total industrial output, but he regards the period since the last war as too short to call for a revision of the hypothesis.

The preceding summary is incomplete, but it touches on the most important results of the investigation. Some of these may not appear surprising, but it should be stressed that for the first time such conclusions are presented on the basis of quantitative research, unprecedented in its breadth and in the length of the period covered.

Hoffmann probably would be the last to deny that the degree of reliability of the results is uneven; that many a shortcut used was unduly daring; and that in general his index can, and in all likelihood will, benefit from corrections and improvements. In fact, one of the special merits of the study is the care with which the author at every juncture discusses the pros and cons of the methods used and tries to arrive at a balanced judgment. It is only in a few cases that this review felt that a fuller treatment of the problems involved would have been in order. In the following, attention may be called to some of them.

The discussion of the net-value series obtained (point 2 above) should have been somewhat less cursory in view of its striking conclusion, which in effect means that, major wars apart, one might just as well measure long-term change in the *volume* of net output by change in its net value at current prices. The difficulty is that the exact meaning of the net-value series produced by the author is rather elusive. First of all, some discrepancy between a value series computed in this manner and one based on actual values is unavoidable, since only a multiplication of a Laspeyres volume index by a Paasche price index or, vice-versa, a multiplication of a Laspeyres price index by a Paasche volume index would yield the correct value index. Second, multiplying an index of output weighted by values added by export prices of finished manufacturing goods (or retail prices) need not give a correct approximation to the actual *net-value* series, because such price indexes reflect behavior of prices (agricultural raw materials) which do not pertain to industrial value added. Third, the use of several weighting junctures means in itself that at every such juncture the volume of the output index is pulled toward the value index. Fourth, it is at least questionable to what extent a volume index of output based on net weights of one year does, within each weighting period, properly reflect such changes in value added: value-of-product ratios as presumably take place within that period and which *must* affect net values at current prices but *cannot* affect the net volume index and *need not* affect any price index by which the volume index is multiplied. For all these reasons, which might have been stated in the text, the correspondence found between the two series may be spurious and need not necessarily mean what Hoffmann thinks it does.

361

Similarly, the weighting problem may have justified a longer and more extensive discussion. The index-number problem is, of course, merely disguised and not eliminated by the use of several weighting periods. One percent of growth, say in 1800–1820, may mean something very different from one percent of growth during, say, 1900–1913. Hoffmann's readers would have benefited from at least a general expression of his views on the subject. Such a discussion would have thrown some useful additional light on the nature of long-term change, in addition to providing the reader with some idea about the possible direction and extent of the bias imparted to the index by alternative weight choices. At any rate, one of the great advantages in having Hoffmann's index is the possibility for testing the effect of varying weights, even though such tests probably would involve recomputing the author's index by the use of the geometric mean.

One might wonder how far the author has succeeded in establishing the validity of his twenty-year cycle — a counterpart of the Kuznets-Burns fluctuation. That some rhythmical sequence of this sort is observable seems fairly clear. Still, even apart from the possibility that the results have been influenced by the specific methods used in smoothing the series, the degree of the regularity involved is open to question, and one cannot help feeling that, in some passages at least, Hoffmann's language in referring to those regularities is more categoric than is warranted by his material. An inspection of the curves (Diagram P) reveals *inter alia* considerable variation in the intensity of the fluctuations. Hoffmann believes that these variations depend upon the rate of growth in the sense that fluctuations tend to become less pronounced in periods of rapid growth. But the causal nexus might just as well be tied from the other end because absence of fluctuations may have been one factor accounting for the high speed of industrialization in the periods concerned. Furthermore, the author's explanation of his cycle (point 4 above) seems to presuppose a constant average durability of machinery over a very long period, an assumption that does not appear too plausible *prima facie*.

The foregoing remarks are not meant, of course, to detract from the pioneering achievement of this book. It is a major contribution to the study of British industrial history. Its importance even transcends the spatial limits of the investigation. Hoffmann surmises that "the statistical methods employed could be used to extend our inquiries to the history of other industrial economies" (p. 225). This reviewer, who in his own work already has profited from Hoffmann's methods, must agree emphatically. To duplicate Hoffmann's performance, at least for the major countries on the European continent, would immeasurably increase our grasp of the processes of industrial development. What is available in this field now is still quite inadequate, in comparison with this book. Perhaps the appearance of this translation will inspire some English economist to reciprocate and to embark upon a similarly ambitious quantative study of long-term growth in Germany.

On the other hand, one will agree perhaps less wholeheartedly with Hoffmann's opinion that "it would be an important addition to our knowledge of the evolution of industrial economies if it could be shown that the British experience was typical of all industrial economies." This view may set an unduly narrow framework for further research. That many features of the British industrial development were in fact reproduced elsewhere may be taken for granted. But it would seem important to understand that the very existence of previous British experience tended to influence and to alter the course of subsequent industrializations in other countries, and to do so in a rather typical fashion and in a number of very significant respects. This appears fairly clear even on the basis of our present knowledge. The student of these problems should, therefore, be just as interested in deviations from, as in conformities to, the British pattern. And it is quite possible that, from a study of other industrializations as *belated* processes, new hypotheses might be derived even for the study of British experience, and the recent reversal of the rate of growth in Britain might come to be usefully regarded not as an exceptional or temporary phenomenon but as a typical repetition of the catching-up processes which had in the past characterized the course of industrialization in countries other than England. Awareness of such a broader historical framework for research would lend further significance to Hoffmann's most valuable study.[4]

4. A few words on the translation of this study should be added. Once the translators get beyond the first sections of the book, the rendition improves greatly and

THE CONQUEST OF THE MATERIAL WORLD *

It is a pleasure to be able to reread consecutively the series of beautiful essays John Nef has published over the last thirty-odd years. They contain solid and purposeful research, original ideas, and stimulating polemics. Since the individual essays first appeared as self-contained pieces, the volume is in some measure repetitious; but this should not bother the reader, since the restatements help to emphasize the unifying thesis of the book: the significance of the industrial upsurge in England during the hundred years between 1540 and 1640, which the author describes, somewhat waveringly, either as the "major rehearsal" for the "elder Toynbee's industrial revolution" which began in the last decades of the eighteenth century, or as the "real" start of which the later development was but a natural and not more impressive continuation.

The collection is introduced by an essay on "Mining and Metallurgy in Medieval Society," which is an illuminating and far-ranging piece, even though in his eagerness to stress the rising dominance of the continental governments over the extraction of metals, Nef tends to play down — unjustifiably and unnecessarily — the immense contribution made by South German capital, not just to the financing but to the technological progress in mining and metalmaking. In the concluding part of the volume, the essay on "Genesis of Industrialism and Modern Science" makes some interesting, though perhaps some-

---

becomes quite readable. But the first sections have been allowed to remain in a pretty woeful state. The question is not just one of style but of elementary intelligibility. Crucial sentences dealing with the description of the basic methods employed in the construction of the index are garbled beyond recognition. For instance, the phrase (in a correct translation) "of constructing index numbers from the respective sums of products of quantity and price" has been rendered on p. 9 as, "of constructing adjusted [?] prices [?] from cumulative [?] totals of quantities and values [?] of products [?]." Other important sentences, particularly in the first paragraph on p. 17, defy understanding just as boldly. In addition, some misprints of figures force themselves upon our attention (for example, pp. 30, 150). No doubt, upon the occasion of a second printing, a thorough revision of the initial sections and the correction of misprints will be carried out. This will happily remove the present strain on our gratitude to the translators for making this study available in English.

* Review of John U. Nef, *The Conquest of the Material World: Essays on the Coming of Industrialization* (Chicago–London: University of Chicago Press, 1964).

what superficially treated, points on the different position of science in England and in France, and particularly on the differences in orientation of French and English mathematicians in the sixteenth and seventeenth centuries; however, not much more emerges than the appearance of mere simultaneity, rather than any intimate connection, between progress in industry and science of the period. Not everybody will be able to appreciate the alternatives of the epilogue, with its assertion that religious faith is more important than the fruits of scholarship for "the things that are closest to our hearts," and that the danger of pseudoscientific beliefs is greater than that of dogmatic perversions of true religion. These pages will be read with respect as an expression of deeply felt personal views and of the urgent need for simple absolute truths in a world of relativism, where any one of the very uncivilized "civilizations" and very uncultured "cultures" is readily regarded as a civilization or a culture. But the relation of those things to the essays is tenuous, save perhaps for Nef's sense of loss of spiritual and aesthetic values that occurred in the process of "conquering the material world."

The heart of the book lies in the comparison between English and French industrial growth from 1540 to 1640. The main fact of a rapid spurt in England, centering upon mining and "heavy industries," is very convincingly established. The attempt to assess the quantitative differences in the rates of growth and volumes of per capita industrial output is somewhat less successful. Although a good deal of factual material is adduced, it is on the whole impressionistic (especially for France), so that very precise questions receive rather tentative and imprecise answers. The clearest case for England's advantage over France is that of coal output, an area that no one is better qualified to treat than Nef, the author of a classic monograph on the subject. With regard to other branches of English industrial endeavor, modern research has arrived at less impressive results. On the whole, it appears very likely indeed that, during the period, England's industry grew at a faster clip than that of France. Whether, as Nef believes, English industrial output by 1640 came to equal that of France is much less certain.

In interpreting his results, Nef is rather skeptical about attributing much importance to the spiritual effect of Protestant doctrines. He sees the main effect of the Reformation upon growth in the dissolution of monasteries, which transferred lands, rich in coal and iron ore, into private hands that were eager to exploit the resources, as well as in a basic change in the nature of demand. The demise of the Roman Catholic Church reduced the demand for "things of beauty" and created a "vacuum" filled by the new demand for utilitarian goods. This change in general economic orientation from "beauty to utility," from "quality to quantity," Nef regards as crucial for the emergence of modern industrialism and considers it more revealing than any measurable dimensions of industrial progress. Incidentally, while Nef the scholar continues pounding on the significance of the change, Nef the individual keeps deploring it, and at one point even raises the remarkably inappropriate question as to whether the beauty of a modern automobile can stand comparison with a medieval cathedral, a painting of Botticelli's, or a play of Shakespeare's.

Nef's well-known attack on the Hamilton-Keynes thesis, "Prices and Industrial Capitalism in France and England," has been included in the present volume, and rightly so since it too deals with the origins of "industrialism" and has an important bearing upon the comparisons of industrial growth in the two countries. The thesis claimed that the influx of precious metals and the resulting price revolution with its lag of wages (the "profit inflation") were largely responsible for the economic upswing of the period. Nef questions the validity of this monetary explanation, just as earlier in the book he was much too reluctant to attribute the depression of the fourteenth century to the exhaustion of easily accessible silver mines on the Continent. Nef certainly succeeds in showing that the picture was much more complex than Keynes presented it in his *Treatise on Money*. As Nef argues, the indices used by Keynes tended to exaggerate the fall in real wages. Some portion of the laborer's wage was paid in kind; some of the laborer's foodstuffs came from his own plots of land; the soaring timber prices may have raised the cost of production above the general level of prices; bread prices did not rise as much as grain prices; and, above all, France, which showed roughly the same degree of profit inflation, did not experience an upswing comparable to that of England. It would seem that Nef has been indeed able to cast some doubt on the thesis, but has hardly succeeded in refuting it.

Some of his points are telling, others are obviously weak. If prices of bread — and beer — rose somewhat less because (as Nef claims) of cost-reducing technological improvements, this would mean that the wage earners' levels of consumption fell less than Keynes's figures indicated, but it would also mean that it had become possible to sustain a larger number of industrial workers on a given quantity of staple foodstuffs. And it still remains to explore to what extent the new technology in milling and brewing, as indeed in industry at large, was not the result of investments first induced and then increasingly rendered possible by the "profit inflation."

Moreover, only the *extent* of the fall of real wages is in dispute. The fact itself is generally accepted. The available information shows that prices of cereals rose more than those of converted products, a natural enough effect in conditions of falling real wages. Nef comments on this circumstance by saying, "As the price of bread apparently increased more than that of other foods, it is possible that the poor replaced bread, cakes, and porridge to some extent by other kinds of nourishment, such as herrings, beef, mutton, eggs, cheese, and small beer" (p. 253). This statement, which gratuitously disturbs the ghost of Marie Antoinette, almost certainly reverses the causal nexus. During the period, inferior goods showed higher price rises not only within the whole group of foodstuffs, but also within the group of bread grains (rye versus wheat, which incidentally may explain the plantings of rye on less suitable soils under the late Tudors); and elements of this pattern can be observed all over Europe from the shores of the Atlantic to the plains of Russia. In fact, it is extremely rare that an economic historian can travel so far and so safely on so simple a hypothesis.

As far as the comparison with France goes, Nef does tend to shift the argument when he claims that the lower rates of growth in France, despite a similar degree of "profit inflation," prove that the price revolution did not *inevitably* lead to a commensurate spurt of industrial development. Inevitability is not an operation concept in historical research, and the thesis was not argued in these terms. There are, however, excellent reasons why England could utilize the opportunities afforded by the price revolution more effectively than France. There is the absence of the religious wars that continued in France until the last decade of the sixteenth century. More important, however, is the basic fact of England's relative economic backwardness at the start of the period. As Nef himself points out, England's "concentration of capital in mining and metallurgy from 1540 to 1640 was stimulated by the application of technological processes introduced with the help of skilled foreign artisans" (p. 132); the blast furnace probably came to England from France (p. 177). And the area of productive borrowings from abroad was not confined to mining and metalmaking. France, much more advanced, had no comparable possibilities at her disposal. Similarly, the English stress on "utilitarian" goods, of which Nef rightly makes so much, is in general a characteristic of modern industrializations in conditions of backwardness. At any rate, such differences in the rate of growth as existed between England and France are unlikely in themselves to detract from the Hamilton-Keynes thesis. As far as the latter is concerned, we now have some studies dealing with the problems involved, and a great deal more research is necessary which will have to utilize very thoroughly for a larger number of countries the mass of price information which has been collected since the initial publication of Nef's paper. But whatever the final judgment, there is no doubt that all such research will greatly benefit from the probing questions raised by our author.

HOW ECONOMIC GROWTH BEGINS *

Everett Hagen, a well-known economist with an interesting predictive record in the field, feels that "economic theory has rather little to offer towards an explanation of economic growth" (p. 8). He believes that in order to understand economic growth, and particularly "how it begins," one needs a broad system analysis which combines the findings of psychology, sociology, and anthropology, the major contribution coming from psychology through a theory of personality formation. The purpose of the book is to offer and to test

* Review of Everett E. Hagen, *On the Theory of Social Change: How Economic Growth Begins* (London: Tavistock Publications, 1964).

such a theory which provides "a more comprehensive, accurate, and logically simple explanation of the facts of life than an alternative theory" and in addition "coincides closely with outcomes so far observed" and, hopefully, "also will predict future outcomes accurately" (p. 19). Economic factors may serve as parameters in such a theory, but the author suggests the possibility that "the most fruitful and simple hypotheses of how growth begins may omit them" (p. 52).

Economic growth is defined as a "series of advances in technology and a rise in per capita output, rapid enough so that marked change occurred within each generation and indeed during each decade" (p. 10). Such a growth requires "concentration of leadership" supplied by individuals from some "distinctive social group" and endowed with "creativity." Traditional society which consists of an "upper elite" and the "simple folk," with the possible addition of great traders as a third element, is "custom-bound, hierarchical, ascriptive [based on inherited status], and unproductive" (pp. 55-56). It is unable to produce the "innovational personality"; instead it produces the "authoritarian personality." Personality in any society is essentially formed by child training during a crucial period extending from infancy through the first six or eight years. In a traditional society, childrearing is characterized first by excessive indulgence and toleration which prevents the infant from relying on his own resources and using his initiative; later on, the child is submitted to a set of strict rules because he is regarded as mischievous, ignorant, incapable, and helpless. He is treated roughly, made afraid of his parents, taught deference toward older people, is threatened with, and submitted to, grave punishments, while praise is withheld from him. All this is reinforced during the Oedipal period when the child becomes the domineering father's easily defeated sexual rival. A man so raised likes both to submit to superiors and to lord it over his inferiors; he does not make his own decisions and neither seeks affection of others nor is prepared to love them. This system of training produces deep anxieties and rages which are so strong that they must be entirely repressed, and the individual's subconscious processes are sealed off and cannot become a source of "creativity." Such an individual views the world as incomprehensible and not amenable to change by initiative. By contrast, an innovational personality receives in early childhood a sense of being loved and valued; such a child is encouraged in his explorations of the world without being pushed beyond his capabilities, is confronted with manageable tasks (such as toilet training, which, however, we are told, "is not the almost absolute key to some aspects of personality which it once was thought to be," p. 157); during the Oedipal period, a child so raised is willing to identify with his father because he is sure of the latter's affection for him.

The problem now is to show how the trammels of the traditional society can be shaken off and the personality transformed so that growth can begin. The mechanism is said to operate as follows. In a traditional society every group has its established and respected position. But at some point "status respect" is withdrawn from the "simple folk" by a respected upper group. This change ushers in a period of "retreatism." In the long run — over a number of generations — it undermines the position of the father while that of the mother is enhanced. Humiliated by the weakness of her own father and her husband, she wishes her son to become strong and accordingly begins to require of him performances which he must accomplish as his capacities develop. The weakness of the father makes it easier for the son to pass through the Oedipal period without losing the mother's comfort and aid. The child's initially strong aggressive urges become moderate and can be applied to creative tasks. Thus, "retreatism" is not a dead end. Eventually it creates a situation which is propitious for the formation of creative innovational personalities in sufficiently large numbers. When they fuse into a more or less distinctive group, economic development can begin. Thus Hagen sees the process as a sequence of stages. "The historical sequence seems to be authoritarianism, withdrawal of status respect, retreatism, creativity" (p. 237).

This, then, is Hagen's theory. All of it is presented in a surprisingly apodictic fashion. The author's faith in the theories he has absorbed is unshakeable, and doubts about the decisive significance of childhood experience never seem to cross his mind. Hagen likes to charge economists with "ethnocentricity," but he himself has no scruples at all in applying a personality theory based on modern Western and particularly American material to very different societies and remote historical periods. At any rate, as one turns to the second half of the long book, devoted to "Cases in Point" (England, Japan, Colombia, Burma, Indonesia, Colonial Problems, and Sioux Indians), it is in vain that one looks for some evidence for the assertions made so confidently in the theoretical part. In general, Hagen is a sharp observer and provides many interesting insights into conditions in the countries and regions he has visited. Similarly, Hagen's demonstration that the mere disruption of the traditional society in the colonial areas need not necessarily lead to economic growth is quite convincing. The presentation in tabular form of the religious affiliations of innovators during the Industrial Revolution and of the socioeconomic background of their fathers is a real contribution to entrepreneurial history. But as far as support for the theory as a whole is concerned, the empirical offerings are disappointing to say the least. Several points appear to be in order.

(1) The author claims to have discovered "retreatist" periods. The interesting cases naturally are those where such a period was clearly followed by a period of economic development. The test is in the historical record. In England, the "withdrawal of status respect" is claimed to have occurred some seven or eight centuries before the Industrial Revolution, the interval being filled by retreatism. In Japan, the retreatist time span is said to have lasted about as long, while in Colombia it was limited to four hundred years. Russia is not discussed as a "case in point," but the information is freely offered that there retreatism was confined to a mere three hundred years. In none of these cases is the author able to provide any information on what happened within the lap of the family and what changes the parent-child relationship and methods of child training underwent during those historical periods. There is, as he blandly admits, "no evidence one way or the other" to support his theorizing in this respect. By the same token, there is also no evidence to show that whatever changes had taken place were causally related to the subsequent economic development in the countries concerned. The probability is strong indeed that historical evidence of the type needed to corroborate Hagen's theoretical propositions simply does not exist and the validity of his stage theory cannot be tested. Among many other things, for instance, Hagen would have to demonstrate that the

anxieties resulting from child rearing of average persons in a given historical situation were neither too strong nor too weak but just right to produce "creative" personalities. Dead men tell no tales on an analyst's couch, and a theory dealing with alleged mass phenomena would require a very large sample and very many couches.

(2) While there is no evidence "one way," it would seem that on closer inspection of the historical record Hagen would find many indications pointing "the other way." I think he would be surprised to see how closely the position of the child and the character of his training in countries like Germany or Austria or Sweden, say before the First World War, resembled in many respects what he quotes to be the situation in a country like Burma. He would have discovered the same aversion to letting an infant cry; inculcation of the fear of parents and of extreme deference to older people, including injuncitons against use of personal pronouns in addressing superiors; threats of punishment by dark forces (*der schwarze Mann, der Wauwau*, the gypsies); distrust of the child's mischievousness and enforcement of strict rules; quick recourse to corporal punishment, to say nothing of the severe discipline imposed subsequently in the primary and secondary schools and a system of instruction there that seemed deliberately designed to stifle creative impulses. One must seriously wonder whether early childhood and personality formation, upon which Hagen's theory is built, are really as relevant to economic growth as he would wish us to think. He himself says at one point: "There must be deviance at all times both because the random play of human intelligence will cause some new ideas to seem attractive in spite of all the sanctions that exist, and, more important, because random differences in family environment produce deviants of various types" (p. 179). One wonders again whether this admission does not suffice to conclude that, at least in Europe of the eighteenth and nineteenth centuries, whenever a favorable situation obtained (because of, say, the lowering of an institutional barrier, or the emergence of great profit opportunities in view of increased availability of foreign technological progress or increased availability and cheapening of foreign capital, or the initiation of government policies designed to promote economic growth), the relatively small number of creative

individuals needed would not step forward whatever the methods of childhood training in the society at large.

(3) Hagen's dichotomy of authoritarian and innovational individuals, too, is open to doubt. On the one hand, in several European industrializations the existence of masses of people willing to submit obediently to the discipline of the factory proved a great boon to economic growth. On the other hand, the innovating European entrepreneur, with a few notable exceptions, certainly was an "authoritarian personality" in the sense of fully acting the part of an absolute master in his own house, while very often quite willing to submit meekly to the traditional powers (court, aristocracy, army, and the like).

(4) Hagen's picture of the traditional society is based on a sweeping generalization: "Traditional society persists because it is satisfying to all concerned" (p. 84). "If a hierarchical authoritarian social structure persists for centuries (as it has in traditional societies) it must be concluded that the members of the society found it satisfactory, and did so because in childhood they found such a structure of relationships the best solution to a problem they faced" (p. 6). These assertions appear to be at variance with the author's own concept of retreatism, a period which according to him can and did last for centuries and is characterized by the humiliation that comes in the wake of "withdrawal of status respect." Nor do they take into account the role of power as a perpetuating element of the "traditional society." At one point Hagen touches on the problem, but only to brush it aside by saying that even continued submission to force must have satisfied certain needs of personality (p. 262). Once one begins to argue this way, anything goes and it is hard to see why "withdrawal of status respect" too, since it persisted for centuries, did not satisfy certain needs of personality. If people enjoyed being held down by brute force, they might also have enjoyed being humiliated and despised. Obviously, the problems of mass satisfaction or dissatisfaction are much too complex to allow of easy answers even for any contemporary society, be it developed or underdeveloped. It is little short of fantastic to believe that a single glib generalization can be made to gauge the extent of social discontent, or the absence thereof,

in different societies over tremendously long historical periods. And it is no less fantastic to assume that the most complex and variegated story of the social position of the "simple folk" — not a simple concept either — can be meaningfully and adequately described over several centuries under the title of "withdrawal of status respect" with the latter accepted as a universal historical fact, necessarily preceding as a link in the causal chain the "beginning" of economic development.

(5) Hagen admits in the concluding paragraph of his book that the speed of the development from stage to stage cannot be predicted on the basis of his constructs and findings. What can be predicted, he says, is that all presently underdeveloped countries will eventually blossom forth in an upsurge of rapid economic growth. This is so because in all of them has occurred withdrawal of status respect from the simple folk and lesser elite. This, no doubt, is very reassuring, and the question whether the countries concerned will have to linger for thirty or eight hundred years in the limbo of retreatism may be considered a trifling detail from the point of view of a grandiose theoretical construct. Still, since the theory has been introduced as possessing considerable predictive quality (ability to foretell "accurately future outcomes"), some readers may feel that here as elsewhere the gap between promise and fulfillment is far too wide for comfort.

They may also feel that for the time being economists may safely continue their attempts to clarify, in their own small way, the concrete problems of economic development. For in facing prosaic matters such as capital and labor availabilities, market size and structure, complexity of interindustrial linkages, size of plant and enterprise, or role of financial institutions, they deal with observable and measurable phenomena in terms of demonstrable or refutable propositions. This in the field of scholarship would seem much preferable to mere speculation about things that are unknown and in all likelihood unknowable. Miracles, of course, are always possible. Should Hagen discover methods to obtain convincing evidence in support of his theory, economists will indeed come upon evil days. "Status respect" will be withheld and centuries of "retreatism" may be in store for them. But for the moment, happily enough, the danger is quite remote.

POPULATION PROBLEMS *

This collection of conference papers augmented by discussants' comments is presented in the customary style of a National Bureau volume. The authors are divided between demographers and economists. "The papers are of first-rate quality," says A. J. Coale in his introduction. Coming from the chairman of the planning committee of the conference and the contributor of an important paper, the statement has a curious ring. But it is quite correct. Most of the papers, taking each by itself, are very good. It is another question what degree of unity attaches to the volume as a whole. Conferences of this sort being what they are, modesty of expectation is in order. It is indeed fortunate that the area covered turns out to be narrower than originally intended. For the title is misleading and reaches out farther than the contents. This is not really a book on population problems in developed countries in general. The first — demographic — part of the volume contains two papers on countries other than the United States: "An International Survey of Recent Fertility Trends" by Halvor Gille and an essay on "Differential Fertility in Europe" by Gwendolyn Z. Johnson. Both are highly competent and informative pieces, but they cannot change the character of the volume. The remaining papers in the demographic part and the entire economic part — to the extent that they have an empirical locus — deal almost exclusively with the United States. Even so, the material presented is so variegated and at times so specialized as to defeat any attempt at a unified review. It must suffice therefore to advert to some of the papers and to discuss some of the views and conclusions offered.

It is not surprising to find that in a symposium of this kind central attention is directed to the problem of rising fertility in the United States. It is in this area that the disconcerting changeability of the rates conspired with the imperfection of the tools to falsify the demographers' predictions. One will appreciate, therefore, Norman Ryder's contribution to this volume in which he describes his ingenious method for estimating, from data on period fertility, the complete fertility of cohorts who are still in the childbearing age. But improve-

* Review of *Demographic and Economic Change in Developed Countries*, National Bureau of Economic Research (Princeton: Princeton University Press, 1960).

ment in the ability to predict is only part of the problem. Looking back at the completed records, one cannot help being struck by the discrepancy between the wealth and solidity of the empirical data and the elusiveness of the interpretive problems. Here no doubt lies one of the reasons for the weak internal coherence of the volume. The demographer's craft yields tangible results. But the economist's art deals with factors that are highly uncertain as to their relative significance and direction.

It is understandably tempting, therefore, to try to escape from complex problems into a simple exercise in the economics of choice. That is what Gary S. Becker has done in his contribution. Children are regarded as a durable good, primarily a consumers' durable. The cost of children is computable essentially as present value of expected outlays (with some appropriate additions and deductions); at the same time, this cost determines the "quality" of children; separating quantity and "quality," Becker arrives at the conclusion that quantity-income elasticity for children is small but positive, while quality-income elasticity is large. Thus, comfortingly enough, the demand for children turns out to be very much like that for motor cars. If the conclusion appears to contradict historical evidence, the reason, Becker assures us, lies in the uneven diffusion of knowledge regarding contraceptive practices. Once the latter is kept constant, a direct relation between income and number of children appears.

This is a suggestive little model. It would be attractive to extend it to related areas, such as matrimonial (and other) choices, a wife being clearly elected, or rather selected, as a durable consumers' good (whereas a mistress might qualify as a semidurable). Still, there are certain dangers in pushing the analogy between a child and an automobile too far. In the case of the child, the act of shopping has felicific aspects not fully duplicated in buying a car or a refrigerator. This is a fairly familiar fact, which a theorist will ignore at his own peril in appraising the *totality* of the choices involved. Historically, many other relevant factors in addition to contraceptive knowledge have varied across a stratified population and over time, drastic differentials in time horizons being one of them. As Duesenberry points out in his Comment, the empirical evidence adduced by Becker is far from overwhelming, and the assumption of free rational choice among children of different "quality" is hardly realistic. Quite apart from social custom and social pressure, there is the problem of parental identification with the children. This, too, is a familiar fact, bound to confuse, if not erase, Becker's demand and cost schedules. Outlays on, say, a child's winter coat, unlike the cost of putting anti-freeze into a car, can be indistinguishable from a father's expenditure on his own coat or hat. It would not be much more artificial to let a man view himself as his own durable consumers' good.

Once we move away from the charming simplicity of Becker's procreative economics, the picture becomes more blurred, but also more significant. One may single out A. J. Coale's article on "Population Change and Demand, Prices, and the Level of Employment." This is probably the central piece in the economic part of the volume. Coale examines the effect of changes in population upon the principal components of national income. He discusses, one by one, population growth in relation to the consumption function, investment other than housing, investment in housing, and finally government expenditures. The author combines theoretical considerations with the results of other writers' correlation analyses and serves up an estimate of the hypothetical employment situation in 1940 under the assumption of the dependency burden and growth rate of 1957. The result is an increase in demand large enough to absorb at least 60 percent of the unemployment that prevailed in the earlier year; taking the effect of government expenditures into account, as much as 90 percent of unemployment may have been wiped out. The contingency of causal effects proceeding in the opposite direction cannot be excluded, but Coale's results agree so well with this reviewer's preconceptions as to be quite safe from criticism. In his introduction to the volume, Coale supplies what amounts to a broadened summary of his own article by saying (p. 14): "When viewed in aggregate terms, the effect of demographic variables on the economy form a paradox of sorts: the growth arising from high fertility increases aggregate demand, but reduces the full employment capability of the economy to increase output per head."

This statement does less than justice to Simon Kuznets' contribution, "Population Change and Aggregate Output." Kuznets starts from the general impression that, at least in modern times, secular rise of population was generally associated with a marked secular rise in per capita output. He does not assert an inevitable causal connection. Nor does he deny the likely presence of the oft-discussed unfavorable effects on output. He wishes simply to redress the balance of the debate by theorizing — "speculating" is his term — about the possible positive effects of population growth, having in mind, as almost everybody else in the volume, primarily growth caused by high fertility (and possibly immigration). The discussion proceeds under three heads, separating the role of the population as producers, savers, and consumers. The individual factors adduced are not all equally significant or plausible. One may doubt, for instance, the supposition that in any population the share of geniuses and highly talented men is constant, so that growing population implies larger absolute numbers in the two categories. Once this is granted, however, it does not seem implausible to surmise, as the author does, that injection into the economy of men of genius and great talent yields increasing returns. In addition to stressing the advantages of bigness in a couple of other areas, Kuznets discusses a number of cases in which growing population elicits output-raising responses on the part of workers, savers, and consumers. A possible reduction of leisure is one of the suggested possibilities. Another is an interesting saving-increasing sequence via something that may be described as "keeping *down* with the Joneses" on the part of the earners of upper incomes. Milton Friedman in his Comment persists to regard such effects as merely partial offsets to the unfavorable consequences of population growth. But Kuznets obviously thinks in terms of dynamic processes changing the basic givens of the economy, such as labor's attitude to work or consumers' receptiveness to new products. It is a moot question whether, and if so to what extent, such effects actually occur. But they cannot be refuted or their magnitudes limited by logical reasoning, as Friedman has tried to do. "Speculations" offered by Kuznets should be regarded as a stimulating and challenging program for empirical research.

In the light of Kuznets' essay, Coale might well have surrounded his paradox with some reservations and qualifications. On the other hand, Coale's own expectation of a positive influence of population growth on effective demand finds some further moderate support in the essay by Jean A. Crockett, in which she examines the effects of rising population on demand for food; and a rather strong corroboration in Robert Ferber's study on "Population and Demand for Services." Yet it is Ferber who, while stressing the role of population in stimulating consumers' expenditures, warns against assuming an automatic nexus between population and consumption. It seems that anything might happen.

This feeling of uncertainty expressed at the end of the last paper of the volume is a fitting conclusion to the 500-odd pages of the symposium. Despite all the efforts, the economics of demography remains an elusive business, and the accumulated stock of reliable empirical knowledge appears distressingly small. When it comes to the final count, the most significant things said on the subject of "the great fertility reversal and the sustained rise since" are contained in the few comments Coale makes in his introduction. And they are very much in the nature of "speculation." But perhaps impatience is out of place. It is possible that we stand at the beginning of a new era. It is possible that the future lies with formidable, multidirectional stochastic models, which operate with the immediate decision units and the solution of which is obtained by simulation on large electronic computing machines. A fascinating preliminary view of such a model was presented to the conference by Guy H. Orcutt and Alice M. Rivlin in their piece on the Household Sector. But the road is long and arduous. And it is not absolutely clear that moving along it will bring us closer to testing some of the more alluring hypotheses with which this volume is sprinkled.

ITALIAN ECONOMIC HISTORY, 1861–1914 *

For a long time, economic history in Italy meant something that had happened ages before the advent of the nineteenth century. It is a welcome sign of the modern shift in emphasis that the doyen of Italian economic historians has been willing to devote years of study

* Review of Gino Luzzatto, *L'Economia italiana dal 1861 al 1914*, I, 1861–1894 (Milan: Banca Commerciale Italiana, 1963).

to economic developments in Italy during a period beginning with the Unification and ending with the outbreak of the Great War. Gino Luzzatto's book was originally conceived as a copestone to a series of monographs, sponsored — as is the present volume — by the Banca Commerciale Italiana. Unforeseeable delays in the preparation of the monographs induced Luzzatto to attempt his survey without waiting for the completion of the supporting studies. This was a happy decision. For a general survey of this kind was badly needed and, in fact, may give useful directions to the monographic efforts still in process.

For the period under review, the mid-nineties supply a natural breaking point. The time before it was filled with monetary and financial troubles, unbridled speculations, false starts in industrial development, severe agricultural slumps, and the dramatic bank collapses of the early nineties. Thereafter came the great spurt of Italian industrialization and a rapid transformation of the economic structure of the country. The present first volume, which treats the unhappy years before 1895, offers an admirably lucid and surprisingly comprehensive story. It begins with a terse description of the economic backwardness of the country in 1861 as well as of the first attempts to let the political unification be followed by its economic counterpart. The emergence of what Luzzatto calls a national market was a slow and painful process. In this connection, the author rightly criticizes the overhasty extension of the low Sardinian tariff to the whole territory of the newly created state, which placed enterprises in many regions outside of Piedmont under intolerable pressure. In addition, given the paucity of communications within the Peninsula (no throughgoing railroad connections south of Bologna) and the inferiority of the Italian merchant marine, the tariff actually impeded economic intercourse between the north and the south.

Whereas in dealing with railroad construction, imports of capital from abroad, monetary unification, budgetary problems, and the temporary abandonment of currency convertibility (1866–1883), the author treads fairly uncontroversial ground, he has a thesis of his own to propound in rejecting the assertion of considerable agricultural progress in the sixties, followed by stagnation and decline in the seventies. Luzzatto has assembled a good deal of direct and indirect evidence in support of his view that the earlier decade was as unfavorable to agriculture as its successor. This view is strikingly at variance with a pioneering study on Italian national income (*Indagine sullo sviluppo del reddito nazionale dell'Italia dal 1861 al 1956*) which was published in 1957 by the Central Institute of Statistics. Luzzatto regards the agricultural statistics of the period as completely untrustworthy. Still, it is curious that the trail-blazing effort of the Institute is never even mentioned in this book, be it with regard to agriculture or in any other connection. Luzzatto's thesis is of considerable general interest in view of the recent debates in Italy on the role of agriculture in preparing the industrial upsurge in the country.

At times, in reading Luzzatto's description of governmental policies, one wishes it were somewhat less straightforward and contained a more extensive discussion of possible alternatives. Thus, in weighing the pros and cons of the resumption of specie payments, the author might well have mentioned the possibility of stabilizing the lira at a lower level, which in all probability would have enabled the government to return to convertibility at an earlier time. This would have eliminated sooner a barrier to capital imports, the most serious disability of the *corso forzoso* with its wide fluctuations of the exchange rate.

There is also some inconsistency in the author's treatment of the tariff reform of 1887. He is very right in criticizing the irrational structure of that tariff and in describing its grave effects upon the commercial relations with France. Still, he is willing to admit that the tariff at least served to postpone the crisis and suggests that recourse to agricultural protection was inevitable. This is not very convincing, considering that Italy was in a much poorer position than other countries to afford the luxury of a highly protected agriculture and remembering that, in Luzzatto's own view, the cessation of capital imports from France and the disastrous fall of agricultural exports to that country were a direct consequence of the tariff, as was therefore the greatly increased emigration to European countries and overseas.

In general, the author does not make much use of archival materials. The only and very welcome exception is his scrutiny of the archives of the Banca d'Italia with regard to the dismal story of the great banking crashes of the nineties. Of particular interest in this connection is the revelation of the support which, at Bismarck's prompting, a syndicate of German bankers extended, in 1880–1890, to the faltering prices of Italian government securities. This action adumbrated the arrival in Italy a few years later of German investment banking which was to prove such a decisive factor in the much happier story of the following two decades.

BASIC DATA ON ITALIAN ECONOMIC HISTORY *

The previously issued four volumes of the Economic Archive of the Italian Unification were devoted to government budgets and money and exchanges in the seven Italian states; in addition, there was a comprehensive analysis of the Tuscan population census of 1841 (vols. III–IV). With the present volume, the Archive expands into a new and significant area. Of the five reports contained in this volume, one deals with "Money and Mint in the Papal States from the Restoration till 1870," but its main interest lies in the four studies of prices in Florence, Turin, Milan, and in the Papal States and Rome.

The price series presented refer to food and feedstuffs and in some cases to fuels (wood, charcoal, and oil). Their number is by no means inconsiderable. There are 27 series for Florence, 28 for Turin, 19 for Milan, and 15 for the Papal States, and 5 for Rome after 1861. Most of the series extend over very long periods. Of the Milan series, 15 begin in 1801 and the remaining four start within the first decade of the century; for Turin, 18 series begin in 1815 and 10 in 1858; all of the series for the Papal States begin between 1823 and 1825; in Florence, on the other hand, only 5 series begin in 1800; 12 start between 1839 and 1849, and the remaining 10 in 1873. The Turin series contain some gaps, particularly in the fifties; in a few cases prices of the province of Turin, as distinguished from the city market, were substituted for the years 1852–1857, for which information on city market prices was lacking. All in all, the volume of price data supplied is impressive, even though they refer to a limited number of commodities.

* Review of *Archivio economico dell'unificazione italiana*, V (Rome: Industria Libraria Tipografica Editrice, 1957).

In each of the four reports, the statistical tabulations are prefaced by a concise description of the sources used and the nature of the material. The reader receives a fairly clear idea of what is known of the procedures through which market quotations were currently ascertained by the authorities. The bulk of the data must be presumed — largely on the basis of the weights and measures used — to represent wholesale prices. In some cases, however, the exact nature of the price remains doubtful, and several series clearly refer to retail dealings. Some of these, for some portions of the period, were fixed by the authorities, but since rigid fixing was avoided and the prescribed prices were continually adjusted to follow changes in the wholesale markets, the respective series retain economic significance.

An effort has been made to assure, over the whole period, the constancy of type and quality of the commodities for which prices have been gathered. Difficulties in this respect seem to have been confined to the Florence market. In general, the individual reports follow as far as possible the same outline. All of them contain a most useful section on conversion coefficients for the old weights, measures, and currencies. Each report shows a diagram of wheat prices over the whole period, both in original currencies and in Italian lire. All the reports contain some photo offsets of original materials; curiously enough, only the Florence report contains illustrations that bear directly on the subject matter (original price records), while the other reports carry some rather extraneous materials (contemporary travel documents and the like).

The usefulness of having these price data carefully collected, collated, and published in this very attractive form is, of course, unquestionable. As was originally envisaged by the Scientific Committee in charge, the individual reports eventually will add up to an impressive "Statistical and Economic Handbook of the Italian Risorgimento." They will shed much light on the specific economic problems of Italian unification and provide a better grasp of the general problem of economic integration; it will become possible to treat Italian economic history of the nineteenth century in terms of significant economic concepts rather than, as has been mostly true so far, within some vague and often irrelevant institutional framework. As a result, important insights into the specific retarding factors in Italy's economic development will be gained. All this was clearly outlined in the original "Presentation" of Volume One of the Archive by I. Bonini of IRI, the organization which has originated and sustained the project. What has been published so far, and in particular the material assembled in this volume, goes a long way to justify those expectations. Still, it might be in order to wonder whether some improvements in the presentation of the material would not render it even more serviceable from the point of view of future users.

In fact, it would seem that a somewhat greater effort at elaboration and refinement might save much additional labor later. To give an example: the annual price series contained in this volume (and only annual data are given) represent as a rule *unweighted* averages (computed over unweighted monthly averages) of variously averaged daily or weekly quotations. Since most of the data refer to agricultural produce, one would assume large seasonal variations in quantities traded in wholesale markets. Under these circumstances, to give the same weight to the immediate post-harvest sales as to later marketings may distort the price picture considerably and, as likely as not, impart a considerable upward bias to the annual averages. If some data on the seasonal distribution of the turnover were uncovered in the course of research, at least for some years, it would be most desirable to have them included along with the price information and to have some alternative weighted series constructed. On the other hand, if such information be unavailable, a statement to that effect would be disappointing but useful.

Apart from price averages of individual commodities, one naturally thinks of the possibility of constructing an aggregate price index for all the commodities presented. Again, it would be most helpful for future research if the reports contained some indication concerning the availability of information on quantities traded. If such information can be obtained, at least for some selected years, it would seem to be quite consonant with the basic aims of the Archive to publish it and to have some tentative index computations presented. Similarly, it would be desirable to include at an early point as much of interspatial comparisons of price levels as the accumulated materials would permit. In general, the usefulness of the reports would be greatly increased if it were possible, every time the reports on a certain subject matter have been completed for all the seven states, to issue a summary report containing interstate comparisons. It is a common experience in research that too strict a division of labor between collection of raw material and its processing tends to diminish the final yield. No one can treat and interpret the raw material as well as those who have been in intimate contact with it, and it is in the process of interpretation that additional data which otherwise would be overlooked may come to be recognized as eminently relevant and a search for them instituted. It is possible of course that, as the work progresses, further reports quite naturally will tend to develop in this direction. At any rate, this reviewer must hope that his plea for somewhat less modesty and self-restraint on the part of the able scholars who are responsible for the project will not be misunderstood. It stems from the interest aroused by the venture rather than from any desire to belittle what already has proved to be a most fruitful effort in research.

TUSCAN INDUSTRY, 1900–1911 *

Most of this book consists of a survey of the industrial development in Tuscany during the first decade of the present century. Interest in the modern industrial history of Italy is still a rather recent phenomenon, and a regional study of this kind, short as it is (115 pages), offers valuable insights and indicates many directions in which further research can proceed. It is true that the data utilized by the author do not allow of any deeper penetration into matters such as cost-price structure, capital intensity, and productivity of labor, and there is no attempt at constructing an aggregate index of industrial output for the region. But the book does contain a wealth of well-documented material on the individual industries, dealing with their whole range from mining and production of ferrous metals to ceramics and straw processing. It gives a very clear general impression of the progress made, placing a good deal of emphasis on technological

* Review of Giorgio Mori, *L'Industria Toscana fra gli inizi del secolo e la guerra di Libia* (Florence: no. pub., 1963).

innovations, changes in business organization, and, particularly and most relevantly, on the role of banks in financing industrial growth and in constituting the centers of many entrepreneurial decisions. The author, however, is not content to limit himself to a more or less factual presentation of processes of industrial change in one region. He believes that the story of Tuscan development can shed additional light on broad economic and noneconomic aspects of Italian history of the period. This makes for stimulating reading, but opens the door to a number of critical objections.

Among other things, the author looks for an answer to the question why, only a short time after the successful creation of the country's industrial basis, its "liberal bourgeois" framework collapsed under the attack of Fascism; and he rejects the "naive determinism" that attributes the event to the tensions and conflicts created by the war and its aftermath. But an alternative explanation is never given, unless one is willing to take for an answer the brief references to growth of trade unions, the "dualistic" character of the Italian economy, and the general spread of economic imperialism. If this be "sophisticated determinism," an effective case for it is hardly made by the author. Labor conflicts no doubt did affect the rate of industrial growth between 1896 and 1914 (although very much less so in Tuscany than elsewhere in the country), but it was surely not a foregone conclusion that in the absence of war Giolitti's conciliatory policies would have found their "limits" in the radicalization of the trade unions. And as to the "dual economy," the backwardness of the Italian south no doubt constituted a grave problem, but no country in Europe ever showed a spatially uniform development, which is scarcely surprising given the regional variations in comparative advantages, conjoined with factor mobility across regional boundaries. In fact, the dualistic character of European industrialization was much more than a merely regional problem. Max Weber's pronouncement, that in the German economy around 1900 only the "top" was modern and everything beneath it still medieval, was indeed an exaggeration, but a most illuminating one.

Tuscany, as the peripheral, southernmost region of the Italian "north," lagged in its industrial drive very considerably behind Lombardy, Piedmont, and even Veneto. This is well shown by Mori. It is, therefore, hardly surprising that the region can provide little enlightenment for the understanding of the great spurt of Italian industrialization. This is particularly clear for the case of the protective tariff, which the author regards as a very positive factor. The strong protection given to iron and steel no doubt benefited Tuscany where — given the lack of national coal resources — the strong locational pull of Tuscan iron ore was responsible for a considerable growth of iron and steel making. But on a national scale, the author's praise of the tariff is hardly convincing. There is little doubt that the Italian iron and steel industry was created at the price of retardation in the engineering industries, the area of greatest promise for the country's industrial development. The author presents no evidence for the implausible assertion that the growth of the highly protected Italian iron and steel industry *reduced* the prices of ferrous metals. A comparison of Italian steel prices with those in contemporaneous Danish or Dutch markets should have convinced him of the contrary. And it is, therefore, no argument against Schumpeter's or Rostow's general views when the author finds that the Tuscan iron and steel industry failed to play the part of a "leading sector." The grave crisis of the industry at the end of the period under review, both in Tuscany and elsewhere in Italy, to which Mori refers, shows clearly the organic weakness of that ill-begotten child of the tariff. To take this position, incidentally, is not, as the author believes, to preach the blessings of free-trade policy. Italy could then have derived great benefits from a rational tariff. But the absence of protection was much preferable to an irrational protection of iron and steel or cotton textiles, which latter industry was also headed for a severe crisis and of which, as the author shows, "no trace" remained in Tuscany after World War I.

In discussing the great industrial upsurge in Italy of these years, the author somewhat obscurely refers to saturation of markets and the consequent imperialist policies of capital export. While this *might* explain why German banking capital came to Italy, it cannot detract from the author's very excellent treatment of the activities of the Banca Commerciale Italiana and the Credito Italiano — the German banks — whose amazing scope and intensity in Tuscan industrialization he brings out so well, including, it should be added, the banks' ability to mobilize the capital of the traditionally anti-industrial landed interests in Tuscany, thus making it available for industrial investment. Moreover, a much more plausible explanation for the German capital export can be found in the fact that, toward the end of the century, German industry was becoming increasingly independent of the banks, which naturally sought new areas for the application of the techniques of industrial promotion they had developed so effectively in Germany. In this sense, certain parts of Hilferding's classic study, to which the author keeps referring, were anachronistic at the very time of the book's publication (1910). And as to the imperialist character of the German economic penetration into Italy, this reviewer must record his impression gained from scrutiny of the archives of the Banca Commerciale. After a very short time, the German directors of the bank became quite italianized and proceeded — in their correspondence with the German mandators — to defend the interests of Italian industry with great vigor and effectiveness.

FRANCE AND THE ECONOMIC DEVELOPMENT OF EUROPE *

The thesis of this important book is a simple one: France made a signal contribution to the economic development of Europe in the nineteenth century. The core of the study lies in the five chapters of Part Two entitled "Sinews of Growth, Credit and Transportation." It is supported by several case histories assembled in Part Three (Belgium, Germany, Italy, and the Near East). The brief survey of French lending to governments is also housed in Part Three, but is hardly a case history. Presumably it would have been placed in Part Two, except for the author's belief that borrowings by foreign governments did little to strengthen the "sinews of growth" and often tended to weaken them.

In order to establish his thesis, the author provides an immense

* Review of Rondo E. Cameron, *France and the Economic Development of Europe, 1800–1914: Conquests of Peace and Seeds of War* (Princeton: Princeton University Press, 1961).

array of factual detail, the rich harvest of assiduous work in the Archives Nationales and other public and private French archives as well as in various archives in other countries (mainly Belgium, Holland, and Austria). In addition, a great deal of information has been extracted from the files of the *Journal des chemins de fer* and many other contemporaneous sources. The detailed presentation actually stops in the early 1880's, the rest of the period until 1914 being treated cursorily. But for the main period under study, the wealth of evidence cannot fail to convince the most skeptical reader. Frenchmen did perform great feats of daring investment and feverish entrepreneurship over wide areas of the Continent. After Cameron's skillful transformation of congeries of facts into a lively and well-written story, it will become altogether impossible to cling to the faded image of sluggish French entrepreneurs, inseparably wedded to routine and security and mortally afraid of risk and innovation. As Cameron keeps unfolding one episode after the other, one can only marvel at the vigorous daring and the enormous amplitude of the French effort.

And yet, as one closes the long book, one is somewhat uncertain as to the exact limits of what has been demonstrated. Of the crucial importance of the French contribution to railroad construction in countries such as Spain, Italy, and Austria, there can be no doubt. Nor can there be any hesitation in recognizing the impetus which continental banking received from France. It is also certain that French entrepreneurs successfully promoted important mining activities in several countries. But when it comes to manufacturing, one cannot help feeling that there is a certain discrepancy between the tone of the author's statements and the factual evidence he offers. Beyond that, a few reservations apart, the book leaves a strong impression that France was the most significant outside factor in the economic development of European countries. The study naturally contains no quantitative assessment of the French contribution in comparison with that of England and Germany.[1] Such a comparison is not easy, and

1. The author has made a valiant effort to evaluate the total magnitude of French capital exports for the period under study. Some of the estimates are very ingenious, but also rather uncertain. He combines estimates of surpluses in the balance of payments on current account with direct estimates of the aggregate lending abroad. The derivation of the former is described, but since the basis of the latter is never

there was no reason why the author should have added to his prodigious labors. But many things in the book are written as though such a comparison had been made and France's predominant role established.

Moreover, it is not merely French investment and technical assistance in foreign parts that Cameron is concerned with. In his introductory chapters, he paints a broad picture of French ideological, intellectual, legal, and institutional impact upon the rest of the Continent, which he sees as a part of what he calls the determinants of Europe's economic development. In particular, he assigns in this respect a crucial role to the French Revolution and the Napoleonic era. But the economic effects of what happened during that quarter century are a very complex story which defies any simple interpretation. The author himself must admit that the agrarian conditions which were sealed by the revolution proved a strong retarding force upon the subsequent economic development of France; and that by contrast, "ironically," as he says (p. 27), the very un-French turn given to the Prussian agrarian reform in the period of reaction proved a very positive factor in the industrial development of Germany. The irony is rather on the author, who has been carried away by his otherwise very appealing enthusiasm for the glories of 1789. It is all right to praise the beneficial effects of the *Code Napoléon* and of the metric system. But Cameron's references to the continental system are decidedly too mild. In a more balanced account, for instance, the lasting damage inflicted by Napoleon's narrow-minded economic nationalism upon Italy would deserve a good deal of weight. Nor does the author mention Napoleon's persistent attempts to discriminate against the new *départements* within his empire. In addition, it would be surely wrong to ascribe all liberalizing tendencies in Europe to the effects of the French Revolution. The reforms of Joseph II in Austria, for instance, antedated the French Revolution, and his plans for commutation of peasant obligations remained unfulfilled at least in part because of the revolution.

In his conclusion, Cameron tries to deal with the question of the effect of the large French capital exports upon the economic develop-

revealed, it is very difficult if not impossible for the reader to form an independent judgment of the results of these computations.

ment of France. The present book is a fine study of French economic activities beyond the borders. To gauge their impact on France would have required a thorough examination of the French economy. Such an examination — a subject for another voluminous study — quite naturally has not been included in the present book. The brief attempt undertaken here is therefore probably ill advised. A mere reference to the all-justifying existence of interest differentials which made foreign investment more profitable is surely not good enough. There is the problem of adequate appreciation of foreign risks and of an appropriate time horizon on the part of the investors. Moreover, if the capital dispositions offered abroad had been properly utilized for the increase of capital stock in France, it is conceivable and perhaps even probable that dynamic sequences would have been unleashed in the course of which the pattern of relative profitabilities may have been drastically changed. On the other hand, without a special and difficult analysis it is impossible to ascertain to what extent the export surpluses resulting from capital exports were truly additional to the French national product.

In this connection, the French failure to reimport the French innovation in banking in the creatively adjusted form of the mixed bank may have deserved strong emphasis. The author regards the specialization in French banking as inevitable (p. 195). It is safe to assume that the reasons for this development were manifold and not confined to the policies of French bankers, but it is difficult to see why something that did *not* occur in a large number of continental countries should have been inevitable in France. But the point is that existence in France of powerful mixed banks closely concerned with industrial enterprises may have produced strong dynamic effects and greatly accelerated the French rate of growth, at the same time probably reducing the flow of capital from the country. Pending further research, the judgment on the merits and demerits of French capital exports must be suspended. But even apart from this thorny problem, the author's conclusion does not seem to do full justice to his study. He says: "The generalization which emerges most clearly from the study of French contributions to the economic development of Europe relates to the role of capital. It may be stated simply, categorically, and unequivocally: capital is a necessary but not a sufficient condition for economic development" (p. 507). Despite the forceful language, this is a rather trivial observation, which also suffers from the fact that necessity and sufficiency become extremely elusive terms when used in historical contexts. The significant generalization that does emerge from the study is the successful establishment of the author's thesis concerning the powerful role of France in European economic development. It would have been better if some exaggerations of that role had been avoided. But no one can read this book without a feeling of indebtedness to the author for the vast increase in our knowledge of highly important aspects of the economic history of Europe in the nineteenth century.

THE MÉLINE TARIFF *

In the words of Eugene Golob, the Méline Tariff of 1892 was "part of the fundamental economic law of the Third Republic." It was the answer of French agriculturists to the structural changes in production and transportation which took place in the second half of the past century. In the course of this momentous transformation, grain production in the industrialized countries of Europe became a high-cost area within the framework of the world economy. Adjustment to new conditions or protection was the alternative. In France, as in Germany, the latter was chosen.

A tax on food, and particularly on bread, is the most unpopular of all taxes. Moreover, the French agriculturists could not convincingly plead that what they wanted was only *temporary* protection. Therefore, vindication on a broader basis was necessary to make the country acquiesce in agricultural protection. Such vindication was found in the ideas of economic nationalism.

Autarkic, or semi-autarkic, ideas became and remained an integral part of the agricultural ideology. Therefore, during and after the Great Depression, agricultural protectionism contributed to the general process of disintegration of world trade to an extent which cannot

* Review of Eugene Owen Golob, *The Méline Tariff: French Agriculture and Nationalist Economic Policy* (New York: Columbia University Press, 1944).

be measured solely in terms of the restrictive effects of the various protectionist devices. No less, and perhaps more, important was the role of agriculture as a source of autarkic ideas. Thus, the theme of the present study may claim a wider significance than is usually attached to inquiries into a special field of economic history.

The first chapter of the book gives a brief but well-organized sketch of the history of French agriculture during the nineteenth century prior to the depression of the eighties. It is followed by an account of the impact of the agricultural depression. The chapter on Syndicats Agricoles shows how the professional organizations of French farmers became imbued with the spirit of economic nationalism; in this process the author emphasizes the role of the antiliberal and antisocialistic ideas of Social Catholicism. The presentation of the nationalist economic theory is essentially devoted to Paul-Louis Cauwès, whose work, as Golob suggests, "represents a refinement and advance of nationalist economics far beyond List." The author goes on to describe the protectionist campaign. The leading role of the Société des Agriculteurs, the organization of large landowners, before and during the campaign, is duly brought out, and emphasis is placed on the importance of the alliance between protectionists in industry and agriculture. The parliamentary struggle which ended in the passage of the Méline Tariff receives a rather detailed account. In the final chapter, Golob tries to deal with some of the effects of this tariff on the development of French agriculture between 1892 and 1910. His main conclusion is that the Méline Tariff was unable to bring to a halt the process of the relative decline of agriculture within the French economy but that it was able to attenuate and to retard this decline.

Golob has collected a considerable amount of factual material. The numerous references to contemporary speeches and articles afford a better and more intimate understanding of the atmosphere of the struggle for and against protection. Throughout the book, there are scattered indications of certain of the broader issues involved — as, for instance, the interrelation between protectionism and the democratic development of France.

Yet the book leaves a certain feeling of disappointment. In part, this is due to the somewhat disconcerting willingness of the author to

393

accept the doctrines and the programs of agricultural protectionists, or rather his unwillingness to lift the discussion above the level of the protectionist argument. Thus, he gives the impression that the alternatives faced by French agriculture were only protection or defeat in the competitive struggle. It is on one of the last pages of the book that one finds the following remark: "The whole policy of agricultural protection is nevertheless open to the accusation of timidity. Augé-Laribé writes that a nation courageous and conscious of its strength would have entered the competitive world of the late 19th and 20th centuries and accommodated itself to the necessities of the new day." But Golob hastens to add that "the question transcends economic policy and raises a question of national attitudes." It is difficult to approve of this self-restraint.

Even the sentence just quoted does not make it fully clear that the author is really aware that between the two alternatives — great shrinkage of the volume of agricultural production and the protection of its *traditional pattern* — there may have been a third solution; that is to say, an agriculture adjusted to competitive conditions by a change in its structure from the production of staples to that of converted products. The failure to raise this question prevents Golob from fully appreciating the *economic* significance of the role played by the Société des Agriculteurs as representatives of large landowners. In this respect, comparisons with the parallel development in Germany may have been quite instructive. For the same reason, the author does not inquire at all into the highly important question of the distribution of protection as among grains and high-grade products. A closer analysis of the table of tariff rates he gives on page 174 would have shown that the tariff actually protected grains *at the expense* of converted products. A comparison of the tariff rate on barley with that on hogs, for instance, shows that the foreign hog-raiser was given in the French market an advantage of about 7 francs per quintal over the French producer. Thus, the tariff not only was not placed in the service of the adjustment to competitive conditions in agriculture; it actually made such adjustment more difficult and, in fact, almost necessarily led to further upward revisions of the tariff rates.

In a certain sense, these deficiencies of the book are related to the "synthetic method" in history, as used by Golob. This method, as

Golob explains in the foreword, implies a many-sided treatment of the subject. The Méline Tariff is to be viewed from the point of view of theoretical economics and as a culmination of a long protectionist campaign; as one phase in the development of French commercial policies *as well as* in the light of French political history.

In the concluding paragraph of the book, Golob seems to regard the irreconcilable character of the controversy between nationalist and liberal economics as a justification of the synthetic method. He seems to think that if the economist has to take value judgments for granted, the presentation of economic history must faithfully register all positions. Far from becoming an effective synthesis, economic history, if it follows this course, grows into an agglomeration of facts and attitudes in which the reader, and perhaps the author, is likely to become hopelessly submerged.

Freedom from value judgments must not prevent the historian from selecting a significant angle under which the material is collected and arranged. Only in this way can the parts of the inquiry be "synthesized," that is, meaningfully related to each other. Golob's subject may have suggested a number of such approaches. The question of how the adjustment of agriculture to competitive conditions could have been achieved, and to what extent and from what causes this was prevented by the adoption of the Méline Tariff, is only one of them. To be sure, to obtain an intelligent answer a number of various data, economic, political, social, are necessary, and Golob is certainly correct in trying to widen the scope of his inquiry. But this variety of data can result in a "synthesis" only if they are subordinated to a leading point of view. Golob's failure to work out such an approach results first in the fact that a number of important issues are raised only in order to be dropped abruptly, thus providing hints rather than serious treatment; and, second, that a discrepancy arises between the amount of material assembled and the scope of its interpretation. It would seem that the same basic deficiency limits the author in the discussion of the effects of the tariff merely to the question whether the expectations or predictions of the one or the other side were justified by subsequent developments. In other words, the effects of the Méline Tariff are largely treated in terms of arguments and counterarguments used during the protectionist campaign.

Golob has performed a service in collecting a great deal of material worth rescuing from oblivion. A greater degree of independence from the actors of his drama, and a more generous use of the tools of economic analysis, would have made it a more significant book.

AN ECONOMIC HISTORY OF SOUTHEASTERN EUROPE *

This is a collection of extracts from contemporaneous writings and legal enactments concerning the economic conditions in the nineteenth century in Hungary, Bulgaria, Rumania, and in the regions of present-day Yugoslavia. The purpose is twofold: to cast some light into a remote corner of European economic history and to provide some basis for comparisons with currently underdeveloped countries. Doreen Warriner's essay on "Contrasts and Comparisons" serves as a general introduction to the volume, and the material for each country is prefaced by a shorter statement of the contributing editors.[1] The preface, signed by all five editors, says with reference to the history of the countries concerned: "The experience was very varied, and should be studied from contemporary sources, because the diversity and intricacy of the social fabric may easily be obliterated by modern methods of packaging history. The advantage of approaching the subject through the eyes of contemporaries is that their eyes were fresh; they observed detail and diversity. Powers of observation were undimmed by academic disciplines; minds were uninhibited in making judgments of value" (p. vii). Those are good points, even though somewhat peevishly expressed. They would have been still better had the editors added that at times the contemporary observer may suffer from bias or ignorance, from lack of perspective or a propensity to generalize with undue intrepidity — all of which may reduce the value of his "judgments of value." Partly for this reason, many

---

* Review of Doreen Warriner, ed., *Contrasts in Emerging Societies, Readings in the Social and Economic History of South-Eastern Europe in the Nineteenth Century* (London: University of London, 1965).

1. G. F. Cushing for Hungary; V. de S. Pinto for Bulgaria; E. D. Tappe for Rumania; and Sonia Bičanič for Yugoslavia.

extracts in the present volume can be read, but could be "studied" only if accompanied by a very thorough editorial annotation, apprising the reader of the reliability of the figures quoted, calling his attention to and explaining the inconsistencies among different writers, and pointing out errors of commission and omission. The editors' attempts in this direction seem far from adequate. It is, therefore, not surprising that the most useful and enlightening pieces in the book are either longish excerpts from writings of highly reputable academic scholars, such as K. J. Jirecek and Karl Grünberg, or extracts from legal acts on the peasant emancipation in Croatia (1848) or Rumania (1864). The editors would have done well by relying more heavily on this type of material; in particular they may have included the important Article 35 of the act of the Hungarian Diet of 1790–91. It is another matter that with regard to legal stipulations editorial help was needed in order to enable the reader to gauge the magnitude of the burdens imposed upon the peasants in connection with land redemptions, say in Croatia, rather than merely to tell him in an editorial footnote that the "annual rents . . . were capitalized for 20 years" (p. 340), which misleading statement is meant to say that the present value of the rents was computed by capitalizing them at 5 percent for an infinite number of years. (This, incidentally, is not the only case of arithmetic sloppiness in the volume. When Doreen Warriner informs the reader that Hungarian national income increased, between 1899–1901 and 1911–1913, 75 percent and per capita income about 70 percent, she does not stop to wonder what rate of population growth the two figures imply; taking the correct rate, per capita income must have grown less than 59 percent.) Where the relevant legal texts are not given, as in the case of the Organic Regulation in Rumania, the reader must piece together its contents from several dispersed extracts, and he still remains ignorant of the important fact that by this measure the Russian legal principle of the lords' ownership of the land was firmly established in the principalities.

Understanding is also impeded by certain gaps in the book, particularly with regard to pertinent basic data. For Hungary, at least, a brief statistical appendix is included. But the relatively good Bulgarian statistics for the later part of the period are not utilized at all. Rumanian statistics of the time are not better than they should be. But G. D. Creango's 1907 data on size of farms by number and area ought to have been included as an indispensable aid to the comprehension of the texts. Some information on the Rumanian cooperative movement (both land-leasing and credit cooperatives) would have been welcome, as would have been a brief statement on governmental measures taken in the aftermath of the 1907 peasant rebellion. Here extracts from, say, Jon Ghitescu's 1913 pamphlet would have been an obvious choice. In the case of Serbia, the problem of village usury is touched upon lightly, but there is no mention of the policy of government which protected peasants from usurers to such an extent as to make it virtually impossible for them to obtain productive credits, thereby not only retarding the differentiation in the villages (though not preventing the emergence by 1897 of landless peasants, numbering 11 percent of the total, a fact not mentioned in the volume), but also impeding technological progress in agriculture. It is also a pity that the Bulgarian editor failed to include an excerpt from the works of D. Blagoev, far and away the most important Marxian writer in Southeastern Europe. His writings provide a striking illustration of the inapplicability of Marxian analysis to the problems of the area, and a well-chosen extract would have illuminated some points Doreen Warriner makes in her introduction.

As far as concerns the second object of the book, its value for the current problems of underdevelopment, serious doubts are in order. Doreen Warriner, after making some excellent remarks about the weaknesses of Marxian and Rostovian approaches to economic development, and after somewhat contradicting herself on whether or not the coming of railways was a "good thing" for the peasants (pp. 11, 19) and whether or not Bulgarian cooperatives were in need of governmental support (pp. 16, 17), arrives at the unexciting general conclusion that "economic development is a long slow process, much impeded by large landownership, and not easy for peasant economies" (p. 25). In reality, in order to make the historical experience treated in this book relevant for current problems and, in fact, in order to place the economic history of Southeastern Europe in proper perspective, a different approach, a somewhat different selection of material as well as time period, would have been needed. The basic fact was that despite agrarian reforms and the decline of handicrafts, most of the region still lacked elements which in more advanced countries were usually regarded as prerequisites of economic development. The problem then was whether Southeastern Europe could find effective and sufficient substitutions for the missing prerequisites, suitable for the degree of backwardness of the countries concerned. Putting the question in this manner would have helped us to see the economic history of the region as an integral part of the economic history of Europe, and would have thrown into sharp relief the need for sustained demand for industrial goods and capital dispositions for the entrepreneurs. Either aspect of the problem would have led to a discussion of the role of banks and, particularly, of governmental policies. It is, therefore, regrettable that the nature and effects of government aid to Hungary's industry — the only country where considerable industrialization took place — are passed over in silence. Nor can the reader of the book get a clear idea of the Bulgarian government's measures to promote industrial development or judge the reasons for their inadequacy. To enable him to do so would have required extending the period under review a good deal beyond the end of the nineteenth century. In the whole region, but particularly in Serbia, Bulgaria, and Rumania, no understanding of the possibilities for economic development, and of obstacles thereto, can be formed without an analysis of government budgets, and especially of choices that determined their expenditure side. This crucial aspect of the problem is entirely neglected in the book.

GROWTH AND STAGNATION IN THE EUROPEAN ECONOMY *

Eminently "modern" in its approach, this book derives its inspiration from two primary sources: the current preoccupation with problems of economic development and the current stress on quantitative

* Review of Ingvar Svennilson, *Growth and Stagnation in the European Economy*, United Nations Economic Commission for Europe (New York: Columbia University Press, 1954).

research. Both growth and stagnation are defined in quantitative terms as (relatively) high or low rates of long-term change. The study is an attempt to measure and to interpret this change for Europe of the interwar period. The interpretation is placed within a definite framework. Europe, at the end of the First World War, is said to have stood in need of a thorough economic transformation if its economic growth was to continue. The problem, as the author sees it, was essentially threefold: to modernize Europe's industry by introducing new products and new technology; to adapt its exports to the changes in world demand in the direction of an increased stress on machinery and transportation equipment; and to adjust its economic structure to the new political boundaries and to changes in the centers of population growth. The central theme is a discussion of the extent to which Europe's economy responded to that challenge. The main body of the book consists of a series of essays on population, agriculture, a number of key industries in manufacturing, transportation, and foreign trade. The investigation comprises the whole of Europe with the exception of Russia and the Baltic States — 23 countries in all. The statistical apparatus includes 72 tables and 61 charts in the text and 75 tables in the appendix. The appended notes on sources and statistical procedures are exemplary in their completeness and lucidity.

Because the study has been conceived as one of long-term growth, the basic period under investigation (1913–1938) has been extended for certain statistical series back to 1880 and often brought up to 1950. But historical "long term" is not simply a matter of a sufficiently long term series. The author rightly refuses to accept the view that because "changes . . . over a long period cannot be more or less than the integrated net result of the changes in each of the shorter periods" (p. 3), a study of short-term changes will yield comprehension of long-term growth. He stresses that the problem is one of emphasis. It is a "question of bringing out more clearly the nature and impact of those factors and relations whose effect on economic development appears mainly in the long-run." Since long-term changes in productive capacity reveal themselves in boom periods, the author consistently views the economic evolution in Europe from peak to peak of the cycle. At the same time, he rejects "a separation of cyclical variations and long-term changes by mechanical devices" which would transcend the peak years. He argues that such methods were useful for the period before 1914 but are inappropriate for the interwar period, with its lower rate of long-term change and much greater amplitude of short-term fluctuations. Accordingly, all the rates of change are computed simply by using the successive boom periods as the initial and terminal members of a compound-interest formula.

At this point, some doubts may be vented. On the one hand, for nineteenth-century Europe a mere peak-to-peak approach has also often yielded valuable insights into the nature of long-term change; if for no other reason because in several important instances what lay between two boom years was not just a short-term fluctuation but a specific "long-term" initial upsurge of industrialization in a backward country. On the other hand, if the statistical picture of the interwar period is so strongly dominated by short-term fluctuations (and the question of output-capacity ratios in the individual boom years after all defies precise statistical answers), then the value and validity of a long-term approach might well require some special justification. As the author remarks, such a justification must lie in historical continuity. But the degree of such continuity is liable to differ in different historical periods. There can be fairly long periods of quantitative change in which long-term factors are rather inoperative, and the development is dominated by a series of short-term sequences. "Europe" of the interwar period, with its wartime burdens, its violent inflations, its social and political unrest, its economic disintegration in the Great Depression, and its preparation for the coming war, seems to be strongly overshadowed by the play of specifically short-term factors. It is not clear that long-term analysis can be as fruitfully applied to such a period as it can to nineteenth-century Europe.

Presumably, the answer is that a comprehensive historical analysis, and particularly one extending to institutional factors, lies outside the scope of this book. This appears perhaps most clearly in the last chapter where output, investment, and exports of the individual countries are correlated. The author himself remarks that the "comparison of national developments," as carried out in that chapter, "should . . . be regarded as merely a registration . . . of the configuration of some of the principal elements in long-term growth. Such an analysis cannot hope to provide more than a bare framework to be covered later by the fabric of all the manifold developments in each particular country" (p. 222).

Deceived by the modesty of the author, one might be tempted to regard this study mainly as a highly refined preparation of quantitative data for the purposes of subsequent interpretation. But the temptation must be resisted. For throughout the book there is dispersed a great deal of most enlightening historical observation and generalization with regard to the basic problem of Europe's economic transformation. Perhaps one of the finest features of the book is the stress Svennilson places upon the degree of economic backwardness of the individual economic areas. He sees the process of long-term development as being decisively influenced by the opportunities for more backward countries to import capital and technology from the more advanced countries. He shows a very keen comprehension of the mechanics of both the catching-up and the falling-behind processes. A part of the same historical framework is the author's acceptance of the view that a relatively high rate of growth must be regarded as an independent factor of long-term change, having important consequences for the character of industrial structures resulting from that rate. The excellent chapters devoted to individual industries are illuminated by a series of empirical illustrations of those processes. The resistance to road transportation and electrification, the retarding role of old capital in the struggle against the development of water power (Chapter 6), but also the catching-up process in the field of motor-vehicle production (Chapter 8) displaying all the usual features of creative imitation, may be mentioned in this connection. This, no doubt, is the stuff long-term growth and stagnation are made of. While the applicability of these ideas to interwar Europe is somewhat limited, Svennilson does succeed in exploiting fully the opportunities that were available to him. His discussion of these matters certainly is most pertinent to problems of long-term development in other areas and periods.

Perhaps a word on the author's "Europe" is in order. It is true that most of the statistical material presented is broken down by countries; it is further true that time and again a serious attempt is made to separate and to compare developments in individual countries and groups of countries. The author is quite conscious of the "basic fact" of "very large divergencies in the long-term growth of various national units," and he states explicitly that "it would be meaningless to discuss . . . [Europe's] development as if national frontiers did not exist" (p. 41). And yet at times one has the feeling that Europe is treated either as a homogeneous economic entity or at least as a *totum pro partibus*. Thus the usefulness, within the context of the book, of the statistical aggregates for the whole area as given in the chapters on population and agriculture, appears quite elusive. When the author says that "Europe was suffering from the arteriosclerosis of an old-established, heavily capitalized system, inflexible in relation to violent economic change" (p. 52), the statement is, of course, meaningless in terms of a Europe that includes Bulgaria, Yugoslavia, Spain, and Portugal. But even Svennilson's concept of the "three leading countries," which includes Germany, would not fit the diagnosis too closely, quite apart from the fact that the somewhat infelicitous pathological image is at variance with the author's own insight into the specific sequences of long-term change: rejuvenation is an important aspect of the processes of economic development.

At times, this tendency to think in terms of too large an area seems to blur the view for important causal connections. In discussing the significance of a high rate of growth, the author stresses that the share of output devoted to capital goods will be higher in a rapidly expanding than in a stationary economy. "The more rapidly an economy is expanding, the more the capacity of its capital goods industries will exceed current requirements for the renewal of its capital equipment" (p. 206). This is certainly generally true for a large area where, even in the absence of autarkic policies, a high rate of net investment is likely to result in a high share of producers' goods in total output. But for a smaller area, where foreign trade could obviate domestic output of capital goods, the connection does not necessarily hold. If as an empirical fact many smaller areas, such as some European countries of the nineteenth century, did show a strong leaning toward rapidly increasing output of heavy industries, there was a specific reason: it was within the field of those industries that the contemporaneous technological progress had been most vehement, and backward countries often did tend to favor branches of industrial endeavor in which the most modern technology could be applied.[1]

1. I am somewhat dubious about the author's view that advanced countries must

This tendency was frequently strongly reinforced by state and banking policies, which again cannot be understood in terms of Europe as a whole. Fortunately, the propensity of the author to take an unduly comprehensive view does not pervade the whole book, and the reader has no reason to be surprised when, toward the very end of his text, in a chapter devoted to the discussion of national units, the author concludes: "Between the less advanced countries and the more highly developed parts of Europe there were such large differences in the consumption of investment goods that there is some justification in speaking of two different Europes" (p. 211). This is certainly very true, except that the statement need not be confined to the sphere of investment and that for many purposes it is quite appropriate and, in fact, imperative to operate with an even larger number of "Europes."

Svennilson's very interesting attempt to construct an index of investment in Europe based on steel and cement consumption should not go unmentioned. The author has a good deal of distrust toward indices based on value aggregates (although he could not altogether avoid their use for individual countries). Apparently he feels that an index based on raw-material consumption is indeed subject to some bias through the changing composition of inputs of investment goods industries, but that bias, he feels, need not differ from country to country and should not influence comparisons of national trends. This may seem unduly optimistic. Furthermore, in support of his method, the author states that it "has the advantage of eliminating or reducing errors derived from . . . uncertainties over relative national price levels" (p. 208). This, however, is an advantage only if we decide to regard the differences between such price levels as fortuitous, which in all likelihood they are not. Without detracting from the value of the task performed by the author in constructing his index (to which there is little alternative anyway because of lack of data), it would seem an illusion to try to eliminate the index-

explore the "frontiers of technology" while more backward areas may be content to imitate existing technology (p. 206). Quite apart from the fact that imitation is rarely pure, I believe that historical experience suggests a strong propensity on the part of backward countries to apply the most modern technological processes, not yet introduced in more advanced countries. That there are both exceptions and limits to this is another matter. Besides, there are advanced countries and advanced countries.

number problem by looking the other way. The changing relation of prices of investment goods to those of total output is in itself a significant long-term process and at times quite revealing of the nature of long-term growth. It would seem preferable therefore, wherever possible, to face the problem squarely,[2] and Svennilson might have a special reason for doing so. Early in his study he comes to lament the "unhappy division between the cost and price theory on the one hand and the theory of growth and employment on the other" (p. 8). A closer study of the index-number problem in relation to economic development could contribute to an empirical rapprochement between the two and stimulate attempts at reconciliation.

For the rest, this reviewer must confess to a feeling of helplessness in the face of this tremendous effort. The book contains such a wealth of empirical material and of mature thought; it touches on so many important problems and deals with them in such a sophisticated way; its methodology is so explicit and so deliberate that it seems quite impossible within the scope of this review either to communicate to the reader a comprehensive idea of its contents or to criticize it in a consistent fashion. The foregoing remarks should be regarded as the reviewer's admission of failure on both counts.

THE GREAT DEPRESSION IN GERMANY *

Impressed by Kondratiev's concept of "long waves" in modern economic growth, Hans Rosenberg believes that the alternating sequence of upswings and downswings of this type produces simultaneous long waves in political and social history. The thesis is presented first in a more general form, but the actual purpose of the book is to illustrate it in the light of the so-called Great Depression in Germany — Kondratiev's downswing of 1873–1896. Accordingly, the far-reaching political and social changes that occurred during those years

2. The author's rather cursory remark that production indices tend to suffer from a downward bias constitutes, I fear, an undue simplification which does not begin to allow for the complexities of the situation.

* Review of Hans Rosenberg, *Grosse Depression und Bismarckzeit: Wirtschaftsablauf, Gesellschaft und Politik in Mitteleuropa* (Berlin: Walter de Gruyter and Co., 1967).

are seen as a consequence of the long period of economic instability ushered in by the great crash of 1873. The list is impressive. The aversion from laissez-faire policies, the rise of protectionism, the end of the political apathy of the populace and, in particular, the *Politisierung* of the business community, the stagnation of the liberal parties, the regrouping of conservative forces, the upsurge of the Social Democratic Party as well as Bismarck's attempt to obstruct the labor movement by the twin strategy of ruthless (for nineteenth-century standards) suppression and social reforms (the workers' insurance system) — all these are presented as specific products of the Great Depression. And so is Bismarck's cautious foreign policy, which is said to have been dictated by the grave domestic problems; by contrast, the aggressive policies of Wilhelm II are interpreted as a fruit of the subsequent "long upswing" from 1896 to 1913.

All this makes most interesting reading. Professor Rosenberg's mastery of the relevant literature, his sharp eye for the revealing significant trifle, and his vivid and lucid style deserve high praise. In particular, his description of changes in ideologies and social attitudes (including the rise of anti-Semitism) is quite admirable. But the main thesis, alas, remains unconvincing. In fact the author himself, in his clear-headed objectivity, inflicts considerable damage upon it by his numerous qualifications and admissions. The trouble is that the concept of a Great Depression in Germany of the period is a rather dubious one and holds mainly with respect to the prevailing price trends. As far as industrial output is concerned, the remainder of the seventies was indeed a period of stagnation (although virtually of no decline), but thereafter, during the fourteen years from 1882 to 1896, industrial output grew at the high annual rate of about 4.5 percent, which was about equal to the rate achieved during the preceding long upswing (1849–1873) and actually a good deal higher than the rate of industrial growth during the following long upswing of 1896–1913 (3.1 percent per year). It is true that population grew more slowly in 1849–1873 than in 1873–1896 (0.7 percent versus 1.0 percent per year), but it grew much faster (1.4 percent per year) between 1896 and 1913. Faced with difficulties of this sort, the author first asserts that growth of output was largely the consequence of sharpened competition and greater pressure to innovate in a period of falling prices and, as such, quite compatible with a depression. But then, despairing of economic indicators, he says that criteria of depression which are relevant for social historians or historical sociologists need not be those of an economist — which probably is true but, unfortunately, quite detrimental to a thesis originally based on economic criteria. The heart of the difficulty lies in the fact that the actually depressed segment of the German economy throughout the period was agriculture, most notably, the large estates east of the River Elbe. But the depression there was not a cyclical but a structural phenomenon, resulting from the expansion of grain output overseas in conjunction with the cost-reducing technological progress in ocean transportation.

Nor is it plausible to explain the rise of a mass labor movement in those years by reference to the Great Depression. Industrial employment increased by some three million during the period (which incidentally represents a somewhat higher rate of growth than in the preceding period 1849–1873). This increase probably was the most direct cause of the phenomenal rise in Social Democratic votes. To argue, as the author does, that the great crash and the following cyclical depression led to the political by-product of Bismarck's *Sozialisten-Gesetz*, and that this in turn "created" the mass labor movement, is hardly plausible. For this view neglects more than just the natural effects of an enormous numerical growth of industrial labor. In the specific German conditions, deeply rooted social discrimination by the middle class against the factory worker was at least as potent a factor of labor discontent and political protest as was economic distress. This is an instance of the long survival of premodern value systems, a parallel to Schumpeter's theory of imperialism which explains the phenomenon in terms of Marxian superstructure lagging behind the changed infrastructure. Similarly, the dogged insistence of the German entrepreneur on remaining absolute "master in his own house" was but a replica of the traditional position of the East Elbian Junker on his estate. No depression, great or little, was responsible for this deeply ingrained attitude.

Equally implausible is the author's attempt to explain the revisionist movement within the Social Democratic Party by reference to the "long wave." To the extent that Bernstein, beginning in 1896, based his theories on the experience of the preceding years, it was not the long depression but the positive elements, such as the diminished severity of cyclical recessions, that attracted his attention and made him doubt the validity of orthodox Marxism. The overriding fact is that there had been revisionist tendencies before Bernstein (Vollmar!) in the very midst of the "Great Depression," and that much of Revisionism is explicable not by long or short waves, but by the preceding enormous success of the movement: by the impossibility, that is, of keeping a rapidly growing political mass party, whose members were burdened with grave but remediable grievances, in a state of inactive waiting for the day of the revolution. What is true, however, is that the rise of the labor movement presumably would have been delayed without Bismarck's introduction of general franchise in 1866 and 1871, that is to say, well before the great crash. Witness the case of Austria where, in the absence of franchise, no significant labor movement developed until 1889.

To make these points is not to deny, of course, the importance of the year 1873 in German history. The collapse of *Gründerzeit* left a permanent trauma. Nor is it to be gainsaid that much of the German political history of the period can be explained in economic terms. Most significant in this respect is Rosenberg's insight that the very rapidity of the German industrialization created strong tensions within the country's social system. This is a general phenomenon in industrialization in backward countries. Moreover, the conjunction of rapid industrial growth and an agrarian depression greatly enhanced those tensions. In particular, the plight of the Junkers, whose economic basis was shrinking and whose status was being jeopardized by the triumphant industrialization, certainly was a crucial factor in shaping the history of the period. All this has little to do with long waves and great depressions. And yet one has every reason to welcome this book. The thesis, although unsubstantiated, is a very original one, its heuristic value beyond doubt. In the course of elaborating it, the author offers innumerable perceptive observations, many of which are suggestive guidelines for further research. It is to be hoped that this courageous attempt to build bridges between quantitative economic analysis and political and social history will be imitated and emulated.

APPENDIX II

Reviews: Russian Economic History

A. Before 1917

AN ECONOMIC HISTORY OF RUSSIA *

A comprehensive presentation of Russian economic history from its origins till modern times should claim considerable interest. The peculiar features of the country's economic development (particularly the specific recurring patterns which characterize that development) can be gleaned from such a presentation, and it is in this way that students of the Soviet economy may be able to derive from the story of past centuries suggestive material for interpretation and reinterpretation of contemporary processes. Moreover, a consideration of Russian economic history over a very long period tends to open up new vistas for the contemplation of European economic history. Much of that history has been written with the "norm" of the English development in mind. It is quite likely that comparisons with the evolution that proceeded in the east of the Continent would throw into relief some significant factors in continental history which otherwise could not have been easily perceived.

The list of books dealing with the whole sweep of Russian economic history is, however, extremely short in any language, including the Russian. There are, of course, the volumes of Klyuchevski's *History of Russia*, from which those interested in economic history will always receive much enlightenment. But Klyuchevski's work peters

* Review of Peter I. Lyashchenko, *Istoriya narodnogo khozyaystva SSSR* (History of the National Economy of the USSR), vol. I (Ogiz, 1947), 663 pp., and vol. II (Ogiz, 1948), 738 pp.; Peter I. Lyashchenko, *History of the National Economy of Russia to the 1917 Revolution*, trans. L. M. Herman, Intro. Calvin B. Hoover (New York, 1949), 880 pp.

out in the first half of the nineteenth century, and was conceived, after all, as a course in general rather than in economic history. There are, furthermore, the works by Kulisher and Dovnar-Zapolski, but the former does not carry the treatment of the subject beyond the seventeenth and the latter ends in the fourteenth century.[1] Actually, for decades, James Mavor's work remained the solitary attempt at describing the whole flow of Russia's economic development.[2] While this study is not entirely without merit, its sketchy character, its extensive reliance for long periods of earlier history on a single — even though excellent — secondary source (Klyuchevski), its propensity to escape into purely political irrelevancies in treating more recent periods, and its lack of independent judgment and analytical penetration greatly detract from the value of the book. Quite recently, a short sketch of Russian economic history from the ninth to the twentieth century appeared in France, but its brevity makes it comparable neither to the works just mentioned nor to that of Lyashchenko.[3] For the sake of completeness, one might also mention two studies devoted to Russian economic history in the nineteenth century. One of them, by Picheta, is little more than a pamphlet and covers only the first half of the nineteenth century; the other, by Khromov, is a more detailed and original piece of work, which, however, has not yet become available to Western readers.[4]

In these circumstances, Lyashchenko's voluminous opus has very few competitors in the field, and the American Council of Learned Societies undoubtedly acted wisely in deciding to sponsor Leon Herman's English translation of the book. The translation was made from the 1939 one-volume edition. In 1947–48 Lyashchenko issued a

1. M. V. Dovnar-Zapolski, *Istoriya russkogo narodnogo khozyaystva* (History of the Russian National Economy; Kiev, 1911), vol. I. I. M. Kulisher, *Istoriya russkogo narodnogo khozyaystva* (History of the Russian National Economy; Moscow, 1925), vols. I and II. See also the German one-volume version of the two volumes: Josef Kulischer, *Russische Wirtschaftsgeschichte* (Jena, 1925), vol. I.

2. James Mavor, *An Economic History of Russia* (London-Toronto, 1914).

3. Bertrand Gille, *Histoire économique et sociale de la Russie du moyen-âge au vingtième siècle* (Paris, 1949), p. 236.

4. V. I. Picheta, *Istoriya narodnogo khozyaystva v Rossii XIX–XX vekov* (History of the National Economy in Russia of the Nineteenth and Twentieth Centuries; Moscow, 1923); P. A. Khromov, *Ekonomicheskoye razvitiye Rossii v XXIX–XX vekakh* (Economic Development of Russia in the Nineteenth and Twentieth Centuries; Gospolitizdat, 1950).

new and considerably expanded two-volume edition. Although Herman is right in intimating in his Translator's Note that, in both basic structure and main substance, the 1939 edition does not differ too much from its successor, it seemed advisable to base this discussion on the latest Russian edition and to append a few comments on the English edition. Accordingly, unless otherwise stated, page references given in the following relate to the 1947–48 Russian edition.

The organization of the book can be described briefly. The presentation is divided into two main parts: the first volume is devoted to what the author calls the "Pre-Capitalist Formations" — a period of about fifteen centuries; the second, to the five or six decades of Russian "Capitalism," the abolition of serfdom in the 1860's forming the dividing line. The first volume begins with a sketch of prehistoric development; Lyashchenko then proceeds to deal with what he calls the "Period of Early Feudalism of the Peoples of the USSR." Thereafter, the author concerns himself with the "Period of the Developed Feudal Serfdom Economy," continues with a description of the decline of that economy; goes on to treat the "Serfdom Economy in the Period of the Absolutist State"; and concludes the volume with a discussion of the "Disintegration of the Serfdom Economy in the Nineteenth Century." The second volume proceeds from a description of "Industrial Capitalism" to one of "Imperialism"; devotes by way of an excursion and elaboration a fair amount of space to the development of the country's major economic regions; and winds up with a discussion of the economy during the period of World War I until the downfall of the Provisional Government in 1917.

As is suggested by this structure of the work, it is designed to present itself as a Marxian interpretation of Russian economic history. This, of course, is to be expected from a standard work which has been published in Soviet Russia. Lyashchenko introduced himself as a Marxian in his *Sketches of the Agrarian Evolution in Russia,* published more than four decades ago. But while in the early years of the century it made definite sense to describe a historical book as Marxian, such a designation contributes little to the understanding of a work published in present-day Russia. It is legitimate to ask to what extent the use of Marxian terminology is accompanied by anything that might be termed a Marxian analysis of economic development.

This question is prompted by the growing recognition that the relationship between official Soviet ideology and Marxism cannot be adequately expressed by a simple sign of equality.

Official Soviet ideology is a complex phenomenon. Its function is essentially one of vindicating changing policies of the Soviet government through reference to an ostensibly invariant philosophy. Since the actions of the government are determined by changing practical needs, the ideology can perform its justifying function only by being subject to a steady process of change and adaptation. The result is a rather heterogeneous mass of doctrines and fragments of doctrines. Where no pragmatic need for revision has been at work, original Marxian propositions have remained undisturbed; in other cases only the shell of the original language has been preserved, but the contents have been rather radically changed; certain chunks of the original doctrine have been discarded altogether. In addition, a whole panoply of formal injunctions and rites, the observance of which is required, has become part and parcel of the ideological structure. And this agglomeration, which in various ways pervades all spheres of Russian intellectual life, is then referred to as Marxism, thus evoking the vision of a clear-cut and consistent system. The sociological rationale of the process is as obvious as is its logical meaninglessness.[5]

Accordingly, a good deal of Lyashchenko's Marxism is not Marxism at all, but represents the trammels and the trimmings of the official ideology. First of all, there are the silences of the taboos and the clamors of veneration. These may be illustrated by comparing the introduction to the first edition of the book to that of the present edition. The earlier introduction, written at the time of "NEP liberalism," contained respectful references to Kant and to men like Bücher, Brentano, and Sombart.[6] Two decades later, all such refer-

---

5. Those who find such a development surprising may do well to refer to the brilliant essay by Rosa Mayreder, *Der typische Verlauf sozialer Bewegungen* (Anzengruber Verlag, Vienna-Leipzig), and particularly to her fine discussion of the heterogeneous nature of ideologies in what she calls the "power phase" of social movements (p. 28). This most illuminating essay (written in the spring of 1917) reads now, after more than four decades, like a historical sketch of ideological developments in Soviet Russia in the intervening period.

6. P. I. Lyashchenko, *Istoriya russkogo narodnogo khozyaystva* (History of the Russian National Economy; Moscow-Leningrad, 1927), p. 13.

ences have been mercilessly eradicated. On the other hand, it was still possible in 1927 to publish a book of this sort without mentioning Stalin even once. In 1947, references to Stalin, his works, and his contributions to the study of economic history are abundant.

A Soviet economic historian must avoid the appearance of "subservience" to Western scholarship and, in general, he must tread very warily where Russian nationalism is concerned. Thus, Lyashchenko must reject the theory of Varangian origins of the Russian state (I, 109–116). It is true, of course, that Marxian theory of the origin of the state stresses the factor of social differentiation as against the conquest theory of such scholars as Gumplowicz, Ratzenhofer, and Oppenheimer. But in this case the motivation is clearly nationalistic rather than Marxian. Lyashchenko is quite ready to emphasize the importance of conquest as long as it proceeds within the milieu of the Slavic tribes (I, 114). What he must reject is the implication of inferior ability of the Russians to act as a state-forming force. For the same reason, Lyashchenko has to go out of his way — and certainly out of the way of any *economic* history — to claim that the term *Rus'* (Russia) is of Slavic rather than Scandinavian origin, a task, incidentally, which Lyashchenko performs with rather conspicuous reluctance (I, 52–54).[7] And, finally, in order to prove the same thesis Lyashchenko has to exaggerate out of all proportion the importance of agriculture in Slavic tribal economy by the ninth century. It is not enough simply to correct the earlier impressions of the *absence* of agricultural activities during that period; the Varangians must be shown to have found a settled and economically advanced population (I, 83–89). Once the ulterior motive is clear, the reader is not much surprised to find later in the book a candid statement that in the fifteenth century — six centuries later — hunting and apiculture constituted the primary economic activities in the Kiev area (I, 352).

Similarly, the process of Russian territorial expansion, and in

7. This moderation is to Lyashchenko's credit. At the time when he was preparing the present edition, altogether fantastic interpretations of the term *Rus'* were given currency in Soviet Russia in connection with N. Marr's theories. See, for instance, N. S. Derzhavin, *Proiskhozhdeniye russkogo naroda* (The Origins of the Russian People; Moscow, 1944), where the word is derived from "Etruscan" (p. 52ff). At that time to show restraint in following Marr (as Lyashchenko does expressly, I, 22) required in Russia as much civil courage as it did later, after Stalin's rejection of his theories, to refrain from a wholesale condemnation of that curious figure.

particular the annexations of the Ukraine and White Russia, must be claimed to have brought to the respective populations freedom from the yoke of local nobilities and, in addition, to have been "progressive" in the sense of opening up new economic possibilities for the development of the regions concerned (I, 361, 538). Those are sweeping and, on the whole, quite unfounded assertions, and after having made them Lyashchenko calmly proceeds to show, at least by implication, that the formerly Polish territories were much further advanced economically than the Russian "heartland." In the very special case of Georgia, Lyashchenko even has to contradict himself rather bluntly by describing Transcaucasia first as less advanced than Russia (I, 538) and then stating that Georgia at the time of annexation was much further advanced than Russia (I, 556).

All this either is quite neutral as far as Marxian analysis of economic history is concerned or else is in direct opposition to Marxism in the fundamental methodological sense that the specific relativism of Marxian dialectics is replaced by the assumption of constancy of relationship among individual factors (thus an increase in the power of the Russian state is at all times economically "progressive"). Karl Mannheim once pointed out a strictly parallel development within the democratic Marxian movements in Central Europe: "Marxian proletarian groups rise to power, shake off the dialectical elements of their theory, and begin to think in the generalizing methods of liberalism and democracy." [8] The difference lies only in the absolute values for the sake of which the methodological transformation takes place, and in the fact that in Soviet Russia this process has been greatly accelerated by the formidable pressures of a dictatorial government.

There are, however, other fundamental characteristics of a Marxian approach to economic history which one would expect to encounter in a basic Soviet publication of this kind. At the very least, one might anticipate an attempt at an endogenous interpretation of economic history, with great stress laid on productive forces and production relations as the basic agents of economic change and on class interest and class struggle as the social mediums through which the change asserts itself. Such interpretations can indeed be found in Lyashchenko's book, but curiously enough time and again they appear almost as afterthoughts.

8. Karl Mannheim, *Ideology and Utopia* (New York–London, 1949), p. 118.

The fact is that while, for certain periods and areas of Western economic history, Marxian interpretations succeeded along with others in making a significant contribution to the understanding of economic development, Russia, with its economic backwardness, the much more independent role of the state, and the subordination of a good deal of economic processes to the play of political force, provided over certain crucially important periods a singularly infertile ground for the application of Marxian models.

This is intimated in the introduction, where Lyashchenko speaks of the sharp differences that exist between Western European and Russian economic history, mentions the inapplicability of a general theoretical scheme to all times and climes, and insists that social superstructure (that is, political institutions, legal framework, ideologies, etc.) exert a "tremendous degree of influence" upon the infrastructure of the society.

These views are reflected throughout the book but to a varying extent. Perhaps least of all have they influenced Lyashchenko's treatment of the earlier periods of Russian history, particularly the thirteenth and fourteenth centuries which the author defines as the time of developed feudalism in northeastern Russia. In describing that period, Lyashchenko places far too much emphasis on the role of certain juridical instruments, such as the immunities, and tends to exaggerate the degree to which at that time "black" soils changed over to seignorial possession as well as the degree to which the peasantry became enserfed. Despite some qualifications (I, 190), it is not made sufficiently clear to the reader that during the period concerned a not inconsiderable part of the peasantry still occupied lands which were unencumbered by feudal obligations (although they were under tax obligation to the respective princes) and that such "serfdom" as had developed was essentially in the nature of contractual obligations capable of being dissolved by the peasants. It hardly could have been otherwise in conditions of extremely low density and high fluidity of the population, a factor to which Lyashchenko devotes very little attention. To tie the peasants to the soil under such conditions required the intervention of political rather than economic power.

As a result of this distribution of emphasis, the reader may find it difficult to appreciate fully the tremendous revolutionary significance of the transformation of these conditions which was brought about by

the action of the rising and expanding Moscow state. This transformation entailed more than just a curtailment of the hereditary allodial
estate (*votchina*) and emergence of the temporary landholding
(*pomestye*) predicated upon performance of services to the state on
the part of the holder. In the course of the process, considerable areas
of formerly "black" peasant lands were reassigned by the state to
its servants.

This eminently political process is quite incomprehensible save
within the framework of the expanding state and its growing needs.
It took place under economic conditions wherein the imposition of
burdens upon the tillers of the soil, to sustain the military and the
bureaucratic servants of the state, was the only method available to
the latter for financing its budget. The serfdom of the peasants, in
the sense of their becoming indissolubly tied to the soil, stands at
the far end of this protracted process and must again be understood
as essentially brought about by the state in the interest of the state.
Lyashchenko does not try to disguise the role of the state in this
crucial development, but his description of the preceding period tends
to detract from the scope of the transformation that took place. In
addition, he blurs the clarity of his presentation by remembering
suddenly that "behind" the political change there must have been
a "real cause" in the form of an economic change. Thus, after describing the changes that took place, he says: "At the basis of these
changes in social relations and in the nature of the serfdom economy
of the Moscow state lay the growth of the social division of labor,
the deepening separation of the city from rural areas, the development of city handicraft, development of markets and money economy"
(I, 236).

This gratuitous twist to an otherwise straightforward description
of the evolution that occurred during the fifteenth and the sixteenth
centuries is quite inconsistent with the statement made only a few
pages later, that markets remained altogether undeveloped and that
the economy preserved its "closed" character until at least as late as
the seventeenth century (I, 247). Equally misleading is the assertion
that the *pomestye* was economically more "progressive," than the
votchina (I, 256, 260). Because the *pomestye* corresponded to the
political needs of the government and rendered possible its expan-

sionist policy, Lyashchenko feels that it was "progressive." The use of the word is, of course, perfectly harmless in itself. But then comes the unfortunate desire to be "theoretical" about it, that is, to show that political progressiveness must have developed on the basis of economic progressiveness. Accordingly, he proceeds to speak of the great improvements in agricultural techniques which reputedly accompanied the change in seignorial land tenure. There is little or no evidence for such claims, except for the fact that the *pomestye* presumably involved greater demands upon the labor of the peasants. And Lyashchenko himself admits elsewhere (I, 234, 254) that there was no difference between the *pomestye* and the *votchina* with regard to "modes of production."

Similarly, in dealing with the process of enserfment, Lyashchenko places due stress on the decisive role played by the government in restricting and finally abolishing the peasants' rights of free exit from the estate; and, incidentally, the author greatly improves his description of the process by introducing references to the 1580 act concerning the "forbidden years," that is, years during which the peasants' right to dissolve the service relationship was for the first time suspended; (the first edition did not carry any reference to that crucial government action). But here again Lyashchenko weakens his presentation considerably by insisting that these government policies reflected class struggles between the seigneur and the peasant. Thus, very implausibly, the state is presented as an executive committee of the pomeshchik class, and the fact that the process of enserfment reflects more than anything else the powerful interest of the state itself is allowed to be obscured (I, 260).

On the whole, the superimposed layers of artificial formulas and generalizations can be quite easily separated from the underlying main trend of the story as told by Lyashchenko. Still, this dualistic method, involving as it does recurring reinterpretations of the material, not only taxes the patience of the reader but also prods the author into discovery of imaginary problems. Thus, after having claimed that the new form of land tenure was economically more efficient than its predecessor, Lyashchenko finds himself forced to explain why this more "progressive" form of agriculture led, toward the end of the sixteenth century, to a near collapse of the Russian economy (I,

256). In reality, of course, there is no problem at all. Quite on the contrary, the whole process presents a series of sequences which constitute a typical pattern of Russian economic development: whenever the military needs of the state became pressing, an institutional economic framework was adopted that was designed to make it possible for the government to support its foreign policy and its military ventures despite the hopelessly backward economy; in the process, heavy burdens were placed on the shoulders of the peasant population, and the pressure continued to a point where the physical and the human resources of the country were so greatly depleted that the economy was no longer capable of sustaining the government's policy. This pattern of development is as clearly visible in the Russia of Ivan IV as in the Russia of the early eighteenth century during the reforms of Peter the Great. In fact, some elements of the same pattern can be discerned even as late as the nineties of the past century, under Witte's policies of rapid industrialization. The further back in history these sequences occur, the less likely do they appear to provide compensations in terms of increases in the productive capacity of the economy. As a result, the longer was the period of stagnation and decline that followed the original outburst of governmental activities and the greater was its impact upon the economy.

Viewed in this way, the economic decline in the closing years of the sixteenth century did not take place *despite* the economic transformation wrought by the government, but *because* of it. If Lyashchenko had decided to accept without tergiversation the role of the government as the primary *agens movens* of the institutional economic change he described, he would have spared himself the chore of finding imaginary solutions to sham problems. Again, it is not the author's inability to see the actual connections — he states them explicitly enough (I, 257); it is rather that sensible interpretations appear continually commingled with artificial ones.

The treatment of the economic policies under Peter the Great reveals the same features. The role of the government as the primary factor responsible for the economic change taking place is clearly shown. But then this presentation is mechanically conjoined with a statement claiming that the state of Peter's time was "a state of *pomestye* holders and merchants." Particularly for the first half of the reign, the opposite statement would have been less of an ex-

aggeration: At a time when the government was creating by bureaucratic appointments not only the *pomestye* nobility but also many a
merchant and industrialist, it would have been much more reasonable
to say that these classes were called to life by acts of the government.
Presumably, the author recognizes that, since he drops a few remarks
concerning the "contradictory and inchoate class structure" of Peter's
empire (I, 380) — which remarks naturally come as a surprise after
his earlier unqualified blunt statements on the subject.[9]

Lyashchenko provides a good sketch of Peter's industrialization
policies. He describes them as mercantilistic, but then hastens to add
that Peter did not borrow them from Western models (I, 365). This
is a rather inane statement, presumably designed to avoid the charge
of "groveling before the West." But it would have been quite in
order if Lyashchenko had stressed the peculiar features of Russian
industrial mercantilism, that is, its much greater stress upon the role
of the state as entrepreneur and manager rather than mere promoter
of industrial enterprises as well as its much greater interest in producers' goods and military-goods industries and its lack of interest in
luxury production.

At the same time, it should be noted that Lyashchenko's treatment of such questions as craft-guild organization and city policies in
earlier Russian history appears a very model of restraint and reasonableness, compared to what now is being said on the subject in some
Soviet historical studies. Thus, Smirnov presents a picture of complete
similarity between the medieval city in France or Germany and in
Russia, of, say, the sixteenth century; he claims that, as in the West,
the "air of the Russian city made its inhabitants free" (without
bothering to explain, however, why strict government measures were
necessary to prevent the flight *from* Russian cities); and even goes
so far as to speak of *Zunftzwang* and *Bannmeile* as typical for Russian cities. Another scholar, Rybakov, without going quite so far, tries

9. It is indeed not easy to form a clear idea of Lyashchenko's real views on the
matter. He dismisses as unfounded the views of M. N. Pokrovski, the Soviet historian
who was posthumously purged in the later thirties and who regarded the absolute
monarchy between the sixteenth and the nineteenth centuries as an instrument of "commercial capitalism." Lyashchenko's position makes very good sense, but the first
(1927) edition of his present work contained a rather elaborate presentation of the
same conception of the period as one characterized by commercial capitalism. Lyashchenko, pp. 123–184.

hard to establish the existence in Russia of at least certain elements of craft-guild organization in order to show that "Russian handicraft was subject to general historical laws valid for the West and the East." [10] Against the background of the boundless exaggerations and distortions in these studies (which, incidentally, contain a great deal of new and valuable research material, unconnected with the generalizations just mentioned), it is salutary to read Lyashchenko's clear and unambiguous statement: "In Moscow of the fifteenth and sixteenth centuries, there existed neither a craft-guild organization of the artisan population . . . nor craft-guild regulation of handicraft." (I, 268.) Later on, Lyashchenko describes the complete failure of Peter's attempts to introduce craft-guild organization by imperial decree (I, 406). It is only regrettable that Lyashchenko leaves it to the reader to surmise how the absence of the craft-guild experience may have affected the subsequent course of the country's industrial development.

Lyashchenko's appraisal of Russia's economic position in the second half of the eighteenth century is perhaps somewhat less unambiguous, but on the whole quite reasonable. Such an appraisal has been controversial ever since the appearance of Tarle's paper, "Was Russia of Catherine the Great Economically Backward?" [11] The present tendency in Soviet Russia is to answer the question in the negative, as did Tarle some forty years ago. Lyashchenko has a statement to the same effect (I, 446), but this apparently is another instance of his usual way of conforming on a verbal level. For he proceeds to state explicitly that the rates of economic growth of the period and its degree of technological progress were very low in comparison to those of Western Europe (I, 454). And he makes it clear that the maintenance of serfdom (which in the interval had lost all its earlier functional relation to the government's policies of economic develop-

10. P. P. Smirnov, *Posadskiye lyudi i ikh klassovaya bor'ba do srediny XVII veka* (Burgesses and Their Class Struggle before the Middle of the Seventeenth Century; Moscow–Leningrad, 1947), I, 61, 134, 172, 177; and B. A. Rybakov, *Remeslo drevney Rusi* (Handicraft in Ancient Russia; Moscow, 1948), pp. 729ff, 781.

11. E. Tarle, "Byla li Yekaterininskaya Rossiya ekonomicheski-otslaloy stranoy?" (Was Russia of Catherine the Great Economically Backward?), *Sovremenny Mir* (The Contemporary World), no. 5 (1910), pp. 3–29. Reprinted in E. V. Tarle, *Zapad i Rossiya* (The West and Russia; Petrograd, 1918), pp. 122–149.

ment and had evolved into personal bondage) decisively prevented Russia's participation in the great industrialization movement that was then in the making in Western Europe. He might have added that even a static snapshot view of the second half of the eighteenth century fully reveals Russia's economic backwardness in relation to the West.

This is true with regard to techniques employed in agriculture, where the problem still lay in the general extension of the three-course rotation. Lyashchenko makes it clear that Russian agriculture of the period was in a state of stagnation, if not decline, and it is only unfortunate that he quotes with apparent approval certain views according to which the depression of agriculture was caused by a shift of population to the cities (I, 410–411). From all we know, the ratio of town population to rural population remained fairly constant between the death of Peter the Great and the end of the eighteenth century, and the very enormity of the percentage of the rural population in the total — over 96 percent — should have effectively dispelled any idea of Russia's having been anywhere near Western levels in its economic position. The *pièce de résistance* of such claims is the very high level of pig-iron production in the Urals. But the very fact that more than one half of that output did not find opportunities for further processing within the country and was exported should have bespoken the backwardness of the country with sufficient clarity. What can be said is that, as a result of Peter's reforms, Russia was probably not inferior militarily to its opponents in the West. But that meant precisely that the great impetus for the state to concern itself with the country's economic development was lacking. A clear discussion of these points would have improved Lyashchenko's treatment of the problem, but the reader will find in his presentation a sufficient amount of material to form his own judgment.

The center of attention in Lyashchenko's story of the first six decades of the nineteenth century is naturally held by the problem of serfdom and of the chain of events that led to the emancipation of the peasants. This is the field where the author has done most of his independent research, and the pertinent chapters, including those on the effects of the emancipation, are probably the best in the whole book. Nevertheless, his thesis that the serfdom economy was in the state of "general crisis" (I, 563ff), and that this crisis caused the emancipation, should not be accepted without qualification.

That the serfdom economy in the non-black-earth region was under considerable stress is, of course, generally admitted. Maintenance of serfdom relations there was not in the interest of the serf-owning nobility, as was fully shown by the attitude of that group during the discussions that preceded the reform and by the contribution it made to the adoption of a much more far-reaching emancipation than had been originally planned. But it would be very difficult to say the same of the black-earth region. That the competition of the virgin southern steppes began to be felt in central black-earth areas is true, but the extent of this pressure should not be exaggerated. As long as the railroad network remained so small, the region's markets in the north were rather effectively protected by the high cost of transportation. There is little evidence for any decline of agriculture in that region. Thus, to speak blandly of a "general crisis" is rather misleading. On the other hand, from the end of the forties the rapidly growing exports of Russian grain undoubtedly strengthened agriculture as a whole and, while the slow development of railroads prevented full utilization of export possibilities, there was little indication that by the mid-decades of the century serfdom agriculture had already become incompatible with increasing sales on wide markets.[12] Nor is there sufficient evidence that use of free labor was necessarily more profitable than that of serf labor in central black-earth regions.[13] The primary force leading to the emancipation was rather that the Crimean War demonstrated clearly the incompatibility of serfdom with the maintenance of Russia's military position, thus providing a traditional impetus for economic change. In addition, peasant discontent threatened rebellion, jeopardizing the internal power of the government. The causes for the emancipation lay not within but rather outside agriculture, and it was much more a crisis of the Russian state than one of the serfdom economy. But here, as several times earlier, Lyashchenko shows some reluctance to admit that political forces rather

12. See Peter Struve, *Krepostnoye khozyaystvo, izsledovaniye po ekonomicheskoy istorii Rossii v XVIII i XIX vekakh* (The Serfdom Economy, an Inquiry into the Economic History of Russia in the Eighteenth and Nineteenth Centuries; Moscow, 1913), p. 159.

13. *Ibid.*, pp. 103–112.

than endogenous economic development were responsible for great economic transformations.

Perhaps for similar reasons, Lyashchenko tends to go too far in assessing the direct effects of the emancipation upon subsequent industrial development. His computations yielding a figure of four million persons available for industrial occupations as a result of the reform itself is undoubtedly greatly exaggerated. It includes a substantial number of persons already engaged in industrial pursuits and also persons who were to become agricultural rather than industrial laborers (II, 24ff). On the other hand, Lyashchenko hardly mentions the great restrictions upon the formation of a permanent industrial labor force which were inherent in the technique of the emancipation — that is, the fact that, through the reform and the subsequent legislation, the peasants were placed within the reinforced trammels of the village commune and that a powerful impediment was erected thereby against permanent migration of labor to the cities. All Lyashchenko does is to refer in a dependent clause (II, 26) to certain "artificial conditions" that prevented the efflux of labor without explaining at all what those conditions were.

This failure to point up a fundamental element in the postreform situation is probably connected with Lyashchenko's basic tendency to disregard the significance of the village commune. After having treated the commune in the earliest periods of Russian history, he allows it to disappear completely from his pages until, after a gap of several centuries, a brief remark occurs to the effect that with the intensification of serfdom relations the repartitional commune revived and developed in the nineteenth century (I, 503) — not a word is said on the connection between the commune and the poll tax introduced by Peter the Great; thereupon the subject is dropped again, to be mentioned only in passing in connection with the effects of the commune upon agricultural output in the postreform years. As a result, the reader is quite unable fully to understand the import of the belated relaxation of the commune restrictions, culminating in the reforms carried out by Stolypin after the 1905 revolution. The techniques of those reforms are described, but their meaning and potential significance for the country's economic development remain blurred (II, 261ff).

All this tends to create the impression that the emancipation in itself was sufficient to unleash considerable and sustained industrial development. This impression is strengthened by Lyashchenko's discussion of the problem of capital supplies. The introductory chapter to the second volume contains an interesting statement on the various sources of preindustrial ("original") accumulation of capital in Russia (II, 7–17), which leads to the conclusion that the paucity of such original accumulations required large imports of foreign capital (and it might be added that there is no attempt on Lyashchenko's part to underrate the role of foreign capital in the process of Russian industrialization). The concept of "original accumulation of capital" is rather dogmatically accepted, and it is not explained at all that the concept makes sense only on the assumption of discontinuities in industrialization processes, although the sudden break occasioned by the abolition of serfdom in Russia might have been used to provide special justification for the use of the concept. The important point, however, is that in this connection Lyashchenko might have mentioned the role of the Russian state, upon which, in conditions of Russian economic backwardness, devolved the task of compensating for the lack of existing claims on income and wealth in the hands of persons willing to use them for investment purposes, by channeling through the means of taxation much larger portions of national income into investment than otherwise would have been made available.

That Lyashchenko does not see the connection detracts from his — in many respects very excellent — description of the industrial development following the reforms of the sixties. Although in the important chapters dealing with the subject, "The Industrial Upswing of the Nineties" and "State Economy and Economic Policy" (II, 147–217), the basic facts regarding the government's policies of industrialization are fully detailed, the tendency remains to explain the industrialization of the nineties as a phase in the cycle. Thus, the crucial fact is obscured that, even after the reform, rapid industrial growth was premised upon sustained intervention of the government. Lyashchenko does criticize the policy of low tariffs pursued by the government in the first two decades following the emancipation. But this misses the real point. In the panoply of the governmental measures of the nineties, the high protective tariff played a relatively subordinate, and in some of its portions even a negative, role as far as industrial development was concerned.

Because he has not properly emphasized the essential connection between government policies and industrialization in the nineties, Lyashchenko finds it difficult to appreciate the importance of the government's retreat from industrial promotion in the period between the 1905 revolution and the outbreak of the First World War: the economic progress born out of the policies of the nineties had been so great that, in the years 1907–1914, a high rate of industrial growth could be maintained despite the greatly diminished scope of governmental participation in the economy.

For the same reason, Lyashchenko fails to appreciate the importance of concomitant developments in Russian banking, although he presents a good deal of pertinent material on the subject (II, 346ff). What escapes him is that, as the government retreated, the banks began to take over some of the functions previously performed by the government. This involved the extension of banking operations from the mere provision of working capital to that of long-term industrial capital. As the backwardness of the economy diminished, adoption of a banking system shaped upon the German model of universal banks became possible. Lyashchenko, starting as he does from the preconceived view that capitalist industrial development leads everywhere to the domination of "industrial capital" by "financial capital," believes that the English "investment trusts" and "financial companies" provided "the most consummate form" (II, 365) of this connection and does not realize that the ascendancy of banks over industry is essentially a result of certain phases of economic backwardness, that such ascendancy was negligible in the advanced English economy, that it was particularly developed in more backward Germany, and that industry in the latter country began to liberate itself from this system at just about the time that Russian industry became mature enough for its adoption.

Lyashchenko's tendency to overemphasize the effects of the emergence of cartels in Russian industry after the turn of the century may stem from similar preconceived ideas. The pertinent chapters contain some original research on the subject and, in general, make very worth-while reading. But the author's charges that these organizations had considerable restrictive effects on the output of basic industries (particularly coal and iron), and thereby retarded the rate of industrial development of the country, have a very slender basis in fact. The rapid growth of coal and iron output between 1900 and 1913 belies the author's thesis; in addition, prices of coal did not rise any faster than the general price index, while prices of iron and iron products fell over the period, some of them very considerably indeed. This emerges clearly also from the very useful statistical appendix which Lyashchenko includes in the second volume of his work. This, incidentally, is not the only example of discrepancies between statements in the text and statistical tabulations. On the whole, statistical materials have been rather imperfectly incorporated; as a rule, Lyashchenko does not bother to enlighten the reader about the comparability of his statistical series and the degree of reliability that attaches to them.

To conclude: Lyashchenko's is not an easy book to read. A superficial perusal will perforce confuse the reader. Lip service to accepted formulas must be separated from the author's own views, and dogmatic ideas time and again succeed in stifling the guarded reasonableness of the author's general approach. But a reader who has succeeded in working his way through the maze of largely verbal contradictions and inconsistencies will be well rewarded. He will find in the book a great deal of valuable empirical material which, on the whole, is well organized, and he will be able, despite all imperfections and preconceptions, to follow the long-range drift of Russia's economic development, to form an idea of important uniformities in that development, and to compare it with the more familiar patterns of Western Europe and with the economic evolution under the Soviets.

A brief postscript on the English translation may be in order. Translation of a voluminous work of this kind, replete with rather complicated technical terms, is of course a very considerable enterprise. Herman must be commended for rendering Lyashchenko's book into very readable and lucid English. At the same time, it is perhaps unfortunate that a number of inconsistencies, slips, and awkward renditions were not caught prior to letting the manuscript go to press.[14]

It would be altogether unfair to hold these shortcomings against the translator alone or even to regard him as chiefly responsible for them. Herman has given throughout the book enough evidence of his competence as a translator, and he has done a fine job. What the English edition lacks is proper editorial supervision. Such a supervision would have removed the inconsistencies and eliminated the errors. It would have done away with some inevitable *lapsus calami* (such as "forbidden days" instead of "forbidden years" on p. 196). A competent editor would have eliminated many a mutilated transliteration of Russian terms (such as *kabal* instead of *kabala* or *pozhiloy* instead of *pozhiloye*). The lack of editorial attention is also reflected in the absence of a glossary of Russian terms or of a table showing conversions of Russian weights and measures into American equivalents. As it is, it is somewhat difficult to assign portions of the book as course readings, because the reader will find time and again numerous transliterations, which may or may not have been translated or explained elsewhere in the book, and he may or may not be successful in hunting down such a translation by a cumbersome journey through the index.

14. To give a few examples: It would have been better to avoid the inconsistency of translating *vykupnyye platezhi* as "ransom payments" in some passages and as "manumission payments" or as "redemption payments" in others. The last rendition is probably much more acceptable than the others and ought to have been used throughout. As it is, the reader has no way of knowing that all these terms mean one and the same thing. It is unidiomatic to use "correlation" instead of "rate of exchange" (II, 562) or "trade turnover" instead of "trade" or "volume of trade" (I, 264). Some historical terms have been misunderstood. *Khamovny* does not mean "common" (I, 290); it is the archaic adjective for "pertaining to weaving." The important term *tyaglo*, the translation of which is admittedly difficult and must vary with the context, has been incorrectly rendered in spots. Thus the phrase *vozvratit' v tyaglo* (p. 208) should not have been translated by "to return to the household"; the phrase there means "to return [a person] to taxpaying status." The terms *zakladchiki*, *dvorniki*, and *zakhrebetniki* have been wrongly translated respectively as "pawnshop keepers," "janitors," and "porters" (I, 207). These terms were essentially not occupational, but referred to personal relationships to third persons which tended to make the subjects exempt from tax paying status. Curiously enough, the cognate term *zakladnichestvo* appears awkwardly but meaningfully translated as "personal mortgaging," on the very next page.

LORD AND PEASANT IN RUSSIA *

To say it at once, Jerome Blum's book is a most impressive piece of work. Here is the history of one thousand years of Russian agrarian relations, presented with a knowledge of the subject and a lucidity in the narration that will make this book a standard work in the field for many years to come. It was a bold enterprise indeed to embark upon the study of such an immense body of literature, replete with uncertain and changeable technical terms and dealing with economic matters which are inextricably connected with the whole flow of the political history of the country and which at the same time reach into the very depths of its social history. It is truly amazing how well the author has acquitted himself of his task.

The ten centuries encompass the protracted and complex process of enserfment and the virtual enslavement of huge segments of Russian peasantry. It continued until the great reversal of emancipation in 1861, which is the terminal point in Blum's presentation. To a very large extent, the process is an integral part of Russian legal history, and again one cannot but admire the clarity with which the author interprets the long series of juridical enactments, many of which have been controversial in intent, meaning, and effect.

Since it is impossible within the confines of this review to do even approximate justice to the richness of the contents of the book, and since in all likelihood subsequent editions will follow, it may be best to devote what follows primarily to a number of critical comments in the hope that some of them may be accepted, or at least dealt with, by the author in later revisions. In this way, it should be possible to convey an idea of some of Blum's crucial interpretations and his distribution of emphasis among the causal factors involved.

No more than passing mention should be made of a few trifling lapses. The interested reader will have no difficulty in recognizing that the captions of a couple of maps are switched, as is their location in the book. Here and there, the author failed to penetrate the deeper mysteries of Russian morphology, so that a plural noun is mistaken for a collective singular, or a genitive case, either singular or plural,

* Review of Jerome Blum, *Lord and Peasant in Russia from the Ninth to the Nineteenth Century* (Princeton: Princeton University Press, 1961).

for the nominative. Some translations into English of Russian technical terms appear to be either wrong or at least infelicitous. Incidentally, the very useful glossary appended to the book could be improved by equipping the transliterations with appropriate pronunciation accents, and the same may be done for the proper names in the index.

More important than these beauty blemishes is another point. Laudably, the author did not shy away from introducing strains of economic analysis into his picture. Still, further elaborations in this direction would seem eminently desirable, particularly in treating the general economic effects of serfdom in the modern era. It is also true that at times the crucial point in economic interpretation is added as an afterthought; this appears to be the case, for instance, in the discussion of monetary phenomena in the fifteenth and sixteenth centuries (pp. 119, 133).

There is a fair amount of quantitative data in the book. Most of the time, they are taken over bodily and without further transformation from Russian sources. (Incidentally, Blum also reprints on p. 317 an 1844 estimate by Le Play of food consumption of Russian workers, based on data for just two families, which is altogether too silly for words.) But the author is careful in pointing out more recent information leading to important revisions of previous figures, as is the case with the earlier underestimates of the share of forced labor in mines and factories in the nineteenth century (pp. 323–325). In another instance, the author uses official data for 1854–1859 and computes the average value of seignorial holdings in various regions. In this connection, he provides very reasonable explanations for the small margins between prices of serf-populated and prices of uninhabited lands and effectively rejects the established view according to which the relative smallness of the differentials in some regions was due to the alleged economic decline of serfdom (pp. 370–375). This is very good, and one could only wish that throughout the author had shown himself somewhat more venturesome in using statistical data for independent estimates of his own. In particular, he might well have tried to relate his data on peasants' obligation to income estimates using productivity data and other information. He reproduces such a computation by a Russian historian for the sixteenth century (pp. 235–236) and also reprints such data for the state peasantry in the nineteenth century (p. 487), and it would have been natural and revealing to indicate at least the corresponding order of magnitude for the seignorial peasantry in the nineteenth century.

To shift from the desirability of more extensive economic and statistical analysis to the crucial matters of historical interpretation raised in the study, the main problem may be approached as follows. Blum insists several times throughout his book that in dealing with the rise of serfdom, as well as with its eventual abolition, one must resist the temptation of assigning the effect to just one causal factor. A variety of forces, varying in importance in different periods, tended to shape the course of events. This is an agreeable attitude which, at least on the face of it, serves to avoid undue simplifications. Nevertheless, it is not without its disabilities. In his eagerness to establish a number of causes, the author isolates them so much as to blur the all-important connections between them, which are essential to the comprehension of the process. In explaining the subjugation of the peasantry, Blum seeks to separate the long swings of economic progress and retrogression from the role of the state, and the latter again from the economic backwardness of the country, which in turn was reflected in the absence of a strong bourgeoisie. There is something artificial about distinctions of this sort. For it seems reasonable to say that the economic backwardness of the country decisively determined the nature of the Russian state, as well as the economic policies pursued by the Russian government. Because the economic environment was so backward, the state for long periods was the primary influence on economic change in the country.

For this reason, it is not very convincing to treat periods of decline and stagnation in Russia of the fourteenth to sixteenth centuries as though they were endogenous economic phenomena. True, the influx of precious metals in the sixteenth century may have in some degree accelerated the pulse of economic life, and it is interesting — though the author does not mention it — that the changes in Russian price structure tended to resemble somewhat those experienced in Western Europe. But it is hazardous to exaggerate the importance of monetary economy in Russia of the period, and there is no substantive evidence presented — beyond mere coincidence in time — that economic development in fairly isolated Russia, particularly in the fourteenth and fifteenth centuries, was induced by the same causes as in European counterparts. In general, it is difficult to combat the impression that, here as in other places, Blum is much too ready to assume identity of historical causations in Russia and the West. Even if it could be admitted that the economic difficulties in Tatar-dominated Russia, struggling to throw off the Mongolian yoke and torn by internal strife, were in any way similar to those experienced in the contemporaneous West, the differences remain overwhelming. The Western decline in the fourteenth century was compatible with rising standards of welfare and was marked by the ascendance of craft guilds — that great school of industrial activities and in many respects the cradle of modern economic values and attitudes. The permanent absence of these factors in Russia is an important element in the totality of phenomena implied in the economic backwardness of the country. At the time when the guilds were rising to power in the West, the Tatars, as Blum mentions (p. 63), were making captives of Russian skilled artisans in order to weaken the forces of resistance to their domination. At any rate, economic stagnation in Russia, when it occurred, had no redeeming positive features.

The main point, however, is that the military policies of the Russian state in themselves go far to explain the ups and downs in the country's economic life. In particular, the great stagnation at the end of the sixteenth and in the early seventeenth century is readily attributable to the exhausting nature of the military ventures in the preceding period and to the great burdens placed upon the shoulders of the peasantry. If the country had not been so backward, the state would have had at its disposal resources other than peasant labor in order to maintain its expansionist policies.

Similarly, the process of enserfment is almost inconceivable without the power of the state. How else could it be achieved in a country so open toward the vast empty spaces in the south and the east as was the great Russian plain? Blum is quite right (pp. 112, 155–156) in casting doubt on the belief — one should not dignify it by calling it "theory" — in some inborn nomadic yearnings in the Russian soul, and he equally rightly explains that self-interest and "catastrophes" (the most important among them clearly being the intolerable pressure of governmental policies) pushed the population into mass flights from the state and from the state-created gentry. But one cannot help wishing that the author had placed more stress upon this aspect of the development. Precisely because he considers his effort "a study in the history of human freedom" (p. 4), more might have been said on the tragic story of the Russian frontier, with the temporary freedom attained by escaped peasants continuing precariously until the state had extended its power to the new regions and proceeded to subjugate the peasantry, as it had done in the heartlands of the country.

It is certainly not outright wrong to say that the state in the sixteenth and seventeenth centuries "only channeled and intensified already existing tendencies" (p. 606 and, almost in the same words, p. 219). The first limitations on the freedom of the peasantry certainly long antedated the intervention of the state. And still, the words just quoted are rather misleading because what they are supposed to cover, in the author's own presentation, is the creation of the "service state" and the forcible alienation, to use the Swedish term, of the masses of "black" peasants into subjection to the lords. It was the state that placed the seal of inescapable finality upon the process, reducing the seignorial peasantry to the position of chattel slaves, and maintaining and protecting the relationship after the connection between serfdom and service to the state had been severed. It is very often perilous to confuse the origins of an historical phenomenon with its subsequent essential characteristics.

Blum is strongly inclined to view this process of enserfment of Russian peasantry as an integral part of the development that occurred over most of East Europe (Eastern Germany, Livonia, Poland, Lithuania, Bohemia, Silesia) and as being primarily the result of "the increase in power of the nobility, and especially of lesser nobility." And he says: "It seems to me that the history of agrarian institutions in Russia would have taken much the same course without the creation of the absolute state" (p. 606). This is a rather bold conjecture. The elements of similarity are, of course, present. This is even true in a sense that Blum does not wish to stress. For instance, the process of enserfment of East Elbian peasants by the Junkers is difficult to describe without reference to central power and the legal measures by which the enserfment was rendered possible. At the same time, however, the differences are formidable. The Russian "service state" is not comparable to anything in Eastern Germany. Nowhere in Eastern Germany was the peasant reduced to the role of a commodity that could be, and generally was, sold severally or in groups, if one abstracts from anecdotal stories of some Mecklenburg Junkers who lost and won peasants in a game of cards. Except for Polish lands along the Dnieper, nowhere in Eastern Europe were the geographic conditions such as to lead to a mass exodus of the oppressed peasantry, had it not been restrained by the forces of the state.

Whatever parallels may be traced for the earlier period, they doubtless are wholly invisible in the eighteenth century. There is nothing in Russia (except in some formerly Polish territories) to serve as a counterpart to Maria Theresa's *Robot Patente* and *Urbaria*, to Joseph II's abolition of serfdom, or to Prussian efforts to stop the engrossing of peasant land by the Junkers. There was nothing, of course, to duplicate the earlier *reduktion* (the reversal of the alienations) in Sweden. In complete divergence from the rest of Europe — be it East or West — in Russia the eighteenth century marked the complete enslavement of the seignorial peasants and, at the same time, enormously expanded their numbers by introducing the system into the more recently acquired regions of the country and by lavish grants of state peasants to nobility and gentry.

Blum's description of this process is excellent, and it is only regrettable that he blurs its significance in his later generalizations and conjectures. Surely, by no stretch of the imagination could the events of the eighteenth century be attributed to any specific economic trends. The driving forces must be sought in the political sphere, that is to say, in the curious situation of the "absolute" state in a backward country, with an immense power superimposed upon a weak and treacherous foundation. One of the functions of serfdom was to make the state militarily strong. Serfdom was an essential cog in the Petrine policy of economic development. But the military successes and the gains in the economic field were achieved at a high price. The peasantry became a reservoir of repressed rebellion, an ever-present threat to the safety of the state. The risk of taking off the lid and unleashing unpredictable cataclysms seemed too great, and the perpetuation of serfdom and continued reliance upon nobility and the gentry was a natural *pis-aller*. It is quite true, as Blum points out, that the whole development must be understood in terms of the country's economic backwardness. But this does not mean that the state was not the primary active agent in making fateful decisions, even though within a narrow framework of alternatives, so that bound by earlier acts it was driven to perpetuate the system of serfdom when, no longer a factor aiding the modernization of the country, that system became one of the main obstacles to economic progress.

Here again I must hesitate to accept the author's appraisal. Blum says: "The relative retardation in Russian economic growth has often been blamed on serfdom, on the grounds that the serf was an inefficient worker who could not — or would not — adapt himself to new techniques of production, while the limitations on his freedom of movement are supposed to have produced a shortage of industrial labor. But this explanation understates the very considerable freedom of movement allowed peasants who were seeking work, and it neglects the technical and commercial skills developed by serf and state peasants who were engaged in *kustar* production and trade." And he goes on to list, as "more cogent explanations for Russian retardation," the low quality and poor distribution of natural resources and the inadequacies of the transportation system (p. 343). While it is perfectly correct that serfdom was not the only disability from which the Russian economy suffered, it does seem that the economic consequences of serfdom are imperfectly presented by the author.

First of all, he is doubtless guilty of exaggeration when he states that by the end of the eighteenth century Russian industry "approximated and in some extent surpassed the industrial development of other European lands" (p. 294). Possibly, he was unduly influenced by some recent attempts in Russian literature to deny the economic backwardness of the country under Catherine II, and to let this rediscovery of Tarle's paradoxical thesis be followed by the discovery of an "industrial revolution" in Russia in the first half of the nineteenth century. Very rightly, Blum refuses to accept the latter (p. 343); but as far as the former is concerned, there is hardly any doubt that taking into account the structure of Russian industry, its absorptive capacity for the raw materials produced (including iron) and its degree of mechanization — as by any other reasonable yardstick — Russia was in the eighteenth century and remained throughout the nineteenth century far and away the most backward among the major European countries

The fact that serfs could seek, and in fact found, industrial employment is undeniable, but it is equally true that their stay in the factories could be terminated by the seignors' order and mostly was of short duration. Blum himself admits that for these reasons serf labor was offered to industry in a "sellers' market and commanded correspondingly higher wages" (p. 322). What he does not observe, but should have said in this connection, is that in a situation where the serf working in industry remained under obligation to pay a quitrent to the lord, the quitrent burden actually represented a tribute paid by industry to agriculture. When one considers how very painful was the process of forming a stable industrial labor force in much more advanced countries, where specific disabilities of this kind were absent, the additional barriers created by the existence of serfdom must be regarded as most serious obstacles to industrialization. The very fact, mentioned by Blum, of the importance of the rural cottage industry and its ability to compete with the factory cannot be separated from the serf status of the *kustari* and in reality is another aspect of the paralyzing effect of serfdom upon the industrial development in the country.

One final point may be in order. The author's treatment of the institution of the Russian village commune belongs among the finest parts of the book. An extremely controversial subject is handled with exemplary clarity of presentation and reasonableness of interpretation. Blum's thesis of the hiatus between the relatively ancient spontaneous commune that tended to disintegrate in the sixteenth century and the modern land-equalizing repartitional commune, created in response to Peter I's *podushnaya podat'* (soul tax), is unexceptionable. It is, however, a flaw in the organization of the book that the chapter dealing with the later-day commune has been placed so far toward the end. It has a clear and momentous bearing on the author's earlier discussion of problems of efficiency of Russian agriculture of the period, as well as on the question of the relationship between agrarian institutions and industrialization. Even in the absence of serfdom,

435

the commune would have militated against modernization of agriculture, kept down the peasantry's demand for industrial goods, and inhibited the flow of labor to industry. Because of the existence of the commune, the gravity of the retarding effects that stemmed from serfdom was greatly enhanced. For the rest, the repartitional commune in Russia, in which the collective elements were pushed so much further than in the open-field system of medieval Europe, is another aspect of the curious Russian sequence: institutions originating in attempts to modernize the country evolved into strong barriers to further modernization. What is true of serfdom is *mutatis mutandis* true of the commune. This is one of the many lessons taught, some of them perhaps unwillingly, by Jerome Blum's admirable book.

THE ORIGINS OF FARMING IN RUSSIA *

This book deals with the early history of farming in the European territory of modern Russia from prehistorical beginnings until the Mongolian invasions of the thirteenth century. The study has two central parts. One is devoted to the techniques of agricultural production; the other to "social relations" in agriculture. The author is at his very best when he describes in fair detail the nature of implements used in farming and their relation to changes in the prevailing systems of land cultivation. The presentation is based on an impressive array of archeological material, a good deal of which has been analyzed with the help of modern electronic devices. It is important to note that the archeological material is treated as continuous, beginning with the earliest available traces of population on the great plains in the east of the European continent. In discussing that material, the author keeps moving back and forth through the centuries so that the point at which the evidence becomes "Russian" in any definite sense of the word is quite elusive.

The book contains what probably is the best available discussion of the various types of tilling tools, from the scratching plow (*ralo*

* Review of R.E.F. Smith, *The Origins of Farming in Russia* (Paris and The Hague: Mouton and Company, 1959).

in Russian, which the author renders as *ard*, a term that is etymologically clear, even though lexically surprising) via the light forked plow (*sokha*), whose shares (*lemekhi*) may or may not have been equipped with iron tips (*soshniki*), to the powerful share-coulter-moldboard combination in the developed heavy plow. The reader is left with a rather clear idea of the potentialities and limitations of each of these implements within the framework of different methods of cultivation: (1) slash and burn farming (*podseka*), (2) shifting farming (*zalezh*), and (3) field farming, including the three-field system. Again, the technical aspects of those systems are presented very lucidly. Thus, the reader is led to appreciate the consequences of the failure to remove the roots of the larger trees which constituted the difference between *podseka* and an assart. It might be noted, however, that in later periods when field farming had grown to be more important, *podseka* came to mean the clearing of forest land for *permanent* cultivation, hence an assart. See, for example, a quotation from a fifteenth-century document in A. D. Gorski, *Ocherki ekonomicheskogo polozheniya severo-vostochnoy Rusi, XIV–XV vekov* (Sketches of the Economic Conditions of Northeast Russia in the Fourteenth and Fifteenth Centuries; Moscow, 1960; p. 38). Incidentally, terminological problems are quite important. The meaning of many technical terms in Russian agricultural history has been confused by shifts over time, regional dialectal variations, and sloppy usage. It is, therefore, not the least merit of this book to have established some firm associations between words and objects. The author has made an attempt to provide some indication of the probable yields in slash and burn farming as compared with field farming, as well as of the variations in the length of the period during which the fertility of the ash cover could be maintained. Once the burnt soil gave out, the land was allowed to revert to forest. Then the changing composition of the forest in the process of regeneration constituted another notable facet of *podseka* farming.

These are crucial problems, and their treatment in the study is illuminating. A major interpretative problem is presented by the degree of association of specific implements with particular systems of cultivation. The author says: "It appears . . . that the implements used in preparing the seed-bed were not decisive in determining the course of development of any system . . . More than one system can be carried out with similar implements . . . the co-existence and simultaneous use of differing evolutionary forms of implements is a characteristic feature of farming" (p. 105). This is a very defensible position. It is prudent to eschew commitment to one-way causal connections. The effect may have run from the implement to the farming system or from the farming system to the implement. Even Soviet historians (like Grekov) have hesitated to espouse wholeheartedly a technological interpretation of changes in farming. In fact, very simple implements can be used in a variety of ways. Within certain limits and with appropriate skill, one share of a twin-share *sokha* can be forced to act as a primitive moldboard. At the same time, the author would not deny that, at least at far ends of given historical periods, there was a natural tendency for progress in implements to be paralleled by progress in the systems of cultivation. Thus the scratching plow would have been of little use on the long strips of the open field; but a developed plow would have been worse than useless on the ash cover of the burnt-over land where, at least in the years immediately after the clearing, no plowing at all was required. On the other hand, something more might have been said on both the conditions that favor an uneven rate of progress in the two branches of agricultural evolution and the effect of such an unevenness upon the nature of farming.

The other main part of the book is somewhat less illuminating. There are certain narrow limits to an attempt to correlate changes in what the author calls "social and agrarian relations" with the changes in the farming system. It would seem that the author tends to go beyond what is reasonable in this respect. The range of social phenomena discussed in this connection is surprisingly wide: division of labor between the sexes and the growth of male importance, changes in marriage customs, and even development of private property in land, advent of serfdom, rise of political entities, and establishment of feudalism. Some segments of this discussion are quite plausible. Thus, the association of a very large patriarchal family commune with slash and burn farming is natural enough because of the massive investment of brute labor required to clear the land. But even here the author is forced to go on and stress that other forms of social organization (nonkinship commune, or serf-worked or slave-worked estate, or combinations of all three) were in fact utilized for the purpose. In general, in dealing with problems of social structure Smith betrays a somewhat stronger inclination to speculate and a greater readiness to deduce the existence of causal or functional relations than is the case in the earlier parts of the study. At times, one has the feeling that crucial problems of Russian economic — and not only economic — history are discussed in a manner that is unduly cursory. But the author is again very convincing when, returning to the question of technology, he concludes that the cheapness of the tools used in farming gave "no basis for dominance by the lords" and that, accordingly, "there appears to be no direct correlation between changes in the types of tools and changes in social structure" (p. 188). This negative conclusion has an obvious and direct bearing upon the problem of the origin and diffusion of serfdom in Russia. Indirectly, it may serve to stress the role of political power in the process. It is important to see this point coming from the pen of a scholar who has versed himself so deeply in the technological aspects of Russian agrarian history.

SOCIAL AND ECONOMIC HISTORIES OF RUSSIA *

The comprehensive study of Russian economic history which Peter Struve had set out to write, and to which his quaintly elaborate title was meant to apply, has remained unfinished. The present volume contains, in addition to two introductory chapters, a fully completed part (seven chapters) on the early medieval period, carrying the story to the time of the Mongolian invasion, and five chapters of the second part dealing with the rise of Moscow; four of these chapters were still in first draft at the time of Struve's death in 1944. A long appen-

---

* Reviews of P. B. Struve, *Sotsial'naya i ekonomicheskaya istoriya Rossii s drev-neyshikh vremen do nashego, v svyazi s razvitiyem russkoy kul'tury i rostom rossiy-skoy gosudarstvennosti* (The Social and Economic History of Russia from Ancient Times to the Present, in Connection with the Development of Russian Culture and the Growth of Russian Statehood; Paris, 1952), and Bertrand Gille, *Histoire économique et sociale de la Russie du moyen âge au XXe siècle* (Paris: Payot, 1949).

dix (occupying more than two fifths of the volume) presents a series of reprints of various papers, including three articles on Russian feudalism and the Russian peasantry and a number of obituaries devoted to Soloviev, Klyuchevski, and other Russian historians.

The book as conceived by the author was designed to reveal the historical roots of the Russian revolution which are "buried deeply in Russia's historical backwardness." The flow of Russian history was to appear as a perennial struggle between freedom and compulsion, between free and regimented economic activities, and the Russian revolution was to emerge as a "grandiose reaction of the traditional forces of compulsion against the equally traditional forces of freedom" (p. 7, preface, written in 1938).

Those are exciting promises, particularly to this reviewer who has come to believe that very important aspects (including the changing degree of economic compulsion) of the economic history of both Russia and the West can be discussed fruitfully in terms of changing levels of economic backwardness. It is, therefore, with a keen sense of regret that one realizes that the promises have remained unfulfilled. The story as presented here stops at such an early point in Russian economic history that one fails to discern more than the vaguest contours of the grand historical conception that was in the author's mind.

There is no need to summarize here the actual contents of the book. It would be impossible to reproduce the wealth of interesting detail and the fascinating discussion of sources. On the other hand, Struve's earlier essay in *The Agrarian Life of the Middle Ages* was essentially in the nature of a brilliant summary of the material collected in the present volume.[1] The balance of this review may be confined, therefore, to a few broad comments. Perhaps the central point in Struve's presentation is the refutation of what he calls the slavophile and the Marxian legends which assume the original existence of the village commune among the Eastern Slavs. Struve believes that such an assumption has no foundation in reality. In taking this position, he continues the work of some distinguished Russian scholars, such as B. N. Chicherin and V. I. Sergeyevich, whose views in some sense were the Russian counterpart of those of a long line of

---

1. *The Cambridge Economic History of Europe* (Cambridge, Eng., 1942), pp. 418–437.

Western scholars from Fustel de Coulanges to Dopsch. Struve's position seems unexceptionable for the very early period, and it may be noted that even a modern Soviet historian has had to admit that "the sources contain no indication concerning the existence of the obshchina in the ninth and tenth centuries." [2]

Much less well founded, however, is Struve's bland identification of the legally free segments of the peasantry with an economically dependent class that occupied lands belonging to members of a small landowning group. The inference is that no loss of land by the peasantry could ever have occurred in the later periods for the simple reason that the peasants had never owned the land. It is obvious that the existence of such a situation under conditions of abundant land resources calls for an explanation. According to Struve, such an explanation is provided by the scarcity of capital, which was concentrated in the hands of the landowners. This view is hardly satisfactory, least of all in the unqualified form in which Struve chooses to present it. On the one hand, it tends to overestimate the importance of capital in an extensive agriculture where the use of capital was kept at a minimum. On the other hand, it overlooks something of which the author is perfectly aware elsewhere in the book (pp. 124–125), to wit, those peasant obligations which were tax payments rather than interest payments on capital advanced. As a result, the author neglects the position of the "black" peasants, occupying nonallodial black lands which, in juridical theory, may have been "owned" by the holder of the political power but, in economic practice, were in the possession of the taxpaying peasants. The obligations of black peasants were in essence political, and it is perhaps significant that Struve has avoided any discussion of capital ownership on black lands.

An important and unfortunate consequence of this generalization from the conditions on allodial or white lands to the peasantry as a whole is the failure to prepare the reader for the understanding of the crucial significance of the transference of the black lands by the Moscow princes to the members of the "serving classes" (army and bureaucracy), a process very much comparable to the alienation of crown lands in seventeenth-century Sweden. In fact, it might

2. See S. B. Yushkov, *Ocherki po istorii feodalisma v kievskoy Rusi* (Essays on the History of Feudalism in Kievan Russia; Moscow–Leningrad, 1936), p. 8.

be quite in accord with the spirit of Struve's general conception to suggest that it is in this alienation (which, unlike the development in Sweden, was *not* followed by a reversion) that the deepest roots of the Russian revolution must be sought.

But one must stop here. Strictures of this nature can hardly be fair when addressed to fragments of what doubtless would have become an outstanding contribution. Had the book been completed, major shifts in emphasis may have been introduced, and those portions now available may have appeared in an altogether changed perspective. At any rate, one has every reason to be grateful to Struve's sons, who by publishing this volume have provided us with this insight into the laboratory of a great economic historian.

Bertrand Gille's brief survey of Russian economic history is based entirely on secondary sources. It contains quite a few minor inaccuracies and some outright errors. Nevertheless, on the whole, it is a very useful contribution. The author has devoted a good deal of thought to what he calls the unique aspects ("les caractères originaux") of Russia's economic development, and, despite certain exaggerations and simplifications, he has succeeded both in discerning the principal traits of that development and in weaving around them a significant factual narrative. The author faced a difficult problem of organization and presentation, and he solved it astonishingly well.

Gille places much emphasis on the low density of population and regards this factor as the main barrier to peasant enserfment during earlier phases of Russian history. This is a very defensible view. Unfortunately, the author pushes it much too far in his extreme and categoric conclusion that "medieval Russia was a free economy" (p. 25). On the other hand, in his discussion of the origins of serfdom he allocates more weight to the economic factor (peasant indebtedness) as against the political factor (governmental policies of creating *beneficia*) than is consistent with his basic emphasis on the low density of population. To reconcile the two views, he would have had either to claim significant changes in density or else to stress changes in capital equipment available to the peasants, as does, for instance, Peter Struve in his important *Social and Economic History of Russia.*

The chapters on the origins of capitalism and mercantilism make very good reading. The writer's insistence that Russian policies of industrialization did not *begin* with Peter the Great is certainly justified. He is much impressed by the "curious phenomenon" which is "perhaps unique in the whole history of the world" — namely, that "capitalism appeared in industry and commerce at a time when the agrarian economy was evolving toward feudalism" (p. 79). The uniqueness of the phenomenon is highly debatable, particularly in view of Asian economic history, but its importance for comprehending the nature of Russian economic development is indubitable.

It is perhaps regrettable that Gille felt impelled to spend time discussing the question of whether "capitalism" did or did not exist in seventeenth-century Russia. His answer is in the affirmative if capitalism means accumulation of considerable wealth and its concentration in a few hands, but in the negative if capitalism means the existence of private industrial enterprise detached from agriculture and based on a developed financial organization (pp. 76–77). All this is in part purely verbal and in part rather dubious. The point concerning accumulation of capital is considerably weakened by the author himself, by his much justified stress on the role of the state and foreign enterprise in providing capital for the country's economic development.

The discussion of developments during the eighteenth century after the death of Peter I is perhaps the least satisfactory part of the book. The designation of the era as the "birth of liberalism" is misleading, since the chief justification for such a designation is negative and lies in the decline of governmental promotion of economic development. This is the period during which occurred the perpetuation of serfdom through the surrender of peasant serfs into virtually unrestrained ownership by the gentry, and it requires a considerable strain on the concept of liberalism to associate it with such a far-reaching absence of freedom in occupational choice. In addition, the author does not stress the economic stagnation that followed Peter I's departure, and he obviously tends to exaggerate the speed of economic development in the second half of the century. He seems also to overestimate greatly the influence upon Catherine II of the views of contemporaneous French *économistes*, and his statement that the "influence of physiocratic ideas which assigned to agriculture a place of central importance prepared the upsurge of [Russian] grain exports" (p. 129) is really quite unfounded.

In characterizing the first half of the nineteenth century, the author says that the industrial transformation in the West oriented Russia toward development of agriculture and caused her to neglect industry. The point would have been more convincing if the great rise in agricultural exports had not begun in the late forties and the early fifties of the nineteenth century (that is, at best, at the very close of the period under review) and if the period of rapid industrialization had not been initiated in Russia in the very wake of that increase in exports. The rise in population (p. 162) hardly can be sufficient to explain the difference between the two halves of the century. Throughout, the author's treatment of the period 1800–1850 suffers from inadequate appreciation of the retarding effects of serfdom upon industrial development. Partly for this reason, he arrives at the unexpected and unguarded conclusion that during the first half of the century "Russia did all she could to further industrial development" (p. 159). The opposite statement would have been much nearer the truth.

The chapter "Liberalism and Its Crises" deals with the period 1860–1914, stretching from the emancipation of the peasantry to the outbreak of the First World War. It contains a succinct description of the emancipation procedure and presents, within its scope of fifty-odd pages, plenty of material on the ensuing industrialization, including railroad building, problems of labor supply to industry, output data, and banking and financial developments. Considering the role played by the state during the nineties, and particularly the high protective tariff of 1891 and the flow of extensive budgetary assistance to industry, the whole period cannot be described as one of liberalism, except with a good many qualifications. The author's failure to make these qualifications and to place sufficient emphasis on the role of governmental policies in the process of industrialization is regrettable, since it results in a somewhat distorted picture of a most important period of economic evolution. The last chapter is devoted to the impact of the war upon the Russian economy and brings the story to the revolutionary year 1917.

In conclusion, some of the more important errors, inaccuracies, and inconsistencies may be briefly noted.

On page 25, we are told that the Mongols arrested the political and economic disintegration of the country. On page 29, it is said that such disintegration was carefully maintained by the invaders. Gille should have made up his mind on the matter. The truth probably is that the rise of the Duchy of Moscow would have been quite unlikely without the constant support and protection of the Moscow princes by the Mongolian overlords.

A little more care might have been employed in assuring consistency in the use of proper names and technical terms. Thus, the reader finds the name of the Moscow prince Ivan Kalita (meaning Ivan the Purse) once correctly spelled on page 31; on the same page he also is described as Ivan d'Escarcelle, which is the correct French translation of Kalita, but the reader has no way of knowing that the two Ivans are one and the same person; finally on page 35 the name is misprinted as Ivan Kalitz.

With reference to the important work of Y. Krizhanich, the Croatian émigré and first literary representative of Russian mercantilism, the reader is told on page 45 that Krizhanich disapproved of monopolies and advocated commercial and industrial freedom; on page 70, the reader is apprised that "from 1650 on, under the influence of the economic ideas of Krizhanich, state monopolies were instituted for the principal items of exports." The reader may well feel confused by the two statements and should have been told that, while Krizhanich objected to monopolistic privileges to private trade or to domestic state trading, he was strongly in favor of a permanent government import and export monopoly.[3] Possibly, the fact that Gille confined his research to secondary sources is responsible for the confusion. In addition, there is no direct evidence for Krizhanich's having influenced Russian economic policy at any time, but least of all "from 1650 on." Except for a very short trip in 1647, Krizhanich did not arrive in Moscow until late in 1659, was sent into Siberian exile (presumably on account of his Catholicism) early in 1661, and did not begin formulating his economic ideas until 1663; and there is no indication of any influence beyond the fact that some of his Siberian writings were, from 1775 on, included in the library of the tsars, and perhaps in that of Prince W. W. Golitsin.[4]

---

3. See *Russkoye gosudarstvo v polovine XVII veka* (The Russian State in the Middle of the Seventeenth Century; Moscow, 1859), pp. 9, 11, 23.

4. S. A. Belokurov, *Yuri Krizhanich v Rossii* (Yuri Krizhanich in Russia; Moscow, 1900), pp. 22, 208.

There is a certain nonchalance in the book with regard to statistical data, none of which, incidentally, is covered by a source reference. On page 49, for example, Fletcher's famous estimate of Russian budgetary revenues is cited without giving the reader any intimation of the grave uncertainties and duplications attached to that estimate.[5] Incidentally, Fletcher's estimate does not, as Gille believes, refer to the middle of the sixteenth century but to the late eighties. Fletcher was in Moscow in 1688 or 1689, which was not, as Gille believes, during the reign of Ivan the Terrible but during that of his son Fedor. In addition, to reproduce Fletcher's most dubious, if not inane, comparison of the taxation burden in Russia with that of contemporaneous England, and to do it without reservations, is unfortunate.

There are also some outright errors. To say that in 1879 two thirds of the industrial workers were occupied in enterprises employing more than 1,000 workers is, of course, plain nonsense, and also at variance with data given by the author himself on the very next page (pp. 197–198). The tabulation of changes in industrial output (p. 202) shows a number of inaccuracies, and some figures in it refer to years other than those indicated. It is certainly quite unjustified to say that the bulk of state-bank deposits and balances on current account around the turn of the century represented moneys of industrial and commercial enterprises (p. 182); by far the larger part of those accounts was held by the Russian treasury. It is very misleading to treat values at current prices as denoting changes in "real" terms. Gille does that with regard both to foreign trade data and to national income data. As a result, he claims on page 213 an increase in Russian national income between 1900–1913 of 79.4 percent. This figure at current prices presumably comes from S. N. Prokopovich's study (no reference given); if this is true, it would have been just as easy to copy from the same page in that source the data on changes in income in terms of the 1900 prices which show an increase of only 39.4 percent.[6]

There are also factual errors and omissions, some of which are not without importance. Thus, the statement that no limitation of

5. See S. M. Seredonin, *Sochineniye Dzhil'sa Fletchera* (The Works of Giles Fletcher; St. Petersburg, 1897), pp. 307ff.

6. S. N. Prokopovich, *Opyt ischisleniya narodnogo dokhoda* (An Attempt at Computing National Income; Moscow, 1918), p. 67.

working hours for adult workers in industry occurred before 1914 (p. 191) is incorrect in view of Witte's act of June 2, 1897, which generally limited the number of working hours per day to eleven and a half.

There are, finally, some curiosities in the interpretation of basic economic concepts. Thus, Mr. Gille states that, while Russia succeeded toward the end of the nineteenth century in having a "favorable," that is, active, balance of trade, she did not succeed at the same time in having an active balance with regard to gold (p. 168). This, of course, is quite confused. What presumably is suggested, but not said at all, is that although Russia's balance of payments on current account showed a deficit, Russia kept importing gold.

LANGUAGE AND ECONOMIC HISTORY *

Over fifty years ago, Van der Meulen published his study on Russian maritime and shipping terms of Dutch origin (Amsterdam, 1909). The number of borrowed terms listed in that study — not counting derivations from borrowings — was close to 1400. The purpose of the present shorter study, in which about 425 words are discussed under some 230 items, has been to revise or to supplement the material relating to some of the words dealt with in the earlier work, and also to expand its scope by including items other than maritime terms. Many terms in both studies are part and parcel of an international vocabulary and appear, in addition to Dutch, in other Germanic and at times also in Romance languages. In many cases, therefore, it required a good deal of close linguistic analysis before the historical attribution of a given foreign word in Russian to a Dutch source could be proved or at least be made plausible. Some of these attributions no doubt must remain conjectural and may be successfully overruled by the claims of competing lenders, as is evi-

---

* Review of R. Van der Meulen, *Nederlandse Woorden in het Russisch. Supplement op de Hollandsche Zee-en Scheepstermen in het Russisch*, Verhandelingen der Koninklijke Nederlandse Akademie van Wetenschappen, Afdelning Letterkunde, new series, part 64.2 (Amsterdam, 1959).

denced by material assembled by other scholars.[1] Information from various sources must be collated in dealing with such questions, but basically these are philological problems, and the present study, like its predecessor, addresses itself primarily to professional philologists. Nevertheless, Van der Meulen's findings should be of considerable interest to economic historians. For the mass of Russian linguistic borrowings from Holland was only a concomitant of the wave of technological and institutional reforms which swept Russia under Peter the Great. The nature of the borrowed vocabulary serves therefore to emphasize the peculiar features of the great spurt of economic development in Petrine Russia.

As might be expected, the newer publication tends to re-emphasize the basic fact that Russia was — and still is — indebted to the Dutch for the bulk of her shipping terminology. As one scrutinizes the *nonmaritime* borrowings, it is easy to notice that they appear to be dominated by terms pertaining to three categories: (1) various textile materials, some of which, incidentally, became very popular with Russian consumers; (2) various species of fish; (3) various fruits, vegetables, and *Genussmittel,* mostly for luxury consumption, but including the name for the crudest, cheapest, and most popular type of Russian tobacco. More important, however, is the negative aspect of the list, that is, the weakness or the near absence of two other categories which as a rule play a very considerable role in the processes of absorption by backward countries of foreign economic terminology: business terms, and names of tools and machinery. Van der Meulen's list shows almost no terms relating to "capital goods" outside the area of shipbuilding; and even the number of designations of shipyard instruments proper is quite small. When it comes to business terms, the paucity of borrowings is even more striking: the terms for stocks, stock exchange, and bankruptcy seem to exhaust the list. This lopsidedness in the composition of Russian verbal liabilities vis-à-vis the Dutch is not fortuitous. First of all, it casts a strong light on the nature of technological borrowings in periods *preceding* modern industrialization. What was being borrowed were "advanced" productive processes that could be executed with the help of the traditional,

1. Clara Thörnqvist, *Studien über die nordischen Lehnwörter im Russichen* (Uppsala, 1948).

relatively primitive tools. At the same time, the absence of business terms from the borrowings serves to illuminate the nature of big spurts of economic development under the tutelage of the state. In the early years of the eighteenth century, the Dutch were in a position to supply commercial terms galore. But the demand was lacking, and Russia during her classical period of mercantilism was not interested in expanding her mercantile terminology by borrowings from Holland or, for that matter, from any other country.

In 1910, one year after the publication of Van der Meulen's earlier work, there appeared in Russian the study by N. A. Smirnov, "Western Influences on the Russian Language during the Petrine Era." [2] That standard work contained a list of some 3500 borrowings. About one quarter of them were shipping terms; another quarter was occupied by terms connected with government administration; the third quarter was held by military terminology; the balance was taken up by miscellaneous words, with a preponderance of luxury terms imported from France, either directly or via Germany or Poland. Even using a very generous interpretation of the concept of business terminology, this reviewer was unable to find more than two dozen borrowed words that could be stretched to suit the concept. In particular, the lack of accounting terms is most revealing. The economic enterprises created during the Petrine spurt were not oriented toward any careful calculus of costs and revenues. The state, that is, the Russian people, was going to foot the bill, and profitability or its absence aroused little interest. The influx into Russian of foreign — mostly Italian — accounting terms was reserved for a later period, in which private enterprise had acquired greater importance and independence. It would seem that economic historians, and particularly those interested in periods of rapid spurts of economic development in backward countries, might find it quite profitable to pay close attention to the philological counterparts of technological and economic borrowings.

2. *Zapadnoye vliyaniye na russkii yazyk v petrovskuyu epokhu*, Imperial Academy of Sciences (St. Petersburg, 1910).

COUNT WITTE *

The last decade of the nineteenth century is one of the most interesting and instructive periods in Russian economic history. Those were the years of the great spurt of prerevolutionary industrialization, in which the government played a central role. Whether one views this spurt against the background of traditional patterns of rapid economic change in the country, compares it with its antecedents in more advanced European countries, or sees it as a lesson for current underdeveloped countries, it stands out as a great challenge to economic analysis and historical interpretation. It is, therefore, a great pity that Theodore Von Laue has not succeeded in doing full justice to his subject.

The book is not without merits. It is well written. It presents a good personal portrayal of Witte, the powerful minister of finance, whose policies, energy, and resourcefulness certainly must be regarded as the strategic factor in the economic transformation of the time. The author's archival research also has added one or two previously unknown features to Witte's biography. Professor Von Laue is fairly successful in describing the various forces that opposed and undermined Witte's influence and eventually led, in 1903, to the dismissal of the minister and to the fall of his system. It is, finally, true that in this book, as compared with his earlier articles on the subject, the author has made considerable progress in seeing the positive aspects of Witte's policies. Nevertheless, the study as a whole is likely to mislead and to confuse the reader, and the main reason is twofold: the technical competence of the author in dealing with economic and statistical problems is inadequate, and his general interpretations are warped by dogmatic preconceptions that make him see inevitabilities and necessities where at most he should be weighing alternatives and assessing probabilities.

Von Laue is quite right, of course, in regarding the budget and the public debt, the balance of payments, and the stability of the rouble as crucial ingredients of Witte's industrial policies. But he is altogether uncertain about the nature of the problems involved. This is true

* Review of Theodore H. Von Laue, *Sergei Witte and the Industrialization of Russia* (New York: Columbia University Press, 1963).

particularly of the balance of payments, where most of the trouble lies simply in his lack of understanding of the elementary concepts. Thus, he does not hesitate to make Witte say, nonsensically, that "he did not approve of preserving an active [sic] balance of payments through continued foreign loans" (p. 142). In another passage the author says that gold purchases from abroad, needed for the establishment of the gold standard (which establishment the author persists in calling "conversion") could be made "*either* . . . from a surplus in government revenues . . . *or*, more effectively" from an active balance of trade, unless one had recourse to the "dubious" solution of "foreign loans negotiated, say, for the construction of Russian railroads" (p. 10, italics added). There is no indication in the book that the author understands that, gold movements apart, a surplus on capital account definitionally means a deficit on current account; nor that, causally, the deficit on current account may be either the cause or the effect of a surplus on capital account. Borrowing, particularly foreign borrowing, is generally viewed by the author as dubious and "deplorable," an evidence of "bondage" and an indication that the Russian government "could not make ends meet" (p. 105). Elsewhere in the book he is willing to admit that the times were very propitious for capital imports; that foreign loans were obtained at relatively low interest rates; that successful conversions reduced the cost of servicing old loans; and that the funds obtained were largely used for productive purposes. But he still charges Witte with the inability to remove a "significant, though indetermined, deficit" in the balance of payments "with all the evil consequences thereof" (p. 111). Apparently, if the evil of foreign borrowing had to continue, Von Laue would have liked to see it at least mitigated by an active balance on current account!

In view of the author's helplessness in dealing with those factors, it is not surprising that in the concluding chapter, where he tries an appraisal of Witte's policies, biased contemporaneous statements are hopelessly interwoven with his own views, without any serious attempt at independent clarification of the qualitative problems involved. For example, first the author quotes some very destructive strictures in terms of roubles and kopeks from the enemies of Witte's budgetary policy — they charged that "underneath the brilliant façade of solvency the government operated at a permanent deficit" and "avoided bankruptcy only by going ever deeper into debt," so that "from this angle railroad construction and even industrialization as a whole were no more than a huge hoax born of an inexorable fiscal necessity" (p. 283). This should have put him under clear obligation to try to enlighten the reader through reasonable comparative estimates as to the orders of magnitude involved in budgetary deficits and foreign and domestic borrowing over the whole period under review. Instead, he prefers to hide behind the statement that, with regard to those things, "finality unfortunately has been irretrievably washed down the river of time" and, instead of presenting figures, he proceeds to refer again to some very general and mutually irreconcilable utterances, this time from contemporaneous foreign sources (p. 293).

However regrettable the inability of the author to go beyond superficialities and to offer a convincing analysis of his own of what happened during the period, the greatest weakness of his book lies in the absence of a considered judgment in appraising the long-term results of Witte's industrialization. After admitting (p. 269) that under Witte "Russia was indeed catching up," he ends what he calls (with some violence to adverb, adjective, and noun) his "purely economic analysis" on a negative note: "But even at best — and this may be readily conceded to Witte's opponents — the utmost effort did not guarantee that the gap between an underdeveloped Russia and the rapidly advancing countries in the West could ever be closed. The more she tried to catch up, the more she fell behind" (p. 302). The point here is not so much that "guarantee" in this context is a fairly meaningless term and "ever" a very long time; or that the author obviously is unable to make up his mind and to liberate himself from his earlier preconceptions. What matters most is that a historian writing more than a half century after the events he describes should have explored how the Russian economy developed once the cataclysms that shook it in the early years of the century were over. The impressive fact is that, in the years between 1906 and 1914, Russian industrial output again grew at the very respectable rate of better than 6 percent a year. This was indeed somewhat lower than the rate of growth achieved under Witte (8 percent), but the successful development in the later period was achieved despite the government's rather restrictive fiscal policy, and despite the appearance of some improvement in the levels of consumption of the population; in short, despite the absence of pressures even remotely comparable to those generated in the nineties. The all-important point is that this burst of spontaneous growth, essentially based on private initiative, is inconceivable except as a result of the development of the country's productive forces, both material and human, which were called to life by Witte's policies of forced-draft industrialization. Perhaps the greatest achievement of those policies was that — seen in their inseparable connection with the subsequent period — they proved a self-liquidating operation. Von Laue's study, which breaks off with the demise of the man, deprives the reader of the historical scope necessary for an appraisal of the historical significance of the "Witte system."

We do not know of course whether, in the absence of war, this process of gradual westernization of the Russian economy and of its diminishing backwardness would have continued for a long time to come. The chain of momentous and tragic events that began in 1914 naturally put an end to the historical chapter, the description of which our author has left unfinished. As we know from views Von Laue expresses in an essay published in the same year as the present book, he is not afraid of the most sweeping generalizations in this respect. It is his opinion that, war or no war, the Bolshevik revolution and the totalitarian policies pursued by the Soviet government, including even the ruthless suppression of freedom in arts and letters, were all inevitable. Von Laue claims that there is "no reason to shun concepts of historical necessity, as long as they are spelled out in some detail." [1] On the contrary, I believe that historical necessity is not an operational concept and has no place in serious scholarly presentation. Nor have I been much impressed with Von Laue's "spelling" proficiency in putting down on paper, with a light heart and a heavy hand, "some details" of the boldest historical speculations, even though, happily enough, economic literacy is not necessarily required in that field.

1. "Of the Crises in the Russian Policy," in John S. Curtiss, ed., *Essays in Russian and Soviet History* (New York, 1963), p. 314.

453

RUSSIAN POPULISM *

This is a monumental effort in painstaking research. The nearly twelve hundred tightly printed pages of the two volumes are based on perusal of innumerable books, articles, pamphlets, leaflets, and minutes of judicial proceedings. This study in its breadth and comprehensiveness is without precedent in the literature of the subject in any language, Russian not included. Franco Venturi's standards of scholarly accuracy are high indeed, and it may be added that I did not notice more than a few errors of fact, which turned out to be much too trifling to deserve mention here.

The importance of the subject matter should fully justify the herculean labor that went into the preparation of these volumes. Russian populism, that specific brand of agrarian socialism, deserves close study for a number of reasons. Populism occupied a central place in Russian intellectual history over several crucial decades of the nineteenth century. Its road was illumined by the brilliance of several great figures, among them Herzen, Bakunin, and Chernyshevski, to name only three. It was, over a long period, the dominating creed of that strange and curious group, the Russian intelligentsia; and it came to play, through a series of dramatic actions culminating in the assassination of Alexander II, a grave role in the political history of the country. Finally, at least in some of its emanations, it created elements of thought and norms of conduct which have become deeply ingrained in twentieth-century Bolshevism.

The author's method is simple and straightforward. His main concern has been to present the thought of his heroes and to unfold the story of their actions without indulging in lengthy interpretations. In a sense, the author is right when, in his preface, he expresses the view that the book may be useful primarily as an anthology. Large parts of it are indeed in the nature of an anthology, and the rest is a straight narrative. But the selection is an excellent one, and it could not have been made had not Professor Venturi tried hard to interpret for himself the nature of Russian populism.

---

* Review of Franco Venturi, *Il Populismo russo*, 2 vols. (Turin: Giulio Einaudi, 1952). [English translation in 1960: *Roots of Revolution. A History of the Populist and Socialist Movements in Nineteenth Century Russia*, trans. F. Haskell, intro. I. Berlin (London, Weidenfeld and Nicolson).]

The very decision to confine the period under study to thirty-three years (1848–1881) is the product of mature understanding. In a sense, Russian populism may indeed be conceived as a reaction to the revolutions of 1848 which caused men like Herzen — originally a staunch "Westerner" — to develop a vision of social development in Russia based on indigenous Russian institutions, the village commune and the producers' cooperative. And Venturi understands equally well that the early eighties marked the end of an epoch in the development of Russian populism, even though he does not make the reasons for it perfectly clear.

And yet one cannot but wish that the author had decided to share his thinking more fully with his readers and by so doing had attempted to make explicit much of what is contained in the book by mere implication and indirection. The point is that, at least to my mind, it is almost impossible to understand Russian populism without reference to the contemporary flow of the country's history and in particular to the basic condition of its economic and political backwardness. Backwardness, of course, is a relative concept, and however loudly the populists may have proclaimed their divergence from the "rotting West," the paradigm of Western development always remained before their eyes and forced them to return time and again to the problem of Russia's position vis-à-vis the West. This is perhaps the crucial dilemma in populist thought. The populists clearly saw the advantages inherent in Russia's being a latecomer upon the modern historical scene. They saw and stressed the possibility of adopting the results of foreign experience without incurring the heavy cost of experimentation, of errors and detours. Both Herzen and Chernyshevski found very felicitous phrases — duly recorded by Venturi — to express the essence of this situation. But they did so only in order to abandon the argument by an almost imperceptible twist and to raise the paradoxical claim that the preservation of the *old* rather than the easy adoption of the *new* constituted the "advantages of backwardness."

The result was a tragic surrender of realism to utopia. Here is perhaps the main reason for the decline of populism. When the rate of industrial growth leapt upward in the middle of the eighties, after the government had committed itself to a policy of rapid industrialization, the divorce between the populist utopia and the economic reality became too great, and the movement proved unable to survive the repressions that followed Alexander III's advent to the throne. In this sense, Venturi's terminal point, the assassination of Alexander II on March 1, 1881 (Julian calendar), is much too abrupt an end to his story, which obviously called for a further concluding chapter.

Similarly, the political radicalism of the populists finds its explanation in the political backwardness of the country. The existence of an absolutist government was unacceptable to minds whose standards of political normalcy were, despite everything, imported from the West. On the other hand, both the absence of constitutional government and the late start of economic development effectively barred the Russian intelligentsia from normal professional pursuits. What was, for decades, left to them (even though left to an astonishing degree by the standards of modern dictatorships) was the field of pure thought uninhibited and untempered by the exigencies of normal practical action. As a result, when at length it came to action, its character was one of absolute radicalism, displaying a most complex bundle of contradictory features: a spirit of self-sacrifice, heroism, devotion, and love of the people conjoined with the idea that the end justified the means and that any method, from forged imperial manifestoes to murderous conspiracy, was justified in the struggle against the absolute evil of absolutism. And equally complex and contradictory was the uneasy to-and-fro within populist thought between radical anarchism and the no less radical apotheosis of the omnipotent Jacobinic state.

This political radicalism was no doubt greatly reinforced by the economic conditions of the country. Because the populists refused to see the "advantages of backwardness" where they actually lay, the coming of capitalism meant for them not a chance for remarkably rapid economic growth (as occurred in fact between 1885 and 1900), but merely a great increase in popular misery and above all the extinction of the village commune. Hence developed the attitude of "now or never" — the race against time — so rightly and so persistently stressed by Venturi. Hence also developed the paradoxical fact that it took a strong injection of Marxism in the 1890's to effect some sort of precarious reconciliation between the intelligentsia and the idea of industrial development of the country. And very soon it appeared that the most radical sectors of Russian Marxism, while formally rejecting populist theories, had adopted a good many populist ideas and attitudes. This influence has never been quite obliterated. Populism as a movement of thought and action belongs to history, but as Venturi mentions in his preface (though not in his text), it is undeniable that many of its most negative features are far from being extinct in the Russia of our time.

This is perhaps the most striking lesson of the book. Venturi likes to regard populism as a special chapter in the history of European socialism, and it is a defensible view. But it is possible that greater interest may attach to the study of populism if it is viewed instead as a chapter in the history of ideologies in conditions of backwardness. Then the story of Russian populism may acquire a note of actuality and may serve better to emphasize the great dangers that are inherent in unduly prolonged periods of economic and political backwardness.

The foregoing remarks, largely drawn from Venturi's own selection of material, are not meant, of course, to detract from the great value of his splendid study. He has written a most reliable and most suggestive book, which in all likelihood will remain for a long time the basic reference source on the subject.

THE 1905 REVOLUTION *

This distinguished contribution to the history of the Russian revolutionary movement is conceived as a massive historical introduction to the study of the revolutionary cataclysm that shook the Russian Empire in 1905. The author begins his story in 1881, the year of the regicide and the terminal point in Franco Venturi's celebrated book on Russian populism. In many respects, the present volume appears to be a deliberate continuation of Venturi's study, upon which at times it relies rather heavily. The events of 1905 are reserved for a second volume, but the author carries his presentation to the very threshold of the great upheavals of that year.

* Review of Valdo Zilli, *La Rivoluzione russa del 1905, I: La Formazione dei partiti politici (1881–1904)*, Istituto Italiano per gli Studi Storici, no 16 (Naples, 1963).

The book deals with the ideological and organizational history of political parties in Russia during their crucial formative years, an extremely complex and variegated subject. It encompasses the crisis and decline of old populism; the rise of Marxism as a dominating ideology; the slow emergence of Social Democratic labor organizations; the brief attempts in the late nineties to confine the labor movement to purely economic concerns; the formation of the national Social Democratic Party and the almost simultaneous regeneration of populism in the shape of the Socialist Revolutionary Party, committed to agrarian socialism and possessing a fairly eclectic program and the appendage of a terrorist organization; the very hesitant formation of a "liberal" (nonsocialist) opposition party; and, finally, the split within the Social Democratic Party into the Menshevik and Bolshevik groups, amounting in fact to the creation of two independent organizations.

The author tells this story in great detail. Hardly anything is marginal enough to escape his attention. The first casual references to Marx in Russian writings are as carefully recorded as are the histories of some tiny and short-lived clandestine organizations. The formidable research effort is based on an impressive range of sources, revealing, incidentally, close acquaintance with the modern American literature in the field. The documentation is so extensive that it would seem petty to reproach the author for his not infrequent use of indirect sources in cases where the primary source was clearly available. Yet there are some hazards to this procedure and, though I did no thorough checking, in at least two cases the meaning of the original was found to be distorted as a result of having been strained through a secondary source. But, given the size of the book and the difficulty of the subject, the book as a whole is a fine testimony to the author's precise and diligent scholarship.

The presentation is essentially factual, and the reader is left to form his own opinion regarding the causal sequences of events. There is, in particular, no clearly articulated explanation of the causes of the unrest that gripped the country toward the end of the century, exploding in rebellious student demonstrations, quickening the pulse of political movements, leading to strikes and widespread acts of peasant violence, and finally culminating in the drama of the 1905 revolution. To be sure, a long and perhaps unnecessarily discursive chapter deals with the origins and the course of the war with Japan and the impact of the defeat on the prestige and power of the government. But the long-term effects of the forced-draft industrialization of the nineties and the government's desperate race against time are touched upon much too lightly. The roots of the revolution that lay in the discontent of the despoiled peasantry, which was forced to bear the cost of the great economic effort, should deserve much more emphasis; so, for that matter, should the growing disaffection of the gentry, whose position within the social structure was being adversely affected by the industrialization. Inadequacies of this sort are then reflected in related matters, such as the lack of a clear explanation for Witte's negative attitude toward the zemstvos; nor is there a sufficiently comprehensive explanation of the motivations that caused the leaders of those organizations to join in the general struggle against autocracy.

There is one point, however, on which the author does offer his own interpretation of what seems to him a crucial aspect of the prehistory of the 1905 revolution, that is, the split in the Social Democratic movement. A large part of the book is devoted to the evolution of Lenin's ideas, and the proceedings of the fateful congress in 1903 are summarized at length with great clarity. In his appraisal, the author views the Mensheviks as the dogmatic representatives of Western Marxism, while the Bolsheviks, whose ideological and organizational continuities with revolutionary populism are rightly stressed, are credited with a creative adaptation of Marxism to Russian conditions. They are said to have turned the very backwardness of the country to good political account and are praised therefore as a truly "Russian" movement. There is probably much truth in this position. The only trouble is that it explains things other than those on the author's agenda. Zilli is writing the history of the 1905 revolution. But the detailed presentation of Lenin's ideas and the story of the split are primarily relevant to a history of Russian Bolshevism as well as to that of the October Revolution and the subsequent history of the Soviet state. For it is not clear at all that the existence of the two Social Democratic groups and the ideological struggles between them before and after the revolution had much to do with the latter's origin, vicissitudes, and outcome. Nor does it seem correct to take the eventual victory of Bolshevism for granted, just because it actually occurred after three years of an unprecedented and disastrous war effort. It was not a foregone conclusion that the development would proceed along "Russian" rather than Western lines, as is shown, *inter alia* by the decline of Bolshevism between 1906 and 1914. For the same reason, it is difficult to accept the author's somewhat condescending treatment of the Socialist Revolutionary Party. It is true that this movement failed to produce an intellectual impact comparable with that of Marxian social democracy. But it was a profoundly democratic movement, exercising a strong appeal to the peasantry — the vast majority of the population. In the absence of war, the party, in all likelihood, eventually would have become one of the pillars of the political edifice in the country. In a very real sense, it was the most Russian of all the political groups at the time. There are clear and by no means negligible disabilities to attempts at writing history backward from the "ineluctable" victory of Bolshevism, which took place in an entirely different period and in entirely different circumstances.

Thus, the main and considerable value of the book lies in the comprehensive, skillful, and competent array of factual information that gives it a unique position in the literature on the subject. Not the least attractive feature of the study is the large number of significant trifles which are very much worth rescuing from oblivion. To let just one example stand for many: I was glad to be reminded that the phrase "cult of personality" was first used in a Russian context in 1901. Revealingly, it occurred in a critical pamphlet directed against Lenin, whose dictatorial ideas and policies caused one of his opponents to hurl at him the sacral term *Personenkult*, which had been previously coined and cast about in the debates of the German labor movement.

THE SOCIALIST REVOLUTIONARIES *

This book on the Russian Socialist Revolutionary Party stems from more than two decades of research and fully reveals the author's incomparable knowledge of the subject. But it is hopelessly marred

* Review of Oliver H. Radkey, *The Agrarian Foes of Bolshevism: Promise and Default of the Russian Socialist Revolutionaries, February to October 1917* (New York: Columbia University Press, 1958).

by unbridled emotions. Professor Radkey's task was to explain the decline of the Socialist Revolutionaries from a peak of immense popularity after the February Revolution to their discomfiture by the Bolsheviks in the October Revolution. Yet, long before Radkey begins to explain the defeat, it becomes clear that he cannot forgive it. Unlike Lucan's Cato to whom *causa victa placuit*, Radkey knows neither mercy nor courtesy in his strictures. The old populists, the venerated figures of the nineteenth century, are brushed aside contemptuously as a "tiny band of adult children." "Folly," "ineptitude," "fatuousness," "nauseous display of hypocrisy," "large child," "aberration," "intellectual snobbishness," "caste prejudice," "feminine venom" — those are the terms in which the author characterizes his heroes. Many an action or attitude is attributed to the Jewishness or membership in Masonic lodges of the persons concerned. This may be quite true, but in absence of any real evidence in support of those imputations one cannot help feeling that they were more in place in the contemporaneous Russian newspapers and pamphlets (whence they possibly came) than they are in a scholarly work published four decades after the event.

Vituperative, scornful, and condescending as Radkey chooses to remain throughout his book, he does make an effort to discuss the problem on a somewhat higher level. He lists a number of factors to explain the course of events, but the analysis is lacking in both depth and range, and in particular the fateful connection between the problem of the war and that of gentry land remains in the dark. The final yield of nearly five hundred pages is astonishingly meager. After having exhausted an inelegant vocabulary in upbraiding the Socialist Revolutionaries, the author suddenly and surprisingly admits, "in justice to them," that for the problem of war and peace "there was no easy solution, perhaps no solution at all." Continuing in his reflective mood, Radkey also admits belatedly that at least some Social Revolutionary leaders could not accept a German victory and had to consider what a Hohenzollern hegemony in Europe would mean for the development of democracy in Russia. Yet he quickly recovers to argue that those fears were unwarranted, because after America's entry into the war its outcome was no longer in the balance. This is an easy hindsight that ignores the formidable impetus of German offensive thrusts in 1918, a full year after the February Revolution. It is on the very last page that the author divulges what would have been the correct policy for the Socialist Revolutionaries to follow: to steer "a middle course of keeping the army in being, but formally suspending operations." But would the soldiers agree to stay put? Radkey admits this to be uncertain but remains undaunted: "Had the front gone to pieces anyway, the party would at least have the consolation of having acted in conformity with its principles and would have emerged with a clear conscience." One must wonder whether the mouse of this alternative policy justifies the mountain of angry rebuke under which the author has buried the actual policy pursued by the Socialist Revolutionaries.

HISTORIES OF RUSSIAN ECONOMIC THOUGHT *

The modest intrinsic value of N. K. Karataev's book lies in its convenient summaries of the contents of periodicals published by the Russian Academy of Sciences (established in 1724) and of various travelogues and geographic or geological surveys containing economic information mostly on the peripheral areas of the country. In addition, the author utilized unpublished archival materials of the Academy and those of the Free Economic Association (established in 1765). Economic historians will find in the book a number of useful bibliographical indications. Yet the main interest of the study does not derive from what it contributes to our knowledge of economic doctrines and economic research in eighteenth-century Russia, but from its illumination of Soviet historical scholarship in the sixth decade of our century.

Karataev's approach to his subject has been prefabricated for

* Reviews of N. K. Karataev, *Ocherki po istorii ekonomicheskikh nauk v rossii XVIII veka* (Essays in the History of the Economic Sciences in Russia in the Eighteenth Century; Moscow: Academy of Sciences of the USSR, Press of the Economics Institute, 1960); John F. Normano, *The Spirit of Russian Economics* (New York: John Day, 1945); *A History of Russian Economic Thought: Ninth through Eighteenth Centuries,* John M. Letiche, ed., trans. with the collaboration of Basil Dmytryshyn and Richard A. Pierce. (Berkeley–Los Angeles: University of California Press, 1964).

him. His task, he says, "is to demonstrate the existence in Russia of the eighteenth century of feudal economics and the beginnings of bourgeois economics." Accordingly, all the writers mentioned are classified as being either feudal or bourgeois. As is the custom in Soviet Russia, the two terms are used as though their meaning were entirely unambiguous. It is therefore worth noting that, even within the narrow context of this book, the term "feudal" appears in at least three distinct connotations. The use of the term "bourgeois" is similarly slipshod. A dichotomy of this kind is particularly ill suited to Russian economic and intellectual history in the earlier parts of the eighteenth century. The considerable modernization under Peter the Great, which Soviet writers describe as the initial stage of Russian capitalism, was indubitably achieved through putting the Russian peasantry under pressures that the selfsame writers describe as feudal. Hence classifying this or that writer as belonging to one of the two groups is neither convincing nor interesting. The period was marked by a drastic change in attitudes, from the stress on economic development in the first quarter of the century (Pososhkov) to radical agrarian populism in its last quarter (Radishchev). The change had momentous consequences for Russia's intellectual history in the nineteenth century, but it entirely eludes the pair of conceptual or preconceptual crudities with which Karataev operates.

On the other hand, Karataev's book bears the mark of a certain return to reason that occurred after the death of Stalin. In the last quinquennium of the dictator's life, any acknowledgment of foreign influences was stigmatized as groveling before the West. Karataev, writing as he does in a somewhat different climate, still has to credit some Russian mediocrities with having anticipated both the physiocrats and Adam Smith, or to assert that in 1825 some (unnamed) "English economists sorrowfully acknowledged England's lag behind Russia in the diffusion of economic knowledge," which of course is sheer nonsense. Nevertheless, Karataev is able to discuss at some length the ties connecting Russian writers with foreign economists, particularly with French and German mercantilism. This is progress. But, again, the most arresting aspect of that discussion is the absence of foreign influences upon Karataev himself. All modern literature on mercantilism seems quite unknown to him. At any rate, he writes as though nothing has been said on the subject since the days of Marx, thus providing striking evidence for the intellectual isolation in which Soviet historians find themselves.

There is plenty of spirit and a modicum of economics in this somewhat pretentious little book by John Normano. Essentially it retells the story of the Russian intelligentsia, its philosophical beliefs and its historical and social ideas. The author tries to separate the French, English, and German influences. Each of them receives a special chapter. Yet time and again the trichotomy breaks down. This is, for instance, the case with Radishchev, the great social critic under Catherine II, and even more strikingly with the Decembrists, who are discussed in the chapter on English influence, although the author is also forced to treat here the ascendancy over them of the ideas of the French Revolution. Moreover, the Decembrists reappear in the chapter on German influence, since it was from German universities that some of them received their ideas of economic and political liberalism. The intellectual goods shipped by any single nation are seldom homogeneous, and the character of the shipments changes from period to period. The author tends to simplify these relationships. After indicating the growing predominance of German thought in Russia from the middle of the nineteenth century onward, he permits his interpretation to culminate in a bizarre description of the Russian revolution "as a reaction against, and prevention of, continued German hegemony in Russian economic life and thought." In making this unguarded statement, the author conveniently forgets certain things of which he is perfectly aware elsewhere, such as the large influx of capital from England, France, and Belgium in the years preceding World War I, as well as the fact that, after all, German Marxism is not entirely unrelated to the ideology of Bolshevism.

The author is on somewhat firmer ground when he regards Bolshevism as a synthesis of the conflicting currents which divided the Russian intelligentsia in the past. In varying guise throughout the decades, it was the struggle between those who wanted Russia to follow the West, or thought this development inevitable, and those who envisaged for Russia an independent social evolution. The author's discussion of the elements of this synthesis, together with his insistence on historical continuity, in the present Russian system makes worthwhile reading, but it contains no attempt at a critical distribution of emphasis and gives little more than a collection of interesting points of view.

But what about Russian economics itself? At times the author reveals that he conceives of his book as a history of economic thought in Russia. This is misleading. The book deals with the general intellectual climate in which certain economic creeds developed. Economic theories are carefully avoided. Thus, the reader may learn that Tugan-Baranovski's "real strength as an economist was in his investigations of England's industrial crises," but not a single word is devoted to his contribution to the theory of business cycles. The influence of the Austrian school of economics on Russian scholars is relegated to a dependent clause, and no mention is made of Chayanov and his school of agricultural economics, which applied the marginal-utility analysis to investigations of peasant economy. The author does list, particularly in the earlier sections of the book, a fair number of Russian economists and some of their works. This bibliographical information may be useful to those who want to obtain a general orientation in the field. Unfortunately, the titles are given in translation only, without transliteration of the Russian original. This may make utilization of the bibliographical data more difficult.

The book is written in a lively style and reads well. It is stimulating and will cause no damage as long as the reader remains on his guard against the author's predilection for sweeping generalizations.

In the 1950s, the Soviet Academy of Sciences sponsored the preparation (under the editorship of A. I. Pashkov) of a voluminous three-thousand-page history of Russian economic thought. The present volume is a translation of the first quarter of the study. The Russian original appeared in 1955, and accordingly in approach, contents, and style it still bears undisguised the disgraceful marks of Soviet historical writings under Stalin. The authors of the individual chapters did not find it difficult to "illustrate" the general conclusions laid down for them in advance by an omniscient and infallible dictatorship, and to show that Russian writers on economic problems were not significantly influenced by the West while offering major original contributions to the history of economic doctrines. The contributors' considerable ignorance of Western economic thought and their analytical helplessness no doubt greatly facilitated their task. Curiously enough, the story begins in the ninth century so that everything, from legal stipulations bearing on economic life to a metaphoric reference to harvesting in an epic poem, becomes an integral part of Russian economic thought. With all its faults, nevertheless, the book might deserve an English translation. Primitive as its level is and despite all distortions, it does provide in its jejune summaries much information about a number of Russian writers, some of whom, particularly in the eighteenth century when more mature economic thinking appears, are figures of considerable interest. Besides, it is useful for readers who are not familiar with the Russian language to see a typical product of totalitarian scholarship in the field of history and economics. Unfortunately, this justification is all but frustrated by the quality of the present translation. The first few chapters are less objectionable, but most of it is amateurish, inconsistent, and sometimes downright wrong. Above all, it lacks the guidance of a careful and competent editor.

In reading the present volume, I stumbled over innumerable mistranslations of all kinds. Technical economic terms have often been rendered inexactly or wrongly. Thus, to give some examples, "accounting" becomes "discount"; "circulation of bills of exchange" becomes first "credit," then "exchange," then "exchange rate," until at the very end of the book an approximation is achieved by rendering "bills of exchange" as "promissory notes"; "debased coins" are converted into their opposite by being called "undervalued money"; "price formation" becomes "price formulation," and the "single tax" of the physiocrats becomes "uniform tax"; at one point "value" is called "cost," "cost" — "losses," "local price differentials" — "price fluctuations," "profitability" — "efficiency," and "goods contracted for" — "price"; because a somewhat unusual technical term is used in the original, "selling" becomes "buying" and later "confiscation" and a "clearly pronounced export surplus" is turned into an "acutely passive trade balance"; "rate of marketing" becomes "production"; "large-scale industry" is "heavy industry" throughout; and "small-scale commodity production" is transformed into "production of small goods." There are also difficulties with specific archaic terms referring to historical institutions, which could and should have been resolved by proper editorial annotations and cross-references. The glossary appended to the book is incomplete and imprecise.

Many deficiencies of the translation stem simply from an inadequate knowledge of Russian vocabulary and idioms, and from a poor grasp of the morphology and the syntactic structure of the Russian sentence. Accordingly, there are numerous erroneous renditions of words and phrases, and the meaning of many sentences is occluded or altogether perverted. Again, a few selected examples should suffice. How could the average reader know that "black lands" meant lands populated by unenserfed peasantry, when the crucial explanatory sentence is mistranslated and particularly when, later on, "black land regions" comes to stand for "black earth regions"? The editor offers no assistance and remains mute even when he confronts the reader with the phrase, "the black city young person," a term referring to taxpaying and social status and requiring, not an absurd literal translation, but an understanding circumscription and proper annotation. Since the original terms are not transliterated, let alone explained, the reader is likely to remain confused as to the important difference between *sloboda* in the sense of a tax-exempt suburb and a *posad* which comprised the taxpaying population of the towns, particularly because either term is frequently translated as "settlement." Obviously, the historically very important term *verkhovniki* (members of the Verkhovnyi Taynyi Sovet — the Supreme Secret Council) should have been explained rather than let the reader wonder about "the 'leaders' of 1730." The reader must be astonished to learn that Peter the Great "forbade poverty" when the reference is simply to the usual mercantilistic measures against beggars. Dictionaries are tricky things, and the effects of Russian homonyms can be devastating, as they are when, for example, an "assembly of the village commune" is translated as "peaceful assembly" because in Russian *mir* means both commune (or world) and peace. For apparently similar though more elusive reasons, a book called "Justification of Legal Limits on Interest Rates" appears under the title "Justification of Encouragement of Sobriety by Laws." In the translators' hands, "injury to honor" (a very broad juridical term in the Moscow codes) becomes "dishonesty"; "indentured peasants" — "mortgagees"; and "red tape" or "the law's delay" — "intriguers." "Peasants *and* cotters" is first rendered as "poor peasants," then "peasants and the poor," before at long last the approximate wording "landless peasants" is hit upon. On the other hand, it is exasperating to see that very often a term is correctly rendered for a number of times, and then suddenly a silly rendition appears. Thus, for instance, the word *chern'* is first properly rendered as "rabble" and "mob," but in a context that required rendition as "common people" the term is translated as "monks," probably because of the association between *chernyi* (black) and the black clergy. Similar lexical fantasies must be responsible for turning "nations in chains" into "entombed people" or for letting a "reliable method" become a "hopeful sign," or a "reliable monetary system" an "active [?] monetary system."

In translations from the Russian, the correct spelling of non-Russian proper names that appear in the Cyrillic script constitutes a problem. At times in this translation they are simply retransliterated. As a result, Charles Dumoulin appears as Diumulen, Mably once and Morelly throughout are Italianized into Mabli and Morelli, and Oncken becomes Onken. Then again the retransliteration can be imaginatively wrong; thus Beardé de l'Abbaye is introduced once as l'Abbé de Bearde and then as Béarde de l'Abbé, whereas Jean Meslier (sometimes spelled Mellier) is unaccountably turned into Jean Mallet. Several Russian place names are garbled because of erroneous derivations from an adjective form in the original.

The volume contains a fairly large number of quotations from, and references to, Russian translations of non-Russian authors. The editor failed to check the quotations with, and to supply references to, the originals, thus producing incongruous results. To give only one example, a phrase from Adam Smith, "stock employed in agriculture," was clumsily translated by the Russians as "capital expended in agriculture." This then is fully nonsensically retranslated into English as "capital dissipated in agriculture." The editor was clearly obliged to inform the reader of the correct English original, all the more so as in this case the careless Russian text converts Adam Smith's reference to the "southern provinces of North America" and the "West-Indian Islands" into "South America" and "India." In this

468

volume, even quotations from Scripture are freely retranslated from Church Slavonic, thus appearing in an unwonted guise, while the "nine beatitudes" of the Sermon on the Mount are unblinkingly translated as "heavenly bliss."

The best thing that can be said about the translation is that on the whole it succeeds fairly well in conveying the drabness and flatness of the original style. But the translation goes too far. For the original text, unattractive as it is, is still graced by many quotations from old Russian or Church Slavonic sources, some of which have force and rhythmic and metaphoric beauty. In the original, moreover, such quotations are often preceded by a circumscription of their contents in modern Russian. When the archaic quotations are rendered in flat, modern English, their original character is lost, and they only accentuate the horrible, repetitive style of the original.

B. *After 1917*

AN ANALYSIS OF SOVIET AGRICULTURE *

Publication of Naum Jasny's monumental attempt to analyze plans and performance in the field of Soviet agriculture is an event of major importance. The volume of Western literature on the Soviet economy is vast, but this review would not be unduly lengthened were it to include a complete list of significant scholarly works in that literature. Serious books on the subject are scarce, and this is particularly true in the field of Soviet agriculture. However much one may disagree with individual portions of Jasny's study and whatever exception one may even wish to take to the main thesis of his work, the fact remains that it is a most comprehensive treatise on a most difficult and elusive subject. After Jasny has broken the path, discussion of the problems involved even by those who may not accept all his conclusions will inevitably be conducted on a much higher level and in a much more pertinent fashion. Jasny's emphasis is essentially quantitative, and therein lies perhaps the greatest significance of his contribution. Careful statistical analysis is both the most needed and the most neglected aspect of economic research on Soviet Russia.

As intimated in the foregoing paragraph, the study is likely to provoke dissent and disagreement. For Jasny's thesis is drastic: the collectivization experiment of the Soviet government has been a failure.[1] It has been a failure measured by the enormous discrepancy

---

* Review of Naum Jasny, *The Socialized Agriculture of the USSR: Plans and Performance* (Stanford: Stanford University Press, 1949).

1. It is true that in an early passage of the book Jasny says: "Much has been written on the great Soviet reorganization drive in general and the collectivization of peasant farming in particular. The appraisals range from enthusiastic acclaim to prophecies of complete failure, with extreme views greatly predominating. The present writer cannot deny having an appraisal of his own, but this study has not been prepared to expound this appraisal. Rather its purpose is to give the reader an opportunity to form his own opinion" (p. 5). But it is difficult to understand what this statement means in light of the contents of the book. For Jasny does not hide his opinions, and there is no reason why he should. Not only the general tone in which

between plan and fulfillment. The First Five-Year Plan of 1926–27 envisaged a gross agricultural output of 20.7 billion roubles (a still higher target was 22.6 billion) for 1932–33, while actual output in 1932 according to Jasny amounted to only 11.7 billion. The corresponding figures for the last year of the Second Five-Year Plan (1937) were 26.2 and 18.2 billion, and 1937 was a quite unusually favorable year. Moreover, output in 1938 and 1940 remained below 1937, even if adjustment is made for the unfavorable weather conditions in those two years (pp. 628, 775). The experiment has been a failure also in comparison with the precollectivization status. In 1938 and 1940, gross agricultural output was only some 11–13 percent higher than in 1927–28 (p. 682); and the picture is even more striking with regard to the evolution of net output (income) from agriculture: if normal weather conditions had prevailed in 1938, income from agriculture in that year would have exceeded that of 1927–28 by a little over 3 percent. The results have been still less favorable if viewed by "the real test of success of economic progress," which "is consumers' satisfaction" (p. 84). Food consumption of the rural population deteriorated between 1928 and 1938, and the same is true, Jasny holds, of the urban population. Finally, the productivity of labor in agriculture on an hourly basis has remained at the same average level as that of the individual peasant before collectivization (p. 53). The much advertised socialized agriculture that is said by the Soviets to be the most mechanized agriculture in the world is, according to Jasny's conclusions, no more productive than the hopelessly primitive agriculture of a backward peasantry. At the same time, the official claims, while indeed admitting underfulfillment of plans, are greatly in excess of the actual results. Thus, income from agriculture in 1937 was 15 percent below the plan according to official claims, but Jasny's figure for the income in that year is no less than 30 percent below the official claims.

A comprehensive critical examination of the methods by which Jasny reached his striking conclusions would exceed the scope of this

the study is written, but numerous explicit statements make the author's appraisal abundantly clear. To cite a few examples: Soviet agriculture is "incompatible with a permanently sound economy" (p. 33); it is "neither efficient nor stable" (p. 37); "new organizational forms would have to be found for agriculture" (p. 38); "the results of the collectivization have been deplorable" (p. 60).

review. But some remarks on the nature of the author's statistical conclusions may be in order.

The great difficulty that confronts any statistical investigation of the Russian economy is the nature of Soviet statistics. There is no doubt that they are presented in such a way as to create the impression of results more favorable than those actually attained. The devices used by the Soviet government for that purpose are manifold. One of the outstanding examples of such a highly misleading presentation is the way in which the series on output of grains was changed, beginning in 1933, from recording the actual crop brought into the barn (barn yield) to the estimated preharvest yield (biological yield), which makes no allowance for harvesting losses. Jasny devotes a good deal of space and effort in his book precisely to an attempt to estimate for the years after 1933 the magnitude of the discrepancy between biological and barn yields so as to obtain a consistent series of the actual grain crops. This is, at least in principle, a possible enterprise because, distorted as the Soviet statistics are, they are not as a rule based on sheer invention; the figures published have meaning and significance. Even though, surprisingly enough, Jasny himself has seemed to deny it elsewhere,[2] his whole study is based on the assumption that Soviet statistics are usable and may serve as a foundation for serious research. In fact, this study provides a good deal of proof for the soundness of that assumption. But the distortions are great and, what is more, a great deal of information is deliberately suppressed. As a result, many gaps in information must be filled out by what often amounts to rather arbitrary estimates. The margin for error of some estimates is perforce considerable.

This may be illustrated by reference to the instance just quoted. Jasny's procedure in trying to ascertain the true barn yield is an example of painstaking and ingenious research. He is not content with using one method of analysis. Along with an estimate of the barn crops on the basis of utilization of the harvest by food, seed, feed, and so on, he also estimates for the four years 1933–1936 the total barn crop by combining some calculations on utilization with data of a different order, such as deliveries of grain to the govern-

2. Naum Jasny, "Soviet Statistics," *Review of Economics and Statistics*, XXXII (1950), 92–99.

ment, the magnitude of distribution of grain to collective farmers, and an estimate of stolen grain. He thus estimates the total collective-farm crop, and then proceeds to estimate the noncollective-farm crops with the help of some Soviet data on the percentage share of collective-farm crops in total crops. Furthermore, he makes still another estimate on the basis of various statements of official Soviet analysts. And, finally, he compares the evolution of actual grain output as computed by himself, with the official data on output of other than grain crops for which barn-yield data were still used by the Soviets.

The material Jasny assembled for the purposes of this analysis is of the greatest possible importance, and anyone interested in these problems must feel indebted to the author. Furthermore, all these approaches yield results which, though they show discrepancies among themselves (in one case the discrepancy is as high as almost 10 percent), are still much closer to each other than to the official data on grain output (p. 544). But at the same time, the reader must not overlook the manifold uncertainties that remain attached to all these estimates. To give a few examples: By far the largest single item of grain utilization is food. How is this item estimated for, say, the period of 1933–34 to 1936–37? "The population averaged about 162 million in 1933/34 through 1936/37. The yearly per capita consumption in this period may be estimated at possibly 230 kilograms" (p. 751). That is all. Few would quarrel with the population figure, and no one should be willing to reject lightly any estimates made by a man of Jasny's authority. But the fact remains that Jasny does not supply any reasons for his estimate of per capita food consumption. Again, within the estimate based on writings of official Soviet analysts, Jasny uses absolute figures for certain portions of the total output (such as compulsory deliveries to the government or payments in kind to machine tractor stations), in conjunction with given data on the percentage share of each of these items in the total, in order to obtain the size of the total crop. If the absolute data and the percentages were correct, computing the total crop on the basis of compulsory deliveries should, of course, yield the same result as a computation on the basis of payments in kind. But the uncertainty inherent in these data is revealed by the fact that "for reasons unknown," as Jasny says (p. 740), each of these operations results in

473

a different figure for the total crop of the same year, the discrepancy between the extreme results again being about 10 percent. Accordingly, there are not only discrepancies in results as among different methods, but within one and the same method. The operation also involves an estimate of the share of the total harvest produced by collective farms. Jasny says (p. 745), "USSR crops for 1935 and 1936 are based on the assumption that the kolkhoz crops were 80 and 82 per cent respectively of the total barn crops," which is terse but not very illuminating.

In his third estimate of the grain crop, Jasny assumes that three million tons of the crop are stolen by the farms, except for additional theft of seed (pp. 741, 745). Again no reasons are given. The quantity estimated as stolen is a little less than 5 percent of the estimated total crop in 1935. This may be reasonable and then again it may not. The relation between the Soviet government and the peasantry is still one of continuous struggle, even though its acute phase has passed. The peasants perpetually try to resist the government's attempts to appropriate a large share of the grain harvest at nominal prices. In the Soviet press and also in various Soviet novels and plays, descriptions of methods of evading delivery obligations by hiding grain, bribing officials, and the like, are encountered galore. Jasny's description of conditions on collective farms fully corroborates this picture. In these circumstances, an estimate of 6 or 7.5 million tons for theft may be just as good and perhaps better than that of three million tons. Jasny's utilization estimates do not seem tight enough to exclude altogether the contingency of an additional utilization of some thirty to forty-five kilograms of grain per capita in the rural populations, as would be implied in such higher estimates of theft. Thus a much larger volume of theft, increasing the harvest in some years by an additional 5 to 7.5 percent, is not altogether implausible on the basis of Jasny's presentation.

What is to be concluded from the foregoing? Certainly not that Jasny's estimates are necessarily wrong. They need not be. But as one reads Jasny's study, the impression grows that the author is riding his thesis too hard. Jasny himself seems astonished at the size of discrepancies between the official biological yield and the barn yield as computed by him. They are considerably in excess of possible harvesting losses (p. 545). From this Jasny infers that the biological yields, too, are overestimated. Possibly so, but there seems to be enough leeway in Jasny's own estimates to keep open the possibility that it is the estimates of barn yield that are too low. It would have been the better part of wisdom and would have revealed a greater kindness to his readers had Jasny consistently called to their attention all the cases of weaknesses, uncertainties, and low probabilities in his estimates, rather than forcing that labor upon the readers. Possibly no better estimates than those by Jasny are feasible, but this is no reason to present them as better than they actually are. The opinion which at least one reader has formed upon the perusal of the book is that its results are less conclusive than would appear from its tone, in the sense that the margin for error may well be a good deal larger than the few percent the author is willing to allow.

Jasny's book is essentially a quantitative analysis of changes in Soviet agriculture. It is not conceived as a historical analysis of the factors that caused the momentous institutional change and transformed an agriculture based on individual peasant households into the "socialized agriculture of the USSR." But the study necessarily provides a most valuable basis for historical treatment of the development; and, furthermore, there are a good many interesting statements that are highly pertinent to such a treatment. On the other hand, it is permissible to judge Jasny's appraisal in the light of a general view of Soviet economic evolution, and the remainder of this review will be devoted to a few considerations of this nature.

One interesting aspect in this connection is the role of Marxism as a factor determining Soviet decisions with regard to the socialization of agriculture. The great and, in fact, decisive importance of this factor is generally assumed. Jasny seems to support this view by saying, "the establishment of large-scale state farms and the collectivization of peasant farming were undoubtedly the outgrowth of the Marxian idea that large-scale farming is much superior to small-scale farming, just as large-scale industry is superior to small-scale industry" (p. 6). No one will want to deny that Marxian ideas of this sort played some role in forming policies. Nevertheless, those who feel, as I do, that the significance of Marxian ideology in Soviet Russia has been immeasurably exaggerated and that many Soviet policies are to be explained primarily by pragmatic rather than ideological factors will find in Jasny's study a good deal of corroborating evidence. In describing the compulsion that was necessary in order to force some 20 million individual producers into the collective farms, Jasny rightly remarks that Lenin and, for a number of years, Stalin were opposed to the use of force against the mass of peasants (p. 30). This is useful to remember at a time [3] when in Soviet Russia Stalin's policy is usually described as a continuous straight line, as one based on an unwavering purpose and perfect knowledge and foreknowledge. The truth is that Stalin was for a long time opposed to a compulsory collectivization, and since it never required any preternatural powers of prediction to understand that none but compulsory collectivization was possible, this perforce meant opposition to collectivization. What changed Stalin's mind? Surely not sudden remembrance of tenets of orthodox Marxism with regard to advantages of large-scale enterprises in agriculture. Jasny says: "It is the writer's profound conviction that the socialization drive was, politically and economically, an inevitable consequence of the triumph of the Bolshevik party on November 7, 1917, rather than a *deus ex machina* that emerged in 1928 as a result of the victory of one wing of the Communists over another" (p. 18). "There was no choice for the Party" (p. 30). He explains later what he has in mind: "When it finally became certain that the price disproportions between farm and non-farm products could not be eliminated, an attempt was made to find a form of farm organization which would function effectively in spite of unfavorable price relationships." And he adds: "Compulsory collectivization was expected to accomplish this miracle, but it failed" (p. 207).

It might be argued that Jasny's presentation is unduly narrow. He does not pay due attention to the critical significance of the fact that, by the beginning of the second half of the twenties, prewar industrial capacity was approaching full utilization and further growth of industry required disproportionately larger investment outlays. Nor does he go into a general analysis of the monetary situation of the time and the existing relationships between spendable incomes of the population and the volume of available consumers' goods. The

3. The reference is to the year 1951.

terms of trade between agriculture and industry that had turned against the former were but one aspect of a very complex situation. But it is true that the economic situation was extremely unstable; that the orthodox equilibrating devices of price increases or tax increases or both were politically impractical; and that, as Jasny shows, the unfavorable price relations caused peasants to reduce the marketing of their produce in the cities. It is presumably true that in the situation then existing any government would have had to carry out readjustments requiring sacrifices. But a non-Bolshevik government would in all likelihood have found a good deal of cooperation on the part of the peasants, and it would have been able to reduce the amount of sacrifices needed by recourse to commercial and financial markets abroad. These opportunities were not open to the Soviet government. It is in this sense that Jasny is right in saying that compulsory collectivization stemmed from the Bolshevik seizure of power in November 1917. To break the deadlock, either the government had to go or the backbone of the peasantry had to be broken. The pressures of that situation carried in themselves a threat to the sustenance of the urban population and to the very maintenance of the Soviet government in power. They caused Stalin to overcome his apprehensions and to embark — very much *malgré lui*, like the hero in Molière's comedy — on the perilous course of a second revolution, which he not inaptly described as a "revolution from above." [4] Once the collectivization was completed and the government's hands untied, it proceeded to impose upon the population the enormous burden of high-speed industrialization. At any rate, compared with the very pressing exigencies of the given situation, Marxian predilections for large-scale farming, it would seem, do not deserve a great deal of emphasis as a codetermining factor.

With a good deal of shrewdness Jasny surmises that "from the very start a certain degree of hypocrisy was involved in all the enthusiasm for large-scale farming" (p. 31), and Jasny's description of the gradual relegation of state farms to a subordinate position is very pertinent in this respect. It seems correct to assume that huge state farms were much more in conformity with general Marxian

4. Stalin, "Otnositel'no marksisma v yazykoznanii" (On Marxism in Philology), *Bol'shevik*, XXVII (June 1950), 12.

preferences than the much smaller collective farms. But when the sovkhoz, as Jasny shows, proved to be a relatively high-cost enterprise and, in particular, when it became clear that members of the collective farms, unlike the employees of sovkhozy, could be made to bear the burden of fluctuations in output, the Soviet government had no hesitation to concentrate on a form of agricultural organization which, though less "Marxian," was more consonant with the aims of the Soviet government. All this should not be surprising, since developments of nonagricultural sectors of the economy show very much the same tendencies. The Soviet government, for instance, did not hesitate to embark, in 1939, on a campaign against "gigantomania" as soon as the shadows cast by approaching war rendered greater regional self-sufficiency advisable.[5]

Jasny's comprehension of the motives that prompted the Soviet government to embark upon the collectivization drive does not agree too well with the dramatic thesis of the book. The study as a whole is bound to leave the reader with the impression that the socialization of Soviet agriculture deserves a place of distinction in any history of human stupidity. The question here is not whether Jasny's estimates of output and income of Soviet agriculture are one hundred percent correct or not. If, despite what was said in the earlier portions of this review, they are accepted without reservations, the fact of a considerable maldistribution of emphasis remains.

Jasny says himself: "The fundamental objective of the collectivization drive was to obtain a large part of the kolkhoz output, regardless of the size of the crop or the needs of the kolkhoz members. Those in power were not too hopeful that the kolkhoz would be the means of creating an abundance of farm products" (p. 279). This undoubtedly is a decisive aspect of the whole development. To secure steady supplies of agricultural products to the growing city popula-

---

5. In the early 1950s, the Soviet government launched an ambitious campaign of kolkhoz consolidations, designed to enlarge substantially the size of the individual collective farm. This was a move in the opposite direction. It would be difficult to argue, however, that Marxian ideas played an important role in initiating the new development. It seems that essentially the need for accelerated transfer of manpower into industry, in conjunction with a desire to tighten even further the government's control over and its supervision of collective farms, must be held accountable for the new policy. As usual, the motivations were pragmatic rather than ideological.

tion, without the necessity of providing a sufficient *quid pro quo* in terms of industrial consumers' goods, was indeed an essential condition of rapid industrialization. In this sense the collectivization drive was, from the point of view of the Soviet government, eminently successful. "By 1937 the perfection of procurement techniques had made the receipts practically independent of the size of the grain crop" (p. 82). But if this was the case, compulsory collectivization achieved precisely what it was expected to achieve, and some of Jasny's statements in the book (such as the one from p. 207 quoted earlier, "Collectivization was expected to achieve this miracle, but it failed") are rather inconsistent with his own appraisals of the results. When, in addition, it is considered that, between 1926–27 and 1939, population engaged in agriculture was not inconsiderably reduced (p. 713), it is difficult to escape the feeling that nothing can be gained in presenting the collectivization drive as an unmitigated failure. To be sure, in view of the propaganda claims of the Soviet government, there is good justification for Jasny's efforts to demonstrate how enormously exaggerated are the claims concerning improvements in the standard of living. But beyond that, an appraisal of the policy in these terms becomes pointless once it is understood that raising the standards of welfare of the population was not the actual objective of the drive for collectivization. If it had been, the compulsory collectivization and what Jasny calls the "man-made famine" that resulted from it never would have taken place.

Jasny's failure to place sufficient emphasis on the role of agriculture within the over-all economic policies of the Soviet government sometimes leads him to unwarranted conclusions. Thus in discussing the rationality of mechanization in Soviet agriculture, he draws the distinction between saving *of* labor (numbers of released workers) and saving *on* labor (amounts of wages saved). He states rightly that level of wages is "the principal and in general decisive factor in the competition between tractor and animal power" (p. 473). But when he goes on to conclude that introduction of tractors into Soviet agriculture was not rational, because "it is hardly possible to find a country in the world where farm labor works for so little remuneration as that of the regular kolkhozniki," he seems to forget something of what he is perfectly well aware elsewhere in the study. The low wage (income) of the kolkhozniki is not the result of the operation of a free labor market or a free market for agricultural products. It is a political wage, artificially held down by the low prices paid to collective farms for compulsory deliveries of their produce. *To the extent that this is true*, it is not that tractors are introduced *despite* low rural wages. The point rather is that wages are as low as they are *because* of large output of nonconsumption goods, including also output of tractors and other farm machinery. It is, of course, most likely that the mechanization of Soviet agriculture has proceeded too rapidly, but this could not be argued on the basis of the artificially low wage of the kolkhozniki alone without taking into account changes in the composition of industrial output and the productive contribution of released laborers outside the field of agriculture. And at the same time it should be noted that even mechanization that appeared excessive on an economic calculus may have been altogether rational from the point of view of the purposes of the government. For mechanization afforded, through the device of machine tractor stations, opportunities for additional control of the collective farms and and an additional leverage for appropriation of agricultural produce by the government.

Similarly, Jasny's failure to view agricultural developments against the background of the aggregate economic development limits somewhat the effectiveness of his attempt to make the reader grasp the present agrarian conditions in Russia by a historical comparison. Jasny states that the analogy of collectivized agriculture to serfdom had become "increasingly justified" (p. 57). What he has in mind is primarily the personal position of the collective farmers. The precise extent to which the analogy holds may be open to doubt, but the elements of resemblance are sufficiently strong to permit its use. Jasny's general emphasis, however, and his tendency to disregard the role of collectivization within the economy as a whole make him overlook an important aspect of historical similarity between the two systems. The connection in several early epochs between serfdom and the pace of economic development in Russia was as undeniable as is the connection now between placing the peasants in the strait jacket of collectivization and rapid industrialization. In many respects, the development of the Soviet economy in the thirties may be conceived of as a recurrence of the historical pattern of Russia's economic development. It is this functional resemblance that Jasny might have stressed. The tragedy of the present situation in Russia lies precisely in the current use of techniques of economic development that ought to have remained peculiar to a long bygone age.

Unless readers keep the limitations of Jasny's presentation in mind, they are likely to receive a mistaken impression of the degree of purposefulness and rationality inherent in Soviet agricultural policies. In following Jasny's computations readers would do well to note the spots where missing links in Soviet information are arbitrarily interposed. Unless they do, they will not be able to form independent opinions of the soundness of the individual estimates. The nature of these opinions may vary, but no reader of Jasny's book can forbear paying admiration to the enormous industry and knowledge that went into the making of the book. And no reader retracing the steps of Jasny's analyses can avoid the feeling of high intellectual satisfaction at the ingenuity and the acumen with which Jasny has molded into meaningful forms the refractory material of Soviet statistics.

THE SOVIET BUDGET *

The most worthwhile portions of this book deal with the trials and errors that punctuated the gradual evolution of the Soviet budgetary system. It is useful indeed to be shown by this well-informed historical account that the development of that system proceeded in response to unforeseen and probably unforeseeable exigencies of given situations, rather than in the execution of a grandly conceived master plan. No general ideology and no specialized theory were available to guide the uncertain steps of the innovators. It is all the more impressive that in the second half of the 1930s there emerged something like a consistent, or at least coherent, complex of policies and arrangements suited to the Soviet dictatorship's basic aim of very rapid and comprehensive industrialization. At the same time,

* Review of R. W. Davies, *The Development of the Soviet Budgetary System* (Cambridge, Eng.: Cambridge University Press, 1958).

the author succeeds well in pointing out the manifold weaknesses of the system. He stresses in particular the inability of the special banks through which the investment funds were channeled to enforce high standards of efficiency in the utilization of those funds by the enterprises engaged in construction, as well as the lack of incentives for greater efficiency within those enterprises (pp. 257–262). Even more important is his general conclusion that by the end of the prewar period in 1941, "the Soviet government had not succeeded in finding a satisfactory method of supervising the day-to-day work of enterprises through either the State Bank or the financial departments — and it is perhaps possible that there is no way of arranging satisfactorily this kind of financial supervision from outside the industry" (p. 276). Most students of the Soviet economy will probably agree that lack of specific knowledge as to what goes on inside the economic enterprises lays the most restraining trammels upon exercise of dictatorial power in economic matters and, by the same token, constitutes the most crucial problem of Soviet planning.

The merits of R. W. Davies' book are very real. If some readers should find it difficult to appreciate them fully, the reason must lie in a certain vagueness of the more analytical parts of the study and in a curious difference in tone and tenor that is noticeable between the first and the second half of the book. In the earlier portions, there is a tendency to be unduly categoric. It is surprising to see the attributes of "inevitable" or "essential" or "necessary" somewhat lightheartedly attached to measures of economic policy. Not unsimilar in effect is the assertion that in a "directly planned economy," as practiced in Soviet Russia, "the method of financing investment is . . . a technical question" (p. 146); or the insistence that financing economic growth through voluntary savings is incompatible with such an economy (p. 145). It is true, of course, that the magnitude of the burden imposed on the population is determined by the basic decision with regard to the volume of investment goods to be produced. But it is equally true that, in a society that was far from being egalitarian, the budgetary emphasis on indirect taxes had a definite social and economic meaning. In view of the propensity of Soviet literature to deny that the turnover taxes are "taxes on the population," a less perfunctory treatment might have been in order.

482

On the other hand, the rate of investment mentioned in one connection is studiously evaded in others. There is no reason in the world why the Soviet type of planning should be *in itself* at variance with finance by voluntary savings, except for the fact that the Soviet government wished to take away from, or not to make available to, the population a good deal more consumers' goods than the population was ready to part with voluntarily. To say, as does Davies (on p. 144), that if "labor and material resources . . . are available and if planners . . . consider the object desirable, there could be no point in making the achievement of the plan dependent on personal savings," unfortunately begs the question. The problem is precisely whether and to what extent resources for investment *should be made available* in excess of spontaneous savings.

The insufficient stress on the high rate of investment also appears to have prevented the author from clearly stating the reasons for which the Soviet government rejected direct taxes in favor of indirect taxes. While he spends much time on discussing the pros and cons of turnover taxes versus profit taxes, he is satisfied to remark (in a footnote on page 147 and then again on p. 342) that "direct taxation has a strong disincentive effect, owing to the money illusion." (The wording is curious — what Davies probably intended to say was that direct taxes were unsuitable because, unlike sales taxes, they did *not* allow deception through money illusion.) The real point is that sales taxes, in addition to eliminating the surfeit of purchasing power in the hands of the population, also made it possible to do something about reducing demand for individual consumers' commodities to the level of the *given* supply of those commodities. The great advantage of sales taxes for Soviet planners was that manipulation of tax rates could be substituted for adjustments in the production program for consumers' goods, so that undivided attention could be paid to output of producers' goods. The book would have gained if these relationships were explained more fully, and in particular if (after a mere hint on p. 145) the reader did not have to wait until the very end of the book (p. 337) before being told plainly that it was the high rate of investment that was mainly responsible for the inflation of the 1930s. (This, incidentally, would have been the proper context for speaking of "money illusion": while the high rate of investment

483

precluded increases in real wages, a semblance of such increases was produced by rising money wages.)

It is only obliquely that the author acknowledges that the high rate of investment stands behind the Soviet system of "direct planning" (that is, specific production and investment plans, quantitative allocation of resources, and ancillary role of prices — see pp. 96 and 327). There is little doubt that Davies tends to exaggerate the "directly allocative" aspects of Soviet planning. If prices, to use his language, were only "determined" and not also "determining," many important phenomena of the Soviet economy would defy understanding. Most notably, it would be incomprehensible why subsidies were ever used or why nonrepayable grants should be preferable to loans as a means of financing industrial growth. The author says this was so because servicing the loans would have raised prices of producers' goods (p. 147). If the role of Soviet prices of producers' goods had been solely passive, this could not have been a serious consideration.

As said before, in the second half of the book these analytical uncertainties give way to a realistic treatment of the Soviet economy. The concluding discussion of Soviet economic limitations and of the ways in which the working of the economy might be improved is quite excellent. Still, it is worth noting that even here perhaps too much emphasis rests on a side issue. The problem is not whether injection of "quasi-market pulls," which the author favors, would be compatible with "direct planning." The main point, rather, is that any permanent relaxation of the grip of the central power upon the economy must be premised on a permanent decline in the rate of investment. In particular, the author's suggestion to simplify the turnover tax by confining it to a few rates would depend on the Soviet government's willingness to begin adjusting output of consumers' goods in sensitive response to fluctuations and shifts in consumers' demand. It is improbable that such a departure from the traditional lopsided preoccupation with investment goods can be carried out without considerable reallocation of national income in favor of consumption. Since in fact the rate of investment appears to have been rising rather than falling, and both Soviet politicians and Soviet economists claim and proclaim that output of producers' goods must grow faster than output of consumers' goods, either in obedience to an "economic law" or at least as a necessary condition of growth, it is not clear at all that economic reforms along the lines suggested by the author are likely to acquire lasting importance. This is not to say, however, that those suggestions can be brushed aside as unimportant. The decentralization measures put into effect in recent years may prove only temporary, and their reversal, perhaps under new inflationary threats, may not be unlikely.[1] Still, a reviewer of Davies' valuable study must point out that, such as they are, those measures have been foreseen, or at least adumbrated, in the concluding chapter of the present book.

WAS STALIN REALLY NECESSARY? *

This collection of Alec Nove's essays is above all an excellent source of information on the vicissitudes of Soviet economic policies since the death of Stalin. The author's interests range over a very wide area. His themes include rates of aggregate growth and the curiosities of statistical measurements (which, he argues, not only distort the results but also affect the nature of economic decisions), labor incentives in agriculture, level and structure of wages, social legislation, the organization and behavior of enterprises, and the dilemmas of Soviet planning. In all these fields — and many others — Professor Nove seems to have read everything worth reading, and he writes about the relevant facts and problems with a freshness and liveliness of style and thought that are most attractive.

The main problem around which most of the essays are woven relates to the economic rationality of the Soviet system. Much of Nove's discussion focuses on the current debates in Russia concerning the role of profits as a "success indicator," the appropriate structure and function of prices, the degree of autonomy to be accorded managers of Soviet enterprises within the framework of central planning, and the inadequacies of the concept of gross value of output both as a yardstick of performance and as a source of irrational decision

1. The reference is to the second half of the 1950's.

* Review of Alec Nove, *Was Stalin Really Necessary? Some Problems of Soviet Political Economy* (London: George Allen and Unwin, 1964).

making. From his vast reading of Soviet materials, the author extracts examples demonstrating manifold inefficiencies. In general, he believes that Soviet prices are meaningless and that as a result resources are used uneconomically; at the same time, employment of inadequate measurements invites additional misallocations and waste that produce undesirable distortions of the product mix, including the output of unduly short-lived commodities, perennial shortages of spare parts, and other disabilities.

There is no doubt that there is much truth in this indictment, and it is a matter of common knowledge that there exists in Russia a body of critical opinion which urges more or less far-reaching reforms of the system. What is less clear is the aggregate weight of the existing deficiencies and the real motivations behind the proposals for reform. The problem has existed for decades. The author himself admits that, to some extent at least, the many complaints of inefficiency which fill the pages of Soviet newspapers and economic journals are the result of a greater freedom to discuss and criticize. Still, however numerous the individual illustrations, they are in their very nature impressionistic. It is not at all certain that the drag of inefficiencies upon the Soviet economy today — both on macro and micro levels — has increased considerably. In fact, it is probably true that, taking it for all in all, the Soviet economy today works more smoothly and effectively than it did in the thirties. Nove argues that the economic establishment in Russia has grown so large and the composition of output has become so variegated that the central authorities find it much more difficult to control, and check upon, the workings of the individual enterprises than used to be the case in the thirties, when a small range of basic industrial materials constituted a rather large segment of total industrial output, and when the newly created machinery industry did not comprise a huge nomenclature of items and types.

Nor is it certain that the Soviet price system now is in a more confused state than in earlier periods. Soviet prices are, of course, no better than they should be, but it seems to go much too far to describe them as entirely meaningless. Over long periods they show a clear connection with cost, as is evident by the pragmatic test of applying changing price weights to the index numbers of Soviet output, yielding differentials in the rates of growth similar to those one would expect on the basis of Western industrial history. This is not much, but it is something. The author rather obscures the significance of such tests by claiming that the "right" answers come from the Russians' adherence to what he calls "the law of comparative disadvantage." But this, I take it, is said with tongue in cheek, because sizable discrepancies between Laspeyres' and Paasche's indices must derive from considerable reductions in cost of output, followed by corresponding price reductions, and every industrialization, involving as it did changes in scarcity relations, continually changed the array of comparative advantages. In this connection, however, the author must be especially commended for his fine attempt to measure in sterling the purchasing power of the consumer's rouble (essay 14), even though he is somewhat unclear, at least verbally, when it comes to a comparison between Soviet and English real wages. In that comparison he does not use, as he believes, Russian weights, but English weights. The use of the former, no doubt, would make the earnings of Russian labor appear even smaller in relation to those of English workers, and it would be most desirable if the author were to expand his study by converting English real wages into roubles.

To return to the main point, Nove defines economic rationality first as the achievement of maximum results at minimum real cost (p. 51). This, of course, is a logically untenable definition, even though it is difficult to upbraid the author for using it because, if I am not mistaken, it was originally perpetrated by no lesser man than Leibniz and also because, many pages later toward the end of the volume, Nove supplies a reasonable definition by speaking of "attainment of given objectives at least cost." In fact, it may be argued that something approaching a faulty concept of rationality actually exists in Soviet economic life: output is being pushed up, while cost is being pushed down. But this is not good enough, since the deficiencies of the price system must render uncertain, if not defeat, attempts to find determinate solutions by discovering the trade-off points between output and cost. This indeed is a serious disability, and there are others. But their proper significance cannot be judged in economic terms alone, and must be seen within the total context of the Soviet system.

To a large extent, the economic irrationalities that exist in the Soviet economy are a consequence of, and inextricably connected with, the mechanics of dictatorial rule. A high degree of autonomy granted to individual enterprises may be expected to remedy many of the present inefficiencies, but it would also deprive the dictatorship of one of its most important raisons d'être. The question thus is a highly political one, and it is not unlikely that both the complaints of inefficiency and the reforming proposals are motivated much more by political than by economic considerations. They are an integral part of the struggle for freedom that is being waged in Russia, in many forms and many areas. For even relatively moderate and seemingly technical proposals designed to place greater emphasis on profit, or to put reasonable prices on capital dispositions, would inject the rule of law into the relations between enterprises and central authorities and, by the same token, loosen the latter's grip on the former.

It is not surprising, therefore, to find the Soviet government reluctant to pay a high political price for the removal of inefficiencies by reforms at the enterprise level. Nove remarks at one point (p. 74) that Khrushchev's "own predisposition towards party-enforced priorities and administrative solutions leads him to lean towards the centralizers." But he does not fully explain the formidable stake the dictatorship has in maintaining a strongly centralized economy. Very similarly, in dealing with the abortive attempt at decentralization, launched in 1958, Nove discusses its failure and reversal in terms of economic expediency rather than political pressures. This is all the more astonishing since, in the first essay in the book, the author is quite willing to accept as an explanation for Stalin's basic decisions in economic policy the dictatorship's need to justify its existence (p. 23). That essay contains a penetrating analysis of Stalinism, and it is unfortunate that Nove chose to give the essay, as well as the whole volume, a highly misleading title that enmeshes him in sham concepts of historical necessity and mysterious distinction between objective and subjective necessities. What he actually asks, and deals with in a very interesting way, is not whether "Stalin was really necessary," but whether Stalin's policy was essential for the continuation of the dictatorship. In the absence of compulsory collectivization and super-industrialization, the Soviet dictatorship was likely to disintegrate.

And it is really a related problem that implicitly dominates the rest of the essays in this stimulating book. For the economic debates in Russia and the fluctuations in economic policies which Nove presents and analyzes so well are primarily an important manifestation of the weakening of the dictatorship that has occurred during the last decade. At any rate, the pressures that exist and the decisions that will be made in the economic field can tell us a great deal more about the direction of the Soviet dictatorship — be it toward further disintegration or renewed consolidation — than exercises in Kremlinological scrutiny of Soviet leaders, which Nove views with well-justified skepticism.

STALINISM *

This book by a well-known economist and economic historian at Handelshögskolan in Stockholm is essentially devoted to Soviet ideology. Considering the brevity of the study, the presentation is amazingly comprehensive without becoming at all superficial. The author has a sure flair for the significant, and he has succeeded in dealing with most of the fundamental aspects of his subject: dialectical materialism, the materialistic conception of history, and attitudes toward economic development, church and morality, art, literature, scholarship, nationalism, foreign policy, and war. With very few exceptions, the material has been gleaned from primary sources. The book is interspersed with flashes of real insight, as when the author uses the phrase "the hated model" (p. 65) in order to characterize the Soviet attitude toward the United States.

The book, however, offers even more than a description and interpretation of the essentials of Soviet ideology. It also contains a main thesis, namely, that Marxian ideology has had an important determining effect upon the Soviet development. Although this thesis is presented in a modest and unobtrusive way, the contents of the book may be viewed as a skillful and balanced defense of that thesis.

* Review of Arthur Montgomery, *Stalinismen* (Stockholm: P. A. Norstedt och Söner Förlag, 1953).

Against those who, like this reviewer, are skeptical as to the operational significance of Marxism in Soviet Russia, Professor Montgomery points to the fact that many things that may seem to contradict his thesis tend to dissolve themselves into short-run tactical deviations, and that such changes in Soviet ideology as have taken place must be ascribed to the process of adaptation to changing conditions without abandonment of the basic Marxian tenets. The author recalls in this connection that Stalin, as far back as 1917, opposed "dogmatic Marxism" in favor of "creative Marxism." On the other hand, the author explicitly stresses the importance of other than ideological factors, such as the historical traditions of Russian policies.

Montgomery is very persuasive. Still, I am not completely convinced. What appears blurred throughout the book is the fundamental distinction between Marxian ideology as a determinant of governmental decisions and ideology as a system of propaganda. That ideology in the latter respect is of considerable importance is, of course, undeniable, although even here one must consider that the Russians have injected many an element into their ideological structure which is quite alien to the spirit of Marxism: the role of great men in history, nationalism, the preservation of the state, inequalities of income, and so forth. One is almost tempted to say that what has been preserved is a thin shell of Marxian terms and very general concepts, while the contents have been most radically changed.

But whatever may be true with regard to propaganda, the role of Marxian ideology as a determinant of Soviet actions seems to have been reduced almost to the vanishing point. Questions of historical imputation are admittedly difficult. Still, the pattern of Soviet behavior over a long period appears to be much more readily and consistently explicable in terms of the mechanics of dictatorship, which have a dynamism of their own. The dictatorial government is unstable in the sense that it must at all times try to maintain and to increase its power. This does not mean that there is no "ideology" behind such policies. But it is the specific ideology of power rather than that of Marxism.

It is instructive to go over Montgomery's study with the foregoing distinction in mind. It emerges then that most of his discussion refers to Soviet attempts to channel the thinking of the population along lines that are desirable from the government's point of view and, at the same time, to evoke a sham impression of ideological continuity. Moreover, there is hardly any reference in the book to concrete examples of Marxian ideology as a determinant of policy decisions.

The foregoing remarks are not meant, of course, to detract from the value of Montgomery's informative and suggestive study. Its translation into English would seem very desirable indeed.

BAD ECONOMICS AND SHREWD POLITICS *

The title of this book (whose author is a corresponding member of the Soviet Academy of Sciences) describes its contents somewhat lengthily but correctly. According to Pashkov, there is an economic law in obedience to which, in a growing economy, output of producers' good necessarily grows at a faster rate than does output of consumers' goods. The law is said to have been discovered by Marx and to have received its final formulation at the hands of Lenin. It is slightly disconcerting that, in the numerical-growth models which Marx produced in Volume Two of *Das Kapital*, the outputs of producers' goods and consumers' goods were assumed to develop at the same rate. Pashkov explains, however, that in those examples Marx was abstracting from technological progress. When this assumption is relaxed and technological progress introduced, "variable" capital, the author says, is steadily replaced by "constant" capital, which necessarily implies that output of producers' good outstrips that of consumers' goods.

Historically, the author explains, the validity of the law dates from the introduction of machinery into the process of production. Pashkov criticizes Stalin, who is said to have erred in believing that the law governed even the premachinery stage of economic growth (p. 19). Yet once that stage is overcome, the law becomes both

---

* Review of A. I. Pashkov, *Ekonomicheskii zakon preimushchestvennogo rosta proizvodstva sredstv proizvodstva* (Economic Law Concerning the Faster Growth of Output of Producers' Goods; Moscow: Gosplanizdat, 1958).

ubiquitous and eternal. It characterized capitalist development in the past and continues to do so because "in the epoch of imperialism and the general crisis of capitalism, technology in capitalist countries continues to develop despite the tendency toward putrefaction" (p. 49). (One must not infer from the use of a term such as putrefaction — *zagnivaniye* — any special predilection of Soviet economists for strong language; such terms are coined at the very top of the Soviet hierarchy and are then frozen into a general usage which seems both obligatory and colorless.) As far as Soviet Russia is concerned, the law has been in force during "the period of transformation from capitalism to socialism," a period extending from 1917 to 1936. It has continued to prevail since 1936, that is, since the "establishment of a socialist economy in Russia" (another verbal icicle), and it will remain valid even in the communist society of the future, as the author informs us with a prescience that is quite unmarred by doubt or reservation (p. 85). On the other hand, if the law were not valid and if outputs of producers' goods and consumers' goods were to develop at the same rate, constant productivity of labor and "complete absence of any technological progress" would be the inevitable result (p. 140).

All this does not make too much sense. Most of the time, it seems, the author has only a vague notion of what he is talking about. The statement just quoted does not, for instance, prevent him from stressing elsewhere in the book (p. 59) that much technological progress can be achieved through replacement of worn-out equipment, that is to say, in principle at a zero rate of growth of producer-goods output. The inference — *a minori ad maius* — that technological progress must be possible at *any* positive rate of output of producers' goods — whatever its relation to output of consumers' goods — eludes him entirely. There is, incidentally, no sign of comprehension on the part of the author that the "law" he expounds with so much vigor implies a steadily *growing* rate of investment, leading eventually to a situation in which — *ceteris paribus* — investment would come to constitute the bulk of national income and the rate of growth of output would tend to approach the output-capital ratio asymptotically.

In discussing the effects of changes in the ratio of constant to variable capital, Pashkov does not allow himself to be perturbed in the least by problems such as the degree of unemployment, consumption by profit receivers, or the index-number problem. Accordingly, it never occurs to him that a labor-saving innovation in a relatively labor-intensive branch of the economy may well result in shifting factors of production to that branch and away from other more capital-intensive branches, making the economy as a whole *less* rather than more capital-intensive. That capital-output ratios may fall not only because of faster growth of branches in which such ratios are low, but also because labor-saving innovations may be more than offset by capital-saving innovations — and that accordingly even a declining rate of investment may in favorable circumstances be associated with a high rate of technological progress and growth of output — is something Pashkov would like to ignore but cannot. For both Polish and East German economists seem to have made the point with much vigor and resonance.

In addition, there has been some criticism of the "law" from indigenous sources, but these were handled more effectively. Pashkov devotes some time to criticizing articles of Soviet economists that have been submitted to *Voprosy ekonomiki*, a leading Soviet economic periodical, or to the Institute of the Academy of Sciences, but *not* published by them. This remarkable trouble-saving innovation in the area of academic polemics is likely to blur and distort the dissenters' views. Still, it seems clear that the suppressed Soviet economists tried to argue that growth and technological progress were quite possible at a constant rate of investment, and also felt that constant rates of investment and consumption were much more consonant with the basic principles of socialism.

Abuse apart, Pashkov has little to reply to those strictures. He has spent some time trying to verify his law. In the case of Russia, Soviet policy would have provided full support for his contentions, even if unsupported by faulty index numbers. For the rest, his statistical compilations, which are confined to manufacturing, are astonishingly primitive and reveal ignorance even of those historical materials he could use most effectively (Walther Hoffmann's well-known study of stages and types of industrialization being an obvious example). Nevertheless, Pashkov is quite willing to consider his statistical ragout as "incontrovertible" evidence in support of his law (p. 46); and yet when faced by dissenting views and, in particular, by empirical data for the more recent economic history of Western countries which are not consistent with his thesis, he is eager to escape at once into generalities and to accuse the critics of confusing a simplified abstract model with a description of complex reality (pp. 180–181). The truth is that he never makes up his mind as to whether his law denotes historical "inevitability," an empirical regularity, or simply a condition of rapid growth.

Pashkov's erudition is less than overwhelming.[1] He does an exceedingly poor job in defending his thesis. But this does not mean that his book should be brushed aside as unimportant. The contrary is true: what he defends and for what he is trying to find some theoretical basis and vindication is nothing less than the official line of Soviet economic policy, in fact, its guiding principle. In his *Theses* (Control Figures for the Development of the Soviet Economy, 1959–1965), Khrushchev referred to "Lenin's doctrine" concerning "the faster growth of heavy industry" and to the need for setting the plan targets for the current seven-year plan accordingly.[2]

Since the inception of the five-year plans, Soviet economic policy has been essentially directed to investment for investment's sake. It is largely by *increasing* the rate of investment that the Soviets have been able, in recent years, to avoid considerable declines in the rate of industrial growth. There is very little doubt that, in any foreseeable future, there is no *economic* reason to prevent the Soviets from continuing that policy, that is, from acting as though there were in fact an economic law of the sort suggested by Pashkov. And there may be very weighty political reasons to make it appear advisable to the Soviet government to continue such a policy more or less indefinitely.

1. He even presents an apologia for the Soviet statistical use of the concept of "gross value of output," which is based on aggregations of values of product of individual factories, involves numerous double-countings throughout the process of production, and varies with changes in the structure of industry and the concept of "factory." The reason given in defense of such a gross concept ("gross" in every sense of the word) is that value-added data do not include the "most important part of the reproduction process," that is, "producers' goods designed to produce producers' goods" (p. 81).

2. *Sovetskaya rossiya*, November 14, 1958. The reader is referred to my Introduction, note 2, for the recent change in Soviet policy.

Thus, the present book is an excellent example of the traditional Soviet policy of using Marxian theory and ideology in order to justify policies which are pursued for eminently practical reasons that have little to do with Marxian theories and beliefs. But Pashkov's book reveals more than that. For it is at the same time a very good example of what happens in this process to Marxian theory and ideology. One of the basic elements of Marxian doctrine used to be the emphasis upon the historical nature of economic laws. The Marxists criticized the Austrian school, for instance, for its concept of general economic laws, those common to all stages of economic development and to all economic systems. In particular, Marxian scholars at all times stressed the specificity of laws of capitalist development. It is indeed most instructive to see how something that is presented as a fundamental law of economic growth is now declared to be common to both capitalism and socialism. Pashkov himself seems at times astonished at his own views and keeps looking for some *differentiae specificae* without being able to find anything more convincing than the law of increasing misery, which, he says, is conjoined with the operation of his law of growth under capitalism (pp. 21, 56, 64). To repeat, the function of ideologies changes with the times. But the content of ideologies changes with their function.

IDEAS AND FOREIGN POLICIES *

This is an ambitious effort in the history of ideas. The first half is devoted to a study of the "Russian idea" or the Russian Nationalgeist; the other half deals with kindred aspects of oriental ideologies. The author assumes (p. 2) that there *is* such a thing as *the* national spirit of Russia, although he does not explain how it can be defined, that is, distinguished from various "non-Russian spirits," both within and without Russia. He rejects the "mechanistic sociological" approaches that he says are popular in Anglo-Saxon countries, and declares himself "in the main" an adherent of the "idealistic philosophy of history" (p. 5). He asserts, however, that the "ideological

* Review of Emanuel Sarkisyanz, *Russland und der Messianismus des Orients: Sendungsbewusstsein und politischer Chiliasmus des Ostens* (Tübingen: J. B. C. Mohr, 1955).

phenomena" that are the object of his study should not be conceived as "primary causes" of historical events but merely as a "working hypothesis" (p. 6), which presumably means as a model in which abstraction is made from other than ideological factors. All this is partly obscure and partly naive. Throughout, there is plentiful reference to the "Russian idea" which constitutes the "deeper reasons" or "deeper forces" in the flow of history. The difference between such reasons or forces and primary causes is elusive.

Nevertheless, the book is more interesting than can be expected from the somewhat confused methodological pronouncements. The main point in the "Russian" half of the study is that the ideology of Marxism per se is quite insufficient for the comprehension of Russian Bolshevism, which must be viewed against the background of "Russian ideology." A large part of the book is therefore devoted to a description of the Russian "world principle." The author stresses the holistic (*ganzheitlich*) character of Russian thinking, its "pan-ethicism," and the specific concept of *pravda* with its threefold inseparable meaning of truth, law, and justice. The "sub-historical" [*sic*] messianistic-chiliastic elements of Russian tradition, the concept of *sobornost'*, of collective guilt and collective redemption, the doctrine of the dissolution of the state in the lap of the church, the flight from the world — all these are described in detail. The author then shows how much of this traditional ideology of old Moscow, continuing in the "old-believing depths" of the Russian people, was taken over by Russian revolutionary ideologies of the nineteenth century, particularly populism — and thence entered Russian Bolshevism. At this point, however, the historical continuity of the "Russian idea" was both reaffirmed and broken. For the Russian revolution was both the acme and the negation of Russian chiliasm (p. 402): Bolshevism, having received its "motive forces" from Russian orthodoxy, turned away from that spiritual source and entered upon a process of *Verbürgerlichung*, of becoming filled with the bourgeois spirit (pp. 149, 152, 402, 405); in this process, Bolshevism reduced human personality to a "mechanical commodity" and thereby "actually joined the general evolution of the West" (p. 406).

Neither these dialectical contortions, nor the quaint terminology, nor the fact that the attitude toward the individual is precisely the area where Bolshevism (to put it gently) failed to "westernize" Russia should disguise the existence of certain fairly obvious similarities or recurrences in the course of Russian history. In the October Revolution, when the Bolsheviks were carried to power on a wave of peasant rebellion, they made generous use of popular slogans borrowed from the value system of the Russian peasantry. Moreover, certain quite unpleasant aspects of populist attitudes and policies appear to have been lastingly duplicated in the values and practices of the Soviet leaders. But the extent to which such duplications represent genuine "continuities" is a moot question to which, unfortunately, our author does not address himself. This should be the central problem of any serious intellectual history.

Unguarded inferences from similarities to continuities can be quite deceptive. Ideas can be rediscovered independently of past history or borrowed from other sources. They may be adopted merely for strategic or tactical reasons and not be an integral part of the value system of the alleged carriers of continuity. Lenin's doctrine of the marcescence of the state is a good example. Sarkisyanz points out that "one of the roots" of Lenin's radical position, as developed in *State and Revolution*, leads via Bakunin to the anarchic position of the "ecclesiastic slavophiles" (p. 68) and presumably thence into the primeval soil and soul of old Moscow. This may be true, but he offers no evidence, nor does he try to compare the relative significance of the individual "roots." Yet only through such comparisons can the idea of continuity be persuasively conveyed to the reader. It is all right to stress the eschatological character of "Russian" thought. But a look at any serious book on Western ideology would have convinced the author of the presence of strong eschatological elements in Western socialism. However much importance one may wish to attribute to a country's own spiritual past, it is advisable not to forget Esaias Tegnér's profound and candid words: "In the last analysis, all culture stands upon leased ground."

Moreover, the Weltanschauung of old Moscow was much less massive and consistent than the author would have us believe. And ideologies that developed during the St. Petersburg period may also provide a reasonable point of imputation for contemporary value

497

systems. In fact, several times (as on pp. 165–167) the author has to draw rather obvious analogies between Soviet Russia and Petrine Russia, oblivious that elsewhere in the book Petrine Russia is presented as negating the true Russian tradition. With intellectual history becoming increasingly popular, it is important to keep in mind that Nationalgeist is far from being a common-sense concept (however well it may lend itself to academic small talk) and that the essence of scholarship consists in clear awareness of conceptual and inferential limitations.

Since our author foregoes any attempt to buttress his thesis by showing its limitations, preferring emphatic assertion to the much more modest and laborious collection of evidence and application of balanced judgment, the book's primary appeal is directed to faith rather than to reason. Moreover, a reasoned approach to the problem of ideological continuity would almost inevitably have called for broader historical models. The problem, of course, is not whether ideas determine circumstances or vice versa, but that it is very difficult to discuss ideas in a sociological vacuum. Many additional insights might have been won if the author had treated his problems in relation to Russia's changing conditions of political and economic backwardness. In particular, it might have been useful to ascertain under what conditions and pressures certain ideas and values not only appear and disappear, but also reappear, on the historical stage.

While the treatment of Russian ideology raises serious objections, the second part of the study has immediate and significant bearing on current policies. In a general review of elements of prevailing ideologies in Islamic countries, India, Burma, and Indonesia, the author shows quite convincingly (though mostly with the help of translated or secondary sources) how many ingredients of "Russian" ideology can be discerned in these countries. The Russians certainly put those ingredients to account in their own propaganda in the early days of Soviet history, and have derived therefrom valuable lessons for their oriental policy. The attempts to connect Islamic or Buddhist ideas, or derivations therefrom, with the Soviet version of Marxism and to place the resulting explosive mixture at the service of Russian political purposes deserve a great deal more attention than they have received so far. It is irrelevant in this con-

498

nection that Soviet Marxism may have very little, if anything, to do with the original commodity. The point is that the ethos of a high rate of industrial growth may turn out to be quite compatible with "messianic yearnings." The author does not see this too clearly. Problems of economic growth seem too mundane for his cogitations; moreover, he insists that the Soviet policy in China is not just a continuation of Empire policy, but is motivated by the "Russian idea" although "in a distorted form." Nevertheless, the emphasis upon the Soviet Realpolitik aspect of those ideological affinities in backward countries constitutes the main value of this book.

APPENDIX III

Review: *Problems of Translation*

A MANUFACTURED MONUMENT?

I've set up to myself a monument not wrought by hands. — PUSHKIN

Vladimir Nabokov's monumental edition of *Eugene Onegin* is the strangest blend, fascinating and exasperating. It has everything: artistic intuition and dogmatic stubbornness; great ingenuity and amazing folly; acute observations and sterile pedantry; unnecessary modesty and inexcusable arrogance. It is a labor of love and a work of hate.

The sheer bulk of the edition is staggering. It has 1,850 pages spread over four elegantly published volumes.[1] The first volume contains prefatory materials and the text of Nabokov's English translation. The second and third are devoted to a detailed commentary, followed by two appendixes: one is a sixty-page study of Pushkin's African ancestor and is just a gloss, grown out of control, to a single line — "beneath the sky of my Africa" (chapter i, stanza 50); in the other appendix Nabokov presents his fine "Notes on Prosody" in which, among other things, he compares the role of the iambic meter in Russian and English poetry. The fourth volume contains an excellent index and a facsimile of the 1837 edition of *Eugene Onegin*, which was published a few weeks before the poet's death.

I. A "THEORY" OF TRANSLATION

Nabokov, whether in Russian or in English, is a most unspontaneous writer.[2] One is not surprised, therefore, to find that Nabo-

1. Aleksandr Pushkin, *Eugene Onegin, A Novel in Verse*, trans. Vladimir Nabokov (New York: Random House, 1964).
2. Very revealingly, a passage in his very memorable memoirs concludes: "I

kov's translation is a deliberate application of his general ideas on the subject of translations of poetry. He says that "attempts to render a poem in another language fall into three categories": (1) paraphrastic, (2) lexical, and (3) literal. The latter means "rendering as closely as the associative and syntactical capacities of another language allow, the exact contextual meaning of the original. Only this is a true translation" (I, vii–viii). In fact, as we are told later, only a literal translation is a translation at all, and hence the term is "somewhat tautological" (III, 185). Definitional ukases are, of course, less interesting than the profit-and-loss account that follows from the concept. Reintroducing the alleged redundancy, Nabokov says that a "translation . . . is literal when it implies adherence not only to the direct sense of a word or sentence but to its implied sense" and "when the precise nuance and intonation of the text are rendered" (III, 185). This, no doubt, is an attractive promise. Assuming for the moment that it can be fully redeemed, one must wonder about the cost of the method. It is high indeed. Nabokov's program involves a great deal more than the elimination of rhymes, and he is quite outspoken about it: "I have sacrificed to the completeness of meaning every formal element save the iambic rhythm . . . In fact to my ideal of literalism I sacrificed everything (elegance, euphony, clarity, good taste, modern usage, and even grammar) that the dainty mimic prizes higher than truth" (I, x).

Truth is a noble word, but it should neither disguise the naiveté of this self-advertisement nor obscure the problem. Surely, the aesthetic truth is a great deal more than correct conveyance of meaning; and what Nabokov sacrifices so lightheartedly and so disdainfully is not his own elegance and clarity and euphony, but Pushkin's. Throughout his work, Nabokov likes to speak of standards of scholarship. But the scholar's truth is a relative one, and it is bound by method and purpose. Obviously, the "truth of literalism" relates at best to a single aspect of that infinitely complex entity which is a work of poetic art. It is avowedly untrue of others. A translation is a little bit like a geographic map which can be true as to distances and areas,

wonder whether anyone will notice that this paragraph has been constructed upon Flaubert's intonations." Vladimir Nabokov, *Drugie berega* (Other Shores; New York, 1954), p. 103.

or distances and angles, or areas and angles, but cannot truly represent all the three elements. This does not make one projection "truer" than the others, although of course there are good and bad maps.

II. The Translation

Dropping the geographic comparison before it starts limping, let us turn to Nabokov's translation. It has admirable qualities. Above all, it reveals a superb understanding of the original text. In saying this, I do not mean merely absence of various misunderstandings of word, idiom, and circumstance which have marred earlier translations. Half a century has passed since I have first read *Eugene Onegin*; I have reread it many times, and most of its stanzas are indelibly impressed upon my memory. But I must confess that it is only now, thanks to Nabokov's help, that I have become aware of certain ambiguities in Pushkin's text and of the possibilities of varying interpretations. Nabokov went to great pains to discover the precise meaning of every term, however trifling, so that meats, pies, and fruit juices, berries and flowers, trees and animals, could all receive their proper gastronomical, botanical, and zoological equivalents. On the other hand, there is Nabokov's incomparable mastery of English vocabulary. The most hidden riches of the dictionary are always at his beck and call. The result is a translation that in some sense is indeed the most correct translation imaginable. But in what sense?

Appraising the translation first in Nabokov's own terms, the lexical fidelity of the rendition is above criticism. This is a considerable achievement — for some purposes. But Nabokov has promised a good deal more: faithful reproduction of "contextual meaning," of the precise "nuances and intonations" of the original. And here indubitable successes alternate with dismal failures. One of the secrets of the novel's irresistible charm lies in Pushkin's ability to mix with magic facility some Church Slavonic and Russian archaisms with Gallicisms and grass-root colloquialisms. Nabokov claims that "terms that are stilted or antiquated in Russian have been fondly rendered in stilted or antiquated English" (I, x). In reality, many archaic words wear an altogether modern garb.[3]

3. For instance, the Old Russian *ochi* (eyes) and the Church Slavonic *lanity* (cheeks), *persi* (breasts), *vezhdy* (eyelids), *usta* (lips), *tsevnitsa* (pipe), *dennitsa*

Apart from the impropriety of rash promises, this failure may be quite forgivable, since in many cases archaic equivalents simply do not exist in English. Much worse is the opposite case, when ordinary words and expressions, the daily bread of the language, appear in strange archaic or outlandish or bombastic forms. Why should, for instance, *obez'yana*, the normal Russian word for "monkey," be transformed into "sapajou"; or *pustynnoe ozero* — a phrase that any Russian today could use in almost casual speech — be rendered as "wasteful lake"? [4] Why should *tsvetki*, the much used endearing diminutive for "flowers," be translated as "flowerets," which no one ever uses? Why is Tatiana's terse colloquialism — *do togo li?* — rendered as "Is this relevant?" which more or less catches the meaning but is ludicrous when addressed to an illiterate peasant woman? Why is the nurse herself made to say "no dearth of" for "quite a few," which is entirely out of character and, by the same token, out of context, even though lexically as correct as can be.

There are several possible reasons for these mistranslations — for this is what they are by Nabokov's own yardsticks. One reason, presumably and somewhat paradoxically, lies in the very obsession with "literalism." This makes him render *golubka* — the common and somewhat folksy endearment (corresponding to "darling" or "honey") — as "doveling," which no English speaker can possibly utter. Nabokov, of course, knows well that the nurse in saying *neponyatna ya* uses a dialectal form of *neponyatliva ya*, meaning "I am dim," "I am slow-witted"; but *neponyatna ya* in standard Russian means "I cannot be understood," and Nabokov does not hesitate to translate the phrase as "I am not comprehensible," thus adding the insult of an inappropriate heavy Latinism to the injury of literalism that perverts the meaning.[5]

(dawn); the last word in Pushkin's context means "sunrise," and hence Nabokov's "ray of dawn" for *luch dennitsy* is curious, since dawns may have cracks but have no rays in the common sense of the word.

4. No one could possibly sense any archaism in Alexander Blok's: "*I vnov' pustynnym stalo more.*"

5. It is still another matter that very often when a Russian postposits the personal pronoun the accented syllable of the preceding verb or adjective is lengthened, and a plaintive or apologetic note is introduced into the phrase. This is certainly true of the present case. Thus *neponyatna ya* is not equivalent with *ya neponyatna*. But it is futile to deplore here the loss of a fine nuance.

At times, Nabokov's belief that the derivation of words offers the key to their meaning leads him astray. The Russian *kolpak* has long lost its Turkic connotation of "sheepskin hat" and has become a simple cap (fool's cap, nightcap); when the Russian word, completely assimilated as it is, is rendered by the outlandish English "calpack," which has retained the original meaning, semantics is cruelly sacrificed to etymology. A similar problem exists with regard to Gallicisms. Modern Russian — like other Slavic and Germanic languages — was formed under strong French influence. Russian poetry of the eighteenth and early nineteenth century bears all the marks of that highly beneficial influence. But two things must be remembered: (1) the penetration into Russian of *calques* (or *Lehnübersetzungen*) from the French started before Pushkin, and (2) most of such permanently retained Gallicisms were subject to a process of Russification in the course of which the values and connotations of words and phrases were subtly, and sometimes not so subtly, changed, and the feeling for their foreign origin was lost.[6] What on the face of it might look like a direct *calque* very often contains strong elements of creative adaptation. Such a change occurred almost inevitably and instantaneously, when the *calque* merely added a new usage to a well-established Russian word. Then, also, the foreign meaning was automatically Russified. Therefore, in retranslating a Russian Gallicism into French, the original French term will not necessarily yield the semantically correct translation.[7] Pushkin's *belyanka* comes indeed straight from André Chénier's "une blanche" (chap. ix, st. 39), but the Russian word carries with it the suggestion of a peasant beauty, which is both most proper and important in the context and is quite lost in Nabokov's so "absolutely accurate" (II, 464–65) rendition: "a white-skinned girl" (no reference to the Caucasian race is intended).

6. Pushkin's predecessor, Batyushkov, certainly used many words whose origin could be traced back to French. But it is interesting that in his very careful and critical marginalia in a volume of Batyushkov's poetry it is only once that Pushkin scribbled a disapproving "Gallicism!" on the margin. See "Zametki na polyakh vtoroy chasti 'Opytov v stikhakh i prose' K. N. Batyushkova" (Notes on the Margins of the Second Part of "Experiments in Verse and Prose" by K. N. Batyushkov), in A. S. Pushkin, *Polnoe sobranie sochinenii* (Collected Works; Moscow, 1949), XII, 260.

7. Nabokov's own attempt to justify the use of "sapajou" (see above), by reference to a letter of Pushkin's, is unconvincing for the same reason.

By contrast, the word *nega* has nothing folksy about it. Nabokov in his Commentary distinguishes beautifully between the various shades of the term and cites their various French counterparts. But the word had become, by Pushkin's time, a common and rather lightweight coin in Russian literary language; morphologically it was well supported by a very simple adjective, and Nabokov's renditions of it as "mollitude" (via the French *mollesse*) or "dulcitude," ingenious as they may be, are infinitely heavier and farther away from ordinary language than is the Russian original. Similarly, and even more disturbingly, plain words like *zhar* or *mirnye mesta* are solemnized respectively into "ardency" and "pacific sites." When *rumyannye usta* is rendered by "vermeil lips," it is forgotten that the Russian word is inextricably connected with the peasant ideal of a woman's red cheeks and rosy lips, as well as with the crust of a well-baked pie served on a peasant's table or the color of an apple grown in his backyard. In all such cases the Russification of the foreign, romantic vocabulary and its fusion with everyday language is ignored, and "literalism" is abandoned in favor of "historical literarism" while always preserving the lexical correctness.

Finally, and perhaps most importantly, one cannot help feeling that very often the choice of the strange and artificial word has been determined by the desire to preserve the iambic meter. It is true that often enough Nabokov abandons the tetrameter, and at times his lines do not scan at all. But it is equally true that time and again "nuances and intonations" are sacrificed to meter. This alone explains certain shortcomings of the translation. Only because of the meter, the very Russian fur coats have been converted into French "pelisses"; "curses" become "imprecations"; and old peasant women have acquired the vocabulary of college students. It is, therefore, difficult to accept Nabokov's assertion that "the retention [of the meter] assisted rather than hindered fidelity" (I, x). It is not clear at all why Nabokov persisted in retaining the meter, and at times only the semblance thereof, since he has shown quite convincingly in his "Notes on Prosody" that iambic tetrameters in Russian and in English are far from being equivalent and accordingly serve different purposes and produce a different impact upon the reader.[8]

8. The three reasons suggested in the text cannot fully account for all the oddities

There is little doubt that Nabokov's "ideal of literalism" would have been better served by a straightforward prose translation. Even then the result would have been no more than an approximation. Even then he would have found many limits to literalism other than merely the avowed impossibility of rendering "national gestures and facial movements" (III, 19). Even then he would have been defeated by the differences in the history of the two languages and the resulting lexical incongruences. And, above all, even then he would have been still plagued by the inconsistencies inherent in his concept of literalism. For it is impossible to combine an exact rendition of contextual meaning with a rendition of the influences that acted upon a poet and of the literary reminiscences that were, or rather may have been, in his mind. One cannot reproduce *uno actu* the complicated process of creation and its results. It is, therefore, not surprising that Nabokov, in his attempt to "re-incarnate" *simultaneously* Pushkin and Chénier (II, 465), does justice to neither.

If we now abandon Nabokov's own framework, we may be allowed — *pace* our translator — to ask the simple and not irrelevant question as to whether his *Eugene Onegin* can be enjoyed in a manner a Russian reader enjoy's Pushkin's *Evgenii Onegin*.[9] In fleeting moments of modesty, Nabokov describes his own translation as a "pony" and a "crib" (I, 7, 8). The self-debasement is uncalled for. There are hundreds of lines and also a fair number of stanzas in Nabokov's rendition that are perfectly admirable. To give some illustrations, here is the first quatrain of a stanza (chap. i, st. 20). The theater performance is about to begin:

> By now the house is full; the boxes blaze;
> parterre and stalls — all seethes;
> in the top gallery impatiently they clap,
> and, soaring up, the curtain swishes.

of the translation. A Russian traveling in a vessel is said to "swim" in it, or "on it." Shakespeare's Rosalind indeed spoke of "swimming in a gondola," but when Nabokov forces Pushkin to duplicate the act, he conjures up visions of a swimming pool in a gondola and does violence to the meaning of a Russian word. Here playfulness and eccentricity are the only explanation (*EO*, chap. i, st. 49).

9. Nabokov spells Pushkin's Christian name *Aleksandr*, but accepts the English form of *Evgenii*; the former is an eccentricity, the latter probably a natural enough concession to the demands of the meter.

This could not be better. Or (chap. iv, st. 40):

> But our Northern summer is a caricature of Southern winters;
> it will glance by and vanish: this is known,
> though to admit it we don't wish.
> The sky already breathed of autumn,
> the sun already shone more seldom,
> the day was growing shorter,
> the woods' mysterious canopy
> with a sad murmur bared itself,
> mist settled on the fields,
> the caravan of clamorous geese
> was tending southward; there drew near
> a rather tedious period;
> November stood already at the door.

With some reluctance, Nabokov had to acquisce in the three "already's" to render the light-footed and semantically not-quite-equivalent Russian monosyllabic *uzh*; but apart from this and, of course, forgetting Pushkin's flowing rhymes, we find that the English stanza has marvellously caught the beauty of the original.

But such lovely flowers are surrounded, if not smothered, by much less fragrant weeds:

> . . . Seeing all at once
> the young two-horned moon's visage
> in the sky on her left,
> she trembled and grew pale.
> Or when a falling star
> along the dark sky flew
> and dissipated, then
> in agitation Tanya hastened
> to whisper, while the star still rolled,
> her heart's desire to it.
> When anywhere she happened
> a black monk to encounter,
> or a swift hare amid the fields
> would run across her path,
> so scared she knew not what to undertake,
> full of grievous forebodings,
> already she expected some mishap.
> (chap. v, sts. 5 and 6)

508

Or (chap. i, st. 37):

> The fairs remained not long
> the objects of his customary thoughts

(Incidentally, the etymology of "fairs" here is Anglo-Saxon rather than Latin; it is only much later in the novel that Eugene Onegin has some transient interest in the famous fair at Nizhni Novgorod.)

Or (chap. vi, st. 3):

> With his unlooked-for apparition,
> the momentary softness of his eyes,
> and odd conduct with Olga,
> to the depth of her soul,
> she's penetrated.

Pushkin once wrote an epigram in which he repeated the first lines of Zhukovski's romantic dialogue (a translation of J. P. Hebel's Allemanian *Vergänglichkeit*). Converting Pushkin's (and Zhukovski's) iambic pentameters into "honest roadside prose," it reads: "Listen, Grandfather, every time I look at that Roettler Castle, the thought crosses my mind: What if this is prose, and a bad one, too?"

In an inflected language like the Russian, the endings of verbs in the present and future tenses and the case endings of nouns and adjectives, varying with the gender as does the past tense, supply sure guides to the reader. Such a language offers greatest freedom for the order of words, and all kinds of inverted constructions can be ventured upon without any loss in terms of lucidity and elegance. In Nabokov's attempts to render the *individual lines* as closely as possible, the sentences lose Pushkin's transparent clarity, to say nothing of elegance which, as often as not, is destroyed altogether. Nabokov's translation can and indeed should be studied, but despite all the cleverness and occasional brilliance it cannot be read. For someone who is not unfamiliar with Russian and can try to read the original, Nabokov's rendition will be of inestimable service. It will do for him, particularly in conjunction with the Commentary, infinitely more than any sublinear "pony." But if he knows no Russian, he may well try, still with Nabokov's help, a rhymed "unliteral" English version of the novel. Nabokov is untiring in his vicious strictures of his predecessors. Balanced judgment is not his forte, and he is not in the habit of stressing his competitors' achievements. It is true that they took excessive liberties with the text and were indeed guilty of many inaccuracies, although most of the time the gravity of the offences is not commensurate with the wrath Nabokov pours over them. But when everything is said and done, it is to the other translations that an English reader must turn if he wants to catch a faint echo of Pushkin's music and get a feeling, however vague, for the airy lightness of his lines. For Nabokov's "true" translation does not happen to come very close to Pushkin's aesthetic truth, just as Lolita, Nabokov tells us, was not as intelligent a child as her IQ might suggest.

Walter Arndt, the most recent translator of the novel, receives the full blast of Nabokov's competitive fury,[10] but much of Arndt's translation does convey crucial things that are lost in Nabokov's. The latter is particularly proud of his rendition of stanza 28 of chapter ii. He says, this time with more restrained modesty: "Whatever accuracy I have achieved in this stanza, I owe to the ruthless and triumphant elimination of rhyme" (II, 286). Let us, therefore, compare his own and Arndt's [11] renditions:

Nabokov

She on the balcony
liked to prevene Aurora's rise,
when, in the pale sky, disappears
the choral dance of stars,
and earth's rim softly lightens,
and, morning's herald, the wind whiffs,
and rises by degree the day.
In winter, when night's shade
possesses longer half the world,
and longer in the idle stillness,
by the bemisted moon,
the lazy orient sleeps,
awakened at her customary hour,
she would get up by candles.

10. Vladimir Nabokov, "On Translating Pushkin, Pounding the Clavichord," *New York Review of Books* (April 30, 1964), pp. 14–16.

11. Walter Arndt, *Eugene Onegin, A New Translation* (New York, 1963), p. 50.

Arndt

Upon her balcony at dawning
She liked to bide the break of day,
When on the heaven's pallid awning
There fades the starry roundelay,
When earth's faint rim is set to glowing,
Aurora's herald breeze is blowing,
And step by step the world turns light.
In winter time, when darkling night
The hemisphere for longer covers,
And sunk in idle quietude,
Beneath a hazied moon subdued,
The languid Orient longer hovers,
Roused at accustomed time she might
Begin the day by candle light.

Nabokov's stanza is one of his best, but I prefer Arndt's version. Neither Nabokov nor Arndt could reproduce Pushkin's lovely alliteration in line 6: *I vestnik utra veter veyet* (v-t-t-v-t-v-t), although both have made the same half-hearted attempt (Nabokov: w-w; Arndt: b-b). I suppose Nabokov would shed a tiger's tear about the loss in Arndt's rendition of Pushkin's *preduprezhdat'* which Nabokov, again making a detour via Paris, has rendered by "prevene." He might grow literally wild over Arndt's somewhat blurred distinction between dawn and sunrise (or rather between *l'aube* and *l'aurore*) — a sin Nabokov himself is guilty of elsewhere. But taking it for all in all, Arndt's stanza is a successful refutation of Nabokov's basic claim. In this case, fairly "triumphantly," you can have the rhymes and the correct meter and be quite close to the original. To be sure, Arndt's translation as a whole is uneven. It has its peaks and troughs — and flats. So has Nabokov's. In the last analysis Pushkin's masterpiece is probably untranslatable,[12] and no one will ever recreate it in all its holistic grandeur. But while Nabokov tells us with great precision what *Eugene Onegin* is all about, it is from Arndt's and some of his predecessors' passages that one can hope to get at least an inkling of what it is really like.

12. As is, for instance, *Gore ot uma*, Griboedov's magnificent comedy in verse, usually called *Woe from Wit*, where the perversion of the text begins with the rendition of the title.

III. The Commentary

Nabokov's Commentary (in which much of the material in Volume One must be included) is altogether stupendous in length, scope, mass of underlying research, and attention to detail. It covers both the original text and the translation. Nabokov explains, first in a brief summary and then in running comment, stanza by stanza, the structure and the action of the novel. He is untiring in searching for sources of Pushkin's phrases, images, characterizations, and descriptions of nature. One thing is clear. After this Commentary the future translators of *Eugene Onegin* will not commit any silly errors; with this Commentary a much more understanding reading of the novel in Russian as well as in English is possible. If, in reading the Commentary, the feeling of admiration and the sense of gratitude are dulled by growing irritation, the reason must be sought in the author's uncontrolled anger, his lack of generosity, his narrow prejudices, eccentricities, inconsistencies, and irrelevancies.

A stanza (chap. viii, st. 25) in Nabokov's translation reads:

> Here was to epigrams addicted
> a gentleman cross with everything:
> with the top-sweet tea of the hostess,
> the ladies' platitudes, the *ton* of men,
> the comments on a foggy novel,
> the badge two sisters had been granted,
> the falsehoods in reviews, the war,
> the snow, and his own wife.

Mutatis mutandis and remembering that a very handsome acknowledgment to Mrs. Nabokov has been made in the Foreword, this is a fair description of the author as seen through the pages of his Commentary. He is indeed angry at everything, from American students' ignorance of names of trees and flowers (III, 9), American steaks, "the tasteless meat of restless cattle" (II, 149), and the "ruminant American speech" (III, 472) — presumably also the speech of tasteless and restless people — to poets, novelists, playwrights, and critics through the ages. The list is long: "Insipid Virgil and his pale pederasts" (II, 55; there is, of course, nothing like an enterprising and murderous pervert); Ariosto's "dreary *Orlando Furioso*" (II,

199); "the conventional, colorless, and banal style of Fénelon and Racine" (III, 169); Corneille's "bombastic and platitudinous *Cid*" (II, 83); "Voltaire's abominably pedestrian verses" (II, 147); "Rousseau's morbid, intricate, and at the same time rather naïve mind" (II, 340); "Sheridan's singularly inept comedy" (II, 102); "a queer strain of triviality" in Goethe's *Faust* (II, 235); "the well-meaning, but *talentlos* August Wilhelm Schlegel" (II, 230); "Madame de Staël's insipid novel" (II, 277); "Stendhal's much overrated *Le Rouge et le Noir*" (II, 87) and his "paltry literary style" (III, 115); "Balzac's — a popular novelist's — much overrated vulgar novelette" (II, 277; III, 335); "the famous, but talentless Belinskii" (II, 136); "the derivative and mediocre Sainte-Beuve" (II, 154); Dostoevski, "a much overrated, sentimental and Gothic novelist of the time" (III, 191); and, in one final sweep, "all the plaster idols of academic tradition from Cervantes to George Eliot (not to speak of the crumbling Manns and Faulkners of our time)" (III, 192).

This, no doubt, was great stuff *pour épater la coed* at Cornell. It should be noted, however, that most of this remarkably foolish abuse is heaped quite gratuitously in that it has no bearing at all on *Eugene Onegin* or Pushkin in general. It is also worth pointing out that the superb Shakespeare translations of the *talentlos* Schlegel have traveled unimpaired through "the envious distance of the ages" (Pushkin), while some more recent translators may (again quoting Nabokov's Pushkin) "glance by and vanish: this is known, though to admit it we don't wish." But the real curiosity is that Nabokov's demolition of the great is so irresistibly reminiscent of a certain preposterous brand of Russian literary criticism of the 1860's, when Pisarev — a "harsh type" (III, 58) — did not shrink from describing Pushkin as "a frivolous versifier." [13]

Given Nabokov's mood, it is no wonder that his remarks on other commentators of *Eugene Onegin* show neither restraint nor fairness. He describes the work of N. L. Brodski and D. I. Chizhevski as "worthless compilations" (I, 60) and continues to pound on them, pointing out every little error in spelling or reference. Brodski, a Soviet popularizer, is indeed not much better than he should be. His

13. D. I. Pisarev, *Sochineniya* (Works; Moscow, 1956), III, 415.

attempts to convert Onegin into a revolutionary are fairly silly, as has been pointed out by serious scholars even in Soviet reviews, a circumstance Nabokov might well have mentioned; [14] just as he might have said that he had followed Brodski, at least in having a section called "Pushkin on *Eugene Onegin*," which has almost identical contents.

Professor Chizhevski, on the other hand, is a very considerable scholar of great erudition. True, his comments contain some errors for which he must be held responsible. Nabokov, however, must have known that Chizhevski had an inadequate command of English and that his commentary was written in Russian and was then translated and proofread for him. In the process, a good many errors of transliteration and many misprints have remained uncorrected. But Nabokov is out to cut throats, and there is no literary fair-practice act to restrain him. The tone of Nabokov's milder strictures may be best illustrated by applying it to Nabokov's own errors. They would sound like this: "The incredible Nabokov manages to make at least three mistakes in his comment on Ochakov (II, 305). He actually writes: At the time and later, the name of this fortified Moldavian [?] town and Russian port, some forty miles west [wrong again: east] from Odessa, was spelled 'Oczakow' in the British press. The fortress was stormed by Suvorov's troops in 1788, during the Turkish Campaign, and became Russian by the treaty of 1792 [wrong again: 1791]." Or: "Nabokov's error in citing a German title completely destroys its grammar" (III, 486–487). Or: "Nabokov's mistake in spelling a Rumanian word (III, 156) shows his ignorance of the etymology of Romance languages." All these are, of course, perfect trifles, and Nabokov's nugatory ire would be fully incomprehensible if one did not know so well its antecedents in Russian and German petty and rude polemical habits.

It is true that Nabokov's Commentary is in many respects, including completeness and probably accuracy, infinitely superior to its predecessors. (Incidentally, I have not looked up Nabokov's references, except one — Juvenal, *Satire X* — where the correct line turned out to be 113 rather than 213, but this, I am willing to assume, was just my own bad luck.) But it is only fair to say that Chizhevski has many a fine comment, which Nabokov would have

14. For instance, the review by A. Ivanenko in *Pushkin, Vremennik* (Pushkin, a Chronicle; Moscow-Leningrad, 1941), VI, 526–527.

been wise to accept and incorporate. In particular, Chizhevski has a keener sense of the evolution of the Russian language and of Pushkin's characteristic blending of archaisms and colloquialisms. He is decidedly more careful and more scholarly in pointing out regional variations in Russian accentuation and pronunciation. From time to time, Nabokov seems to labor under the strange misapprehension that the language spoken in his environment in St. Petersburg was the only correct Russian. It is, therefore, quite funny when he explains that Pushkin was able to rhyme *dushno* with *skuchno* in Tatiana's speech (chap. iii, st. 17) only because of the girl's "maternal Moscovism" (II, 363). For the same rhyme occurs at least twice in *Eugene Onegin* (chap. i, st. 19; chap. vii, st. 48) where the speaker is not Tatiana, but Pushkin himself. Considering that Pushkin spent his childhood in and near Moscow, pronouncing "ch" as "sh" in certain words must have been perfectly natural for him.[15] It was Pushkin who suggested that one would do well to listen to the "astonishingly pure and correct" Russian of a Moscow *prosvirnya* (a *popolana* engaged in baking hosts for the church); and in discussing precisely these features of Moscow pronunciation, Pushkin expressly identified himself with it.[16]

Chizhevski also deals in a more relaxed and balanced way with such questions as the time period in the novel, the possible real-life models of its heroes and heroines, and Pushkin's literary antecedents. With regard to all these matters, to which a large part of the Commentary is devoted, Nabokov's pedantry and inconsistencies are

15. It is indeed an exception when *skuchno* rhymes with a word whose ending *is* pronounced as ". . . . uchno." See chap. ii, st. 13 (*skuchno-nerazluchno*). This for Pushkin was a mere "eye rhyme," of which he expressly disapproved. See his review of *Poésies et pensées de Joseph Delorme* in Pushkin, *Polnoe*, XI, 200.

16. Pushkin, *Polnoe*, XI, 149. In making comments of this sort Nabokov calls to mind the wonderful memoirs by Andrey Belyi, *Na rubezhe dvukh stoletii* (On the Borderline of Two Centuries; Moscow–Leningrad, 1930), where Belyi's uncle — "a disheveled conspirator and nihilist" — arrives from St. Petersburg to annoy the Muscovites by pronouncing *chto* (what) as though the word had five "ch"s (p. 127). Moscow and much of Russia, of course, says *shto*. When Nabokov goes on to denounce angrily the dreadful "Soviet provincialism" *bryuki* (trousers; II, 106), he might have noticed that it occurs in the writings of a pre-Soviet provincial writer called Leo Tolstoy, where even the endearing diminutive *bryuchki* is used (*Detstvo*, [Childhood], chap. xv), just as Tolstoy used quite naturally the word *chubuk* for a long-stemmed pipe (*Yunost'* [Youth], chap. xiii), which Nabokov claims is still South Russian.

striking. He describes the calendar of the novel year by year, month by month, and day by day, accusing Pushkin — this time more in sorrow than in anger — of having committed mistakes. Tatiana's Saint's Day occurred on January 12, 1821, which in that year fell on a Wednesday, but the careless Pushkin unaccountably made it a Saturday (II, 477). Again, Pushkin causes Tatiana, in 1824, to converse with the Spanish ambassador, but Nabokov (with the help of a Russian scholar) found out that in 1824 Spain had no ambassador at the court of St. Petersburg (III, 183).[17]

Much has been written on the possible relation between the characters in the novel and people Pushkin was acquainted with. This is quite natural in a work which is so full of "autobiographizations," to use Nabokov's term. Pushkin himself referred in *Eugene Onegin* (chap. viii, st. 51) to the model or models after whom Tatiana was painted (wavering in his drafts between the singular and the plural, but finally deciding on the singular). At the same time, Nabokov is surely right in objecting — as did many before him — to "the proto-typical quest as blurring the authentic, always atypical methods of genius" (II, 229). The trouble, however, is that Nabokov is neither consistent in this attitude nor clear-headed in his cogitations about the problem. Despite his harsh words about "prototypical sleuths," he lustily plunges into some "prototyping" of his own and devotes several pages to the treatment of Pushkin's relation to a girl who is mentioned, partly in disguised form, not even in the text of the novel but in drafts (III, 199–207), which according to Nabokov's view (expressed earlier, I, 15), should have been ruthlessly destroyed anyhow, "lest they mislead academic mediocrities into thinking that it is possible to unravel the mysteries of genius by studying canceled readings." [18] He has no hesitation in identifying the young wife of a

17. Pushkin of course could have, without damage to the meter, let Tatiana speak to the British or Austrian envoy, but the Spanish ambassador gave him the chance of a fine alliteration: *s poslom ispanskim* (s-p-s-s-p-s), which should be a little bit more important to us — as it probably was to Pushkin — and which Nabokov, fascinated by a perfect irrelevancy, does not notice. It is no less ridiculous when Nabokov carefully collects various hints in the novel in order to determine the approximate longitude and latitude of Onegin's and Tatiana's estates in the country, only to inform us later that Pushkin had no real Russian places in mind, but let the respective chapters of the novel play in imagined "Arcadian" surroundings.

18. Nabokov continues: "In art purpose and plan are nothing, only the result

businessman, when she appears in a fleeting reference in "Onegin's Journey" (III, 299), although he fails to do so in discussing a beautiful stanza (chap. vi, st. 16) that is obviously devoted to her memory (III, 22).[19] He does not mind distinguishing between "more" and "less" reckless "prototypists" and goes to a considerable length to discuss the — possibly divided — ownership in real life of a pair of lovely feet of whose beauty Pushkin sings in what Nabokov calls the "Pedal Digression" (I, 24). It takes him some twenty pages to belabor the point, which he says "is of no interest whatsoever," and he returns to it once more sixty pages later. In the process he also rejects the possibility that those feet might have belonged to Maria Raevski — later the wife of a Decembrist whom she followed into Siberian exile. For at the crucial time when Pushkin could have admired her feet, Maria — "the ugly duckling" — was not fifteen, as she falsely claims, but only thirteen-and-a-half years old (II, 119). It is, incidentally, odd that Lolita's bard, a nymphet's singer, should preclude sensuous interest in a mere child, particularly since Pushkin had some proclivities in that direction.[20]

---

counts. We are concerned only with the structure of a published work for which the author alone is responsible insofar as it was published within his lifetime. Last minute alterations or *those forced by circumstances — no matter what motives affected him* — should stand as he let them stand" (I, 15; italics supplied). This dogmatic position Nabokov borrowed — without reference — from M. L. Gofman, one of the most notable Pushkin scholars. Gofman, however, was very far from suggesting destruction of drafts and variants of which he published the first scholarly edition. See "Propushchennye strofy *Evgeniya Onegina*" (Omitted Stanzas of *EO*), *Pushkin i ego sovremenniki* (Pushkin and His Contemporaries; St. Petersburg, 1922), vols. VIII–IX, nos. 33–35, p. 22. Nabokov himself, of course, comments most extensively on drafts, omitted stanzas, and variants, and even finds the sources of mottoes which Pushkin intended to use and then dropped. To suggest, however, that even obvious and well-known changes made as concessions to censorship, sometimes in response to the censor's demands, must be left untouched is hardly a tenable position. But that is precisely what Nabokov does in his translation. Naturally, any such restorations involve very delicate problems, but these cannot be solved by an unreasonable general rule; what is needed is exercise of thoughtful judgment in each individual case. This is what, in another connection, is suggested by the ever reasonable B. Tomashevski, "Izdaniya stikhotvornykh tekstov" (Editions of Poetic Texts), *Literaturnoe nasledstvo* (Moscow, 1934), XVI–XVIII, 1090.

19. P. E. Shchegolev, *Pushkin, Ocherki* (Essays; St. Petersburg, 1912), pp. 219–220.

20. In the Ukraine he flirted with the twelve-year-old daughter of his mistress Davydova, and in Bessarabia with the thirteen-year-old daughter of a Moldavian

More important than all these inconsistencies about irrelevancies is Nabokov's failure to realize that he uses the term "prototype" in two quite different senses. Hence comes his confusion between "prototypes" and the "typical" quality of characters created by an artist. If Pushkin's Tatiana had been a portrait of a definite living model, she would have been an individual rather than a "type." Therefore, the search for such models, whatever its value, has nothing at all to do with the entirely different questions as to what extent the heroes of the novel can be considered as typical of certain groups of Russian society in the 1820s; and to what extent Onegin, for instance, can be regarded as one of the first incarnations of the "superfluous people" which kept appearing in Russian literature throughout the rest of the century and more recently re-emerged in Pasternak's *Doctor Zhivago*. There exists an immense body of literature devoted to these problems. Very great — and not so great — Russian writers have treated them, including Klyuchevski, probably the most eminent among Russian historians. For obvious reasons, Russian literature, much more than that of other countries, happens to be an integral and crucially important part of Russia's intellectual history; and considering it as such was, therefore, an indeed one-sided but very legitimate way of literary criticism. Nabokov describes this criticism as "the most boring mass of comments known to civilized man" (II, 151). But Nabokov's strictures, which are both sweeping and narrow-minded, are seldom warped by a false ambition of consistency. Their main purpose is to disagree and to lengthen the long list of his disparagements. In this case, as in others, once he has vented his ire, he calmly proceeds to refer to Onegin as a member of a certain minority "set" of Russian society (II, 221) and to connect Tatiana not only with the literary "type" of high-minded Russian girls (say, in Turgenev's novels) but also with the historical heroines of the Russian populist movement (II, 281); in other words, to do himself what he so contemptuously rejected a few pages earlier.

The most original and, in many respects, the most admirable part of the Commentary is the result of Nabokov's unrelenting pursuit, mostly in French and English literature, of parallels to *Eugene Onegin*. Some of those have been traced before, although

---

noble. See V. Veresaev, *Sputniki Pushkina* (Companions of Pushkin; Moscow, 1937), I, 288, 301.

Nabokov does not like to give credit where credit is due.[21] But no one, before Nabokov, has ever gone to such lengths in this respect, and one is awed by the knowledge of literary sources revealed in the process. In the aggregate, his comments provide a fascinating mosaic picture of the literary ambiance within which *Eugene Onegin* can be placed. Here, no doubt, lies Nabokov's most significant contribution. But it is also here that his penchant for pedantry and irrelevancy celebrates its greatest triumphs. What he is after is Pushkin's literary debts. The number of cases in which the respective debit items can be clearly provided is, of course, limited. Some of the connections are plausible and supported by evidence, others much less so. Nabokov seldom tries to attach carefully considered probability coefficients to his assertions. He prefers to be apodictical rather than conjectural even when he speaks of unconscious, subliminal reminiscences, untroubled by the fact that it is difficult enough to establish what was consciously in a poet's mind in the process of creation.[22] And every so often he is content to note mere similarities, mentioning antecedents of which Pushkin avowedly was ignorant, and in some cases even dragging in quotations from works published after the completion of *Eugene Onegin* and even after Pushkin's death. This is supposed to demonstrate "the logic of literary evolution" (III, 53), but it is difficult to see, for instance, the relevance of a much later reminiscence of Chateaubriand's, showing that he too, like a girl mentioned in *Eugene Onegin*, once was fond of playing tag with the ocean surf; or what

21. Very unfortunately, this is true of the Commentary as a whole. A couple of times Nabokov says contemptuously "as is known to Russian commentators" (I, 30, 136), which is quite inappropriate, because he would have to repeat the phrase a hundred times were he to point out every bit of knowledge and every suggestion that he has gleaned from others. In general, his references to his predecessors, unless designed to criticize their shortcomings, are very sparing indeed. Even when credit is given, it is often done grudgingly. "P. Morozov," Nabokov says, "easily broke the clumsy code" of Pushkin's cyphered fragments of chapter x (III, 366). This patronizing tone about a major achievement of a scholar (made possible only by the happy idea to relate the apparently meaningless lines of the cypher to a quatrain in one of Pushkin's poems) comes with exceedingly poor grace from a writer who is ever ready to exult over his own little discoveries. Werner Sombart, in the preface to *Der moderne Kapitalismus*, said: "Zu danken habe ich niemand." Nabokov, in his Foreword, expresses the same sentiment in a different language. He might have considered what his Commentary would have been like without the enormous body of research, conducted through long decades by Pushkinists.

22. Nabokov himself admits that the "pursuit of reminiscences may become a form of insanity on the scholiast's part" (II, 32).

Alice's "curioser and curioser" has to do with "more frightful still and still more wondrous" in Tatiana's nightmare (II, 507). The fact is that Nabokov could not resist making his Commentary a general repository of his learning, just as throughout he is unable to stem the course of his free associations and engages in frequent digressions, interspersed with disagreeing and disagreeable remarks about everything and everybody.[23]

Despite the formidable length of the Commentary and the staggering number of parellelisms, it is curious to see that some most probable instances of borrowings, influences, or allusions have been omitted, presumably because of the commentator's relative neglect of German and sometimes even Russian sources.[24] It seems as though a special effort was made to overlook the obvious in favor of the farfetched and esoteric.

23. Nabokov's inability to suppress any bit of information brings onto the pages of the Commentary one John Metschl who, in 1928, in describing an American collection of firearms, misspelled the make of pistols that happened to be used in Onegin's duel; we are also favored with a very plausible reason for the misspelling (III, 39).

24. To give a few examples: Tatiana's farewell to her country home is very close to Johanna's famous monologue in Schiller's *Die Jungfrau von Orleans*, of which a Russian translation by Zhukovski — who (along with Batyushkov) was young Pushkin's poetic teacher — had appeared a couple of years before Pushkin embarked upon his novel. Chizhevski very properly mentions the likelihood of the connection. Similarly, the concluding stanza of the "established text" (chap. viii, st. 51) bears very great resemblance to *Zueignung* in *Faust*, where Goethe deplores the vanished friends to whom the early fragments of the drama once were read:

Sie hören nicht die folgenden Gesänge
Die Seelen, denen ich die ersten sang.
Zerstoben ist das freundliche Gedränge . . .

and Pushkin:

But those to whom in amicable meetings
its first strophes I read —
some are no more, others are distant . . .

It should be noted that Pushkin probably read *Zueignung* in the original, since he used (twice) for mottoes a line from *Vorspiel auf dem Theater* in *Faust*, and, as Tomashevski shows, Pushin's octaves in his poem on the Crimea (1821) are derived from *Zueignung* (*Tomashevski*, "Strofika Pushkina" (Pushkin's Stanzas) *Issledovaniya i materialy* (Explorations and Materials; Moscow–Leningrad 1958), II, 94–95). In addition Pushkin *could* have read *Zueignung* in one of the three French translations available at the time; but he *must* have read it in Zhukovskii's Russian rendition which appeared in 1817 as an introduction to the ballad "Twelve Sleeping Virgins." Finally, Nabokov might well have mentioned that Pushkin's description of the hustle and bustle on the piazza in Odessa ("Onegin's Journey" st. 25) contains a

Nabokov's propensity to disagree at any price (including that of consistency) finally pushes him into a major disagreement with Pushkin himself. The novel ends with Tatiana's admitting that she still loves Onegin, but rejecting him because "to another I belong, to him I shall be faithful all my life" (chap. viii, st. 47).[25] Nabokov concedes that Pushkin intended Tatiana's "decision to be a final one" (III, 240). And indeed the chapter bears Byron's lines for a motto: "Fare thee well, and if for ever, still for ever fare thee well." It was the finality of Tatiana's decision that prevented Pushkin from returning to the novel, when he toyed with the idea a few years later.[26] But critics whom Nabokov does not like praised Tatiana for her high moral standards.[27] So does Nabokov himself four pages earlier when he speaks of her "uncompromising constancy" (III, 236).[28] But this is quickly forgotten, and in the face of "the amorphous mass of comments produced with monstrous fluency by *ideynaya kritika* (ideological critique)," Nabokov "deems it necessary to point out that her [Tatiana's] answer to Onegin does not at all ring with such finality as commentators have supposed it to do" (III, 241). Thus Pushkin was in error ("Hier irrt Goethe!"), and Onegin's chances with Tatiana looked good. The novel remained unfinished, and Nabokov "cannot help trying to imagine what we should do if called

---

line which Pushkin borrowed almost verbatim, continuing it humorously, from the well-known poem by Batyushkov, *Stranstvovatel' i domosed.*

25. Actually, the Russian *otdana* ("given") does not mean "belong"; it means "I have been made to belong." Therefore, Nabokov's translation, like that of other translators, including Arndt's, misses the crucial point that Tatiana's marriage was not an act of her own choice.

26. Cf. M. L. Gofman, "Istoriya sozdaniya *Evgeniya Onegina*" (History of the Writing of *EO*) in *A. Pushkin, Evgenii Onegin* (Paris, 1937), pp. 221–223.

27. Among these critics Nabokov is probably wrong to include Belinski, who felt on the contrary that faithfulness to an unloved husband was Tatiana's least admirable quality. Cf. V. G. Belinski, *Sobranie sochinenii v trekh tomakh* (Collected Work in Three Volumes; Moscow, 1948), III, 564–65.

28. In his review of Arndt' translation, Nabokov, aghast at a slightly frivolous tone injected by Arndt into Tatiana's speech, exclaims indignantly: "Tatiana, Pushkin's Tatiana!" — thus imitating almost verbatim the hated Dostoevski's ejaculation in his famous Pushkin Speech, over which Nabokov pours the thick venom of his heavy pedantry. F. M. Dostoevski, *Sobranie proizvedenii* (Collected Works; Moscow-Leningrad, 1929), XII, 381. Incidentally, in criticizing Dostoevski, Nabokov repeats — without reference — a point made by N. O. Lerner, *Rasskazy o Pushkine* (Tales about Pushkin; Leningrad, 1929), pp. 213–216.

521

upon to continue the book in his [Pushkin's] name" (III, 311). It is, therefore, not for nothing that in one passage Nabokov calls Pushkin the "unfellowed, unmatchable" Pushkin,[29] a "fellow writer" (I, 59).[30]

In prerevolutionary Russia, there was a man, called Count Amory, I believe, who specialized in writing book-length epilogues to other people's "unfinished" novels. Ready to succeed where Pushkin failed, he would have seized eagerly on Nabokov's idea. It is fairly clear what course he should have taken. Tatiana, Nabokov tells us (II, 298), may have been — because of her maternal connection with Moscow aristocracy [31] — a grandaunt, or a cousin twice removed, of Princess Dolly Shcherbatskaya-Oblonskaya in *Anna Karenina*. But from Nabokov's novel interpretation it follows that Tatiana was related neither to Dolly, the faithful wife of an unfaithful husband, nor to one of Turgenev's virtuous maidens, but rather was the "prototype" of Anna Karenina herself.[32] Pushkin possibly intended in the tenth chapter of the novel (which he burned, lest it be found by the Secret Police) to let Onegin participate in the Decembrist uprising. What would be more natural than letting an adulterous

29. As John Taylor, the Penniless Pilgrim, would have said.

30. It is just possible that some oddities of Nabokov's Commentary stem from his identification with Pushkin. Is this the source of the uncontrolled digressions? Nabokov, too, sprinkles his Commentary with references to his own biography, including his ancestors. He describes the Commentary as "casual notes" (III, 183), thus duplicating Pushkin's very deceptive reference to the "casual strophes" of his novel. And Nabokov places in the Translator's Epilogue his fine translation of Pushkin's lovely poem "The Work," written upon the completion of Eugene Onegin, and accompanies it by the following note: "Pushkin dated this poem: 'Boldino, September 25, 1830, 3:15.' Translated one hundred and twenty-six years later in Ithaca, New York." The day and the hour of the translation are not given.

31. Nabokov says that Soviet commentators miss this "fine point." Whatever its fineness, the point of Tatiana's noble descent is expressly made twice by D. Blagoy, *Sotsiologiya tvorchestva Pushkina, Etyudy* (The Sociology of Pushkin's Work, Studies; Moscow, 1931), pp. 138, 149.

32. A German scholar once did remark on the similarity of the *Endsituation* in *Onegin* with the *Ausgangssituation* in *Anna Karenina* — L. Müller "Der Sinn der Liebe und der Sinn des Lebens," *Zeitschrift für Slavische Philologie* (Heidelberg, 1951), XXI.1, 23; but only because he felt that Tolstoy's novel carried an implicit moral approval of Tatiana's decision. In another piece the same author points out the rather obvious resemblance between the finality in *Onegin* and in Pushkin's *Dubrovski* — "Schicksal und Liebe in Jevgenii Onegin" in A. Luther, ed., *Solange Dichter leben: Puschkin-Studien* (Krefeld, 1949), pp. 160–161.

Tatiana heroically follow Onegin into Siberian exile? In fact, since Pierre Bezukhov too, at the end of the novel, is close to Decembrist circles, both *Eugene Onegin* and *War and Peace* could be "finished" jointly with further possibilities for interesting complications between Tatiana and Pierre and Eugene and Natasha. But Count Amory is dead, *Eugene Onegin* will have to remain a torso, and Pushkin's error will live on in all its uncorrected glory.

It it indeed deplorable that so much of Nabokov's great effort is so sadly distorted by the desire to be original at all cost, by confused theorizing, by promises that never could be redeemed, by spiteful pedantry, unbridled emotions, and, last but not least, unrestrained egotism. All this is bound to annoy some readers; it will revolt others. The work, including the translation with its specious tenets, is a monumental handiwork, patched together from most heterogeneous materials. And yet it is also more than that. It contains real intuitions, numerous flashes of brilliance, and a mass of solid learning. In many respects it is a seminal contribution, and it is to be hoped, therefore, that future translators and commentators of *Eugene Onegin* will not imitate Nabokov's lack of generosity and will gratefully acknowledge their inevitable indebtedness to his findings, clarifications, and interpretations — the fruit of enormous industry, skill, and erudition.

American Research on the
Soviet Economy

Three decades ago, on the eve of the last war, our knowledge of Soviet economic development was small indeed. There was, of course, no scarcity of writings on the subject. The shelves of the Slavic Division in the Library of Congress in Washington and of other great libraries in the country were crowded with books, fat and lean, on the New Economic Policy of the 1920's and the five-year plans that followed it. But the scholarly content of that literature was low. With a few notable exceptions, they contained superficial descriptions of current events. As a rule, depending on the bias of the individual author, statistical data published by the Soviet government were either accepted with childlike faith or rejected *in toto* with equally naive skepticism. Moreover, there were few attempts to address even the most obvious economic questions to the material. Cost structure, methods of price formation, relative prices, determinants of investment decisions, fiscal and monetary policies — to give just a few signal instances — received hardly more than passing mention. Neither interest in those problems nor competence in treating them was in evidence. In many cases, a good knowledge of the Russian language was the only legitimation which the writers concerned could offer in order to justify their posing as specialists on the Soviet economy; and at times even that qualification was wanting.

This unsatisfactory state of affairs began to change during the Second World War, when a number of Soviet economic studies were prepared at the instance of the United States government. In those studies, independent approaches were for the first time applied to calculations of Soviet national income. In addition, much effort was devoted to the investigation of Soviet capabilities in the individual branches of the economy. The bulk of that work has remained unpublished. Nevertheless, the critical methods for the treatment of Soviet statistical data, as developed at the time, strongly influenced the direction and character of later studies, when sustained scholarly research on the Soviet Union began at several universities, first and foremost at the Russian Institute at Columbia University and at the Russian Research Center at Harvard University. Because of the present writer's close connection (particularly between 1948 and 1956) with the latter institution, it is convenient to describe the problems that had to be confronted and the decisions that were reached in terms of the experience gleaned at Harvard.

The first and most important question referred to the nature of the work to be performed. In the last years of the war, the belief was variously expressed that after its termination the Soviet Union would be willing to abandon its autarkic policies and engage in large-scale commercial and financial transactions with foreign countries. Hence, in the mid-forties, great interest was attached to problems connected with Soviet state trading, such as the possibilities of discrimination or dumping on the part of the foreign trade monopoly. A good deal was written on the methods of financing a large and growing volume of trade, its probable composition, and related questions. But within a few months after the fall of Japan, the first Soviet acts of cold war as well as the adoption, early in 1946, of the Fourth Five-Year Plan, showed clearly that the Soviet dictatorship was determined to continue its prewar policy of giving absolute priority to heavy industry and of keeping the volume of foreign trade at a very low level. Accordingly, problems of Russia's international economic relations, and in particular those of Russian-American trade, receded far into the background. By the same token, it became obvious that Russia's domestic economy was to be the main object of study. There were real alternatives, however.

The temptation was to devote attention primarily to the current economic scene in Russia, and to organize and direct research accordingly. This was an attractive possibility for more than one reason. First of all, it promised easy and early accomplishments. Pursuing this course, it would have been natural to engage a number of readily available men, who possessed a thorough knowledge of Russian, had in the past published books and articles on various aspects of the Soviet economy, and could be expected to continue to do so under the auspices of a university research center. Much of the job could be done as teamwork, and publication of a monthly or quarterly bulletin, registering and interpreting important economic events in Russia, would have fitted well into such an arrangement. In addition to yielding very certain results, this way of doing things would have appealed both to government agencies and to broad sections of the public, whose interests quite naturally concentrated on current affairs and the processes of day-to-day change.

But outweighing these advantages was the consideration that this course would have left the field of Soviet economic studies in the charge of journalistic superficiality and analytical incompetence. If serious scholarly work on the Soviet economy was to be done, another road, much longer and more arduous, had to be chosen. Preoccupation with current problems had to be eschewed, at least for a considerable time. Instead, basic research involving painstaking statistical work and generous use of tools of economic analysis was to be the primary objective. This perforce meant concentrating on the period beginning in the late 1920's and continuing throughout the 1930's. The form this research had to assume was a series of monographs devoted to individual significant aspects of the Soviet economy and prepared by well-trained economists.

The next problem, of course, was to find the men qualified to do the work. In the past, American economists had shown an almost complete lack of interest in Soviet economic problems, the two or three exceptions serving to confirm the general neglect. No one could expect seasoned scholars to abandon their research and to spend much time and effort on mastering what is after all a rather difficult language as well as the great deal of background information necessary for any intelligent "area study." Clearly, a new field had to be built up by new people, and graduate students in economics were the obvious source.

The years immediately following the war were particularly propitious for the purpose. The G.I. Bill was attracting large numbers of unusually mature students to the universities. Some of them had acquired a knowledge of Russian during their years of service thanks to the Army Special Training Program, which had used very modern and effective methods of language instruction. Nevertheless, in order to induce a graduate student in economics to convert himself into an "expert on the Soviet economy," special incentives had to be offered. In some cases, the Russian Research Center at Harvard would start financing a prospective research fellow at the time of his graduation from the so-called Soviet Area Program, in which a degree of Master of Arts in Regional Studies was obtained after two years of work. Thereupon, the student, with the generous aid of the center, would spend up to two years preparing for his general examination for the Ph.D. in economics. The quid-pro-quo was the student's obligation to undertake thereafter to write a dissertation in the field of Soviet economy and, upon completion of the dissertation, to spend another year in converting it into a publishable book. This meant that the student's connection with the center at times lasted as long as six years.

This was a protracted business, but the arrangement was fully justified by the results. For the first time, a group of well-trained economists was attracted to Soviet economic studies. Since the center underwrote their period of research for years ahead, they were able to engage in projects that required long and painstaking effort. A great deal had to be learned. In particular, the art of separating the meal from the bran in Soviet statistics had to be mastered, the learning processes in this respect not being helped much by a sham debate as to whether or not the Soviet government falsified its statistics deliberately. But the problem was not merely to assess the degree of reliability of the individual series, to test them for internal consistency, and to discover the true meaning of a statistical figure that was often presented in a deliberately misleading fashion. Even more important was to learn how to combine statistical data so as to obtain information which never was intended to be divulged by the compilers and publishers of Soviet statistics. And statistical analysis was closely connected with economic analysis, producing gradually a fuller understanding of the basic elements of the Soviet economy, its processes of change, and its mode of operation.

This work was guided by still another important decision. The nature of the effort and its scale presupposed an effective research organization. But organized research has its own hazards. There is the frequent desire to organize too much; to foist a research director's favorite topic upon a hesitant, if not unwilling, research worker; to press for teamwork, particularly for interdisciplinary research, which was, and still is, an "o.k. word" with many organization men in research. These temptations, too, had to be resisted. The prospect of joint research would have appealed to lesser talents, but would have been scorned by independent and creative minds. Nor would an excellent student accept work on a subject unless it genuinely excited his curiosity and aroused his research instincts. The ultimate selection of a topic had to come from the student himself. Care had to be exercised lest a relatively insignificant topic were chosen. But in a virgin field there was no dearth of highly important subjects.

Decisions of this sort did not remain peculiar to the Russian Research Center at Harvard. In particular, the RAND Corporation in Santa Monica pursued a very similar policy, making a signal contribution to research on the Soviet economy. Today, as one looks back and reviews the results of those efforts, they appear impressive indeed. Some three hundred years ago a Dutch scholar, now almost forgotten, chose a proud device for his coat-of-arms: *Quantum est quod scimus*. While it is true that there are still many things we do not know about the Soviet economy, the increase in knowledge that has occurred during the past two decades is truly stupendous. At least in these relative terms, the American students of Soviet economic development may well feel justified in appropriating old Boxhorn's self-confident motto.

It would far exceed the scope of this paper to give a complete listing of the important studies that appeared in print during this period, and a partial listing would do injustice to the works omitted. But at least a brief survey of some of the areas in which significant work has been done is in order. In the field of national income and output, an original and effective method was devised for calculating the national income of the Soviet Union within a conceptual framework employed in Western presentations of national accounts. In a series of studies, the computations were first made at current Russian prices, and the magnificent work was crowned by a volume in which the previously computed data were expressed in constant prices, thus offering for the first time a reliable and detailed picture of the rate of aggregate growth of the Soviet economy. In various other studies, special attention was devoted to the rate of growth of industrial output, to productivity of labor in Soviet industry, and to Soviet capital formation. In reference to the entire period since 1928, it is probably no exaggeration to say that, as a result of these studies, our information on the rate of Soviet economic growth is superior even to that available to Soviet planners, who for the earlier parts of the period still operate with patently inadequate yardsticks. Studies of Soviet prices threw light on the peculiarities of the price structure in Soviet Russia and the degree of meaningfulness inherent in the price system.

No less important was a thorough investigation of the evolution of real wages, revealing an astonishing lag of the latter behind the growth of output. A monograph on Soviet taxation presented the relevant material as a problem of eliminating the gap between the purchasing power in the hands of the population and the available supply of consumers' goods at existing prices. The role of the interest rate, and of its substitutes, in determining investment decisions was investigated. The policies of Soviet industrial enterprises were the subject of at least two important studies, showing curious and wide discrepancies between the idealized picture usually presented in Soviet literature and the actual behavior of managers of industrial enterprises. Those studies were illuminatingly supplemented by an investigation of Soviet methods of accounting. A magnum opus written by a productive scholar, unconnected with the main research organizations in the field, offered a thorough examination in quantitative terms of the collectivized agriculture of the Soviet Union. The Soviet iron and steel industry and the railroads became the subject matter of two studies, which in their mastery of the respective materials and in analytical sophistication were fully comparable to monographs on industrial organization in the United States. Soviet economic writings under Stalin were reduced to a jejune regurgitation of the pronouncements of the dictator, but the lively debates in the twenties dealt with real and important alternatives of Soviet economic development. In a significant study, the arguments and counterarguments of those days were translated into the language of modern economics and served to illuminate the complex situation that existed in Russia in the second half of the twenties, out of which emerged Stalin's policy of collectivization of agriculture and superindustrialization.

This enumeration naturally conveys no idea of the depth of analysis reached in the individual studies. But it should give at least some impression of the range of the problems treated and of the vigor and concentration with which the field of Soviet economic studies was attacked. There can be no doubt that the results attained amply testify to the soundness of the original decisions. The roundabout way proved a highly productive one. Thanks to the long series of fundamental investigations, it has become possible to deal with current economic problems of the Soviet Union in a competent and sophisticated fashion, and at the same time to hazard intelligent guesses — conditional predictions — about the path the Soviet economy is likely to travel in the future. One has only to refer to the reports submitted by the community of American students of the Soviet economy to the Joint Committee of Congress, or to study the papers and discussions of some scholarly conferences in which past research and current analysis were deliberately connected, to find plentiful evidence for the progress achieved through first withdrawing into basic research and then returning to the examination of current problems.

The success is obvious. The study of the Soviet economy has been effectively transformed into an integral part of the discipline of economics. In fact, at least in some respects, the preoccupation with the Soviet economy has had effects transcending the limits of a mere area study. In trying to gauge the rate of growth of an economy that grew fast and whose structure was rapidly changing — and in attempting comparisons between the Soviet levels of income and output and those of other countries — students were forced to face up squarely to the problem of the nature of the yardsticks used. It would not have done simply to shrug the index-number problem away by merely referring to its annoying existence, as had been done so often before. Accordingly, there appeared both historical and theoretical interpretations of the index-number problem in industrializing economies, which already have found many an echo in areas quite unconnected with Soviet studies. In addition, the economists working on the Soviet economy had to be particularly conscious of the ways in which results of statistical computations should be published. The Soviet statistical material was often uncertain and most of the time fragmentary. To transform it into usable statistical data, it was necessary to make many arbitrary assumptions and estimates of varying degrees of plausibility. It is not surprising, therefore, that it became the practice to call for the publication of extremely detailed statistical appendices to the texts of the studies. This is something that could and should be imitated in many a field of historical statistics, where the shortcomings of the original data and the problems of treating them are not very different from those in the Soviet Union. A full view into the statistician's kitchen, for instance, would be most desirable in any presentation of long-term income and output series for many Western countries in the nineteenth century.

Although many an important aspect of Soviet economic development has been treated in the studies alluded to here, there is of course a good deal of room for further basic research. The number of monographs devoted to individual Soviet industries could be considerably increased. An area that so far has remained almost entirely outside the purview of scholarly attention is Soviet technology. A series of studies investigating the economic problems involved would be eminently desirable and would take several years to accomplish. In particular, a study of obsolescence in the Soviet economy — of "moral depreciation" as the Soviet economists call it, following Marx — would be enlightening indeed, particularly if it could be presented in comparative terms, using for the purpose the relevant developments in the American or some other Western economy. While we know a good deal about the way in which industrial enterprises are run in Russia, the management of collective farms has not yet been studied in any comparable fashion, and an investigation would certainly prove very rewarding.

These few examples do not begin to exhaust the variety of further significant research projects. But one additional point may be in order. In the past, when the large backlog of purely economic problems pressed for urgent investigation, interdisciplinary research had to be looked upon with misgivings, and attempts in that direction were discouraged. Today, after much of the basic economic work has been done, this is no longer true to the same extent. Sociological, political, and perhaps psychological themes may be profitably conjoined with economic analysis. Most notably, it is to be recognized that in Soviet Russia economic decisions most frequently are a function of the political necessities or desires of the Soviet government. The need to maintain the dictatorship in power makes for the primacy of politics over economics, the tenets of the materialistic conception of history to the contrary notwithstanding. A serious and detailed study of politics as a determinant of economics, and of the resulting deviations from optimal economic solutions, would be extremely useful. Nevertheless, it probably would be illusory to expect that a study of this kind could be successfully carried out as the joint enterprise of an economist and a political scientist. If the focus of such work is to remain economic, a project conducted in its entirety by an economist who has managed to acquire the necessary grasp of Soviet politics would be much more likely to yield significant results.

For the moment, however, the chances that a great deal of interesting and original economic research will be done are less than excellent. In the last few years, the influx of young and promising talent into the field has been slow. There are many reasons to account for this. For one, research on the Soviet economy no longer offers the wide open spaces that invited students twenty years ago. Moreover, a great change has occurred in the American labor market for young economists; it has become a pronounced sellers' market. Universities and colleges throughout the country have been expanding rapidly, and the academic demand for economists seems to have been growing, if anything, at a still higher rate. In contrast to the previous practice, leading universities have been offering assistant professorships to graduate students who have not yet completed the requirements for the doctor's degree. Finally, able graduate students find it very easy today to obtain generous individual grants from various foundations. In these conditions, Ph.D. theses can be prepared without the individual's having to submit to the rhythm of work and the responsibilities which are inevitably imposed even by the most liberal research organization. A bright graduate student in economics can proceed much faster along the conventional road of academic advancement by choosing a thesis topic in economic theory or related areas which does not require the long years of arduous work necessary for successful empirical research in the Soviet field. Obviously, the problem is not an easy one. Much will depend on the imaginativeness and resourcefulness of the men in charge of the larger research organizations; on their ability, that is, to suggest new themes and to find ways and means to compensate outstanding students for the unavoidable retardation in their careers, thus once more making the area of Soviet economic study attractive to them.

To discover appropriate solutions would seem most important for more than one reason. The scholars working in the field of Soviet economic research have come to constitute a closely knit group, even formally organized in a miniature professional organization of their own. This has advantages and disadvantages. The spirit of comradeship and the friendships formed in the years of common apprenticeship in the research centers create many opportunities for consultation and stimulation. At the same time, however, they have produced somewhat excessive loyalties and reticences. It is, for instance, not easy to find reviewers in the United States willing to comment in professional journals frankly and bluntly on books published by their colleagues in the field. There has been much mutual admiration and a curious absence or near absence of public disagreement in what, after all, is an uncertain and controversial subject. An infusion of young talent would blow whiffs of fresher air over the field. It would also generate new stimuli and open up promising vistas for further original work, thus serving to continue what was once a daring venture into the unknown and has proved a successful and highly significant operation in research.

Index

Prepared by Margarita Willfort

545